Lecture Notes in Artificial Intelligence 1620

Subseries of Lecture Notes in Computer Science
Edited by J. G. Carbonell and J. Siekmann

Lecture Notes in Computer Science
Edited by G. Goos, J. Hartmanis and J. van Leeuwen

T0216970

Springer

Berlin
Heidelberg
New York
Barcelona
Hong Kong
London
Milan
Paris
Singapore
Tokyo

Werner Horn   Yuval Shahar   Greger Lindberg
Steen Andreassen   Jeremy Wyatt (Eds.)

Artificial Intelligence in Medicine

Joint European Conference
on Artificial Intelligence in Medicine
and Medical Decision Making, AIMDM'99
Aalborg, Denmark, June 20-24, 1999
Proceedings

Springer

Volume Editors

Werner Horn
Austrian Research Institute for Artificial Intelligence
Schottengasse 3, A-1010 Vienna, Austria
E-mail: werner@ai.univie.ac.at

Yuval Shahar
Stanford University, Department of Medicine and Computer Science
251 Campus Drive, Stanford, CA 94305-5479, USA
E-mail: shahar@smi.stanford.edu

Greger Lindberg
Huddinge University Hospital, Department of Medicine
Karolinska Institutet, Sweden
E-mail: greger.lindberg@medhs.ki.se

Steen Andreassen
Aalborg University, Department of Medical Informatics and Image Analysis
Fredrik Bajers Vej 7D, DK-9000 Aalborg, Denmark

Jeremy Wyatt
University College London, School of Public Policy
29/30 Tavistock Square, London WC1H 9EZ, UK
E-mail: jeremy.wyatt@ucl.ac.uk

Cataloging-in-Publication data applied for

Die Deutsche Bibliothek - CIP-Einheitsaufnahme

Artificial intelligence in medicine : proceedings / Joint European Conference on
Artificial Intelligence in Medicine and Medical Decision Making, AIMDM '99,
Aalborg, Denmark, June 20 - 24, 1999. Werner Horn ... (ed.). - Berlin ;
Heidelberg ; New York ; Barcelona ; Hong Kong ; London ; Milan ; Paris ;
Singapore ; Tokyo : Springer, 1999
 (Lecture notes in computer science ; Vol. 1620 : Lecture notes in artificial
 intelligence)
 ISBN 3-540-66162-X

CR Subject Classification (1998): I.2, I.4, J.3, H.4

ISBN 3-540-66162-X Springer-Verlag Berlin Heidelberg New York

© Springer-Verlag Berlin Heidelberg 1999
Printed in Germany

Typesetting: Camera-ready by author
SPIN 10705254   06/3142 – 5 4 3 2 1 0   Printed on acid-free paper

Preface

The European Societies for Artificial Intelligence in Medicine (AIME) and Medical Decision Making (ESMDM) were both established in 1986. A major activity of both these societies has been a series of international conferences, held biennially over the last 13 years. In the year 1999 the two societies organized a joint conference for the first time. It took place from June 20–24th, 1999 in Aalborg, Denmark.

This "Joint European Conference on Artificial Intelligence in Medicine and Medical Decision Making (AIMDM'99)" was the seventh conference for each of the two societies. This conference follows the AIME conferences held in Marseilles (1987), London (1989), Maastricht (1991), Munich (1993), Pavia (1995), and Grenoble (1997). Previous ESMDM conferences have been held in Leiden (1986), Copenhagen (1988), Glasgow (1990), Marburg (1992), Lille (1994), and Torino (1996).

The AIMDM conference is the major forum for the presentation and discussion of new ideas in the areas of Artificial Intelligence and Medical Decision Making in Medicine. This fulfills the aims of both societies. The aims of AIME are to foster fundamental and applied research in the application of Artificial Intelligence (AI) techniques to medical care and medical research, and to provide a forum for reporting significant results achieved. ESMDM's aims are to promote research and training in medical decision-making, and to provide a forum for circulating ideas and programs of related interest.

In the AIMDM'99 conference announcement, authors were encouraged to submit original contributions to the development of theory, techniques, and applications of both AI in medicine (AIM) and medical decision making (MDM). Contributions to theory could include presentation or analysis of the properties of novel AI or MDM methodologies potentially useful in solving medical problems. Papers on techniques should describe the development or the extension of AIM or MDM methods and their implementation. They should also discuss the assumptions and limitations which characterize the proposed methods. Application papers should describe the implementation of AI or MDM systems in solving significant medical problems, including health care quality assurance, health care costs, and ethical considerations. Application papers should present sufficient information to allow evaluation of the practical benefits of the system.

The call for papers for AIMDM'99 resulted in 90 submissions. Following the traditional format for AIME and ESMDM conferences there were two styles of submission: full papers and abstracts. We received 57 full paper submissions (55 for AIM areas, 2 for MDM areas), and 33 abstract submissions (14 for AIM areas, 19 for MDM areas). Looking at the research areas on which the submitted papers focused, we note that AIMDM was able to maintain its wide scope both in methodology and application compared to the previous conferences. Further, submissions from 23 countries from all the 5 continents make evident that AIMDM is not limited geographically.

Each submission was evaluated carefully by two members of the program committee with support from additional reviewers. The reviews judged the relevance, originality, quality of research, presentation, and the overall impact of the work. As a result 42 submissions were accepted for oral presentation and 32 submissions were accepted for poster presentation. The proceedings volume contains all accepted full paper submissions: 27 full papers (those 47% of full papers accepted for oral presentation) and 19 short papers (the 33% of full papers accepted for poster presentation appearing in a shortened version). In addition, this volume contains extensive analysis papers in four keynote areas of research written by the invited conference speakers: clinical practice guidelines, workflow management systems in health care, temporal reasoning and temporal data maintenance, and machine learning approaches used in mining of medical data.

The high quality of research and application papers in this volume strengthen our belief, that the "Artificial Intelligence in Medicine" series is a worthwhile addition to the literature. This is the seventh volume of a series of AIME proceedings with steadily improving quality. This book continues the dissemination of important results from research and development in the fields of artificial intelligence in medicine and medical decision making.

We would like to thank all those people and institutions who contributed to the success of AIMDM'99: the authors, the members of the program committee and the additional reviewers, the members of the local organizing committee, and the invited speakers Nada Lavrač, Gianpaolo Molino, Yuval Shahar, and Mario Stefanelli. Further, we would like to thank the organizers of the two workshops accompanying the technical conference: Ameen Abu-Hanna, Peter Lucas, and Silvia Miksch, and the presenters of the tutorials: Steen Andreassen, Robert Hamm, Claire Harries, Finn V. Jensen, Nada Lavrač, Leonard Leibovici, Joseph Pliskin, Ehud Reiter, Karla Soares Weiser, and Blaž Zupan. Finally, we would like to thank the institutions which sponsored the conference, namely the Aalborg University (Department of Medical Informatics and Image Analysis), the Austrian Research Institute for Artificial Intelligence, the University of Vienna (Department of Medical Cybernetics and Artificial Intelligence), and the Det Obelske Familiefond.

March 1999

Werner Horn
Yuval Shahar
Greger Lindberg
Steen Andreassen
Jeremy Wyatt

Program Committee

Chair:

Werner Horn (Austrian Research Institute for Artificial Intelligence, Vienna)

For AIME:

Yuval Shahar (USA) [Co-Chair]

Steen Andreassen (Denmark)
Pedro Barahona (Portugal)
Robert Baud (Switzerland)
Jan van Bemmel (The Netherlands)
Carlo Combi (Italy)
Luca Console (Italy)
Michel Dojat (France)
Rolf Engelbrecht (Germany)
John Fox (United Kingdom)
Catherine Garbay (France)
Reinhold Haux (Germany)
Jim Hunter (United Kingdom)
Elpida Keravnou (Cyprus)
Nada Lavrač (Slovenia)
Leonard Leibovici (Israel)
Silvia Miksch (Austria)
Alan Rector (United Kingdom)
Costas Spyropoulos (Greece)
Mario Stefanelli (Italy)
Mario Veloso (Portugal)
Bonnie Webber (United Kingdom)
Jeremy Wyatt (United Kingdom)

For ESMDM:

Greger Lindberg (Sweden) [Co-Chair]

Gianni Barosi (Italy)
Diederik Dippel (The Netherlands)
Jack Dowie (United Kingdom)
Jose I. Emparanza (Spain)
Carmi Z. Margolis (Israel)
Gianpaolo Molino (Italy)
Christian Ohmann (Germany)
Helmut Sitter (Germany)
Charles Sulman (France)
Sarah Twaddle (United Kingdom)
Jef Van den Ende (Belgium)

Additional Reviewers

Elske Ammenwerth (Germany)
Ion Androutsopoulos (Greece)
Riccardo Bellazzi (Italy)
Ekkard Finkeissen (Germany)
Johannes Fürnkranz (Austria)
Klaus Hammermüller (Austria)
Christian Holzbaur (Austria)
Vangelis Karkaletsis (Greece)
Robert Kosara (Austria)

Stefan Kramer (Austria)
Matjaž Kukar (Slovenia)
Giordano Lanzola (Italy)
Dunja Mladenić (Slovenia)
George Paliouras (Greece)
Stavros J. Perantonis (Greece)
Marko Robnik-Sikonja (Slovenia)
Andreas Seyfang (Austria)
Thomas Wetter (Germany)

Organizing Committee

Chair: Steen Andreassen (Aalborg University, Denmark)

Werner Horn
Greger Lindberg
Steve Rees
Yuval Shahar
Jeremy Wyatt

Local Organizing Committee

Chair: Steve Rees (Aalborg University, Denmark)

Kim Dremstrup Nielsen
Johnny Solberg

Workshops

Computers in Anaesthesia and Intensive Care
   Chair: Silvia Miksch (Vienna, Austria)

Prognostic Models in Medicine
   Co-Chairs: Ameen Abu-Hanna (Amsterdam, The Netherlands)
            Peter Lucas (Utrecht, The Netherlands)

Tutorials

Chair: Jeremy Wyatt (London, United Kingdom)

Data Mining Techniques and Applications in Medicine
   Blaž Zupan and Nada Lavrač (Ljubljana, Slovenia)
How to Build a Causal Probabilistic Network
   Finn V. Jensen and Steen Andreassen (Aalborg, Denmark)
Natural Language Generation in Medicine
   Ehud Reiter (Aberdeen, Scotland)
Psychology of Medical Decision Making
   Robert Hamm (Oklahoma City, USA) and Claire Harries (London, UK)
Systematic Reviews: How to Read (and Maybe Perform) a Metaanalysis
   Karla Soares Weiser (Tel Aviv) and Leonard Leibovici (Petah-Tiqva, Israel)
Advanced Tutorial on Utility and Decision Theory
   Joseph Pliskin (Beer-Sheva, Israel)

Table of Contents

Model-Based Systems

Neural Networks, Causal Probabilistic Networks

Knowledge Representation

Temporal Reasoning

Machine Learning

Natural Language Processing

Image Processing and Computer Aided Design

Keynote Lectures

From Clinical Guidelines to Decision Support

Gianpaolo Molino

Department of Medicine
Laboratory of Clinical Informatics
Azienda Ospedaliera San Giovanni Battista
Corso Bramante 88, 10126 Torino (Italia)
Tel/Fax: +39-11-6336665
e-mail: medgen1.molinette@mail.cs.interbusiness.it

Abstract. Medical Informatics applies computer-based technologies to several aspects of medicine, including clinical practice, research and education. In all these fields different trends and interests can be identified, respectively related to methodology, technique, and health care policy, including cost-effectiveness analysis, armonization of efforts, budget management, quality assessment and support to medical decision-making. All the above aspects may take advantage of proper guidelines aimed at minimizing the misuse and unsuitability of health services, at identifying the appropriate strategies for health policy, and at suitably supporting clinical decisions.

1 Basic Definitions

According to Cook et al. [1] clinical practice guidelines can be described as an "attempt to distill a large body of medical expertise into a convenient, readily usable format". In contrast to protocols, which are by definition prescriptive, the major goal of guidelines is to provide all the information needed for discretionary and responsible decisions. In particular, guidelines appear to be the ideal support for decision-making whenever, like in clinical practice, the proper use of data may be essential to achieve efficiently the right conclusion, and ethical as well as legal constraints exist.

Guidelines cannot be dissociated from medical action. This might be defined as any clinical activity, with its many psychological, cognitive, epistemological, and methodological implications, contributing to remove or modify abnormal or unsafe conditions.

2 Typology of Clinical Guidelines

A very large amount of guidelines for clinical practice have been developed during the last years [2, 3] but a minor number among them has been really applied, and a still

W. Horn et al. (Eds.): AIMDM'99, LNAI 1620, pp. 3-12, 1999.

lower number has been certified. As regards guideline availability, large differences exist between the different countries of the world.

With respect to their sources, three major groups of guidelines can be identified, which will be listed here in decreasing order of constraint and increasing order of practicality for the user. A first group includes guidelines certified by laws and institutional regulations, whose application is mandatory. The second category includes guidelines supported by clinical evidence and consensus conferences, which represent a sound suggestion for medical operators. A third class of clinical guidelines consists in programs, in most cases prototypes, developed by experts or societies, usually not certified, and proposed or sold for practical use [4].

On the other hand, as regards technological aspects, clinical guidelines may be: textual guidelines, presented in a written form; graphical guidelines represented as flow-charts or algorithms; computerized guidelines, corresponding to the above third class, which apply advanced methods and technologies of computer science and are developed to support either medical decision-making or workflow management. Unfortunately, only a very small amount of computerized guidelines directly interacts with electronic patient records [5, 6].

3 Needs and Problems

The development and supply of clinical guidelines should be directly related to real clinical needs. The correct utilization of available resources is the key problem, whose most important aspects are related to workflow analysis, decision support, optimization of available procedures, cost-effectiveness analysis, definition of optimum strategies and criteria. The assessment and endorsement of suitable guidelines considering all the above aspects might be very relevant for defining the minimum requirements enabling medical services to provide quality performances [4].

Several additional problems, however, need great attention. A patient-centered approach in medical decision-making is undervalued in most existing clinical guidelines [7, 8], which are too much focused on cost reduction. Another important demand is for anxiety reduction and legal liability of physicians [7, 9]. Lastly, guidelines should provide some support in forecasting the real need of resources, instead of simply analyzing their actual use with respect to quality achievement and cost-effectiveness optimization.

4 Scenario and Contexts

According to the above considerations, clinical guidelines may have quite different *scenarios*. Indeed, they may be applied not only to the solution of specific clinical problems, but also to answering at the best the personal wishes of patients, and to properly manage the existing opportunities with respect to social requirements. Moreover, locally (clinical units) as well as centrally (management offices), the scenario of guidelines should also take into account the many constraints depending on health care policy and financial availability [8].

Another important distinction is the one relating clinical guidelines to the expected *users*. Indeed, while general practitioners usually manage patients whose diagnosis is complex and/or poorly defined, specialists are mainly requested to treat much better defined conditions [4, 10]. These considerations explain why clinical guidelines should not be considered unique and invariable, but should be preferably flexible and context-sensitive, thus resulting in most cases in hierarchies of related guidelines.

Some more distinctions are related to the actual *goal* and *context* of medical action [11, 12]. As an example, in the emergency room the need of computer based tools is very limited, since decision-making must be there immediate and mainly dependent on operator skills. On the other hand, computerized guidelines are somewhat impractical for home care, since the second opinion they provide is expected to occur a-posteriori. In contrast, in ward and ambulatory care the decision support of guidelines might also be very useful when available on-line. Such distinctions obviously imply the existence of quite different goal-related and context-related facilities in clinical guidelines.

5 Basic Requirements

The positive offect of clinical guidelines on medical practice was demonstrated by several studies [3, 13 14]. However, concerns and perplexities have been raised about the actual applicability of guidelines as regards concepts, contents and potential weaknesses [4].

A set of requirements caracterizing clinical guidelines has been previously defined. It includes validity, reliability, applicability, flexibility, clarity, transparency, and upgradability [2, 10]:

validity: guideline goals and outcomes should be explicit, and the real pertinence of the chosen guideline should be checked before using it;

reliability: guidelines should be supported by the literature and/or the consensus of experts; proof of clinical utility should be provided, evaluating the results according to evidence-based criteria;

applicability: a friendly interface is not the only requirement; the model of action the guideline proposes should reflect clinical methodology, and some added value should be tangible;

flexibility: the guideline should be made compliant to context and scenario requirements, but also to clinician needs;

clarity: guideline decisions, conclusions and explanations should be logic, sharp and unambiguous;

transparency: all the knowledge chunks must be carefully defined and described, and explanations should be thorough and convincing;

upgradability: since most guidelines become outdated in a very short time, because of changes in medical knowledge, upgrading should be ensured by competent people at short time intervals.

According to these requirements ideal clinical guidelines appear like structured and dynamic knowledge bases, usually limited to a restricted domain but following a multi-task approach and preferably organized as *metasystems*.

6 Aims and Features

Clinical guidelines are aimed at increasing the effectiveness and quality of clinical practice at the lowest possible cost compatible with available resources. As a side effect they are expected to promote the standardization of procedures.

From several points of view clinical guidelines can be considered as cognitive, behavioral, operational and management models. Indeed, clinical guidelines usually incorporate quite different functions directed at supporting medical action by means of information, expertise, warnings and alarms, and policy suggestions.

Guidelines providers should be political and financial institutions, scientific societies and experts. Potential users are the professional figures related to health management, including hospital care, speciality care and home care. Correspondingly, a lot of expectations are associated with clinical guidelines: rational organization of medical knowledge (e.g., according to a shearable database); recording facilities (including not only facts but also time-dependent events); support in patient management (e.g., assisted medical decision-making); quality assessment and improvement (according to explicit and objective criteria); educational outcomes (obtained by means of simulation, navigation and browsing facilities) [10].

7 Central Role of Medical Action

Clinical guidelines should reflect real life. Thus, the availability of a reliable model of medical action is absolutely important. Generally speaking, the goal of medical action is to solve clinical problems (related to diagnosis, treatment or follow-up). This is made possible by a close interaction among different action models: a knowledge model (reflecting medical culture), a behavioral model (derived from doctor competence), an organizational model (including problems related to workflow management and cost-effectiveness analysis); an information model (supporting recording facilities and data flow); and a psychological model (featuring the emotions and uncertainties of operators).

Medical actions should be carried out according to their relative priorities, which result from the compromise among logical, ethical and financial requirements. Clinical guidelines have a key role in weighing and integrating the preconditions of medical actions, which are facts (to be recognized), contexts (to be identified) and knowledge (to be incorporated). Thus, in addition to their main function of supporting medical decision-making, clinical guidelines can also provide a very important preliminary evaluation of the consistency, reliability and cost-effectiveness of compatible medical actions, whose outcomes eventually represent the substrate of quality assessment, as regards conformity to goals, effectiveness and efficiency [15].

Clinical activity is not a personal task of individual physicians, but needs co-ordination of the many people involved. Indeed, act management has been widely applied to define the broad typology of clinical activities, to support the development of open hospital systems architecture, and to provide a concrete basis for the development of clinical guidelines [16].

8 Guidelines and Patient Management

The clinical guideline may be considered the formal representation of the patient management process: it results from a sequence of actions, which may be clinical (related to nurse or doctor activities), technical (related to the execution of any kind of investigations) and managerial (related to organization and surveillance tasks). Actions may differ considerably, but their sequences or associations should be fully integrated in the patient management process, and should be the natural target of clinical guidelines [15].

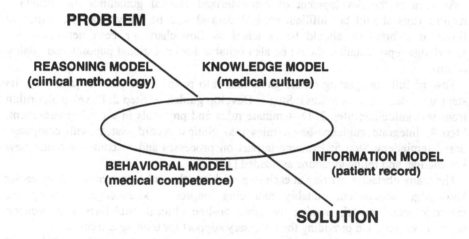

Fig. 1. Clinical guidelines aimed at optimizing the patient management process imply the involvement and integration of different interacting models.

It is worth noting that guideline features may differ in the different medical care contexts (hospital ward, day-hospital, ambulatory, home care). In any case, however, clinical guidelines can be described as a multifactorial process depending on at least three elements: patient caracteristics, tasks features and available resources. The following sequence of operations usually occurs. First, the *action project* is defined according to the task (selected among those considered in the guideline) and the existing clinical situation (extracted from patient record). Thereafter, the action project becomes *real action* in conformity with available (context related) resources. According to such a layout, the major requirements qualifying a clinical guideline are the possibility of direct interaction with the record containing patient data and reporting clinical events, the pertinence of the algorithm with the actual clinical problem, its methodological reliability, and the correspondence between available and needed   resources. As shown in Fig. 1, clinical guidelines aimed at optimizing the patient management process imply the involvement and integration of different interacting models.

9 User Involvement

To be reliably applied to clinical practice a guideline should be grounded on a knowledge base covering a reasonable portion but not necessarily the whole domain related to the expected application. User involvement might be very useful to define the proper dimension of the knowledge base. In addition, guideline functions should be consistent with user needs, outcomes should solve real problems, and messages should be clear and concise.

As regards the development of computerized clinical guidelines the following requirements should be fulfilled: clinical data should be tidily recorded, expected flows of information should be sketched as flow-charts or Petri networks, and knowledge representation should be also suitable for educational puposes and quality control.

Toward fully integrating online guidelines into practice the path is quite long. Its steps were described as follows: Step 1: Develop guideline; Step 2: Develop algorithm from text guideline; Step 3: Disseminate rules and protocols in a local environment: Step 4: Integrate guideline-based rules into clinical record system with computer-based reminders; Step 5: Examine impact on processes and outcomes, monitor new knowledge, and refine guideline as needed [17].

The many obstacles existing at each step of this path can be overcome making easier knowledge acquisition, suitably managing imprecise knowledge, shearing the methodological model, making available on-line clinical guidelines and decision support systems, and providing the necessary support for training activities.

Guidelines may be reliable only if the necessary contributions are provided by all the actors, i.e., the medical staff, computer scientists, technicians, patients and health care managers. It is quite relevant that the different contributions, while eventually fully integrated, should be preferably developed independently to ensure specificity and competence.

While physicians are mainly asked to define goals, clinical methods and interfaces, the help of computer science people is mainly related to providing and integrating strategies that support knowledge browsing, messaging and evaluation procedures [18]. It is worth noting that the result of such a collaboration is *more than a sum*, because of the added value due to the interplay of reciprocal expertises and/or to the emergence of subliminal skills [19]. To this extent, the development of a strategy of interaction shearing concepts, models, experiences and talents is absolutely relevant, and should be applied with the aim of complementing insead of replacing.

10 Impact and Limitations

So far the impact of clinical guidelines on medical practice has been quite poor. Among the many reasons considered to explain this failure the following appear to be the most relevant for the users: time waste, stiffness, ambiguity, misuse of professional skills, disagreement, ethical and legal concerns and fear of automatic decisions. All these obstacles should be overcome to make guidelines accepted and effective [4, 9].

Some apparent conflicts inherent to clinical guidelines need attention. First, as regards context sensitivity, it seems paradoxical to produce practice guidelines to reduce variability, while building expedients facilitating the compliance to local needs [17]. However, since resource availability is an essential feasibility condition, shortage of them should better suggest to dismiss the guideline instead of applying it inappropriately. In no case, indeed, guideline remodeling should lead to illogical or improper solutions.

Changes in medical knowledge suggesting guideline upgrading may also collide with user experience and feeling. In such a case the guideline should be immediately modified according to the criteria of evidence based medicine, instead of simply removing the conflict and applying the old rules.

11 Guidelines and Quality Assessment

Whenever a patient is admitted to the hospital, attending physicians are expected to provide effective and efficient care. The fulfilment of such an obvious requirement implies the organization of clinical information and medical actions. In particular, the physician is asked to identify existing clinical problems, to rank them according to priority criteria, and to make the proper decisions in a reasonable sequence. General principles of clinical methodology and personal competence make this possible in most cases [20]. However, at least for unexperienced physicians, the decison aid provided by guidelines may be very useful for optimizing the clinical management of patients and ensuring high quality outcomes.

This is particularly true in the case of computerized guidelines directly interacting with electronic clinical records, which allow more efficient and shearable information. A computerized approach to the quality control of patient care was previously proposed [15], based on a clinical data architecture directly interacting with clinical guidelines [15, 21]. The program was based on a knowledge-based system which was used in two ways: with on-line hints to ensure effective and efficient medical decisions on a simulated patient for training purposes; and without facilities supporting user decisions to be applied on-line for quality assessment (Fig. 2).

The quality control should include the evaluation of effectiveness and efficiency with respect to the overall process of patient care, as well as to single hypotheses or individual decisions. The evaluation should regard the number and reliability of activated hypotheses, costs, time spent, number and appropriateness of investigations. The process should be recursive, so that results of each cycle can be used to define new goals and indicants for the next cycle. Lastly, the quality control should be *active*, i.e., it should directly involve the physicians in the definition of goals and indicants and in the evaluation of results; and the assessment should be *objective*, i.e., indicants should be predefined and evaluation criteria should be transparent.

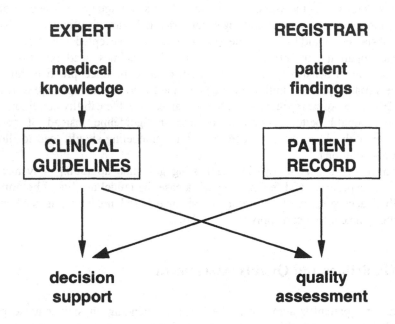

Fig. 2. Interaction between clinical guidelines and patient data to support computer assisted medical decision-making and quality control.

12 The Way Forward

In spite of the considerable results obtained so far by means of clinical guidelines, the way forward appears still long and complicated. Efforts should be paid in modeling clinical guidelines on real medical actions, structured clinical records, different contexts of application, patient and user satisfaction, social needs and network requirements.

Special attention should be paid in properly training potential users. Indeed, the new deals of continuing medical education now include familiarization of physicians with clinical (preferably computer based) guidelines. Tools should include textbooks, demonstrations, seminars, coursewares, training on real cases, and simulations on virtual patients.

Lastly, since the number of domain-independent programs made available to support the development of clinical guidelines is increasing, it seems reasonable to anticipate that in a short time *metasystems* of clinical guidelines, i.e. families of guidelines shearing well assessed strategies and interfaces, will be available.

In summary, three major outcomes may be expected from the use of guidelines: cultural enrichment due to information, improvement of competence due to the training effect, and increased efficiency resulting from decision support to difficult, uncommon, controversial or complex clinical decisions.

Acknowledgements. The author thanks the many collaborators who took part in the activity of the Laboratory of Medical Informatics during the last years, and in particular Fabrizio Bar, Stefania Battista, Oscar Bruschi, Luca Console, Daniele Mantovani, Marina Marzuoli, Francesca Molino, Emma Nicolosi, Paolo Raviola, Crispino Seidenari, Dario Sestero, Paolo Terenziani, Mauro Torchio, Piero Torasso and Katia Vanni.

References

1. Cook, D.J., Greengold, N.L., Ellrodt, A.G., Weingarten, S.R. The relation between systematic reviews and practice guidelines. Ann. Intern. Med. 127 (1997) 210-216
2. Institute of Medicine. Guidelines for clinical practice: from development to use. Washington DC. National Academic Press (1992)
3. Lobach, D.F., Hammond, W.E. Computerized decision support based on clinical practice guidelines improves compliance with care standards. Am J Med. 102 (1997) 89-98
4. Purves, I. Computerised guidelines in primary health care: reflections and implications. In: Gordon, C. and Christensen, J.P. (eds): Health telematics for clinical guidelines and protocols. IOS Press (1995) 57-74
5. Henry, S.B., Douglas, K., Galzagorry, G., Lahey, A., Holzemer, W.L. A template-based approach to support utilization of clinical practice guidelines within an electronic health record. JAMIA 5 (1998) 237-244
6. Glowinski A. Integrating guidelines and the clinical record: the role of semantically constrained terminologies. In: Gordon, C. and Christensen, J.P. (eds.): Health telematics for clinical guidelines and protocols. IOS Press (1995) 207-218
7. Delamothe, T. Wanted: guidelines that doctors will follow. Implementation is the problem. B.M.J. 307 (1993) 218 (Letter)
8. Field, M.J., Lohr, K.N. (eds.). Guidelines for clinical practice: from development to use. National Academic Press, Washington DC (1992)
9. Shortliffe, E.H. Testing reality: the introduction of decision-support technologies for physicians. Methods Inf. Med. 28 (1989) 1-5
10. Gordon, C. Practice guidelines and healthcare telematics: towards an alliance. In: Gordon, C. and Christensen, J.P. (eds.): Health telematics for clinical guidelines and protocols. IOS Press (1995) 3-16

11. Mold, J.W., Blake, G.H., Becker, L.A. Goal-oriented medical care. Fam. Med. 23 (1991) 46-51

12. Hayward, R.S., Laupacis, A. Initiating, conducting and maintaining guidelines development programs. Can. Med. Assoc. J. 148 (1993) 507-512

13. Grimshaw, J.M., Russel, I.T. Effect of clinical guidelines on medical practice: a systematic review of rigorous evaluations. Lancet 342 (1993) 1317-1322

14. Johnston, M.E., Langton, K.B., Haynes, R.B., Mathieu, A. Effects of computer-based clinical decision support systems on clinician performance and patient outcome: a critical apprisal of research. Ann. Intern. Med. 120 (1994) 135-142

15. Nicolosi, E., Molino, F., Molino, G. Computerized approach to active and objective quality control of patient care. Int. J. Biom. Comp. 42 (1996) 59-66

16. Nicklin, P., Frandji, B. Act Management and clinical guidelines. In: Gordon, C. and Christensen, J.P. (eds.): Health telematics for clinical guidelines and protocols. IOS Press (1995) 117- 124

17. Zielstorff, R.D. Online practice guidelines: issues, obstacles, and future prospects. JAMIA 5 (1998) 227-236

18. Duff, L. and Casey, A. Implementing clinical guidelines: how can information help?. JAMIA 5 (1998) 225-226

19. Patel, V.L., Allen, V.G., Arocha, J.F., Shortliffe, E.H. Representing clinical guidelines in GLIF: Individual and collaborative expertise. JAMIA 5 (1998) 467-483

20. Koran, L.M. The reliability of clinical methods, data and judgements. N. Engl. J. Med. 293 (1975) 642-646

21. Beeler, G.W., Gibbons, P.S. and Chute, C.G. Development of clinical data architecture. In Proceedings of 16th Annual Symposium on Computer Applications in Medical Care (SCAMC) (1992) 244-248

Artificial Intelligence for Building Learning Health Care Organizations

M. Stefanelli

Dipartimento di Informatica e Sistemistica, Università di Pavia
via Ferrata 1, I-27100 Pavia, Italy
mstefa@ipvstefa.unipv.it

Abstract. About thirty years of research in Artificial Intelligence in Medicine (AIM), together with a partial failure to disseminate AIM systems despite the significant progress in developing the underlying methodologies, has taught that AIM is not a field that can be separated from the rest of medical informatics and health economics. Since medicine is inherently an information-management task, effective decision-support systems are dependent on the development of integrated environments for communication and computing that allow merging of those systems with other patient data and resource management applications. The explosion of communication networks raised more recently another goal for AIM researchers: the full exploitation of those facilities require to model the organization where health care providers and managers work. This means that the AIM community has to acquire knowledge from other fundamental disciplines, as organization theory, sociology, ethnography, in order to exploit its modeling methodologies to represent behavior within an organization. It will allow the development of systems able to support collaborative work among everybody involved in patient care and organization management. A most promising approach is the exploitation of workflow management systems. They support the modeling and execution of workflows, which focus on the behavioral aspects of personnel involved in clinical processes. Workflow management systems provide tools for the design and implementation of innovative workflow-based Hospital Information Systems. This represents a great challenge for AIM researchers to prove that their theoretical background is essential to build those innovative systems.

1 Introduction

Information and Communication Technologies (ICT) offer society the opportunity to reengineering Health Care Organizations (HCO) into more value-driven, knowledge-based, and cost-effective enterprises. We are benefiting from astounding advances in medical knowledge and technology. At the same time many problems have to be faced by HCO even in developed countries: quality of care is very uneven and costs are rising. Citizens are unhappy with their care; health professionals are unhappy with

W. Horn et al. (Eds.): AIMDM'99, LNAI 1620, pp. 13-29, 1999.
© Springer-Verlag Berlin Heidelberg 1999

the HCO they are working in; payers are unhappy with costs; and governments react by enacting regulations that will fail to introduce any substantial change. Financial resources will never be enough to do all we would like to do. Biomedical research will produce better knowledge and treatments, but these results will be gradual and likely offset by increased demand by an aging society. ICT revolution and better management of HCO offer promise of dramatic help.

To attain this goal HCO must be able to exploit ICT to become learning organizations. Current theories of learning reveal that the process of acquiring knowledge cannot be separated from the process of applying it. Integrating working and learning is a fundamental requirement for HCO to increase the efficiency and effectiveness of their activities.

The integration of working and learning requires the development of tools to support these socially based process-oriented views of representations of work. In medicine representation of work may take many forms: patient record, instrumental and material resources, medical knowledge and expertise available within the organization, as well as the distribution of tasks among people involved in the management of different types of patients. Thus, patient management protocols provide models of medical processes, which can be enriched, by models of the organization to build models of patient workflows. These can be used as the core of Workflow Management Systems (WfMS) which provide a model-based communication infrastructure for health care professionals collaborating in patient management.

The great challenge for researchers in Artificial Intelligence in Medicine (AIM) is to exploit the astonishing capabilities of ICT to disseminate their tools to benefit HCO by assuring the conditions of organizational learning at the fullest extent possible. To do that the AIM community should activate new multidisciplinary research projects, based on mutual respect and willingness to integrate into its culture other disciplines, such as organizational science, sociology, and epistemology in order to design and develop decision support system smoothly integrated into a computer-supported collaborative work framework

This paper seeks to stir debate, discussion, and action towards new research issues within AIM research community.

2   History of Artificial Intelligence in Medicine

In 1992 P. Szolovits, the editor of the first book ever published on AIM, defined this new emerging field as resulting from the combination of sophisticated representations and computing techniques with the insights of expert physicians to produce tools for improving health care [27]. In the 1970s, AIM researchers dealt with research issues which were largely fundamental, such as knowledge representation, knowledge acquisition, causal reasoning, problem-solving methods, and uncertainty management. In the next decade the same issues received further attention, but it became to appear very clear that it was no longer possible to develop AIM research in isolation: the applied issues touch more generally on the broad field of medical informatics. In the late 80' and the early 90' AIM researchers were convinced that the advent of integrated information systems in health care would have paved the way for efficient implementation and fielding of decision support systems. Even in cases where the research project was shaped by careful ethnographic studies of the medical workplace, the practical difficulties in acquiring, filtering and entering clinical knowledge impeded the usability of the resulting decision support systems. Such difficulties were considered a convincing proof that AIM was a multifaceted, multidisciplinary field at the intersection of AI, computer science, biomedical engineering, medicine, and possibly many other disciplines.

Fielded AI systems in other areas of society have tended to be introduced in settings where employees are told by their supervisors that use of the system is part of their job. This is not the common situation in HCO where is still limited the number of settings where someone else can direct them to use a tool unless they want to do so. Most physicians resist such pressure, and it is not clear that external requirements for system use would be wise unless the value of the system can be documented: beside the clinical decision support the system must be used as a routinely to enhance collaboration and cooperation with other health care workers involved in the patient care management. Greenes and Shortliffe [17] stated this argument in a very clear way saying that physicians are 'horizontal' rather 'vertical' users of information technology. They will be attracted to computers when they are useful for every patient and when the metaphor for system use is consistent across the varied applications offered.

The limited success with dissemination of AIM systems is, in my view, due more to this failure of integration than it is to any basic problem with the AI technology that have been developed. Such an integration is not only a technical integration but mostly an organizational integration. To embed AIM systems into real work environments it is essential to combine medical with organizational knowledge. Until now, the largest effort done by AIM researchers was directed to the first issue. We must be aware that the second issue too is essential for dissemination of AIM systems. We must also be aware that the expertise we developed as a research community can be successfully used to accomplish such a complex task. I strongly feel that technology is ready while design and development methodology is still under development for building collaborative systems.

3   The Knowledge Society

One of the most evident consequences of the information society is that *our economic and social life is becoming more and more knowledge-driven*. Recent management literature illustrates this point speaking of: smart products, knowledge-based services, intelligent enterprise, knowledge workers, knowledge-intensive and learning organizations, the knowledge-based economy, knowledge society, etc.

Knowledge has thus come to be recognized and handled as a valuable entity in itself. It has been called *the ultimate intangible*. There are some estimates that intellectual capital now comprises typically 75-80% of the total balance sheet of companies. *Today, knowledge is a key enterprise asset.* This is true in general, but it is particularly true in case of HCO. Managing knowledge is therefore becoming a crucial everyday activity in modern organizations.

What is knowledge? A possible answer to this question can be given by defining what is the different meaning of three often-encountered words: data, information and knowledge [26]. Data are input signals to our sensory and cognitive processes, information is data with an associated meaning, while knowledge is the whole body of data and information together with cognitive machinery that people is able to exploit to decide how to act, to carry out tasks and to create new information.

In the area of the knowledge management, it has been pointed out that large part of knowledge is not explicit but tacit. Following Polanyi's epistemological investigation [23], tacit knowledge is characterized by the fact that it is personal, context specific, and therefore hard to formalize and communicate. Explicit, on the other hand, is the knowledge that is transmittable through any formal and systematic language. Polanyi contends that human beings acquire knowledge by actively creating and organizing their own experiences. Thus, explicit knowledge represent only the tip of the iceberg of the entire body of knowledge. As he puts it, "*We can know more than we can tell*".

Nonaka and Takeuchi [21] investigated the interaction between tacit and explicit knowledge concluding that they are not totally separate but mutually complementary entities. They interact and interchange into each other in the creative activities of human beings. Their dynamic model of knowledge creation is anchored to a critical assumption that human knowledge is created and expanded through social interaction between tacit and explicit knowledge. This process has been called *knowledge conversion*. This conversion is a social process between individuals and not confined within an individual. Nonaka and Takeuchi postulated four different modes of knowledge conversion [21]. They are as follows:

1) **Socialization** is from tacit knowledge to tacit knowledge,
2) **Externalization** is from tacit knowledge to explicit knowledge;
3) **Combination** is from explicit knowledge to explicit knowledge,
4) **Internalization** is from explicit knowledge to tacit knowledge.

The aim of knowledge management is to properly facilitate and stimulate these knowledge processes. The ultimate goal is that of converting as much as possible tacit into explicit knowledge.

Thus, knowledge management can be defined as a framework and a tool set for improving the organization's knowledge infrastructure, aiming at getting the right knowledge to the right people in the right form at the right time. Evidently, knowledge management is not a one-shot activity. It must be daily supported within an organization through the most appropriate methodologies and technologies to foster individual and collective learning within the organization [26].

4   Learning Organizations

Organizations are composed of multiple interacting communities, each with highly specialized knowledge, skills, and technologies. The execution of important tasks require these diverse communities to bridge their differences and integrate their knowledge and skills to create a new, shared perspective [5], that is to create knowledge according to Nonaka and Takeuchi [21].

This active process is often complicated by the fact that a community shared ontology, or domain model, is often tacit, making it uninspectable and difficult for another community to understand. Supporting such long-term, asynchronous collaboration is particularly important in knowledge intensive organizations. This requires systems able to support knowledge sharing across workplace communities and across time. However, sharing knowledge is different to simply sharing information: people need support for interpreting each others' perspective and for negotiating a new, shared perspective.

A learning organization, systematically defined, *is an organization, which learns powerfully, and collectively to better acquire, manage and use knowledge for improving productivity.* It empowers people within and outside the organization to learn as they work. Methodology and technology should be utilized to optimize both learning and productivity.

It is important to note the difference between the terms *learning organization* and the *organizational learning.* In discussing learning organizations, we are focusing on the *what,* and describing the systems, principles, and characteristics of organizations that learn and produce as a collective entity. Organizational learning, on the other hand, refers to *how* organizational learning occurs, i.e. the skills and processes of building and utilizing knowledge. Organizational learning as such is just one dimension or element of a learning organization.

5   Organizational Learning

Organizational learning should be thought in terms of the *organizational environments* within which individuals think and act. Organizations have been conceived as behavioral settings for human interaction, fields for the exercise of power, or systems of institutionalized incentives that govern individual behavior. From one or more of these perspectives, we may be able to describe the conditions under which the thought and action of individuals yield organizational learning. But such an approach still leaves us with the problem of linking individual to organizational learning.

We might consider solving this problem by treating organizational learning as the prerogative of a person at the top that learns for the organization as a whole. Alternatively, we might think of clusters of individual members as the agents who learn for the larger organization to which they belong. However, we are still left with the problem until we are not able of determining under what conditions the thought and action of individuals, independently of their power, role or number within the organization, become distinctively organizational.

Argyris and Schon [2] suggested that the idea of organizational action is logically prior to that of organizational learning: learning itself is a kind of action and the performance of an observable action new to an organization is the most decisive test of whether a particular instance of organizational learning has occurred.

Organizations are systems in which individuals cooperate to perform tasks that arise repetitively. Every cooperative system embodies a strategy for dividing up, according to one principle or another, the tasks it regularly performs and delegating the components to individual members, thereby establishing individual roles. The organization's *task system*, its pattern of interconnected roles, is at once a division of labor and a design for the performance of work.

An agency is a collection of people that make decisions, delegates authority for action, and monitor membership, all on a continuous basis. It is a collective vehicle for the regular performance of recurrent tasks. Since its members can act for it, then it may be said to learn when its members learn for it, carrying out on its behalf a process of inquiry that results in a learning product.

Under what conditions does knowledge become *organizational*? Two distinct but complementary answers to this question can be recognized.

First, organizations function in several ways as *holding environments for knowledge*. Such knowledge can be held in the minds of individual members. If it is held in only this way, it may be lost to the organization when the relevant individuals leave. But knowledge may also be held in an organization's files, which record its action, decisions, regulations, and policies as well as in the maps, formal and informal, through which organizations make themselves understandable to themselves and others.

Second, *organizations directly represent knowledge* in the sense that they embody strategies for performing complex tasks that might have been performed in other ways. This is true not only of an overall task system but also of its detailed components. Organizational knowledge is embedded in routines and practices which may be inspected and decoded even when individuals who carry out them out are unable to put them into words.

Such organizational task knowledge may be variously represented as systems of beliefs that underlie action, as prototypes from which actions are derived, or as procedural prescriptions for action in the manner of a computer program. We may choose to represent such knowledge through *guidelines or protocols that* provide a way of representing *theories of medical action*.

Organizational continuity would not be understandable if it depended exclusively on multiple, parallel, private imaging. When organizations are large and complex, their members cannot rely entirely on face-to-face contact to help them compare and adjust their private images of organizational theory-in-use. Even face-to-face contact, private images of organization often diverge. Individuals need external references to guide their private adjustments.

Such references functions are fulfilled by organizational memories. They include files, records, databases, and financial accounts, as well as physical objects (tools, products, or working materials) that hold organizational knowledge. Programs are procedural descriptions of organizational routines: they include work plans, policies, protocols, guidelines scripts, and templates. Artifacts such these describe existing patterns of activity and serve as guides to future action. Organization memories are motivated by the desire to preserve and share the knowledge and experiences that reside in an organization. As such, most systems focus on capturing the knowledge, storing it, and making it accessible, rather explicitly supporting the creation of new knowledge. By themselves, organizational memories are e necessary but insufficient step towards organizational learning.

By single-loop learning we mean a learning process that changes strategies of action or assumptions underlying strategies in ways that leave the values of a theory of action unchanged. In such learning episodes, a single feed-back loop, mediated by organizational inquiry, connects detected errors, that is an output of action mismatched to expectations and, therefore, surprising, to organizational strategies of action and their underlying assumptions. These strategies or assumptions are modified, in turn, to keep organizational performance within the range set by existing organizational values or norms. The values and norms themselves remain unchanged.

By double-loop learning, we mean a learning process that results in a change in the values of theory-in-use, as well as in its strategies and assumptions. This loop connects the observed effects of action with strategies and values served by strategies. Strategies and assumptions may change concurrently with, or as a consequence of, change in values.

Organizations continually engaged in transactions with their environments regularly carry out inquiry that takes the form of detection and correction of errors. Single-loop learning is sufficient where error correction can proceed by changing organizational strategies and assumptions within a constant framework of values and norms for performance. It is, therefore, concerned primarily with effectiveness: how best to achieve existing goals and objectives, keeping organizational performance within the range. In some cases, however, the correction of errors requires inquiry through which organizational values and norms themselves are modified, which is what we mean by organizational double-loop learning.

6   An Infrastructure Supporting Organizational Learning

Organizational learning depends on the HCO's ability to manage knowledge and to process information to support decision making. Those abilities determine the organization's *agility*, that is capacity to permanently understand new health demands from the society, quickly respond by introducing new biomedical technologies, therapies and services for the patients' health care. In HCO achieving this level of responsiveness interactions among individuals and groups will be managed by dialogue and negotiation, relations will predominantly become peer-to-peer rather than hierarchical and knowledge will be more important than rank. To achieve this sort of organization, collaborative information systems are essential ingredients that help with providing access to information, support decision making and aid in action execution.

Roboam and Fox [24] noticed that such systems span multiple levels from the hardware/software platform to the high-level knowledge-based problem solving activities. They distinguished the following layers.

- *Network communication layer*: it is concerned with providing services for interconnecting heterogeneous equipment and resources.
- *Data related support services layer*: it provides the capabilities to request and send information from/to the nodes of the HCO network.
- *Knowledge and information distribution layer*: it provides services for knowledge and information sharing among the nodes of the HCO network.
- *Organization layer*: it models the structure, goals, roles etc. that define the position of nodes in the HCO network.
- *Coordination layer*: it is concerned with the high level knowledge based problem solving systems used by the nodes to support their problem solving activities.

The development of an information infrastructure along these lines is of course a long-range goal. AIM researchers should play their fundamental role by exploiting agent-based technology to provide suitable solution to the design and development of the knowledge and information distribution and coordination layers.

Agents are software components that support the construction of distributed information systems as collection of autonomous entities that interact according to complex and dynamic patterns of behavior. Although the notion of agent is still debated, there exist clear aspects that distinguish agents from other current models of software systems.

7   Workflows and Workflow Management Systems

While medical processes describe the activities of a medical team in a comprehensive manner for the purpose of defining the most effective and efficient patients' management, *workflows* focus on the behavioral aspects of medical work with regard to a possible support of their execution through information technology. A workflow is an activity involving the coordinated execution of multiple tasks performed by different processing entities [19].

The Workflow Management Coalition (WfMC) defined a basic set of workflows' building blocks: activities to execute tasks, transitions between activities, participants and application performing activities, and workflow relevant data [28]. These building blocks allow us to specify medical processes in terms of complex nets of activities designed to achieve the main goal of the best medical practice.

Workflows can be decomposed hierarchically in sub-workflows. Activities may be assigned to one or more *agents*. They may be health care professionals, machines, and computers, but also organizational units or roles. There are manual and automated activities. Human agents perform manual and partly automated activities, while computers execute automated activities in the form of application programs.

Workflow management is the automated coordination, control and communication of work, as it is required to satisfy workflow process. A *Workflow Management System* (WfMS) is a set of tools providing support for the necessary service of workflow creation (which includes its formal representation), workflow enactment, administration and monitoring of workflow processes. The developer of a workflow application relies on tools for the specification of a workflow process and the data it manipulates. These tools cooperate closely with the workflow repository service, which stores workflow definitions. The workflow process is based on a formalized workflow model that is used to capture data and control flow between workflow tasks. Several formalisms can be exploited to build a workflow model. The use of *high-level Petri nets* [18] seems very promising for modeling and analyzing clinical processes. Petri nets have proven to be useful in the context of logistics and production control. However, the application of these Petri nets is not restricted to logistics and manufacturing, they can also be used to support business process reeingineering efforts. High-level Petri nets extend the classical Petri net model with *"color"*, *"time"* and *"hierarchy"*. These extensions are essential for representing clinical processes. The high-level Petri nets inherit the advantages of the classical Petri nets, such as the graphical representation, the sound mathematical foundation and the abundance of analysis methods. An alternative approach is to build an *"information-centered"* model instead of a *"process-centered"* model. Structural contingency theory and the literature that has developed from it on organizational design is one of the most promising theoretical approaches to understanding organizational performance [22]. Among the various derivatives of contingency theory, organization theorists have used the information processing view of organizational behavior in a broad range of domains. A HCO can be modeled as an information processing and decision making machine: the process model describes the tasks that generate the information and the health care professionals are the agents that process and use that information. The agents are linked through a communication infrastructure and work within an organizational framework that constrains their behavior [11]. To model HCO we need to integrate the two approaches into a unified modeling framework.

The workflow enactment service (including a workflow manager and the workflow runtime system) consists of execution-time components that provide the execution environment. Administrative and monitoring tools are used for the management of user and work group roles, defining policies, audit management, process monitoring, tracking, and reporting of data generated during workflow enactment.

Workflow technology has matured to some extent, and current products are able to support a range of applications. Nevertheless, a majority of the workflow products are directed towards supporting ad-hoc or administrative workflows that serve us office automation types of applications, and primarily involve human tasks supported through forms-based interface.

Support for medical workflows is today limited to more repetitive processes, that is care delivery processes to similar patients. In such a case a guideline or a protocol can suitably describe the process. Many limitations remain to support more demanding applications and to provide a better support of health care professionals' work. Two main issues require to be addressed by workflow technology: support for scalability and support for adaptable and dynamic workflows. There may be a wide range of events or conditions to which the workflows and a WfMS may need to adapt to, including the reasons of exceptions handling and load balancing.

7.1   Web Based Workflow Systems

Most existing WfMS provide very good support for process engineering but limited support for process execution, often requiring additional proprietary desktop applications with limited platform availability. Unfortunately, process engineering cannot be effective unless the results are accessible to the people who must carry out the process. Web based WfMS provide a process mediation service using tools that most users already have and know how to use. Users interact with the system using their Web browser to retrieve a list of tasks for which they are currently responsible. The system may use email and pagers to notify people when they need to do something.

Many productivity applications are emerging on organizations' Intranets, and more are being developed. A Web based WfMS is designed to interoperate seamlessly with Intranet applications. It should allow workflow management to be added to pre-existing data and information management systems without requiring significant modifications to the underlying system.

7.2   Workflow-Based Hospital Information Systems

WfMS provide a new point of view in the design of Hospital Information Systems (HIS). They offer significant advantages [15].

- They enhance the degree of automation in hospitals, because they include manual, partially or fully automated activities in a comprehensive manner.
- Workflow-based HIS may be adapted to changes more easily than conventional HIS. This is the result of the separation between the workflow model and the workflow execution. Changing the former causes changing the latter exactly as in the knowledge-based systems.
- Workflow-based HIS make easier integrating legacy systems in a heterogeneous application environment. Instead of replacing legacy systems or using them in isolation, the workflow approach enables an evolutionary migration strategy: with no or minor changes in the interfaces the activities of the legacy systems may still be used, if they are "wrapped".

8   Knowledge Representation

The effective introduction of ICT in HCO requires the integration of knowledge, expertise and skills from three different domains: medical, organizational and technological domain [1].

By medical domain knowledge we mean any representation of medical work as a set of activities that result from the interaction between patients and heath care professionals. They may be physicians, nurses and any other allied health professional, while medical work is not restricted to activities taking place in a hospital or any other intramural HCO.

Professionals do their work in an organizational setting: their work depend on the material and financial resources made available through the organization they work in. There are rules, regulations, and laws, but also unwritten codes and practices that determine the professionals' behavior in an organization.

The sociological understanding of these complex practices is essential to hope to introduce successfully information and communication technologies into HCO [4]. They represent the third piece of the puzzle we need to compose to build a HIS. We consider all the technologies that support medical work in practice to belong to that domain, whether they are the most advanced decision support systems or more clerical systems.

The above mentioned three domains should integrate each other to obtain the best possible results in patients' care delivery. Berg writes *"that the work of medical personnel is rewritten in the light of the tool and vice versa"* [3].

People must communicate and collaborate within an organization, directly or through IT systems. However, due to different needs and background contexts, there can be varying viewpoints and assumptions regarding what is essentially the same subject matter. The way to address this lack of a *"shared understanding"* is to reduce or eliminate conceptual and terminological confusion. This allows the creation *of* a *"unifying framework"* for the different viewpoints and serves as a basis for communication between people and inter-operability among systems.

Ontology is the term used to refer to the shared understanding which may be used as the unifying framework. An ontology necessarily entails or embodies some sort of worldview with respect to a given domain. The worldview is often conceived as a set of concepts (e.g. entities, attributes, and processes), their definitions and their inter-relationships: this is referred as a *"conceptualization"*. Such a conceptualization may be implicit; e.g. existing in someone's head, or embodied in a piece of software. Shared conceptualizations include conceptual frameworks for modeling domain knowledge; content-specific protocols for communication among inter-operating agents; and agreements about the representation of particular domain theories. Even if the word ontology is sometimes used to refer to the former, the more standard usage and that which we will adopt is that ontology is an explicit account or representation of a conceptualization.

An important motivation for the use of ontologies is to integrate models of different domains into a coherent framework. This arises in business process reengineering (where we need an integrated model of the enterprise and its processes, its organizations, its goals and its customers), multi-agent architectures (where different agents need to communicate and solve problems), and concurrent engineering and design.

8.1   Medical Knowledge

AIM researchers developed a great expertise in representing medical knowledge. These efforts were aimed at building decision support systems to solve knowledge intensive medical tasks. The user-system interaction was considered the main issue to guarantee their dissemination within HCO. However, too little attention was devoted to modeling the overall medical process where single medical tasks are embedded and the collaborative work of many highly skilled professionals, nurses, physicians and other care providers, is requested to pursue the ultimate institutional goal: the delivery of the most effective patient care. Social pressures are driving HCO to increase productivity and reduce costs, while maintaining, or even increasing, the quality of patient care. As in other organizations, development of standards of practice has been used as one method to achieve these goals. There have been significant efforts to define guidelines and protocols to reduce practical variability and to improve the quality of patient care [9]. In many cases, these methods of standardizing medical practices have been successful [7]. Although the words *"guidelines"* and *"protocols"* are often used interchangeably, there are practical differences between them that are useful. Guidelines have been defined as *"systematically developed statements to assist practitioner and patient decisions about appropriate health care for specific clinical circumstances"* [9]. Like guidelines, protocols include information relevant to decisions, but include other kinds of activities as well, such as randomization procedures for informed consent, quality assurance procedures, scheduling patients procedures and so on. In general, protocols represent the final stage of adopting a centrally developed guideline to best practice for local use [14].

Yet systematic reviews have shown that the mere existence of these guidelines or protocols does not necessarily lead to changes in practice [16]. Certainly, if clinicians are unaware of best practice, they cannot implement them; and if they haven't been convinced of their utility, they will not use them. These are goals to be pursued by the medical community. However, there are goals for the AIM community: to increase the power of formal representations of practice guideline taking into account complexity, flexibility and uncertainty management needs and to make them online available to the right person at the right time during her daily work [13].

The most sophisticated form of online guideline or protocols is to today when they are embedded in a computer-based patient record system. In this situation, programmed rules derived from them operate in the background. The rules are triggered by patient data; when necessary data unavailable in the record are sought from the patient record system and patient-specific recommendations are provided to the health care provider. There are only very examples of this advanced form of guideline-based or protocol-based decision support. However, a step forward needs to be done: a practice guideline or a protocol must be viewed and used as a representation of a medical process. Hence they may represent the core of a WfMS able to improve collaboration and communication between all the health care professionals involved in patient care delivery. In such a way also HCO administrators are enabled to properly manage resources allocation and utilization to achieve institutional goals.

Two main problems for guidelines or protocols dissemination and utilization still require considerable research efforts: making them site-specific and managing exceptions.

National guidelines or protocols invariably will require some modification to be useful within a particular clinical setting [12]. How their representation will make easier their adaptation to specific organization and which will be the performance of modified guidelines or protocols within a particular clinical setting are still fundamental research issues. In some instances, guidelines or protocols developed to improve patient care and reduce costs may create additional and unanticipated problems when they are used within a specific organization. This suggests that there can be problems, specific to a particular organization, that can affect the effectiveness of a guideline or a protocol and that cannot be predicted by the population-level analysis. These organization specific problems are related to the process of medical care and can affect the cost and the quality of medical outcomes of patients treated following these guidelines.

One such problem that has been recognized is increased demands for coordination and communication in health care. Nationally developed medical guidelines or protocols are designed for a hypothetical, ideal organization in which all activities are completed without exception, all patients respond in categorical ways, and all interactions within the organization are seamlessly coordinated. Most medical guidelines or protocols do not consider the additional burden imposed by communication, problem resolution, and coordination between organization participants. Exceptions need to be resolved, activities need to be coordinated with other activities to share a common goal, and resources and organizational limitations addressed. The time and cost involved with this coordination is a hidden cost to the organization, and can result in unpredictable results when guidelines or protocols are implemented within the organization.

8.2 Organizational Knowledge

Organizations are diverse and complex, and so it may be useful to adopt a simplifying model focusing on their basic elements. According to the model proposed by Leavitt [20] and adapted later by Scott [25], we can consider the following basic components.

- *Social structure* refers to the relationships existing among participants in the organization. It can be separated into two components. The first component can be called the *'normative structure'*: it includes values, norms, and role expectations. Values are the criteria employed in selecting the goals of the behavior; norms are the generalized rules governing behavior that specify, in particular, appropriate means for pursuing goals; and roles are expected behaviors of participants given their position in the social structure. The second component focuses on the actual participants' behavior, rather than on prescriptions for behavior. Thus, it can be called *'behavioral structure'* and can be represented in terms of activities and interactions. The social structure of an organization varies in the extent to which it is formalized. A formal structure is one in which the social positions and the relationships among them have been explicitly specified and are defined independently of the personal characteristics of the participants occupying these positions.

- *Participants o social actors* are those individuals who contribute to the organization.
- *Goals* may be defined as representations of desired ends, conditions that participants attempt to effect through the performance of task activities.
- *Technologies* consist in part of material resources and equipment but also comprise the domain knowledge and skills of participants.

We can now adopt the following definition of a HCO taking a *'rational system'* perspective: *HCO are 'collectivities oriented to the pursuit of relatively specific health prevention and/or management goals and exhibiting relatively highly formalized structures'*. They are *'purposeful'* in the sense that the activities and interactions of participants are coordinated to achieve specific goals. Goals are specific to the extent they are explicit, are clearly defined, and provide unambiguous criteria for selecting among alternative activities. The cooperation among participants is *'conscious'* and *'deliberate'*; the structure of relations is made explicit and can be *'deliberately constructed and reconstructed'*. A structure is *'formalized'* to the extent that the rules governing behavior are precisely and explicitly formulated and to the extent that roles and role relations are prescribed independently of the personal attributes of individuals occupying positions in the structure.

Thus, to model HCO we need to represent all these elements in some formal way, that is to build an organizational model. Which are its basic entities? We should consider that an organization could be represented through a set of constraints on the activities performed by agents. In particular, an organization consists of a set of divisions and subdivision (recursive definition), a set of organizational agents (said to be member of a division of the organization), a set of roles that the member play in the organization, and an organization goal tree that specifies the goals (and their decomposition into subgoals) the members are trying to achieve.

An agent plays one or more roles. Each role is defined by the goal set that it must fulfill. Each role is also given enough authority to achieve its goals. Agents perform activities in the organizations and consume resources (such as materials, labors, or tools). The constraint set limits to the agent activities. An agent can also be a member of a team created to perform a special task. Moreover an agent has skill requirement and a set of communication links defining the protocol with which it communicates with other agents in the organization.

Although some very promising projects developed an enterprise model [10], only preliminary work has been done specifically for HCO. Falasconi and Stefanelli [8] built a rich model for this purpose which may represent a basis for further research in a large cooperative effort involving the whole AIM community.

9   Conclusions

Clinical knowledge explicitly represented, as well as the organizational knowledge, almost always tacit, represent the core asset for the third millennium HCO. If people are an asset then effective people management is an asset too.

HCO are now facing new fundamental problems. How information and communication technologies can be effectively used to exploit the institutional intellectual capital? Intellectual capital is the term given to the combined intangible assets which enable the HCO to function [6]. It can be split into four categories:

- Care delivery services assets;
- Intellectual skills assets;
- Human-centered assets;
- Infrastructure assets.

Care delivery services assets are the potential a HCO has due to society health demands. They are important because they give a HCO a competitive advantage in acquiring resources, both private and public, to pursue its institutional goals. Intellectual skill assets include medical and professional knowledge of HCO participants. What is essential is to guarantee its continuous acquisition from medical sciences development and its immediate utilization for increasing the quality and clinical efficacy of delivered care. Human-centered assets comprise the collective expertise, creative and problem solving capabilities, leadership, entrepreneurial and managerial skills embodied by the participants of the organization. Human are expensive to hire, train and sustain. As they become proficient and then excel in their employment, they learn more and become more valuable. But knowledge in the head of the individual belongs to the person – not to the organization. So it's important to understand the skills, knowledge and expertise of the individual in order to know how and why someone is valuable and what role they should play within the organization. The optimal position for the organization is to be able to derive maximum benefit from an individual being working within the organization. Infrastructure assets are those technologies, methodologies and processes which enable the organization to function. But we are not talking about the value of the tangibles which comprise the computer systems, the communication networks, the bio-medical instruments and so on, but the way in which they are used in the organization. A good example is the Internet. Its use is free. It also doesn't belong to anyone, so it won't appear on anyone's balance sheet. However, the ability to use the Internet, for example, to deliver new home care services means the potential for the organization to be more effective in achieving its goals. Therefore the Internet may become an asset. Infrastructure assets are important because they bring order, safety, correctness and quality to the organization. They also provide a context for the participants of the organization to work and communicate with each other. Marketing the value of infrastructure assets to the individual within the organization is important, in order to ensure they understand what they are supposed to do in given situations and how they contribute to the achievement of corporate goals. However, infrastructure assets should not be perceived as law and must change and bend to reflect changes in the market and workplace. Organizations, which do not regularly question the value and effectiveness of infrastructure assets, lose the edge which make them win.

Acknowledgements

This work is partially funded by the **European Union** through the project **PatMan** (Patient Management) within the *Health Care Telematics Applications Programme*.

References

1. Aarts, J., Peel, V., Wright, G.: Organizational Issues in Health Informatics: a Model Approach. *International Journal of Medical Informatics* **52** (1998) 235-242.
2. Argyris, C., Shon, D.: Organizational Learning II.   Addison Wesley, Reading, MA (1996).
3. Berg M.: Rationalizing Medical Work-decision Support Techniques and Medical Practices. Cambridge. MIT Press, Cambridge, MA (1997).
4. Berg, M., Langerberg, C., Berg, I.V.D., Kwakkernaat, J.: Considerations for Sociotechnical Design: Experiences with an Electronic Patient Record in a Clinical Context. *International Journal of Medical Informatics* **52** (1998) 243-251.
5. Boland, R., Tenkasi, R.: Perspective Making and Perspective Taking in Communities of Knowing. *Organization Science* **6** (1995) 350-372.
6. Brooking, A.: Intellectual Capital. International Thomson Business Press, London (1996).
7. Ellrodt A.G., Conner, L., Ridinger, M., Weingarten, S.: Measuring and Improving Physician Compliance with Clinical Practice Guidelines: a Controlled Interventional Trial. *Annals of Internal Medicine* **122** (1995) 277-282.
8. Falasconi S., Dazzi, L., Lanzola, G., Quaglini, S., Saracco, R, Stefanelli, M.: Towards Cooperative Patient Management through Organizational and Medical Ontologies. *Methods of Information in Medicine* **37** (1998) 564-575.
9. Field, M.J, Lohr, K.N. (eds.): Clinical Practice Guidelines: Directions for a New Program. IOM Report. National Academy Press, Washington D.C. (1990).
10. Fox, M.S., Gruninger, M.: Enterprise Modeling. *AI Magazine,* Fall (1998) 109-121.
11. Fridsma, D.B.: Representing the Work of Medical Protocols for Organization Simulation. In: Chute, C.G. (ed.): Proceedings of the Annual Fall Symposium of the American Medical Informatics Association (AMIA). Hanley and Belfus, Philadelphia, PE. (1998).
12. Fridsma, D.B., Gennari J., Musen, M.: Making Protocols Site-specific. In: Cimino, J. (ed.): AMIA Fall Symposium. Hanley and Belfus, Philadelphia, PE. (1996).
13. Fridsma, D.B., Thomsen, J.: Representing Medical Protocols for Organization Simulation: an information processing approach. *Computational and Mathematical Organization Theory* (1999) (to appear).
14. Gordon, C.: Practice Guideline and Health Care Telematics: Towards an Alliance. In: C. Gordon, C., Christensen, J.P. (eds.): Health Telematics for Clinical Guidelines and Protocols. IOS Press, Washington, D.C. (1995).
15. Graeber, S.: The Impact of Workflow Management Systems on the Design of Hospital Information Systems. In: D.R. Masys, D.R. (ed.): Proceedings of the Annual Fall Symposium of the American Medical Informatics Association (AMIA). Hanley&Belfus, Philadelphia, PE. (1997).

16. Greco P.J., Eisenberg, J.M: Changing Physicians' Practices, *New England Journal of Medicine* **321** (1993) 1306-1311.
17. Grenees, R.A., Shortliffe, E.H.: Medical Informatics: an Emerging Academic Discipline and Institutional Priority. *JAMA*, 263, (1990) 1114-1120.
18. Jensen, K., Rozenberg, G. (eds.). High-level Petri Nets: Theory and Applications. Springer-Verlag, New York, N.Y. (1992).
19. Krishnakumar N. and A. Sheth, A.: Managing Heterogeneous Multi-system Tasks to Support Enterprise-wide Operations. *Distributed and Parallel Databases* **3** (1995) 155-186.
20. Leavitt, H.: Applied Organizational Change in Industry: Structural, Technological and Humanistic Approaches. In: March, J. (ed.): Handbook of Organizations, Rand McNally, Chicago, MI (1995).
21. Nonaka, I., Takeuchi, H.: The Knowledge-Creating Company. University Press, Oxford, U.K. (1995).
22. Pfeffer J.: Understanding Organizations: Concepts and Controversies. Research Paper No. 1378. Stanford Graduate School of Business (1996).
23. Polanyi, M.: The Tacit Dimension. Routledge & Kegan Paul, London (1996).
24. Roboam, M., Fox, M.S.: Enterprise Management Network Architecture, a Tool for Manufactoring Enterprise Integration. Artificial Intelligence Applications in Manufactoring, AAAI Press/MIT Press, Cambridge, MA (1992).
25. Scott, W. R.: Organizations: Rational, Natural and Open Systems. Prentice-Hall, Englewood Cliffs, N.J. (1992).
26. Schreiber A. Th., Akkermans, J.M., Anjerwierden, A.A., de Hoog, R., Shadbolt, N.R., Van de Velde, W., Wielinga, B.J.: Engineering and Managing Knowledge, the CommonKADS Methodology (1999) (to appear).
27. Szolovits, P. (ed.): Artificial Intelligence in Medicine. AAAS Selected Symposia Series. Westview Press, Boulder, CO (1992).
28. Workflow Management Coalition. Interface 1: Process Definition Language (TC-1016). WfMC: Brussels (1996).

Timing Is Everything: Temporal Reasoning and Temporal Data Maintenance in Medicine

Yuval Shahar

Stanford Medical Informatics
Medical School Office Building x215, 251 Campus Drive
Stanford University, Stanford, CA 94305-5479
shahar@smi.stanford.edu

Abstract. Both clinical management of patients and clinical research are essentially time-oriented endeavors. In this paper, I emphasize the crucial role of *temporal-reasoning* and *temporal-maintenance* tasks for modern medical information and decision support systems. Both tasks are important for management of clinical data, but the first is often approached mainly through artificial-intelligence methodologies, while the other is usually investigated by the database community. However, both tasks require careful consideration of common theoretical issues, such as the structure of time. In addition, common to both of these research areas are tasks such as temporal abstraction and management of variable temporal granularity. Finally, both tasks are highly relevant for applications such as patient monitoring, support to application of therapy guidelines, assessment of the quality of guideline application, and visualization and exploration of time-oriented biomedical data. I propose that integration of the two areas should be a major research and development goal. I demonstrate one integration approach by presenting a new architecture, a *temporal mediator*, which combines temporal reasoning and temporal maintenance, and integrates the management of clinical databases and medical knowledge bases. I present and discuss examples of using the temporal mediator for several of the application areas mentioned. I conclude by reemphasizing the importance of effective knowledge *representation*, knowledge *reuse*, and knowledge *sharing* methods to medical decision support systems in general, and to time-oriented systems in particular.

1. Introduction: Time in Medical Care and Medical Research

It is almost inconceivable to represent clinical data and reason about them without a temporal dimension. Clinical interventions must occur at one or more time points (e.g., appendectomy performed *on March 17 1998*) or over periods (e.g., chemotherapy administered *from April 3 1994 to May 25 1994*). Similarly, patient characteristics and measurements (such as laboratory test results, physical examinations, or a diagnosis) have to hold during time points or time periods (e.g., high fever in the evenings *from December 11 1997 to December 14 1997*). Various qualitative and quantitative temporal relationships (e.g., high fever occurring *after* mumps immunization) can exist between measurements and/or interventions.

W. Horn et al. (Eds.): AIMDM'99, LNAI 1620, pp. 30-46, 1999.
© Springer-Verlag Berlin Heidelberg 1999

From the point of view of medical information systems, time is important for representing information within an electronic medical-record system, for querying medical records, and for reasoning about time-oriented clinical data as part of various decision-support applications, such as diagnosis, therapy, and browsing of electronic patient records for management or research purposes. Representing, querying, and reasoning about time-oriented clinical data is equally important for care providers who need certain information about one or more patient records as it is for automated decision support systems. For instance, during the treatment of a patient by an experimental chemotherapy protocol, either the care provider or an intelligent therapy-support system might need to refer a complex temporal query to the patient's record. Such a query might ask whether the patient had more than two episodes of bone-marrow toxicity of grade II or more (as defined in the context of the experimental protocol), each lasting at least 3 weeks, within the past 8 months. Major examples of tasks that depend heavily on such access to time-oriented data and their interpretations include patient monitoring, management of patients using therapy guidelines, and interactive visualization and exploration of longitudinal patient data.

It useful to distinguish, at least conceptually, between two research directions, distinct with respect to their focus and the research communities pursuing them, that are relevant to the temporal dimension: (1) **Temporal reasoning (TR)**, which supports various inference tasks involving time-oriented clinical data, such as therapy planning and execution, and traditionally has been linked with the artificial-intelligence community, and (2) **temporal data maintenance (TM)** which deals with storage and retrieval of clinical data that have heterogeneous temporal dimensions, and typically is associated with the (temporal) database community. Figure 1 shows a typical conceptual structure for TR and TM modules in a time-oriented clinical decision-support system.

Unfortunately, the TR and TM research communities have been quite separate conceptually and physically, although there is recent progress. However, several themes common to both communities can be readily noted. For example, the necessity for *temporal data modeling* is recognized in both research areas: Without due attention to the time model underlying any framework, data can be neither maintained nor reasoned with. Furthermore, certain tasks are common to both research areas, such as the *abstraction* or aggregation of time-stamped data into meaningful interval-based concepts, and the handling of *variable temporal granularity*.

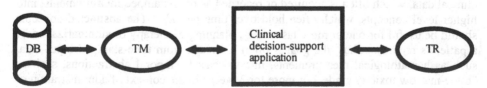

Fig. 1. Typical relationship of time-oriented computational modules in a clinical decision-support system. DB = patient electronic database; TM = temporal data-maintenance module; TR = temporal-reasoning module.

I will argue that there are sufficient similar goals and common grounds to justify an effort for integration of TR and TM in medical information systems, and furthermore, that such an integration is quite feasible. I will also argue for the importance of disciplined representation of knowledge about time-oriented data, in particular in the knowledge-intensive medical domains, as part of this enterprise, and for the importance of the facilitation of the maintenance, sharing, and reuse of such knowledge.

1.1 Structure of the Paper

In Section 2, I focus on the TR area by examining one of its major tasks: The temporal-abstraction task. In Section 3, I discuss the importance of TM. In Section 4, I emphasize the importance of integration of TR and TM in medical decision support systems, and present an architecture that is being developed to address that need, namely, a temporal mediator. In Section 5, I discuss several applications that use the temporal mediator. Section 6 concludes the paper.

2.   Temporal Reasoning: The Temporal-Abstraction Task

Most clinical tasks require measurement and capture of numerous patient data, often on electronic media. Physicians who have to make diagnostic or therapeutic decisions based on these data may be overwhelmed by the number of data if the physicians' ability to *reason* with the data does not scale up to the data-storage capabilities. Most stored data include a time stamp in which the particular datum was valid; an emerging pattern over a stretch of time has much more significance than an isolated finding or even a set of findings. Experienced physicians are able to combine several significant contemporaneous findings, to abstract such findings into clinically meaningful higher-level concepts in a context-sensitive manner, and to detect significant trends in both low-level data and abstract concepts.

In many clinical domains, a final diagnosis is not always the main goal of data abstraction. What is often needed is a coherent intermediate-level interpretation of the relationships between data and events, and among data, especially when the overall context (e.g., a major diagnosis) is known. The goal is then to abstract the clinical data, which often is acquired or recorded as time-stamped measurements, into higher-level concepts, which often hold over time periods. The abstracted concepts should be useful for one or more tasks (e.g., planning of therapy or summarization of a patient's record). Thus, the goal is often to create, from time-stamped input data, such as hematological measurements, interval-based temporal abstractions, such as "bone-marrow toxicity grade 2 or more for 3 weeks in the context of administration of a prednisone/azathioprine protocol for treating patients who have chronic graft-versus-host disease, and complication of bone-marrow transplantation" and more complex patterns, involving several intervals (Figure 2). We call that task the **temporal-abstraction task**. (The term "temporal abstraction" is somewhat misleading, it is the time-oriented data, and not the time itself, which are being abstracted.)

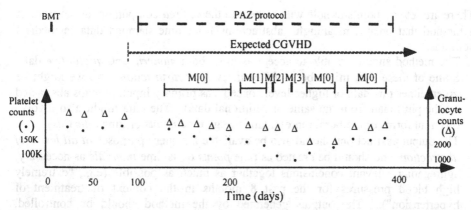

Fig. 2. Temporal abstraction of platelet and granulocyte values during administration of a prednisone/azathioprine (PAZ) clinical protocol for treating patients who have chronic graft-versus-host disease (CGVHD). Raw data are plotted over time at the bottom. External events and the abstractions computed from the data are plotted as intervals above the data. BMT = a bone-marrow transplantation event; PAZ = a therapy protocol for treating chronic graft-versus-host disease (CGVHD), a complication of BMT; ⊢ ⊣ = event; • = platelet counts; Δ = granulocyte counts; ⊢——▶ = context interval; ⊢⊣ = abstraction interval; M[n] = bone-marrow–toxicity grade n.

The ability to automatically create interval-based abstractions of time-stamped clinical data has multiple implications:

1. *Data summaries* of time-oriented electronic data, such as patient medical records, have an immediate value to a human user, such as to a physician scanning a long patient record for meaningful trends [1].
2. Temporal abstractions support *recommendations* by intelligent decision-support systems, such as diagnostic and therapeutic systems [2].
3. Abstractions support *monitoring* of plans (e.g., therapy plans) during execution of these plans (e.g., application of clinical guidelines [3]).
4. Meaningful time-oriented contexts enable generation of *context-specific abstractions*, maintenance of *several interpretations* of the same data within different contexts, and certain hindsight and foresight inferences [4].
5. Temporal abstractions are helpful for *explanation* of recommended actions by an intelligent system.
6. Temporal abstractions are a useful representation for the process and outcome intentions of designers of clinical guidelines, and enable real time and retrospective critiquing and quality assessment of the application of these guidelines by care providers [5].
7. Domain-specific, meaningful, interval-based characterizations of time-oriented medical data are a prerequisite for effective *visualization* and dynamic exploration of these data by care providers [6]. Visualization and exploration of information in general, and of large amounts of time-oriented medical data in particular, is essential for effective decision making. Examples include visualization of periodic patterns in clinical data, and deciding whether a certain therapeutic action has been effective. Different types of care providers require access to different types of time-oriented data, which might be distributed over multiple databases.

There are several points to note with respect to the *desired* computational behavior of a method that creates meaningful abstractions from time-stamped data in medical domains:

1. The method should be able to accept as input both *numeric* and *qualitative* data. Some of these data might be at *different levels of abstraction* (i.e., we might be given either raw data or higher-level concepts as primary input, perhaps abstracted by the physician from the same or additional data). The data might also involve different forms of temporal representation (e.g., time *points* or time *intervals*).

2. The output abstractions should also be available for query purposes *at all levels of abstraction*, and should be created as time *points* or as time *intervals* as necessary, aggregating relevant conclusions together as much as possible (e.g., "extremely high blood pressures for the past 8 months in the context of treatment of hypertension"). The outputs generated by the method should be controlled, sensitive to the goals of the abstraction process for the task at hand (e.g., only particular types of output might be required). The output abstractions should also be sensitive to the context in which they were created.

3. Input data should be used and incorporated in the interpretation even if they arrive *out of temporal order* (e.g., a laboratory result from last Tuesday arrives today). Thus, the past can change our view of the present. This phenomenon has been called a **view update** [7]. Furthermore, new data should enable us to reflect on the past; thus, the present (or future) can change our interpretation of the past, a property referred to as **hindsight** [8].

4. Several possible interpretations of the data might be reasonable, each depending on additional factors that are perhaps unknown at the time (such as whether the patient has AIDS); interpretation should be specific to the context in which it is applied. All reasonable interpretations of the same data relevant to the task at hand should be available automatically or upon query.

5. The method should leave room for some *uncertainty* in the input and the expected data *values*, and some uncertainty in the *time* of the input or the expected temporal pattern.

6. The method should be generalizable to other clinical domains and tasks. The domain-specific assumptions underlying it should be explicit and as declarative as possible (as opposed to procedural code), so as to enable *reuse* of the method without rebuilding the system, *acquisition* of the necessary knowledge for applying it to other domains, *maintenance* of that knowledge, and *sharing* that knowledge with other applications in the same domain.

One example of a temporal-abstraction framework is the **knowledge-based temporal-abstraction (KBTA) method** [9]. The KBTA method decomposes the temporal-abstraction task into five subtasks; a formal mechanism is proposed for solving each subtask. The five temporal-abstraction mechanisms depend on four domain-specific **knowledge types**: structural, classification (functional), temporal-semantic (logical), and temporal-dynamic (probabilistic) knowledge. Domain values for all knowledge types are specified when a temporal-abstraction system is developed. An example of temporal-semantic knowledge is that, unlike two anemia periods, two episodes of 9-month pregnancies can never be summarized as an episode of an 18-month pregnancy—even if they followed each other—since they are not *concatenable*, a temporal-semantic property.

The KBTA framework emphasizes the explicit representation of the knowledge required for abstraction of time-oriented clinical data, and facilitates its acquisition, maintenance, reuse, and sharing. The KBTA method has been implemented by the **RÉSUMÉ** system and evaluated in several clinical domains, such as guideline-based care of oncology and AIDS patients, monitoring of children's growth, and management of patients who have insulin-dependent diabetes [7].

The KBTA method proposes particular **ontology** (a theory of concepts and relations among them) of time, time-oriented objects, and temporal-reasoning knowledge. Another example of such a general ontology is Keravnou's **time-object ontology** for medical tasks [10].

Other approaches have been applied to the task of abstraction of time-oriented medical data into higher-level concepts [11; 1; 12; 13; 8; 14; 15; 16]. Most approaches, however, do not emphasize the need for a formal representation that facilitates acquisition, maintenance, sharing, and reuse of the required temporal-abstraction knowledge. Such an emphasis, however, is essential for the widespread dissemination and maintenance of time-oriented medical decision-support systems.

3. Maintenance of Time-Oriented Medical Data

For any realistic decision support system, it is not sufficient to be capable of reasoning about time-oriented medical data. It is also necessary to be able to effectively and efficiently store and retrieve the time-oriented data.

Initially, systems that were designed to manage time-oriented clinical data were based on the flat relational model. These systems were based on stamping the database tuples with the appropriate time stamp. Thus, the date of the patient's visit was added to the specific attribute values. Later work has proposed the use of specific temporal-query languages for clinical data that are structured by a temporal-network model. Even though such languages were oriented to individual patient records and were not based on a generic data model, they were early attempts to address the need for an extension of query languages so as to enable the system to retrieve complex temporal properties of stored data. Most query languages and data models used for clinical data management were application-dependent; thus, developers had to provide ad-hoc facilities for querying and manipulating specific temporal aspects of data.

Recent work on temporal clinical databases presents a more general approach and highlights the true requirements for storage and maintenance of time-oriented medical data. An issue that was explored in depth in the general temporal-database area is the one concerning what *kinds* of temporal dimensions need to be supported by the temporal database. Three different temporal dimensions have been distinguished [17]:

1. The *transaction time*; that is, the time at which data are stored in the database (e.g., the time in which the assertion "The white blood-cell (WBC) count is 7600" was entered into the patient's medical record)
2. The *valid time*; that is, the time at which the data are true for the modeled real world entity (e.g., the time in which the WBC-count was, in fact, 7600)
3. The *user-defined time*; whose meaning is related to the application and thus is defined by the user (e.g., the time in which the WBC count was determined in the laboratory).

Using this temporal-dimension taxonomy, four kinds of databases can be defined:

(a) *snapshot databases*, based on flat, timeless data models;

(b) *rollback databases*, which represent explicitly only the transaction time (e.g., a series of updates to the patient's *current* address stamped by the time in which the modification was recorded)

(c) *historical databases*, which represent explicitly only the valid time (thus, they represent the best current knowledge about the WBC value on 1/12/97, and allow future updates referring to data on 1/12/97, but keep no record of the updates themselves)

(d) what are now called *bitemporal databases*, which represent explicitly both transaction time and valid time and thus are both historical and rollback.

Thus, in a bitemporal database it can be represented explicitly that, on January 17, 1997 (transaction time), the physician entered in the patient's record the fact that on January 12, 1997 (valid time) the patient had an allergic reaction to a sulpha-type drug.

The bitemporal database is the only representation mode that fulfills all requirements for time-oriented medical databases, although historical and rollback databases are currently most common. There are multiple advantages for the use of bitemporal databases in medical information systems, including the ability to answer both research and legal questions (e.g., "When another physician prescribed sulpha on January 14 1997, did she know at that time that the patient had an allergic reaction to sulpha on a previous date?").

3.1 Maintenance of Both Clinical Raw Data and Their Abstractions

Several recent systems allow not only the modeling of complex clinical concepts at the database level, but also the maintenance of certain inference operations at that level. For example, active databases can also store and query derived data; these data are obtained by the execution of rules that are triggered by external events, such as the insertion of patient related data [18]. Furthermore, integrity constraints based on temporal reasoning [19] can often be evaluated at the database level, for example to *validate* clinical data during their acquisition. This validation, however, requires domain-specific knowledge (e.g., height is a monotonically increasing function, and should never decrease, at least for children).

3.2 Management of Different Temporal Dimensions of Clinical Data

Typically, only the *valid time*, at which the clinical data or conclusions were true, has been considered in medical-informatics research. However, storing also the *transaction time*, at which the data were inserted into the patient's record, has multiple benefits, such as being able to restore the state of the database that was true (i.e. what was known) when the physician or a decision-support system decided on a particular therapeutic action, an ability that has significance both for explanation and legal purposes. Another temporal dimension of information considered recently is the *decision-time* [20]: the decision time of a therapy, for example, could be different from both the valid time during which the therapy is administered and from the transaction time, at which the data related to the therapy are inserted into the database.

3.3 Storage and Retrieval of Time-Oriented Clinical Data

An example of a TM system that accesses time-oriented relational clinical databases and enables the formation of complex temporal queries is the **Chronus** temporal-maintenance system [21]. In the general TM area, researchers are developing several versions of (bi)temporal databases, which can manage time-oriented data, such as systems based on SQL3 [22] and TSQL2 [23].

4. Integration of Temporal Reasoning and Temporal Maintenance: A Temporal Mediation Service

Several issues are common to the TR and TM research communities. For instance, from the theoretical point of view, several basic choices have to be made when modeling time for management of or reasoning about time-oriented clinical data. Examples include the use of time points or time intervals as the primitive temporal objects; modeling time as linear, branching, or circular; and using absolute (e.g., date and time) versus relative (e.g., days since start of therapy) time.

Two commonly recurring and closely related tasks in both the temporal-reasoning and the temporal-maintenance research areas are (1) the temporal-abstraction task mentioned in Section 2, and (2) the handling of variable temporal granularity. Since these tasks are highly relevant to both the TR and TM research communities, they might be viewed as one of the potential bridges between them (besides fundamental theoretical issues, such as the time model).

Temporal abstraction provides a concise, context-sensitive description of a collection of time-stamped raw data. *Management of variable temporal granularity* deals, in fact, with an abstraction of the time primitives themselves; it concerns the level of abstraction (e.g., time unit, such as a day or a month) at which the time element (instant, interval, and so on) associated with the relevant data is represented. Note that the tasks of temporal abstraction and of handling variable temporal granularities are interconnected. When reasoning about various temporal-granularity levels, emphasis is placed on the abstraction of the representation of the *time component* of a time-oriented assertion; when performing a temporal-abstraction task, the emphasis is placed on the abstraction of the time-oriented *entity* itself.

Real decision-support applications that involve time-oriented medical data require to some extent both maintenance of the data and reasoning about them. Thus, an integration of the TR and TM projects is imperative, at least at the application level. Furthermore, as I show below, such an integration is quite possible, at least within certain reasonably general frameworks and assumptions.

The integration of the two functions necessary for medical decision-support systems, TR and TM, within one architecture, can be accomplished within a *temporal mediator*, a transparent interface that can be created to the patient's database. Database mediators have been proposed by Wiederhold [24; 25] as a solution to the problem of providing to applications certain services that involve the integration of different sources of data and/or knowledge.

An example of ongoing research in temporal mediators is the **Tzolkin** temporal-mediation module [26]. The Tzolkin module combines the RÉSUMÉ temporal-abstraction system, the Chronus temporal-maintenance system [21], a temporal-query parser and a controller into a unified temporal-mediation server (Figure 3). The Tzolkin server answers complex temporal queries of care providers or clinical decision-support applications, hiding the internal division of computational tasks from the user (or from the clinical decision-support application). When users or applications ask complex temporal queries including abstract (derived) terms that do not exist in the database, the Tzolkin controller loads the necessary raw data from the database using the Chronus module, uses the RÉSUMÉ module and the appropriate domain knowledge to abstract the data, stores the results, and uses the Chronus module again to access the results and answer the original temporal query.

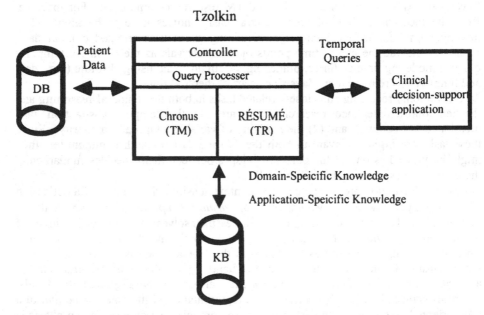

Fig. 3. The Tzolkin temporal-mediation architecture. The Tzolkin mediator enables care providers and decision-support systems to query patient records for complex temporal patterns, possibly involving high-level clinical abstractions. Tzolkin incorporates several modules to support this functionality: The Chronus access method for temporal databases, the RÉSUMÉ temporal-abstraction module, a temporal-query preprocessor, and the system-control structure. DB = patient electronic database; KB = domain- and application-specific knowledge base; TM = temporal data-maintenance module; TR = temporal-reasoning module.

The RÉSUMÉ temporal-abstraction module has been described in Section 2. The Chronus [27] temporal-maintenance module is Tzolkin's interface to the underlying standard relational database. Chronus communicates with the database via standard SQL; thus, any relational database containing time-stamped intervals of data can be integrated easily into the Tzolkin system. Chronus uses the query-processing engine of the relational database to maximize efficiency. The Tzolkin **query preprocessor** detects and informs the system of abstractions to be computed (i.e., it specifies when the temporal-reasoning module is needed). It also processes requests for Tzolkin's auxiliary services, such as data caching and batch processing (e.g., computing all possible abstractions given a set of patient data). Finally, the Tzolkin **controller** is the top-level module that coordinates the interactions of all other Tzolkin modules. It is responsible for calling each module in the proper order, for ensuring that each module has the necessary information to complete the task, and for returning the results of a query.

The Tzolkin knowledge base provides domain- and application-specific knowledge to the system. The domain-specific knowledge specializes Tzolkin to a particular medical domain (e.g., oncology). Besides domain-specific temporal-abstraction knowledge, such as properties of different clinical parameters in different contexts, the application-specific knowledge specializes Tzolkin to a particular database. The application-specific knowledge includes a data model that tells Tzolkin the database schema and the name and location of relevant patient data. Both sets of knowledge define the data requirements of each module and ensure that all abstractions from RÉSUMÉ are computed in a manner that is semantically consistent with the needs of the user (either the health-care provider or the calling process). The temporal-abstraction knowledge is acquired from expert physicians via a graphical knowledge-acquisition tool [28; 29].

5. Uses of a Temporal Mediator Within Clinical Decision-Support Applications

To demonstrate the use of a temporal mediator, I will describe briefly three applications: Automated support to the application of clinical guidelines; automated quality assessment of guideline-based therapy; and visualization and exploration of time-oriented clinical data.

5.1 Automated Support of the Application of Clinical Guidelines: The EON Project

The **EON** project [3] is a component-based architecture for the support of the application of guideline-based therapy. The EON architecture includes a therapy planner (the episodic skeletal-plan–refinement method), the Tzolkin temporal mediator, an eligibility-determination module (Yenta) that matches patients to appropriate clinical guidelines, and a domain knowledge base server. The EON modules use the Common Object Request Broker Architecture (CORBA) as a communication protocol (Figure 4). All temporal queries and assertions in the EON architecture are mediated through the Tzolkin mediator.

5.2 Automated Quality Assessment of Guideline-Based Therapy: The Asgaard Project

The **Asgaard** project [5] is a general framework for the representation, application, and critiquing of clinical guidelines. The Asgaard project uses the **Asbru** guideline-specification language, which enables the representation of both the prescribed actions of time-oriented therapy guidelines and their underlying *process* and *outcome intentions*. Thus, the Asgaard quality assessment module can critique (either in real time or retrospectively) care providers' actions in a much more flexible fashion. The critique considers the intentions of the guideline designers with respect to temporal and value constraints on both the pattern of *actions* that the provider was expected to create, and the pattern of patient *states* expected as outcome from the application of the guideline. Asbru intentions are temporal abstractions to be achieved, avoided, or maintained. All conditions, such as guideline eligibility and abort conditions, are temporal expressions as well.

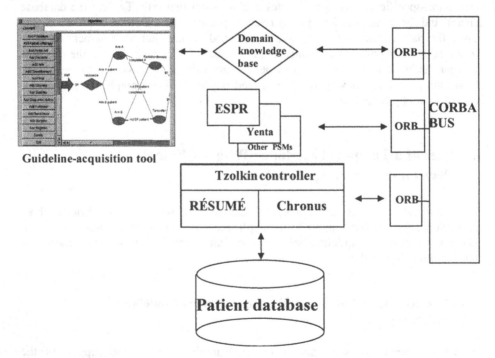

Fig. 4. The EON architecture. Several different problem-solving methods (PSMs), such as the episodic skeletal-plan refinement (ESPR) method that is used for therapy-plan execution, communicate with the patient database and the domain knowledge base using a Common Object Request Broker Architecture (CORBA) bus.

As in the EON architecture, all temporal queries are mediated through the Tzolkin temporal mediator (Figure 5). In the Asgaard architecture, the temporal-mediation module (Tzolkin) is one of several task-specific reasoning modules. Like other reasoning modules, the temporal-mediation module requires domain-specific (temporal-abstraction and other) knowledge.

5.3 Intelligent Visualization and Exploration of Time-Oriented Clinical Data: The KNAVE Project

A major challenge to medical informatics is to provide care providers with graphical temporal-query interfaces that enable them to take advantage of the sophisticated architectures that are being built on top of the clinical, time-oriented electronic patient records [30]. Indeed, many queries might be unnecessary if useful visualization interfaces exist. The semantics of these interfaces (e.g., deciding automatically which abstraction level of the same set of parameters to show and at what temporal granularity) might draw upon the domain-specific knowledge base. An early example was a framework for visualization of time-oriented clinical data [31], which defined a small but powerful set of domain-independent graphic operators with well defined semantics, and a domain-specific representation of appropriate temporal-granularities for the display of various entities in the specific clinical domain.

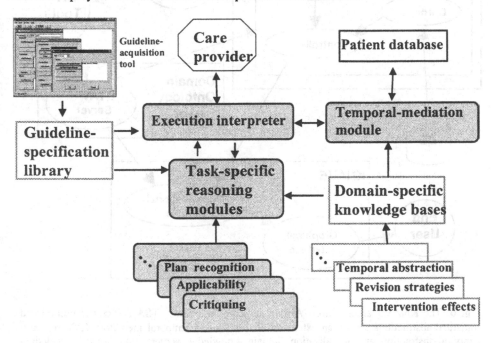

Fig. 5. The Asgaard Architecture. Several task-specific reasoning modules, such as the critiquing (quality assessment) module, support the guideline-execution interpreter when necessary. The task specific modules require various types of domain-specific knowledge. Note that the temporal-mediation module (Tzolkin) is a special task-specific reasoning module and requires domain-specific temporal-abstraction knowledge.

More sophisticated interfaces can be built by taking advantage, for instance, of formally-represented knowledge about time-oriented properties of clinical data in specific clinical areas, such as the ontology provided by the KBTA temporal-abstraction method, to build powerful graphical interfaces for visualization of and exploration of multiple levels of abstractions of time-oriented clinical data. Indeed, this approach is being taken by the developers of the **Knowledge-based Navigation of Abstractions for Visualization and Explanation** (KNAVE) architecture [6] (Figure 6).

In the KNAVE architecture, the local visualization and exploration module enables care providers and other users to formulate queries about time-oriented patient data interactively. The queries, typically involving abstractions such as "levels of anemia in the past 5 months," are referred to a temporal-mediation service. The output abstractions are displayed by the KNAVE visualization and exploration module. KNAVE then enables exploration of the abstractions by direct manipulation of a representation of the domain's temporal-abstraction ontology (Figure 7). Examples include drilling down the dependency (DERIVED-FROM) hierarchy (Figure 8),

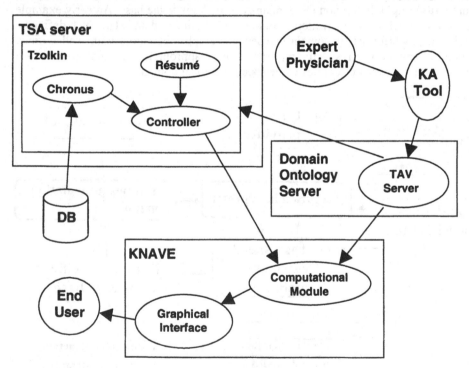

Fig. 6. The KNAVE architecture. Arrows indicate data flow. TSA server = temporal-and statistical-abstractions server, an extension of the Tzolkin temporal mediator; TAV server = temporal-abstraction and visualization domain--knowledge server; KA tool = knowledge-acquisition tool. Users interact with the graphical interface, which draws the computational module. Queries are answered by the TSA server using data from the patient DB and knowledge from the domain-ontology server. Exploration is enabled through direct access to the domain-specific knowledge through the TSA server.

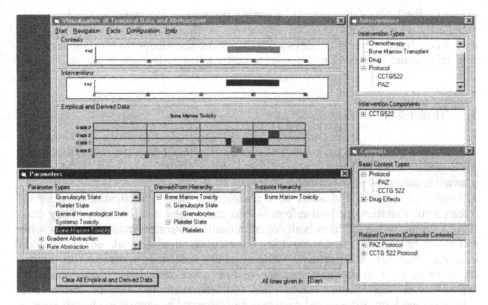

Fig. 7. The interface to the dynamic semantic-exploration operators in KNAVE. The seven browsers access directly the domain-specific knowledge through the domain-ontology server. The display window reflects the results of a query to the temporal mediator, which accesses the patient's database. The ABSTRACTED-INTO relation had been split into a "Derived-From Hierarchy" and a "Supports Hierarchy" exploration operators to facilitate browsing.

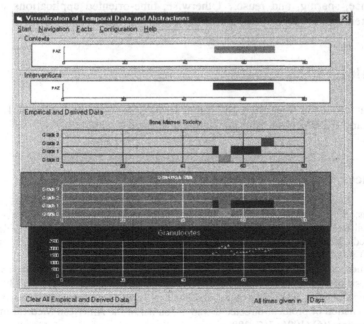

Fig. 8. The result of an ABSTRACTED-FROM exploration in the KNAVE visualization and exploration module, starting from the abstractions shown in Figure 7.

exploring the PART-OF hierarchy, zooming in and out by changing the temporal-granularity (e.g., from DAY to MONTH) while automatically changing the abstraction level, retrieving relevant classification knowledge to explain temporal abstractions, and asking What-If queries to perform interactive sensitivity analysis.

6. Summary

Maintenance of and reasoning about time-oriented clinical data are two research and development areas that are important for multiple clinical tasks, all of which are relevant to medical decision support systems.

Although the TR and TM areas have traditionally been investigated by different research communities, medical informaticians cannot ignore either area. They must strive to combine results from both communities in integrated architectures, to solve real-world problems. As an example, I presented ongoing work on the Tzolkin temporal mediator architecture. The Tzolkin mediator is useful in diverse applications, such as therapy planning, quality assessment, and visualization and exploration of time-oriented clinical data and their multiple levels of abstractions. Additional work on (bi)temporal databases and temporal mediators in clinical areas is necessary.

Finally, it is important to realize that a large amount of temporal-abstraction knowledge already exists in informal formats in multiple medical domains. Often, this knowledge exists as text or as general common-sense medical knowledge. This knowledge can be and should be acquired and represented formally to facilitate its maintenance, sharing, and reuse. Otherwise, time-oriented applications would be forced to reinvent the wheel over and over again.

Acknowledgements

Dr. Shahar has been supported by grants LM06245 from the National Library of Medicine and IRI-9528444 from the National Science Foundation.

References

1.   Downs, S.M., Walker, M.G., and Blum, R.L.: Automated summarization of on-line medical records. In: Salamon, R., Blum, B., and Jorgensen, M. (eds.): MEDINFO '86: Proceedings of the Fifth Conference on Medical Informatics. North-Holland, Amsterdam (1986) 800–804.
2.   Keravnou, E.T., and Washbrook, J.: A temporal reasoning framework used in the diagnosis of skeletal dysplasias. Artificial Intelligence in Medicine 2 (1990) 239–265.
3.   Musen, M.A., Tu, S.W., Das, A.K., and Shahar, Y.: EON: A component-based approach to automation of protocol-directed therapy. Journal of the American Medical Informatics Association 3(6) (1996) 367–388.
4.   Shahar, Y.: Dynamic temporal interpretation contexts for temporal abstraction. Annals of Mathematics and Artificial Intelligence 22(1-2) (1998) 159-192.

5. Shahar, Y., Miksch, S., and Johnson, P.: The Asgaard project: A task-specific framework for the application and critiquing of time-oriented clinical guidelines. Artificial Intelligence in Medicine 14 (1998) 29-51.
6. Shahar, Y. and Cheng, C. (1998). Knowledge-Based Visualization of Time-Oriented Clinical Data. Proceedings of the 1998 AMIA Fall Symposium, Orlando, FL.
7. Shahar, Y. and Musen, M.A.: Knowledge-based temporal abstraction in clinical domains. Artificial Intelligence in Medicine 8(3) (1996) 267-298.
8. Russ, T.A.: Using hindsight in medical decision making. In: Proceedings of Symposium on Computer Applications in Medical Care. IEEE Computer Society Press, New York NY (1989) 38-44.
9. Shahar, Y.: A framework for knowledge-based temporal abstraction. Artificial Intelligence 90 (1) (1997) 79-133.
10. Keravnou, E.T.: A multidimensional and multigranular model of time for medical knowledge-based systems (submitted).
11. Fagan L.M., Kunz, J.C., Feigenbaum, E.A. and Osborn, J.J.: Extensions to a Rule-Based Formalism for a Monitoring Task. In: Buchanan, B.G. and Shortliffe, E.H., (eds.): Rule-Based Expert Systems. Addison-Wesley, Reading, MA (1984) 397-423.
12. De Zegher-Geets, I.M.: IDEFIX: Intelligent Summarization of a Time-Oriented Medical Database. M.S. Dissertation, Program in Medical Information Sciences, Stanford University School of Medicine, 1987; Knowledge Systems Laboratory Technical Report KSL-88-34, Department of Computer Science, Stanford University, Stanford, CA, 1988.
13. Kohane, I.S.: Temporal reasoning in medical expert systems. Technical Report 389, Laboratory of Computer Science, Massachusetts Institute of technology, Cambridge, MA, 1987.
14. Kahn, M.G.: Combining physiologic models and symbolic methods to interpret time-varying patient data. Methods of Information in Medicine 30(3) (1991) 167-178.
15. Larizza, C., Moglia, A,. and Stefanelli, M.: M-HTP: A system for monitoring heart-transplant patients. Artificial Intelligence in Medicine 4(2) (1992) 111-126.
16. Haimowitz, I.J. and Kohane, I.S.: Automated trend detection with alternate temporal hypotheses. In: Proceedings of the Thirteenth International Joint Conference on Artificial Intelligence. Morgan Kaufmann, San Mateo (1993) 146-151.
17. Snodgrass, R. and Ahn, I.: Temporal databases. IEEE Computer 19(9) (1986) 35-42.
18. Caironi, P.V., Portoni, L., Combi, C., Pinciroli, F., Ceri, S.: HyperCare: A prototype of an active database for compliance with essential hypertension therapy guidelines. In: Proceedings of the 1997 AMIA Annual Fall Symposium (formerly the Symposium on Computer Applications in Medical Care). Hanley & Belfus, Philadelphia, PA (1997) 288-292.
19. Horn, W., Miksch, S., Egghart, G., Popow, C., and Paky, F.: Effective data validation of high-frequency data: time-point-, time-interval-, and trend-based methods. Computers in Biology and Medicine, Special Issue: Time-Oriented Systems in Medicine 27(5) (1997) 389-409.
20. Gal, A., Etzion, O., Segev, A.: Representation of highly-complex knowledge in a database. Journal of Intelligent Information Systems 3(2) (1994) 185-203.
21. Das, A.K., and Musen, M.A.: A temporal query system for protocol-directed decision support. Methods of Information in Medicine 33 (1994) 358-370.
22. Melton, J.: An SQL3 Snapshot. In: Proceedings of the Twelfth International Conference on Data Engineering. IEEE Computer Society Press, Los Alamitos, CA (1996) 666-672.
23. Snodgrass, R.T.: The TSQL2 Temporal Query Language. Kluwer Academic Publishers, Boston (1995).
24. Wiederhold, G.: Mediators in the architecture of future information systems. IEEE Computer 25 (1992) 38-50.
25. Wiederhold, G. and Genesereth, M.: The Conceptual Basis of Mediation Services. IEEE Expert 12(5) (1997) 38-47.

26. Nguyen, J.H., Shahar, Y., Tu, S.W., Das, A.K., and Musen, M.A.: Integration of temporal reasoning and temporal-data maintenance into a reusable database mediator to answer abstract, time-oriented queries: The Tzolkin system. Journal of Intelligent Information Systems (in press).
27. Das, A.K., Shahar, Y., Tu, S.W., and Musen, M.A.: A temporal-abstraction mediator for protocol-based decision support. In: Proceedings of the Eighteenth Annual Symposium on Computer Applications in Medical Care (1994) 320–324.
28. Stein, A., Musen, M.A., and Shahar, Y.:. Knowledge acquisition for temporal abstraction. In: Proceedings of the 1996 AMIA Annual Fall Symposium (formerly the Symposium on Computer Applications in Medical Care) (1996) 204–208.
29. Shahar, Y., Chen, H., Stites, D.P., Basso, L., Kaizer, H., Wilson, D.M., and Musen, M.A.: Semiautomated Acquisition of Clinical Temporal-abstraction Knowledge. Stanford Medical Informatics Tech Report SMI-98-0735 (1998).
30. Combi, C., Pinciroli, F., Musazzi, G., and Ponti, C.: Managing and displaying different time granularities of clinical information. In: Ozbolt, J.G. (ed.): The 18th Annual Symposium on Computer Applications in Medical Care., Hanley & Belfus, Philadelphia, PA (1994) 954-958.
31. Cousins, S.B. and Kahn, M.G.: The visual display of temporal information. Artificial Intelligence in Medicine 3(6) (1991) 341–357.

Machine Learning for Data Mining in Medicine

Nada Lavrač

J. Stefan Institute, Jamova 39, 1000 Ljubljana, Slovenia
nada.lavrac@ijs.si

Abstract. Large collections of medical data are a valuable resource from which potentially new and useful knowledge can be discovered through data mining. This paper gives an overview of machine learning approaches used in mining of medical data, distinguishing between symbolic and sub-symbolic data mining methods, and giving references to applications of these methods in medicine. In addition, the paper presents selected measures for performance evaluation used in medical prediction and classification problems, proposing also some alternative measures for rule evaluation that can be used in ranking and filtering of induced rule sets.

1 Introduction

Large collections of medical data are a valuable resource from which potentially new and useful knowledge can be discovered through data mining. Data mining is an increasingly popular field including statistical, visualization, machine learning, and other data manipulation and knowledge extraction techniques aimed at gaining an insight into the relationships and patterns hidden in the data.

Machine learning methods [51] described in this paper can be classified into symbolic and sub-symbolic methods. Examples of symbolic methods are rule induction methods such as learning of if-then rules [13], decision and regression trees [57] and logic programs [37], and case-based reasoning. Examples of sub-symbolic methods are instance-based learning methods [17,3], artificial neural networks [60] and Bayesian classification [33,34]. These induction methods are mostly concerned with the analysis of classificatory properties of data tables. Data represented in a tables may be collected from measurements or acquired from experts. Rows in the table correspond to objects (training examples) to be analyzed in terms of their properties (attributes) and the class (concept) to which they belong. In a medical setting, a concept of interest could be a set of patients with a certain disease or outcome. Supervised learning assumes that training examples are classified whereas unsupervised learning concerns the analysis of unclassified examples.

In medical problem solving it is important that a decision support system is able to explain and justify its decisions. Especially when faced with an unexpected solution of a new problem, the user requires substantial justification and explanation. Hence the interpretability of induced knowledge is an important property of systems that induce solutions from medical data about past

W. Horn et al. (Eds.): AIMDM'99, LNAI 1620, pp. 47–62, 1999.

solved cases. Symbolic data mining methods have this property since they induce symbolic representations (such as decision trees) from data. On the other hand, sub-symbolic data mining methods typically lack this property which hinders their use in situations for which explanations are required. Nevertheless, when the classification accuracy is the main applicability criterion, sub-symbolic methods may turn out to be very appropriate since they typically achieve accuracies that are at least as good as (or frequently better than) those of symbolic classifiers.

The first part of this paper gives an overview of machine learning approaches used in mining of medical data, distinguishing between symbolic and sub-symbolic data mining methods. Due to space restrictions this overview does not contain illustrative examples; for a subset of described methods, these can be found in [39]. It also gives references to applications of these methods in medicine, some of which are described in detail in an edited volume on intelligent data analysis in medicine and pharmacology [38]. The second part of this paper describes selected measures for performance evaluation used in medical prediction and classification problems, proposing also some alternative measures for rule evaluation that can be used in ranking and filtering of induced rule sets. Some other measures not discussed here are described in [39,41].

2   Symbolic Data Mining Techniques

2.1   Rule Induction

If-Then Rules Given a set of classified examples, a rule induction system constructs a set of rules of the form IF Conditions THEN Conclusion, or, if using a different notation, Conditions → Conclusion. The condition part of a rule is a conjunction of attribute tests of the form $A_i = value$ for discrete attributes, and $A_i < value$ or $A_i > value$ for continuous attributes. The conclusion part is class assignment $C = c_i$.

An example is *covered* by a rule if the attribute values of the example fulfill the conditions of the rule. An example rule induced in the domain of early diagnosis of rheumatic diseases [36,22] assigning the diagnosis crystal-induced synovitis to male patients older than 46 who have more than three painful joints and psoriasis as a skin manifestation, is represented as follows: "IF Sex = male AND Age > 46 AND Number-of-painful-joints > 3 AND Skin-manifestations = psoriasis THEN Diagnosis = Crystal-induced-synovitis".

The well-known algorithms of the AQ falimy of rule learners [48] use the covering approach to construct a set of rules for each possible class c_i in turn: when rules for class c_i are being constructed, examples of this class are positive, all other examples are negative. The covering approach works as follows: AQ constructs a rule that correctly classifies some examples, removes the positive examples covered by the rule from the training set and repeats the process until no more examples remain. To construct a single rule that classifies examples into class c_i, AQ starts with a rule with an empty antecedent (IF part) and the selected class c_i as a consequent (THEN part). The antecedent of this rule is satisfied by all examples in the training set, and not only those of the selected class. AQ then progressively refines the antecedent by adding conditions to it, until only examples of class c_i satisfy the antecedent. To allow for the handling of imperfect data, some if-then rule learning algorithms may construct a set of rules which is imprecise, i.e., does not classify all examples in the training set correctly.

If-then rule induction algorithms, such as AQ15 [49] and CN2 [13,12] have been frequently applied to the analysis of medical data. Examples of medical applications include [49,22,35].

Rough Sets If-then rules can be also induced by using algorithms based on the theory of rough sets introduced by Pawlak [54,55]. Rough sets (RS) are concerned with the analysis of classificatory properties of data aimed at approximations of concepts. RS can be used both for supervised and unsupervised learning.

The main goal of RS analysis is the synthesis of approximations of concepts c_i. The basic concept of RS is an *indiscernibility* relation. Two objects x and y are indiscernible if their object descriptions have the same values of attributes. A main task of RS analysis is to find minimal subsets of attributes that preserve the indiscernibility relation. This is called *reduct* computation. Decision rules are generated from reducts by reading off the values of the attributes in each reduct. The main challenge in inducing rules lies in determining which attributes should be included in the conditional part of the rule. Rules synthesized from the (standard) reducts will usually result in large sets of rules and are likely to over-fit the patterns of interest. Instead of standard reducts, attribute sets that "almost" preserve the indiscernibility relation can be generated.

The list of applications of RS in medicine is significant. It includes extracting diagnostic rules, image analysis and classification of histological pictures, modeling set residuals, EEG signal analysis, etc. Examples of RS analysis in medicine include [26,32,63].

Association Rules The problem of discovering association rules [2] has recently received much attention in the data mining community. The problem is defined as follows: Given a set of transactions, where each transaction is a set of *items* of the form *Attribute = value*, an *association rule* is an expression of the form $B \rightarrow H$ where B and H are sets of items. The intuitive meaning of such a rule is that transactions in a database which contain B tend to contain H.

An example of such a rule is: `Diagnosis = pneumonia` $\rightarrow$ `Fever = high` `[C=80,S=10]`. The meaning of this rule is: "80% of patients with pneumonia also have high fever. 10% of all transactions contain both these items." Here 80% is called *confidence* of the rule, and 10% support of the rule. Confidence of the rule is calculated as the ratio of the number of records having true values for all items in B and H to the number of records having true values for all items in B. Support of the rule is the ratio of the number of records having true values for all items in B and H to the number of all records in the database. The problem is to find all association rules that satisfy minimum support and minimum confidence constraints. To do so, all itemsets that satisfy the minimum support level are first generated, and then all frequent itemsets are combined with each other to produce all possible rules satisfying the minimum confidence constraint.

Association rule learning was applied in medicine, for example, to identify new and interesting patterns in surveillance data, in particular in the analysis of the Pseudomonas aeruginosa infection control data [8]. An algorithm for finding a more expressive variant of association rules, where data and patterns are represented in first-order logic, was successfully applied to the problem of predicting carcinogenicity of chemical compounds [18].

Ripple Down Rules The knowledge representation of the form of ripple down rules allows incremental rule learning by including exceptions to the current rule set. Ripple down rules (RDR) [14,15] have the following form:
IF Conditions THEN Conclusion BECAUSE Case EXCEPT IF... ELSE IF...

There have been many successful medical applications of the RDR approach, including the system PEIRS [23] which is an RDR reconstruction of the hand-built GARVAN expert system knowledge base on thyroid function tests [28].

2.2   Learning of Classification and Regression Trees

Systems for Top-Down Induction of Decision Trees (TDITD) [57] generate a decision tree from a given set of examples. Each of the interior nodes of the tree is labeled by an attribute, while branches that lead from the node are labeled by the values of the attribute.

The tree construction process is heuristically guided by choosing the 'most informative' attribute at each step, aimed at minimizing the expected number of tests needed for classification. A decision tree is constructed by repeatedly calling a tree construction algorithm in each generated node of the tree. In the current node, the current training set is split into subsets according to the values of the most informative attribute, and recursively, a subtree is built for each subset. Tree construction stops when all examples in a node are of the same class. This node, called a leaf, is labeled by a class name. However, leaves can also be empty, if there are no training examples having attribute values that lead to a leaf, or can be labeled by more than one class name (if there are training examples with same attribute values and different class names), together with the probability assigned to each class.

The best known decision tree learner is C4.5 [59] (C5.0 is its recent upgrade) which has also been incorporated into commercial data mining tools (e.g., Clementine and Kepler). The system is is widely used since it is well maintained and documented, reliable, efficient and capable of dealing with large numbers of training examples.

There have been numerous applications of decision tree learning in medicine, e.g., [35,40,38].

Learning of regression trees is similar to decision tree learning: it also uses a top-down greedy approach to tree construction. The main difference is that decision tree construction involves the classification into a finite set of discrete classes whereas in regression tree learning the decision variable is continuous and the leaves of the tree either consist of a prediction into a numeric value or a linear combination of variables (attributes). An early learning system CART [7] featured both classification and regression tree learning.

2.3 Inductive Logic Programming

Inductive logic programming (ILP) systems learn relational concept descriptions from relational data. In ILP, induced rules typically have the form of Prolog clauses. Compared to rules induced by a rule learning algorithm of the form IF Conditions THEN Conclusion, Prolog rules have the form Conclusion :- Conditions, denoting Conclusion ← Conditions. Conclusion is a target predicate to be learned, and Conditions a conjunction of literals.

The best known ILP systems include FOIL [58] and Progol [52] and Claudien [19]. LINUS is an environment for inductive logic programming [37], enabling learning of relational descriptions by transforming the training examples and background knowledge into the form appropriate for attribute-value learners.

ILP has been successfully applied to medical data analysis, including early diagnosis of rheumatic diseases [37] and carcinogenesis prediction in the predictive toxicology evaluation challenge [62].

2.4 Case-Based Reasoning

Case-based reasoning (CBR) uses the knowledge of past experience when dealing with new cases [1,43]. A "case" refers to a problem situation — although, as with instance-based learning [3], cases may be described with a simple attribute-value vector, CBR most often uses a richer, often hierarchical data structure. CBR relies on a database of past cases that has to be designed in the way to facilitate the retrieval of similar cases.

Several CBR systems were used, adapted for, or implemented to support reasoning and data analysis in medicine. Some are described in the Special Issue of *Artificial Intelligence in Medicine* [44] and include CBR systems for reasoning in cardiology, learning of plans and goal states in medical diagnosis, detection of coronary heart disease from myocardial scintigrams, and treatment advice in nursing. Other include a system that uses CBR to assist in the prognosis of breast cancer [45], case classification in the domain of ultrasonography and body computed tomography [29], and a CBR-based expert system that advises on the identification of nursing diagnoses in a new client [6].

3   Sub-symbolic Data Mining Methods

3.1 Instance-Based Learning

Instance-based learning (IBL) algorithms [3] use specific instances to perform classification tasks, rather than generalizations such as induced if-then rules.

IBL algorithms assume that similar instances have similar classifications: novel instances are classified according to the classifications of their most similar neighbors.

IBL algorithms are derived from the nearest neighbor pattern classifier [25,16]. The nearest neighbor (NN) algorithm is one of the best known classification algorithms and an enormous body of research exists on the subject [17]. In essence, the NN algorithm treats attributes as dimensions of an Euclidean space and examples as points in this space. In the training phase, the classified examples are stored without any processing. When classifying a new example, the Euclidean distance between that example and all training examples is calculated and the class of the closest training example is assigned to the new example.

The more general k-NN method takes the k nearest training examples and determines the class of the new example by majority vote. In improved versions of k-NN, the votes of each of the k nearest neighbors are weighted by the respective proximity to the new example [21]. An optimal value of k may be determined automatically from the training set by using leave-one-out cross-validation [64]. In our experiments in early diagnosis of rheumatic diseases [22], using the Wettschereck's implementation of k-NN [65], the best k was chosen in this manner.

3.2 Artificial Neural Networks

Artificial neural networks may be used for both supervised and unsupervised learning.

For unsupervised learning — learning which is presented with unclassified instances and aims to identify groups of instances with similar attribute values — the most frequently used neural network approach is that of Kohonen's self organizing maps (SOM) [31]. Typically, SOM consist of a single layer of output nodes. An output node is fully connected with nodes at the input layer. Each such link has an associated weight. There are no explicit connections between nodes of the output layer.

For supervised learning and among different neural network paradigm, feed-forward multi-layered neural networks [60,24] are most frequently used for modeling medical data. They are computational structures consisting of a interconnected processing elements (PE) or nodes arranged on a multi-layered hierarchical architecture. In general, PE computes the weighted sum of its inputs and filters it through some sigmoid function to obtain the output. Outputs of PEs of one layer serve as inputs to PEs of the next layer. To obtain the output value for selected instance, its attribute values are stored in input nodes of the network (the network's lowest layer). Next, in each step, the outputs of the higher-level processing elements are computed (hence the name feed-forward), until the result is obtained and stored in PEs at the output layer.

Multi-layered neural networks have been extensively used to model medical data. Example applications areas include survival analysis [42], clinical medicine [5], pathology and laboratory medicine [4], molecular sequence analysis [66], pneumonia risk assessment [10], and prostate cancer survival [30]. There are fewer applications where rules were extracted from neural networks: an example of such data analysis is finding rules for breast cancer diagnosis [61].

Other types of neural networks for supervised learning include Hopfield recurrent network and neural networks based on adaptive resonance theory mapping (ARTMAP). For the first, an example application is tumor boundary detection [67]. Example studies of application of ARTMAP in medicine include classification of cardiac arrhythmias [27] and treatment selection for schizophrenic and unipolar depressed in-patients [50]. Learned ARTMAP networks can also be used to extract symbolic rules [9,20].

3.3 Bayesian Classifier

The Bayesian classifier uses the naive Bayesian formula to calculate the probability of each class c_j given the values of all the attributes for a given instance to be classified [33,34]. For simplicity, let $(v_1..v_n)$ denote the n-tuple of values of example e_k to be classified. Assuming the conditional independence of the attributes for the given class, it can be shown that $p(c_j|v_1..v_n)$ is proportional to $p(c_j)\prod_i \frac{p(c_j|v_i)}{p(c_j)}$; these probabilities can be in turn estimated from the training set, using the relative frequency, the Laplace estimate [53] or the m-estimate [11]. Given the above formula for $p(c_j|v_1..v_n)$, a new instance is classified into the class with maximal probability.

The Naive Bayesian formula can also be used to support decisions in different stages of a diagnostic process [46,47] in which doctors use *hypothetico-deductive reasoning* gathering evidence which may help to confirm a diagnostic hypothesis, eliminate an alternative hypothesis, or discriminate between two alternative hypotheses. As shown by [46], Bayesian computation can help in identifying and selecting the most useful tests, aimed at confirming the target hypothesis, eliminating the likeliest alternative hypothesis, increase the probability of the target hypothesis, decrease the probability of the likeliest alternative hypothesis or increase the probability of the target hypothesis relative to the likeliest alternative hypothesis.

4 Evaluation Measures for Predictive Data Mining in Medicine

Predictive induction deals with supervised learning for prediction and/or classification tasks.

4.1 Performance Evaluation

Given a set of training examples, quality of classifications can be tested in two ways.

1. Testing on a training set. This case applies in the construction of rules where heuristic measures are used for rule evaluation and/or feature selection. This

approach is used also when we want all the available information to be used for learning. Moreover, assigning a quality measure to a rule allows for their ranking, and consequently, for rule filtering.

2. Testing on a separate test set. In this case standard approaches to quality evaluation can be applied like leave-one-out, cross-validation, etc.

The evaluation measures developed below are appropriate for both evaluation frameworks.

4.2   Confusion Matrix

Consider a binary classification problem (given only two classes: positive and negative). In this case, a *confusion matrix* is used as a basis for performance evaluation.

	predicted positive	predicted negative	
actual positive	TP	FN	P_a
actual negative	FP	TN	N_a
	P_p	N_p	N

Table 1. A confusion matrix.

In the confusion matrix shown in Table 1 the following notation is used. P_a denotes the number of positive examples, N_a the number of negative examples, P_p the examples predicted as positive by a classifier, and N_p the examples predicted as negative. The fields of the confusion matrix contain the numbers of examples of the following four subsets (between brackets the symbol denoting the number of examples in each subset is indicated):

True positives (TP): True positive answers denoting correct classifications of positive cases.

True negatives (TN): True negative answers denoting correct classifications of negative cases.

False positives (FP): False positive answers denoting incorrect classifications of negative cases into class positive.

False negatives (FN): False negative answers denoting incorrect classifications of positive cases into class negative.

In the fields of the confusion matrix, for the convenience of computation, the absolute numbers may be replaced by the relative frequencies, e.g., TP by $\frac{TP}{N}$, and P_a by $\frac{P_a}{N}$. This may be more convenient when relative frequencies are used as probability estimates.

4.3   Standard Performance Evaluation Measures

The *classification accuracy* is the most popular performance evaluation measure used in predictive knowledge discovery where the goal of learning is prediction or classification. The classification accuracy measures the proportion of correctly classified cases.

In binary classification problems using the confusion matrix notation, the accuracy is computed as follows:

$$Acc = \frac{TP + TN}{TP + TN + FP + FN} = \frac{TP + TN}{N} \tag{1}$$

Notice that this performance evaluation measure is symmetric w.r.t. the accuracy of predictions of the positive and negative examples.[1]

If in binary classification problems we were only interested in the correct predictions of the target class, accuracy could also be defined as the fraction of predicted positives that are true positives. Let R be the induced classifier, and $Acc(R)$ the accuracy of correct predictions.

$$Acc(R) = \frac{TP}{TP + FP} = \frac{TP}{P_p} \tag{2}$$

This measure, if applied to single rules, is called *confidence* in association rule learning, and *precision* in information retrieval. *Accuracy error*, derived from accuracy, is defined as $Err(R) = 1 - Acc(R) = \frac{FP}{P_p}$. Accuracy can also be used to measure the *reliability* of the classifier in the prediction of positive cases since it measures the correctness of returned results.

The *reliability of negative predictions* is defined as follows:

$$NegRel(R) = \frac{TN}{TN + FN} = \frac{TN}{N_p}$$

Sensitivity is a measure frequently used in medical applications. It measures the fraction of actual positives that are correctly classified. In medical terms, maximizing sensitivity means detecting as many ill patients as possible.

$$Sens(R) = \frac{TP}{TP + FN} = \frac{TP}{P_a}$$

This measure is identical to *recall* known from information retrieval (recall of positive cases).

Specificity is also a measure frequently used in medical applications. Specificity can be interpreted as recall of negative cases:

$$Spec(R) = \frac{TN}{TN + FP} = \frac{TN}{N_a}$$

---

[1] For multi-class problems (k classes), let TP_j denote the fraction of correctly classified instances of class c_j; then the classification accuracy can be computed as follows: $Acc = \frac{1}{N} \sum_1^k TP_j$.

Maximizing specificity is equivalent to minimizing the false alarm rate, where $FalseAlarm(R) = 1 - Spec(R) = \frac{FP}{TN+FP}$. In medicine, this measure is aimed at minimizing the fraction of healthy patients declared as ill.

4.4   Rule Set versus Single Rule Evaluation

In this section we consider only symbolic learning, where the outputs are prediction or classification rules, induced from classified examples.

A learner usually induces a set of rules and not a single rule. Consider a set of rules of the form $H_i \leftarrow B_i$, where H_i is class assignment $C = c_i$ and B_i is a conjunction of attribute tests. Notice, however, that the form $H_i \leftarrow B_i$ also covers association rules, in which H_i does not represent class assignment but typically a conjunction of attribute tests.

1. If all the H_i are identical, i.e., $\forall i: H_i = H$, this set of rules can be considered as a hypothesis about H. In this case, a hypothesis can be written in the form of a single rule $H \leftarrow B$, where B is a disjunction of all B_i. Under these circumstances, the evaluation of a hypothesis (a set of rules) can be elaborated in the same framework as the evaluation of single rules.
2. If H_i are not identical, one can not form a hypothesis as a single rule. In this case the evaluation of a set of rules can not be elaborated in the same framework as the evaluation of single rules, and evaluation measures for a set of rules have to be defined.

4.5   Non-standard Measures for Rule Evaluation

The measures outlined in Section 4.3 can be used for the evaluation of classifiers performance (e.g., performance of a set of rules), as well as the evaluation of single rules. In addition to the above standard measures, other measures that evaluate the quality of single rules can be defined [41]. In data mining these measures may turn out to be important when trying to extract individual rules representing meaningful regularities hidden in the data.

Let us use the notation in which $n(X)$ denotes the cardinality of X, e.g., $n(H_i B_i)$ is the number of instances for which H_i is true and B_i is true (i.e., the number of instances correctly covered by the rule), $n(\overline{B_i})$ is the set of instances for which B_i is false (instances not covered by the rule, etc.) N denotes the total number of instances in the sample. The relative frequency $\frac{n(X)}{N}$ associated with X is denoted by $p(X)$.

Accuracy of rule $R_i = H_i \leftarrow B_i$ is here defined as the conditional probability that H_i is true given that B_i is true:

$$Acc(H_i \leftarrow B_i) = p(H_i|B_i)$$

$Acc(H \leftarrow B)$ defined as $p(H|B)$ indeed measures the fraction of predicted positives that are true positives in the case of binary classification problems, as defined in Equation 2:

$$Acc(R) = \frac{TP}{TP + FP} = \frac{n(HB)}{n(HB) + n(\overline{H}B)} = \frac{n(HB)}{n(B)} = \frac{\frac{n(HB)}{N}}{\frac{n(B)}{N}} = \frac{p(HB)}{p(B)} = p(H|B).$$

Relative accuracy, defined as

$$RAcc(H_i \leftarrow B_i) = p(H_i|B_i) - p(H_i)$$

is the accuracy gain of a rule $H_i \leftarrow B_i$ relative to a rule $H_i \leftarrow true$ that would classify every instance into H_i (i.e., class c_i). This measure indicates that a rule is only interesting if it improves upon the 'default' accuracy $p(H_i)$.

The point about relative measures is that they give more information about the utility of a rule than absolute measures. For instance, if in a prediction task the accuracy of a rule is lower than the relative frequency of the class it predicts, then the rule actually performs badly, regardless of its absolute accuracy.

It is now useful to provide another view on performance evaluation. In predictive induction it is well understood that a rule may be considered useful only if its predictive accuracy is higher than the accuracy of the classifier that classifies all examples into the majority class. This understanding is incorporated also into building an ordered list of rules by a rule learner CN2 [13] which stops building new rules once their accuracy drops below the accuracy defined by the majority class threshold. If H_0 denotes the majority class in predictive induction dealing with multi-class problems, the majority class threshold is defined as $p(H_0) = \frac{n(H_0)}{N}$.

Relative threshold accuracy is defined as follows:

$$TRAcc(R) = p(H|B) - p(H_0)$$

where H_0 denotes the majority rule head.

There is however a problem with relative accuracy as such: it is easy to obtain high relative accuracy with highly specific rules, i.e., rules with low generality $p(B)$ (low proportion of examples covered by the body of a rule). To overcome this problem, a weighted variant of the relative accuracy measure is introduced.

Weighted relative accuracy trades off generality and relative accuracy. It is defined as follows:

$$WRAcc(H \leftarrow B) = p(B)(p(H|B) - p(H)).$$

It was shown in [41] that rules with high weighted relative accuracy also have high novelty. High novelty is achieved by trading off generality and rule accuracy gained in comparison with a trivial rule $H \leftarrow true$. This also means that having high relative accuracy is not enough for considering a rule to be interesting, since the rule needs to be general enough as well.

4.6   Other Rule Evaluation Measures

With new tasks being addressed in knowledge discovery, the development of new evaluation measures is important. Additional measures are needed as many knowledge discovery tasks involve the induction of a large set of redundant rules and the problem is the ranking and filtering of the induced rule set. It was shown in previous work [41] that relative and weighted relative measures can be introduced not only for accuracy but also for the reliability of negative predictions, as well as for sensitivity and specificity. The utility of these measures for data mining in medicine still needs to be empirically evaluated in further work.

The paper [39] presents also some other evaluation measures, including post-test probability (which is appropriate for stepwise diagnostic processes), information score (which is similar in spirit to the above discussed relative accuracy for classifiers giving probabilistic answers), and misclassification costs.

5   Conclusion

Traditionally, data analysis was the final phase of experimental design that, typically, included a careful selection of patients, their features and the hypothesis to test. With the introduction of data warehouses, such a selective approach to data collection is altered and data may be gathered with no specific purpose in mind. Yet, medical data stored in warehouses may provide a useful resource for potential discovery of new knowledge.

The process of hypothesis generation and knowledge discovery is supported by data mining tools, among which the use of machine learning tools turns out to be advantageous; their use may namely result in logical rules that can be easily interpreted by medical experts. The aim of this paper is to present a variety of data mining methods and to discuss some of the evaluation criteria appropriate for supporting medical problem solving.

Acknowledgments

I am grateful to Blaz Zupan and Peter Flach for their contribution to this overview; Blaz Zupan provided the information on CBR and neural networks, and Peter Flach contributed to the development of non-standard measures for rule evaluation described in this paper. Thanks to Jan Komorowski and Claude Sammut for their help in describing rough set and ripple-down rules approaches, respectively.

The work on this paper was financially supported by the Slovenian Ministry of Science and Technology. In part it was also supported by a Joint Project with Central/Eastern Europe funded by the Royal Society.

References

1. Aamodt, A. and Plaza, E.: Case-based reasoning: Foundational issues, methodological variations, and system approaches, *AI Communications*, 7(1) 39–59 (1994).
2. Agrawal, R., Mannila, H., Srikant, R., Toivonen, H. and Verkamo, A.I.: Fast discovery of association rules. In U.M. Fayyad, G. Piatetski-Shapiro, P. Smyth and R. Uthurusamy (Eds.) *Advances in Knowledge Discovery and Data Mining*, AAAI Press, 1996, pp. 307–328.
3. Aha, D., Kibler, D. and Albert, M.: Instance-based learning algorithms, *Machine Learning*, 6: 37–66 (1991).
4. Astion, M.L. and Wielding, P.: The application of backpropagation neural networks to problems in pathology and laboratory medicine, *Arch Pathol Lab Med*, 116: 995–1001 (1992).
5. Baxt, W.G.: Application of artificial neural networks to clinical medicine, *Lancet*, 364(8983) 1135–1138 (1995).
6. Bradburn, C., Zeleznikow, J. and Adams, A.: Florence: synthesis of case-based and model-based reasoning in a nursing care planning system, *Computers in Nursing*, 11(1): 20–24 (1993).
7. Breiman, L., Friedman, J.H., Olshen, R.A. and Stone, C.J.: *Classification and Regression Trees*. Wadsworth, Belmont, 1984.
8. Brossette, S.E., Sprague, A.P., Hardin, J.M., Waites, K.B., Jones, W.T. and Moser, S.A.: Association rules and data mining in hospital infection control and public health surveillance. *Journal of the American Medical Inform. Assoc.* 5(4): 373–81 (1998).
9. Carpenter, G.A. and Tan, A.H.: Rule extraction, fuzzy ARTMAP and medical databases. In: *Proc. World Cong. Neural Networks*, 1993, pp. 501–506.
10. Caruana, R., Baluja, S., and Mitchell, T.: Using the Future to Sort Out the Present: Rankprop and Multitask Learning for Medical Risk Analysis, *Neural Information Processing* 7 (1995).
11. Cestnik, B.: Estimating Probabilities: A Crucial Task in Machine Learning, In: *Proc. European Conf. on Artificial Intelligence*, Stockholm, 1990, pp. 147-149.
12. Clark, P. and Boswell, R.: Rule induction with CN2: Some recent improvements. In: *Proc. Fifth European Working Session on Learning*, Springer, 1991, pp. 151–163.
13. Clark, P. and Niblett, T.: The CN2 induction algorithm. *Machine Learning*, 3(4):261–283 (1989).
14. Compton, P. and Jansen, R.: Knowledge in context: A strategy for expert system maintenance. In: *Proc. 2nd Australian Joint Artificial Intelligence Conference*, Springer LNAI 406, 1988, pp. 292–306.
15. Compton, P., Horn, R., Quinlan, R. and Lazarus, L.: Maintaining an expert system. In: *Applications of Expert Systems* (Quinlan, R., ed.), Addison Wesley, 1989, pp. 366–385.
16. Cover, T.M., Hart, P.E.: Nearest neighbor pattern classification, *IEEE Transactions on Information Theory*, 13: 21–27 (1968).
17. Dasarathy, B.V., ed.: *Nearest Neighbor (NN) Norms: NN Pattern Classification Techniques*. IEEE Computer Society Press, Los Alamitos, CA, 1990.
18. Dehaspe, L, Toivonen, H. and King, R.D.: Finding frequent substructures in chemical compounds. In: *Proc. 4th International Conference on Knowledge Discovery and Data Mining, (KDD-98)* (Agrawal, R., Stolorz, P. and Piatetsky-Shapiro, G., eds.), AAAI Press, 1998, pp. 30–37.

19. De Raedt, L. and Dehaspe, L.: Clausal discovery. *Machine Learning*, 26:99–146 (1997).

20. Downs, J., Harrison, R.F., Kennedy, R.L., and Cross, S.C.: Application of the fuzzy ARTMAP neural network model to medical pattern classification tasks, *Artificial Intelligence in Medicine*, 8(4): 403–428 (1996).

21. Dudani, S.A.: The distance-weighted k-nearest neighbor rule, *IEEE Transactions on Systems, Man and Cybernetics*, 6(4): 325–327 (1975).

22. Džeroski, S. and Lavrač, N.: Rule induction and instance-based learning applied in medical diagnosis, *Technology and Health Care*, 4(2): 203–221 (1996).

23. Edwards, G., Compton, P., Malor, R., Srinivasan, A. and Lazarus, L.: PEIRS: A pathologist maintained expert system for the interpretation of chemical pathology reports, *Pathology* 25: 27–34 (1993).

24. Fausett, L.V.: *Fundamentals of neural networks: Architectures, algorithms and applications*, Prentice Hall, Upper Saddle River, NJ, 1994.

25. Fix, E., Hodges, J.L.: Discriminatory analysis. Nonparametric discrimination. Consistency properties. Technical Report 4, US Air Force School of Aviation Medicine. Randolph Field, TX, 1957.

26. Grzymała-Busse, J.: Applications of the rule induction systems LERS, In: [56], 1998, pp. 366–375.

27. Ham, F.M. and Han, S., Classification of cardiac using fuzzy ARTMAP, *IEEE Transactions on Biomedical Engineering*, 43(4): 425–430 (1996).

28. Horn, K., Compton, P.J., Lazarus, L. and Quinlan, J.R.: An expert system for the interpretation of thyroid assays in a clinical laboratory, *Austr. Comput. Journal* 17(1): 7–11 (1985).

29. Kahn, C.E., and Anderson, G.M.: Case-based reasoning and imaging procedure selection, *Investigative Radiology*, 29(6): 643–647 (1994).

30. Kattan, M.W., Ishida, H., Scardino, P.T. and Beck, J.R.: Applying a neural network to prostate cancer survival data. In: *Intelligent data analysis in medicine and pharmacology* (Lavrač, N. Keravnou, E. and Zupan, B., eds.), Kluwer, 1997, pp. 295–306.

31. Kohonen, T.: *Self-organization and associative memory*, Springer-Verlag, New York, 1988.

32. Komorowski, J. and Øhrn, A.: Modelling prognostic power of cardiac tests using rough sets, *Artificial Intelligence in Medicine*, 1998 (in press).

33. Kononenko, I.: Semi-naive Bayesian classifier. In: *Proc. European Working Session on Learning-91* (Kodratoff, Y., ed.), Porto, Springer, 1991, pp. 206–219.

34. Kononenko, I.: Inductive and Bayesian learning in medical diagnosis, *Applied Artificial Intelligence*, 7: 317–337 (1993).

35. Kononenko, I., Bratko, I., and Kukar, M.: Application of machine learning to medical diagnosis. In *Machine Learning and Data Mining: Methods and Applications*, R. S. Michalski, I. Bratko, and M. Kubat (Eds.), John Willey and Sons, 1998, pp. 389–408.

36. Lavrač, N., Džeroski, S., Pirnat, V. and Križman, V.: The utility of background knowledge in learning medical diagnostic rules, *Applied Artificial Intelligence*, 7: 273–293 (1993).

37. Lavrač, N. and Džeroski, S.: *Inductive Logic Programming: Techniques and Applications*. Ellis Horwood, Chichester, 1994.

38. Lavrač, N., Keravnou, E. and Zupan, B., eds.: *Intelligent Data Analysis in Medicine and Pharmacology*, 1997, Kluwer.

39. Lavrač, N.: Selected techniques for data mining in medicine. *Artificial Intelligence in Medicine*, Special Issue on Data Mining Techniques and Applications in Medicine, 1999 (in press).

40. Lavrač, N., Kononenko, I., Keravnou, E., Kukar, M. and Zupan, B.: Intelligent data analysis for medical diagnosis: Using machine learning and temporal abstraction. *AI Communications*, 1999 (in press).

41. Lavrač, N., Flach, P.A. and Zupan, B.: Rule evaluation measures: A unifying view, 1999 (submitted to Int. Workshop on Inductive Logic Programming, ILP-99).

42. Liestøl, K., Andersen, P.K. and Andersen, U.: Survival analysis and neural nets, *Statist. Med.*, 13: 1189–1200 (1994).

43. Macura, R.T. and Macura, K., eds.: Case-based reasoning: opportunities and applications in health care, *Artificial Intelligence in Medicine*, 9(1): 1–4 (1997).

44. Macura, R.T. and Macura, K., eds.: *Artificial Intelligence in Medicine: Special Issue on Case-Based Reasoning*, 9(1), 1997.

45. Mariuzzi, G., Mombello, A., Mariuzzi, L., Hamilton, P.W., Weber, J.E., Thompson D. and Bartels, P.H.: Quantitative study of ductal breast cancer–patient targeted prognosis: an exploration of case base reasoning, *Pathology, Research & Practice*, 193(8): 535–542 (1997).

46. McSherry, D.: Hypothesist: A development environment for intelligent diagnostic systems. In: *Proc. Sixth Conference on Artificial Intelligence in Medicine* (AIME'97), Springer, 1997, pp. 223–234.

47. McSherry, D.: Avoiding premature closure in sequential diagnosis, *Artificial Intelligence in Medicine*, 10(3): 269–283 (1997).

48. Michalski, R.S.: A theory and methodology of inductive learning. In: *Machine Learning: An Artificial Intelligence Approach* (Michalski, R., Carbonell, J. and Mitchell, T.M., eds.), volume I, Palo Alto, CA, Tioga, 1983, pp. 83–134.

49. Michalski, R., Mozetič, I., Hong, J. and Lavrač, N.: The multi-purpose incremental learning system AQ15 and its testing application on three medical domains. In *Proc. Fifth National Conference on Artificial Intelligence*, Morgan Kaufmann, 1986, pp. 1041–1045.

50. Modai, I., Israel, A., Mendel, S., Hines, E.L. and Weizman, R.: Neural network based on adaptive resonance theory as compared to experts in suggesting treatment for schizophrenic and unipolar depressed in-patients, *Journal of Medical Systems*, 20(6): 403–412 (1996).

51. Michie, D., Spiegelhalter, D.J. and Taylor, C.C., eds.: *Machine learning, neural and statistical classification*, Ellis Horwood, 1994.

52. Muggleton, S.: Inverse entailment and Progol, *New Generation Computing, Special Issue on Inductive Logic Programming*, 13(3–4): 245–286 (1995).

53. Niblett, T. and Bratko, I.: Learning decision rules in noisy domains. In: *Research and Development in Expert Systems III* (Bramer, M., ed.), Cambridge University Press, 1986, pp. 24–25.

54. Pawlak, Z.: Information systems – theoretical foundations. *Information Systems*, 6:205–218 (1981).

55. Pawlak, Z.: *Rough Sets: Theoretical Aspects of Reasoning about Data*, volume 9 of *Series D: System Theory, Knowledge Engineering and Problem Solving*. Kluwer, 1991.

56. Polkowski, L. and Skowron, A., eds.: *Rough Sets in Knowledge Discovery 1: Methodology and Applications*, volume 18 of *Studies in Fuzziness and Soft Computing*. Physica-Verlag, 1998.

57. Quinlan, J.R.: Induction of decision trees. *Machine Learning* 1(1): 81–106 (1986).

58. Quinlan, J.R.: Learning logical definitions from relations, *Machine Learning* 5(3): 239–266 (1990).
59. Quinlan, J.R.: *C4.5: Programs for Machine Learning*, San Mateo, CA, Morgan Kaufmann, 1993.
60. Rumelhart, D.E. and McClelland, J.L., eds.: *Parallel Distributed Processing, Vol. 1: Foundations.* MIT Press, Cambridge, MA, 1986.
61. Setiono, R.: Extracting rules from pruned networks for breast cancer diagnosis, *Artificial Intelligence in Medicine*, 8(1): 37–51 (1996).
62. Srinivasan, A., King, R.D., Muggleton, S.H. and Sternberg, M.J.E.: Carcinogenesis predictions using inductive logic programming. In *Intelligent Data Analysis in Medicine and Pharmacology* (Lavrač, N. Keravnou, E. and Zupan, B., eds.), Kluwer, 1997, pp. 243–260.
63. Tsumoto, S.: Modelling medical diagnostic rules based on rough sets, In: *Proc. First International Conference on Rough Sets and Soft Computing – RSCTC'98* (Polkowski, L. and Skowron, A., eds.), volume 1424 of *Lecture Notes in Artificial Intelligence, Springer Verlag.* Springer, 1998, pp. 475–482.
64. Weiss, S.M., Kulikowski, C.A.: *Computer Systems that Learn.* Morgan Kaufmann, San Mateo, CA, 1991.
65. Wettschereck, D.: A study of distance-based machine learning algorithms, PhD Thesis, Department of Computer Science, Oregon State University, Corvallis, OR, 1994.
66. Wu, C.H.: Artificial neural networks for molecular sequence analysis, *Computers & Chemistry*, 21(4): 237–56 (1997).
67. Zhu, Y. and Yan, H.: Computerized tumor boundary detection using a Hopfield neural network, *IEEE Transactions on Medical Imaging*, 16(1): 55–67 (1997).

Guidelines and Protocols

Guidelines-Based Workflow Systems

S. Quaglini, C. Mossa*, C. Fassino, M. Stefanelli, A. Cavallini**, G. Micieli**

Dipartimento di Informatica e Sistemistica, Università di Pavia
Via Ferrata 1, I-27100 Pavia, Italy
sil@ipvaimed2.unipv.it
*Consorzio di Bioingegneria e Informatica Medica, Pavia, Italy
Via Ferrata 1, I-27100 Pavia, Italy
mossa@aim.unipv.it
**Stroke Unit, IRCCS Istituto Neurologico "C. Mondino" Pavia, Italy
Via Palestro, 11 I-27100 Pavia, Italy
micieli@cpbim1.unipv.it

Abstract. This paper describes a methodology for achieving an efficient allocation of resources while using clinical practice guidelines. The resulting system can be classified as a "guideline-based patient workflow management system". Both medical and organisational knowledge are represented through computational formalisms, from relational tables to Petri net. Human and technological resources, necessary to guideline-based activities, are represented within an organisational model. This allows running the Petri net for simulating the implementation of the guideline in the clinical setting, in such a way to validate the model and to suggest an optimal resource allocation, before the workflow system is installed. Finally, we are experimenting the real setting implementation. For illustrating the methodology, an application concerning the management of acute ischemic stroke is presented.

1 Introduction

To exploit the great potentiality that clinical practice guidelines (GLs) [5] offer to improve health care outcomes, it is essential to develop a methodology that allows their effective and efficient implementation within the clinical routine. It has already been shown that connection with the electronic patient record (EPR) improves the compliance with the GL, together with care delivery quality [8]. For this reason, we developed a framework for a formal computerised representation of GLs, and for their integration with the EPR [10]. It has also been shown that implementation of GLs is often impaired by organisational constraints [6], and that a site-specification of the GL is almost always necessary. In addition, improving communication among professionals has been recognised as one of the most important goals of modern hospital information systems, being lack of communication facilities a major bottleneck in health care organisations. To face these problems, it is clear that, as well as the GL medical knowledge, also health care organisational knowledge must be modelled [9]. Modelling medical knowledge establishes *what* to do, modelling organisational knowledge establishes *how* and *by whom* to do. Eventually, we realised that a Workflow Management System (WFMS) could be the correct tool to fully

W. Horn et al. (Eds.): AIMDM'99, LNAI 1620, pp. 65-75, 1999.
© Springer-Verlag Berlin Heidelberg 1999

implement a GL and to control its outcomes. In fact, a WFMS is defined as "a system that completely defines, manages, and executes workflow processes through execution of software whose order of execution is driven by a computer representation of the workflow process logic" [2,3]. When the medical process model is provided by a GL, we refer to the system as a GL-based WFMS. Through such a system, we could be able to answer questions as *Is there any bottleneck in the hospital structure that impairs the GL implementation ?, How much does it cost to implement the GL ?, Is any human or technological resource over- or under-loaded?*, and so on.

An important aspect, to save time and resources from the development point of view, is that WFMS are very common in real world settings other than health care. Thus, we tried to exploit results achieved in those contexts, by importing the sharable technology into the health care context. In other words, we propose a methodology for integrating research tools developed in our laboratories with available commercial tools able to manage classical workflow models. As a bench-test we illustrate the implementation of a GL for the acute ischemic stroke management, developed within the American Heart Association [1], and actually under evaluation in four Italian Stroke Units. This project aims at evaluating the benefit of GLs for the management of a disease that represents the third cause of death in industrial countries, and the first cause of permanent disability, so being a source of both direct and indirect social costs. On the other hand, it has been shown [4] that standardised diagnostic procedures for stroke may decrease cost, maintaining the quality of care. The opinion of the experts is that a further introduction of standardised therapeutic procedures and improved co-ordination among the different health care operators involved, could increase the benefit, by decreasing mortality and improving quality of life of survivors.

2　The Proposed Methodology

Fig 1 shows the main methodological steps to build a guideline-based patient WFMS. The basic idea has been to use the Petri net formalism [2,3] to represent GLs, in order to exploit the Petri Net computational properties for performing simulations. Very briefly, classical Petri nets represent processes, and are made up of two types of nodes, places and transitions, connected by directed arcs. Arcs can not link nodes of

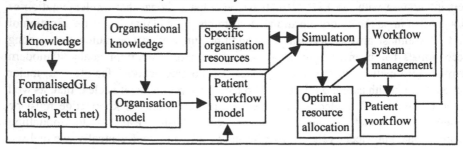

Fig. 1. The process of building a patient workflow management system

the same type. Transitions may fire when *tokens* are present in the corresponding input place(s). When a transition is fired, tokens are consumed from its input places and produced for its output place(s).

Token distribution in a certain time represents the state of the system. Classical Petri nets allows for the modelling of states, events, conditions, synchronisation, parallelism, choice and iteration. To efficiently describe real processes, these features are not sufficient, thus many extensions have been proposed. The so-called "high level" Petri nets allow to add colours, hierarchy and time to this basic representation, so that we can model data, simulate time spent in each transition, and structure large models. With these extensions, Petri nets can embed all the necessary knowledge to represent GLs and their implementation. Unfortunately, it should be very difficult, for non-expert users, to directly represent guidelines using Petri nets. Thus, we propose, as an intermediate step, a graphical editor oriented to the medical experts, by means of which a textual GL may be easily formalised. This intermediate representation itself may be used as well for other kinds of applications, but if a workflow management system is needed, an automatic translation into a Petri net is performed. Finally, from the objects representing the Petri net, a translation into the Workflow Process Definition Language (WPDL) is performed. Using such a standard (WPDL is the language recommended by the Workflow Coalition), it is possible exploit different existing products for the subsequent phases. As a matter fact, workflow simulations are performed using INCOME™, and real-world imple-

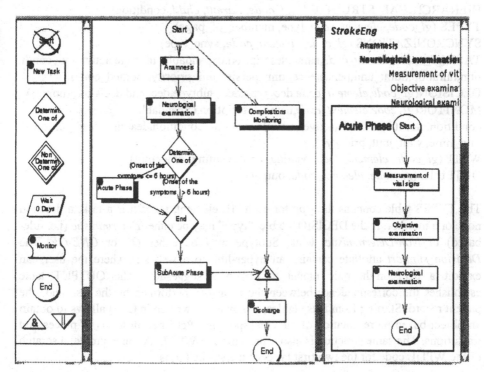

Fig. 2. The main page of the GL for the stroke management. Shadowed blocks are expandable blocks: on the right the expansion of the "acute phase" block is shown

mentations are being experimented using ORACLE WORKFLOW™. The purpose of the simulation is to verify and to validate the workflow model, and to find the optimal resource allocation, before the workflow system is implemented in the real setting. The optimal resource allocation is suggested after different simulations. Then, as long as real-world results and statistics are collected implementing the workflow management system, additional problems, not previously considered, may be highlighted and possibly fixed.

3   Guidelines Formalization

The graphical editor for building formalised GLs, extensively described in [10], exploits a terminology server drawn from UMLS (Unified Medical Language System) [7], and in particular from the SNOMED thesaurus. It is used to label tasks in such a way that different GLs, that possibly run in the same environment, share a common terminology. The same conceptual model should be shared by the database storing the electronic patient record, to allow an easy integration with the GLs. Figure 2 shows the main page of the GL for the Acute Ischemic Stroke. The GL is structured in "pages" that represent different abstraction levels (i.e. non-atomic tasks may be represented, and their expansion will be in an inner page). The internal representation consists in nine relational tables (italic attributes are the relation keys).
GUIDELINE (*gl_code*, description, eligibility criteria, first_task, intention, source)
HIERARCHICAL_STRUCTURE (*gl_code, parent, child*, condition)
TYPES (*gl_code, element_code*, type, member_of_page)
SYNCRONIZATIONS (*gl_code, element_code*, sync_type)
TASK(*gl_code,element_code*,name,description,expandable_in_page,activation_condition,duration,durat_unit,persistence_time,persist_unit,priority,snomed_code)
DECISION(*gl_code,element_code*,dec_type,dec_subtype,dec_end,decision_support)
MONITOR(*gl_code,element_code*,name,description,expandable_in_page,activation_condition,monitor_module,active_module,monitor_condition,deadline,deadl_unit,waiting_time, wait_unit, priority)
WAIT (*gl_code, element_code*, waiting_time, waiting_time_unit)
OUTPUTS (*gl_code, element_code*, output)

The TYPES table contains the *type* for each GL element, i.e. if it is a task, a decision node or a monitor. In the DECISION table, "type" may be either *Deterministic* (i.e. rule-based) or *Non-Deterministic*, while Subtype may be either *OR* or *ONE-OF*. The *Decision_support* attribute contains an hyper-link to a web site where the user can exploit a decision-theoretic model to obtain a suggestion. The OUTPUT table establishes the correspondence between the measures performed by the task and the patient record. Starting from these tables, a translator (written in C++) allows to obtain an object-based representation of the corresponding Petri net, in terms of places and transitions. The same structure is also represented in WPDL. As an example, a scratch of the WPDL code for the two first tasks of the stroke GL is:

```
WORKFLOW MT0
        DESCRIPTION        "Petri Net for Stroke_Eng"
        ACTIVITY T2068
                IMPLEMENTATION        ATOMIC
                DESCRIPTION    "Onset Modalities Deficit Duration Deficit Type"
                EXTENDED_ATTRIBUTE NAME      Anamnesis
                EXTENDED_ATTRIBUTE TIME_UNITMINUTES
                EXTENDED_ATTRIBUTE PROC_TIME          0
        END ACTIVITY
        ACTIVITY T4602
                IMPLEMENTATION        WORKFLOW "MT4602"
                DESCRIPTION "Main signs and symptoms to assess a preliminary diagnosis"
                EXTENDED_ATTRIBUTE NAME "Objective and Neurological examination"
                EXTENDED_ATTRIBUTE TIME_UNITMINUTES
                EXTENDED_ATTRIBUTE PROC_TIME          0
        END ACTIVITY
        TRANSITION T1
                FROM    T2068
                TO      T4602
                EXTENDED_ATTRIBUTE STORE_SHORT_NAME          "PT2068"
                EXTENDED_ATTRIBUTE STORE_NAME        "Anamnesis"
        END TRANSITION
```

This description may be interpreted by the Income package, and the resulting Petri net is shown in Fig. 3. The Petri net is the so-called "behavioural model" of the WF, because it represents the sequence of activities to be performed. The next step for

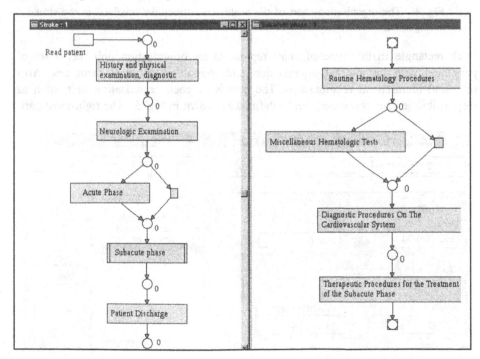

Fig. 3. The translation of the first page of the GL into the corresponding Petri-Net. The right part of the figure shows the expansion of the task "subacute phase"

building a WFMS is to allocate the resources necessary to perform these activities. Resources are represented in the organisational model, as explained in the following paragraph.

4   The Organisational Model

The organisational knowledge is represented by organisation charts, i.e. organisation units and hierarchies describing the structure of the hospital (in general, of the health care organisation). The organisation chart of the health care structures involved in the implementation of the GL for the stroke management is shown in Fig. 4.

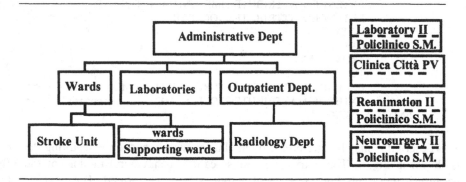

Fig. 4 . The organisation chart of the health care structures involved in the stroke management

Each rectangle in this type of chart represents an organisation unit, i.e. a set of personnel with an internal organisation and, possibly, technical resources. Arcs represent hierarchical relationships. The details of each organisation unit, such as responsibilities and resources, can be defined as shown in Fig. 5. The right-most part

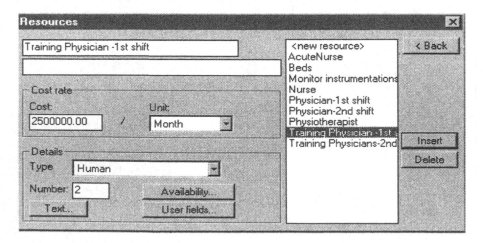

Fig. 5. Details of the stroke organisation unit: the resource specification

of of Fig. 5 shows the resources assigned to the stroke unit: they are both human resources (six nurses, one responsible physician, two assistant physicians) and technical resources (six beds, instruments for rehabilitation, ECG, PA and O2 monitoring instrumentation). The other necessary resources are external to the stroke unit: some instrumentation (TAC, RNM) belong to other units in the same hospital, while some consultants (cardiologists, logopedist, neurosurgeon) belong to other hospitals (namely Clinica Citta' di Pavia and Policlinico San Matteo).

5   Dynamic Simulation and Analysis of Health Care Processes

It is very important to verify the soundness of the workflow model before putting the workflow management system into practice. By using Petri nets this can be done by simulation runs. During simulations, concrete objects are added into the process model: in our context, the objects are the patients admitted to the stroke unit. These

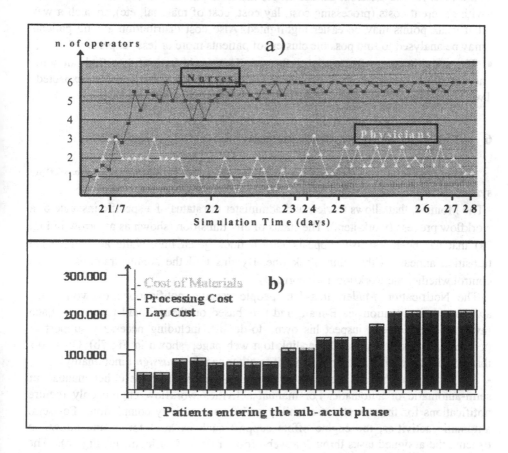

Fig. 6. (a) the workload of two different human resources **(b)** the cost allocation (Lit)

objects are described into a database (the so-called "information model"), in such a way that realistic patient records may be provided to the simulator. The main purpose of simulation runs is to find time, amount and cost of the used resources. Some useful information that can be derived is:

- at which time (if any) certain resources have a high or low work-load. This should allow to re-allocate both the number and the shifts of the operators
- bottlenecks or capacity reserves at certain times: each place in the Petri net has a predefined capacity (for example no more than six patients may be in the stroke units at the same time) in such a way that its "load", i.e. the ratio between the capacity and the actual number of objects, may be computed
- time spent by patients in the phases of their management. Execution time associated to each activity is sampled from a random normal distribution estimated from real data or by the expert opinion. Both single values and statistics can be produced
- the costs for the different patients in the different phases. An activity is associated with different costs (processing cost, lay cost, cost of material, etc), in such a way that weak points may be easier highlighted. Also cost distribution among patients may be analysed to find possible clusters of patients more or less "expensive".
- The activities more frequently performed. This could be useful to find out some activity that, for reasons to be explained, is not performed as frequently as expected.

Two exemplars of these reports are illustrated in Fig. 6a-b.

6   The Workflow Implementation

Through Oracle Workflow, we are experimenting the installation of the workflow system in the clinical setting. The main modules of the system are:

- The Monitor, that allows to view and administer the status of a specific instance of a workflow process (work-item). The status of any transition (shown as an arrow in Fig. 7a) that has been traversed appears with a thick green line, while an untraversed transition appears with a thin black line. By this tool the administrator is able to control whether the workflow runs correctly.

- The Notification Mailer, that lets people receive notifications of work-items awaiting their attention via E-mail, and acts based on their E-mail responses. Each involved operator can inspect his own to-do list, including necessary support to perform the task(s) (exg: an hyper-link to a web page, shown in Fig 7b). Operators that do not accept the task can forward it to other people (*reassign* functionality)

- The Activities, that are the real-world tasks. Activities may be either manual, or semi-automatic or automatic. For manual activities workflow engine only require notifications for the operator availability and for the activity completion. For semi automatic activities, the engine offers support such as html forms and allows to execute the assigned tasks through a web browser (exg: data input in Fig 7c). The automatic activities are transparent to the users and are completely executed by the engine.

By these modules it is possible to check the workflow status and the resource availability, to assign tasks to people according to their roles, defined in the organisation model, and to monitor the task execution. Information about the performed tasks are stored into the workflow database, in such a way that statistics can be performed on times, costs, and workloads.

7   Conclusion

In this paper we proposed a methodology for modelling and implementing clinical workflow processes where expertise in medical care can be completely separated from expertise in organisational structure. This separation allows an easier maintenance of the system in face of changes in either the medical knowledge or the resource allocation. The tools developed, integrated with commercial technological solutions, support:

• knowledge acquisition, in terms of medical knowledge (contained in clinical practice GLs) and in terms of site-specific working formalities;

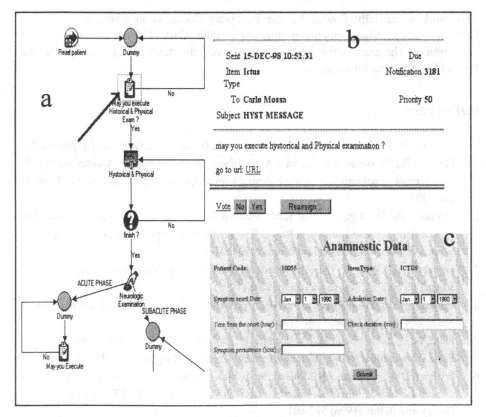

Fig. 7. The workflow implementation. (a) the monitor console (the arrow indicates the current task), (b) a message sent to a human resource (in this case a physician), and (c) the form for data input that automatically appears to the physician when accepting the

- optimal resource allocation, through the simulation of a workflow model, based on the sound Petri net theory
- real-life patient workflow implementation, through a workflow engine.

Of course, as for any other information tool, interaction with the system may rise problems if a user needs analysis has not been carefully performed before the implementation, as well as an analysis of the already existing information flows. Barriers to real usage of computerised systems are common experiences, mainly due to the unavoidable impact onto the health-care personnel daily work. Special attention must be paid in order to reduce overburden to the users and to identify and guarantee all possible benefits. In terms of workflow, this imply for example to assess the number and the timing of the messages sent to the operators, avoiding unnecessary messages and annoying computer interaction. Keeping attention to these issues, we believe this methodology will improve health care delivery by facing the problems due to user non-compliance with GLs and to difficulty of communication and co-operation among health care professionals.

Acknowledgements

This work is partially funded by the European Commission through the project PatMan (Patient Management) within the Health Care Telematics Applications Programme. The authors thank S.K. Andersen and the other partners of the Patman Project for their helpful comments.

References

1. Adams H.P., Brott T.G., Crowell R.M., Furln A.J., Gomez C.R., Grotta J., Helgason C.M., Marler J.R., Woolson R.F., Zivin J.A., Feinberg W., Mayberg, M. Guidelines for the management of patients with acute ischemic stroke. Special Report. Stroke, 25, 9 (1994), 1901-1911

2. van der Aalst W.M.P., van Hee K.M., Houben G.J. Modelling and analysing workflow using a Petri-net based approach, Proc. 2nd workshop on Computer-Supported Cooperative Work, Petri-nets and related formalisms (1994) 31-50

3. van der Aalst W.M.P. The Application of Petri Nets to Workflow Management. The Journal of circuits, systems and computers (1998)

4. Bowen J., Yaste, C. Effect of a stroke protocol on hospital cost of stroke patients. Neurology 44 (10) (1994) 1691-1694

5. Field, M.J., Lohr, K.N. (Eds). Institute of Medicine. Guidelines for Clinical Practice. From Development to Use, National Academy Press, Washington D.C. (1992)

6. Fridsma, D.B., Gennari, J.H., Musen, M.A. Making generic Guidelines Site Specific. In: Cimino J.J. (ed) J. Am. Med. Inform. Assoc., Proc. 1996 AMIA Fall Symp., Philadelphia, Hanley and Belfus (1996) 597-601

7. Humphreys, B.L., Lindberg, D.A.B., Schoolman H.M., Barnett G.O. The Unified Medical Language System: An Informatics Research Collaboration. J. Am. Med. Inform. Assoc., 5 (1998) 1-11

8. Lobach D.F., Hammond W.E., Development and Evaluation of a Computer-assisted Management Protocol (CAMP): Improved Compliance with Care Guidelines for Diabetes Mellitus Proc. SCAMC, 18 (1994) 787-791

9. Prietula, M.J., Carley, K.M. and Gasser, L. (Eds) Simulating Organisations – Computational models of institutions and groups, AAAI Press/The MIT Press, Menlo Park, California (1998)

10. Quaglini, S., Dazzi, L., Gatti, L., Stefanelli, M., Fassino, C., Tondini, C. Supporting tools for guideline development and dissemination, Artificial Intelligence in Medicine, 14 (1998) 119-137

Enhancing Clinical Practice Guideline Compliance by Involving Physicians in the Decision Process

Brigitte Séroussi[1], Jacques Bouaud[1], and Éric-Charles Antoine[2]

[1] Service d'Informatique Médicale, AP–HP & Département de Biomathématiques,
Université Paris 6, Paris, France
{bs,jb}@biomath.jussieu.fr
[2] Service d'Oncologie Médicale, Groupe Hospitalier Pitié-Salpêtrière, Paris, France
eric.antoine@psl.ap-hop-paris.fr

Abstract. Despite the proliferation of implemented clinical practice guidelines (CPGs) as decision support systems, there is still little evidence of changes in physicians behavior. The reasons usually evoked to explain the low physicians compliance consider the incompleteness of guidelines knowledge, the impreciseness of the terms used and the physicians psychological reluctance. Another reason comes from the original verbal design of CPGs as well as the impossibility to enumerate all the contexts in which a guideline applies, which avoid the automatised control of all CPGs interpretations and therefore the design of robust formal models. The ONCODOC approach proposes a decision support framework for implementing guidelines where the context-based interpretation is controlled by clinicians. The first application deals with breast cancer therapy. Experimented in real size at the point of care, the system demonstrated significantly high scores of theoretical agreement with CPGs recommendations and compliance.

1 Introduction

Recently, to reduce high health costs and practice variation among physicians, there has been a growing emphasis in the development of clinical practice guidelines (CPGs). However, despite the proliferation of computer-based CPGs as decision support systems (DSSs), there is still little evidence of changes in physicians behavior. To explain the low physicians compliance to CPGs, there are commonly admitted reasons, either psychological with the reluctance of physicians to loose their autonomy and clinical freedom [1], or practical with the strongly criticized incompleteness of CPGs knowledge, and the lack of precision in the categorisation of clinical situations. Another reason comes from the context-free automatisation of a medical knowledge that needs a contextual interpretation to generate acceptable inferences. Medical decision making in the context of actual clinical settings is indeed a complex process that can hardly be modelled [2].

W. Horn et al. (Eds.): AIMDM'99, LNAI 1620, pp. 76–85, 1999.
© Springer-Verlag Berlin Heidelberg 1999

Developed in collaboration with the "Service d'Oncologie Médicale Pitié-Salpêtrière" (SOMPS), ONCODOC [3] is a computer-based CPG system elaborated in a document-based paradigm with a knowledge-based approach. Rather than providing automated decision support for guideline-based medical care, the system involves the physician in an active medical reasoning process although following CPGs. As opposed to usual fully computerised approaches [4,5,6], the clinician has thus the opportunity to control the knowledge operationalisation by his free interpretation of the information provided, and can participate to the therapeutic decision by building the patient-specific clinical context and by choosing among the proposed recommendations. Tested in a real-size experimentation and routinely used at the point of care by the oncologists of the SOMPS in the management of breast cancer patients, ONCODOC demonstrated significantly high scores of both adherence defined as a theoretical agreement with CPGs recommendations and compliance.

2   Clinical Practice Guidelines

2.1   CPGs as Decision Support Systems

The current development of evidence-based medicine has lead to the multiplication of CPGs. CPGs are expected to provide practitioners accurate, relevant, and updated decision support to normalise patient care. Most of them have been developed, edited, and validated by governmental or professional organisations. They are usually written as textual documents with a logical structure including an objective, a review of the state of the art supported by scientific references, and recommendations for medical actions. They are often published as paper-based documents. The recent deployment of information technologies allows for the widespread dissemination of their computerised versions over computer networks (internet, intranets, or HIS). Although such technologies solve the problems of dissemination and of knowledge access at the point of care, on-line delivery of textual documents is not sufficient to provide effective practical answers in daily clinical situations. The text-based implementation strategy does not allow the physician to retrieve easily and to apply straightforwardly the knowledge contained in the CPGs to solve a given medical problem: obtaining individualised recommendations is time consuming and often unfruitful.

In order to enhance the use of CPGs, numerous attempts have been made to design knowledge-based systems capable of implementing CPGs to provide in daily practice actual DSSs in various medical domains. The challenge of this approach pertains to artificial intelligence, that is to build a computational formal model that accounts for all the facets of CPGs knowledge. The underlying methods are those of decision making and knowledge representation: elementary state-transition tables, situation-action rules, reflex logic modules (Arden syntax), decision-tables [7], action plans [8,9], etc. More recently, generic guideline representation languages, with a clear syntax and semantics, such as PROforma [5] and GLIF [4] have been designed to handle the various concepts that care formalisation implies. Depending on their goals, these new DSSs may be consulted interactively by a clinician or automated from computerised patient data.

However, despite the proliferation of experiments with implemented CPGs, there is still little evidence of physicians compliance (often less than 50%) to guideline recommendations. Additional developments such as computer-generated reminders or individualised feedback to clinicians [10] have been shown to enhance guidelines utilisation but still, median compliance remains very low.

2.2   Common Pitfalls

Several works [1,11,12] have analysed the multiple reasons for physicians' low compliance to CPGs. The reasons commonly admitted come from the fact that medicine is not an exact science: there is no formal model for medical knowledge which is mainly expressed in natural language. Common problems in implementing CPGs as DSSs are dependant on CPGs features inherent to the writing mode, on the formalisation process from text to formal representations [2,13], and of physicians' attitudes towards CPGs in the context of a particular patient.

CPG Knowledge Is Incomplete. A first pitfall is due to the incompleteness of CPG knowledge. Mostly because of the textual writing mode, which is simply linear, there is no systematised description of medical problems. As a result, some clinical situations, potentially under the scope of the CPG, may not be considered, thus missing recommendations. These knowledge gaps may not necessarily be a problem depending on the level of expertise of the reader who may fill the gaps with implicit knowledge. But, in the knowledge acquisition process from a textual guideline, such gaps are transferred to the knowledge base. Patel *et al.* [12] showed that knowledge base designers with distinct competence and level of expertise built different formal representations of a textual guideline. Designers with background knowledge were able to fill the gaps with their own knowledge. To eliminate such gaps in the translation of CPGs from text to computer-based formats, Shiffman and Greenes [7] have suggested to use decision tables which can be viewed as a method to both detect such gaps and fill them.

CPG Knowledge Is Difficult to Formalise. Another identified pitfall is due to the use of "imprecise" terms to describe medical knowledge. Natural language terms are often the only access to the underlying notions. The semantics of these notions is not always strictly formally defined, that is, in a unique and universal manner. For instance, the term "good cardiac function" does not have strictly the same meaning for a young woman or for an older one, depending on her taking or not anthracyclins. Some of the terms used in textual guidelines may thus lack specificity, may be ambiguous or not clearly defined [1].

Impreciseness of medical terms is not a problem for humans (physicians) who generally understand textual CPGs. For a given patient case, the actual context helps them to disambiguate these terms and to give them a correct interpretation, that is, an interpretation that allows the accurate operationalisation of the knowledge. But, such "imprecise" notions must be defined in a context-free manner, *i.e.* valid in every possible context to be formalised. Since every possible context cannot be envisioned, formalisations may appear then as arbitrary reductions of initial knowledge: "[Computer-based guideline applications] may not capture all the nuances and uncertainties expresses in natural language [4]" In some situations, the formal categorisations of encoded CPGs do not cater for their intended meaning in textual CPGs. In individual situations, an *a priori* out-of-context correct category assignment may be defaulted for contextual reasons. The known result is the possible mismatch between clinician's and system's inferences [12]. To deal with this problem of discrete categorisation, some authors propose the use of fuzzy logic [14] or of probabilities and utilities [9].

Clinicians' Attitudes towards Recommendations. Last, but not least, is physicians' attitudes towards CPGs, be they paper-based or computer-based. Among the barriers to their use, psychologic resistance comes from physicians' concerns about clinical freedom, doctor autonomy [15] and importance of ownership in guideline implementation [16]. But, beyond these "sociological" problems, deeper reasons may be invoked due to the untractability of CPGs taking into account all possible contexts: "[...] guideline specifications can never anticipate all the variations physicians see in treating particular patients [17]". In individual situation, the context is formed of the physician own experience and knowledge, and of the patient's state [12]. Both kinds of contexts influence the way CPG knowledge has to be interpreted. It may lead a physician to make decisions that differ from those prescribed by a strict literal application of a guideline, *i.e.* what a DSS would recommend. Such deviations may be justified.

To assess physicians' deviations from a guideline, Advani *et al.* [17] propose a meta-analysis of guideline recommended actions and actual physician actions based on their both intentions at higher levels of abstractions. Details may be different while intentions are identical. So, abstract (out-of-context) agreement with CPGs knowledge for a typical patient and compliance, *i.e.* concrete agreement for an actual individual patient, must be distinguished.

3   The OncoDoc Approach

3.1   Rationale

Medical knowledge, including CPGs, is mostly expressed is natural language. However, if this mode of expression is suited for human to human communication, it is hardly captured in a formal framework. The main property of natural language is to allow interpretation variations depending on the actual context in which this knowledge is applied. Such a property allows for flexibility in CPG use [17], that, by essence, formal models do not have. We consider that low compliance results may be explained by the incapacity of encoded CPGs to anticipate all possible contexts, necessarily unattainable at design time, and to offer sufficient flexibility in interpreting guideline knowledge.

In order to preserve the flexibility in interpreting CPGs, the methodology we adopted in ONCODOC's design aims at delegating the knowledge interpretation task to the physician at the time it is needed when the context of an actual patient is available. The physician is then involved in the decision process which he keeps control over and he is responsible of. Our proposal presents both formal and informal aspects, and is halfway between knowledge representation and literary writing. The clinician is proposed a structured encoded knowledge base (KB), but has the freedom of interpreting this knowledge for a given patient according to his decision task. The points mentioned in section 2.2 are addressed as follows:

- Therapeutic knowledge is encoded in a decision tree which constitutes the formal skeleton of the KB. Decision tree's properties are similar to those of decision tables [7]. Exhaustivity and mutual exclusivity of parameter modalities ensure that the KB is complete, and that its use is unique and non ambiguous. There are no knowledge gaps.
- Decision parameters and their possible modalities are specified using physicians terminology. Additional quantitative or qualitative definitions are specified in natural language to delineate the interpretation space. Although the meaning of the notions that are used is explicited, there is no attempt to formalise them.
- The KB is not supposed to be run by a program (expert system shell, classifier, etc.), but it is aimed at being browsed, *i.e.* "read" by the physician. He has thus the opportunity to operationalise step by step the guideline knowledge while controlling every inferences through his own contextual interpretation.

3.2 OncoDoc in Practice

The first application deals with breast cancer therapy. Therapeutic expertise of ONCODOC has been developed by two domain experts to serve as a CPG. When using the system, the right diagnosis is first selected. Then questions expressed in natural language based on the decision parameters and their definition are displayed. Within the closed but exhaustive choice of mutually exclusive values, the clinician chooses the appropriate answer by a simple mouse click (Fig. 1). In some cases, when needed, context-based comments may be added locally to restrict the interpretation space. When answering the questions, the clinician is actively involved in the knowledge operationnalisation of CPG since he has to control the instantiation of the clinical context of the guideline according to his perception of the physiopathological reality of his patient. During the hypertextual navigation, he interactively builds a specific path in the decision tree that best matches the patient's case summarised as the "recapitulative".

4 Method

A real size experimentation of ONCODOC has been carried out at the SOMPS and lasted 4 months from December 15th, 1997 to April 15th, 1998. It involved an

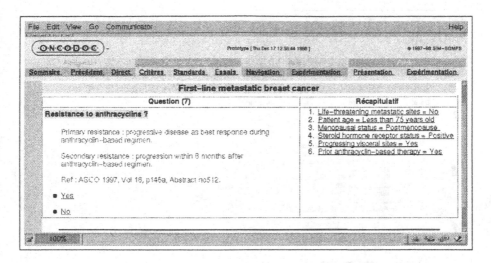

Fig. 1. Hypertextual navigation through the decision tree.

intranet web server, 6 client workstations located in medical consultation offices, and concerned the 8 department residents and attendings. For breast cancer patients, the objective of the consultation had to be specified and discriminated in either "therapeutic decision" or "monitoring" of a previously established therapeutic care plan. For each breast cancer therapeutic decision, the clinician had to use ONCODOC to get the appropriate CPG recommendations for his patient. When reaching a leaf, the corresponding page with the recapitulative clinical context and the list of appropriate therapeutic recommendations is displayed. The printed corresponding "experimentation form" (Fig. 2) was then to be filled in by the clinician to validate the CPG recommendations relevance.

To estimate how clinicians were in theoretical agreement with the CPG recommendations (the "intention" agreement of [17]) and how they complied in practice to the CPG recommendations, two different types of validation were introduced :

— *the theoretical validation* is carried out through the evaluation of how appropriate is each therapeutic proposition to the theoretical clinical context described by the recapitulative alone, disregarding the patient case. To handle the theoretical validation, the clinician has to indicate if he agrees with each therapeutic proposition by checking the boxes on the right side of the experimentation form. When he does not agree, he has to explain why.
— *the practical validation* is carried out through the choice of one CPG recommendation for the patient case, disregarding the recapitulative. The clinician has then to check on the left side of the experimentation form the treatment plan he decides to prescribe. If he finds that none of the CPG recommendations is appropriate, he indicates his own therapeutic decision for the patient.

The quantitative aspect of theoretical and practical validations has allowed the definition of two different criteria : *adherence*, defined as the frequency of

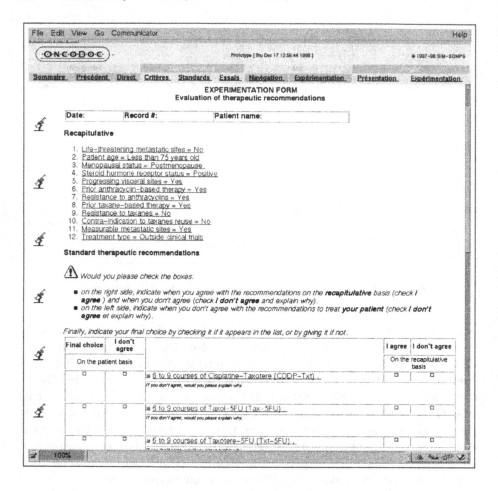

Fig. 2. Experimentation form for both theoretical and practical validations.

physicians theoretical agreement with the CPG recommendations, and *compliance*, as the frequency with which physicians actually followed the recommendations.

5   Results

5.1   Experimentation

Table 1 summarizes the activity of the department during the experimentation. We got 95 experimentation forms corresponding to breast cancer therapeutic decisions. Among them, 17 forms concerned what we called "Partial Navigations", meaning that the hypertextual navigation has been interrupted because some patient information was missing to answer a given question and that the therapeutic prescription has to be delayed, waiting for complementary laboratory tests results. On the 78 remaining experimentation forms, 8 were out of the study and concerned two kinds of breast cancers, intraductal or in situ carcinoma and locoregional relapse, that were not yet implemented at the moment of the experimentation. We got finally 70 exploitable forms, which corresponded to a total of 236 CPG recommendations.

Table 1. Distribution of oncological patient encounters during the experimentation period.

Reason	#	% breast encounters	% overall encounters
Breast cancer therapeutic decision	95	15%	8%
Breast cancer treatment monitoring	536	85%	40%
Breast total	631	100%	48%
Other	698	—	52%
Total	1329	—	100%

Physicians adherence has been measured at 96.60%. There were 8 theoretical disagreements: some CPG recommendations were refused because of lesser therapeutic efficiency as compared to the others propositions of the list, some were rejected on the basis of explanations that were judged as non relevant by the expert in charge of the knowledge base.

Physicians compliance reached 64.28%. Clinicians chose to deviate from the CPG recommendations in 25 cases : 11 cases concerned hormonotherapy treatment schemes not supported by the department medical culture which is essentially chemotherapy-based; 8 cases were "singular" propositions; 2 cases were unacceptable dosage variations, and the last 4 cases dealt with non officially approved therapy schemes.

5.2   Users Satisfaction Survey

At the end of the experimentation, we handle a users satisfaction survey with the distribution of a questionnaire to the involved department clinicians. Among the questions, we were interested to know how the clinicians estimated their adherence and compliance to ONCODOC's recommendations. The results are summarized in Table 2 and show that clinicians really trust the system with an estimated adherence of 92%, and think they do follow the CPG, estimated compliance of 80%. The study of the answers we got also confirmed the suitability of the implementation choices adopted in ONCODOC. Ranked on the Likert scale with 1 for NO and 5 for YES, the preference for expert systems has been rated 2, the preference for the automatic process of patient data (extracted for instance from a computer-based medical record) has been rated 1.86, and the preference for clinical parameters input through entry forms has been rated 1.71.

Table 2. Comparison of both observed and estimated adherence and compliance.

	Observations	Estimations
Adherence (# 236)	96.60%	92.00%
Compliance (# 70)	64.28%	80.00%

6   Discusion and Perspectives

Apart from psychological considerations, physicians compliance to CPGs is low because of context-free computer-based formalisation of context-dependent medical notions that cannot be strictly formalised [2]. The results of our experimentation prove indeed that "black box" systems usual approaches where physicians reduced to medical data providers passively obtain a solution to a given medical problem are not welcomed and that they want, on the contrary, to be actively involved in the decision-making reasoning process. Besides, clinicians have understood how important is the contextualisation of medical data in the interpretation of these data. That is why they dislike global entry forms which lose the fullness of the incremental building of a patient-specific context. From these conclusions it appears that the main issue to increase physicians compliance to CPGs and thus to reduce variation among clinical practice and improve health care, is to build clinical systems that will guide rather mislead, bringing knowledge to physicians fingertips, and let physicians control the medical decision process.

Since the experimentation, the knowledge base has been further developed. In the last version, ONCODOC uses 64 clinical parameters organised in a decision tree made of 1,863 intermediate nodes and 1,906 leaves which cover the CPGs implementation of therapeutic decisions for non metastatic breast cancer (early and locally advanced tumors), first-line metastatic breast cancer, second-line or more metastatic breast cancer, intraductal or in situ carcinoma, and locoregional relapse. After the knowledge base update, we potentially reach a compliance of 80% which is significantly higher than the best figures found in the literature. We have indeed integrated the two last types of breast cancer, as well as the "missing" hormonotherapy schemes not supported by the SOMPS culture. This was done to get closer a therapeutic consensus that we know unreachable. Medical oncology state of the art is indeed nowadays unable to discriminate between some therapeutic options and recommendations are somehow a matter of factions. ONCODOC was initially designed to reduce practice variations among SOMPS physicians and to disseminate the SOMPS therapeutic expertise outside the SOMPS. That is why SOMPS experts elaborated the KB. They have the responsibility of CPGs validity and accuracy. Playing the role of the editorial committee, they are in charge of updating the KB as new oncology information is scientifically acknowledged.

Another real-size experimentation is planned to test the decision tree robustness and to evaluate encoded therapeutic breast cancer recommendations validity in another medical oncology department.

References

1. Tierney, W. M., Overhage, J. M., Takesue, B. Y., Harris, L. E., Murray, M. D., Vargo, D. L., McDonald, C. J. Computerizing guidelines to improve care and patient outcomes : The example of heart failure. *J Am Med Inform Assoc* 1995; 2(5): 316–22.
2. Aliferis, C. F., Miller, R. A. On the heuristic nature of medical decision-support systems. *Methods Inf Med* 1995; 34(1/2): 4–14.
3. Bouaud, J., Séroussi, B., Antoine, E.-C., Gozy, M., Khayat, D., Boisvieux, J.-F. Hypertextual navigation operationalizing generic clinical practice guidelines for patient-specific therapeutic decisions. *J Am Med Inform Assoc* 1998; 5(suppl): 488–92.
4. Ohno-Machado, L., Gennari, J. H., Murphy, S. H., Jain, N. L., Tu, S. W., Oliver, D. E., Pattison-Gordon, E., Greenes, R. A., Shortliffe, E. H., Barnett, G. O. The Guideline Interchange Format: A model for representing guidelines. *J Am Med Inform Assoc* 1998; 5(4): 357–72.
5. Fox, J., Johns, N., Rahmanzadeh, A. Disseminating medical knowledge: the PROforma approach. *Artif Intell Med* 1998; 14(1,2): 157–82.
6. Zielstorff, R. D., Teich, J. M., Paterno, M. D., Segal, M., Kuperman, G. J., Hiltz, F. L., Fox, R. L. P-cape : A high-level tool for entering and processing clinical practice guidelines. *J Am Med Inform Assoc* 1998; 5(suppl): 478–82.
7. Shiffman, R. N., Greenes, R. A. Improving clinical guidelines with logic and decision-table techniques: Application to hepatitis imminization recommendations. *Med Decis Making* 1994; 14: 245–54.
8. Shahar, Y., Miksch, S., Johnson, P. The Asgaard project: a task-specific framework for the application and critiquing of time-oriented guidelines. *Artif Intell Med* 1998; 14(1,2): 29–52.
9. Quaglini, S., Dazzi, L., Gatti, L., Stefanelli, M., Fassino, C., Tondini, C. Supporting tools for guideline development and dissemination. *Artif Intell Med* 1998; 14(1,2): 119–37.
10. Lobach, D. F. Electronically distributed, computer-generated, individualized feedback enhances the use of a computerized practice guideline. *J Am Med Inform Assoc* 1996; 3(suppl): 493–7.
11. Zielstorff, R. D. Online practice guidelines : Issues, obstacles, and future prospects. *J Am Med Inform Assoc* 1998; 5(3): 227–36.
12. Patel, V. L., Allen, V. G., Arocha, J. F., Shortliffe, E. H. Representing clinical guidelines in GLIF: individual and collaborative expertise. *J Am Med Inform Assoc* 1998; 5(5): 467–83.
13. Degoulet, P., Fieschi, M., Chatellier, G. Decision support systems from the standpoint of knowledge representation. *Methods Inf Med* 1995; 34(1/2): 202–8.
14. Liu, J. C. S., Shiffman, R. N. Operationalization of clinical practice guidelines using fuzzy logic. *J Am Med Inform Assoc* 1997; 4(suppl): 283–7.
15. Tierney, W. M., Overhage, J. M., McDonald, C. J. Computerizing guidelines : Factors for success. *J Am Med Inform Assoc* 1996; 3(suppl): 562–6.
16. Berger, J. T., Rosner, F. The ethics of practice guidelines. *Arch Intern Med* 1996; 156: 2051–6.
17. Advani, A., Lo, K., Shahar, Y. Intention-based critiquing of guideline-oriented medical care. *J Am Med Inform Assoc* 1998; 5(suppl): 483–7.

Application of Therapeutic Protocols:
A Tool to Manage Medical Knowledge

C. Sauvagnac [1], J. Stines [2], A. Lesur [2], P. Falzon [1], P. Bey [2]

[1] Laboratory of Ergonomy, CNAM, 41 rue Gay-Lussac. 75005 Paris. France
[2] Alexis Vautrin Center. Avenue de Bourgogne. 54511 Vandoeuvre-les-Nancy Cedex France

Abstract. This paper stress on the possible role of protocols for making evolve medical knowledge. This study is situated in the frame of evidence-based medicine, and shows the necessity of allowing the treatment of particular cases. Therapeutic rules used in the decision group are briefly set out. The field studyshows the main role of usig accurate criteria and of giving values to these criteria.Using criteria allows to specialise the rule for fitting with particular cases. The view shared is that when similar specialisations occur repeatedly this may be potential modifications in the written rule.

1   Introduction

Medicine tends to improve the quality of its decisions by acting both on the relevance and the regularity of courses of action. To do this, medical decisions are made following therapeutic protocols. As a consequence, practices become regular and the best course of action is suggested because it is supported by explicit scientific knowledge. It may seem paradoxical to consider protocols can also be a tool to manage medical know-how. When used by a group, however, they offer an opportunity to exchange and elaborate knowledge; such is the purpose of this paper, to describe the way knowledge is managed in a group during the decision-making process.

The use of therapeutic rules follows a trend that began in the 80's toward a medicine based on research evidence (Evidence based medicine working group, 1992).

The benefits of evidence based medicine are undeniable: decisions are supported by better grounded results that are recognised as valid by the scientific community. However there are certain limitations to this approach. Though the protocols may allow to identify case categories, they level out special cases. Because it is concerned with improving the reliability of its decisions, cancerology has acted as a pioneer in setting up good practice guides (called protocols here) supported by scientific studies. This accounts for the setting up of the Therapeutic Decision Committees or TDC's (Comité de décision thérapeutique) whose function is to have problem cases looked into by a multidisciplinary group. The study related below was conducted in a "breast" TDC to describe the way it operates on one hand, and to suggest a way of recording decisions in order to use the knowledge acquired and produced to elaborate such decisions, on the other.

W. Horn et al. (Eds.): AIMDM'99, LNAI 1620, pp. 86-90, 1999.
© Springer-Verlag Berlin Heidelberg 1999

2   Guide for Medical Decisions

In practice, medical decisions are guided by recommendations based on an analysis of the existing literature and the modelisation of expert appreciations. These are only required if the level of evidence of the references is low.

The FNCLCC Standards Options Recommendations (SOR) are designed to guide choices by offering therapeutic courses of action selected according to the degree of unanimty reached on their beneficial, inappropriate or harmful effect; the standards are unanimous decisions, the options are agreed on by majority, whereas the recommendations are the expression of appreciations (Fédération nationale des centres de lutte contre le cancer, i.e. National Federation of Centres Fighting Cancer, 1996).

The protocols drafted at the Centre Alexis Vautrin are inspired by the SOR's, though they are less detailed to be more broadly used, (they are more precise because the data available is restricted).

Pluridisciplinary decisions occur when the recommendations are to be applied to specific cases; in cases where protocols do not clearly apply, the opinion of different specialists is called for to determine the course of action. Pluridisciplinarity implies confronting appreciations of people who have acquired different expertise in a variety of medical specialties. Visser and Falzon have shown that different tasks lead to a different representation of the same object (1992).

3   Field Study

3.1   Material and Methods

The study covers 86 cases gathered from 13 meetings over a period of 3 years. During that period, 150 meetings were held dealing with a total of 1030 cases.

A prior classification of the cases had been carried out according to the nature of the decision reached. Criteria were divided into 3 categories and were then studied to see how they were treated during the discussions. The 3 categories of criteria are the (case) characterisation criteria, the action criteria, and the rules criteria. During the discussion the criteria are associated with qualitative or quantitative values, or qualifying criticism ; 3 categories of associations were found. Furthermore, criteria are either used separately or in association; such associations were identified.

3.2   Results

The analyses conducted allowed to list the number of decision categories the nature of criteria applied and the use of such criteria.

Categories of decisions
The TDC committee in charge of contentious cases makes the same amount of protocol decisions (28/86) as of decisions requiring adjustments (29/86). The other decisions are elaborated decisions (13/86) and cases without decision (16/86).

Decision criteria

The decision criteria were divided into 3 categories: characterisation, action and rule.

The characterisation criteria relate to the case; they can be "protocol" criteria, that is to say the ones thats are explicitly used to classify cases (size of tumor, status of hormonal receptors) or criteria invoked by practitioners (such as case history or associated pathology). They are used 386 times.

Action criteria relate to the possible actions to be taken for the case under consideration (225 times).

Rule criteria are the ones that explicitly apply a written rule to make a decision (for such a decision to be made, there must be more than 3 nodes). They are used 66 times.

Values assigned to the criteria

To take a decision, that is to decide whether or not to include the case in a protocol category, it is necessary to consider the specific value of the characteristics generally taken into account for a breast cancer (its size, the node status or the existence of metastases) ; but other criteria are also used concerning the specificity of the case at hand. This whole set of criteria must be located on a scale of value.

When the criteria are stated, they are most often assigned a value for the decision to be taken ; this value can be either qualitative, quantitative or critical.

A quantitative value is assigned most frequently (see table II) and is often stated together with the criterion.

Examples of criteria with their corresponding qualitative, quantitative or critical values are shown hereafter.

Example of a qualitative value
she suffers from pain in the pelvis or in the back

Example of a quantitative value (p1 and p2 are two physicians)
-p1: has she had 60 grays (in radiotherapy)?
-p2: 50 grays

Example of a critical value
-p1: "analog of LHRH protects the ovarian stock"
-p2: "yes, but you can't extrapolate at age 45"

Criteria associations

Criteria can be associated either by adding them together (several criteria are considered jointly) or by establishing a hierarchy (one criteria has a prevailing importance over the others). Such associations are not very frequent, only 14 out of the 86 cases.

– the addition of criteria implies that the significance of two criteria combined is different from their significance when isolated.

Example
"if it is 2 cms big, it's not worth operating"
" yes, but since she is 36, it is worth it"

In this case, age is the factor that reinforces the criterion "size of a node."
- the hierarchy is defined by a differential weighting of criteria: these are cases in which two criteria with conflicting prognostic values oppose each other and a choice is made on the relative importance of such criteria.

In summary

The decisions thus appear to focus on the use of the stated criteria that have been assigned values. The criteria are carefully examined in the course of the group decision process; they are assigned values so as to better define them and also, to locate them on quantitative scales of value; they are also reviewed to ensure the validity of the decision being made.

In general, criteria are used separately and are equally weighted. However, in group decisions, some criteria are associated or compared in importance.

3.3 Discussion

The results are used to characterise the TDC committee's role in sharing the different types of knowledge and developing such knowledge.

The protocol can be verified and reinforced

A protocol decision may be taken for cases in which the protocol did not seem applicable at first; this implies that the scope of the protocol was checked beforehand. When some criteria show limit values for a case included in one of the protocol decision categories, the protocol is further defined and reinforced. Similarly, some criteria have ambiguous values: if the decision resorts to the protocol, it will reinforce it by specifying how it should be applied.

Questions may arise as to the limitations in the application of treatments prescribed. If the treatment is ultimately applied as is recommended by the protocol, this will reinforce the protocol.

The use of criteria can be further specified

When a criterion is assigned a critical evaluation, the context in which it can be used is further specified. This critical evaluation gives extra information on the way to characterise cases, on the possible actions to take and the conditions in which rules are applicable:
- a characteristic-critical evaluation combination further defines the conditions in which a characteristic can be deemed certain and can be taken into account,
- an action-critical evaluation combination further defines the conditions in which the proposed therapy applies,
- a rule-critical evaluation combination further specifies the conditions in which the rule applies.

When practitioners adapt a therapy in response to a specific criterion, they establish a sub-category within the protocol thereby specializing it. Sub-categories are also created within a protocol when criteria are associated or compared.

The view shared is that when similar specialisations occur repeatedly this may justify potential modifications in the written rule. When categories of specialisation are detected, a potential modification of the rule may be suggested. This proposal can only be considered if a sufficient level of evidence is provided by literature findings, or even by the development of a therapeutic trial.

4   Conclusion

At the Centre Alexis Vautrin, the TDC committee appears to fulfill two immediate functions: decision-making for contentious cases and recording of such decisions. It also fulfills two other functions with a differed effect: it adjusts the state of knowledge and constantly enhances protocols.

On the basis of the data acquired, it is worth determining how specialisations of protocols can be used to write new ones or modify existing ones. The TDC committee is not only required to achieve immediate functional objectives it must also reach meta-functional objectives (Falzon, 1994) in the medium or long run (fine-tuning of protocols). The resulting knowledge derives from two sources, corresponding to the two different forms of medical practice; the systematic form of practice in research, the therapist's practice based on adjustements.

Supporting the second position leads to different choices in analysis and action. In particular, it implies richer contents in the recordings of TDC discussions. It not only must refer to the decision ultimately reached but must also include the justifications thereof, the alternative hypotheses envisaged, the reasons why they were rejected, the knowledge that was not shared by all (because it was over-specialised) but was nonetheless brought up in the course of the discussion

A project to design a case-based system is currently underway. Its objective is to propose new rules by classifying the successive adjustments made in practice.

References

Evidence based medicine working group. (1992) Evidence-based medicine. A new approach to teaching practice for medicine. *JAMA*, November 4, Vol 268, n°17

Falzon, P., (1994) Les activités méta-fonctionnelles et leur assistance. In *Le travail humain*, vol.57, N°1, pp 1-23.

Federation Nationale des Centres de Lutte Contre le Cancer (1996). *Standards, Options, Recommandations*. Paris.

Visser, W. & Falzon, P. (1992) Catégorisation et types d'expertise. Une étude empirique dans le domaine de la conception industrielle. Intellectica, *15:27-53*.

Decision Support Systems, Knowledge-Based Systems, Cooperative Systems

From Description to Decision:

Towards a Decision Support Training System for MR Radiology of the Brain

Benedict du Boulay[1], Briony Teather[2], George du Boulay[3], Nathan Jeffrey[2],
Derek Teather[2], Mike Sharples[4], and Lisa Cuthbert[1]

[1] School of Cognitive and Computing Sciences, University of Sussex
[2] Department of Medical Statistics, De Montfort University, Leicester
[3] Institute of Neurology, London
[4] School of Electronic and Electrical Engineering, University of Birmingham

Abstract. We have developed a system that aims to help trainees learn a systematic method of describing MR brain images by means of a structured image description language (IDL). The training system makes use of an archive of cases previously described by an expert neuroradiologist. The system utilises a visualisation method – an Overview Plot – which allows the trainee to access individual cases in the database as well as view the overall distribution of cases within a disease and the relative distribution of different diseases. This paper describes the evolution of the image description training system towards a decision support training system, based on the diagnostic notion of a "small world". The decision support training system will employ components from the image description training system, so as to provide a uniform interface for training and support.

1   Introduction

We have developed an image description training system [19, 20] that aims to help radiology trainees learn how to describe MR brain images in a systematic way by means of a structured image description language (IDL). This language allows clinically meaningful features of MR brain images to be recorded, such as the location, shape, margin and interior structure of lesions. The training system makes use of images from an archive of about 1200 cases, previously described in detail using the terms of the IDL by an expert neuroradiologist.

The image description training system employs a visualisation method – an Overview Plot – which allows the trainee to view and access (i) the images themselves, (ii) the written descriptions of the individual lesions in the image, and (iii) a two dimensional representation of the multi-dimensional distribution of all cases of a disease chosen from the archive. The two dimensional representation relates to, and is calculated from, the descriptions of the lesions. Thus one can view the overall distribution of appearance of cases within a disease and the relative distribution of different diseases, one against another. To this extent it is

W. Horn et al. (Eds.): AIMDM'99, LNAI 1620, pp. 93–102, 1999.
© Springer-Verlag Berlin Heidelberg 1999

a kind of case-based training system that provides a visual indexing mechanism to cases similar to the case in hand.

This paper describes the development of the image *description* training system to include a second stage, namely a *decision support* training system, which we see as its immediate role with future potential as a decision support tool.

Two principles have guided the development of the system so far. First, the system is deliberately aimed to support and train the radiologist's inferences from what can be observed *in the images*. In particular, the two dimensional representation is currently based on lesion appearance and confirmed diagnosis, but not on clinical signs and symptoms. The reconciliation of those inferences with other sources of data, such as the clinical history, is a matter for the user. Second, the design exploits as far as possible radiologists' visual-spatial reasoning rather than simply offering numerical or quasi-numerical information about diagnostic probabilities.

In the next section we briefly outline the nature of radiological expertise as it informs the design. A comparison is then made with other knowledge-based learning and teaching environments for radiology that offer substantial adaptivity to the individual or are based on a careful analysis of the training task. The body of the paper briefly describes the image description language and the overview plot, and then outlines the decision support methodology. It concludes with a discussion of our initial evaluation of the component tools and future work.

2 Background

2.1 Medical and Radiological Expertise

Medical experts possess highly structured knowledge that informs the small set of hypotheses that need to be considered in order to make accurate diagnoses. Their reasoning is generally data driven [16] and does not appear to work directly from scientific first principles so much as from an "illness script" that encapsulates various levels of knowledge (including, at base, the scientific) in a schema associated with a particular pathology [18]. When presented with a new case experts rapidly home in on a number of "critical cues" that guide them to consider that small set of possible hypotheses which best explains the data (a "small world") [11, 12]. Experts are also strongly guided by "enabling conditions", i.e. crucial factors in the patient data or clinical history. Experts have schemata that are augmented with vivid, individual cases that they have seen and use these in dealing with new cases [8]. Experts have an excellent appreciation for the range of normality but have a propensity to pay attention to and recall abnormal cases better than normal ones [9].

Expert radiologists are able to identify much of the abnormality in an image very quickly (an initial gestalt view) and this is followed by a more deliberative perceptual analysis, though both stages incorporate data-driven and hypothesis-driven activity [2]. More importantly they have undergone a combined perceptual/conceptual change, evolving from recognising salient image intensities towards recognising diagnostically significant image features. They are better than novices at identifying the 3D location and physical extent of the abnormality (i.e. responding to "localisation cues") [13].

Both experts and novices are sensitive to the skewing effect on diagnosis of other information about the patient [15]. Consulting this prior to viewing the images affects not only what they see but also what they diagnose and therefore recommend. This raises the difficult issue of when in the analysis the radiologist should look at the clinical data and case history.

2.2   Computer-Based Training

While there are many computer-based training aids for radiology (including neuroradiology), most are essentially electronic books or collections of images together with some kind of indexing mechanism, normally based primarily on disease. There have been relatively few systems that attempt to either model the domain or the evolution of knowledge and skill of the student in a detailed way. Of these, Azevedo and Lajoie [2] describe an analysis of the problem solving operators used in mammography as applied by radiologists of various levels of skill. They also analyse the nature of teaching as it occurs in radiology case conferences and particularly the way that experts articulate their diagnostic reasoning. Both these analyses are used as part of the design process for RadTutor [1]. A similar careful analysis in the domain of chest X-rays has been carried out by Rogers [17] as part of the design process of VIA-RAD tutor. Macura and Macura and their colleagues [14] have taken a case-based approach that is similar to our own in a tutor for CT and MR brain images. Their system offers a case-retrieval and decision-support mechanism based on descriptors but does not employ a detailed image description language nor offer an overview plot. However their system does employ an atlas and contains tutorial material and images of normal brains as well as those displaying lesions. It can act as a decision support system by offering a range of possible diagnoses and access to the images of related cases, given the textual information that has been entered.

3   Visual Decision Support Training

3.1   Image Description Language

The basic domain representation underpinning the system is an archive of cases with confirmed diagnoses, all described by the same expert (G. du Boulay) using the IDL. These include separate descriptions for each image sequence/echo as well as detailed descriptions (e.g. the *region, major position, exact location, margin, structure, shape, area, conformity to anatomical feature, interior pattern* (if any) and its *intensity*) of the lesion (or the largest of each type of lesion visible, where there are multiple lesions), as well as *correspondence* between described parts of lesions seen under different sequences and descriptions of *atrophy, other signs* and other *abnormal signals* for the case as a whole [4].

The image description language for MR was derived using an iterative prototyping approach, utilizing experience gained in a similar enterprise for CT brain images and a menu-based computer advisor (BRAINS) to aid in image interpretation and cerebral disease diagnosis [21, 22].

Subsequent to the process of validation and refinement, G. du Boulay employed an interactive description tool (MRID, running under X-Windows for Unix workstations) to describe an archive of some 1200 cases using the terminology of the IDL. These represent a sample of the abnormal cases captured at two different imaging centres dealing with very varied disease.

The IDL describes the appearance of the images rather than the underlying disease, though the ontology of the language is influenced by a knowledge of diagnostically important disease processes. The IDL has been constructed to be as complete and detailed as possible, taking account of the wide range of diagnostic problems that occur in neuroradiology and the variation of image appearance according to sequence type. It should be noted that one of the difficulties found in earlier work is still of major importance. The process of exhaustive description is long and painstaking, and the more recent gains in selecting terms by menu on a computer screen are offset by the more extensive and detailed descriptors made possible by MRI.

For the purposes of the prototype description training system a simplified version of the description language has been used. It provides an initial set of terms to support discussion and sharing of knowledge amongst trainee neuroradiologists and their supervisors. It also serves as a structured representation of knowledge for the MR Tutor, enabling it to generate remedial responses to student errors.

3.2 Display of Small Worlds

We can consider a case as occupying a point in a many-dimensioned space of description features. For the simplified language this space has some 30 dimensions, where each point is a vector of binary values, each representing the presence or absence of a particular feature[1]. Multiple Correspondence Analysis (MCA) is a statistical technique for data reduction and visualisation [7]. It is used here to reduce the dimensionality down to two so as to provide a ready means of overviewing the data. It does this by finding that plane which best spreads out the subset of cases under consideration. MCA is similar to principal components analysis but is applied to categorical/binary data as opposed to scalar data and assesses all possible pairwise associations in the data. Whilst the technique treats ordinal values such as as "tiny", "small", "medium" or "large" as separate dimensions, it has the advantage of not depending on the allocation of arbitrary scale values to these categories.

Effectively, a set of X-Y weightings for each feature value is derived that can be used to position any case in the 2-D space. The first dimension selects those

---

[1] A potential disadvantage of this is that zero means that a feature is not present, so partial descriptions are problematic.

high weighted features that account for the highest proportion of the variability and the second dimension selects less strongly weighted features.

A property of the analysis is that disease contours can be superimposed on the 2-D plot indicating degrees of typicality for cases of each disease. A case near the centre of the contours is highly typical of the disease whereas cases nearer to the periphery are less typical. A further property of the plots is that the proximity of two cases of a particular disease in the plot, i.e. their perceptual proximity, indicates the similarity of the two descriptions in the original multi-dimensional space, see Fig. 1 and also Section 4.2. The overview space has the property that the same perceptual distance between cases represents an increasing degree of similarity as one moves out from the centre of typicality, i.e. this matches the psychological finding that people can make finer similarity discriminations for more typically encountered cases.

In displaying cases for many diseases we adopt a largely hierarchical approach exploiting the "small worlds" metaphor [3]. We divide the diseases up into "small worlds" corresponding to small sets of confusable diseases, and compute separate composite weightings for each small world.

At present, subdivision of diseases into small worlds is based on the opinion of a single expert, but empirical work is in progress to verify these choices. Having computed the MCA weightings for the diseases in a particular small world, we can then use the MCA analysis to compute the separate likelihood contours for each disease in the chosen small world, see Fig. 1. The small world shown involves two broad categories of lesion. For more expert users the small world would need to be at a finer level of diagnostic discrimination.

By repeating this analysis for several small worlds, we have a set of possibilities against which a new case can be viewed. Just as a single small world can be displayed as a single overview plot, so a set of small worlds can be displayed in a composite form which presents the spatial relationship of one small world with another. Some distortion of the overall space may be needed to allow zooming in and out to visualize from the best viewpoint both the relationship between small worlds as well as the relationship between diseases within a small world.

3.3   Decision Support Methodology

Experts rapidly home in on a small world of possible diagnoses that explain most of the data; their visual and diagnostic reasoning are deeply intertwined and they try to reconcile clinical and case history information with data in the images after an initial detailed viewing of the images. In accordance with this view of radiological expertise, the following decision support methodology can be applied (with minor variations) whether the system is acting in the mode of "tutor" and offering a trainee an analysed case from the archive to diagnose, or whether the user (possibly more expert) is attempting to diagnose a case that is unknown to the system, essentially by comparing it to the others in the archive.

View MR case images. The first stage is to view and window the set(s) of image slices. The set is shown in the top left of Fig. 1. If case notes are available, e.g. for a case in the archive, these will not be accessible in the training system at

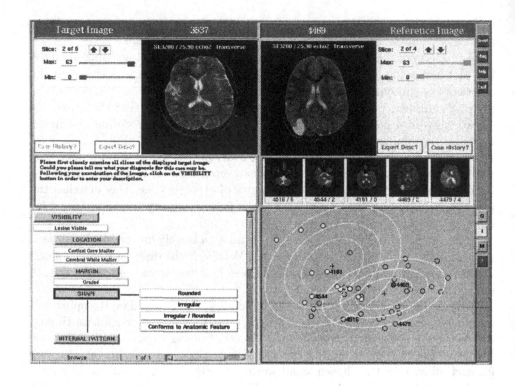

Fig. 1. The image description tutor. The small world of Glioma and Infarct is shown on the bottom right. Infarct cases are shown as lighter coloured dots. A partially completed image description is shown on the bottom left.

this point, so as to reinforce the primacy of the image over other data. Whether they should remain inaccessible, if available, in a decision support system for use by experts is a point of debate that careful user trials will help resolve.

Select and view small world from menu. In the current version of the system the overview plot can display a single small world (see Fig. 1), such as Glioma and Infarct, chosen from a set of small world possibilities. The rapid initial selection of hypotheses is accommodated by the user selecting and clicking on a single button to bring the chosen small world into the overview plot, see the bottom right of Fig. 1. We may have to enable the possibility of the user choosing more than a single small world at this stage, especially if it turns out that some diseases occur in more than a single small world.

Compare related cases from database. The overview plot is populated by dots, each dot representing a case from the archive. These dots are mouse sensitive and can be clicked on to bring the set(s) of image slices up on the screen, (see the top right of Fig. 1). The user can visually compare the images for cases from the archive with the case under examination. Moreover the position of the dot in the overview plot indicates, through its distance from the centroid for a particular disease, how typical that case is in comparison to the population for that disease. For example, Case No. 4161 in Fig. 1 indicates that, on the basis of how the images for this case appear, this is a very typical Infarct and similarly that case No. 4469 is a very typical Glioma.

Read clinical and presentation data. At this point it is important that the radiologist takes all the available data/information into account, if s/he has not already done so. Where a strict regime of delaying access to this data is in operation, access is now permitted to the clinical history and other case data if available.

If case is no longer problematic then exit. The images and the case data may render the case in hand unambiguous and at this point the user can exit, without further action other than to discriminate between the diseases in the selected small world if s/he can. In a future implementation, where the user is a trainee, and when the case under examination is known to the system, a reflective follow-up dialogue that is sensitive to the trainee's history of interaction with the system, the accuracy of their final diagnostic choice(s) and the process they went through as far as this is available to the system will be initiated e.g. which small worlds they explored in the overview plot, which cases within those worlds they called up in the comparison process and the manner in which they explored the images for the case in hand.

Describe case to system. Where the case is more problematic, either because of the trainee's lack of experience or because of its inherent difficulty, the user can engage in the additional task of describing the appearance of the lesion(s) on different sequences using the menu-driven structured image description language, see bottom left of Fig. 1.

See where the description lies in the small world. Using the same coefficients derived from the MCA analysis that produced the small world plot in the overview plot, the position of the case described by the trainee can be shown in the overview plot. Nearby and distant cases can then be examined by clicking on them to examine points of similarity and difference.

Check whether any other small world offers competing possibilities. At present there is only a single small world implemented, so the following steps represent future work. It may be that the position of the dot representing the current case lies in a region of difficulty such that it is either far outside the range of typicality for any of the diseases in the small world, or in a region equidistant from two or more disease centres.

In the former case, the user can investigate other small worlds to see if there are any which are both plausible, given what is known about the case, and display the dot for the current case nearer a disease centroid.

In the latter case, the ambiguous case, the system can offer advice as to which parts of the description have led to diagnostic uncertainty and/or to which further tests might be employed to reduce ambiguity.

Read off relative likelihoods from chosen small world. When the user agrees the description for the case under consideration and the best fitting small world is in view in the overview plot, then the relative likelihoods of the different diseases can be inferred from the position of the case relative to the disease contours of the different diseases in the small world. If required the system can compute diagnostic probabilities and display these to the user.

4   Evaluation

4.1   Description Language

The analytical power of the IDL has been partly tested by its application to the differentiation of multiple sclerosis (MS) from vascular disease [5] and the effects of HIV infection on the brain [6] Further insights into the predictive power of combinations of features will emerge as part of the continuing statistical analysis of the data, including the application of Multiple Correspondence Analysis.

4.2   Overview Plot

We have conducted a limited evaluation of the overview plot, based on the display of cases for a single disease. The evaluation [10] was carried out to investigate whether the statistically derived measures of typicality and similarity presented in the overview plot match the typicality and similarity judgements of radiologists.

A total of seventeen subjects took part in the experiment. These comprised four novices (with no knowledge of radiology), nine intermediates (4th year medics and radiographers with some knowledge of anatomy and imaging) and four expert neuroradiologists. The subjects were presented with the overview plot for a single disease, Glioma, on a computer screen with six cases removed. They were asked to fully explore all the presented cases by clicking on the points to bring up case images and associated descriptions. They were then shown the images and descriptions of each of the six cases previously removed and asked to place a marker representing each case at an appropriate position in the overview plot. Scores were derived for the similarity of each of the six test cases to all the other cases by computing their scaled Euclidean distances from the other points.

An ANOVA of the log distances showed significant differences between the novice, intermediate and expert placement of the cases in the overview plot ($F2, 60 = 3.150 for P < .05$). The average degree of agreement between human and MCA placement was in the expected order of expert (0.97), intermediate (0.95), novice (0.94).

Interviews with the subjects based on a structured questionnaire indicated that they found the overview plot easy to use and acceptable as a means for retrieving cases from the image archive. The evaluation suggests that the overview plot can provide a useful teaching device, to assist a trainee in forming a mental representation of the distribution of cases of a disease comparable to that of an expert.

5 Conclusion

We have described the main components of a largely visual decision support training system derived from an existing system to teach MR image description. This is based on implementing the notion of a small world as an interactive overview plot, based on an MCA analysis of cases from an archive. At present the components described are being re-implemented in Java to improve their portability and their modularity[2].

Much work is yet to be done. This includes choosing in a principled way the small worlds and including within the system some knowledge of the cues that evoke them; evaluating the decision-making leverage (if any) provided by the system, and evaluating the training potential of the system.

Acknowledgements

The work has been supported by ESRC Cognitive Engineering grant L127251035 and by EPSRC Medical Informatics grants GR/L53588 and GR/L94598. The original system was developed in POPLOG.

References

[1] R. Azevedo, S. Lajoie, M. Desaulniers, D. Fleiszer, and P. Bret. RadTutor: The theoretical and empirical basis for the design of a mammography interpretation tutor. In *Artificial Intelligence in Education: Knowledge and Media in Learning Systems, Proceedings of AI-ED97*, pages 386–393. IOS Press, Amsterdam, 1997.

[2] R. Azevedo and S. P. Lajoie. The cognitive basis for the design of a mammography interpretation tutor. *International Journal of Artificial Intelligence in Education*, 9:32–44, 1998.

[3] C. Bishop and M. Tipping. A hierarchical latent variable model for data visualisation. *IEEE Transactions on Pattern Analysis and Machine Intelligence*, 20(3):281–293, 1998.

[4] G. du Boulay, B. Teather, D. Teather, M. Higgott, and N. Jeffery. Standard terminology for MR image description. In M. Takahashi, Y. Korogi, and I. Moseley, editors, *XV Symposium Neuroradiologicum*, pages 32–34. Springer, 1994.

[5] G. du Boulay, B. Teather, D. Teather, N. Jeffery, M. Higgott, and D. Plummer. Discriminating multiple sclerosis from other diseases of similar presentation - can a formal description approach help? *Rivista di Neuroradiologia*, 20(7):37–45, 1994.

[6] G. du Boulay, B. Teather, D. Teather, C. Santosh, and J. Best. Structured reporting of MRI of the head in HIV. *Neuroradiology*, 37:144, 1994.

[7] M. Greenacre. *Correspondence Analysis in Practice*. Academic Press, London, 1993.

[8] F. Hassebrock and M. Pretula. Autobiographical memory in medical problem solving. In *Proceedings of the American Educational Research Association Meeting*, Boston, Massachusetts, 1990.

---

[2] by Fernando De Andres Garcia at De Montfort University.

[9] A. Hillard, M.-W. M., W. Johnson, and B. Baxter. The development of radiologic schemata through training and experience: A preliminary communication. *Investigative Radiology*, 18(4):422–425, 1985.

[10] N. P. Jeffery. *Computer Assisted Tutoring in Radiology*. PhD thesis, De Montfort University, Leicester, 1997.

[11] G. Joseph and V. Patel. Domain knowledge and hypothesis generation in diagnostic reasoning. *Medical Decision Making*, 10:31–46, 1990.

[12] A. Kushniruk, V. Patel, and A. Marley. Small worlds and medical expertise: Implications for medical cognition and knowledge engineering. *International Journal of Medical Informatics*, 49:255–271, 1998.

[13] A. Lesgold, H. Rubinson, R. Feltovich, P.and Glaser, D. Klopfer, and Y. Wang. Expertise in a complex skill: Diagnosing X-ray pictures. In M. Chi, R. Glaser, and M. Farr, editors, *The Nature of Expertise*, pages 311–342. Erlbaum, Hillsdale, NJ, 1988.

[14] R. Macura, K. Macura, V. Toro, E. Binet, and J. Trueblood. Case-based tutor for radiology. In H. Lemke, K. Inamura, C. Jaffe, and R. Felix, editors, *Computer Assisted Radiology, Proceedings of the International Symposium CAR'93*, pages 583–588. Springer-Verlag, 1993.

[15] G. Norman, L. Brooks, C. Coblentz, and C. Babcook. The correlation of feature identification and category judgments in diagnostic radiology. *Memory & Cognition*, 20(4):344–355, 1992.

[16] V. Patel, G. Groen, and C. Fredicson. Differences between students and physicians in memory for clinical cases. *Medical Education*, 20:3–9, 1986.

[17] E. Rogers. VIA-RAD: A blackboard-based system for diagnostic radiology. *Artificial Intelligence in Medicine*, 7(4):343–360, 1995.

[18] H. G. Schmidt and H. P. Boshuizen. On acquiring expertise in medicine. *Educational Psychology Review*, 5(3):205–221, 1993.

[19] M. Sharples, B. du Boulay, D. Teather, B. Teather, N. Jeffery, and G. du Boulay. The MR tutor: Computer-based training and professional practice. In *Proceedings of World Conference on Artificial Intelligence and Education, AIED'95*, pages 429–436, Washington, USA, 1995.

[20] M. Sharples, N. Jeffery, D. Teather, B. Teather, and G. du Boulay. A sociocognitive engineering approach to the development of a knowledge-based training system for neuroradiology. In *Artificial Intelligence in Education: Knowledge and Media in Learning Systems, Proceedings of AI-ED97*, pages 402–409. IOS Press, Amsterdam, 1997.

[21] D. Teather, B. Morton, G. du Boulay, K. Wills, D. Plummer, and P. Innocent. Computer assistance for C.T. scan interpretation and cerebral disease diagnosis. *Neuroradiology*, 30:511–517, 1985.

[22] D. Teather, B. Teather, K. Wills, G. du Boulay, D. Plummer, I. Isherwood, and A. Gholkar. Initial findings in the computer-aided diagnosis of cerebral tumours using C.T. scan results. *British Journal of Radiology*, 54:948–954, 1988.

Internet-Based Decision-Support Server for Acute Abdominal Pain

H.P. Eich, C. Ohmann

Theoretical Surgery Unit, Dept. of General and Trauma Surgery,
Heinrich-Heine University Düsseldorf, Germany
{eich, ohmannch}@uni-duesseldorf.de

Abstract. The paper describes conception and prototypical design of a decision-support server for acute abdominal pain. A user survey was initiated in three surgical departments to assess the user requirements concerning formal decision-aids. The results of this survey are presented. For scoring systems a work-up to separate terminological information from structure is described. The terminology is separately stored in a data dictionary and the structure in the knowledge base. This procedure enables a reuse of terminology for documentation and decision-support. The whole system covers a decision-support server written in C++ with underlying data dictionary and knowledge base, a documentation module written in Java and a Corba middleware (ORBacus 3.1) that establishes a connection via internet.

1. Introduction

In acute abdominal pain (AAP) various formal decision-aids are available. Computer-aided diagnostic systems, guidelines, algorithms, expert systems, decision trees, teaching programs, structured forms and scores are recommended for diagnostic decision-support. The clinical benefit of many of these decision-aids has been proven in prospective studies, e.g. for computer-aided diagnosis and scoring systems [1]. Nevertheless, the majority of these decision-aids is not used in clinical practice. Computer-aided diagnosis is used only in a few hospitals in the United Kingdom in clinical routine. The main reasons for not using formal decision-aids in acute abdominal pain are non-user friendly isolated computer systems with a high work load for data entry. In addition, many of the scores, guidelines and algorithms are only available as paper-based decision-aids. There is no system available integrating different types of decision-support for acute abdominal pain (figure 1). It is the aim of the project to integrate different forms of formal decision-aids in acute abdominal pain in a decision-support-server to be used via Internet and to allow the use of decision-support modules in clinical routine.

W. Horn et al. (Eds.): AIMDM'99, LNAI 1620, pp. 103-112, 1999.
© Springer-Verlag Berlin Heidelberg 1999

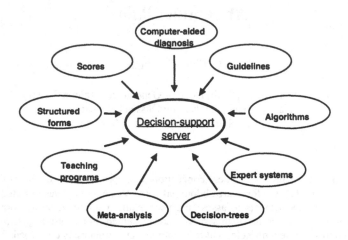

Fig. 1. Types of knowledge resources to be integrated in the internet-based decision-support server for AAP

2. Methods

a) Work-Up of Decision-Aids

Any system to be accepted by clinicians must be based on user requirements. Therefore a survey was planned to assess the user requirements concerning formal decision-aids from surgeons. The questionnaire covering formal decision-aids in general and computer-based decision-aids in particular was sent to 102 doctors of three surgical departments. The questions dealt with application of decision-aids, assessment of areas for use, availability and integration of decision-aids in hospital computer systems, etc. In addition there were questions covering dangers and benefits of computer-based decision-aids.

Separately for the different types of formal decision-aids (e.g. scores, algorithms, guidelines) a structural analysis was performed. This was necessary in order to achieve an adequate implementation in a computer system. The structural analysis of scores is described here. Existing scoring systems were analysed with respect to internal structure and a general object-oriented score model was set up (figure 2). The model can be divided in a structural and administrative part. The administrative part covers an abstract class "knowledge module" from which a "score module" is derived. Therefore, each "score module" has exactly one reference to literature where it was published and may have some references to evaluation studies. In addition a "score module" is characterised by different categories (area of application, population to be applied on, target for use). Special recommendations from the authors may be added. The structural part of the score module covers specific parameters (e.g. leucocytes) with sub-parameters (e.g. sex, age groups), a condition for the relevance of a parameter and the codes or weights which have to be added to calculated the result of a score.

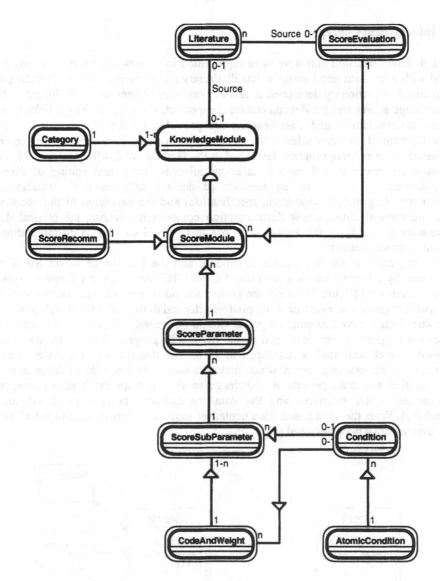

Fig. 2. Problem domain component for scores

A similar procedure was performed for other types of decision-aids using formal representations from the literature (e.g. guideline interchange format (GLIF) [2], standard description of formal clinical algorithms [3]). For integration in the knowledge server only those decision-aids were selected, which were adequately evaluated in prospective studies. Therefore evaluation studies were identified and systematically analysed.

b) Informatical Concept

The different decision-aids have to be represented in a knowledge server. In order to deal with a uniform terminology a data dictionary has to be introduced. Therefore an existing data dictionary developed in another research project has to be linked to the knowledge server and the documentation component. For data exchange links to external nomenclatures and classifications are provided by the data dictionary. The development of the knowledge server covers object-oriented analysis and design and is based on an existing program developed in the German MEDWIS program [4]. The knowledge server should include an editor allowing entry and editing of formal decision-aids, a context driven selection of decision-aids based on standardised parameters (e.g. target, population, specification) and the execution of the decision-aids on clinical data. A new documentation component covering the clinical data necessary for applying the decision-aids has to be developed based on international documentation standards.

The integration of the documentation module and the knowledge server has to be provided by adequate middleware using CORBA (Common Object Request Broker Architecture) [5] (figure 3). Use of the system should be possible via Internet with no restrictions (access at every time, no platform-dependability). For the development of the knowledge server, existing programs should be reused. This covers the core of a decision-support system developed in the MEDWIS program and a data collection module for clinical studies developed in Java. The decision-support system has a modular object-oriented design, which makes it easy to separate the problem domain (application and management of knowledge modules), from the human-interaction component (GUI interface) and the data management component (interface to database). With the Java-based documentation module different form-based clinical documents have been designed [6].

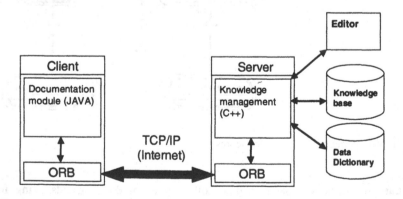

Fig. 3. Informatical conception of an internet-based decision-support server for AAP with a CORBA middleware approach

3. Results

a) Preparation of Decision-Aids

Response rate in the user survey was 73 % (table 1). More than half of the 72 survey participants already use decision-aids. Among them guidelines are used most often (46 %) whereas other instruments (algorithms, scores, decision-trees) are used less frequently (10 to 17 %). Computer-based decision-aids are hardly used at all (7%). These results are in contrast to the strong request for more decision-aids especially for computer-based systems (39 %). Clinicians who already use decision-aids are more interested in additional systems. The standardised questions about attitudes towards computer-based decision-aids revealed more positive than negative appraisal, whereas the answers to open questions focus more on objections. Attitudes towards decision-aids are influenced by the way the instruments are introduced and the way users are informed and involved in the process of implementation.

Table 1. Results of user survey [7] (multiple answers possible)

Which decision-aids <u>do you use</u> in your daily routine?	Number of Surgeons n=72
guidelines	46% (33)
algorithms	17% (12)
scores	15% (11)
decision trees	10% (7)
computer programs	7% (5)
Which decision-aids <u>would you like to use</u> in your daily routine?	
guidelines	46% (33)
algorithms	29% (21)
scores	31% (22)
decision trees	26% (19)
computer programs	39% (28)
no answer	1% (1)
In <u>which area(s)</u> should decision-aids mainly be used?	
student education	50% (36)
physicians education	69% (50)
medical care	56% (40)
clinical studies	63% (45)
no answer	1% (1)
How should decision-aids be <u>available</u>?	
written document	27% (19)
integrated computer program	55% (39)
internet / WWW	30% (21)
hospital information system	66% (47)
no answer	1% (1)

At which **location** should decision-aids be available?	
physicians room	**93% (67)**
ward room	**44% (32)**
intensive care unit	**56% (40)**
operating theatre	**31% (22)**
during patient visit (mobile station)	**10% (7)**
no answer	**1% (1)**
In which way should the **interface to clinical computers** be organized?	
electronic dictionary	**65% (47)**
connected with patient data	**47% (34)**
no answer	**1% (1)**

In a structural analysis 19 scoring systems for acute abdominal pain were identified and characterised by the given criteria (table 2). For every scoring system, clinical parameters, conditions, codes and weights were extracted. In addition 25 studies dedicated to evaluation of the scores were identified and also classified according to the defined criteria. The medical terms used in the scoring systems were analysed and characterised with respect to integration into a data dictionary. The structure of every single score (e.g. parameters, conditions, codes, weights) was stored in the knowledge server.

Table 2. Characterization of scores for AAP

Author	Year	Population	Target
Alvarado	1986	Suspected Appendicitis	Appendicitis
Lindberg	1988	AAP	Appendicitis
Eskelinen I	1992	AAP	Appendicitis
Fenyö	1987	Suspected Appendicitis	Appendicitis
Izbicki	1990	Suspected Appendicitis	Appendicitis
Christian	1992	Suspected Appendicitis	Appendicitis
van Way	1982	Appendectomy	Appendicitis
Teicher	1993	Appendectomy	Appendicitis
Arnbjörnssen	1985	Appendectomy	Appendicitis
Ohmann	1995	AAP	Appendicitis
de Dombal	1991	Appendicitis, NSAP	Appendicitis
Anatol	1995	AAP in Children $\leq$ 10 years	NSAP, App., Gastro-enteritis, Obstruction
Anhoury	1989	AAP in Children $\leq$ 15 years	Appendicitis
Pain	1987	Ileus in small bowel	Strangulation
Ramirez	1994	Appendectomy	Appendicitis
Deltz	1989	Ileus	Operation
Eskelinen II	1993	AAP	Cholecystitis
Eskelinen III a	1994	AAP in men	Appendicitis
Eskelinen III b	1994	AAP in women	Appendicitis

b) Development of a Prototype

The prototype of the decision-support server covers three modules: a data dictionary, a documentation module and a knowledge server. A data dictionary editor was developed according to the specification, allowing data entry, editing and deactivating of terminology. To handle different names and attributes of clinical parameters, the data dictionary has two types of objects: terminology objects and document objects. Terminology objects contain the clinical terminology with internal links (semantic network) and external links to nomenclatures (SNOMED, ICD). Document objects describe how a terminology object has to be documented in a specific situation (e.g. name, value domain, unit). Every document object has a link to one terminology object. With this approach it is possible to handle minor differences between documentation and references in literature (e.g. number of leucocytes per µl and white cell blood count with ml as unit). The data dictionary was implemented in Borland C++ running under Windows 95 on IBM-compatible PC's. The documentation module covers three clinical documents: history, clinical investigation and laboratory. Similar to a C++ program used in a multi-centre trial, the documentation component was developed for form-based data-entry according to international standards [8]. The three clinical documents were implemented in Java as a client application for remote use via Internet. Clinical data to be entered by users are stored in a Microsoft Access database. The knowledge server covers different types of formal decision-aids and the interface to use them. In the prototype application scores and rule-based systems are integrated. A program module is available to enter structure and logic of the different scores and the rule-based systems. As database system the Borland database engine was used, the program modules were developed with Borland C++ and are executable under Windows 95. There is an online access from the knowledge server to the data dictionary. The Java documentation module is linked to the knowledge server via Corba (ORBacus 3.1)[1].

The procedure for use of knowledge modules is the following: first clinical data have to be entered into the clinical documents. Then decision-aids can be selected according to the problem specified (e.g. scores for diagnosis of appendicitis). A specific decision-aid (e.g. Fenyö score) can be selected and the score is executed, if all the clinical data are available. If data are missing additional parameters have to be documented. This procedure can be repeated as often as desirable. In a first step the system is applicable via Internet isolated from any clinical information system. An interface to clinical information systems will be provided in the future using standard interfaces (e.g. HL7, communication servers). Figure 4 shows a part of the history document for AAP. With the documentation module it is possible to carry out international multi-centre studies. All terminological information is imported from the data dictionary. The clinical parameters are ordered in documents, sub-documents, parameters and values, which make it possible to design a document automatically from the data dictionary.

A further feature of the Java client is the display of decision-aids (figure 5). For a single decisions-aid (e.g. score) it is possible to enter the data independent of the documentation module and to execute the score directly.

---

[1] http://www.ooc.com/ob

4. Discussion

The prototype decision-support server is unique in the way that only evaluated decision-aids with proven clinical benefit are integrated in the program. The concrete implementation of the decision-aids is controlled by clinical experts. For that reason an European group has been formed covering experts in the development of decision-support for acute abdominal pain and clinical users. This group monitors the development and use of the system. A major obstacle against the use of decision-aids is the availability. By implementing the system via Internet it can be used by everyone from everywhere without any limitation. Specific software is not necessary, standard browsers can be used. The informatical approach is elegant because new components such as the documentation module implemented in Java and existing programs such as the knowledge server written in C++ have been integrated using a new middleware approach (Corba). The program is much more powerful and flexible than other solutions based on Common Gateway Interface (CGI) and HTML. If necessary other program modules covering medical decision-aids can be implemented and integrated via this approach. This covers also programs running under different operating systems (e.g. Unix, Windows).

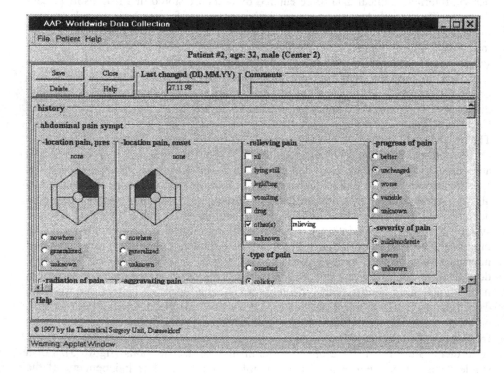

Fig. 4. Documentation component of the internet-based decision-support server for AAP (screen shot of the history document for acute abdominal pain).

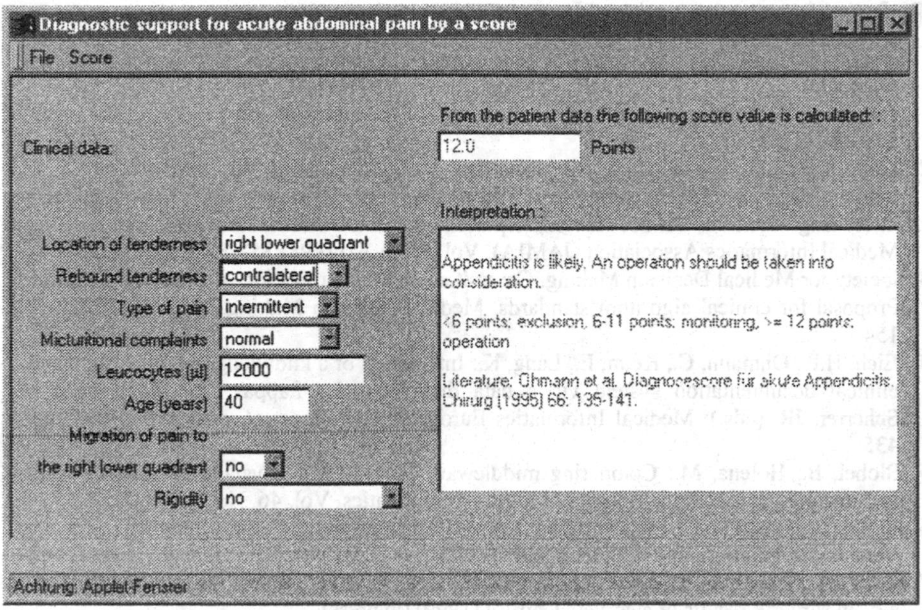

Fig. 5. Prototypical application of a score for AAP

The major advantage of the system is the separation of the terminology in a data dictionary. This allows the definition of clinical terms once, but any term can be used several times in different decision-aids. If another documentation system has to be linked to the knowledge server only a mapping of the terminology to the data dictionary has to be performed. By this procedure the amount of work is considerably reduced. Furthermore, a data dictionary enables multilingual documentation in international clinical trials [9] by translating the single medical term point-to-point. Since only form-based documents with defined possible answers are use, this task is not too time consuming. A shortcoming of the existing system is that it is not integrated in clinical information systems. This is a difficult procedure especially if data safety and data protection are taken into consideration. For safety reasons many clinical information systems are separated from the Internet or the access is limited by Firewall systems. Nevertheless the integration of the knowledge server into one clinical information system is underway. A research project funded by the German Ministry of Education, Science, Research and Technology deals with this issue. The next step would be to bring the system into use and to get it evaluated by clinicians.

Acknowledgements

The work was supported by grant from the North-Rhine-Westphalian Ministry of Schools and Education, Science and Research (Hochschulsonderprogrammm III: Multimedia Projects in Medicine) .

References

1. Ohmann, C., Yang, Q., Franke, C. and the ABDOMINAL PAIN STUDY GROUP: Diagnostic Scores for Acute Appendicitis. European Journal of Surgery, Vol. 161. (1995) 273-281
2. Ohno-Machado, L., Gennari, J.H., Murphy, S.N., Jain, N.L., Tu, S.W., Oliver, D.E., Pattison-Gordon, E., Greenes, R.A., Shortliffe, E.H., Barnett, G.O.: The GuideLine Interchange Format: A Model for Representing Guidelines. Journal of the American Medical Informatics Association (JAMIA), Vol. 5, No. 4. (1998) 357-372
3. Society for Medical Decision Making. Committee on Standardization of Clinical Algorithms. Proposal for clinical algorithm standards. Medical Decision Making. Vol. 12 (1992) 149-154
4. Eich, H.P., Ohmann, C., Keim, E., Lang, K.: Integration of a knowledge-based system and a clinical documentation system via a data dictionary. In: Pappas, C., Maglaveras, N., Scherrer, JR. (eds.): Medical Informatics Europe'97. IOS Press, Amsterdam. (1997) 431-435
5. Blobel, B., Holena, M.: Comparing middleware concepts for advanced healthcare system architectures. International Journal of Medical Informatics, Vol. 46, No. 2. (1997) 69-85
6. Sippel, H., Ohmann, C.: A web-based data collection system for clinical studies using Java. Medical Informatics, Vol. 23, No. 3. (1998) 223-229
7. Aust, B., Ganslandt, T., Sitter, H., Prokosch, U., Zielke, A., Ohmann, C. Formal decision-aids in surgery: results of a survey. Chirurg (1999) (in press)
8. Dombal, F.T. de. Diagnosis of acute abdominal pain, 2ⁿᵈ edn. Churchill Livingstone, Edinburgh. (1991)
9. Ohmann, C., Eich, H.P., Sippel, H. and the COPERNICUS study group: A Data Dictionary Approach to Multilingual Documentation and Decision Support for the Diagnosis of Acute Abdominal Pain (COPERNICUS 555, An European Concerted Action). In: Cesnik, B., McCray, A.T., Scherrer, J.R. (eds.): Proceedings of the Ninth World Congress on Medical Informatics (MEDINFO'98), Vol. 1. Amsterdam, IOS Press. (1998) 462-466

Multi-modal Reasoning in Diabetic Patient Management

Stefania Montani[1], Riccardo Bellazzi[1], Luigi Portinale[2], Alberto Riva[1], and
Mario Stefanelli[1]

[1] Dipartimento di Informatica e Sistemistica, Università di Pavia
via Ferrata 1, I-27100 Pavia, Italy tel. +39-382-505511
stefania@aim.unipv.it,
http://aim.unipv.it
[2] Dipartimento di Scienze e Tecnologie Avanzate, Università del Piemonte Orientale,
Alessandria, Italy

Abstract. We present a decision support tool for Insulin Dependent
Diabetes Mellitus management, that relies on the integration of two
different methodologies: Rule-Based Reasoning (RBR) and Case-Based
Reasoning (CBR). This multi-modal reasoning system aims at providing
physicians with a suitable solution to the problem of therapy planning
by exploiting the strengths of the two selected methods. RBR provides
suggestions on the basis of a situation detection mechanism that relies on
structured prior knowledge; CBR is used to specialize and dynamically
adapt the rules on the basis of the patient's characteristics and of the
accumulated experience. Such work will be integrated in the EU funded
project T-IDDM architecture, and has been preliminary tested on a set
of cases generated by a diabetic patient simulator.

1 Introduction

Nowadays, the advances of Information Technology make it possible to define a
new generation of cooperating decision support systems, able to integrate different modules, based on different methodologies, in a workstation that provides
final users with a valuable help "at the point of use". In this paper we will con-
centrate on the tight coupling of different reasoning paradigm, and, in particular,
on the definition of a system able to integrate Rule-Based and Case-Based Reasoning [1] to support the physician's decision making process.

The basic philosophy underlying this work is to overcome the limitations of
the two approaches. On one side, we aim at providing a Rule-Based system with
the capability to *specialize* the rules on the basis of the patient's characteristics,
without highly increasing the number of rules (the so-called *qualification problem*); moreover we would like some rules (or part of them) to be *dynamically*
adapted on the basis of the past available experience. On the other side, we
would like to provide a Case-Based Reasoning system with a module for giving suggestions based on structured prior knowledge, and not only on the case

W. Horn et al. (Eds.): AIMDM'99, LNAI 1620, pp. 113–123, 1999.

library; this capability is particularly important for medical applications, since final decisions should be always based on established knowledge.

Following such approach, we have defined a multi-modal decision support tool for the management of Insulin Dependent Diabetes Mellitus (IDDM) patients. IDDM management is structured as follows. Patients are visited by physicians every 2/4 months; during these control visits the data coming from home monitoring are analyzed, in order to assess the metabolic control achieved by the patients. The results of such analysis are then combined with other available information, such as laboratory results and historical and/or anamnestic data, in order to finally revise the patient's therapeutic protocol. During this complex process, the physician may *detect some problems* and *propose a solution* relying on some *structured knowledge* (i.e. the pharmacodynamic of insulin, the main drug provided in the protocol) as well as on the *specific patient behaviour* (i.e. young or adult patient) and on *previous experience* (i.e. the information that a certain protocol has been applied on that patient in the past with a particular outcome). When dealing with automated decision support in IDDM management, the combination of different reasoning tools seems a natural solution: the widely-recognized scientific knowledge is formalized in our system as a set of rules [2], while additional knowledge, consisting of evidence-based information, is represented through a database of past cases.

In this paper we present the overall architecture of the multi-modal reasoning system, as well as a first implementation developed within the EU-project T-IDDM. In particular, the Rule-Based system has been defined in collaboration with the Department of pediatrics of the Policlinico S. Matteo Hospital of Pavia, and has been revised on the basis of the suggestions of the medical partners of T-IDDM [3]. The case-base has been derived from the clinical records of 29 patients, for a total of 147 cases collected at the Policlinico S. Matteo Hospital in Pavia.

2   Background of the Work

Rather interestingly, while Rule-Based systems have been largely exploited in the context of medical problems, and in particular in IDDM management [4,5,6], no examples of Case-Based Reasoning (CBR) systems for diabetes therapy can be found in the literature, although, being IDDM a chronic disease, it would be possible to rely on a large amount of patient data, coming both from periodical control visits and from home monitoring.

For what concerns multi-modal reasoning, only a few applications to medicine exist [7], although the general ideas reported in the literature can be easily adopted in the biomedical context. In the previously published experiences, Rule-Based Reasoning (RBR) and CBR can cooperate at different levels. In some applications, a Rule-Based system, that deals with knowledge on standard situations, is applied first. When it is not able to provide the user with a reliable solution, the CBR technique is used, by retrieving similar cases from a data-base of peculiar and non-standard situations [8]. A different approach suggests to use rules as an "abstract" description of a situation, while cases represent a further "specialization". Cases assist RBR by instantiating rules, while rules assist CBR by permitting the extraction of more general concepts from concrete examples [9]. It is possible to decide "a priori" which method should be applied first, or to select the most convenient one in a dynamic way, depending on the situation at hand [9,7]. In particular, the rule base and the case memory can be searched in parallel for applicable entities. Then the best entity (i.e. rule or case) to reuse (and therefore the reasoning paradigm to apply) can be selected on the basis of its suitability for solving the current problem [7]. Finally, RBR can support CBR after the retrieval phase, during the adaptation task: if the memory does not contain suitable examples of adaptations of past cases to situations similar to the current one, the system relies on some general adaptation rules [10].

In the majority of the described examples, RBR and CBR are used in an exclusive way. On the contrary, our approach, which is in some sense similar to Branting's idea [9], defines a proper solution to the current problem through the Rule-Based system, whose rules have been specialized on the basis of the specific patient's context identified exploiting the CBR methodology. Details of the proposed architecture are presented in the following sections.

3   The CBR System

CBR is a problem solving paradigm that exploits the specific knowledge of previously experienced situations, called *cases* [1]; the method consists in retrieving past cases, similar to the current one, and in adapting and reusing past effective solutions; the current case can be retained and put into the base of cases. A case is described by a set of feature-value pairs (F), by a solution (s) and by an outcome (o).

In IDDM management, we interpret a periodical control visit as a case. In this context, F summarizes the set of data collected during the visit. The features are extracted from three sources of information: *general characterization* (e.g. sex, age, distance from diabetes onset), *mid-term information*, (e.g. weight, HbA1c values), and *short term (day-by-day) information* (e.g. the number of hypoglycemic episodes). The solution s is the array of insulin types and doses prescribed by the physician after the analysis of the feature values, and the outcome o of the therapeutic decision is obtained by inspecting HbA1c and the number of hypoglycemic events at the following visit.

It is well known that situation assessment and case search are strongly influenced by the organizational structures the case memory is based on. To make retrieval more flexible we have structured the case memory resorting to a taxonomy of prototypical classes, that express typical problems that may occur to patients. Retrieval is hence implemented as a two-step procedure: a *classification* step, that proposes to the physician the class of cases to which the current case could belong, and a proper *retrieval* step, that effectively identifies the "closest" past cases.

Classification. By exploiting the medical knowledge on the prototypical situations that may occur to IDDM pediatric patients, we were able to build a taxonomy of mutually exclusive classes, whose root (*Patient's problems*) represents the most general class including all the possible cases we may store into the case memory. The root's subclasses are prototypical descriptions of the set of situations they summarize. The classification process aims at limiting the search space for similar cases to the context (i.e. the class, or a small number of classes in the taxonomy), into which the problem at hand can be better interpreted.

Our tool implements a Naive Bayes strategy [11], a method that assumes conditional independence among the features given a certain class, but that is known to be robust in a variety of situations [11]. In our application, the prior probability values were derived from expert's opinion through a technique described in [12], while posterior probabilities were learnt from the available case base (147 cases) by using a standard Bayesian updating technique [13].

Retrieval. By exploiting the classification results, the system performs the retrieval step relying on a nearest-neighbor technique. The physician is allowed to choose whether to retrieve cases belonging only to the most probable class identified by the classifier (*intra-class retrieval*), or to a set of possible classes (*inter-class retrieval*). In the first hypothesis, distance is computed using the Heterogeneous Euclidean-Overlap Metric (HEOM) formula; in the second hypothesis, using the Heterogeneous Value Difference Metric (HVDM) formula [14]. Both methods are applicable not only for numeric and continuous variables, but also for symbolic ones. Moreover, since HVDM may be computationally inefficient when working with large data-bases, we have also implemented a non exhaustive search procedure, that exploits an anytime Pivoting algorithm (see [15] for details).

4   The Rule-Based System

The Rule-Based system exploits the knowledge embedded in a set of production rules, organized in a taxonomy of classes; the rules are fired through a forward chaining mechanism.

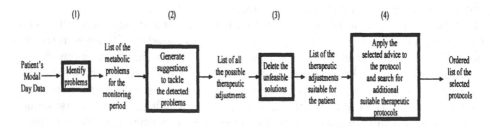

Fig. 1. Steps of the Rule-Based reasoning process.

The system performs a series of steps (see figure 1), each one relying upon a specific rule class.

Data analysis and problem identification.

During home-monitoring, patients collect a large amount of time-stamped data, from Blood Glucose Level (BGL) measurements, to insulin doses and diet information. The data are temporally contextualized according to a time scale obtained by subdividing the day into seven non-overlapping time-slices, that are centered on the injection and/or meal times. The raw data are then abstracted through a Temporal Abstractions (TA) technique [16]: in particular, STATE abstractions (e.g. low, normal, high values) are extracted and aggregated into intervals called *episodes*. After having identified the most relevant episodes, we derive the **modal day** [16], an indicator able to summarize the average response of the patient to a certain therapy. In particular we obtain the BGL modal day by calculating the marginal probability distribution of the BGL state abstractions in each time slice, through the application of a Bayesian method [17] able to explicitly take into account the presence of missing data.

After the BGL modal day has been calculated, the **problem detection rule class** is exploited, to identify the patient's metabolic alterations. In particular, when the frequency of a certain BGL abstraction (called *minimum probability*) is higher than a given threshold, and when the number of missing data (called *ignorance*) is sufficiently small to rely on such information, a *problem* is identified. For example, the following rule detects a hypoglycemia problem in a generic time slice Y using the information contained in the relative modal day component X:

```
IF X IS A BGL-MODAL-DAY-COMPONENT
   AND THE TIME-SLICE OF X IS Y
   AND THE BGL-LEVEL OF X IS LOW
   AND THE MINIMUM-PROBABILITY OF X >= alpha
   AND THE IGNORANCE OF X <= beta
THEN GENERATE-PROBLEM HYPOGLYCEMIA AT Y
```

where *alpha* and *beta* are two parameters that can be instantiated at run-time. Their default values where derived from medical knowledge, and are equal to 0.3 and 0.8 respectively.

Suggestions generation.

In order to cope with the problem it found, the Rule-Based system generates a set of suggestions. Each rule in the **suggestion generation rule class** has a premise which is satisfied when a certain metabolic problem exists. Rules are divided into subclasses on the basis of the advice they generate: a specific problem might be solved by adjusting the insulin doses, or by revising the diet, or the physical exercise plan. Therefore, every time more than one rule fires, so obtaining a set of alternative solutions to be further evaluated.

Suggestions selection.

Among all the generated suggestions, the system selects the most effective ones, always verifying their suitability for the patient at hand. Such step relies upon the activation of two rule classes, the **suggestion selection rule class** and the

filtering rule class. The antecedents of the *suggestion selection* rules take into account the patient's characteristics (e.g. age, associated diseases). As an example, for a pediatric patient with hyperglycemia problems the reasoner would select a suggestion about an increasing meal intake, instead of prescribing the introduction of an additional insulin injection. The *filtering* rules are applied after the deletion of suggestions that resulted to be not admissible for the patient at hand, to filter the remaining ones in order to perform just the most effective action in a single time slice. When comparing two insulin suggestions the rules exploit insulin activity (see [3] for details).

Protocol revision.

Insulin suggestions are applied to the current insulin protocol by the **protocol rule class**, obtaining a revised therapy for the patient at hand. Moreover, the reasoner searches for other suitable protocols, even if defined for different patients, and presents them as an ordered list: the more the retrieved protocol is similar to the current one (in terms of number of injections and of insulin doses for every injection), the higher level it takes in the list: the similarity is calculated using the HEOM method [14]. The physician is able to evaluate the system choices step by step, and finally to choose a suitable solution among the proposed ones.

5   Integration between CBR and RBR

As previously noted, the rule base is partitioned into a set of rule classes that perform the above outlined reasoning steps, and the order in which the rule classes are activated is determined by a set of *metarules*. The integration of CBR into this framework is achieved by defining additional metarules that guide the interaction between the results of the CBR procedures and the rule system. The first metarule states that CBR is applied, at the beginning of the reasoning process, to the patient's visit data. During this step, the user of the system can choose whether to exploit only the results of the CBR classification step, if the output is considered reliable, or to analyze the "closest" cases obtained through intra-class or inter-class retrieval. In this situation, a second metarule evaluates the relationships between the features describing the metabolic state of the patient and the therapeutic actions in the retrieved cases. For example, the HbA1c trend and the insulin requirement trend are jointly analyzed to determine whether an increase in the former is treated with an increase in the latter. The results of retrieval will then be used only if the relationship is statistically significant (with a p-value of 0.1).

A third metarule uses the outcome of the CBR process, if any, to tailor the Rule-Based system according to the identified context. In our implementation, rules are represented as objects characterized by an activation condition, an action and a set of parameters that influence both the activation condition and the action. In this phase, the parameters of the rules can be changed in order to obtain a more effective and more suitable definition of a therapy for the patient at hand. In particular, the behaviour of two rule classes is affected.

Problem detection rules can be specialized by:
1. setting a proper value of the *threshold* for the frequency of BGL abstractions; 2. defining the maximum admissible *number of missing data* so that the information may be relied upon.

For example, when dealing with patients suffering from anorexia, it is important to be able to promptly detect all hypoglycemic episodes, even when few data are available. This is motivated by the fact that such patients run a higher risk of hypoglycemia, due to their nutritional disorder. Therefore, the rule described in section 4 becomes:

```
IF X IS A BGL-MODAL-DAY-COMPONENT
   AND THE TIME-SLICE OF X IS Y
   AND THE BGL-LEVEL OF X IS LOW
   AND THE MINIMUM-PROBABILITY OF X >= 0.2
   AND THE IGNORANCE OF X <= 1
THEN GENERATE-PROBLEM HYPOGLYCEMIA AT Y
```

Suggestion generation rules can be specialized by modifying:
1. the *number of insulin doses* to be added or eliminated to tackle a metabolic alteration; 2. the overall *variation in daily requirement*; 3. the quantitative *variation in a single insulin dose*.

To summarize, CBR influences steps (1) and (2) in figure 1. Finally, the RBR proceeds with suggestions selection and with the definition of a list of alternative protocols, as described above. The integration, by making the system more effective in the detection of patient's problems, and in prescribing insulin modifications that can be stronger or milder, depending on the context in which the RBR is operating, can enhance the RBR performance; in particular we expect the time needed for problem resolution to be reduced, through the definition of a therapy properly tailored on the patient's peculiar needs.

From an implementation point of view, the RBR and the CBR systems are fully integrated in the distributed, Web-based environment, on which the T-IDDM architecture is based. The T-IDDM prototype is composed of two main units, a Medical Unit (MU), devoted to assist physicians in IDDM patients management, and a Patient Unit (PU), meant to help patients in day by day self monitoring; the communication between the two units exploits an extension of the HTTP protocol. Details on the architecture can be found in [18]. The MU modules, and in particular the reasoning ones, rely on *Lispweb*, an extended, special-purpose Web server, written in Common Lisp, that makes it possible to create more "intelligent" and "secure" applications while remaining in the context of Web-based systems [18].

6   Results

To provide a first evaluation of the multi-modal reasoning system performance, we made some tests on a simulated patient, whose characteristic features have been derived from a real pediatric patient case of our case memory, and whose

BGL measurements were generated by an IDDM patient simulator, integrated in the T-IDDM architecture [19]. In particular, we have compared the performances of the multi-modal reasoning system and of the RBR alone, in stabilizing the patient's metabolism through an iterative procedure, consisting in simulating 15 days of monitoring data and then in revising the insulin protocol on the basis of the collected information. The test patient was a boy of 17, with a weight of 52 kg and a height of 170 cm; his metabolic control was characterized by HbA1c = 8% with an increasing trend, and an increasing insulin requirement.

The CBR system classified the above case as a situation of *typical puberal problems*. We chose to retrieve the closest cases from such class, and we found 10 cases, on which the system performed some statistical analysis. The only significant result derived was related to the average variation of regular insulin doses in each injection. In particular such variation was of 2 units, while the default variation proposed by the Rule-Based system is of 1 unit. Therefore, the integration between CBR and RBR in this situation would influence the *suggestion generation rule class* by setting the quantitative variation in a single insulin dose to 2 units, permitting a more aggressive action in insulin treatment. As previously explained, to verify the suitability of this indication, we compared the functionality of the Rule-Based system with the performances of multi-modal reasoning. At first, the IDDM patient simulator was used to generate 15 days of BGL data, with an average of three measurements per day and including also some post-prandial data. To introduce intra-patient variability, the data were derived adding a 10% noise on the simulation results. The obtained BGL values were analyzed both by the Rule-Based system and by the multi-modal reasoning system. The revised protocols were acquired by the simulator and used to obtain the data for the following monitoring period. Such procedure ended when the simulated patient metabolic condition was stabilized. Figure 2 (a) shows the outcome of the Rule-Based system, while figure 2 (b) shows the outcome of the integration approach. It can be easily noted that the Rule-Based system, being more conservative and "cautious", took 6 weeks to regulate the patient's state (2 protocol adjustments, one every 15 days). On the other hand, the integrated system normalized the patient's glycemic levels with just one protocol revision, in a total time of 4 weeks. These first validation results proved to be encouraging, although we aim at exploiting real patients' BGL measurements to get more reliable information.

As a future step in the system evaluation, we plan to include the multi-modal reasoning system here described in the running prototype of T-IDDM. As a matter of fact, the T-IDDM project validation phase has already started, involving ten pediatric patients and two diabetologists at the Policlinico S. Matteo Hospital in Pavia, and will be extended to the other project validation sites. At the moment the T-IDDM prototype just includes the Rule-Based system and the CBR one, working independently. We plan to make the multi-modal reasoning methodology available for the testing sites, in order to get a feedback of its performance directly from the end users.

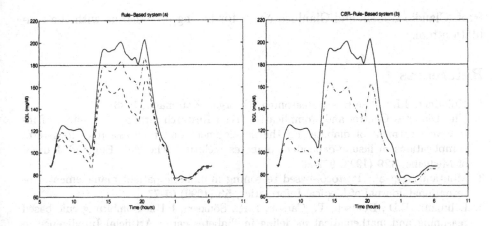

Fig. 2. (a): the 24 hours profiles of blood glucose in response to the different therapeutic protocols proposed by the Rule-Based system. The figure shows the progressive stabilization (within normal BGL ranges, i.e. 70-180 mg/dl) of the patient's metabolism, that moves from the continuous line to the dashed one. (b): the 24 hours profiles of blood glucose in response to the different therapeutic protocols proposed by the multi-modal reasoning system. The BGL values fall into the normality range just with one protocol revision (dash-dotted line).

7 Conclusions

In this paper, we have described a system that integrates CBR and RBR to provide suggestions on insulin therapy planning for IDDM patients. The proposed approach could be extended in several directions. From a methodological point of view, CBR could be a valuable support also for model-based reasoning system. For example, a CBR system may allow a Causal Probabilistic Network based system dynamically deriving probabilities, or expressing preferences towards certain decisions among others; finally, it may suggest some hints on how to reduce the decision space. From the application point of view, multi-modal reasoning could be helpful in a variety of situations, and in particular in the management of chronic diseases where each patient's data are accumulated over time. More generally, such systems would be helpful in trying to combine established structured knowledge with the "operative" knowledge of experts and with the past experience collected in a certain health care institution. In the future we will continue investigating the management and integration of medical knowledge, as we believe that it represents one of the most interesting application areas of AI in medical informatics.

Acknowledgments This paper is part of the EU TAP project T-IDDM HC 1047. Dr. Stefano Fiocchi and Dr. Giuseppe d'Annunzio are gratefully acknowledged their support in the CBR and in the RBR systems definition. We thank

Prof. Claudio Cobelli and Gianluca Nucci for having provided us with the simulation tool.

References

1. Kolodner, J.L.: Case-Based Reasoning, (Morgan Kaufmann, 1993).
2. The Diabetes Control and Complication Trial Research Group: The effect of intensive treatment of diabetes on the development and progression of long-term complications in insulin-dependent diabetes mellitus, The New England Journal of Medicine, **329** (1993) 977-86.
3. Montani, S. et al.: Protocol-based reasoning in diabetic patient management, International Journal of Medical Informatics, **53** (1999) 61-77.
4. Lehmann, E.D., Deutsch, T., Carson, E.R., Sönksen, P.H.: Combining rule-based reasoning and mathematical modeling in diabetes care, Artificial Intelligence in Medicine, **6** (1994) 137-160.
5. Zahlmann, G., Franczykiva, M., Henning, G., Strube, M., Huttls, I., Hummel, I., Bruns, W.: DIABETEX- a decision support system for therapy of type I diabetic patients, Comp. Meth. and Prog. in Biomed., **32** (1990) 297-301.
6. Deutsch, T., Roudsari, A.V., Leicester, H.J., Theodorou, T., Carson, E.R., Sönksen, P.H.: UTOPIA: a consultation system for visit-by-visit diabetes management, Medical Informatics, **21** (1996) 345-358.
7. Bichindaritz, I. et al.: CARE-PARTNER: a computerized knowledge-support system for stem-cell-post-transplant long-term-follow-up on the World-Wide-Web, JAMIA, Symposium supplement 1998, 386-390.
8. Surma, J., Vanhoff, K.: Integrating rules and cases for the classification task, In: Proceedings of the first ICCBR, Lecture Notes in Artificial Intelligence 1010, pp. 325-334 (Sesimbra, 1995).
9. Branting, L.K., Porter, B.W.: Rules and precedents as complementary warrants, In: Proceedings of the 9th National Conference on Artificial Intelligence (AAAI 91) (Anaheim, 1991).
10. Leake, D.B.: Combining rules and cases to learn case adaptation, In: Proceedings of the 17th Annual Conference of the Cognitive Science Society (Pittsburgh, 1995).
11. Kononenko, I.: Inductive and Bayesian learning in medical diagnosis, Applied Artificial Intelligence, **7** (1993) 317-337.
12. Montani, S., Bellazzi, R., Portinale, L., Fiocchi, S., Stefanelli, M.: A case-based retrieval system for diabetic patients therapy, In: Proceedings of IDAMAP 98 workshop, ECAI 98, pp. 64-70 (Brighton, UK, 1998).
13. Mitchell, T.: Machine Learning, (Mc Graw Hill, 1997).
14. Wilson, D.R., Martinez, T.R.: Improved heterogeneous distance functions, Journal of Artificial Intelligence Research, **6** (1997) 1-34.
15. Portinale, L., Torasso, P., Magro, D.: Selecting most adaptable diagnostic solutions through pivoting-based retrieval, In: Lecture Notes in Artificial Intelligence, 1266, pp. 277-88 (Springer Verlag, 1997).
16. Larizza, C., Bellazzi, R., Riva, A.: Temporal abstractions for diabetic patients management, In: Lecture Notes in Artificial Intelligence, pp. 319-330 eds. E. Keravnou, C. Garbay, R. Baud and J. Wyatt, (Springer Verlag, 1997).
17. Ramoni, M., Sebastiani, P.: The use of exogenous knowledge to learn Bayesian Networks for incomplete databases. In: Advances In Intelligent Data Analysis, Lecture Notes in Computer Science, pp. 537-548, eds. X. Liu, P. Cohen and M. Berthold, (Springer Verlag, 1997).

18. A. Riva, R. Bellazzi, M. Stefanelli, A web-based system for the intelligent management of diabetic patients, MD Computing, 14 (1997) 360-64.
19. Cobelli, C., Nucci, G., Del Prato, S.: A physiological simulation model of the glucose-insulin system in Type 1 Diabetes, Diabetes Nutrition and Metabolism, 11 (1998) 78.

Experiences with Case-Based Reasoning Methods and Prototypes for Medical Knowledge-Based Systems

Rainer Schmidt [a], Bernhard Pollwein [b], Lothar Gierl [a]

a) Institut für Medizinische Informatik und Biometrie, Universität Rostock
Rembrandtstr. 16 / 17, D-18055 Rostock, Germany
e-mail: [rainer.schmidt / lothar.gierl]@medizin.uni-rostock.de
b) Institut für Anästhesiologie, Ludwig-Maximilians Universität München
Marchioninistr. 15, D-81377 München, Germany

Abstract. In this paper we discuss the importance to create prototypes automatically within Case-Based Reasoning systems. We present some general ideas about prototypes deduced from analyses of our experiences with prototype designs in domain specific medical CBR systems. Four medical Case-Based Reasoning systems are described. As they use prototypes for different purposes, the gained improvement is different as well. Furthermore, we claim that the generation of prototypes is an adequate technique to learn the intrinsic case knowledge, especially if the domain theory is weak.

1 Introduction

Cases are the most specialised form of knowledge representation. The knowledge of physicians consists of general knowledge they have read in medical books plus their experiences in form of cases they have treated themselves or colleagues have told them about. Not all cases are of the same importance. Some are typical while others are rather exceptional, e.g. a paediatrician does not remember all his patients with measles, but maybe those with serious complications or those where his measles diagnoses were surprisingly wrong. Especially in diagnostic tasks the thoughts of physicians circle around typical cases. They consider the differences between a current patient and typical or known exceptional cases. For diagnostic tasks cases are usually described by a list of syndromes or symptoms (syndromes are described by symptoms which can be called features). These syndromes and symptoms are of different importance for typical cases, some are essential while an often occurrence of others may be only coincidental.

We believe that especially for diagnostic tasks medical Case-Based Reasoning systems should take the reasoning of physicians into account [1]. Such systems should not only consist of general medical domain knowledge plus a flat case base, but the case base should be structured by typical case generalisations called prototypes [2]. The main purpose of such generalised knowledge is to guide the retrieval process and sometimes to decrease the amount of storage by erasing redundant cases. In domains with rather weak domain theories another advantage of case-oriented techniques is their ability to learn from cases. Only gathering new cases may improve the systems

W. Horn et al. (Eds.): AIMDM'99, LNAI 1620, pp. 124-132, 1999.
© Springer-Verlag Berlin Heidelberg 1999

ability to find suitable similar cases for current problems, but it does not elicit the intrinsic knowledge of the stored cases. To learn the knowledge contained in cases a generalisation process is necessary. As physicians reason with prototypical and exceptional cases anyway, the creation of prototypes seems to be an adequate learning technique at least for medical domains.

In the following we describe the general form of prototypes in case-oriented medical systems. Subsequently, we elaborate the role of prototypes in our domain specific medical CBR systems for dysmorphology [3], liver transplantation [4], antibiotic therapy advice for infectious diseases [5], and early warnings concerning the kidney function [6] .

2   Prototypes as a Form to Describe Medical Knowledge

The use of case oriented generalised knowledge presents the opportunity to structure case bases. Cases can be clustered into groups, prototypical diseases or schema. Clancey [7] distinguishes between prototypes that represent specific expressions of diseases or therapies and schema that contain essential features of diseases or therapies. As Selz [8] characterises a schema as a description of an entity where at least one part remains vague, the distinction between prototypes and schema seems to be fluid. We only use the term prototype and refer to a hierarchy of prototypes where the most general prototypes that contain only the most common features are situated at the top and the most specific ones are placed at the bottom.

As humans look upon cases as more typical for normal cases as more features they have in common [9], distances between prototypes and cases usually consider the shared features. Tversky [10] determines the similarity between a case and a prototype by adding up the shared features and subtracting the features of the prototype which the case does not share and the features of the case which the prototype does not share. Rosch and Mervis [9] determine the similarity between prototypes and cases as the shared features relative to all features of the prototype. That means, in contrast to Tversky they ignore those case features which the prototype does not share.

The generalisation from specific cases to prototypes has the advantage of abstracting general knowledge that sometimes might improve the domain theory. The drawback is the loss of specific information. However, within a weak domain theory medical cases very often contain too much specific information and the problem is to elicit typical or important features.

In the field of instance-based learning [11], in which learning is performed by accumulating examples of each category, and subsequent classification is done by finding the stored examples most similar to the candidate to be classified, some efforts have been made to define typical examples for each category [12]. Typical attributes or typical values are identified by their low variability within the category.

Biberman [13] investigates the role of prototypicality in the field of concept learning. Following Rosch and Mervis [9] he argues for two factors affecting the prototypicality of an item: The numbers of properties it shares with other members of its concept, and the numbers of properties it shares with members of contrasting concepts. The second factor seems to be only party practicable for medical applications. If a hierarchy of diagnoses exists in a domain, inside this hierarchy the diagnoses can be viewed as contrasting concepts, but outside this hierarchy exists an open world of other diseases that are not considered in the application and sometimes are even still unknown. Bibermans results of applying concept learning algorithms to some example domains suggest that prototypicality is a successful classification and storing criterion in structured domains that contain more or less prototypical members.

In the overlapping field of Case-Based Reasoning and Machine Learning some systems using generalisation hierarchies of prototypes for classification tasks have been developed. REFINER [14] which is in principle domain-independent but was mainly applied in medical domains and PROTOS [15] which is designed for clinical audiology are knowledge acquisition tools too. REFINER classifies new cases with the help of the user while PROTOS classifies according to similar cases and only if this fails the user has to support the classification process.

3   Medical CBR Systems and Prototypes

We have not created a general prototype tool, but we have used different prototype designs within a few medical cases-based systems we developed for various domains and tasks. As these systems contain such distinct tasks as diagnosis, therapy advice and time course analysis, it seems too ambitious to attempt to develop a general prototype tool that can handle all these tasks. Here we present and summarise our experiences with these systems.

3.1   Antibiotics Therapy Advice

The antibiotics therapy adviser named ICONS [5] attempts to find calculated antibiotics therapy combinations for intensive care patients who got an infection disease as additional complication. A calculated pathogen spectrum is determined by the affected organ and the group of patients the current patient belongs to. ICONS considers the contraindications of the patient by reducing the set of applicable antibiotics and subsequently uses rules to generate antibiotics combinations to cover the calculated pathogen spectrum. The cases are distinguished by their affected organs, groups of patients and contraindications.

From a medical point of view, prototypes correspond to typical antibiotic treatments associated with typical clinical features. At the top level, a prototype is created for each affected organ and each group of patients. All cases of a prototype belong to the same group of patients, the same organ is affected and the same pathogen spectrum deduced from background knowledge has to be covered. The cases are discriminated by their contraindications. These are antibiotic allergies, reduced organ functions (e.g. kidney, liver), specific diagnoses (e.g. acoustic distortion or diseases, the central nervous system), special blood diseases, pregnancy and the patient's age group (e.g. adult, child, infant).

First, all cases are stored below a prototype (a possible prototype hierarchy is shown in Fig. 1). Only upon reaching the threshold "number of cases" the prototype is filled, i.e. the contraindications of the associated cases are inspected, and every contraindication reaching the relative frequency of the second threshold "minimum frequency" are included in the prototype. Subsequently, the prototype is treated like a case and the resulting suggestible antibiotic therapies are stored. Those cases that have no additional contraindications in comparison to the prototype are erased.

We create an alternative prototype below an existing prototype, if enough (threshold "number of cases") cases exist for the latter, that have at least one contraindication in common the prototype does not include. The alternative prototype is constructed from the deviating cases of the superior prototype. The difference between the alternative and the superior prototype consists of other contraindications, other antibiotic therapies and a different position within the prototype hierarchy.

Our aim was to reduce the amount of storage and to guarantee efficient retrieval time, because the case base grows incrementally. We used the prototype idea of clustering typical common features and keeping the deviating cases. However, as it is no diagnostic but a therapeutic task where the contraindications play the role of constraints and as only those cases are adaptable that have got no additional contraindications in comparison to the current case, sometimes useful cases are erased. That means, this prototype design is not only advantageous in this application, but also has a slight drawback.

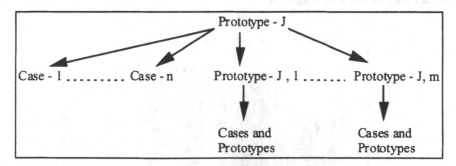

Fig. 1. Possible relationships of a prototype

3.2 Dysmorphic Syndromes

GS.52 is a prototype-based expert system that is routinely used in the children's hospital of the University of Munich for many years. It is a diagnostic support system for dysmorphic syndromes. Such a syndrome means a non-random combination of different disorders. The major problems are the high variability of the syndromes (hundreds), the high number of case features (between 40 and 130) and the continuos modifications of the knowledge about dysmorphic syndromes.

Each syndrome is represented by a prototype that contains its typical features. The prototypes are acquired by an expert consultation session. The physician selects a new or an existing syndrome and typical cases for the syndrome. Subsequently, GS.52 determines the relevant features and their relative frequency (Table 1 shows an example for such a learned prototype).

Table 1. Portion of an example of a generated prototype. The numbers are the relative frequency in percentages the features occurred in the cases of the prototype.

Heart murmur	30%	Depressed nasal bridge	23%
Diminished postnatal growth rate	77%	Anteverted nares	63%
Hypercalcaemia	30%	Prominent lips	17%
Prenatal onset	75%	Long philtrum	17%
Mild microcephaly	67%	Full. of peri-orb. region	75%
Full cheeks	46%	Medial eyebrow flare	25%

The diagnostic support occurs by searching for the most adequate prototypes for a current case. A similarity value between each prototype and the current case is calculated and the prototypes are ranked according to these values. We evaluated the similarity measure of Tversky and the measure of Rosch and Mervis (see section 2.). The result (Fig.2.) indicates to present the ten most probable syndromes rather than to produce the one and only diagnosis.

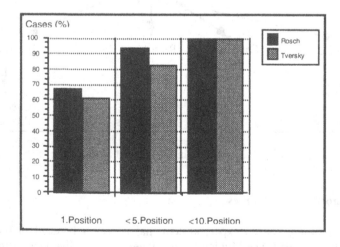

Fig. 2. Sensivity of GS.52 using cases of trisomy-21

For both measures the correct diagnosis was always among the first ten, mostly among the first five and majoritiely the first position. The measure of Rosch and Mervis performed better which indicates to ignore those features of the current case the prototype under consideration does not share.

3.3   Postoperative Management of Liver-Transplanted Patients

Liver-transplantation and the following postoperativ management is a domain with an extreme weak domain theory. If liver-transplanted patients get postoperative complications, they usually get a lot of them and it is yet only very partly known which of these complication causes other complications, because the pathophysiological concepts of relevant complications are not well understood. The idea of our system COSYL is to give some diagnostic advice for the task of finding out the main underlying complications. We search for the most similar case and present his diagnoses. Although the case base contains only slightly more than 200 cases the retrieval time is very time consuming because the amount of each patient record is enormous.

To guide the retrieval we use two classification levels. At the top level we consider the reasons for the transplantation. The further classification depends on that reason, e.g. the number of retransplantations is one classification feature at the second level. As we have clustered some groups of patients, the retrieval has to take only a part of the case base into account. Another main advantage is the fact that for each group it is known which sorts of features are worth to look at.

We only use predefined classifiers and do not create or learn prototypes, because the features are clinical parameter values whose relevance is unknown. Of course it is possible to generate confidence intervals for the various features and to create a prototype that agglomerates these intervals. Such a prototype would have no medical meaning, because most of the features may be unimportant and because no medical facts (diagnoses, therapies) are described. However, we guide the retrieval by known classifiers and the reduction in the consultation time is tremendous.

3.4   Kidney Function Analysis

Recently, we have developed an early warning system [6, 16] that performs multiparametric time course analysis concerning the kidney function for intensive care patients. We have designed a method (Fig.3.) that consists of two abstraction steps plus case-based reasoning retrieval. First, we abstract many daily parameters into a single daily kidney function state. Subsequently, we generate three main trend descriptions for the course of the kidney function states within a time period of seven days. The parameters of these trend descriptions are the features for the retrieval.

Prognosis of multiparametric courses of the kidney function for intensive care patients is a domain without a medical theory. Moreover, we can not expect such a theory to be formulated in the near future. So we attempt to learn prototypical course pattern. Therefore, knowledge on this domain is s tored as a tree of prototypes with

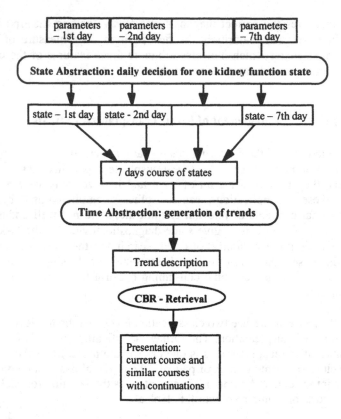

Fig.3. Abstractions for Multiparametric Prognoses in ICONS

three levels and a root node. Except for the root, where all not yet united courses are stored, every level corresponds to one of the trend descriptions. These are the short-term trend T1, the medium-term trend T2 and the long-term trend T3. As soon as enough courses that share another trend description are stored at a prototype, we create a new prototype with this trend. At a prototype at level 1, we unite courses that share T1, at level 2, courses that share T1 and T2 and at level 3, courses that share all three trend descriptions. We can do this, because regarding their importance, the three trend descriptions T1, T2 and T3 refer to hierarchically related time periods. T1 is more important than T2 and T3, because they are additional extensions into the past and because the current course is more relevant for the further development of the kidney function than the course some days ago.

4   Conclusion

In medical decision making it is very important to focus on patients seen in a special facility of a hospital or at a practitioner. The use of CBR systems in a special health care facility forms automatically a facility adapted knowledge base. This is the main advantage of CBR systems in medicine.

In ICONS and in COSYL the main purpose of prototypes is to structure the case base and to guide the retrieval. The part of the prototype design in ICONS that goes beyond this purpose is ambivalent, because the general drawback of prototypes occurs, namely the loss of information by generalisation. In GS.52 prototypes are used in a typical medical diagnostic task. They directly correspond to the physicians sense of prototypes. As comparisons with single cases are unable to identify typical features, in this application that is characterised by a lack of knowledge about typical features of the syndromes the use of prototypes is not only sensible, but even necessary. Apart from guiding the retrieval and structuring the case base prototypes mainly serve a different purpose in our early warning system. In a domain where the relevant kidney parameters are known but no knowledge about their temporal course behaviour exists we attempt to learn typical course pattern. As the prototypes are of the same form as the courses they are appropriate for this learning task.

Summarising our experiences we would like to make quite clear that the role of prototypes depends on the application and the task. For medical diagnoses as in GS.52 they even seem to be necessary because of their correspondence to medical prototypes which guide the physician's diagnoses. In domains with very poor domain theories they guide the retrieval. This is very important if the amount of the cases is enormous (COSYL). Furthermore they may help to learn general knowledge (kidney early warning).

Table 2 gives an overview about our systems, their medical tasks, the existing knowledge of each domain, the main purposes of prototypes and the improvements gained by them.

Table 2. Overview of our systems and the improvements gained by prototypes

Program	Task	Knowledge	Purpose	Improvement
ICONS	Therapy Advice	Alterations of Influence Factors	Structure the Case Base	Ambivalent
COSYL	Diagnostic Advice	Nearly None	Structure the Case Based (+ Learning)	Enormous Retrieval Speed up
GS.52	Diagnosis	Continuos Modifications	Define Typical Diseases	Impossible without Prototypes
Kidney	Time Course Analysis	Very Weak	Learning	Retrieval Speed up + Learning

References

1.   Strube, G., Janetzko, D.: Episodisches Wissen und fallbasiertes Schließen: Aufgaben für die Wissensdiagnostik und die Wissenspsychologie. *Schweizerische Zeitschrift für Psychologie 49* (4) (1990) 211-221

2.   Swanson, D.B., Feltovich, P.J., Johnson, P.E.: Psychological Analysis of Physician Expertise: Implications for Design of Decision Support Systems. In: Shires, D.B., Wolf, H. (eds.): *Proceedings of MEDINFO 77* , North-Holland, Amsterdam, (1977) 161-164

3.   Gierl, L., Stengel-Rutkowski, S.: Integrating Consultation and Semi-automatic Knowledge Acquisition in a Prototype-based Architecture: Experiences with Dysmorphic Syndromes. *Artificial Intelligence in Medicine 6* (1994) 29-49

4.   Swoboda, W., Zwiebel, F. M., Spitz, R., Gierl, L.: A case-based consultation system for postoperative management of liver-transplanted patients. In: Barahona, P.,Veloso, M., Bryant, J. (eds.): *Medical Informatics Europe, Proceedings of the 12th International Congress of the European Federation of Medical Informatics* , IOS Press, Amsterdam (1994) 530-534

5.   Schmidt, R., Boscher, L., Heindl, B., Schmid, G., Pollwein, B., Gierl, L. : Adaptation and Abstraction in a Case-Based Antibiotics Therapy Adviser. In: Barahona, P., Stefanelli, M., Wyatt, J. (eds.): *Artificial Intelligence in Medicine, Proceedings of the 6th Conference on Artificial Intelligence in Medicine Europe, AIME'95* , Lecture Notes in Artificial Intelligence, Vol. 934, Springer -Verlag, Berlin Heidelberg New York (1995) 209-217

6.   Schmidt, R., Heindl, B., Pollwein, B., Gierl, L.: Multiparametric Time Course Prognoses by means of Case-Based Reasoning and Abstraction of Data and Time. *Medical Informatics 22* (3) (1997) 237-250. And in: van Bemmel, J.H., McCray, A.T. (eds.): *Yearbook of Medical Informatics 98* , Schattauer-Verlag, Stuttgart (1998) 407-420

7.   Clancey, W.J.: Heuristic Classification. *Artificial Intelligence 27* (1985) 289-350

8.   Selz, O.: Über die Gesetze des geordneten Denkverlaufs. Stuttgart (1913)

9.   Rosch, E., Mervis, C.B.: Family Resemblance: Studies in the Internal Structures of Categories. *Cognitive Psychology 7* (1975) 573-605

10. Tversky, A.: Features of Similarity. *Psychological Review 84* (4), 1977, 327-352

11. Aha, D.W., Kibler, D., Albert, M.K.: Instance-based Learning Algorithms. *Machine Learning 6* (1991) 37-66

12. Scott, P.D., Sage, K.H.: Why Generalize? Hybrid Representations and Instance-Based Learning. In: B.Neumann (ed.): *Proceedings of the 10th European Conference on Artificial Intelligence, ECAI 92* , John-Wiley, New York (1992) 484-486

13. Biberman, Y.: The Role of Prototypicality in Exemplar-Based Learning. In: Lavrac, N., Wrobel, S. (ed.): *Proceedings of the 8th European Conference on Machine Learning, ECML 95* , Lecture Notes in Computer Science 912, Springer -Verlag, Berlin Heidelberg New York (1995) 77-91

14. Sharma, S., Sleeman, D.: REFINER: A Case-Based Differential Diagnosis Aide for Knowledge Acquisition and Knowledge Refinement. In Sleeman, D. (ed.): *Proceedings of EWSL 88* , Pitman Publishers, London (1988) 201-210

15. Bareiss, R.: Exemplar-based Knowledge Acquisition. Academic Press, San Diego, (1989)

16. Schmidt, R., Heindl, B., Pollwein, B., Gierl, L.: Abstractions of Data and Time for Multiparametric Time Course Prognoses. In. Smith, I., Faltings B. (eds.): *Proceedings of the third European Workshop on Case-Based Reasoning, EWCBR-96* , Lecture Notes in Artificial Intelligence, Vol. 934, Springer -Verlag, Berlin Heidelberg New York (1996)

Exploiting Social Reasoning of Open Multi-agent Systems to Enhance Cooperation in Hospitals

Samir Aknine

LAMSADE, Université Paris Dauphine
Place du Maréchal De Lattre De Tassigny
75775 Paris Cedex 16, France
Aknine@lamsade.dauphine.fr

Abstract The Virtual Hospital Patient Scheduling System (VHPSS) focuses on building multi-agent cooperative systems. We have chosen to build Intelligent agents that perform coordination tasks for the users, i.e. the medical staff. An agent in VHPSS system has a limited information. To solve some problems, the agent has to cooperate with the other agents of the surrounding environment. This article presents this scheduling system based on our principal contributions in research on multi-agent systems. (1) At the architectural level, the system is based on a multi-agent software agent architecture which has several advantages: parallelization of agent's tasks, reusability of agent's components, partial mobility and partial cloning of agent's code. (2) At the cooperative level, the system uses a new agent negotiation protocol making it possible to accelerate the process of task allocation.

Keywords: Multi-agent systems, negotiation protocol, multi-agent software agent model, medical assistance.

1 Introduction

This article explains how agents can exploit their capacity in order to support the medical staff in a hospital complex specialized in the treatment of burnt patients, either by cooperating with other agents, or with human actors that they represent in the virtual system.

For instance, when a doctor receives a patient in an emergency state, he must perform several radiological tests, blood tests, etc., before starting any surgical operation. To confirm his diagnostic, the doctor must transfer his patient in different services so that the patient undergoes the necessary tests. Fulfilling these tests requires the availability of the necessary material for all operations and qualified staff. In general, these tests are carried out after a long time. To accelerate the patient pretreatment process, the doctor can collect some of this information from other services or hospitals that have been already visited by the patient. In order to give for the doctor a software support, we have chosen an agent oriented design approach to solve this problem.

W. Horn et al. (Eds.): AIMDM'99, LNAI 1620, pp. 133-137, 1999.
© Springer-Verlag Berlin Heidelberg 1999

At a cooperation level, the problem is to reason on the other agent capacity in the system. To select in an effective way, i.e. as soon as possible, the agent depending on a certain task in order to answer to the environment's dynamics, we apply the contract net protocol extension that we have developed [Aknine, 98b]. At the architectural level, we propose in this article a multi-agent architecture and an agent model which are based on the functionalities of the hospital treatments.

This article is organized as follows: in section 2, we present the paradigm of reactive coordination of the medical care systems. In section 3, we detail the VHPSS agent model proposed and its operations. In section 4, we present our agent negotiation protocol. Finally, we conclude in section 5.

2 Application Context

In a hospital processing center, the medical staff is often confronted to treat several patients at the same time. So a patient can be treated by various doctors and nurses. Thus, the medical staff is organized in a cooperative group sharing the same resources, i.e. patients. Because of the strong dynamicity of the system and the great quantity of information handled by the medical staff, sometimes it happens that one medical personal neglects one of the tasks which was allocated to him. This weakens the human actors cooperative process. The intervention of an artificial system is essential in this first level in order to organize and to supervise the activities of the human actors cooperative system.

The cooperative medical care system proposed is composed of doctors and of medical personal who take part in the process of a patient's treatment. To relieve the various actors from some coordination tasks, we have designed a cooperative work system composed of software agents. For each actor is associated a software agent. The actor of the system carries out the task of the medical process (processing, analyzing, regulating, etc.), as for the agent, it assists and represents the actor in the artificial system. It checks the task activation conditions which will be announced to the other agents of the system when these conditions are satisfied.

Knowing the profile of the actor which corresponds to the tasks that he/she can perform, the agent proposes the actor whom it represents to carry out the announced tasks. Once a task is assigned to the respective actor, a cooperative problem solving process begins between the agent and the actor to whom the task is allocated. For instance, when a doctor prescribes the patient's treatment, the software agent can analyze the knowledge collected on the patient's health state and then propose the corresponding treatment to the doctor which will be able to apply it.

3 Agent Model

The agent model that we propose is a generic agent model. It is composed of various primitive agents: two agents of decision (ManagerAgent and PlannerAgent), an agent of execution (ExecutorAgent), an agent of perception/communication and a working memory. The first control agent (the ManagerAgent) integrates the behaviors which manage the execution of the domain tasks. The second control agent (the PlannerAgent) plans dynamically the sequence of the tasks which implies a dynamic generation of the actors' activity plans. Both the ExecutorAgent and its actor participate in the execution of the selected tasks. Each primitive agent of the basic agent communicates with the other agents through the shared working memory.

This multi-agent structure of an agent has several advantages. On one hand, it allows an agent to accomplish several tasks at the same time and thus the reactivity in taking the decisions caused by the fast evolution of the environment, advantages underlined by various authors; in addition, it makes it possible to fulfill the requirements of confidentiality.

On the other hand, The multi-agent character of the agent allows the partial migration of its programs, i.e. the ExecutorAgent is able to migrate from one site to an other in order to perform the solicited task. For instance, the agent can seek in other medical complexes, medical information on the diseases already contracted by a patient and to carry out the necessary processing in the concerned site whereas the other basic agent components (ManagerAgent, PlannerAgent and SupervisorAgent) not directly implied in the execution of this task can remain in the initial site. They can exchange messages with the ExecutorAgent through their communication modules. The partial migration of code is particularly interesting in the sense that it can reduce the network submersion risk with an unusable code.

Moreover, while referring to the arguments provided in (Rothermel and al, 1997), the authenticity of the data transferred via the network without a constant monitoring can sometimes be questioned. In our application, the displacement of the agents ensures us the confidentiality and the authenticity of the data, requirements imposed by any patient for its doctor. Indeed, some necessary data to the processing of the agent can not be transferred through the network; the agent treats them directly in their storage sites. From these sites, it returns its own results (For more details see [Aknine, 98c]).

4 Agent Cooperation

In a hospital complex, a robust cooperation is essential between all the members in order to offer the best services because of the vital character of the acts achieved by these members. The cooperation of these members is carried out through the cooperation of the artificial agents integrated in the assistance system. A significant question to ensure this cooperation between the agents is: which protocol to use to ensure an effective allocation of the system's tasks?

The contract net protocol is often used for coordinating the agents during the problem solving. In the definition provided by Smith and Davis [Smith, 80][Smith & al 81], the CNP is essentially a collection of nodes, which cooperate to solve a problem. A node can be a manager, who controls a task's execution or a contractee who performs it. When a task cannot be executed by an agent for reasons such as the lack of information, it can be proposed to other agents. At the receiving of an announce, the agent evaluates its interest for this task. If it is interested enough, the agent submits a bid to the manager for this task. The latter bases on the agents' bids for selecting the appropriate agents. Then, the manager sends an acknowledgment message to the best bidder. Moreover, as we have shown in our previous experiments done on the contract net protocol and the extension of the CNP in [Aknine, 98b], the task allocation mechanism by using the contract net protocol is long. For this reason, we have applied the CNP extension that we have developed.

In our protocol, we insert two levels of propositions and commitments for the CNP, by introducing four new phases, which we call: Pre-Bidding, Definitive-Bidding, Pre-Assignment and Definitive-Assignment. These steps replace Bid and Assignment phases of the traditional CNP.

When a manager announces a task for the contractees, he receives PreBids, i.e. temporal propositions from these ones. These PreBids evaluates the contractees' capacities for executing the task when they receive an announce. To the best one, the manager sends a PreAccept and PreRejects for all the others. For each evolution of the contractees' situation, they can postulate with new PreBids. So they can evolve to a PreAccept state, or stay in the PreReject state. At the receiving of a PreAccept message, the potential contractee can send his DefinitiveBid. This one can be questioned by the manager if during the Bidding phase, a prerejected contractee has sent a better PreBid, whose value exceeds the potential contractee's DefinitiveBid. It can also result in the signing of the contract and then in a definitive rejection of all the other agents. The negotiation ends with the execution of the task by the selected contractee.

Using several levels of propositions and allocations to negotiate the execution of tasks (1) allows an agent to manage several negotiation processes simultaneously and so reduces the global length of the negotiation between the agents. (2) An agent can propose himself with a temporary bid (PreBid) to perform a task as soon as it receives an order. Afterwards, if the agent receives new orders, it can modify its previous proposition as long as it has not sent a DefinitiveBid. (3) The length of the PreBidding phase allows an agent to make the best choice among the proposed tasks before postulating definitively for the tasks. So after the acceptation of the execution of the tasks, the risk of disengagement is free. (4) The manager and its contractees do not incur any penalty risk, as the first proposition is only a temporary one. The contract is signed once they have come to a definitive agreement. Actually, the manager does not definitively reject all the contractees as long as it has not received a definitive bid from the potential contractee which confirms its intention to perform the task both parts agreed on and it informs the other contractees of the existence of a potential contractee to perform the task.

5 Conclusion

In this article, we have proposed a Virtual Hospital Patient Scheduling System allowing an effective cooperation between human actors treating patients. The system is based on our two principal contributions: a new intelligent agent negotiation protocol and a multi-agent software agent architecture. The architecture is centered on the three principal aspects of the new applications: mobility, reusability and flexibility. This architecture is perfectly reusable for other cooperative systems, in the sense that the description and the implementation of the software agents are totally independent of the application domain. The agents' control is totally independent of the domain tasks that they execute.

A first experimentation of this architecture was done on an application of technical specification writing in the telecommunication domain. [Aknine, 98c]. A first application of our protocol was done on goods delivery applications. The virtual medical system is especially conceive to meet the requirements of the recent applications by proposing an interesting solution of a partial cloning and migration of the agent's code.

Acknowledgement

We would like to think all the doctors who helped us during this work particularly Aknine H.

References

Aknine, S. "Exploiting Knowledge Ontology for Managing Parallel WorkFlow Systems", International Conference on Expert Systems and Applied Artificial Intelligence, Springer Verlag, 1998a.

Aknine, S., "Issues in Cooperative Systems: Extending the Contract Net Protocol", A Joint Conference on the Science and Technology of Intelligent Systems, USA, 1998b.

Aknine, S. "A Reflexive Agent Architecture applied to Parallel WorkFlow Systems", CE'98, 5th ISPE Int. Conf. on Concurrent Engineering Research and Application, Japan, 1998c.

Decker, K.& Li, J. "Coordinated Hospital Patient Scheduling", ICMAS, Paris, 1998.

Dojat, M. Pachet, F., Guessoum, Z. et al. "NéoGanesh: A Working System for the Automated Control of Assisted Ventilation in ICUs", AI in Medicine, 11, 97-117, 1997.

Huang, J., Jennings, N. R. and Fox, J. "An Agent Architecture for Distributed Medical Care", Wooldridge, M. J. & Jennings, N.R. (eds.), Intelligent Agents, Springer, 1995.

Nwana, H., S. et Azarmi, N. Software Agents and Soft Computing : Toward Enhancing Machine Intelligence : Concepts and Applications, Springer, 1997.

Parc, A. S. and Leuker, S. "A Multi-agent Architecture Supporting Service Access", First International Workshop on Mobile Agents, MA'97, Berlin, Germany, 1997.

Smith, R., G. et Davis, R. "Frameworks for co-operation in Distributed Problem Solving", IEEE Transaction on System Man and Cybernetics, 1981.

Influence Diagrams for Neonatal Jaundice Management*

Concha Bielza, Sixto Ríos-Insua, and Manuel Gómez

Decision Analysis Group, Madrid Technical University, 28660 Madrid, Spain
{mcbielza,srios,mgomez}@fi.upm.es

Abstract. Influence Diagrams (ID) are widely known to be a useful tool in Decision Analysis (DA). However, when facing a complex real-world problem, we often encounter many difficulties. Namely, the evolution of the ID skeleton until a final version is attained, provides interesting issues related to problem modelling. We also come up against computational difficulties caused by the size of the problem. Our motivation is a real medical problem of neonatal jaundice management, and we present the solution we have implemented in the Decision Support System (DSS) developed.

1   Introduction

Jaundice develops in a healthy baby when the blood contains an excess of bilirubin. Newborns tend to have higher bilirubin levels because they have extra oxygen-carrying red blood cells, and their young livers cannot metabolize the excess bilirubin. The infants are then usually exposed to special lights that break down excess bilirubin –*phototherapy*–. But when bilirubin levels are extremely elevated, jaundiced newborns may suffer damage to the nervous system (including irreversible brain damage), and all their blood needs to be replaced –*exchange transfusion*–. An important challenge is to distinguish between what is known as physiological jaundice and the more serious version, pathological jaundice, related to the development of kernicterus (bilirubin-induced encephalopathy) and the baby having risk factors. Current recommendations try to balance out the risks of undertreatment and overtreatment [7]. However, it is not very clearly stated at which point bilirubin levels are high enough to require treatment and which treatment to administer.

The Neonatology Service at the Gregorio Marañón Hospital in Madrid was interested in studying the problem of jaundice in newborns. We agreed and started to develop a DSS called IctNeo. It represents and solves the problem by means of an ID, an acyclic directed graph to represent and solve DA problems under uncertainty, see [9]. The main objectives are to include a large number

* Paper supported by DGESIC project PB97-0856 and CAM project 07T/0009/1997. We are grateful to doctors M. Sánchez Luna and S. Caballero, the experts in the structuring and elicitation processes.

W. Horn et al. (Eds.): AIMDM'99, LNAI 1620, pp. 138–142, 1999.

of uncertain factors and decisions, to better define when treatment is required and/or should be changed, to decrease costs and risks due to, e.g., blood exchange, and to take into account the preferences of parents and doctors. As a result, the hospital will have an automated problem-solving tool as an aid for improving jaundice management.

This paper outlines the methodology used to construct IctNeo. Some difficulties were encountered when reasoning on the structure and content of the ID that represents the problem (Section 2) and when solving the ID (Section 3). The conclusions are set out in Section 4.

2 Constructing the Influence Diagram

2.1 Towards the Final Structure

The scope of the problem was delimited by considering infants born at the hospital during the early days of their life, and who were aged 3 days or less, because this is the critical period of time when the most harmful effects take place.

The sequence of the problem follows. The doctor first decides whether or not to admit the baby to hospital and, possibly, confine it to the Intensive Care Unit. If the baby is admitted, it is necessary to control the bilirubin levels, carrying out different tests and giving the patient some of the prescribed treatments: phototherapy, exchange transfusion or observation, depending on a series of characteristics of the newborn baby, like age, weight, bilirubin and hemoglobin levels. After each treatment stage, the effects on the baby are observed, repeating the process as many times as necessary until the problem is over, i.e., the infant is discharged or she receives a treatment that falls outside the scope of the problem with which we are concerned, again delimiting our problem. We started to structure the problem as a generic ID, clustering the nodes which belong to the same logical group into sub-models.

The following step was to disaggregate nodes and decide how many stages there were in the problem. As regards the first issue, the knowledge before admission consists of certain characteristics of the mother and baby, clinical findings, like hemoglobin and bilirubin serum concentrations, and the results of a series of tests, see Fig. 1 below. The pathologies which have an influence on hyperbilirubinemia are stated at the top of Fig. 1; see [8] for further details.

The second issue concerning the number of stages of which the problem is composed is more interesting. In principle, every decision node would be identical, its domain containing the different treatment actions and hospital discharge. Since doctors consider that the time between one treatment and the next lasts 6 hours, it would be necessary to have a sequence of 12 decision nodes to account for at most 72 hours. This, however, would entail an intractable ID, due to the size of the set of nodes and arcs. Apart from this, there are a number of constraints placed by doctors on the chain of treatment decisions, e.g., not to perform more than two exchange transfusions per full treatment, the exchange transfusion must be followed and preceded by phototherapy, among others. Also, the length of the jaundice process varies. If the baby is not admitted, the length of time will be the minimum, because the sequence of treatment decisions does not make sense. The ID considering all these issues is highly asymmetric, that if evaluated as traditionally [9], its optimal policy includes sequences of decisions that do not meet the constraints.

But we observed that treatments were very often referred as a combination of the initial 6-hour therapies, e.g. 6-, 12-, or 18-hour long phototherapy, and we decided to redefine the domains at the decision nodes. We identified three types of treatment decisions: (1) decisions made in the initial phase of the treatment (alternatives allowed when starting the treatment, such as phototherapies of different lengths and observations); (2) decisions made in the main part of the treatment (some grouped treatments, e.g., 12-hour phototherapy, plus exchange transfusion, plus 6-hour phototherapy, always satisfying the constraints); and (3) decisions made in the final phase. This led to 4 treatment nodes. In this manner, we solved the problems mentioned above, at the expense of increasing the difficulty of decision domains definition.

2.2 Quantitative Information of the ID

The ID is complete when the quantitative information obtained via an elicitation process has been entered. Most probability tables were assigned with the aid of subjective judgements according to the SRI protocol and its extensions [6]. The main problem was, for chance nodes with many predecessors, how to obtain the tables with so many entries from the experts and how to store so much information. For this purpose, we used generalized noisy OR-gates [1] based on a causal model, requiring a number of assignments that is linear in the number of causes rather than exponential, as is usually the case. Our saving was of 70%.

The preferences of the experts were represented by means of a multi-attribute utility function [4]. With the aid of experts, we first constructed an objectives hierarchy, whose goals included minimizing financial, social and emotional costs, as well as risks and injuries, all of which measured the preferences of parents and doctors. We then constructed the scales of the attributes and derived a functional form of the multi-attribute utility function that was consistent with the assumptions investigated. Readers are referred to [3] for a detailed explanation, where, in addition, all the assignments are allowed to be imprecise, as a means of sensitivity analysis. The final ID is shown in Fig. 1.

3 Evaluating the Influence Diagram

The storage space requirements grow enormously due to node inheritances during chance node removal and arc reversal operations, during the problem-solving process. Our ID requires a maximum storage capacity of 1.66×10^{14} storage positions, where the average size of the problem is 1.79×10^{13} storage positions. Therefore, the process becomes unmanageable. We provide several ways to alleviate that computational burden.

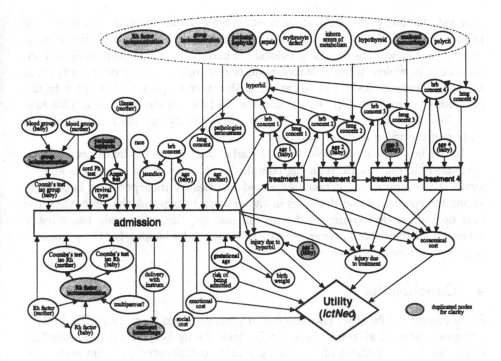

Fig. 1. Final ID of our problem.

The algorithm for evaluating IDs [9] proceeds by reducing nodes and we know that all possible deletion sequences lead to the final solution, but they may involve different computational efforts. So, our first contribution is to search for a *good* node deletion sequence, since finding an *optimal* sequence has been shown to be a *NP-hard* optimization problem. The one-step-look-ahead heuristic [5] recommends that the next node to be deleted is the one that leads to computations over the smallest domain, taking into account only one operation (ahead).

Our proposal improves on that heuristic. First, we use Kong's heuristic to choose only two candidates. Second, the system qualitatively constructs a search tree from these two nodes, and decides to stop the exploration if, after the evaluation of one million possibilities, we have achieved a reduction in problem storage of at least 50% compared to Kong's heuristic. Otherwise, it continues exploring solutions until they are exhausted or until four million trials have been conducted. In this manner, the storage space required in the problem-solving phase is divided by at most two, as compared with Kong's heuristic. The search is improved by pruning the search tree when identical IDs are reached along certain paths from the root, thus reducing the size of this tree.

Our second contribution is as follows. The operation of chance node removal may produce an increase of the expected utility tables because the value node inherits the predecessors (if any) of the removed node. Nevertheless, the computation of the expected utility is not essential at that point, and we propose to postpone computation until it is necessary, i.e., at the time of a decision node removal. At that point the system must remember the chance nodes that have been removed and the arcs that have been reversed, carrying out all the computations that were not made previously. Therefore, a mixed approach is more advisable, in which, when a chance node is removed, we compute the expected utilities whenever this implies a saving in the storage space with respect to the previous diagram. Let $C(i)$ be the conditional predecessors of node i. This saving takes place whenever $C(i) \subset C(v)$, where i, v designate the removed chance node and the value node, respectively.

In our last version of IctNeo, we take advantage of the evidence propagation operation [2], once again reducing complexity. Moreover, the system is able to avoid the computation of many expected utilities by incorporating knowledge about the constraints on decisions in the grammar script: at the time when the first decision node is removed during the process, the value node has already inherited all the decision nodes, and its table is cut by looking for the sequences that do not meet the constraints.

4   Conclusions

Some common difficulties encountered in practice when using large IDs include features related to all the steps in the Decision Analysis cycle. At the modelling stage, we had to address an increasingly more complicated problem structure, while at the evaluation stage, we had to find solutions to cope with our large problem that was otherwise unsolvable. The manner in which these issues were addressed will provide insights to the community involved in the design and solution of decision models by means of IDs.

References

1. Díez, F.J.: Parameter Adjustment in Bayes Networks. The Generalized noisy OR-gate. In Heckerman, D., Mamdani, A. (eds.): Uncertainty in AI: Proc. of the 9th Conference. Morgan Kaufmann, San Mateo (1993) 99–105
2. Ezawa, K.J.: Evidence Propagation and Value of Evidence on Influence Diagrams. Oper. Res. **46**, 1 (1998) 73–83
3. Gómez, M., Ríos-Insua, S., Bielza, C., Fdez del Pozo, J.A.: Multi-attribute Utility Analysis in the IctNeo System. Work. Pap. Dept. of AI, Madrid Tech. Univ. (1998)
4. Keeney, R.L., Raiffa, H.: Decisions with Multiple Objectives. Preferences and Value Tradeoffs. Wiley, New York (1976)
5. Kong, A.: Multivariate Belief Functions and Graphical Models. PhD. Dissertation. Dept. of Statistics, Harvard Univ., Cambridge, Mass (1986)
6. Merkhofer, M.W.: Quantifying Judgmental Uncertainty: Methodology, Experiences, and Insights. IEEE Trans. on Sys., Man and Cyber. SMC **17**, 5 (1987) 741–752
7. Newman, T.B., Maisels, M.J.: Evaluation and Treatment of Jaundice in the Term Infant: A Kinder, Gentler Approach. Pediatrics **89** (1992) 809–830
8. Ríos-Insua, S., Bielza, C., Gómez, M., Fdez del Pozo, J.A., Sánchez Luna, M., Caballero, S.: An Intelligent Decision System for Jaundice Management. In: Girón, F.J. (ed.): Applied Decision Analysis. Kluwer, Norwell (1998) 133–144
9. Shachter, R.D.: Evaluating Influence Diagrams. Oper. Res. **34** (1986) 871–882

Electronic Drug Prescribing and Administration – Bedside Medical Decision Making

I.R. Clark[1], B.A. McCauley[1], I.M. Young[1], P.G. Nightingale[1], M. Peters[1], N.T. Richards[2], D. Adu[2]

[1] Wolfson Computer Laboratory, Queen Elizabeth Hospital, Edgbaston, Birmingham, B15 2TH, U.K.
[2] Department of Nephrology, Queen Elizabeth Hospital, Edgbaston, Birmingham, B15 2TH, U.K.

Abstract. A rules-based electronic drug prescribing system is described, which by means of radio-linked mobile terminals allows bedside entry of drug prescription and administration data to be evaluated in real-time against wide-ranging clinical data including interactions and allergies. Results of a questionnaire assessing the acceptability of the system are summarised, and preliminary analysis of data gathered as part of routine operation is presented, showing doctors' responses to warning messages of differing severity.

1. Introduction

A rules-based drug prescribing system (RUMPS), developed by Wolfson Computer Laboratory (WCL), Division of Medical Sciences, University of Birmingham, is in routine use within the Renal Unit, University Hospital Birmingham NHS Trust (UHB). The system is generic in concept, and includes radio-linked mobile terminals, enabling rules-based drug prescribing and administration at the bedside.

The system both proposes actions, and queries or denies user-initiated proposals, based on the continuous assessment of patient data available to it and on medical knowledge represented within it. The bedside availability of the system means that it is capable of impacting decisions relating to the appropriate and effective use of resources at the point at which the clinical decision is made. The system therefore provides an important mechanism by which best practice (as defined by the medical knowledge contained within the system) can be applied routinely within a clinical setting and offers a clear route for the implementation of evidence based medicine and reduction of risk from prescribing errors.

1.1 Background

The 64-bed Renal Services Unit within UHB is an internationally recognised centre for the provision of medical and surgical services for patients with renal disease,

W. Horn et al. (Eds.): AIMDM'99, LNAI 1620, pp. 143–147, 1999.

including: nephrology; the treatment of acute renal failure; all modes of dialysis and associated access surgery; and renal transplantation. The rules-based drug prescribing and administration system is an extension of an earlier rules-based system that has provided a successful strategy for improving the appropriateness of laboratory testing and has resulted in: significant saving in medical staff time; significant reduction in the number of laboratory investigations requested; and improved continuity of care. Evaluation of radio-linked terminals began in early 1996 and allowed the trial of a character-based system [1,2,3,4] in July 1996. The current graphical version of the system was introduced into full routine clinical use on the Renal Unit in January 1998.

2. The System

Laboratory results and X-ray reports may be reviewed, drugs prescribed and their administration recorded at the bedside, using hand-held wireless thin-client terminals. Doctors and nurses carry these devices on their rounds, using them to enter or retrieve data anywhere within the ward areas. The same programs are available on desk-top PCs around the hospital, enabling access to the system from consultants' and ward offices, pharmacy and theatre areas.

When prescribing, the system considers contra-indications such as potential drug–drug, serological and/or clinical state interactions and where a drug is found to be inappropriate for a specific patient, therapy is prohibited and an alternative drug must be sought. Where a contra-indication is not too severe (as defined within the drug data dictionary), warnings are issued but may be overridden. Those considered more serious require that the prescriber's password is re-entered. The system also applies rules whilst recording administration data, for example warning if an attempt is made to administer a PRN drug with a frequency greater than that prescribed. More complex rules access relevant laboratory results, acquired on-line, to monitor serological trends and to manage therapeutic monitoring, etc. Additionally, rules within the prescribing module express protocols for drug therapy in specific areas of renal disease and transplantation. In this situation drug therapy (often a panel of drugs with appropriate routes, forms, doses) is 'proposed' by the system, for authorisation by medical staff, these protocols being initiated by medical staff on the basis of the patient's disease state. A further series of rules automatically highlights scripts for review by medical staff, an important example of this function being the monitoring of the duration of antibiotic therapy.

3. Methodology

3.1 Overall Architecture

The application is client-server based, with a central M (MUMPS) database server communicating via TCP/IP with Delphi GUI clients. All rule evaluation is server-based. A mixture of thin-client hand-held terminals and conventional desk-top PCs (thick-client) are used by the system. The radio-linked terminals communicate with the server via a number of radio access-points, each connected to the hospital's wired LAN and located around the ward areas. Doctors and nurses may move between the influence of different access points whilst maintaining a continual link to the server. Radio links operate in the 2.4 GHz band, which is licensed for this technology, at power levels much less than those used for mobile phones. No problems relating to radio-borne interference have been encountered during use of the terminals in a hospital environment.

3.2   Rules

All rules within the system are of Boolean form and fall into two distinct groups known locally as 'simple' and 'complex'. Simple rules are driven exclusively from tables within the data dictionary, and are real-time comparisons of current patient data and pre-defined dictionary parameters. These rules are applied at the point where a doctor or nurse uses the system to change the patient record by, for instance, adding a drug prescription or administering a drug, and may result in the user being warned of a possible problem resulting from their action, or in some cases, in the action being denied. Examples of checks made by such rules are: various interactions, as already outlined; dosing levels; route/form compatibility; dose/strength availability; time between administrations; total number of administrations; etc. Complex rules are routines compiled from Medical Logic Modules (MLMs) written in Arden Syntax, which are processed through the inference engine [5,6] within the central server. Since these rules have access to all data within the patient record and are 'time-aware', they allow more sophisticated and/or longer-term checks to be made on prescribing and other processes, by, for instance: warning if a patient's biochemistry or haematology appears to be adversely affected by a particular current prescription, or automatically proposing a drug level assay at an appropriate time after the prescribing of certain antibiotics and immunosuppressants. Evaluation of such rules is most often an asynchronous background process, triggered by, for instance, the reception of result data from a laboratory feeder system. Synchronous foreground operation of the rulebase is also possible.

4.   Results

The general assessment of the system by 14 doctors and 24 nurses, 3 months after installation, indicated a good degree of acceptability of the system. Legibility and availability of data, both of which contribute to patient safety, were scored highly by both groups. Whilst these might be considered obvious by-products of electronic systems, when implementing such systems the routine operational effort required by users to obtain such benefits must not be perceived to be significant if they are to find acceptability. It is pleasing therefore that both groups found the system easy to use.

More detailed analysis indicated that doctors perceived benefit in terms of prescribing (warning messages, default scripts and protocol prescribing), and nurses in terms of administration (24-hour availability of administration data, clear indication of previously not-administered drugs, drugs allocated to appropriate ward rounds): neither group felt that the time now required for these activities was significantly greater than before introduction of the system.

As a part of routine operation the system retains substantial 'audit-trail' data to allow details of prescriptions and administrations and any changes to these to be retrieved for clinical and medico-legal purposes. These data also enable significant audit of usage:

- 49.8% of new prescriptions displayed warning messages to the prescriber.

- In 13.2% of these cases a doctor started to prescribe a drug, was shown warning messages and did not complete the prescription.

- Where high level warnings were issued, 64% of scripts were not completed.

- 86.5% of drug doses were administered, 66.1% within one hour of the prescribed time and 88.4% within two hours.

- 13.6% of PRN drug administrations were paracetamol, of which 1.7% were given within 4 hours of the previous administration.

Further analysis of these real-time data is beginning to give insight into a wide range of clinical and nursing practices, in a level of detail which is not generally available to paper-based or off-line, 'open-loop' prescribing systems. In light of these data, approaches are now being evaluated whereby the rule-based aspects of the system may be used to improve the clinical and cost-effectiveness of prescribing, by, for instance: suggesting antibiotics based on organism and sensitivity data from laboratory feeder systems, ending scripts automatically when patients have been on certain antibiotics for pre-defined periods or directing junior doctors towards the use of those drugs preferred by their more senior colleagues.

5. Conclusion

The high level of acceptability expressed by clinical and financial managers and users shows that such systems, when made available at the point of care, not only offer a powerful mechanism for the introduction of clinical protocols and decision support, but also provide an everyday tool to clinical and nursing staff which is highly valued, improves patient care and operational efficiency, and gathers transparently information as part of the electronic patient record.

6. Acknowledgements

The authors would like to thank the staff of the Queen Elizabeth Hospital Renal Unit and Pharmacy for their advice during the design and development of the system, and for their patience and commitment during the early prototyping phase.

References

1. Peters M, Neuberger JM. A knowledge-based system for electronic drug prescribing utilising wireless terminals. In Waegemann CP, ed. Toward an electronic health record Europe '96:267-270. Centre for the Advancement of Electronic Health Records, 1996.
2. Peters M, Lambert ME, McCauley BA, Clark IR, Machell TA, McCoy HM, Mayer AD, Neuberger JM. A knowledge-based system for electronic drug prescribing utilising wireless terminals. In Richards B, ed. Current Perspectives in Healthcare Computing 1997. Br J Healthcare Computing, 1997.
3. Nightingale PG, Neuberger JM and Peters M. Rules-based drug prescription and administration by use of wireless terminals. Health Trends 1997 29(3):83-88.
4. Clark I, Peters M, Neuberger JM A knowledge-based system for electronic drug prescribing utilising wireless terminals. In Waegemann CP, ed. Toward an Electronic Patient Record '97:226-230. Centre for the Advancement of Electronic Health Records, 1997.
5. McCauley BA, Parekh J, Clark IR. A MUMPS application of rule based processing. In: Dayhoff RE, ed. Proceedings of the MUMPS Users' Group Meeting 1991 New Orleans. Maryland, USA: MUMPS Users' Group.
6. McCauley BA, Young I, Clark IR, Peters M. Incorporation of the Arden Syntax within the re-implementation of a closed-loop decision support system. Comput Biomed Res.1996 29(6) 507-518.

Neonatal Ventilation Tutor (VIE-NVT), a Teaching Program for the Mechanical Ventilation of Newborn Infants

Werner Horn[1,2], Christian Popow[2,3], Christoph Stocker[2], and Silvia Miksch[4]

[1] Austrian Research Institute for Artificial Intelligence
Schottengasse 3, A-1010 Vienna
werner@ai.univie.ac.at, http://www.ai.univie.ac.at/~werner
[2] Department of Medical Cybernetics and Artificial Intelligence, University of Vienna
[3] Department of Pediatrics, University of Vienna
[4] Institute of Software Technology, Vienna University of Technology, Austria

Abstract. We developed a computer assisted program for training the medical staff in ventilating newborn infants. The Java-based client-server program consists of two modules: the instructor module enabling the domain expert to create courses of virtual patients, the tutorial module running consultations with virtual patients. The tutorial module displays the course of the transcutaneous blood gases and a table of the ventilator settings which can interactively be adjusted by the trainee to provide an adequate gas exchange to the virtual patient. VIE-NVT is currently tested at our neonatal intensive care unit.

1 Introduction

Mechanical ventilation of newborn infants needs expert knowledge, clinical experience and a high clinical sensibility for the vulnerable immature patients. Within the last years, a better understanding of the mechanisms involved in the development of chronic (ventilator induced) lung disease has led to reassessment and a more careful definition of ventilation strategies. Moreover, the number of newborn infants ventilated and of the time they spend on the ventilator has been greatly reduced. New members of the medical staff thus have less possibilities to acquire the necessary skills for ventilating newborn infants. Various ventilation simulators have been developed for the training of adult mechanical ventilation ([3,6,7,8]) but not for newborn infants and not including transcutaneous monitoring. We developed a computer assisted training program for ventilating newborn infants based on a simple physiologic lung model and virtual patients.

2 The VIE-NVT System

The neonatal ventilation tutor VIE-NVT is a system which allows a trainee to simulate the mechanical ventilation of virtual newborn infants. It consists of two components: an instructor allowing the expert to define virtual patients, and a tutorial model which is used by the trainee to adjust the ventilation of a patient.

W. Horn et al. (Eds.): AIMDM'99, LNAI 1620, pp. 148–152, 1999.
© Springer-Verlag Berlin Heidelberg 1999

2.1   The Instructor Module

The instructor module is used by the expert neonatologist to define clinical courses of prototypical patients for use by the tutor system. Each virtual patient is defined by a set of parameters to be loaded by the tutorial system. Each data set consists of the (virtual) patient name, the body weight, a diagnosis, the initial ventilator settings, and of time-stamped values for the various physiologic parameters of the lung model. These values define the state and course of the "lung pathology" of the virtual patients. The following parameters may be modified by the instructor:

- compliance (C): the ratio between tidal volume (VT) and inflation pressure, a measure of the ventilation part of lung pathology; it determines the amount of peak inspiratory pressure needed to generate the VT
- lung factor (LF): determines the oxygenation part of lung pathology
- shunt (Q_s): defined as right to left shunt reducing the efficacy of oxygenation
- circulation factor (k_{CIRC}): determines the relationship between PO_2 and S_aO_2, the two measures of oxygenation
- spontaneous minute ventilation (Ve_{spont}): the amount of minute ventilation performed by the patient without the aid of the ventilator. Ve_{spont} reduces the amount of mechanical ventilation needed to achieve a certain PCO_2
- initial ventilator settings: inspiratory oxygen concentration (F_iO_2), peak inspiratory pressure (PIP), endexpiratory pressure $(PEEP)$, ventilation rate (f), inspiratory time (t_i)
- NO responder: NO, nitric oxide, is a smooth muscle relaxant acting on the peripheral pulmonary vessels; the switch NO responder (yes/no) determines if the oxygenation improves when NO is added to the inspiratory gas.

2.2   The Tutorial Module

Thetutorial module simulates the course of a selected patient. It uses a lung model defined by a set of equations. The lung model is divided into two interconnected tasks, ventilation and oxygenation. The results of the simulation and the outcome of (virtual) therapeutic actions are presented to the trainee using a graphical interface.

Ventilation, removal of CO_2 from the circulating blood, determines the P_aCO_2, the arterial partial pressure of carbon dioxide which is directly related to the transcutaneously measured $P_{tc}CO_2$. The following equation is motivated by a correlation study [2] and derived from the analysis of 442 cases with corresponding carbon dioxide measurements [1].

$$P_{tc}CO_2 = 2.226 + 1.039 * P_aCO_2 \tag{1}$$

Ventilation is directly related to the minute ventilation (Ve) which is determined by the product of the tidal volume (VT) and the ventilation rate (f). Finally, an increased shunt (Q_s) adds to the P_aCO_2.

$$P_aCO_2 = f_{CO2}(Ve_{total}/kg) + \begin{cases} 0 & \text{if } Q_s \leq 0.1 \\ 50 * Q_s - 5 & \text{if } Q_s < 0.9 \\ 40 & \text{if } Q_s \geq 0.9 \end{cases} \tag{2}$$

$$Ve_{total}/kg = Ve_{total}/Weight \tag{3}$$

$$Ve_{total} = Ve_{spont} + Ve_{resp} \tag{4}$$

$$Ve_{resp} = VT * f \tag{5}$$

$$VT = C * (PIP - PEEP) \tag{6}$$

The function f_{CO2} relates decreasing P_aCO_2 to increasing Ve. Characteristic values are given below:

Ve_{total}/kg	100	150	200	250	300	400	500	600
P_aCO_2		150	80	60	50	40	35	25	10

An improvement of the compliance (C) can be achieved in "immature lungs" by giving exogenous surfactant. The surfactant increases C by a factor between 4 ($C \leq 0.1$) and 1 ($C \geq 0.8$).

Oxygenation, the transfer of oxygen from the alveolar gas into the circulating blood, determines the P_aO_2, the arterial partial pressure of oxygen. P_aO_2 is directly related to the transcutaneously measured $P_{tc}O_2$ and the – also transcutaneously measured – S_aO_2, the oxygen saturation of hemoglobin which carries oxygen in the blood. Oxygenation may be changed by changing the inspiratory oxygen concentration (F_iO_2), the mean airway pressure which depends on the peak (PIP), the endexpiratory pressure ($PEEP$), and the inspiratory and expiratory time (t_i, t_e). It also depends on other therapeutical measures like giving exogenous surfactant or nitric oxide (NO).

The correlation between $P_{tc}O_2$ and P_aO_2 is derived from a pulse oximetry study [5]:

$$P_{tc}O_2 = k_{CIRC} * \begin{cases} P_aO_2 - 10 & \text{if } P_aO_2 \leq 90 \\ 69.672 + 0.115 * P_aO_2 & \text{otherwise} \end{cases} \tag{7}$$

The correlation between S_aO_2 and P_aO_2 is based on an equation with the following characteristic values (derived from [4]):

P_aO_2	10	20	30	40	50	60	70	80	90	100
S_aO_2	13.5	35.0	57.0	75.0	83.5	89.0	92.7	94.5	96.5	97.4

The arterial partial pressure of oxygen is approximated by a function derived from physiological and experimental clinical knowledge:

$$P_aO_2 = ((760 - 42 - P_aCO_2) * F_iO_2 + F_{MAP}) * (1 - \overline{Q_s}) * LF \tag{8}$$

There are four main parameters which influence the P_aO_2: the F_iO_2, the mean airway pressure (MAP), the shunt Q_s, and the lung factor LF. The "severity of the lung disease" is represented by the lung factor. It characterizes the diffusion part of the oxygenation. A low LF represents a high diffusion barrier resulting in a low P_aO_2. The LF is ideally compensated by an optimal MAP and a compensating F_iO_2 setting as shown in the following table:

Lung disease	LF	MAP_{OPT}	$F_iO_{2\ COMP}$
none	0.75	0	.21
light	0.33	7	.45
medium	0.25	10	.60
severe	0.2	14	.80

The MAP characterizes the contribution of mechanical ventilation to oxygenation. There is an optimal MAP characterized by the highest attainable P_aO_2. At lower and higher MAPs the P_aO_2 is lower because of a disturbed ventilation–perfusion relationship. A (hypothetic) MAP function (F_{MAP}) reflects this influence:

$$F_{MAP} = 13.2 * MAP * k_{MAP} \qquad (9)$$

$$MAP = \frac{PIP * t_i + PEEP * t_e}{t_i + t_e} \qquad (10)$$

The function value is a result of the ventilator settings ($PIP, PEEP, f, t_i$) and a factor k_{MAP}. This factor is one if the optimal MAP is set, but it decreases with increasing difference between the actual and the optimal MAP:

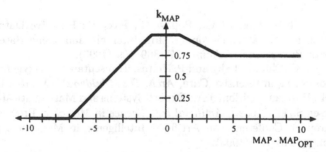

Finally, the perfusion part of oxygenation is characterized by the intra- and extrapulmonary shunt Q_s. The higher the R-L shunt, the lower the P_aO_2. In severe cases a decrease of the intrapulmonary shunt can be effected by switching on NO. This decreases the shunt $\overline{Q_s}$ by 50% if the patient is a NO-responder.

The User Interface The trainee is guided by a user interface which resembles an ICU monitor (with some enhanced features). It continuously displays the "actual" PO_2 and PCO_2 values which are calculated according to the physiologic values defined in the patient data set and the actual ventilator settings which are displayed in a spreadsheet. The user is asked to vary the ventilator settings aiming to appropriately "ventilate" the virtual patient under the changing conditions defined in the patient data set. Appropriate ventilation is defined as keeping the PCO_2 and PO_2 values within the normal range. Additional therapeutic options are the administration of exogenous lung surfactant for improving lung compliance or of nitric oxide for reducing pulmonary vascular resistance thus improving the ventilation perfusion relationship and oxygenation.

3 Conclusion

Appropriate tools for training the medical staff are an essential part in assuring the quality of care in critical situations. Virtual patients specified by data sets offer the advantage to define a wide range of easy to master to very complex situations. The trainee has a chance to react to various situations he/she has rarely seen before without endangering a "true" patient.

The Java-based neonatal ventilation tutor VIE-NVT provides an easy to use interface to learn adequate control of ventilators in neonatal ICUs. The model VIE-NVT uses is both influenced by physiological parameters and by practical experience of experts at our neonatal ICU. VIE-NVT sucessfully has completed its technical evaluation. It is currently clinically tested at our NICU.

Acknowledgement. We greatly appreciate the support given to the Austrian Research Institute of Artificial Intelligence (ÖFAI) by the Austrian Federal Ministry of Science and Transport, Vienna.

References

1. Horn W., Miksch S., Egghart G., Popow C., Paky F.: Effective Data Validation of High-Frequency Data: Time-Point-, Time-Interval-, and Trend-Based Methods, *Computers in Biology and Medicine*, **27**, 389–409 (1997).
2. D. Marsden, M.C. Chiu, F. Paky and P. Helms, Transcutaneous Oxygen and Carbon Dioxide Monitoring in Intensive Care, *Arch. Dis. Childhood* **60**, 1158–1161 (1985).
3. Müller L.M., Hasman A., Blom J.A.: Expert Systems and Mathematical Simulation, in Andreassen S., et al.(eds.), *Artificial Intelligence in Medicine*, Proceedings of the Fourth European Conference on Artificial Intelligence in Medicine Europe, IOS, Amsterdam, pp.110–124 (1993).
4. Niemer M., Nemes C., Lundsgaard-Hansen P., Blauhut B.: *Datenbuch Intensivmedizin*, Fischer, Stuttgart (1992).
5. Paky F., Köck C.M.: Pulse Oximetry in Ventilated Preterm Newborns: Reliability of Detection of Hyperoxaemia and Hypoxaemia, and Feasibility of Alarm Settings, *Acta Paediatr.* **84**, 613–616 (1995).
6. Rutledge G.W., Thomsen G.E., Farr B.R., Tovar M.A., Polaschek J.X., Beinlich I.A., Sheiner L.B., Fagan L.M.: The Design and Implementation of a Ventilator-management Advisor, *Artificial Intelligence in Medicine*, **5**, 67–82 (1993).
7. Thomsen G., Sheiner L.: SIMV: An Application of Mathematical Modeling in Ventilator Management, in Kingsland L.C.(ed.), Proceedings of the Thirteenth Annual Symposium on Computer Applications in Medical Care, IEEE Computer Society Press, Washington, D.C., pp.320–324 (1989).
8. Tovar M.A., Rutledge G.W., Lenert L.A., Fagan L.M.: The Design of a User Interface for Ventilator-Management Advisor, in Clayton P.D.(ed.), Proceedings of the Fifteenth Annual Symposium on Computer Applications in Medical Care (SCAMC-91), McGraw-Hill, New York (1992).

A Life-Cycle Based Authorisation
Expert Database System

Ying-Lie O*

University Medical Centre, Utrecht, The Netherlands
Y.O@dit.azu.nl

Abstract. Authorisation is a compulsory function in information systems that contain patient data. The proposed authorisation model is a refinement of a role-based content-dependent authorisation model. The access permissions are inferred from authorisation rules based on the role of the health care consultant, the association of the consultant with the patient, the security level and the state of the information object within the life-cycle. The design of the system is based on a three-level access control, and a combination of the existing information system with an expert database system.

1 Introduction

Authorisation is a compulsory function in information systems that contain patient data. Patient data contain sensitive information and can for instance be classified into 3 levels [3]: extremely sensitive, sensitive, and least sensitive. The requirements of the authorisation can be summarized as follows [7]:

- Primary access to a functionality is determined by the user's position (for instance physician, nurse, secretary).
- Access to a functionality and associated information is within the scope of the involved unit. A unit is an organisational part that provides specific health care or supporting processes, such as out-patient department, nursing ward, medical secretary, and also external contacts such as the GP.
- Access to information is determined by the association of the health care consultant to the patient during a care episode. For instance, the treating physician has access to all information, while the laboratory may only see the information related to the request.
- The access mode on information is determined by the state of that particular information. For instance, authorized reports may not be altered.

The realisation of the above requirements as an integrated functionality requires careful consideration of the design. The design presented in this paper is partly based on the authorisation model specified in [8].

---

* The author is indebted to P. Verpalen, coauthor of a previous paper, and to B.E. Voeten and H.M. Blanken, University of Twente, Enschede, The Netherlands, for their valuable contribution.

W. Horn et al. (Eds.): AIMDM'99, LNAI 1620, pp. 153–157, 1999.

2   The Authorisation Model

The permissions of users to access information in the information system are defined in an *authorisation model*. *Discretionary access control* (DAC) is based on authorisation for a transaction on an object. In *protection mode* each access must be authorised. *Role-based* authorisation models organise users with similar tasks into roles, and the authorisation is assigned to roles. In *content-dependent* authorisation the conditions for authorisation depend on stored information. A *role-based content-dependent* authorisation model has originally been proposed for object-oriented databases [1]. Similar approaches for health care information systems have also been proposed [6,4]. The requirements pose the following concepts on the authorisation model:

- The access control is discretionary with a role-based content-dependent model, the roles are explicitly defined.
- The content-dependent part of the authorisation depends on the temporal association of the user to the object, within the scope of the unit.
- The information is classified into three security levels: extremely sensitive, sensitive, and least sensitive. Extremely sensitive information is set in protection mode.
- The access mode is determined by the state of the object within its life-cycle. A higher level of access mode implicitly implies lower levels.

The employed *role-based content-dependent authorisation* model is structured according to the phrases

1. "Users have roles" as *organisational authorisation*: role assignment.
2. "A role may perform a number of transactions on certain object types" as *technical authorisation*: role-based authorisation.
3. "A role may perform a number of transactions on certain objects under certain conditions" as *technical authorisation*: base authorisation and content-dependent authorisation.

The logical design is based on the relational database, using predicate logic to represent the rules [2]. A *rule* has the form **if** *body* **then** *head* or *head* ← *body*. If the rule head is absent, then the formula is a *fact*. Attributes with known value (bound variable) in a rule are indicated.

2.1   Organisational Authorisation

Organisational authorisation handles the phrase "users have roles", and is based on administrative information. *User identification* is the registration of a person as a user of the system. The identification is unique, and generally accompanied by identification control for login such as a password.

The *position* (*User_position*) is determined by the organisational position and unit as registered in the personnel system. Permissions are according to health care certificates and specific tasks with respect to patients. A user may have several positions and work for a number of units. The *role* (*Unit_role*) is based on the position and type of information that is generally valid in the unit. An actor is a specialisation of the role with respect to the task, such as requester and performer. There may be several roles associated with a position. The *role assignment* (*User_role* (1)) assigns roles to users, and is stored as a fact.

$$User\_role\ (user, role, unit, valid\_flag) \leftarrow$$
$$User\_position\ (user, position, unit) \land$$
$$Unit\_role\ (role, position, unit, object\_type, actor)\ . \tag{1}$$

An *administrative* part manages the validity of the role assignment (1) as indicated by a validity flag *valid_flag*. The most common assignment is *standard authorisation* which is granted for a long period of time until changes regarding the role assignment occur.

2.2 Technical Authorisation

Technical authorisation comprises the internal structure of facts, authorisation rules, and additional data for content-dependent authorisation. The *role-based authorisation* regards the phrase "a role may perform a number of transactions on certain object types".

The *transaction* (*Trans_mode*) on an object type consists of an associated set of permitted actions according to the state of the object. Most object types have a generic life-cycle {*initiated, active, inactive, filed, archived*} in which the states are directly related to permitted actions. For several object types, the *active* state is further refined, for instance satisfying the following partial orderings of implicit rules: *view* < *print* < *copy* < *update*.

The *role-based authorisation* (*Role_auth* (2)) assigns permitted transactions on object types to roles, and is stored as a fact.

$$Role\_auth\ (role, unit, object\_type, transaction, state) \leftarrow$$
$$Unit\_role\ (role, position, unit, object\_type, actor) \land$$
$$Trans\_mode\ (object\_type, transaction, state, action)\ . \tag{2}$$

The specific part concerns the phrase "a role may perform a number of transactions on certain objects under certain conditions". Object types are classified into 3 security levels (*Object_security*): extremely sensitive, sensitive, and least sensitive. The state of the object (*Object_state*) must be explicitly available. For *content-dependent authorisation* the additional information is stored as data in the object header (*Object_header*).

Two types of authorisation [1] can be distinguished: *base authorisation* and *content-dependent authorisation*. A *role* is granted to perform a *transaction* on an *object* if it has base authorisation or content-dependent authorisation.

Base authorisation (*B_auth* (3)) is an explicit content-independent authorisation that is derived from the role-based authorisation (2) and the state of the object. It is usually assigned to least sensitive information.

Content-dependent authorisation (*C_auth* (4)) is an expression with predicates that must be evaluated. It is assigned to sensitive and extremely sensitive information. *The role predicate* (*Role_p* (5)) evaluates whether there is a valid relation between the role, the unit, and the object. *The transaction predicate* (*Trans_p* (6)) evaluates whether the transaction is valid, and handles the protection mode. *Protection mode* applies to extremely sensitive object types or individual objects, indicated by (*Object_prot*).

B_auth (role, *object*, *transaction*) ←
  $Role\_auth$ (role, unit, object_type, *transaction*, *state*) ∧
  $Object\_security$ (object_type, *security_level* = least_sens) ∧
  $Object\_state$ (*object*, object_type, *state*) ,   (3)
C_auth (*Role_p*, *object*, *Trans_p*) ,   (4)
$Role\_p$ (role, *object*, transaction) = TRUE ←
  $Role\_auth$ (role, unit, object_type, transaction, *state*) ∧
  $Object\_security$ (object_type, *security_level* = sensitive ∨ extremely_sens) ∧
  $Object\_state$ (*object*, object_type, *state*) ∧
  $Object\_header$ (*object*, unit, role) ,   (5)
$Trans\_p$ (role, *object*, transaction) = TRUE ←
  $Object\_security$ (object_type, *security_level* = extremely_sens ∨ sensitive) ∧
  ∃ $Object\_prot$ (*object*, role, transaction) ,   (6)

where ∃ indicates that the evaluation is only carried out if the occurrence exists.

3   Design of the Authorisation System

The authorisation system is designed in a generic way as a supplementary *authorisation EDS* (expert database system) to the existing information system. The EDS is a knowledge base combined with a database [5]. The *authorisation EDS* consists of *facts* in the database, *rules* in the rule base, and procedures for retrieval and evaluation.

3.1   Access Control

The *access control* manages the flow control of the sequence of forms. A *three-level access control* [7] is proposed:

0th *order* login and initial access according to "users have roles". Retrieves the roles from *User_role*, limited by the current unit and acting position.

1st *order* access to functionalities presented by forms according to "a role may perform a number of transactions on certain object types" (form-level constraint). Retrieves the role-based authorisation from *Role_auth*.

2nd order access to objects within the forms is according to "a role may perform a number of transactions on certain objects under certain conditions" (data-level constraint). The evaluation provides a list of objects with permitted transactions, allowing the user to make a sensible choice.

3.2   Concluding Remarks

The combination of three-level access control and the authorisation EDS provides a strict but user friendly system. The additions to the existing information system are data for *content-dependent authorisation* concerning the properties of the objects. Another important design aspect is that the forms are composed in accordance with the role-based authorisation. Instead of programming the constraint procedures, the authorisation EDS is invoked.

The use of a role-based authorisation has administrative advantages. It ensures that users with similar positions and tasks have the same authorisation according to regulations. Also, there are less roles than individual users. Proper adoption in the organisation requires a central service that defines the roles and the authorisation, and assigns these to users. Further implementation is then carried out by system administrators. Although the EDS has not been implemented, this administrative organisation has found to be satisfactory.

The logical design of the EDS allows technical *verification and validation* of the content of the rules and facts by inference and detection of inconsistencies. The rules and associated facts can be implemented as tables in a relational database. Most of the evaluation can be carried out by SQL using the SELECT statement, thus ensuring rapid performance. The content-dependent authorisation (4) requires a simple procedure to control the evaluation of the predicates.

References

1. Bertino, E., Weigand, H.: An approach to authorization modeling in object-oriented database systems. Data & Knowledge Engineering **12**(1994) 1–29
2. Date, C.J., Darwen, H.: Relational Database Writings 1989-1991. Addison-Wesley (1992)
3. Dick, R.S., Steen, E.B., editors: The Computer-Based Patient record: An Essential Technology for Health Care. Institute of Medicine, National Academy Press (1991)
4. Khair, M., Pangalos, G., Andria, F., Bozios, L.: Implementing security on a prototype hospital database. In Pappas, C. et al., editors: Medical Informatics Europe 97, IOS Press (1997) 176–180
5. Missikoff, M., Wiederhold, G.: Towards a unified approach for expert and database systems. In Kerschberg, L. editor: Expert Database Systems, Benjamin Cummings (1986) 383–399
6. Vassilacopoulos, G., Peppes, D. A front end authorization mechanism for hospital information systems. Medical Informatics **21** (1996) 93–103
7. Verpalen, P., O, Y.-L.: Definable confidentiality of information in patient records. In Harnu, A., editor: Proceedings of the 8th European Health Record Conference, NVMA (1995) 311–318
8. Voeten, B.E.: Content-dependent authorisation for a patient hospital information system. Master's thesis, University of Twente, The Netherlands (1996)

A Decision-Support System for the Identification, Staging, and Functional Evaluation of Liver Diseases (HEPASCORE)

Mauro Torchio[1], Stefania Battista[1], Fabrizio Bar[1], Cristina Pollet[1], Marina Marzuoli[1], Maria Cesira Bucchi[1], Roberto Pagni[2], Gianpaolo Molino[1]

[1]Division of General Medicine A and Clinical Informatic Laboratory
San Giovanni Battista Hospital of Turin
C.so Bramante 88, 10126 Turin – Italy
Tel/Fax: +39 11 6336665
e-mail: medgen1.molinette@mail.cs.interbusiness.it
[2]"Baldi & Riberi" Laboratory,
San Giovanni Battista Hospital of Turin
C.so Bramante 88, 10126 Turin – Italy
Tel: +39 11 6336380

Abstract. HEPASCORE has been developed to optimize the application of objective criteria for qualitative and quantitative assessment of liver function. Early recognition of abnormal liver states is performed according to a sequential approach, based at first on clinical rules using data from history and physical examination, then confirming or denying the hypothesis by means of selected laboratory tests. Once an abnormal condition is defined, clinical severity can be evaluated using suitable scores. In addition, selected sets of biochemical tests can be used to score one or more functional aspects. HEPASCORE has been successfully applied to exclude liver abnormalities in subjects at risk, to follow-up liver patients, to predict the natural outcomes of severe liver diseases, to foresee the adverse effects of drugs undergoing first-pass liver extraction and the side effects of invasive procedures.

1 Introduction

An accurate evaluation of clinical data in their pathophysiological meaning is a key step in the follow-up of liver diseases, aimed at characterizing liver damage both qualitatively (different kinds of functional impairment) and quantitatively (clinical severity) [1]. *Functional evaluation* is a multistep process depending on the natural history and the treatment of disease. The study of *clinical severity* is based on the computation of indexes derived from the combination of clinical and/or biochemical selected data. This analysis, mainly used for disease staging and prognostic evaluations, frequently relies on complex calculations requiring the use of a computer. The classical approach to *screening* programs, based on the determination of biochemical parameters without a preliminary clinical examination, is questionable in terms of methods and costs. Therefore, an approach adapting the biochemical and instrumental evaluation to real clinical problems (identified by history and physical examination) is advisable. Finally, an important aspect is *residual liver function* quantification, a feature independent from both the aetiology and type of liver damage

W. Horn et al. (Eds.): AIMDM'99, LNAI 1620, pp. 158-162, 1999.

and relying on the evaluation of specific pathophysiological aspects. In this case, dynamic tests are able to measure particular functional relations of the liver with the whole organism [2].

The system presented in this paper, HEPASCORE, was constructed with the aim of supporting the physician in the *screening* process of liver damage, in the assessment of the *clinical severity* of liver diseases, and in the evaluation of *liver function* and calculation of the *residual functional capacity* of the liver.

2 Materials and Methods

2.1 Selection of Parameters

The decisional model applied for *screening* patients at risk of liver disease is directed to exclude every type of abnormality [3], whereas the procedure applied for the identification and *functional evaluation* of liver alterations consists in the recognition of the abnormalities and in the quantification of damage for each functional aspect. Obviously, in both cases utilised tests should be as much precise and accurate as possible. Nevertheless, in the former case the selected parameters must be mainly sensitive to minimize false negative results, whereas false positive results are of minor importance. In the latter case clinical data must be mainly specific to reduce false positive results (leading to an overestimation of the damage). Moreover, since *screening* procedures are applied to subjects with low expected prevalence of disease whereas functional evaluation is applied to subjects with confirmed disease, the fitness of the tests has not to be evaluated with respect to specificity and sensitivity only, but also must be taken into account their negative and positive predictive values. Such values vary according to the prevalence of a disease in an inverse and direct proportional way, respectively.

Then, the parameters were chosen on the basis not only of their methodological validity (accuracy, precision, specificity, positive and negative predictive values, etc.), but also of the meaning and limitations of their possible association (complementary, redundancy, etc.). The calculation of clinical scores was entirely based on well-established and universally accepted data from the literature. The *screening* section derives from previous works of our group in collaboration with several Hospitals in Turin and with the Technology Institute and the Science Faculty of the University of Turin [4]. In these studies, clinical parameters and diagnostic tests were selected following both experts' opinion and accurate researches utilizing several calculation methods (probabilistic, statistic and fuzzy logic). The selection of biochemical parameters used for the *functional evaluation* and for indexing cholestasis, cytolysis, biosynthesis and immunoreactivity was based on the same studies. The evaluation of fibrosis and induction was based on the literature and on the opinion of some experts. The section regarding *dynamic tests* derives from our direct experience in this particular field of research. Tests included in the program (D-sorbitol clearance and Galactose Elimination Capacity, GEC), were chosen according to their pathophysiological meaning and to the accuracy and clinical value of the results.

2.2 Functions of the System

1. Evaluation of *clinical severity*. With HEPASCORE the physician can automatically calculate some quantitative indexes of clinical severity [5]: the Child-Pugh Score, used for chronic liver diseases; the Mayo Score, a well-established prognostic index for patients affected by primary biliary cirrhosis; the hepatic encephalopathy severity index and the porto-systemic shunt score [6]. A brief explanation about utilized parameters, calculation formalisms and clinical meaning of each index is available, if requested.

2. *Screening* procedure. A sequential approach is used for this purpose, beginning from the history and clinical examination and proceeding to the evaluation of biochemical parameters, as explained by the algorithm reported in Figure 1. Clinical data are used following criteria derived from previous studies in which available data were classified and „weighed" according to their informative content, then selected on the basis of their diagnostic value and finally grouped in rules eventually activating the hypothesis of „absent", „possible" or „likely" liver alteration. This approach was validated according to a clinical point of view. When the disease is „possible", the program applies rules allowing the confirmation or exclusion of the disease. These rules are based on a few biochemical parameters (alanine-aminotransferase, gamma-glutamyltranspeptidase, and albumin) whose normal limit is assumed to be the threshold value. When the disease is „likely" the hypothesis is confirmed by using a wider number of biochemical analyses grouped according to their functional meaning and with less restrictive threshold value. In these steps HEPASCORE acts as a true decision support system able to simplify and standardize the diagnostic process.

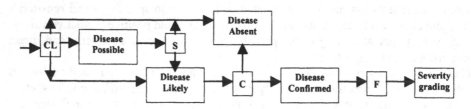

Fig. 1. Diagnostic algorithm of HEPASCORE. CL: clinical rules; S: exclusion rules; C: confirming rules; F: functional evaluation

3. *Functional* Evaluation. This section allows the characterization of hepatic damage through separately considering one or more different functional aspects: cholestasis, cytolysis, biosynthesis, immune reaction, induction and fibrogenesis. The severity degree (*absent, border-line, mild, medium, severe*) of each considered aspect is identified by analysing two or more biochemical parameters: in the case of *undefined alteration* the system utilizes an additional finding in order to obtain the final result.

4. *Residual Liver Function* Evaluation. This task is performed by using the GEC (an index of functioning liver mass [2]) and the hepatic D-sorbitol clearance, which evaluates the functional liver plasma flow [7]. The program immediately calculates and displays the final results indicating also the test accuracy.

2.3 General Features of the System

HEPASCORE has been implemented on Microsoft Access 7.0 for Windows '95. For installation and correct running of the program at least 16 MB RAM are necessary. The user can choose among several utilities: 1) rapid interaction with the system with easy creation of a database which contains anagraphical and clinical data of the patients and the results of the applied procedures. 2) selection of one or more tests and introduction of the requested data. 3) start of the computation procedures. 4) display and print of the results and explanation about the applied rules and the conclusions.

3 Preliminary Evaluation of the System

A preliminary retrospective analysis to assess the agreement of the system conclusions with the observed clinical situations has been performed on 127 consecutive patients, between December 1997 and May 1998, in collaboration with the Department of Gastroenterology of our Hospital. Studied patients were grouped in 4 diagnostic classes: 1) chronic hepatitis (CH); 2) post-viral and/or alcoholic liver cirrhosis (LC); 3) primary biliary cirrhosis (PBC); 4) liver metastases (LM). In patients with biopsy-proven CH the most striking alteration was cytolysis, whereas in patients with LC fibrogenesis index was the major alteration, followed by cholestasis and cytolysis. Cholestasis and immune reaction were the more relevant alterations in PBC patients, whereas in patients with LM they were fibrogenesis and cholestasis indexes (Tab. 1). Such conclusions are in accordance with available knowledge on each considered disease.

Table 1. Functional evaluation: preliminary results of HEPASCORE on a retrospective cohort of 127 patients affected by different liver diseases.

Mean Value of Functional Indexes

Diagnostic Classes	Number of cases	Impaired biosynthesis	Cytolysis	Cholestasis	Immune Reaction	Fibrogenesis
CH	31	0	1.29±0.77	0.29±0.42	0.34±0.44	0.20±0.61
LC	26	1.35±1.23	1.40±0.82	1.42±1.09	0.85±0.38	2.24±0.89
PBC	31	0.37±0.84	1.45±0.71	2.02±0.96	1.90±0.83	n.e.
LM	39	0.13±0.52	0.47±0.74	0.65±0.89	n.e.	1.51±0.94

The table was realized computing the mean value (±SD) of each index for all diagnostic classes after converting textual values in numeric values (absence of alterations = 0; border-line alteration = 0.5; mild alteration = 1; medium alteration = 2; severe alteration = 3); n.e.: not evaluated.

A prospective evaluation is in progress with the aim of testing the reliability of HEPASCORE in the screening of subjects at occupational risk of liver diseases, in the prognostic evaluation and qualitative and quantitative measure of liver damage in chronic liver patients.

4 Discussion

In a previous work from our group the diagnostic efficacy of the sequential approach has been applied to a sample of 288 patients, by comparing it with different diagnostic protocols for liver disease identification; at that time the sequential process based on clinical rules followed by two sets of laboratory investigations yielded the best diagnostic efficacy (4.1% false negative and 18.5% false positive). This model, integrated with new concepts, has been used for building HEPASCORE, thinking that a choice of the procedures and functional aspects to investigate is always preferable to diagnostic routine (problem-oriented approach). HEPASCORE is based on this methodological model, which allows to express the observed alteration according to the kind and severity of liver injury. It is worth noting the possibilty of excluding or recognizing early liver function alterations in subjects at risk utilizing an effective and cheap protocol.

The system represents an useful reference model to adopt standardized criteria in the identification and functional evaluation of liver diseases. Among the several possible applications of the system there are: 1) ruling-out early liver dysfunction in subjects exposed at specific risk; 2) study of new drug hepatotoxicity; 3) investigation of possible effects on liver function by different pharmacological treatment; 4) follow-up of chronic liver diseases and monitoring patients submitted to liver transplantation; 5) evaluation of possible liver function alterations following invasive procedures such as porto-systemic shunt placement and hepatic resection.

References

1. Belforte, G., Bona, B., Cravetto, C., et al.: Selection and assessment of laboratory tests for the evaluation of liver functional impairment. Methods Inf. Med. **24** (1985) 39-45.
2. Tygstrup, N.: Determination of the hepatic elimination capacity of galactose by single injection. Scand. J. Clin. Lab. Invest. **18** Suppl 92 (1966) 118-125.
3. Molino, G., Cramp, D.G.: The diagnosis and management of liver diseases: a systems approach. In: Cramp, D.G., Carson, E.R. (eds.): Measurements in medicine: liver function. Chapman and Hall, London (1989) 224-257.
4. Lesmo, L., Marzuoli, M., Molino, G., Torasso, P.: An expert system for the evaluation of liver functional assessment. J. Med. Syst. **8** (1984) 73-85.
5. Christensen E.: Prognostic models in chronic liver diseases: validity, usefulness and future role. J. Hepatol. **26**(6) (1997) 1414-1424.
6. Molino, G., Battista, S., Bar, F. et al.: Determination of functional portal-sytemic shunting in patients submitted to hepatic angiography. Liver **16** (1996) 347-352.
7. Molino, G., Avagnina, P., Belforte, G., Bircher, J.: Assessment of the hepatic circulation in humans: New concepts based on evidence derived from a D-sorbitol clearance method. J. Lab. Clin. Med. **131** (1998) 393-405.

Model-Based Systems

A Model-Based Approach for Learning to Identify Cardiac Arrhythmias

G. Carrault[1], M.-O. Cordier[3], René Quiniou[2], M. Garreau[1], J.J. Bellanger[1], and A. Bardou[1]

[1] LTSI, Campus de Beaulieu, 35042 Rennes Cedex FRANCE
[2] IRISA, Campus de Beaulieu, 35042 Rennes Cedex FRANCE
[3] IRISA/Université de Rennes 1, Campus de Beaulieu, 35042 Rennes Cedex
currently at INRA, Unité Rennes-Quimper, 35042 Rennes Cedex FRANCE

Abstract. ECG interpretation is used to monitor the behavior of the electrical conduction system of the heart in order to diagnose rhythm and conduction disorders. In this paper, we propose a model-based framework relying on a model of the cardiac electrical activity. Due to efficiency constraints, the on-line analysis of the ECG signals is performed by a chronicle recognition system which identifies pathological situations by matching a symbolic description of the signals with temporal patterns stored in a chronicle base. The model can simulate arrhythmias and the related sequences of time-stamped events are collected and then used by an inductive learning program to constitute a satisfying chronicle base. This work is in progress but first results show that the system is able to produce satisfying discriminating chronicles.

1 Introduction

Researchers have been paying attention to arrhythmia identification for a long time. Two main steps are clearly established i) the signal processing step which produces pertinent information such as P and QRS wave features, ii) the diagnosis step which attempts to explain the abnormal features discovered during the first step. Classically, deterministic tests, Bayesian networks or decision trees have been used for the last issue [Bla86]. More recently, artificial intelligence techniques have been proposed, such as knowledge-based approaches using expert rules [Shi85, Lon96], sometimes combined with fuzzy logic as in [KNB98]. In order to overcome the problem of expertise acquisition, model-based approaches, relying on a heart model instead of expertise knowledge, were experimented ([BML89, TW93, Gue96]). A typical study in this direction is described in [SCLB95] where a cardiac model such as those developed in theoretical cardiology [BABC96] is used for detection as well as diagnostic tasks.

Our work is part of this model-based framework. It relies on a model of cardiac electrical activity. The model can simulate a large number of arrhythmias and outputs the associated signal and its description as a sequence of time-stamped events. Arrhythmia features, learnt from these simulations, are used to analyze on-line ECG signals, and to classify them. A major strength of this

W. Horn et al. (Eds.): AIMDM'99, LNAI 1620, pp. 165–174, 1999.

project is to bring together specialists in the three following fields: signal processing, artificial intelligence (diagnosis, and machine learning) and theoretical cardiology. This is highly desirable when the objective is to build an operational system. Another originality is the fact that the heart model used is not an ad hoc one, developed only for the sake of our project. On the contrary, it was intended to be used as a cardiac simulator in pharmacology and teaching experiments [SCLB95]. Furthermore, the time occurrences of events for atria and ventricular activities in normal and disorder cases, have been validated by clinicians.

An overview of the architecture of CALICOT (Cardiac Arrhythmias Learning for Intelligent Classification of On-line Tracks) is presented in section 2 as well as the cardiac model on which the approach is based. The on-line analysis of the ECG signals is sketched in section 3. It relies on a chronicle base which is acquired off-line by using inductive learning programming techniques as explained in section 4. This work is in progress but the first results, mainly related to chronicle learning, are promising. They are analyzed in section 4.2. The last section is devoted to a comparison of our work with related approaches.

2   A Model-Based Approach

2.1   CALICOT Architecture

The architecture of CALICOT, given in figure 1, separates on-line and off-line treatments. The on-line part includes the signal processing module (1) which outputs the symbolic representation of the analyzed signal in terms of time-stamped events, and the chronicle recognition module (2) which analyses the stream of events and identifies arrhythmia disorders by detecting characteristic patterns.

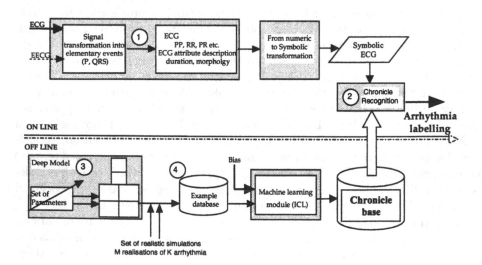

Fig. 1. Architecture of the proposed approach

The off-line part aims at building a set of relevant chronicles (the chronicle base) from cardiac model simulations. The cardiac model (3) is used to generate sequences of events corresponding to normal as well as pathological signals. The learning module (4) relies on inductive logic programming (ILP) to extract the most discriminating patterns which identify the normal and pathological ECGs.

2.2   The Electrical Heart Model

The heart model Cardiolab [SCLB95] is central to our approach. It was originally designed to be a cardiac simulator and explicitly integrates anatomophysiological and electrophysiological knowledge. The model combines a qualitative and quantitative modeling of the electrical heart function and is based on the propagation of action potentials in myocardium. This approach is in fact close to the semi-quantitative approach proposed by [BK92] where numerical information is used in addition to qualitative constraints.

The heart behavior is described according to two abstraction levels. The first level provides a structural model based on macro-cells and the elementary interactions between them as receiving and transmitting delayed impulses to their neighboring cells. These cells (21 in total) correspond to the nodal and the myocardium tissue elements. A cell is mainly characterized by its states phase duration during the cardiac cycle namely resting state (muscle tissue only), depolarization, absolute refractory, relative refractory, slow diastolic depolarization (nodal tissue only). The second level is concerned with all the electrophysiological concepts such as conduction fronts, reentry, blocks. This level combines the elementary events produced at the first level and constructs more complex events. The resulting model is able to simulate a large variety of rhythms by tuning the parameters of the myocardium cells (mainly phase durations). The generic character of the simulation makes the model well adapted for intelligent monitoring.

3   On-Line Arrhythmia Identification

As explained before, the ECG signals are analyzed on-line to identify arrhythmia phenomena. This is achieved by two main modules, the signal processing module and the recognition module.

3.1   The Signal Processing Module

This module processes the signal and outputs its symbolic representation in terms of time-stamped events: i) it detects and identifies markers of the cardiac revolution (P wave, QRS complex) ii) it determines their descriptive attributes (duration, morphology amplitude...) iii) determines temporal relations between these events.

Figure 2 illustrates the functionalities of the module with the analysis of an ECG signal corresponding to a *ventricular couplet*. P_i and R_i are the detected time occurrences of the P and QRS waves. It can be noticed that the ventricular

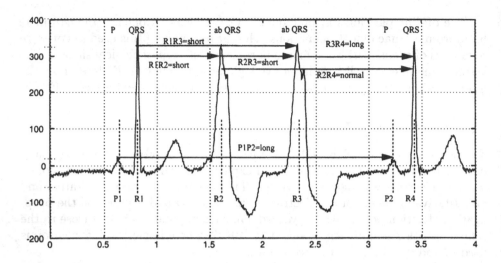

Fig. 2. A signal and its characterization as produced by the signal processing module (the actual coded description is similar to the example described in table 1)

activities $R2$ and $R3$ were not preceded by corresponding P waves. The qualitative values qualifying the wave duration (normal, short or long) and morphology (normal, *ab*normal) are computed by comparing their observed time occurrence to reference values found in [BH80]. In the example, $R2$ and $R3$ are premature (intervals $R1R2$ and $R2R3$ are short) and abnormal (*ab* feature of QRSs) while $P2$ occurs lately (interval $P1P2$ is long).

3.2 Chronicle Recognition

The sequence of symbolic events produced by the signal processing module is then analyzed to identify potential arrhythmia troubles. The chronicle recognition approach was specifically designed to analyze a flow of time-stamped events under real-time constraints [Gha96, RDF97]. A chronicle is a set of events constrained by quantitative or qualitative temporal relations (e.g. *before*, *after*, *500 ms before*). It describes a temporal pattern which characterizes the phenomenon to be identified.

The following chronicle, expressed in Prolog, describes the *bundle branch block* disorder. p_wave and qrs_complex denote events occurring in the ECG. Their arguments stand respectively for the time occurrence and the qualification of the wave shape. The brace brackets specify the temporal constraints on the time occurrence of events. Here, the temporal constraints are qualitative and pp, pr and rr denote the intervals between two successive P waves, a P wave and the next QRS complex and two successive QRS complexes, respectively.

```
bundle_branch_block :-
    p_wave(T1, normal), qrs_complex(T2,abnormal),
    p_wave(T3, normal), qrs_complex(T4, abnormal),
    {pp(T1, T3, normal), pr(T1, T2, normal),
     rr(T2, T4, normal)}
```

This chronicle states that the four specified events must occur and satisfy the following constraints: a first *p_wave* at time T1 followed by a *qrs_complex* at time T2 and again a *p_wave* at time T3 followed by a *qrs_complex* at time T4; the shapes of *p_waves* are normal but those related to *qrs_complexes* are abnormal ; the duration of the *pp*, *pr* and *rr* intervals must be normal (close to the nominal rate). In the bundle branch block case, inter-wave durations are normal but the two *QRS* shapes are abnormal.

Chronicle recognition consists in skimming the flow of events coming from an observed process and detecting the specific events that belong to a chronicle. Once a chronicle has been evoked, the recognizer checks the presence of the remaining events and their temporal constraints. This process is very similar to pattern-matching associated with temporal constraint satisfaction.

4   Off-Line Chronicle Base Acquisition

On-line chronicle recognition is very efficient but chronicle acquisition from experts is often difficult and raises completeness and soundness problems. Deep models are usually simpler to build because they rely on the theoretical or practical knowledge relating to the process itself. Our approach consists in using such a model as a simulator and to generate the observed events resulting from determined situations (usual failures or pathologies). In our application, the cardiac model is used to generate sets of examples, one set per arrhythmia under interest. As these examples cannot be directly used as a rule base (they are in general too numerous and complex), they are processed by an inductive learning tool in order to produce a set of characteristic patterns, which identify the classes (here a set of discriminating chronicles[1]); these patterns are then used for on-line recognition of phenomena from the flow of observations.

4.1   Learning Chronicles

ICL [LRD97] is a classification system that learns clausal theories (first-order representations) which discriminate, as well as possible, between several classes of examples. Positive examples have to be models of the target theory and negative examples must not be models of this same target theory. ICL also makes use of a background theory which contains what is already known and useless to learn. Such a theory improves the efficiency of machine learning.

---

[1] A chronicle is discriminating if it expresses a sufficient condition for the recognition of the related phenomenon with respect to the other chronicles.

In our case, a class corresponds to a normal rhythm or to some disorder. Positive examples are instances of the particular class to be characterized and negative examples are all the other instances.

Multi-class learning in ICL is formally defined as follows:

- Given
    - B a background theory (containing only definite clauses) ;
    - E the whole set of examples ;
    - $C_P \subset E$ the set of positive examples related to class C ;
    - $C_N = E - C_P$ is the set of negative examples ;
    - L_H a language which defines the syntax of acceptable clauses for characterizing the classes
- For each class C, find a clausal theory $H_C \subseteq L_H$ such that
    - $\forall p \in C_P, M(B \cup p)$ is a true interpretation of H_C (completeness) ;
    - $\forall n \in C_N, M(B \cup n)$ is a false interpretation of H_C (consistency).

4.2   Coding Sequence of Events

Cardiac data coming from an ECG have interesting features that must be taken into account for representation. Firstly, cardiac data are highly structured: the normal cardiac activity may be seen as a sequence of beats, each of which is composed of a series of events corresponding to the electrical activation of different areas of the heart. Furthermore, these events are temporally constrained. Secondly, the number of beats necessary to represent and then to detect an arrhythmia is variable: some can be detected on one cycle, from one beat to the next, while some need several beats.

The ECG is coded as a sequence of P waves and QRS complexes. The duration of an ECG used as an example is about 5 seconds corresponding to 5

wave name	P or QRS	time in ms	dur.	1st P 1st R	PP1 RR1	2nd P 2nd R	PP2 RR2	1st R 1st P	PR1	2nd R	PR2
p1	p_wave	17	n	p2	n	p3	n	r1	n	r2	n
r1	qrs_complex	137	n	r2	n	r3	n	p2			
p2	p_wave	807	n	p3	n	p4	n	r2	1	r3	1
r2	qrs_complex	982	n	r3	1	r4	1	p3			
p3	p_wave	1591	n	p4	n	p5	n	r3	1	r4	1
r3	qrs_complex	1983	n	r4	1	r5	1	p4			
p4	p_wave	2374	n	p5	n	p6	n	r4	1	r5	1
p5	p_wave	3157	n	p6	n	p7	n	r4	n	r5	1
r4	qrs_complex	3277	n	r5	1	r6	1	p6			
p6	p_wave	3940	n	p7	n	p8	n	r5	1	r6	1
r5	qrs_complex	4237	n	r6	1	r7	1	p7			
p7	p_wave	4723	n	p8	n	p9	n	r6	1	r7	1

Table 1. A Wenckebach ECG coded as a positive input example for ICL

to 8 beats. Table 1 gives an example of coded ECG. The description attributes associated to waves are the following:

P wave
- duration qualified as short(s), normal(n) or long(l),
- pointer to the next P wave and length of the temporal interval between the current one and the next one (qualified as short, normal or long),
- pointer to the second next P wave and length of the related temporal interval,
- pointer to the next QRS wave and length of the temporal interval between the current P one and this next QRS one,
- pointer to the second next QRS wave and length of the related temporal interval.

QRS complex
- duration qualified as short(s), normal(n) or long(l),
- pointer to the next QRS wave and length of the related temporal interval between the current one and this next one,
- pointer to the second next QRS wave and length of the related temporal interval,
- pointer to the next P wave.

4.3 First Results

As a first experiment, the approach has been used to learn 5 rhythm and conduction disorders: normal, Wenckebach 4:3 (wenckebach in the sequel), Wolff-Parkinson-White (kent), left bundle branch block (lbbb) and trigeminy. Due to space limitations, the language bias and the background theory used to process these examples is not given.

In order to demonstrate the feasability of the approach, an initial learning set containing 25 examples (5 examples per class, each modeling 5 seconds ECGs), has been provided to ICL. Below are the rules that were learnt from the set of simulated sequences. They are given under a disjunctive normal form. ICL proposed one rule per class except for the wenckebach class which is characterized by the disjunction of three rules. These rules are quite satisfying with respect to the restricted set of arrhythmias and the low size of the learning set.

```
normal: p_wave(P,normal), pr1(P,R2,normal), pr2(P,R3,normal),
   qrs(R,normal), rr2(R,R2,normal),
   p_wave(P1,normal), pr2(P1,R2,normal).
lbbb: p_wave(P,normal), pr1(P,R,normal), qrs(R,long).
kent: p_wave(P,normal), pr1(P,R,short).
trigeminy: p_wave(P,normal), pr2(P,R1,short).
wenckebach: p_wave(P,normal), pr2(P,R2,long), qrs(R2,normal).
wenckebach: p_wave(P,normal), pp2(P,P2,short).
wenckebach: p_wave(P,normal), pp1(P,P1,normal),
   succ_P(P1,P2,correct), pr1(P,R2,normal), pr2(P,R3,normal),
   qrs(R,normal), rr2(R,R2,normal).
```

5 Related Work

Much work has been done in the field of qualitative cardiac modeling for ECG recognition. The earliest ones used a knowledge base as a model. More recently hybrid models using quantitative and qualitative temporal constraint propagation were proposed. Our own model, Cardiolab, belongs to this class. We did not retain approaches based on cellular model [BABC96] because we are interested in more abstract events such as the time sequence of the atria and ventricular activities.

[Shi85] presents a knowledge-based approach for the interpretation of arrhythmias. One of the interesting points is the use of causal knowledge about the cardiac conduction system. It can take missing information (missing waves for example) into account. A prototype system named CAA (for Causal Arrhythmia Analysis) using a representation language based on semantic networks, the PSN language, has been implemented.

Kardio ([BML89]) shares several features with our own approach. The goal of Kardio is to recognize cardiac arrhythmias from a coded ECG. The system relies on a purely qualitative electrical model of the heart which cannot actually be considered as a cardiac simulator. Our system, Cardiolab, has a model of electrical heart conduction which combines quantitative and qualitative simulation and is closer to cardiac reality than Kardio, actually it can generate pretty realistic cardiac sequence events. The qualitative model of Kardio has been simulated in order to generate surface (diagnostic and predictive) rules which were then processed by an inductive engine in order to produce compact rule databases (a diagnostic one and a predictive one). The main difference between Kardio and our own approach is that Kardio uses feature-based induction whereas we use ILP. Thus, Kardio can only learn predefined propositional structural relations. By using ILP, we can learn first-order relations which may not be given before induction [SMKS96]. The learnt rules are much simpler and better suited to the chronicle recognition approach. Also, as far as we can see, Kardio uses a hand-coded ECG. Our goal is to devise an integrated system in which the signal processing module that labels the ECG can interact with the chronicle recognizer in order to better detect arrhythmias.

Einthoven [TW93] was designed for ECG interpretation. It uses an extensive quantitative as well as qualitative knowledge base. Einthoven suffers from the classical drawbacks of a knowledge-based approach: the knowledge-base must be extensive in order to provide good diagnoses but it is very difficult to acquire and maintain - we used machine learning for chronicle generation to avoid this drawback; rule-based reasoning is not very efficient and hardly usable for on-line monitoring if not associated with methods such as chronicle recognition.

Ticker [HK95] aims at teaching non-specialists to interpret ECG. The cardiac qualitative model is a directed graph in which the nodes represent states (electrical state of a region) and the arcs possible transitions with associated qualitative temporal contraints (flow of electrical conduction between regions). Different abstraction levels can be defined in order to tailor the explanation to the user's knowledge. As mentioned by the authors, the Ticker model is closer to reality than Kardio's but is too abstracted to produce correct traces.

The heart model of Guertin's Holmes system [Gue96] uses quantitative temporal constraints on intra-beat events as well as inter-beat events and thus can be considered as an extension of Ticker. Temporal abduction is used for diagnosis and the combinatoric explosion of possible explanations is controlled by temporal constraint propagation. The system is not integrated into a monitoring system and processes hand-coded ECG. Though constraint propagation improves the efficiency of abductive inference, we think that such an approach cannot be used on-line. Chronicle recognition is much more efficient from this point of view.

6 Discussion and Conclusion

We have presented an integrated approach for automatic ECG interpretation. Our proposition relies on two points: 1) an on line chronicle recognizer detects arrhythmias on the symbolic labeling of the surface ECG produced by the signal processing module; 2) the specification of the searched arrhythmias as chronicles are learnt from classified example ECGs representing typical arrhythmias obtained from simulation traces of a heart model. For efficiency reasons, this model is not used directly for (abductive) diagnosis as in model-based approaches.

The benefits of learning chronicles over expert associative rules are: an easier acquisition and the fact that discriminating chronicles are learnt, thus insuring an efficient recognition. Other benefits include easy knowledge maintenance which could occur, for example, when more precise diagnoses are expected and some classes of arrhythmias must be split into several. As ICL is based on a formal learning model showing soundness and completeness properties, it guarantees that if the learning set is good (relevant and representative) the set of learnt chronicles will be good (discriminating and not overgeneralised). In our approach, the fact that the model has been validated insures that examples will be correctly classified. But, this says nothing about the completeness or representativity of the learning set. We are now working on model parameter tuning in order to build realistic learning bases.

The work is still in progress. The first results are very promising. As assessed by experts, the features retained in the learnt chronicles are relevant and adjusted to the level of detail that is intended: if few classes are to be discriminated, the learnt chronicles are very simple; if more classes are desired, a new learning step can add discriminating details into the chronicles. We plan the addition of the following disorders encountered in coronary care unit: ventricular asystole, atrioventricular dissociation, complete heart block or accelerated idioventricular rhythm. Another perspective is to confront the learnt chronicles to a real ECG database such as the MIT-BIH.

Up to now our work was focused on the signal processing module and the learning module independently. A further step will be devoted to linking the signal processing module and the chronicle recognizer. It must be emphasized that current available monitoring devices are far from ideal. False alarms and breakdowns are inevitable. The idea is to use the predictions made by the chronicle recognizer to reinforce hypotheses on which the signal processing module works, in order to increase the accuracy of the labeling process.

References

[BABC96] A. Bardou, P. Auger, P. Birkui, and J.L. Chasse. Modeling of cardiac electrophysiological mechanisms : From action potential genesis to its propagation in myocardium. *Critical Reviews in Biomedical Engineering*, 24:141–221, 1996.

[BH80]   M. Blondeau and M. Hiltgen. *lectrocardiographie Clinique*. Ed. Masson, 1980.

[BK92]   D. Berleant and B. J. Kuipers. Combined qualitative and numerical simulation with Q3. In B. Faltings and P. Struss, editors, *Recent advances in qualitative physics*, pages 3–16. MIT Press, 1992.

[Bla86]   R. Le Blanc. Quantitative analysis of cardiac arrhythmias. *CRC: Critical Review in Biomedical Engineering*, 14(1):1–43, 1986.

[BML89]   I. Bratko, I. Mozetic, and N. Lavrac. *Kardio: A Study in Deep and Qualitative Knowledge for Expert Systems*. MIT Press, 1989.

[Gha96]   M. Ghallab. On chronicles: representation, on-line recognition and learning. In *Fifth international conference on knowledge representation and reasoning (KR'96)*, pages 597–606, Cambridge (USA), 1996.

[Gue96]   M. Guertin. Abductive inference of events: Diagnosing cardiac arrhythmias. In *Proceedings of the Florida Artificial Intelligence Research Symposium*, May 1996.

[HK95]   J. Hunter and I. Kirby. Ticker: A qualitative model of the electrical system of the heart. In *Research and Development in Expert System XII (Proc. of Expert Systems'95)*, pages 293–307. Information Press, 1995.

[KNB98]   M. Kundu, M. Nasipuri, and D.K. Basu. A knowledge based approach to ECG interpretation using fuzzy logic. *IEEE Trans. Sytems Man and Cybernetics*, 28(2):237–243, 1998.

[Lon96]   W. J. Long. Temporal reasoning for diagnosis in a causal probabilistic knowledge base. *Artificial Intelligence in Medicine*, 8:193–215, 1996.

[LRD97]   W. Van Laer, L. De Raedt, and S. Dzeroski. On multi-class problems and discretization in inductive logic programming. In Zbigniew W. Ras and Andrzej Skowron, editors, *Proceedings of the 10th International Symposium on Methodologies for Intelligent Systems (ISMIS97)*, volume 1325 of *Lecture Notes in Artificial Intelligence*, pages 277–286. Springer-Verlag, 1997.

[RDF97]   N. Ramaux, M. Dojat, and D. Fontaine. Temporal scenario recognition for intelligent patient monitoring. In *Proc. of the 6th Conference on Artificial Intelligence in Medecine Europe (AIME'97)*, 1997.

[SCLB95] P. Siregar, M. Chahine, F. Lemoulec, and P. Le Beux. An interactive qualitative model in cardiology. *Computers and Biomedical Research*, 28(6), 1995.

[Shi85]   T. Shibahara. On using causal knowledge to recognise vital signals : Knowledge-based interpretation of arrhythmia. In *Proc. of IJCAI'85*, pages 307–314, 1985.

[SMKS96] A. Srinivasan, S. Muggleton, R. King, and M. Sternberg. Theories for mutagenicity: a study of first-order and feature based induction. *Artificial Intelligence Journal*, 85(1,2):277–299, 1996.

[TW93]   D. A. Tong and L. E. Widman. Model-based interpretation of the ECG: A methodology for temporal and spatial reasoning. *Computers and Biomedical research*, 26(3):206–219, 1993.

A Model-Based System for Pacemaker Reprogramming

Peter Lucas[1], Astrid Tholen[2], and Geeske van Oort[2]

[1] Department of Computer Science, Utrecht University
P.O. Box 80089, 3508 TB Utrecht, The Netherlands
lucas@cs.uu.nl
[2] Research and Development Department, Vitatron Medical B.V.
P.O. Box 76, 6950 AB Dieren, The Netherlands
{Astrid.Tholen,Geeske.van.Oort}@vitatron.com

Abstract. The process of reprogramming a cardiac pacemaker can be described in terms similar to those used for describing diagnostic problem solving. In this paper, the process of reprogramming a pacemaker is formalised as a special form of abductive diagnostic reasoning, where observable findings are interpreted with respect to results obtained from diagnostic tests. The dynamics of this process is cast as a diagnostic strategy, where information is gathered in a structured fashion. This abductive theory of pacemaker reprogramming has been used as the basis for a system that in its present form is capable of assisting cardiologists in dealing with problems in atrial sensing and pacing. The performance of the system has been evaluated using data from actual patients.

1 Introduction

Modern cardiac pacemakers are sophisticated electronic devices, capable of providing assistance when the excitatory and conductive system of the heart fails to operate normally, a condition known as *arrhythmia*. In order to accommodate specific patient needs, modern pacemakers can be programmed by setting particular parameters in such way that the resulting pacemaker therapy is optimal for the patient. Changing previously set pacemaker parameters is called *re*programming. Unfortunately, reprogramming a pacemaker is not an easy task: both sufficient time and knowledge of pacemaker functionality and possible pacemaker therapy must be available. It has been observed that due to a lack of one or both of these factors, in many patients, a given pacemaker therapy is suboptimal; in many implanted pacemakers even the original factory settings are kept unchanged. On the one hand, pacemaker technology is moving fast, and the role of software in pacemaker functioning is increasing, yielding pacemaker devices that are almost annually enhanced in their capabilities. On the other hand, pacemaker equipment producers are confronted with the limitations of what clinicians can and are willing to do; they are beginning to realise that some form of intelligent decision support is needed in order to let patients benefit from further advances in pacemaker technology.

W. Horn et al. (Eds.): AIMDM'99, LNAI 1620, pp. 175–184, 1999.

The process of reprogramming a pacemaker consists of observing symptoms and signs in the patient, supplemented with information of past and present electrical behaviour of heart and pacemaker, stored within the device. Based on this information, decisions can be made with respect to desirable changes to pacemaker settings, or with respect to the presence of pacemaker faults. This process appears to have much in common with the process of diagnostic problem solving [3]. In this paper, we present a theory of model-based diagnosis, based on earlier work in the field of abductive diagnosis, that has been adapted to deal with problems of pacemaker reprogramming. Based on this theory, a system has been implemented that is one of few medical, model-based intelligent systems that have moved from academia to industry.

The structure of this paper is as follows. Some basic (patho)physiology of the heart and principles of the structure and function of cardiac pacemakers are briefly reviewed in Section 2. In Section 3, we present a theory of model-based diagnosis used for pacemaker reprogramming, and its implementation. Preliminary evaluation results are given in Section 4. Finally, in Section 5, the achievements and limitations of this research are discussed.

2   Cardiac Pacemakers

We first review the principles of the electrical activity of the heart before discussing the structure and function of cardiac pacemakers.

2.1   Electrical Activity of the Heart

The heart can be viewed as a pump, responsible for maintaining blood pressure and flow within the vascular system. Pressure and flow are the results of a rhythmic contraction of the cardiac muscle, the *myocardium*, which is under control of specialised excitatory and conductive cardiac tissue. This system generates and spreads an electrical impulse, called an *action potential*, through the atrial and ventricular muscular walls, causing contraction of the muscle fibres. A schematic picture of the excitatory and conductive system of the heart is shown in Fig. 1. It consists of the *sinoatrial node*, which is the natural pacemaker of the heart, the *atrioventricular node*, and the left and right bundle branches.

There are a number diseases that may cause the excitatory and conductive system of the heart to fail. This may give rise to low heart rate, referred to as *bradycardia*. Failure of the atrioventricular pathway to conduct electrical impulses from the atrium to the ventricle, called *artrioventricular block*, is a very common cause of bradycardia. Long-term treatment of bradycardia is accomplished by an implantable pacemaker, although there is some place for pharmacological therapy in the early stages [2].

2.2   Structure and Function of a Pacemaker

A pacemaker consists of a *can*, which contains a microprocessor, a battery and an impulse generator. Impulses are transmitted to the heart by means of a *lead*,

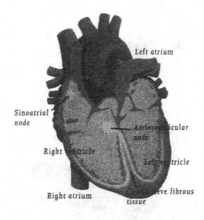

Left atrium

Sinoatrial
node

Atrioventricular
node

Right ventricle

Left ventricle

Right atrium

valve fibrous
tissue

Fig. 1. The excitatory and conductive system of the heart.

which is attached to the can's connector. An example of a modern, advanced pacemaker is Vitatron's *Diamond II* pacemaker (See Fig. 2).

A pacemaker is programmed by means of a *programmer*, a computer with special software that controls an external magnet. Fig. 3 shows an example of a pacemaker programmer. The magnet is placed above the location of the pacemaker; information from the programmer to the pacemaker, and back, is transmitted by means of telemetry.

A modern pacemaker is capable of stimulating, or pacing, the heart, of sensing the intrinsic activity of the heart, and also of automatic adaptation of the pacing rate to the patient's needs, which is called *rate responsiveness*.

A pacemaker like the Diamond II stores and collects a lot of information used to diagnose problems, called *diagnostics*, such as *patient-specific information* (the patient's name, age, and date of implantation), information on the frequency of occurrence of certain events, collected by *counters*, which is sometimes collected over a period of time (then called *holters*). In addition to diagnostics, the pro-

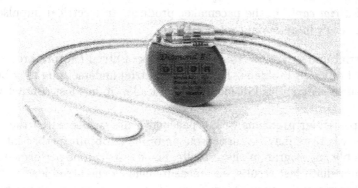

Fig. 2. The Diamond II pacemaker.

Fig. 3. Pacemaker programmer.

grammer also shows the programmed *pacemaker settings*, which determine the operation of the pacemaker.

2.3   Pacemaker Problems and Diagnostic Tests

Cardiac symptoms and signs in a patient with an implanted pacemaker may be due to medical problems, inappropriate pacemaker settings, or pacemaker faults. We focus on problems with atrial sensing and pacing, for which there are three main causes:

- *atrial undersensing*: impulses generated by the sinoatrial node have not been sensed, causing the pacemaker to give inappropriate therapy;
- *atrial oversensing*: the pacemaker senses and reacts to a signal, which, however, has not been generated by the sinoatrial node, e.g. muscle noise;
- *loss of atrial capture*: the pacemaker produces an electrical impulse, which fails to result in an atrial contraction.

In turn, atrial under- and oversensing, and loss of atrial capture are caused by a number of different problems. For example, atrial undersensing may be due to problems such as atrial lead dislocation (the lead's tip has lost contact with the surface).

When particular problems with a pacemaker are suspected by the cardiologist, diagnostic tests may be carried out in order to obtain further information about possible misprogrammings or faults. Some tests can be performed directly, yielding immediate test results, e.g. measurement of the atrial lead impedance, whereas others results, such as an X-ray of the chest, are available only after some delay.

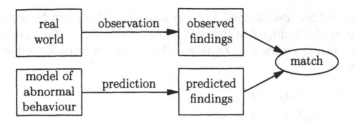

Fig. 4. Matching-abnormal-behaviour diagnosis.

3 Model-Based Pacemaker Reprogramming

Pacemaker reprogramming can be viewed as the process of finding appropriate values for pacemaker settings that avoid the occurrence of abnormal symptoms and signs in the patient. This process can be seen as a form of diagnostic problem solving: when there are particular symptoms or signs in the patient, indicating suboptimal pacemaker settings, pacemaker faults or a medical disorder, the possible causes should be determined and dealt with. The theory of model-based diagnosis offers several ways in which such a diagnostic process can be described. Conceptually, this diagnostic process may be described in terms of *matching abnormal behaviour* (MAB) diagnosis, as schematically shown in Fig. 4 [3]. In MAB diagnosis, there is a model of abnormal behaviour available, which is used to predict abnormal findings that may or must be observed; these predictions are next matched with findings actually observed. A collection of causes described in the model and associated with predictions that best match the findings observed, is taken as a diagnosis. MAB diagnosis is a conceptual model; it is typically formalised in terms of abductive reasoning.

3.1 Theory of Abductive Diagnosis

Our theory of abductive diagnosis is inspired by earlier work by L. Console and P. Torasso [1]. In their theory of diagnosis, the abnormal behaviour of a system is represented as causal knowledge, relating abnormal states and resulting abnormal findings. We shall refer to abnormal states in this article as *defects*, which may be anything, varying from medical disorders, to incorrect pacemaker settings and pacemaker faults.

In this paper, it is assumed that causal knowledge can be represented in Horn formulae of the following two forms:

$$d_1 \wedge \cdots \wedge d_n \rightarrow f \tag{1}$$
$$d_1 \wedge \cdots \wedge d_n \rightarrow d \tag{2}$$

where d, d_i, $i = 1, \ldots, n$, represent defects and f represents an *observable finding*.

Console and Torasso have also proposed a simple mechanism to weaken the causality relation, by means of literals α. These literals represent incompleteness of knowledge with respect to the underlying causal mechanisms relating causes

and effects, and are used to model uncertainty [3,4]. They can be used to block
the deduction of a finding f or defect d if the defects d_i, $i = 1, \ldots, n$, hold true,
but the literal α is assumed to be false. The weakened Horn formulae have the
following form:

$$d_1 \wedge \cdots \wedge d_n \wedge \alpha_f \rightarrow f \tag{3}$$
$$d_1 \wedge \cdots \wedge d_n \wedge \alpha_d \rightarrow d \tag{4}$$

The literals α are called *incompleteness-assumption literals*, abbreviated to *assumption literals*; every assumption literal occurs uniquely within a Horn formula. Formulae of the form (1) and (2) represent certain causal relationships;
formulae of the form (3) and (4) represent uncertain causal relationships.

In the following, the convention is adopted that present findings are denoted
by positive finding literals; absent findings are denoted by negative finding literals. A similar convention is used for defect literals.

Now, let $C = (\Delta, \Phi, \mathcal{R})$ stand for a *causal specification*, where:

- Δ denotes a set possible (positive and negative) defect and assumption literals;
- Φ denotes a set of possible (positive and negative) finding literals;
- $\mathcal{R}$ stands for a set of Horn formulae of the form (1) – (4).

A causal specification can be employed for the prediction of observable findings
in the sense of Fig. 4.

Definition 1. If $C = (\Delta, \Phi, \mathcal{R})$ is a causal specification then, a set $H \subseteq \Delta$ is
called a *prediction* for a set of observable findings $F \subseteq \Phi$ if

(1) $\mathcal{R} \cup H \vDash F$, and
(2) $\mathcal{R} \cup H$ is satisfiable.

Obviously, the notion of prediction formalises the arrow in the lower half of
Fig. 4; the resulting set of findings F corresponds to the predicted (observable)
findings in the same figure.

An *abductive diagnostic problem* $\mathcal{A}$ is now defined as a pair $\mathcal{A} = (C, E)$,
where $E \subseteq \Phi$ is called a *set of observed findings* if all findings in E are positive
(negative findings are dealt with below). A set of observed findings corresponds
to the box in the upper half of Fig. 4.

Formally, a solution to an abductive diagnostic problem $\mathcal{A}$ can be defined as
follows.

Definition 2. Let $\mathcal{A} = (C, E)$ be an abductive diagnostic problem, where $C = (\Delta, \Phi, \mathcal{R})$ is a causal specification with $\mathcal{R}$ a set of Horn formulae of the form
(1) – (4), and $E \subseteq \Phi$ a set of observed findings. A set of defect and assumption
literals $H \subseteq \Delta$ is called a *solution* to $\mathcal{A}$ if:

(1) $\mathcal{R} \cup H \vDash E$ (*covering condition*);
(2) $\mathcal{R} \cup H \cup C \nvDash \perp$ (*consistency condition*)

where H is minimal with respect to set inclusion, and C, called the *constraint set*, is a set of formulas in first-order logic, consisting of defect and finding literals only.

An entire solution H may be taken as a diagnosis, but it is more natural to take a *diagnosis* to consist of the defect literals in a solution H only; we shall do so accordingly.

There are many possible ways for defining a constraint set C. Usually, the constraint set stands for findings assumed to be false, because they have not been observed (and are therefore assumed to be absent); this is an application of the closed world assumption (CWA) [7], restricted to observable findings. However, it may not always be justified to assume negative findings in this way; sometimes, it is more natural to take the findings as being unknown. When we use predicate logic and let particular predicates associated with findings stand for tests, the following definition is obtained (we take $C = C_E$):

$$C_E = \{\neg\pi(t) \in \Phi \mid \pi(s) \in E, t \neq s, \text{ or } \neg\pi(t) \text{ has been observed}\}$$

where π stands for predicate symbols, and t and s are constants. With this definition of the constraint set, only negative literals concerning tests done are included, if not positively observed, supplemented with findings explicitly observed to be absent. Other findings are assumed to be unknown.

In the domain of pacemaker reprogramming it was known beforehand that particular combinations of defects cannot occur. Such impossible combinations can be represented as a set of additional domain constraints D, e.g. $\neg(d_1 \wedge d_2)$ indicates that d_1 and d_2 may not occur together, imposing a further limitation on the number of possible solutions. The final definition of the constraint set that appeared suitable in the present case was therefore as follows: $C = C_E \cup D$.

3.2   Interpretation of Observables

The description above suggests a dynamic, diagnostic process where preliminary diagnoses and the proposal of additional tests are generated by the system; when new test information becomes available, the old diagnoses may need revision. The manner in which old diagnoses are revised, is the subject of the present section.

Proposing tests Using the definition of abductive diagnosis given above, and using the definition of a constraint set as consisting of absent findings, either observed or inferred, it is straightforward to add test selection to the abductive reasoning scheme considered so far. Let $\mathcal{A} = (\mathcal{C}, E)$ be an abductive diagnostic problem, with E the set of observed findings and $\mathcal{C} = (\Delta, \Phi, \mathcal{R})$ a causal specification, then if H is a solution to $\mathcal{A}$ it may hold that $\mathcal{R} \cup H \vDash F$, where $F \supset E$. Since the solution H predicts findings that have not, as yet, been observed, and since all findings resulting from tests are included, either positively in E or negatively in C, the observable findings in the difference set $F \backslash E$ pertain to tests that have not yet been carried out. Using this information, the system may suggest to the user to perform particular diagnostic tests.

Hypothesis revision Now, suppose that a particular test, as suggested by the system, has been carried out, and that a (positive) test result has been entered into the system. Of interest are the effects of this additional information on the diagnostic solutions.

Let H be a solution to $\mathcal{A} = (\mathcal{C}, E)$, such that $\mathcal{R} \cup H \vDash \pi(t_i)$, where $\pi(t_i) \notin E$. Then, H is also a solution to $\mathcal{A}' = (\mathcal{C}, E \cup \{\pi(t_i)\})$ if $\mathcal{R} \cup H \cup C' \nvDash \perp$ for $C' = C \cup \{\neg\pi(t_1), \ldots, \neg\pi(t_{i-1}), \neg\pi(t_{i+1}), \ldots, \neg\pi(t_n)\}$. This result suggests that it is sufficient to check the consistency condition as soon as information corresponding to a suggested diagnostic test result becomes available. We also have that if H is a solution to $\mathcal{A}'$, then H is also a solution to $\mathcal{A}$ if for each $H' \subset H$ it holds that $\mathcal{R} \cup H' \nvDash E$. Practically spoken, this last proposition implies that solutions computed by taking a test result into account will be either identical to old solutions or be supersets of old solutions.

The next property concerns the situation where the actually observed finding turns out to be different from the one previously predicted. Let H be a solution to $\mathcal{A} = (\mathcal{C}, E)$, such that $\mathcal{R} \cup H \vDash \pi(t_i)$, and let $\mathcal{A}' = (\mathcal{C}, E \cup \{\pi(t_j)\})$, $j \neq i$. Furthermore, let $C' = C \cup \{\neg\pi(t_1), \ldots, \neg\pi(t_i), \ldots, \neg\pi(t_{j-1}), \neg\pi(t_{j+1}), \ldots, \neg\pi(t_n)\}$, where C and C' are the constraint sets of $\mathcal{A}$ and $\mathcal{A}'$, respectively. Then, for any solution H' it holds that $H' \not\supseteq H$ and $H' \not\subseteq H$. This result is rather weak, but note that from this proposition, it follows that a solution H' should be different at least in one defect d from a previous solution H if the test result observed is different from the one predicted.

3.3   Diagnostic Strategy

Until now, we have refrained from making assumptions about the order in which diagnostic tests may be performed, as suggested by the system to the user. In reality, it is usually mandatory to do test selection and hypothesis generation in a structured fashion, taking information already gathered into account.

As has been discussed above, diagnostic solutions that are causally related to findings that have as yet not been observed, may give rise to requests for further information. Since new, incoming information may or may not affect the validity of previous solutions, it seems natural to distinguish between various types of solutions. The theoretical background of this distinction has been developed above. *Suspected* solutions predict at least one finding that may be obtained by a test that has not yet been carried out. *Rejected* solutions are solutions to a previous problem, which are now rejected because of the availability of new evidence, that somehow refutes the previous solution. Finally, in the case of a *confirmed* solution, all predicted, associated tests have been carried out, and the observed results appear to correspond to the results predicted.

In the case of reprogramming an artificial pacemaker, the gathering of *evidence* during problem solving may be structured in such way that pacemaker settings and diagnostics, which are readily available from a pacemaker device, are always requested first. Next, information from the follow-up, i.e. information that requires some extra tests, yielding results that are also immediately available, are requested. Finally, information obtained from additional tests, such as a chest radiograph, could be taken as a last source of evidence.

3.4 Resulting Model and System

The resulting system consists of a causal model, an abductive inference engine and a graphical user interface. The causal model was represented as a logical, causal specification, as described above. The abductive inference engine of the system was built on top of the Theorist system. *Theorist* is a Prolog program, developed by David Poole and colleagues, that supports a form of hypothetical reasoning quite similar to reasoning with defaults [5]. The key to mapping abductive diagnosis to reasoning in Theorist appeared to be that defect and assumption literals may be assumed during the diagnostic process; they, therefore, are interpreted in a way similar to defaults [3,8]. We just had to add an engine for strategic inference control to Theorist, in order to implement the reasoning strategy as described in the previous section.

4 Evaluation

It almost goes without saying that an intelligent system that is aimed at assisting cardiologists in reprogramming a pacemaker must be highly reliable. Part of the reliability requirements have been fulfilled by using mathematically sound techniques, and by following a model-based approach to design.

For an evaluation study of the performance of the pacemaker reprogramming advisory system, 126 patients were selected retrospectively from the files, having a total of 143 problems. Only 19 of the 126 patients had sensing or pacing problems of the atrium, which concern problems currently covered by the system. Only one of the 19 patients appeared to have symptoms caused by a combination of problems (far field R-wave sensing combined with a too low P-wave amplitude). The only incorrect advice produced by the system concerned the single patient who had a combined problem. Actually, in this particular case the system diagnosed that there was a far field R-wave sensing problem, but the system did not reach the conclusion that the P-wave amplitude was too low in this patient. In 79% of cases, the expert's conclusions corresponded exactly to the diagnoses produced by the system. Three cases were unclassified due to missing data. In 94% of cases, the diagnostic conclusions produced by the system were correct, leaving out the three unclassified cases.

Finally, in only 8 of the remaining 107 patient cases (7.5%) without atrial pacing or sensing problems, the diagnosis produced was incorrect. Of course, these diagnoses were still sensible, because the clinical evidence also pointed in the direction of atrial pacing and sensing, although it appeared that the actual problem was different from the diagnosis. These results offer information of the risk of diagnosing problems that in reality are absent in the patient.

5 Discussion

In this paper, we have described a model-based system that is capable of assisting cardiologists in reprogramming an implanted pacemaker. In designing the system we have used formal, logical techniques, yielding the advantage that several aspect of the system could be formally investigated.

Although diagnostic problem solving usually involves dealing with uncertain knowledge, we have refrained from using a quantitative probabilistic representation of uncertainty in the final model, and used a qualitative representation instead. In the course of the research, we have designed a number of Bayesian networks that were similar in structure to the logical specifications. However, the advantages gained by the ability to explicitly specify probabilistic information were small, mainly because symptoms and signs in a patient that are possibly related to suboptimal pacemaker settings or pacemaker faults must be clinically investigated anyway. Since diagnostic test selection is carried out in a clearly structured fashion, there was also no need for decision-theoretic techniques to guide test selection as employed in some probabilistic systems. The balance between qualitative and quantitative information may change as the models grow in size. However, the formalism of probabilistic Horn clauses, which is formally equivalent to Bayesian networks [6], may offer a suitable extension when adding quantitative, probabilistic information is required.

At present, the system only covers part of the entire domain. In the near future, the system will be extended by including other parts of the problem domain as well. Furthermore, the current implementation is being replaced by a program that can be integrated with the pacemaker programmer software, so that the user will view the system as a functional addition to the programmer software. Integration also has the advantage that pacemaker data need not be entered by hand, but can be extracted automatically from the pacemaker device.

References

1. L. Console, D. Theseider Dupré and P. Torasso, A theory of diagnosis for incomplete causal models, in: *Proceedings of the 10th International Joint Conference on Artificial Intelligence*, Los Angeles, USA (1989) 1311–1317.
2. K.J. Isselbacher, et al., *Harrison's Principles of Internal Medicine*, 13th edition, McGraw-Hill, New-York, 1994.
3. P.J.F. Lucas, Symbolic diagnosis and its formalisation, *The Knowledge Engineering Review* 12(2) (1997) 109–146.
4. P.J.F. Lucas, Analysis of notions of diagnosis, *Artificial Intelligence* 105 (1998) 295–343.
5. D. Poole, *Local Users Guide to Theorist*, Report, Department of Computer Science, University of British Columbia, Vancouver, 1990.
6. D. Poole, Probabilistic Horn abduction and Bayesian networks, *Artificial Intelligence* 64 (1993) 81–129.
7. R. Reiter, On closed world data bases, in: H. Gallaire and J. Minker, eds., *Logic and Databases* (Plenum-Press, New York, 1978) 55–76.
8. R. Reiter, A logic for default reasoning, *Artificial Intelligence* 13 (1980) 81–132.

Integrating Deep Biomedical Models into Medical Decision Support Systems: An Interval Constraint Approach

Jorge Cruz[1], Pedro Barahona[1], and Frédéric Benhamou[2]

[1]Departamento de Informática, Universidade Nova Lisboa, 2825 Monte Caparica, Portugal
{jc,pb}@di.fct.unl.pt
[2]IRIN, Université de Nantes, 2 rue de la Houssiniere, Nantes cedex 3, France
Frederic.Benhamou@irin.univ-nantes.fr

Abstract. Knowledge representation has always been a major problem in the design of medical decision support systems. In this paper we present a new methodology to represent and reason about medical knowledge, based on the declarative specification of interval constraints over the medical concepts. This allows the integration of deep medical models involving differential equations developed in biomedical research (typical in several medical domains) which, due to their complexity, have not been incorporated into medical decision support systems. The methodology which enables reasoning both forward and backward in time, is applied to a specific domain, electromyography. The promising results obtained are discussed to justify our future work.

1. Introduction

Knowledge representation has always been a major concern in the design of decision support systems, namely in the medical domain. Early medical knowledge based systems were designed to accomplish some specific medical task (e.g. diagnosis) and the medical knowledge was mostly embedded in the procedures used to accomplish that task. This led to problems of consistency (the medical knowledge reflected the views of the medical experts that advised the design of such systems, which by no means was consensual within the health care community) and also of reuse (the same knowledge could not be used in two different tasks – e.g. diagnosis and treatment).

Several approaches were proposed to overcome this problem, namely to represent medical knowledge declaratively. Such systems represent medical knowledge proper (i.e. anatomic, physiologic or pathologic) separately from task related knowledge (i.e. the steps to perform diagnosis, treatment or monitoring tasks). Moreover, task knowledge could be formalised and (re)used in several specific medical domains.

Such view was particularly useful for systems based in logic [1], where useful relations between medical concepts are stored as facts (e.g. causal relations, associations, risk factors) that could be handled by the reasoning process. Nevertheless, the medical concepts and relations represented were usually relatively high level abstractions of the underlying medical and biological processes, and that led to the problem of handling uncertain knowledge.

W. Horn et al. (Eds.): AIMDM'99, LNAI 1620, pp. 185-194, 1999.
© Springer-Verlag Berlin Heidelberg 1999

This problem is alleviated if less abstract concepts are used, where the underlying uncertainty is more controlled. This is the approach taken by the systems with "deep medical knowledge" [2], [3]. In contrast with systems that represented causal but "shallow" relations, say between a disease and a symptom, they represent a more detailed set of pathophysiologic states and processes to explain that shallow relation.

This approach has to handle certain difficulties. On the one hand, the network of concepts and relations is larger, imposing efficient methods to explore them. On the other hand, the deeper the knowledge is, the more dependent it is in numerical data.

Reasoning with this kind of information is, in principle, very costly. Nevertheless, some formalisms may be quite efficient to handle it, namely belief networks [4]. Eliciting all the conditional probabilities in such a belief network is however a difficult problem, made only harder when several diseases are considered, due to the explosion of the required number of conditional probabilities [5].

An alternative (or perhaps complementary) approach is to adopt "deep" biomedical models proposed and accepted in the medical community, but not incorporated into the decision support systems, for example, Cardiovascular [6], Respiratory [7] and Compartment models [8]. But these are often highly non-linear, based on differential equations, and difficult to reason about by simple "logical" procedures.

Simulation of these models can be used to validate some hypotheses. However the usual simulation methods have difficulties to cope with uncertain data (e.g. they might provide "wrong" approximate solutions), and they are "time-directed": given the initial conditions the state of the system can be computed at some later time, but not at some previous time. As such they may only play a "passive" role in a task such as diagnosis, where the goal is to find a problem that has occurred in the past.

In this paper we explore constraint solving over intervals, a recently proposed technology to handle non-linear numerical models, and its use in neurology. Next section presents the model we are using (based on differential equations). Section 3, addresses the advantages of constraint technology in the medical domain with some very simple examples. Section 4 discusses the handling of differential equations and highlights our contributions in this area. Section 5 shows preliminary results obtained with the use of this technology in modelling local nerve lesions. Finally, section 6 presents the major conclusions and discusses our plans for future work.

2. A Biophysical Model for Local Neuropathies

The Peripheral Neuromuscular System (PNS) is a very complex medical domain where uncertainty still plays a major role in spite of a reasonable understanding of the basic underlying physical phenomena. It is responsible for the propagation of nervous impulses between the Central Nervous System (CNS) and muscles or sensory regions.

Several neuromuscular disorders are responsible for anatomical problems in the PNS, namely local neuropathies, i.e. lesions in a specific point of a nerve. The physical damage induced in the nerve by the local neuropathy depends on the severity of the lesion and on degeneration and regeneration phenomena that take place over time. A realistic biophysical model of a local neuropathy should thus take into account three lesion parameters: the local, the severity and the time (how long ago did the lesion happen).

To obtain information about the nerve condition, several electrophysiological studies (EMG) can be performed [9], inducing nervous impulses by stimulation of a nerve point and recording the electrical wave form produced in another point. The form of the wave is directly related to the impulse propagation and consequently to the physical condition of the nerve between the stimulation and the recording point. Latency and Amplitude of the wave are commonly used by physicians for diagnosis.

The major goal of EMG diagnosis is to identify anatomical problems capable of explaining the results observed in a set of electrophysiological studies. In this context the goal would be to predict the values of the lesion parameters from the values of Latency and Amplitude observed in studies performed in the nerve segments. A related goal consists of simulating the effects of a diagnostic hypothesis, i.e. to predict the Latency and Amplitude from the lesion parameters. A biophysical model, useful for the diagnosis/simulation of local neuropathies should hence relate the lesion parameters, Local, Severity and Time to the observable Latency and Amplitude.

A "deep" model should take into account that a nerve is composed of thousands of parallel nerve fibers. By stimulating a nerve point, electrical waves are induced in each nerve fiber and independently propagated towards the recording point. All these electrical waves have the same wave form (the Action Potential) the only difference being the speed of propagation. This velocity is related to the fiber diameter (thick fibers propagate faster) and the physical condition of the fiber (damage can delay or block the propagation). This condition depend on degeneration and regeneration phenomena and the damage is then obtained from their opposite effects. Finally, the electrical wave recorded in an EMG examination is the compound effect of all the action potentials arriving at the recording site with different propagation delays.

Fig. 1 summarises the relations considered in the model, based on several biophysical studies on nerve conduction [10], [11], that we have adopted. Notice its complexity (namely the differential equations it contains) and non-linear nature, which makes it very difficult for conventional techniques to reason about it both forward and backwards in time.

$\text{Amplitude}_{SR}(L,S,T) = |\text{wave}_{SR}(t_{min},L,S,T)|$ $\text{Latency}_{SR}(L,S,T) = t_k$

$\therefore \forall t \; \text{wave}_{SR}(t,L,S,T) \geq \text{wave}_{SR}(t_{min},L,S,T)$ $\therefore \; \text{wave}_{SR}(t_k,L,S,T) = k_1$

$\forall t < t_k \; \text{wave}_{SR}(t,L,S,T) \neq k_1$

$\text{wave}_{SR}(t,L,S,T) = \int \text{potential}(t-\text{delay}_{SR}(D,L,S,T)) \times p(D) \, \partial D$

$\text{potential} \equiv \text{ODE in } \Re^4 \text{ from [10]}$ $\text{delay}_{SR}(D,L,S,T) = \int_{S}^{R} \dfrac{\partial X}{\text{velocity}(X,D,L,S,T)}$

$\text{velocity}(X,D,L,S,T) = \text{if damage}(X,L,S,T) < k_2$
$\qquad\qquad\qquad \text{then} \quad \text{normal\_velocity}(D) \times (1-\text{damage}(X,L,S,T))$
$\qquad\qquad\qquad \text{else} \quad 0$

$\text{normal\_velocity} \equiv \text{from [11]}$

$\text{damage}(X,L,S,T) = \text{degeneration}(X,L,S,T) \times (1-\text{regeneration}(X,L,S,T))$

$\text{degeneration}(X,L,S,T) = S \times e^{-\frac{|L-X|}{\alpha_d + \beta_d \times T}}$ $\text{regeneration}(X,L,S,T) = k_r \times e^{-\frac{X}{\alpha_r + \beta_r \times T}}$

Variables:
L ≡ Local
S ≡ Severity
T ≡ Time
S ≡ Stimulation Site
R ≡ Recording Site
D ≡ Fiber Diameter
X ≡ Fiber Point

Constant Parameters:
$k_1, k_2, k_r, \alpha_d, \alpha_r, \beta_d, \beta_r$

Fig. 1. A biophysical model for local neuropathies

3. Interval Constraints

Constraint systems allow a declarative expression of models as sets of constraints, arranged in a constraint network, and offer sound techniques (constraint propagation) to efficiently find solutions to the constraints. Although successfully applied in other areas, these systems had little use in the biomedical domain (notwithstanding some pioneering work in the modelling of blood circulation and gas exchange [12]).

Modelling complex systems, namely that described in the previous section, requires the use of more complex constraints with variables over the reals and non-linear relations between them, and to represent the uncertainty of biophysical phenomena.

The Interval Constraints framework (introduced by Cleary [13]) is adequate for handling non-linear constraints over continuous variables. Its propagation mechanism starts from a set of constraints over real variables, using Interval Arithmetic [14] to reduce the domains of some variables. This is propagated to other constraints that further reduce the domain of other variables until a stable state is reached.

In this paper we propose an Interval Constraint approach for an adequate representation of biophysical knowledge with sound and efficient capabilities for diagnosis and simulation. In this models uncertainty on some parameters is represented by representing their values as intervals. Reasoning is performed through efficient constraint propagation assuring that intervals are kept as narrow as possible.

3.1. An Example

Suppose we want to model a relation between two variables, one representing a disorder (D) and the other an observable (O) associated with the disorder. All the knowledge we have about this relation is based on previous cases with particular values for the observable associated with particular value for the disorder (see Fig. 2). The above relation could be modelled by the interval constraint

$$O = P_1 \times D + P_2 \qquad \text{w/ } P_1 \in [2,3], \ P_2 \in [0,5] \text{ and } O, D \in [0, +\infty]$$

where P_1 and P_2 are parameters that express the uncertainty about the linear correlation between variables O and D. Notice that, as long as the parameters are treated as ordinary intervals, this model is no longer a linear model. Fig. 2 shows the solutions considered in this model lying in the region delimited by the grey lines.

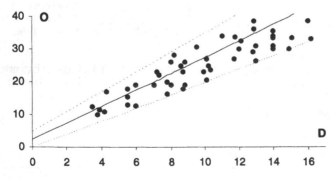

Fig. 2. A relation between variable O (observable) and variable D (disorder). The example is based on a study relating the Conduction Velocity of individual fibers and its diameter [11].

One technique to handle interval constraints decomposes complex constraints into sets of primitive constraints. In this case the constraint would be decomposed into:

$$C=P_1 \times D \qquad\qquad O=C+P_2$$

Simple interval arithmetic rules [14] can then be applied to reduce the domains of the variables and the results propagated. For instance, they can be used to calculate the bounds of C given the bounds of P_1 and D, or else the bounds of P_1 or D from those of the other two variables (P_1=C/D and D=C/ P_1).

Diagnosis can be performed by propagating the bounds of the observable variable. For example, given O=20 and P_2=[0,5] the bounds of C can be calculated and this would trigger the other constraint involving variable C, resulting in a predicted value for the disorder variable to be between 5 and 10:

$$C=O-P_2=[20,20]-[0,5]=[20-5,20-0]=[15,20]$$
$$D=C/P_1=[15,20]/[2,3]=[15/3,20/2]=[\ 5,10]$$

To simulate the effect of a disorder, the information about the disorder is propagated to the observable variable. From a disorder with a value between 18 and 20, a value between 36 and 65 would be predicted for the observable variable:

$$C=P_1 \times D=[2,3] \times [18,20]=[2 \times 18,3 \times 20]=[36,60]$$
$$O=C+P_2=[36,60]+[0,5]=[36+0,60+5]=[36,65]$$

Notice that other simulation methods need the specification of exact values for the variables and provide no safe conclusions in the neighbourhood of these values. The interval constraint approach deals with ranges which can be more or less precise according to the simulation requirements. Either in simulation or in diagnosis the final results are uncertain, given the uncertainty on the value of P_1 and P_2, but the reasoning is sound as the constraints are satisfied and only inconsistent solutions are discarded.

If instead of a single disorder several disorders were affecting the value of a single variable (observable or not) this could be easily represented by a constraint model where at least one variable would be associated to each disorder and an aggregation function would combine the composed effects (this was done in section 2 to combine the degeneration and regeneration into the damage inflicted upon a nerve fiber). The propagation would reduce the domains of the involved variables making the single disorder case just a special case of the multiple disorder case.

The propagation of non-linear constraints over real intervals can be extremely inefficient in complex domains and is an important research area in the constraint community [15], [16]. Techniques to handle interval constraints are usually incomplete in that they cannot discard all the inconsistent solutions, they just assure that no possible solution is discarded, but some inconsistent solutions can still remain after propagation. Different methods can assure different kinds of consistency and they can be more or less appropriate depending upon the constraint characteristics.

The model presented in section 2 included two integral expressions and an ordinary differential equation. An important issue in the Interval Constraint framework is the definition of an adequate methodology to deal with constraints expressed as ordinary differential equations (common in biophysical models [6], [7], [8]), though little work as been done on the context of decision support. This is discussed in the next section.

4. Ordinary Differential Equations

An Ordinary Differential Equation (ODE) defines the derivative of **u** (a vector) with respect to a variable t by means of a function of t and **u** [17]:

$$\frac{\partial \mathbf{u}}{\partial t} = \mathbf{f}(\mathbf{u},t) \tag{1}$$

Even equations with higher order derivatives on the same variable can be transformed into an ODE by including new variables (one for each higher order derivative). Given an ODE and a value for **u** at a given t_0, the initial value problem aims at determining the value of **u** for other values of t; techniques to handle ODEs can also be used to solve integrals, since these problems can be reformulated as initial value problems.

4.1 Existing Approaches

Differential equations is a relatively recent field in constraint programming [18], [19]. All the approaches are based on interval approximations (the interval approximation of **u** is denoted by **û**) of the integral trajectory (**u**(t)) in some intermediate points (t_i), as in the finite differences method of approximation. Such interval approximations have the advantage relatively to other numerical approaches of defining bounds that must necessarily contain the exact solution (**u**(t_i) ∈ **û**(t_i)). These bounds are calculated through a set of constraints (that we call step) relating each point (t_i) and the interval value **û**(t_i) with the subsequent point (t_{i+1}) and the interval value **û**(t_{i+1}).

The various possibilities for the characterisation of this step are generally based on the approximation steps of numerical approaches (Taylor Series, Runge Kutta), but with the error controlled in terms of interval bounds. Some approximation steps can lead to better results than others, and the choice of a particular one, should take into account the complexity of the associated set of constraints.

Independently of the chosen approximation step, the more points are considered the better precision is obtained, albeit with an increased propagation time. In general, the relationship between precision and number of points is difficult to obtain and the number of points needed to obtain a given precision may not be quantified. The existing approaches assume fixed number of intermediate points: if they are too few, there is a lack of precision, if too many, there is an unnecessary waste of time.

This can be a disadvantage, namely if the ultimate goal is to check the consistency of some result with its hypothetical value: all that is required is to check whether the result bounds overlap the bounds of the hypothetical value, rather than some a priori specified precision.

4.2 Our Alternative Incremental Proposal

To overcome this difficulty, we propose an alternative approach for the interval approximation of a differential equation trajectory by considering new intermediate points incrementally. Whenever necessary, a new intermediate point is considered and its associated set of constraints is added, which will eventually narrow, through propagation, the bounds of the trajectory. The uncertainty about the trajectory is thus incrementally reduced with the necessary number of intermediate points rather than with some pre-fixed number of points (possibly found only after a costly generation and test process). Specifically, the new point is chosen as the mid point of the interval which contributes the most to the trajectory uncertainty, thus guaranteeing convergence to the exact trajectory. The algorithm stops whenever the aimed precision is achieved or the consistency check is solved.

We have applied these ideas for the implementation of the model presented in section 2. Since propagation alone gives poor results when the domains of the variables are wide, it was necessary to complement this propagation with a narrowing algorithm similar to the one used to implement box-consistency in the Newton language [15]. The key idea of this algorithm is to narrow the bounds of the domains of all variables until it becomes impossible to further shrink the bounds of any variable without loosing solutions. This is achieved by making partitions on the variable domains and checking the consistency of the constraint network. The narrowing of a variable domain is possible whenever an inconsistent partition is detected near its bounds.

This algorithm performs consistency checks quite and this is where our approach can take advantage relatively to the previous approaches, by detecting inconsistencies sooner. With the previous approaches, when several variables are constrained by an ODE, conclusions about the inconsistency of their domains can only be made after computing all the pre-fixed intermediate points used in the ODE interval approximation. In contrast, our approach detects inconsistencies in early phases of the incremental algorithm with less intermediate points and better performances.

5. Preliminary Results

We performed a number of tests in order to analyse the behaviour of our constraint model for Local Neuropathies. The values we worked with (for Latency and Amplitude) are not tuned yet with real Electromyography values, but the examples shown below can give a first insight of the possibilities of our approach.

All examples are based on studies performed in a nerve (fiber bundle) 100 centimetres long and the electrical wave induced in the EMG tests travels along the nerve segment between centimetre 45 and centimetre 55. This could be the case, for instance, of an EMG study of the Ulnar nerve (the bundle of fibers that connect the muscle abductor digiti minimi to the CNS) between the proximal and the distal sulcus (the Ulnar nerve is an upper limb nerve that is about 100 centimetres long; the proximal and distal sulcus are two sites near the elbow).

Simulation and diagnosis was performed on three cases: a normal nerve; a nerve moderately injured; and one severely damaged. In all cases we focussed on diagnosis or assumed (in simulation) neuropathies localised in the elbow (near centimetre 50).

5.1 Simulation

In simulation, the goal is to obtain narrow bounds for Latency and Amplitude, by constraint propagation on the knowledge model of the disorder parameters (Local, Severity and Time). In the following, we will just mention the Latency results.

To simulate a normal case the Severity variable was set to zero and no further information was given to the system. The Latency obtained for the normal case was between 2.19 and 2.23 milliseconds. To compare the obtained values with real EMG examination values a few considerations are necessary. Firstly, the examination parameters from existing tables of normal values depend on the patient age, country as well as EMG school. Secondly, what is tabled in the tables of Ulnar nerve studies between the proximal and distal sulcus is not Latency but Conduction Velocity. However, from the propagation time (between 2.19 and 2.23 ms) and the distance between stimulation and recording sites (10 cm), the Conduction Velocity is easily obtained (between 44.84 and 45.66 m/s). This is close to tabled values. For instance, in a table used within the ESTEEM project [20], the expected normal value for this Conduction Velocity on a 55 years old patient would be 50 m/s and the lower limit accepted as a normal value is 40 m/s.

To simulate a moderate lesion in the elbow, variable Local was set to 50 cm (the elbow), Severity was set to 0.5 (moderate), and Time was set to 0 (i.e. today). The result obtained for Latency ranged between 2.3 and 2.7 ms, i.e. a Conduction Velocity between 37.03 m/s and 43.48 m/s. As expected, the simulation of a moderate lesion predicts a decrease on the Conduction Velocity (increase on Latency). In reality, this is due to dispersion of action potentials propagated along the different nerve fibers.

A simulation of a severe lesion in the elbow was tested by setting the Severity variable to 1 (the maximum possible value in the model), keeping the other lesion parameters (Local=50 and Time=0). Propagation results in an inconsistency, as expected, since it makes no sense to consider parameters of an electrical wave propagated along the nerve segment when propagation is certainly blocked.

5.2 Diagnosis

In diagnosis our goal is to obtain possible bounds for the disorder parameters from the observations of Latency and Amplitude. To test the diagnostic capabilities of our system, the Latency and Amplitude were set according to the previous simulations (specifically, to the mid values of the predicted bounds). Parameter Local was set to 50 cm as we are interested in lesions localised in the elbow. Severity was left unspecified, to be bound by the system performing diagnosis. Three different Time constraints were investigated: 1) with no Time constraint; 2) Time set between 0 and 2 (within two days of the lesion); and 3) with Time set to zero (today).

In the normal case, the results of test 1 indicate that when nothing is known about the time when the possible disorder has occurred, then a normal observation is compatible not only with no disorder at all (Severity=0), but also with a disorder with a Severity up to 0.666. The Severity cannot exceed 0.666, since beyond this value there are permanent damages and the regeneration effect is insufficient to allow an impulse propagation compatible with the normal observation. For milder lesions, and given sufficient time, nerve regeneration will eventually normalise the physical condition of the affected nerve. For example a lesion with Severity 0.5 will require a regeneration time of at least 136 days. Conversely, if the Time is constrained so becomes the Severity of the lesion. Tests 2 and 3 show that by reducing the bounds of variable Time the Severity is constrained to mild values (less that 0.185 and 0.148 respectively), because the time for regeneration is also reduced.

In the moderately injured case, test 1 shows that there must have existed a disorder with Severity at least 0.371 (not a mild lesion) within a Time of 592 days. As before, a stronger lesion imposes greater regeneration time. In particular, the immediate effects of a moderate injure are similar to those observed with the most severe lesion if enough time (about 592 days) are allowed for regeneration. In tests 2 and 3 the specification of narrow bounds for the Time parameter constrained the upper bound for the lesion Severity (0.651 and 0.581 respectively) due to limitations on the regeneration effect.

In the case of propagation block, all three tests indicate a severe disorder, the Severity value must be at least 0.63 which, in the knowledge model, is the minimum value high enough to block the impulse propagation. In tests 2 and 3, given the small regeneration Time, all Severities above 0.63 justify the blocking. In the first test, even without any information about the time course of the disorder, the system predicts that it must had happened less than 500 days ago (with more regeneration time some impulse propagation would be observed). Moreover, if the Time is constrained to the range 400 to 500 (no propagation after 400 days) then the lesion must have been more severe (Severity above 0.741).

6. Conclusions

In this paper we presented a new methodology to represent and reason about medical knowledge, which is based in the declarative specification of interval constraints over the medical concepts. This approach allows the integration of deep medical models, developed in biomedical research, which due to their complexity, have not been incorporated into medical decision support systems. In particular, the paper addresses a model based in differential equations, quite common in various medical specialities.

The preliminary results obtained are quite encouraging. Despite the complexity of the model, the interval constraint technology we developed is able to elicit significant quantitative information, useful in medical tasks such as diagnosis and treatment. Our methodology allows the specification of some goal state and reasons both forward and backward in time to find compatible posterior/previous states that satisfy the model constraints (which is beyond traditional simulation, that can only reason forward).

We have so far been exploiting a particular domain, electromyography. Regarding our previous work in this domain [3], the new methodology extends knowledge representation to include quantitative and time information within a sound framework. Compared with other approaches to this domain, namely, belief networks, we think our representation can more easily accommodate deep models from biomedical research. It should also ease the handling of multiple disorders, as the aggregation functions used do not explode in complexity with the number of disorders. However, we do not handle well probability/likelihood statements. Future work should address a comparison of these approaches and assess their complimentary or alternative nature.

Future work should also address the application of our methodology to full clinical cases. This includes, in a first phase, to tune the examples to real medical cases for which we have available the ESTEEM database. The second and more challenging phase, relates the integration of the reasoning capabilities enabled by our methodology within a full EMG decision support system.

References

1. O'Neil, M., Glowinski, A. and Fox, J.: A Symbolic Theory of Decision Making Applied to Several Medical Tasks, Lecture Notes in Medical Informatics, Springer, 38 (1989) 62-71.
2. Horn, W.: Utilizing Detailed Anatomical Knowledge for Hypothesis Formation and Hypothesis Testing in Rheumatological Decision Support. In: E. Keravnou, eds., Deep Models for Medical Knowledge Engineering, Elsevier, (1992) 27-50.
3. Cruz, J. and Barahona, P.: A Causal-Functional Model Applied to EMG Diagnosis, Proceedings of the 6th Conference on Artificial Intelligence in Medicine Europe, AIME'97, Springer, Grenoble, France (1997) 249-260.
4. Andreassen, S., Falck, B. and Olesen, K.G.: Diagnostic Function of the Microhuman Prototype of the Expert System MUNIN, Electroencephalography and Clinical Neurophysiology 85 (1992) 143-157.
5. Suojanen, M., Olesen, K.G. and Andreassen, S.: A Method for Diagnosing in Large Medical Expert Systems Based on Causal Probabilistic Networks, Proceedings of the 6th Conference on Artificial Intelligence in Medicine Europe, AIME'97, Springer, Grenoble, France (1997) 285-295.
6. Timmons, W.D.: Cardiovascular Models and Control. In: The Biomedical Engineering Handbook. CRC/IEEE Press, Connecticut (1995) 2386-2403.
7. Poon, C.-S.: Respiratory Models and Control. In: The Biomedical Engineering Handbook. CRC/IEEE Press, Connecticut (1995) 2404-2421.
8. Cobelli, C. and Saccomani, M.P.: Compartment Models of Physiologic Systems. In: The Biomedical Engineering Handbook. CRC/IEEE Press, Connecticut (1995) 2375-2385.
9. Aminoff M.J.: Electrodiagnosis in Clinical Neurology. 3th edn. Churchill Livingstone, New York (1992).
10. FitzHugh, R.: Mathematical models of excitation and propagation in nerve. In: Biological Engineering, chap I, McGraw-Hill, New York (1969) 1-85.
11. Tasaki, I.: Conduction of the Nerve Impulse. In: Handbook of Physiology, section I: Neurophysiology Vol. I. American Physiological Society, Washington (1959) 75-121.
12. Van Denneheuvel, S et al: Reduced Constraint Models. In: E. Keravnou, eds., Deep Models for Medical Knowledge Engineering, Elsevier, (1992) 89-100.
13. Cleary J.G.: Logical Arithmetic. In Future Generation Computing Systems, 2(2) (1987) 125-149.
14. Moore R.E.: Interval Analysis. Prentice-Hall, Englewood Cliffs, NJ (1966).
15. Benhamou, F., McAllester, D. and Van Hentenryck, P.: CLP(intervals) revisited. In Proceedings of the International Logic Programming Symposium (1994).
16. Haroud, D. and Faltings, B.: Consistency techniques for continuous constraints. In Constraints 1(1 and 2) (1996) 85-118.
17. Hartman, P.: Ordinary Differential Equations. Wiley, New York (1964).
18. Older, W.: Application of Relational Interval Arithmetic to Ordinary Differential Equations, in Workshop on Constraint Languages and their use in Problem Modelling, Int'l Logic Programming Symposium, Ithaca, New York (1994).
19. Deville, Y., Janssen, M. and Van Hentenryck, P.: Consistency Techniques in Ordinary Differential Equations. In: Proceedings of the 4th International Conference on Principles and Practice of Constraint Programming – CP98. Pisa, Italy (1998) 162-176.
20. Veloso, M. et al, ESTEEM: European Standardized Telematics Tool to Evaluate EMG Knowledge Based Systems and Methods, in Health in the New Communication Age, Laires, M.F., Ladeira, M.J. and Christensen, J.P. (Eds.), IOS Press, pp. 348-356, 1995

Neural Networks,
Causal Probabilistic Networks

A Decision Theoretic Approach to Empirical Treatment of Bacteraemia Originating from the Urinary Tract

Steen Andreassen[1], Leonard Leibovici[2], Henrik C. Schønheyder[3],
Brian Kristensen[3], Christian Riekehr[1], Anders Geill Kjær[1], and Kristian G. Olesen[1]

[1] Department of Medical Informatics and Image Analysis, Aalborg University, Denmark
sa@danablue.vision.auc.dk
[2] Department of Medicine B, Rabin Medical Center, Petah-Tiqua, Israel
leibovic@post.tau.ac.il
[3] Department of Clinical Microbiology, Aalborg Hospital, Aalborg, Denmark
bkr@danablue.vision.auc.dk

Abstract. Empirical antibiotic treatment with broad-spectrum antibiotics provides a high probability of covering treatment, but is associated with unnecessary costs as high drug prices, side-effects, and facilitated development of antibiotic resistance. A decision support system (DSS) based upon a causal probabilistic network (CPN) was constructed from a database with 491 cases (1992-94) of urosepticaemia and validated on 426 cases (1995-96). The CPN uses decision theory to balance the gain in life-years due to therapy against the costs of the antibiotic therapy, i.e. price, side-effects and ecological cost. The DSS selected antibiotics of an overall lower price, higher coverage and less ecological cost than the antibiotics actually chosen for empirical treatment. Thus, a DSS incorporating the CPN could achieve a desirable antibiotic policy, and it holds promise for improving empirical antibiotic therapy.

1   Introduction

When a clinician is faced with a decision on therapy, then the decision process can be seen as a two stage process. In the first stage the clinician must collect data describing the patient's condition, and in the second stage the data collected must be analysed to arrive at a decision on a therapy. In some cases the analysis of the data may be simple, but in many the analysis can be quite complex, requiring the clinician to draw on knowledge from many different areas. This process, seeing data in the light of knowledge, we refer to as intelligent data analysis.

Fig. 1 lists some of the types of knowledge that are required to arrive a medical decision. To make it concrete we shall focus at "bed-side decisions", decisions that have to be made with some urgency, and we shall use the treatment of bacteraemia with antibiotics as an example. The data available to the clinician when the decision about empirical antibiotic treatment must be made consists of signs, symptoms and laboratory data that confirms that the patient is septic, i.e. has an infection that has caused the patients condition to deteriorate severely. The treatment is called empirical, because it typically must be initiated before any microbiological evidence is available to help in the selection of antibiotic. To select an antibiotic, the first step

W. Horn et al. (Eds.): AIMDM'99, LNAI 1620, pp. 197-206, 1999.
© Springer-Verlag Berlin Heidelberg 1999

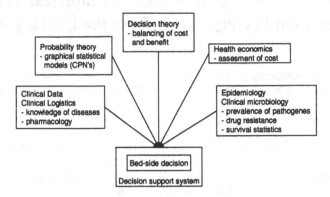

Fig. 1. Types of knowledge required to reach a balanced bed-side decision.

is to guess the identity of the pathogen. Here the clinician can only be guided by fairly soft data: underlying diseases and risk factors, such as surgery and prolonged hospital stay, along with symptoms indicating the source of the infection. Epidemiological knowledge about the prevalence of pathogens at the department combined with the clinical data and knowledge of probability theory will ideally allow the clinician to derive the probabilities for the infection being caused by a range of pathogens. Next the clinician has to make a prognosis, which to a large extent depends on whether the treatment is covering, i.e. if the pathogen infecting the patient is susceptible to the antibiotic used to treat the infection. Prognosis thus requires knowledge about the susceptibility of pathogens to different antibiotics at the department and about the survival statistics for patients receiving covering and non-covering therapy. Again with the use of probability theory, this information will allow the clinician to predict the probability of death, the case fatality rate.

In most cases it is possible to select antibiotics that give close to complete coverage. Clinical practice shows that this is not done, because the therapeutical benefits of antibiotic therapy must be balanced against the cost of the therapy. The clinician must take at least three components of cost into consideration: the cost of purchasing and administering the antibiotic, the cost incurred by side-effects of the antibiotic and the ecological cost. The ecological cost can be described as the cost borne by future patients due to reduced susceptibility of the pathogens to antibiotics. It is believed that the repeated use of an antibiotic, and in particular broad-spectrum antibiotics, gradually reduces the prevalence of pathogens susceptible to that antibiotic [1], and eventually this development of resistance will decrease the possibilities for effectively treating future patients. This type of assessment requires the clinician to be familiar with health economics as well as with the decision theoretical tools required to balance the benefits against the cost.

A clinician must carry out the reasoning outlined above within a fairly short time span, in most cases aided by a departmental or hospital-wide guideline for the use of antibiotics. In practice this process is only partially successful, in the sense that the antibiotic therapy selected is only covering in about 60% of the cases [2], [3], [4]. Medically this represents a problem, since the mortality is high, 20-42% [3], [5], [6] and is related to whether the empirical treatment is covering or not [3]. A Decision Support System (DSS) that could increase the coverage provided by empirical therapy would thus have considerable clinical interest, provided this could be achieved without excessive use of broad-spectrum antibiotics, which may facilitate the development of resistant bacteria [1].

Several DSSs have been designed to help clinicians choose antimicrobial therapy [7], [8], [9], [10], [11], and it seems that DSSs have the potential for markedly improving antibiotic therapy [10], [11], [12].

In this paper a new approach to empirical antibiotic therapy is explored. A DSS is constructed where statistical methods and in particular Causal Probabilistic Networks (CPNs) are used to perform the probabilistic calculations that may not be easy to do accurately as mental calculations.

2   Materials and Methods

During 1992-1994, 505 cases of urosepticaemia were identified at the Department of Clinical Microbiology at Aalborg Hospital. The Department of Clinical Microbiology provides clinical microbiological services to the hospitals of the County of Northern Jutland. Fourteen cases were excluded because of missing data, and 491 cases with 531 isolates were available for study. Of all pathogens, *Escherichia coli* made up 64%, *Klebsiella* spp. 12%, *Proteus* spp. 6%, *Citrobacter* spp. (including *Enterobacter* spp.) 4%, *Pseudomonas aeruginosa* 3%, *Enterococcus* spp. 3%, and other pathogens (including *Candida* spp.) 8%. These 491 cases were used as the derivation set, and a further 426 cases from 1995-1996 were used for validation.

Pathogens were classified into the above mentioned seven groups in order to determine their a priori probability (see Table 1) and for each group a logistic regression model was constructed.

Logistic regression models were chosen because they, like linear multiple regression, only have moderate demands on the number of cases in the database used to construct the equations. The models included 11 clinical variables given in Table 1, which have been shown previously to be independent predictors of bacteraemia [13], [14] and which were available to us. In each model the dependent variable was the infecting pathogen, e.g. *Proteus* spp. (yes/no), and the predictor variables were selected by stepwise backward elimination. In stepwise backward elimination, a model containing all predictor variables is constructed. Subsequently variables are eliminated from the model, one variable at a time using the likelihood ratio test [15]; the level of significance for not eliminating a variable was set to $p<0.15$, which was equivalent to $(\chi^2 >2.12$ (f=1). The odds-ratios for the predictor variables retained in the models are listed in Table 1. Thus, the probability (P) of e.g. *Proteus* spp. is as follows: $P/(1-P) = 0.04 * 1.86^{male} * 2.13^{chronic\ renal\ failure}$

The probabilities obtained for each of the seven pathogen groups were inserted as a priori probabilities in a causal probabilistic network (CPN) (see below).

Table 1. Odds ratios derived form the logistic regression models for the seven bacterial groups

	Escherichia coli (n=340)	Klebsiella spp. (n=65)	Proteus spp. (n= 30)	Citrobacter spp.[*] (n=22)	Pseudomonas aeruginosa (n=17)	Enterococcus spp. (n=16)	Other pathogens (n=41)
Intercept	11..33 (6.17-20.79)[b]	0.06 (0.03-0.1)	0.04 (0.02-0.08)	0.02 (0.006-0.04)	0.002 (0.0002-0.02)	0.009 (0.003-0.03)	0.04 (0.02-0.08)
Malignancy[c]	-	1.65 (0.88-3.08)	-	-	-	-	-
Male[c]	0.42 (0.27-0.67)	2.62 (1.43-4.79)	1.86 (0.83-4.18)	-	-	-	-
Age > 65 years[c]	0.61 (0.35-1.06)	-	-	-	3.88 (0.51-29.49)	-	-
Nosocomial infection[c]	0.38 (0.24-0.58)	-	-	2.39 (0.78-7.27)	8.78 (2.01-38.42)	3.25 (0.86-12.26)	2.69 (1.33-5.44)
Medical patient[c]	-	-	-	-	-	-	-
Stay in ICU[c]	0.30 (0.11-0.83)	2.84 (0.96-8.43)	-	4.51 (1.13-17.97)	-	-	4.30 (1.43-12.89)
Chronic renal failure[c]	0.26 (0.11-0.62)	3.04 (1.21-7.65)	2.1 (0.60-7.58)	-	-	-	-
Urinary tract surgery[c]	-	-	-	3.41 (1.3-8.95)	-	-	-
Urinary tract catheter[c]	0.60 (0.37-0.96)	-	-	-	-	3.64 (1.21-10.88)	-
Chronic liver disease[c]	-	-	-	-	-	-	-
Bedridden[c]	-	2.32 (0.95-5.63)	-	-	-	-	-

[*]This group included *Enterobacter* spp. (n=17). [b]95% confidence limits.
[c]The coded value was 1, if the variable was confirmed.

2.3 The Causal Probabilistic Network

CPNs make it possible to build highly structured stochastical models. A CPN is a graph, where the nodes in the graph represent stochastic variables and the directed edges represent conditional probabilities. The structure of the stochastic model is shown in Fig. 2, with the simplification that only three of the seven groups of pathogens in the model are shown.

In the graphical descriptions of the CPN we used the following unconventional abbreviations of bacterial names: Ecoli for *E. coli*, Citro for *Citrobacter* and *Enterobacter* spp., Kleb for *Klebsiella* spp. The dotted line from the box labelled REQ Ecoli implies that the probability of an *E. coli* infection, derived from the logistic regression equation, is used as the a priori probability in the node "Ecoli" in the CPN. The node "EradEcoli" indicates whether or not the patient harbours an *E. coli* infection after therapy has been initiated. The conditional probability table for "EradEcoli" in the bottom right corner of Fig. 2 specifies that the infection can be considered eradicated if the therapy covered *E. coli* ("CovEcoli" = yes) or if the patient never was infected by *E. coli* ("Ecoli" = no). It can be seen that the conditional probabilities in this case assumed only the values 0 or 1, which means that the conditional probabilities have degenerated into specifying "EradEColi" as a logical function of its "parent-nodes", "Ecoli" and "CovEcoli".

The CPN allows for combination therapy by assigning one antibiotic to the node "Treat1" and another antibiotic to the node "Treat2". The list of antibiotics in question is given in the upper right table in Fig. 2. Coverage for *E. coli* can therefore be obtained by the first antibiotic covering for *E. coli*, represented by the node "Cov1Ecoli", by the other antibiotic covering for *E. coli*, represented by "Cov2Ecoli", or by both. Therefore, the node "CovEcoli" has a conditional probability table that specifies it as the logical OR function of its parents, "Cov1Ecoli" and "Cov2Ecoli". Only combinations of gentamicin and one of the other antibiotics were tested.

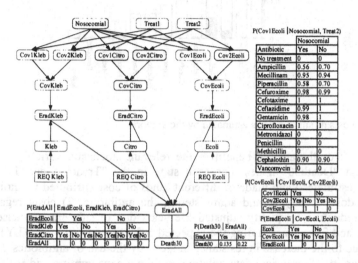

Fig. 2. Structure of the stochastic model. See text for explanation

The conditional probability table for "Cov1Ecoli" is given in the top right corner. It can be seen that the coverage depends on whether the infection was nosocomial or not. The conditional probability table for "Cov2Ecoli" is not given, but is identical to the table for "Cov1Ecoli".

The probability of covering the infection is indicated by "EradAll". The infection has been covered if all present pathogens have been covered, and the conditional probability table for "EradAll" is thus the logical AND function of its parents, "EradEcoli", "EradCitro" and "EradKleb". The last node in the CPN, "Death30", indicates the patient's risk of dying within 30 days after onset of the bacteraemic episode. Based on the case-database it was determined that the probability of death after 30 days was 22.0% for patients who had received non-covering antibiotic therapy, and 13.5% for patients who had received covering antibiotic therapy.

2.4 Costs

The intention was to use a decision theoretic approach to the selection of antibiotic therapy. The combination of logistic regression equations and the CPN described above permitted calculation of probabilities for all the stochastic variables. To convert this to decisions about antibiotic therapy it was necessary to assign utilities in the

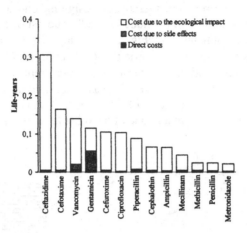

Fig. 3. The costs of antibiotics as estimated by the authors

form of cost or therapeutic benefit to the relevant stochastic variables, i.e. to the "Treat" and "Death30" nodes. For each state in the "Treat" nodes, i.e. for each antibiotic, estimates were made of different kinds of cost attributed to antibiotics: 1) costs per dose of buying and administering the antibiotic, 2) costs regarding the expected reduction in quality adjusted life-years due to side-effects caused by the antibiotic, and 3) costs regarding the expected reduction in life years (LY) of future patients due to the increase in resistance induced by the use of antibiotics. Due to the current scarcity of empirical data, relating antibiotic consumption and resistance, the calculation of ecological cost was based on a qualitative ranking, reflecting the current beliefs of the participating clinical microbiologists. As for many other medical decisions, considerations of economy and life-years form part of the decision. The subjective choice was made to equate one LY to 50,000 ECU. With this assumption the cost and the reductions in life-years can be plotted on the same axis and effectively constitute a "price list" for antibiotics (Fig. 3).

Estimated costs of combination therapy was based upon addition of cost for each antibiotic. The variable Death30 had an associated negative health benefit of 5 LY. This corresponds roughly to the average life-expectancy of patients with bacteraemia [3].

3   Results

The first question was to which extent the logistic regression equations could actually predict the presence of a given pathogen. Fig. 4 gives two cases where the probabilities of *E. coli* and *Klebsiella* spp. are substantially different.

For example, in Fig. 4A the probability of *Klebsiella* spp. has been reduced from the a priori probability of 12% to 6%, and in Fig. 4B the probability has been increased to 52%. These predictions are not strong, but suffice to make *Klebsiella* spp. either a consideration of minor importance or to bring it into consideration. The next step was to use the CPN to predict the effect of different therapies. Using the case from Fig. 4A as an example, Fig. 5A shows that treatment with ampicillin would have a 65.3% probability of eradicating the infection, which is associated with an estimated 16.4% risk of dying within 30 days. Fig. 5B shows that if a combination therapy consisting of ampicillin and gentamicin is used, the corresponding figures are 99.7% and 13.5% due to the improved coverage for *E. coli*.

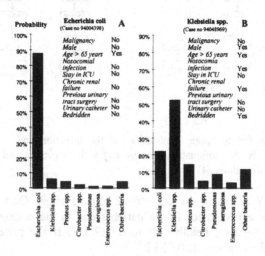

Fig. 4. The probabilities for pathogens calculated by the logistic regression equations for two cases.

The regression equations and the CPN were tested retrospectively as a decision support system. As a reference point we considered the empirical therapy that had actually been given to the patients (Fig. 6). Ampicillin was given in 138 cases as monotherapy and in a further 117 cases in combination with gentamicin. Other combinations of antibiotics, was given in 31 cases. Penicillin as monotherapy was given in 23 cases, cephalosporin in 16, and sulphonamides in 12. In 55 cases the patient did not receive any empirical antibiotic therapy. The results for the empirical therapy are summarised in the first line of Table 2. The coverage achieved by the empirical therapy was 60.8% (95% c.l.: 56.2-65.4). The coverage of 60.8% was achieved by purchasing and administering drugs that on average have a price of 219 ECU per patient. Using the probabilities of death in the derivation set, it can also be calculated that the 60.8% coverage gives a 16.8% probability of death within 30 days of the bacteraemic episode, which was not significant different from the observed death-rate of 14.3% ($\chi^2 = 1.1$ (f=1), $p = 0.30$). While these numbers can be calculated from the case database, the numbers in the remaining columns depend on the assumptions stated in Material and Methods. With the assumption of a life-expectancy of 5 years, it can be seen that the average loss of life-years of an episode of bacteraemia to a patient receiving empirical antibiotic therapy is 0.840 LY.

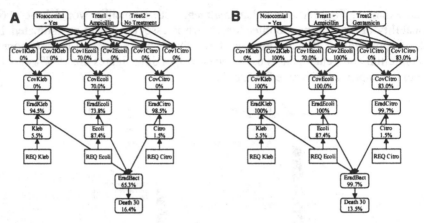

Fig. 5. Probabilities for coverage, eradication of the infection and death within 30 days calculated by the CPN. A combination therapy (*B*) with ampicillin and gentamicin is more effective than ampicillin alone (*A*)

A further 0.018 LY is lost due to side-effects of the therapy. On top of that a cost of 0.071 LY must be expected for future patients due to the ecological effects of the therapy, bringing the total health cost to 0.929 LY. If the price of the antibiotic therapy is added, the total cost is 0.933 LY.

Table 2. Predicted financial and health impact of the different antibiotic policies

Antibiotic policy	Coverage (%)	30 days mortality[b] (%)	Loss of life-years (LY)	Side-effects (LY)	Ecology (LY)	Total health cost (LY)	Price of drugs (ECU)	Total cost (LY)
			------------ Average costs per episode[a] -------------					
Empirical	60.8	16.8	0.840	0.018	0.071	0.929	219	0.933
Max. coverage	96.0	13.8	0.690	0.068	0.180	0.938	373	0.945
Minimum cost	86.4	14.7	0.735	0.020	0.05	0.805	207	0.809

[a]See text for details. [b]The average of the calculated probabilities of death within 30 days associated with the antibiotic therapy proposed by the DSS. The figures are based upon numbers from the derivation set

If the DSS was asked to maximise coverage, it did this by suggesting a combination therapy with gentamicin and vancomycin for all patients. These suggestions yielded a coverage of 96.0%. Although the expected 30-days mortality would be lower than for the original empirical therapy, the corresponding expected costs more than doubled due to side-effects and ecological cost (Table 2). This made the total health cost for this maximum coverage policy (0.938 LY) larger than the total health cost of the empirical therapy currently given (0.929 LY). The total cost which also includes the price of the antibiotics (373 ECU) is also higher (0.945 LY) for the maximum coverage policy than for the empirical therapy currently given. Applying the price list in Fig. 3, the system was requested to minimise total cost. As shown in the right panel in Fig. 6 this minimum cost policy mainly resulted in monotherapies with mecillinam as the most frequent choice (58.9% of all cases), followed by gentamicin (34.7%) and ciprofloxacin (2.6%). The coverage was 86.4%. The expected 30-days mortality was somewhat lower than for the empirical therapy, as given in the Table 2.

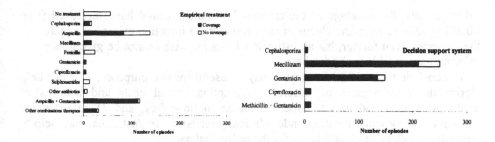

Fig. 6. Usage of antibiotics for the empirical treatment and as proposed by the decision support system when requested to minimise total cost. For each antibiotic, or combination thereof, the number of cases receiving the antibiotic is shown. The bar giving the number of cases is divided into a filled part showing the number of cases where the antibiotic is covering and an open part, showing the number of cases where the antibiotic is not covering

Furthermore, the projected costs due to side-effects were at the same level as for the empirical therapy, and the projected ecological costs were lower. Both total health cost (0.805 LY) and total cost (0.809 LY) were considerably lower than for the other two policies.

4 Discussion

In the decision support system described above, knowledge from a number of areas was incorporated, using mainly a CPN to represent knowledge. The decision support system performed an "intelligent" analysis of the data describing the patient's condition, drawing on the knowledge in the system.

Retrospective testing on a case database of patients with urosepticaemia indicated that this approach may be useful. The most striking observation is that the decision theoretic approach can accurately select a therapeutic policy. When the DSS was requested to minimise total cost, it achieved this by selecting antibiotics with a lower price, higher coverage and lower ecological cost, thus providing potential health benefits both to present and future patients. The DSS did not suggest combination therapies. This is most likely due to our assumption of adding the ecological costs of each antibiotic, when giving combination therapy. This assumption probably does not fit all kinds of combination therapies as it has been suggested e.g. that a combination of a beta-lactam antibiotic and an aminoglycoside gives a lower frequency of resistance among enteric Gram-negative rods than aminoglycosides alone [16]. We are aware of the subjective nature of this price list, but the list is valid in the sense that it reflected our current beliefs.

When assessing the extent of the improvement of coverage from 60.8% to 86.4%, it must be remembered that the DSS had two advantages, compared to the clinician who instituted the empirical therapy. The DSS knew that the patient had a positive blood culture and that the focus of the infection was the urinary tract. Knowledge of a positive blood culture would most likely have caused the group of patients who received either sulphonamides or no empirical antibiotic therapy (16%) to be treated more aggressively. Had these patients been treated with a success rate comparable to other patients, the coverage of the empirical treatment would have increased from 60.8% to 72%. Certain knowledge of the source of the infection might have increased the coverage even further, but an estimate of this increase cannot be given based on information available in the database.

We conclude that a DSS of this type may be useful for two purposes: 1) it can help clarify the consequences of different assumptions about costs and benefits of antibiotic therapy and thus to ascertain an antibiotic policy, and 2) an expanded version of the system, operating under clinically realistic circumstances, may help to optimise the selection of antibiotics for the individual patient.

References

1. McGowan, J.E. Jr.: Antimicrobial resistance in hospitals organisms and its relation to antibiotic use. Rev. Infect. Dis. 5 (1983) 1033-1048
2. Bryan, C.S., Reynolds, K.L. Brenner, E.R.: Analysis of 1,186 episodes of gram-negative bacteraemia in non-university hospitals: the effect of antimicrobial therapy. Rev. Infect. Dis. 5 (1983) 629-638
3. Leibovici, L., Samra, Z., Konisberger, H., Drucker, M., Ashkenazi, S. Pitlik, S.D.: Long-term survival following bacteremia or fungemia. JAMA 274 (1995) 807-812
4. Schønheyder, H.C., Højbjerg, T.: The impact of the first notification of positive blood cultures on antibiotic therapy. APMIS 103 (1995) 37-44
5. Weinstein, M.P., Murphy, J.R., Reller, L.B., Lichtenstein, K.A.: The clinical significance of positive blood-cultures: A comprehensive analysis of 500 episodes of bacteremia and fungemia in adults. Rev. Infect. Dis. 5 (1983) 54-70
6. Pedersen, G., Schønheyder, H.C.: Patients with bacteraemia dying before notification of positive blood cultures: A 3-year clinical study. Scand. J. Infect. Dis. 29 (1997) 169-173
7. Shortliffe, E: Computer-based Medical Consultations: MYCIN. North-Holland, New York (1976)
8. Deutsch, T., Carson, E., Ludwig, E.: Dealing with medical knowledge. Plenum Pres, New York (1994)
9. Dybowski, R., Gransden, W.R., Phillips, I.: Towards a statistically oriented decision support system for the management of septicaemia. Artif. Intell. Med. 5 (1993) 489-502
10. Pestotnik, S.L, Classen, D.C., Evans, R.S., Burke, J.P.: Implementing antibiotic practice guidelines through computer-assisted decision support: clinical and financial outcomes. Ann. Int. Med. 124 (1996) 884-890
11. Leibovici, L., Konisberger, H., Pitlik, S.D., Samra, Z., Drucker, M.: Predictive index for optimizing empiric treatment of Gram-negative bacteremia. J. Infect. Dis. 163 (1991) 193-196
12. Leibovici, L., Gitelman V., Yehezkelli Y., Poznanski O., Milo G., Paul M., Ein D.P.: Improving empirical antibiotic treatment: Prospective, non-intervention testing of a decision support system. Journal of Internal Medicine, 242 (1997) 395-400
13. Leibovici, L. Greenshtain, S., Cohen, O., Mor, F., Wysenbeek, A.J.: Bacteremia in febrile patients: a clinical model for diagnosis. Arch. Intern. Med. 151 (1991) 1801-1806
14. Leibovici, L. Greenshtain, S., Cohen, O., Wysenbeek, A.J.: Toward improved empiric management of moderate to severe urinary tract infections. Arch. Intern. Med. 152 (1992) 2481-2486
15. Hosmer, D.W., Lemeshow, S.: Applied logistic regression. Wiley, New York, (1989)
16. Péchère, J.-C.: Antibiotic resistance is selected primarily in our patients. Infect. Control. Hosp. Epidemiol. 15 (1994) 472-477

An ECG Ischemic Detection System Based on Self-Organizing Maps and a Sigmoid Function Pre-processing Stage

E.A. Fernandez[1], J. Presedo[2], and S. Barro[2]

[1] Favaloro University, Buenos Aires, and Nat.Univ. of EntreRios, Argentina
[2] University of Santiago de Compostela, Spain

Abstract. The detection of ischemia from the electrocardiogram is a time-consuming visualization task requiring the full attention of the physician.This task may become inviable when many patients have to be monitored, for example in an Intensive Coronary Care Unit.

In order to automate the detection process and minimize the number of misclassified episodes we propose the use of an Artificial Neural Net (the Self-Organizing Map - SOM) along with the use of extra parameters (not only ST segment and T wave deviation) measured from the ECG record. The SOM is a widely used Neural Network which has the ability to handle a large number of attributes per case and to represent these cases in clusters defined by possession of similar characteristics.

In this work we propose a three-block ischemic detection system. It consists of a pre-processing block, a SOM block and a timing block. For the pre-processing block we use the sigmoid function as a smoothing stage in order to eliminate the intrinsic oscillation of the signals. The SOM block is the ischemic detector and the timing block is used to decide if the SOM output meets the ischemic duration criteria.

With this strategy, 83.33% of the ischemic episodes (over 7 records) tested were successfully detected, and the timing block proved to be robust to noisy signals, providing reliability in the detection of an ischemic episode. The system could be useful in an Intensive Coronary Care Unit because it will allow a large number of patients to be monitored simultaneously detecting episodes when they actually occur. It will also permit visualisation of the evolution of the patient's response to therapy.

1 Introduction

Coronary ischemia is one of the consequences of atherosclerosis, a pathology which is frequently found in the industrialised world. It has a serious economic impact if undetected at an early stage or if left untreated.

Coronary ischemia usually appears in the left ventricle when myocardial oxygen demand cannot be supplied by coronary artery blood flow. If this situation occurs for a period of time the myocardium can suffer electrical alterations and/or loss of functional muscle mass (myocardial infarction). The detection of an ischemic episode is therefore crucial in order to initiate therapy as early as possible.

W. Horn et al. (Eds.): AIMDM'99, LNAI 1620, pp. 207–216, 1999.
© Springer-Verlag Berlin Heidelberg 1999

Detection of ischemia is usually a visualization task performed by physicians who look for ST segment and/or T wave deviations in the electrocardiogram (ECG). This is not an easy task in an Intensive Coronary Care Unit (ICCU) where various patients must be monitored simultaneously and continuously.

To automate this task, different approaches have been taken in the Artificial Intelligence field, most of them only use the usual ECG parameters (ST segment and/or T wave deviation) in the detection process [6,8,9,10,17,20]. In previous work we showed that the QRS waves information can be used in the ischemia analysis. We also showed that Self-Organizing Maps are useful tools in the detection of ischemic process [2,3]. The Self-Organizing Map (SOM) is an Artificial Neural Network (ANN) model developed by Teuvo Kohonen [1]. This ANN has nodes arranged in a one or two-dimensional array which through an unsupervised learning algorithm represents input space characteristics as a topologically ordered map, where zones or clusters in the map (output space) represent similarities in the input space. This ANN is trained with a training set extracted from different ECG records. Each input vector has 12 parameters measured from the ECG signal. These parameters represent ventricular electrical activity and will be described in section 2.1. After the training stage, the SOM ANN is used as an ischemic detector that can be integrated into an appropriate information system in order to detect automatically ischemic episodes on ECG records.

2   Material and Methods

2.1   The Input Data

Myocardial ischemia is most likely to appear in the left ventricle, so its effects on the ECG record can be seen in the QRS complex, the ST segment and the T wave since they represent ventricular electrical activity. When ischemic episode detection from ECG records is attempted, the usual parameters analyzed are the ST segment and T wave evolution over time [6,8,9,10,17,20]. In the European ST-T Data Base (EDB)[11] a multinational group of cardiologists made the following definition of an ischemic episode:

Definition 1.

- The absolute value of the deviation of the ST segment (T wave) relative to the isoelectric reference value must be more than one (ST) or two (T) millimeters $\{0.1(0.2)mV\}$.
- This change must be maintained for at least 30 sec.
- For two episodes to be considered different, the interval between them must be at least 30 sec.

In order to diminish the number of false positives and false negatives, and to detect those episodes that have no clear bearing on the deviation of the ST segment and T wave, we use not only ST and T wave deviations but also other ECG parameters such as Q wave height, R wave height, S wave height and

ST segment slope (STsl). All these parameters are measured beat to beat from two leads of the ECG and each of these parameters constitutes a time series called a Trend Diagram (TD). These TDs are interpolated, sampled at 1Hz and smoothed with an averaging filter. The TDs are time-dependent signals, so for each instant in time we have a time parametric vector as follows:

$$X(t) = \{Q_0(t), Q_1(t), R_0(t), R_1(t), S_0(t), S_1(t), STs_0(t), \qquad (1)$$
$$STs_1(t), T_0(t), T_1(t), STsl_0(t), STsl_1(t)\}$$

Where 0 and 1 mean $lead0$ and $lead1$ respectively. This parametric vector (after normalisation) will be used to feed the SOM net.

2.2   Pre-processing the Input Data

The TDs are normalised to achieve independence from the record which origi- nated them, and to represent the data on the same shared scale. To do this we propose a new normalization method using a sigmoid function.

$$x_i(t) = \frac{1}{1 + e^{|p_i(t) - \bar{p}| - th_i}} \qquad (2)$$

Where $x_i(t)$ is the normalised parameter i ($i : Q_k, R_k, S_k, STs_k, T_k, STsl_k$; $k : lead0, lead1$), $p_i(t)$ the measured parameter, $\bar{p}_i$ its mean value and th_i is the threshold for parameter i .The th_i parameter is selected under the following assumptions:

Taking into account the ischemic episode definition (Definition 1), we set the thresholds to $0.1mV$ and $0.2mV$ for STs and T respectively. To establish the threshold for the other parameters we assume that TDs have a Gaussian distribution of their values [3,2], so 95.4% of them lie in the $[\bar{p} \pm 2\sigma]$ inter- val and every value outside this interval, is then, interpreted as a "variant value" or as an "abnormal value". Under this assumption we set th_j ($j = Q_0, Q_1, R_0, R_1, S_0, S_1, STsl_0, STsl_1$) to $2\sigma_j$ (standard deviation of parameter j). σ_j was calculated from the first 7 minutes of the corresponding record that, we suppose, are free from ischemic edpisodes.

This kind of normalisation gives us a very uniform signal without significant oscillations, which means a good signal-noise ratio (Figure 1).

2.3   The Training Set

We randomly chose a set of records from the European ST-T Database (EDB), and we manually extracted different ischemic and normal segments from these records. The ischemic segments were checked with the ischemic episode informa- tion available on EDB. The records and segments listed in Table 1 were chosen. In this set, we tried to achieve a wide range of different episodes according to the information on EDB.

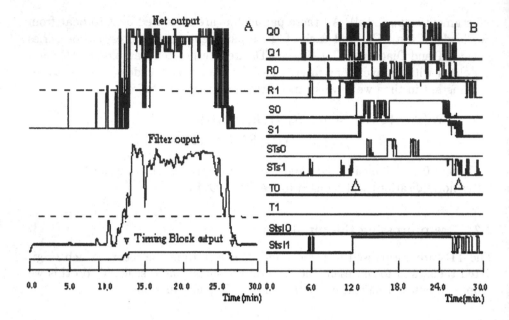

Fig. 1. Panel A shows the different outputs from the from the net in response to the normalized Trend Diagram shown in Panel B. In B an EDB marked episode is shown. Panel A plots a winning node position against time. In the upper two traces together with the threshold node. The detected episode is shown between Δ symbols.

Table 1. Files and time intervals (minutes) selected to build the trainig set

File	Time interval	File	Time interval
E0106	(68-84)	E0154	(31-36)
E0108	(30-50) (60-67)	E0163	(35-42) (113-117)
E0112	(10-20)	E0203	(50-65)
E0123	(79-94)	E0204	(44-55)
E0129	(45-53)	E0211	(14-52)

2.4   The Net

The Self-Organising Map is a widely used ANN model that creates a representation of a high-dimensional input space through an unsupervised learning [5]. The representation has the form of a one-dimensional or two-dimensional array of nodes (map). Each node, after training, is characterised both by its position in the array and by its vector value known as its "codebook " vector. The codebook vectors of each node are compared to any new input vector (new case) using the Euclidean distance between them in order to decide which node corresponds most closely to the new case. The node which corresponds most closely with the new case is considered the "winning" node [1]. SOMs allows us to handle a great amount of information (number of parameters) without an excessive increment in problem complexity. In addition this automatic process reduces problem dimensionality, making the detection of the ischemic episodes much easier than in the case of direct interpretation of the ECG record. The unsupervised learning of the SOM is very appropriate in this problem because we use others parameters in addition to those which are included in the ischemic episode definition (Definition 1). This allows us to reveal any role played by these extra parameters [2], which would not have been possible if we had used a ANN with supervised learning. The SOM structure also preserves the information on the vector weights in the same form as in the input space where as supervised learning ANN does not. Another advantage of SOM is the use of the winning position as output, because it is possible to associate the relative position of the winning node in the net structure to either an ischemic episode or a normal situation in the patient.

In the present study we use a one-dimensional SOM and we follow the winning position over time to detect an ischemic episode. We trained different net sizes with a linear learning rate coefficient and a Gaussian neighborhood, using the SOM_PACK software package [4] and an in-house MS-Windows 95® SOM training software (still under development).

In the initial phase, different one-dimensional arrays were tested to see which of them showed the best order in their vector weights. From this, we chose the 1x15 nodes net (15NN) and 1x18 nodes net (18NN) to be used in the testing stage. As mentioned above, we followed the winning position over time to detect an ischemic episode, so we needed to identify those nodes which map an ischemic episode and those which map a normal situation on the ECG record. We made a distance map and an energy map ($energy = \sum_{j=1}^{n} w_{ij}^2$ where w_{ij} means j-th attribute of the i-th node and N is the input dimension) so that can identify two clusters with a transition zone. Modelling the net as an 1D array from 1 to k nodes, we found that those nodes positioned from 1 to 5 (1 to 7) in the 15NN (18NN) have lower energy and they were labeled the "normal interval", and the nodes from 10 to 15 (12 to 18) were labeled the "ischemic interval" because they have greater energy than the others. The node number 8 for the 15NN and 10 for 18NN were chosen as the limits between the two zones because they showed the best results in the detection process.

To select the winner position we use the following formulae:

$$wp(t) = outputnet(X(t)) = \arg\min_i \{|X(t) - W_i|\}$$

were $X(t) \in R^n$ is the input vector as described in section 2.1, $i : 1..k$, $wp(t) \in R$ is the winner position, $W_i \in R^n$ the vector weight of the node "i", and to detect an ischemic episode we made the following definition

Definition 2.

– The winner position ($wp(t)$) should lie beyond the normal interval.
– The first must be maintained for at least 30 sec.

- For two episodes to be considered different, the interval between them must be at least 30 sec.

Figure 1 shows the net's output signal, where it is seen that, sometimes, it is a very noisy signal because it is oscillating between both intervals. In order to have a more stable signal and to facilitate inspection by the physician, we post-process the net's output in two different ways. In the first case we use a recursive low pass filter with the following characteristics: According to definition 1 and 2, a minimal ischemic episode is a 30 second abnormal signal separated from the next episode by 30 seconds, so we can imagine an episode as a periodic signal with a minimal period of 60 seconds. A second order Butterworth low pass filter was designed with a cutoff frequency at 0.02Hz $\left(\frac{1}{50}\right)$ (to filter the signal with out appreciable distortion at 60Hz), achieving the transfer function formulae:

$$H(z) = \frac{y[z]}{wp[z]} = \frac{0.00431416 + 0.00862831 \cdot z^{-1} + 0.00431416 \cdot z^{-2}}{1.19421 - 2.17695 \cdot z^{-1} + 1.0 \cdot z^{-2}} \quad (3)$$

where wp is the net 's output and y is the filter output.

This kind of post-processing strategy gives a smoother net output as seen in Figure 1 A.

The other post-processing strategy (called a "*timing block*") is quite simple and gives us better results. It consists of measuring the time over which the $wp(t)$ is in the ischemic interval, so:

$$y[0] = 0 \quad (4)$$
$$y[n] = y[n-1] + 1/28 \text{ if } wp[n] > 8 \ \{\text{for the 15NN }\} \quad (5)$$
$$y[n] = 1 \text{ if } y[n] \geq 1 \quad (6)$$
$$y[n] = y[n-1] - 2.5/28 \text{ if } wp[n] < 8 \ \{\text{for the 15NN}\} \quad (7)$$
$$y[n] = 0 \text{ if } y[n] \leq 0 \quad (8)$$

where condition 6 means an ischemic episode and condition 8 means a normal ECG. In equation 5 value 28 means that $y[n] = 1$ after 28 secs., and ratio $\frac{2.5}{28}$ was selected for both robustness to noise inputs and for speed to the end of a detected episode.

As you can see this algorithm is much simpler, faster and visually better than the other. Figure 1 A shows the output of this strategy.

3   Results

All the training sessions were faster (from one to five minutes on a PC Pentium® 120MHz under MS-Windows® 95 and 16 Mbytes RAM) even more so when the net was used as a detector. We randomly chose 7 records from the European ST-T Database (EDB) (listed in table 2), which were not included in the training set, to evaluate the nets. In these records we have 30 ischemic episodes marked by the EDB. All the Trend Diagrams (TD) were pre-processed as stated in sections 2.1 and 2.2. After that they were processed by the SOM net and the output (winning position over time "$wp(t)$") was post-processed by the "*timing block*" and by the "*filter block*" as seen in figure 2. The upper limit of the normal interval was modelled as a threshold node.

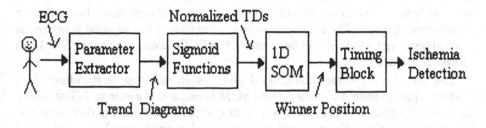

Fig. 2. System Block Diagram of the Ischemic Detector

The detection performance was tested with the EDB ischemic episode information, where the beginning and end of each episode in the records are seen. Those files chosen to train the net were excluded in the validation process. We use the definitions proposed by Jager et al. in [14] to measure the performance of our algorithms. In this work, the interested reader can find the "matching" and "overlapping" criteria for ischemic detection and Sensivity (Se) and Positive Predictivity (+P) measures of performance. Only the "*timing block*" results will be presented because they are the best. The results can be seen in Table 2. The filtered strategy shows lower results than the "*timing block*" in the majority of the cases.

Table 2. Records used to test the nets, TP: True Positive, FP : False Positive, Se : Sensivity, +P : Positive Predictivity

Record	No. of episodes	15NN with timing block TP	FN	FP	Se	+P
e0107	5	5	0	1	100	83.33
e0113	11	7	4	3	63.63	70
e0151	4	4	0	1	100	80
e0202	3	3	0	2	100	60
e0204	2	2	0	4	100	33.33
e0305	2	1	1	1	50	50
e0607	3	3	0	0	100	100
Total	30	25	5	12		
Gross					83.33	67.56
Average					87.66	68.09

4   Conclusions

The sigmoid function seems to be very useful for pre-processing because it gives a good signal-noise ratio and eliminates intrinsic oscillations of state. This is the first time we have employed threshold selection and we feel that more work should be done on this in order to select deviation levels related to an ischemic episode for those parameters not included in the clinical definition 1. The sigmoid function is a very common function in the Neural Network field, but not as a pre-processing stage. The next step in the validation of the sigmoid function as a pre-processing technique will be to check the ECG records where the SOM has a lower performance.

The use of a one-dimensional SOM gives us an easier understanding of an ischemic episode than a bi-dimensional SOM because it is easier to follow a one-dimensional signal over time than a map-trajectory over time. Furthermore, the classification of the different zones (ischemic and normal zones) is simpler and the limits between the different zones easier to recognize.

Many authors handle the ischemic detection problem taking into account only the ST information and all their results are based on detecting ST segment deviations related to ischemic episodes [6,7,8,9,10,15,17,20]. Taddei et al.[13] proposed the use of others parameters such as ST segment slope and ST segment area, Reddy et al.[16] made use of the QRS information detecting Anterior myocardial infarction and Tachor et at [18] shows enhancement of QRS amplitude working with dogs. Our approach tries to handle the detection of ischemic episodes despite their origin. The EDB only gives us the chance to validate performance in the detection of ST and T episodes, so all the results should be analyzed with this in mind. More studies should be made in the interrelation between the QRS information and ischemic episodes in order to achieve a better understanding of myocardial ischemic process.

Our results are comparable with those shown in others works and a validation over all the EDB records should be made to make an exhaustive comparison with the results showed by Jager et al.[20] Laguna et al.[17] and Taddei et al.[13,21]. The main advantage of our work is that from one training of the net it is possible to analyze a wide range of records. It is also possible to implement all the system in-line. The system seems to be robust to noise inputs, especially with the "*timing block*" as seen in figure 1 A where the net's output oscillates and the output of the timing block does not. This improves the detection process, suggesting that it would not be necessary to filter the Trend Diagrams.

The system could be useful in an Intensive Coronary care Unit because it will allow a large number of patients to be monitored simultaneously detecting episodes where they actually occurs, and it will also permit visualisation of the evolution of the patient's response to therapy via the system (pre-processing; net-processing and timing block) output.

Many authors suggest limitations on EDB and have begun to develop new databases for ischemia analysis[15,12]. Aside from that it is necessary to further investigate the relationship between ischemic episodes and QRS waves. The last obstacle is the one with the most difficulties in the evaluation of the methodology proposed in this work.

Acknowledgements

This study was partially supported by grant BID802/OC-AR-PICT N°05-00000-00667 of the Argentina Government.

The authors wish to thank Dr. Peter Willshaw for his help with the manuscript and Mrs.M.E. Torres for the use of her laboratory.

References

1. T. Kohonen, Self-Organizing Maps, Springer, Second Edition, 1987
2. E.A. Fernández, B. Drozdowicz, J. Presedo, S. Barro, "Self-Organizing Neural Network Approach in Ischaemic Detection on ECG Records", Proc. EIS'98, pp.243-249
3. J. Presedo, E.A. Fernández, J. Vila, S. Barro, "Cycles on ECG Parameter Evolution during Ischaemic Episodes", Comp.in Card.1996, pp. 489-492
4. T. Kohonen, J. Kangas, J. Laaksonen, "SOM_PACK, The Self-Organizing map program package" Available via anonymous ftp at cochlea.hut.fi (130.233.168.48), 1992
5. S.L. Joutsiniemi , S. Kaski , T.A. Larsen, "A Self-Organising Map in Recognition of Topographic Patterns of EEG Spectra" IEEE Trans. on Biom. Eng., 42(11), Nov. 1995
6. J. Presedo, J. Vila, S. Barro, F. Palacios, R. Ruiz, A. Taddei, M. Emdim, "Fuzzy Modelling of the Expert's Knowledge in ECG-based Ischaemia Detection", Fuzzy Sets and Systems, 1996, pp.63-75
7. F. Badilini, M. Marri, J. Benhorim, A.J. Moss, "Beat To Beat Quantification and Analysis of ST segment Displacement from Holter ECGs: A New Approach To Ischemic Detection", Comp. in Card., 1992, pp.179-182
8. T. Stamkopoulos, M. Strintzis, C. Pappas, N. Maglaveras, "One-Laed Ischemia Detection Using a New Backpropagation Algorithm and The European ST-T Database", Comp. in Card., 1992, pp.663-666
9. K.I. Diamantaras, T. Stamkopoulos, N. Maglaveras, M. Strintzis, "ST Segment Nonlinear Principal Components Analysis for Ischemia Detection", Comp. in Card., 1996, pp.493-496
10. T. Stamkopoulos, N. Maglaveras, K.I. Diamantaras, M. Strintzis, "Ischemia Clasification Techniques Using an Advanced Neural Network Algorithm", Comp. in Card., 1997, pp.351-354
11. A. Taddei, A. Biagini, G. Distante, M. Emdin, M.G. Mazzei, P. Pisani,N. Roggero, M. Varinini, R.G. Mark, G.B. Moody, L. Braaksma, C. Zeelenberg, C. Marchesi, "The European ST-T Database : Development, Distribution and Use", Comp. in Card., 1991, pp.177-180
12. A. Taddei, M. Emdin, M. Varinini, G. Nassi, M. Bertinelli, C. Carpeggiani, E. Picano, C. Marchesi, "A new Cardiovascular Signal Database for Assessing Methods for Analysis of Ischemic Heart Disease", Comp. in Card., 1996, pp.497-500
13. A. Taddei, M. Varanini,, A. Macerata, M. Emdim, C. Marchesi, "Detection of Ischemic Episodes Through Principal Component Analysis", Biotelemetry XII, 1992, pp.77-84

216   E.A. Fernandez, J. Presedo, and S. Barro

14. F. Jager, G.B. Moody, A. Taddei, R.G. Mark, "Performance Measures for Algorithms to Detect Transient Ischemic ST Segment Changes", Comp. in Card., 1992, pp.369–372
15. F. Jager, G.B. Moody, A. Taddei, G. Antolic, M. Zabukovec, M. Skrjanc, M. Emdim, R.G. Mark, "Development of a Long Term Database for Assessing the Performance of Transient Ischemia Detectors", Comp. in Card., 1996, pp.481–488
16. M.R.S. Reddy, L. Edenbrandt, J. Svensson, W.K. Haisty, O. Pahlm, "Neural Network versus Electrocardiographer and Conventional Computer Criteria in Diagnosis Anterior Infarct from the ECG", Comp. in Card., 1992, pp.667–670
17. P. Laguna, G.B. Moody, R. Mark, "Analysis of the Cardiac Repolarization Period Using the KL Transform: Application on the ST-T Database", Comp. in Card., 1994, pp.233–236
18. N. Thacor, B. Gramatikov, M. Mita, " Multiresolution Wavelet Analysis of ECG During Ischemia and Reperfusion", Comp. in Card., 1993, pp.893–898
19. J. Vila, J. Presedo,M. Delgado, S. Barro, R. Ruiz, F. Palacios, "SUTIL: Intelligent ischemia monitoring system" Int.J. of Med. Informatics, 47,193–214, 1997.
20. F. Jager, R. Mark, G.B. Moody, S. Divjak, "Analysis of Transient ST Segment Changes During Ambulatory Monitoring Using the Karhunen-Loeve Transform", Comp. in Card., 1992, pp.691–694
21. A. Taddei, G. Costantino, R. Silipo, M. Emdim, C. Marchesi, "A System for the Detection of Ischemic Episodes in Ambulatory ECG", Comp. in Card., 1995, pp.705–708

Neural Network Recognition of Otoneurological Vertigo Diseases with Comparison of Some Other Classification Methods

Martti Juhola[1], Jorma Laurikkala[1], Kati Viikki[1], Yrjö Auramo[1], Erna Kentala[2], and Ilmari Pyykkö[3]

1 Department of Computer Science, University of Tampere. P.O. Box 607, Tampere, Finland
2 Department of Otorhinolaryngology, Helsinki University Central Hospital, Finland
3 Department of Otorhinolaryngology, Karolinska Hospital, Stockholm, Sweden

Abstract. We have studied computer-aided diagnosis of otoneurological diseases which are difficult, even for experienced specialists, to determine and separate from each other. Since neural networks require plenty of training data, we restricted our research to the commonest otoneurological diseases in our database and to the very most essential parameters used in their diagnostics. According to our results, neural networks can be efficient in the recognition of these diseases provided that we shall be able to add our available cases concerning those diseases which are rare in our database. We compared the results yielded by neural networks to those given by discriminant analysis, genetic algorithms and decision trees.

1 Introduction

Otoneurology considers diseases that affect the function of the inner ear and some certain parts of the brain associated with hearing and equilibrium of a human. These diseases or disorders involving vertigo are frequent, not only for elderly people. Their diagnostics are difficult even for specialized otologists. Recently, we constructed an expert system [1-11] for their computer-aided diagnosis. In order to promote such research it is useful to compare the results produced with different methods. As a matter of fact, to further increase the accuracy of the correct decisions made by the expert systems we could enlarge it by combining several decision making techniques to facilitate and verify decisions in difficult cases.

At the beginning, we constructed the expert system called ONE [1-11] by using a kind of intelligent scoring system where the determination of the most plausible disease was executed by a technique somewhat resembling the nearest neighbour search in pattern recognition. This expert system consists of 17 diseases or disorders, but some of them are very rare and some quite rare in the case database of the expert system. It would be impossible to try to discover such diseases by using neural networks that definitely presuppose an abundant training set of cases. Thus, we chose the six most frequent diseases from the database for the current study. These diseases

W. Horn et al. (Eds.): AIMDM'99, LNAI 1620, pp. 217-226, 1999.

are Meniere's disease, vestibular schwannoma, benign positional vertigo, vestibular neuritis, traumatic vertigo, and sudden deafness [5-11].

Neural networks are a frequently utilized method in the classification of medical and other applications as well as in other areas. We are interested also in other machine learning techniques, especially in genetic algorithms and decision trees that we investigate in connection with medical informatics [12-15]. The former techniques are, for the present, seldom applied to medical problems, but the latter is already "traditional". In addition, we employed a well-known statistical method, i.e. discriminant analysis which is functionally and theoretically straightforward and clear.

2 The Six Otoneurological Diseases and Vertiginous Patients

First, we specify the six diseases involved [9,10]. The definition of Meniere's disease varies which affects reported incidences. Commonly, vertigo, hearing loss and tinnitus are supposed to be premises for it. Sudden deafness or progressive hearing loss and unilateral tinnitus are typical symptoms in vestibular schwannoma. Its some properties sometimes resemble those occurred in Meniere's disease. In general, Meniere's disease is known to be hard for otologists to verify reliably and its etiology is still open, even if it is frequent; its complicated detection will later be perceived also from our results. Benign positional vertigo is common for the elderly, females in particular. Vestibular neuritis includes clinical symptoms and signs such as acute unilateral loss of vestibular function without simultaneous hearing loss. Infections and vascular or immune-mediated disorders are mentioned as its etiological factors. Traumatic vertigo consists of various peripheral labyrinthine or central vestibular disorders when symptoms begin immediately after a head injury. Symptoms and signs of sudden deafness vary and, therefore, it is often difficult to distinguish from the other disorders.

We collected data of more than 1000 patients to our database at the vestibular laboratory of the Department of Otorhinolaryngology, in Helsinki University Central Hospital, Finland. Information about the clinical symptoms and signs, various laboratory tests and other meaningful factors was stored into the database. Definite diagnoses had been performed by the otoneurologists of the vestibular unit for 872 cases from whom those concerning the mentioned six diseases were selected. Confounding factors, such as noise-induced (e.g. caused by work environment) hearing loss, were discarded and 564 cases were thus taken ultimately to our current study. They are listed in Table 1. The mean age of the patients was 44 years and these 203 males and 361 females were between 13 and 82 years old. All the patients were thoroughly examined by the physicians, not only for this research, but as randomly selected ordinary clinical cases in the vestibular unit of the hospital. Consequently, some patients had missing values in the database.

Table 1. Numbers of different cases in the study.

disease	number of patients
Meniere's disease	243
vestibular schwannoma	128
benign positional vertigo	59
vestibular neuritis	60
traumatic vertigo	53
sudden deafness	21

In our database there is information of maximally 170 issues of symptoms, signs, laboratory tests etc. Several of them are normally excluded depending on the type of a possible patient's problems. There are namely abundantly laboratory and scanning tests, e.g. MRI, that may seldom be conducted if a physician in charge sees some of them necessary in order to make a diagnosis. Thus, a combination of pieces of information about a patient can be rather varying, and for some patients there are a lot of information, but for some other only few issues are sufficient to explain a diagnosis. As mentioned, neural networks cannot use several input parameters in this study because of the relatively small number of the cases. Thus, we were compelled to use the far most essential parameters from the whole assortment of 170 parameters (A_{170}). We could reduce parameter selections in the subsequent form:

$$A_5 \subset A_{13} \subset A_{38} \subset A_{110} \subset A_{170} \tag{1}$$

From the maximum number of A_{170} the specialized otologists determined 110 meaningful issues; those others were very rare questions or seemed to be insignificant for a majority of patients. In our recent research [14,15] we found that, however, a much more condensed selection of A_{38} is often enough for the processing of decision trees. These parameters were also defined by the otologists of our group to be more important than the others in A_{110}. Also discriminant analysis was used to sort the significance of the parameters [10]. In that group even the most important parameters of A_{13} were defined by the otologists. Nevertheless, also this quantity of input parameters would have been too much for neural networks to make their training process possible. Thus, the otologists finally determined the innermost core of five parameters in A_5. These parameters consist of the imperative issues that have to be known in case of any vertiginous patient so that a diagnosis can be given. Although we were able to generate reasonable results by employing solely A_5, it does not imply the other parameters unnecessary. Any piece of information may be useful in diagnostics. For instance, computer tomography can be very important in case of brain tumours. At least up to A_{110} the parameters can give significant hints about the diagnosis of a case [14,15]. The parameter set of A_5 is listed in Table 2.

Table 2. The five parameters seen as the innermost core of all [9,10].

parameter	categories
duration of hearing loss	no hearing loss, a few days, 1-4 weeks, 1-4 months, <1 year, 1-4 years, >4 years
duration of vertigo	no symptoms, a few days, 1-4 weeks, 1-4 months, <1 year, 1-4 years, >4 years
frequency of vertigo attacks	no spells, only once, 1-2 annually, 3-12 annually, 1-4 monthly, 2-7 weekly, several times a day, constant dizziness
duration of vertigo attacks	no attacks, 1-15 s, 15 s – 5 min, 5 min – 4 h, 4 –24 h, 1-5 days
occurrence of head injury in relation to the onset of symptoms	no, yes

As seen from Table 2, the five parameters are of category type. Two first parameters include 7 categories and the following ones consist of 8, 6 and 2 categories, respectively. These parameter types seem to be very suitable for neural network processing. Overall means of parameter values were, excluding the last (binary) parameter, close to an arithmetic mean of the categories when they were counted from zero upwards. Values of the last parameter were mostly 'no injury', i.e. zero. Nevertheless, it was significant, as was assumed, to traumatic vertigo in particular whether the injury was present.

Missing parameter values in the set of A_5 were infrequent, being $1.2 - 8.7$ % depending on the parameters. Altogether, 454 cases were complete, one parameter value was missing in 76 cases, two parameter values were absent in 31 cases, three values in two cases, and four values in one case. Thus, the values of these most important parameters were well represented in the database. Nonetheless, neural networks require complete input values. We replaced the missing values by the corresponding means of the parameters, which is a simple and common technique to generate missing values. There exist more sophisticated imputation methods [16], but this was not an important issue here, since the number of missing values was small. Replacement or imputation of missing values by the parameter means was accomplished merely for the set of A_5 since the decision trees and genetic algorithm did not presuppose it.

3 Recognition Methods Employed

As mentioned above, we chose two machine learning methods, genetic algorithms and decision trees, the results of which are compared to those generated by neural networks. Besides, discriminant analysis was utilized. All the three machine learning methods are accepted in decision making in various fields. Genetic algorithms, however, still seem to be rather rare in medical informatics. In any case, we found them successful in our late studies [12,13]. Also decision trees showed to produce reliable results in our investigations [14,15]. We do not describe them in detail here, since our implementations of the mentioned methods are mostly according to the known theories concerning these methods and we refer to the given references from which any details are found. We briefly give also results generated by our expert system ONE that was the starting point of our research. It is not used as a regular part in this comparison, since it is necessary and characteristic for ONE to use all given input in its recognition process.

We applied perhaps the commonest type of neural networks, a feedforward network in which the training process is handled with the backpropagation algorithm. To maximize the probability to reach a minimum in an error surface we took advantage of momentum term. Adaptive learning was applied as well, to fasten the learning process of the network. The networks were programmed within the Matlab environment [17]. In the neural network literature this ordinary network type is considered most suitable for classification problems [18,19]. In our recent comparison among some neural network structures we did not detect any considerable difference between the neural networks in a medical decision making task [20].

4 Results of the Methods

To apply neural network we divided the cases into a test set (223 or 40 %) and a training set (341 or 60 %). When a neural network is at least partially nondeterministic, several different runs have to be performed. Therefore, we varied the content of the test set and that of the training set as well. Various initial values were also used for the weights of the neural networks.

It would have been optimal to be able to recognize all the six diseases with a neural network after that we first strove. When the distribution of the six diseases was far from uniform (see Table 1), we experimented with a possibility to extend the material by copying those small sets of the diseases to establish a uniform distribution [19]. Nevertheless, several different efforts did not produce good results. The cases of vestibular schwannoma were recognized at a level of 68 %, those of sudden deafness at 40 %, and those of benign positional vertigo, traumatic vertigo and vestibular neuritis practically at 100 % on average. However, the cases of Meniere's disease were always lost entirely. Thus, the total number of correct recognitions (true positive) was only 50 %.

These weak results, after all, support our previous observations and experience on these diseases; e.g. traumatic vertigo is the easiest one to detect, because it is defined almost merely by the parameter of head injury (its presence or not). A head injury was present in all 53 cases of the traumatic vertigo, but only in 4 cases of the other 511. In 21 cases of the others this parameter value was missing. Benign positional vertigo and vestibular neuritis can effectively be found, too. Vestibular schwannoma and sudden deafness are hard cases, and especially the latter one is difficult to separate from Meniere's disease [9]. Vestibular schwannoma can be differentiated by imaging investigations. Meniere's disease has, according to our experience, been one of the worst types to determine. This test well ensures the present comprehension. Its properties seem to cover many other diseases to some extent.

In order to achieve sufficiently qualified results we had to unite the four least disease groups from Table 1 to form three groups: vestibular neuritis, Meniere's disease and the others. This grouping made it possible to obtain good recognition results. A network of three layers (input layer and two processing layers) included 5x6x3 nodes where the six hidden nodes were enough to facilitate the recognition process. For this network, there were sufficiently many training cases in our data to yield an efficiently learnt network.

The results produced by the neural network for the selection of the three disease groups are listed in Table 3. They are average results of ten test runs, but their variation was slight including typically 0-2 more or less correct cases in either of the three groups. Also results of decision trees and genetic algorithms are given in Table 4. All these tests were run with the parameter set of A_5.

Table 3. Results of the neural networks.

disease	number of correct recognitions from all group cases
Meniere's disease	82 / 91
vestibular schwannoma	37 / 47
others	76 / 85

Average results of the neural network were 90 % for Meniere's disease, 79 % vestibular schwannoma, and 89 % for the others. Altogether, 87 % of all the cases were classified right. Vestibular scwannoma is difficult to determine very reliably, at least only with these five parameters. Results of the other diseases were very high, although the cases of the sudden deafness had to be separated from Meniere's disease.

Table 4. Results of decision trees and genetic algorithms.

disease	number of correct recognitions for decision trees and genetic algorithms	
Meniere's disease	93 %	92 %
vestibular schwannoma	73 %	79 %
benign positional vertigo	98 %	98 %
vestibular neuritis	100 %	98 %
traumatic vertigo	98 %	92 %
sudden deafness	-	48 %

For decision trees we performed 10 test runs, each of them including 10-fold cross validations (100 tests altogether). Meniere's disease, benign positional vertigo, vestibular neuritis, and traumatic vertigo could be found effectively. Once again, vestibular schwannoma was quite awkward. Decision trees were not able to detect sudden deafness by using only the five parameters of A_5. The genetic algorithm was also effective. A test series of 10 runs for every disease (60 in all) was performed because of its nondeterministic character. For each run 70 % of the cases were randomly chosen to the training set and 30 % to the test set. Results of the genetic algorithm were almost similar to those of the decision trees, except in the case of sudden deafness that was a hard disease to recognize. This weakness came at least from the fact that there were so small a number of 21 cases (Table 1) of sudden deafness. Earlier, we noticed that small sets are particularly difficult for the genetic algorithm [12,13]. On average, 90 % true positive of the cases excluding sudden deafness were solved by the decision trees and 88 % including all diseases by the genetic algorithm.

To use discriminant analysis we moved to a larger set of parameters of A_{13} [10]. However, in this test we could not apply the same set of the 564 cases, but were compelled to restrict it to a smaller set of 405 cases for which there were parameter values. Discriminant analysis solved this test set reliably on an average of 90 % (Table 5) when the whole data set was considered as a test set.

Table 5. Results of discriminant analysis by using 13 parameters and 405 cases.

disease	number of correct recognitions in percents	from cases
Meniere's disease	87 %	172
vestibular schwannoma	77 %	86
benign positional vertigo	100 %	48
vestibular neuritis	100 %	44
traumatic vertigo	100 %	42
sudden deafness	100 %	13

The results in Table 5 show that Meniere's disease and vestibular schwannoma are still at the same level as before notwithstanding more information was utilized in the process than in the preceding tests. The others, including the difficult sudden deafness, were solved surprisingly well. However, we have to remember the more selected test set as above; these cases consisted of more parameters (information) and more complete data (not imputed). In addition, there was not a separate test set, but the whole data set was employed instead which obviously improves results. Usually a separate test set produces a little weaker results. Although four of the six diseases were found perfectly in this test, the total result did not surpass the achievements of the preceding tests.

Trying to reach even better gains we extended our tests of decision trees and genetic algorithm to the 38 parameters of A_{38}. Even larger sets are fully applicable to rapid decision tree processes, but the genetic algorithm consumed hours already for the concise sets of A$_5$ and A$_{38}$. In Table 6 there are results of A$_{38}$ of decision trees and genetic algorithm when using the set of 564 cases. The test runs were almost similar to those described above, except that no imputation of missing values was carried out. Some of the parameters in A$_{38}$ (unlike in A$_5$) are not of the category type; the continuous parameters were directly used for the decision trees, but were categorized for the genetic algorithm.

Table 6. Results of decision trees and genetic algorithm with 38 parameters.

disease	number of correct recognitions for decision trees and genetic algorithms	
Meniere's disease	86 %	76 %
vestibular schwannoma	74 %	62 %
benign positional vertigo	83 %	74 %
vestibular neuritis	98 %	90 %
traumatic vertigo	96 %	28 %
sudden deafness	71 %	11 %

Decision trees solved 85 % of all 564 cases on average. Note, however, that the difficult sudden deafness was involved in this case. In our previous study [14,15] we were able to obtain results that the set of A$_{38}$ was quite close to the larger sets in recognition accuracy, but in those we did not perform imputations of missing values. The imputation by using parameter means (depending on each disease) can naturally achieve better results, since it generates 'new data', although synthetic. This seeming contradiction as we enlarged to the larger parameter set (more information), but obtained slightly worse results, is a consequence of having excluded the imputation process. The genetic algorithm recognized 66 % (true positive) on average. Again, the small sets of traumatic vertigo and especially sudden deafness did diminish otherwise good results. Of course, leaving out the imputation had also weakening influence on the results. In the tests of the genetic algorithm we emphasized the general accuracy that includes also true negative results instead of solely true positive percents. Taking both into account the accuracy increases above 90 %, since the genetic algorithm is very good at the detection of true negative cases.

5 Comparison and Discussion

To summarize, the neural network strategy chosen was principally as effective as the decision trees and genetic algorithm in the situation of the first test series when using only the five absolutely most crucial parameters. It is very probable that after having received more patient data for the four 'rare' diseases in our database we can achieve for them as effective results as was the situation for Meniere's disease and vestibular schwannoma. This thought is strongly supported by our very first test with the neural network of all six diseases as output nodes. The results gained by the decision trees and genetic algorithm show that the preceding claim is well possible in principle as far as how many correct recognitions (true positive) can surely be yielded from otoneurological material of the six diseases.

The traditional technique of discriminant analysis reached the similar level (90 %) of correct recognitions, but its test situation was better than that of the former three test series. For the last test series of the set of the 38 parameters the decision trees gave also good results (85 %). The genetic algorithm slightly weaker (66 %) coped with since the small sets of some case types are rather disadvantageous to it. In practice, these are at the similar level as those preceding results since also the small set of difficult sudden deafness was involved and no imputation was carried out.

Our expert system ONE generated 79 % entirely correct recognitions and 18 % partially correct for a test set of 365 cases [2]. Partially correct means that it gave also the correct disease, but as the second or third plausible disease instead of the first (most plausible) disease. ONE can suggest at most three diseases in order of their plausibility (like certainty, not statistical probability). However, ONE took advantage of all information input to the database of the cases of the 365 patients. Any given information depended a lot on a patient. Therefore, there were very varyingly missing values, but ONE was implemented to exclude such parameters where a patient had missing values.

Clearly, vestibular schwannoma and sudden deafness are the hardest diseases to differentiate. Meniere's disease is also often troublesome to isolate from the others. These findings support the 'human' experience of the physicians in our research group.

The next step in our research will probably be to widen the case database. This is especially reasonable to improve the results in the case of the four diseases that have the least numbers of cases in the database. This will promote the construction of highly effective computer-aided software to support specialists in the difficult diagnostic field of otoneurology.

References

1. Auramo, Y., Juhola, M., Pyykkö, I.: An expert system for the computer-aided diagnosis of dizziness and vertigo. Med. Inform. 18 (1993) 293-305.
2. Auramo, Y., Juhola, M.: Comparison of inference results of two otoneurological expert systems. Int. J. Bio-Med. Comput. 39 (1995) 327-335.
3. Juhola, M., Auramo, Y., Kentala, E., Pyykkö, I.: An essay on power of expert systems versus human expertise. Med. Inform. 20 (1995) 133-138.
4. Auramo, Y., Juhola, M.: Modifying an expert system construction to pattern recognition solution. Artif. Intell. Med. 8 (1996) 15-21.
5. Kentala, E., Pyykkö, I., Auramo, Y., Juhola, M.: Database for vertigo. Otolaryngol. Head Neck Surg. 112 (1995) 383-390.
6. Kentala, E., Pyykkö, I., Auramo, Y., Juhola, M.: Computer assisted data collection in vestibular disorders. Acta Otolaryngol. Suppl. 520 (1995) 205-206.
7. Kentala, E., Pyykkö, I., Auramo, Y., Juhola, M.: Reasoning in expert system ONE for vertigo work-up. Acta Otolaryngol. Suppl. 520 (1995) 207-208.

8. Kentala, E., Pyykkö, I., Auramo, Y., Juhola, M.: Otoneurological expert system. Ann. Otol. Rhinol. Laryngol. 105 (1996) 654-658.

9. Kentala, E. A neurotological expert system for vertigo and characteristics of six otologic diseases involving vertigo. MD thesis. University of Helsinki, Finland. 1996.

10. Kentala, E.: Characteristics of six otologic diseases involving vertigo. Am. J. Otol. 17 (1996) 883-892.

11. Kentala, E., Auramo, Y., Juhola, M., Pyykkö, I.: Comparison between diagnoses of human experts and a neurotological expert system. Ann. Otol. Rhinol. Laryngol. 107 (1998) 135-140.

12. Laurikkala, J., Juhola, M.: A genetic-based machine learning system to discover the diagnostic rules for female urinary incontinence. Comp. Meth. Progr. Biomed. 55 (1998) 217-228.

13. Kentala, E., Laurikkala, J., Pyykkö, I., Juhola, M.: Discovering diagnostic rules from a neurotologic database with genetic algorithms. Accepted to Ann. Otol. Rhinol. Laryngol.

14. Viikki, K., Kentala, E., Juhola, M., Pyykkö, I.: Decision tree induction in the diagnosis of otoneurologic diseases. Submitted to Med. Inform.

15. Kentala, E., Viikki, K. Pyykkö, I. Juhola, M.: Production of diagnostic rules from a neurotologic database with decision trees. Accepted to Ann. Otol. Rhinol. Laryngol.

16. Schafer, J.L.: Analysis of incomplete multivariate data. John Wiley & Sons, New York (1997).

17. Neural network toolbox for use with MATLAB. MathWorks, Inc., Massachusetts (1992).

18. Fu, L.M.: Neural networks in computer intelligence. McGraw-Hill, Singapore (1994).

19. Swingler, K.: Applying neural networks. Academic Press, London (1996).

20. Pesonen, E., Eskelinen, M., Juhola, M.: Comparison of different neural network algorithm in the diagnosis of acute appendicitis. Int. J. Bio-Med. Comput. 40 (1996) 227-233.

A Comparison of Linear and Non-linear Classifiers for the Detection of Coronary Artery Disease in Stress-ECG

Georg Dorffner[1], Ernst Leitgeb[2], and Heinz Koller[3]

[1] Austrian Research Institute for Artificial Intelligence
Schottengasse 3, A-1010 Vienna, Austria
and Dept. of Medical Cybernetics and AI, Univ. of Vienna
georg@ai.univie.ac.at
[2] Leitgeb Company, Strasshof, Austria
[3] LKH Klagenfurt, Austria

Abstract. In this paper we report about a retrospective comparative study on three classifiers (multilayer perceptron, logistic classifier, and nearest neighbor classifier) applied to the task of detecting coronary artery disease in variables obtained from stress-ECG (treadmill exercise). A 10-fold cross-validation on all three methods was applied and the results were compared to expert performance. The results indicate that the multilayer perceptron had significantly higher specificity (correctly classified normals) than both the other classifiers and experts. In addition, they perform with lower standard deviation than experts, pointing to a more reliable, objective measure for diagnosis.

1 Stress-ECG and Coronary Aartery Disease

The electrocardiogram (ECG) provides direct evidence of cardiac rhythm and conduction and indirect evidence of certain aspects of myocardial anatomy, blood supply and function. Electrocardiography has been used for many years as a key non-invasive method in the diagnosis and early detection of ischemic heart disease (coronary artery disease, or CAD), which is the leading cause of mortality in Western countries [2,3].

To improve the accuracy of the electrocardiogram and obtain more information on the dynamic state of the heart, exercise testing was introduced [2]. During stress testing not only the electrogardiogram is continously registered but also other physiological parameters are monitored (blood pressure, physical symptoms and angina pectoris). According to different established protocols, the workload is increased step by step and the changes of parameters during stress and recovery are recorded and analysed. Skilled cardiologists achieve around 66 % specificity (correctly classified normals) and 81 % sensitivity (correctly classified CAD cases) in detecting CAD based on the resulting data [1].

The design of optimized automatic classifiers is an important contribution to the diagnosis and treatment of this wide-spread disease. In this study, we evaluated three linear and non-linear classifiers applied to this task.

W. Horn et al. (Eds.): AIMDM'99, LNAI 1620, pp. 227–231, 1999.

2 DATA

For the retrospective comparison study, a data set of 550 subjects, including 318 patients with CAD and 132 normals were available. From this, a set of 200 subjects (175 CAD and 25 normals) came from a different recording setting and was used as an independent test set. The remaining 350 subjects ("cross-validation set") were used in a 10-fold cross-validation using the different classifiers. Among the 107 normals in that group, 31 were athletes with no suspicion of CAD whatsoever. Subjects in the cross-validation set were aged from 18 to 89 years and included 283 males and 67 females.

Stress-ECG was done on a standard treadmill setting. The stress program consisted of 11 steps with increasing power, starting with no stress, and increasing by 25 Watts at each step, up to 250 Watts. After this, four more recording steps at rest (immediately after stress, 1, 3, and 5 minutes after stress) followed. During each step several psychological variables were registered and recorded, such as systolic and diastolic blood pressure, and heart rate; symptoms (like fatigue, sweating, etc.), and angina pectoris; different types of arrhythmia; ST-depressions in the ECG signal.

These variables were observed and judged by a cardiologist, the latter two based on the on-going ECG. In each case, the stress part of the program was either completed (up to 250 Watts) or interrupted at severe contra-indications (e.g. severe arryhtmia). In addition, for each subject a number of demographic data was recorded, such as age, height, weight, sex, and an indication of prior infarction. Coronary angiography was used in all cases as the gold-standard reference method for deciding whether CAD was present or not.

3 Preprocessing

The raw data consisting of the above variables was preprocessed by following as closely as possible expert knowledge about the most informative parts in the observed data. For instance, instead of using the heart rate directly, an allowable interval (based on the age and weight of the subject) was computed, and the heart rate increase or decrease was compared to this interval at each time step. This corresponds to the analysis routinely applied by expert cardiologists. Symptoms and types of arrhythmia were categorized into two classes (according to severity), since each symptom occurs too rarely to be encoded spearately. With respect to the time structure of the variables, we again abided by the general routine, separating between stress and rest periods, and summing the contributions of each time step for each of the two parts (see, for instance, [4]).

This preprocessing scheme resulted in 29 numerical values (10 for the stress part, 10 for the rest part, and 9 for the time-independent patient-demographic data) used as input for the classifiers.

4   Classification Methods

The goal of this study was to show whether linear or non-linear classification methods would perform best on detecting CAD based on the above variables over standard methods, and how it compared to expert performance. It was decided to use a logistic disciminator, a nearest neighbor classifier, and a multilayer perceptron (MLP) with one hidden layer for comparison. Expert performance was available in two respects: First, from a meta-study evaluating performance on several experts on diagnosing stress-ECG [1]; and secondly, from the judgements of the cross-validation set by one cardiologist (i.e. the third author) unaware of the results of automatic discrimination.

The MLP consisted of one input layer with 29 units, according to the 29 numerical values obtained from preprocessing, one hidden layer and one output layer. Given the fact that only a little over 300 patterns can be used for training, it was decided that a hidden layer of size 5 was the maximum model complexity the training process could reliably estimate. This number was kept fixed for all training runs. The output consisted of 3 units, encoding normal (all zeros), one-, two- and three-vessel diseases (1, 2, or 3 units set to 1, respectively). For evaluation, all three disease classes were collapsed into one ('pathological'). The decision with respect to 'normal' vs. 'pathological' was made based on whether the average of the activation of all three output units exceeded a threshold (e.g. 0.5). This threshold can be varied to make the classifier either more sensitive (recognizing more positives correct) or more specific (recognizing more negatives correctly). For training it turned out that a simple backpropagation gradient descent method with momentum term sufficed to converge into a minimum at around 3000 training steps (early stopping criterion), where each step consisted of a single presentation of a randomly selected pattern. The learning rate was 0.01, and a momentum rate of 0.9 was used.

The logistic discriminator was realised as a perceptron with 29 inputs and 3 outputs, with a sigmoid transfer function at the output, trained by a delta rule. The nearest-neighbor method was used in the standard way of picking the pattern in the training set with smallest Euclidean distance to a test pattern and returning the corresponding class label.

For comparing the performance of the three automatic classifiers, a 10-fold cross-validation method was used, leading to 10 different training sets of 315 pattern each, and 10 different (disjunctive) corresponding test sets of size 35. The assignment of patterns to sets was random, with the constraint that the distribution of pathologicals vs. normal non-athletes vs. athletes was about the same for all training and test sets. Since equal distribution of pathologicals vs. normals was not possible, a priori probabilites were accounted for by a rudimentary ROC-analysis - i.e. by varying the decision threshold, and basing the comparison upon one fixed threshold for each method (except for nearest-neighbor).

5   Results

Fig. 1 lists the results of the cross-validation on the three automatic methods, as well as an expert diagnosis of the 350 patterns in the cross-validation sets (split into the 10 test sets), and results from literature on expert performance on diagnosing stress-ECG in general [1]. Mean and standard deviation are given for the sensitivity (correctly classified pathologicals) and specificity (correctly classified normals) for all methods (except in the case of external experts, where no specificity distribution was available). The bar graphs illustrate the distribution of the performances over the different test sets. The x-axis shows percentage correct, and the y-axis depicts the relative number of times a method scored in this range. For instance, a bar value of 20 over the value 70 % means that in 20 % of the cases, the method scored around 70 % correct (between 67.6 and 72.5).

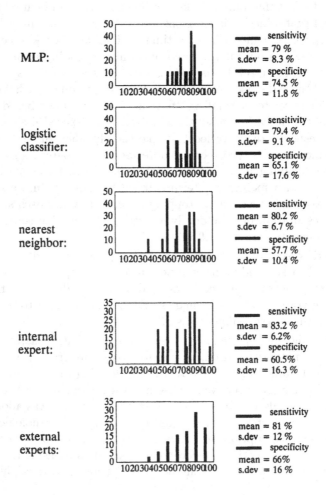

Fig. 1. The comparative results from the 10-fold cross-validation

6 Discussion

The results from the cross-validation show that all three methods reach about the same performance on mean sensitivity (79 to 80.2 %) as the expert diagnosing the same data (83 %). This is also in the range of the published performance of experts in general (81 %). With respect to mean specificity, however, the MLP fared much better (74.5 %) than both the other classifiers (65.1 % and 57.7 %, respectively: the difference to the MLP is significant with $p < 0.1$ and $p < 0.05$, respectively) and the experts (60.5 % for the internal expert judging the same data, 66 % for the external experts). Moreover, the MLP exhibits a decisively lower standard deviation (11.8 %) than the experts in either study (16.3 %, and 16 %, respectively).

An ROC analysis on the independent test set confirmed the ranking among the classifiers. Since this test set was acquired in a slightly different recording setting, overall performance dropped to about 79/70 %. Therefore, the results still have to be taken with caution with respect to routine application.

Still, one can conclude that automoatic classification with expert performance is possible, and that the MLP appears to have an advantage in specificity, both as compared to alternative classifiers and as compared to expert performance. This performance, as the test set indicates, in addition seems to be more robust than for the other classifiers. Moreover, a lower standard deviation on performance points to a more reliable and objective diagnostic method than what human experts with a large inter- and intraobserver variability can achieve.

7 Conclusion

From this study, we view the MLP as a powerful tool in diagnostic support for cardiologists. Since stress-ECG is a relatively cheap, non-invasive, and widespread method, MLPs as non-linear classifiers are likely to contribute to better detection, as well as monitoring, of this prevalent disease.

Acknowledgements The Austrian Research Institute for Artificial Intelligence is supported by the Austrian Federal Ministry for Science and Transport. We thank Harry Burke and Stephen Roberts for valuable comments and input.

References

1. Detrano R., et al.: Exercise-induced ST segment depression in the diagnosis of multivessel coronary disease: a meta analysis. J. Am. Coll. Cardiol. 14(1989) 1501-1508
2. Hurst W.: The Heart, 7th ed., McGraw Hill, New York (1990)
3. Julian D.G., Camm A.J., Fox K.M., Hall R.J.C., Poole-Wilson P.A.: Diseases of the Heart. Bailliere Tindall, London (1989)
4. Koller H., Leitgeb E.: Ist eine Verbesserung der Aussagekraft und Reproduzierbarkeit des Belastungs-EKG erzielbar?. Wiener Medizinische Wochenschrift 143 (1993) 110-117

The Case-Based Neural Network Model and Its Use in Medical Expert Systems

Wayne Goodridge[1], Hadrian Peter[1], Akin Abayomi[2]

[1] Faculty of Science and Technology, University of the West Indies,
Cave Hill Campus
[2] School of Clinical Medicine and Research, University of the West Indies,
Queen Elizabeth Hospital, Bridgetown Barbados

Abstract. A theoretical model called the Case-Based Neural Network Model is introduced that captures selected patient cases into a data structure which incorporates the fundamental components of expert systems. This data structure is made up of a discrete pattern associative neural network of frames. The Case-Based Neural Network Model is implemented as a computer system called MED2000. This system generates appropriate questions and suggestions based on a notion of diagnosis developed by its neural network and knowledge base. When tested by medical experts, the system was found to be accurate and reproducible.

1 Introduction

Case-Based Reasoning (CBR) is a technology that is increasingly gaining popularity with expert system developers. CBR is a cyclic paradigm [1] that consists of the following four stages: retrieve the most similar case or cases; reuse the retrieved case or cases to solve the problem by analogical reasoning; revise the proposed solution; retain the parts of this experience likely to be useful for future problem solving.

CBR is applicable in medicine for the following reasons[6]:

- Clinicians tend to use experiences gained from their clinical practices to treat a current case
- Easy adjustment to requirements of clinics since the Case Base can be maintained
- The subjective knowledge of one or more clinicians can be simultaneously incorporated
- Integration of the Case Base with other sources of data (e.g patient records)

The CBR applied to medical diagnosis systems can however lead to the following concerns:
- Concentration on reference rather than diagnosis and thereby only acting as a source of previous experience if that source is available in the knowledge base.
- Lack of intelligent dialog may result in missing information which may decrease the accuracy of diagnosis.
- Inability of most similarity algorithms to handle attributes that are unknown

W. Horn et al. (Eds.): AIMDM'99, LNAI 1620, pp. 232-236, 1999.
© Springer-Verlag Berlin Heidelberg 1999

- If the Case Base contains cases of varying degrees of attributes then Case-Based representation will be complex requiring large numbers of predicates, relations, constraints and operators [2].
- Adaptation (revise stage) requires complex algorithms and/or highly skilled users
  To address these concerns, this paper introduces a novel approach called the *Case-Based Neural Network (CBNN)* model.

2 Background of the Case-Based Neural Network Model

The Case-Based Neural Network (CBNN) model uses the notion of case-based reasoning, incorporated within a neural network, and the concept of representing knowledge using frames [4]. This model presumes that a knowledge base, and learning and reasoning mechanisms can be incorporated in the same data structure and used for diagnostic problem solving. The key component of the model is the *Heteroassociative* memory neural network [4] that is used as a retrieval mechanism to get the most similar cases that match the symptoms of the current problem. This substitutes the use for the similarity measure and retrieval techniques such as kd-trees and the Case Retrieval Nets (CRNs) [6] used in CBR.

Compared to the traditional CBR model, the CBNN model does not represent a case using an ordered pair (problem, solution) [6]. In CBR a problem is represented as a set of information entities usually of attribute-value pair types. The CBNN model places all the solutions in layer 2 of the neural network, and all the information entities (nodes) related to problem identification in layer 1. This eliminates the problem of case representation [2] that currently exists with the CBR, since the information entities related to the problem in the CBNN are independent of the case.

The CBNN model like the CBR has a learning mechanism. However, the CBNN does not follow the CBR-cycle all the way. Case adaptation is never done in the CBNN model. Instead, new *pure* cases are added to the case base, where a pure case is one involving only one disorder. Because adaptation is a part of the CBR-cycle, learning is a natural part of the CBR. On the other hand, with the CBNN learning is done at selected points in time.

Training with pure cases is necessary in the CBNN because when a case is selected during a diagnostic process the disorder of this case is used to generate a hypothesis. This hypothesis is then used to generate a question whose answer is used to generate another hypothesis. Theoretically, faulty hypotheses may be generated when multiple disorders are coexisting in a case. However, the purity training of the system does not imply that the CBNN model can diagnose only conditions with single disorders. All cases in the CBNN are checked for eligibility (Axiom 3 next section) of being possible candidates for the problem being examined. Once a disorder is eligible it should be listed in the definitive diagnosis

The hypotheses generated in the diagnostic process depend heavily on observed findings and the *Notion of Diagnosis* [7]. The Notion of Diagnosis can be viewed as a case-based reasoning mechanism that determines a set of cases that match the observed findings from which possible disorders (hypotheses) are drawn. Mathematically, this can be expressed as

$$R_\Sigma(E) = H .\tag{1}$$

where $\Sigma = (\Phi, \theta, \omega, e, r)$ is a diagnostic specification
             θ = set of patient cases
             Φ = set of findings
             ω = set of disorders
             e = evidence function (maps findings to cases)
             r = relation between cases and disorders
             R_Σ. = Notion of Diagnosis

3 Methods of Building the Case Base

Let the findings associated with a case be represented with a vector $s(p)$ where $p = 1, 2, \ldots, P$. Each vector $s(p)$ is an n-tuple. Let the case associated with findings be represented with a vector $t(p)$. Each $t(p)$ is an m-tuple, and each $s(p)$ is associated with a $t(p)$.

To store a set of bipolar vector pairs $s(p):t(p)$, $p = 1, \ldots, P$
Where $s(p) = (s_1(p), \ldots, s_i(p), \ldots, s_n(p))$ and
             $t(p) = (t_1(p), \ldots, t_j(p), \ldots, t_m(p))$.
A *weight matrix* $W_e = \{w_{ij}\}$ is given by $w_{ij} = \sum_p s_i(p) t_j(p)$.

The heteroassociative memory neural network can be described as a discrete network where the input and output nodes take values from the set $\{-1, 0, 1\}$. The following meanings can be applied to these values: -1 for findings that are absent, 0 for unknown findings, and 1 for findings that are present.

Now $E \subseteq \Phi$ (observed findings) can be represented as an n-tuple input vector say k. Vector k will then be mapped to the θ domain by the W_e matrix. That is,
             $k . W_e \subseteq \theta$
or $k . W_e = t$
where $t \subseteq \theta$
Thus W_e can be viewed as the notion of diagnosis represented as R_Σ.

Example
If the output layer contains 3 nodes then some of the following mappings are possible:

             $k . W_e = (1,0,0)$ Map 1
             $k . W_e = (0,1,0)$ Map 2
             $k . W_e = (2,4,2)$ Map 3

Every time new findings are presented to the current case, k is changed and a multiplication on W_e is made to ascertain $t(p)$ which is then used to determine a set of cases from the case base that matches the observed findings.

The following axioms are formulated so that the neural network can act as a retrieval mechanism to get the most similar cases.

Axiom 1. If a node in vector t has a positive value then this node represents a case in which the disorder associated with it matches the current observed findings. For example, in Map 1 the disorder associated with case 1 is a possible candidate.

Axiom 2. If a mapped vector t contains nodes that have varying positive integer values, then the node that has the largest positive value is most likely to be the case that has the most possible associated disorder for the given findings observed.

Example: If t = (3,1,-1) then disorders associated with cases 1 and 2 are likely. However, the disorder associated with case 1 is the more likely candidate.

Axiom 3. A disorder , say k, is a part of a definitive diagnosis only if the available findings that will lead to a diagnosis of k exceeds the findings that are unknown.

Let $CURRENT_j = \Sigma\ w_{ij}\ x_j$,   unknown input nodes not included
And $UNKNOWN_j = \Sigma\ |w_{ij}|$, only unknown nodes included

If $|CURRENT_j| > UNKNOWN_j$, then k can be a part of the definitive diagnosis.

4 Preliminary Evaluation

To test the CBNN model a medical expert system prototype is developed as a windows 95/98 based system called MED2000. This system is written in MS Visual Basic.

To test MED2000, 14 pure cases of Haematological conditions and related disorders were added to the case base. Two medical experts in the specialty of Haematology independently simulated 30 classical Haematological cases within the scope of the system.

At the end of each history and examination stage of simulated cases, MED2000, was asked to produce its opinion. This was noted as stage 1 differential diagnosis. After the results of investigations are provided to MED2000, the system, depending on the completeness of information, provided either a definitive diagnosis, with or without further recommendations for strengthening investigations. This was noted as stage 2 diagnosis. At the end of each simulated case scenario the medical expert grades MED2000 as either being accurate or inaccurate in its leading differential diagnosis at stage 1 and its definitive or differential at stage 2, when applicable. Critical comments are also made on the relevance of leading differential diagnosis generated by the system.

5 Results and Discussion

Table 1 below shows the results of five out of 30 randomly selected simulated interactions. These results illustrate that the CBNN is accurate and reproducible at all stages of the diagnostic process, and therefore is a useful model for representing the components of medical diagnostic reasoning which are the knowledge base, the notion of diagnosis and observed findings.

Table 1. Results and key of medical experts' simulated cases generated by MED2000

	Case Simulated	Stage 1	Stage 2	Opinion-Stage 1	Opinion-Stage 2	Comments on DD
1	CML	CML, MF	CML, MF	✔	✔	+++
2	MM	MM, NHL	MM	✔	✔	+
3	PRV	PRV, TB	PRV	✔	✔	-
4	ALL	ALL, AML	ALL	✔	✔	+++
5	AA	AA, AML	AA	✔	✔	+++

	Disease Abbreviations

DD = Differential Diagnosis,
 ✔ = Accurate
 +++ = DD Relevant
   (Related Disorders) ,
 ++ = DD Relevant
   (Unrelated Disorders),
 + = DD Possibly Relevant,
 - = DD Irrelevant
	MM = Multiple Myeloma
	 NHL =Non Hodgkins Lymphoma
	 CML=Chronic Myeloid Leukaemia
	 MF = Myelofibrosis
	 PRV = Polycythaemia Rubra Vera
	 TB = Tuberculosis
	 ALL = Acute Lymphoblastic Leukaemia
	 AML=Acute Myeloid Leukamia
	 AA = Aplastic Anemia

References

1. Aamodit, A., Plaza, P.: Case-Based Reasoning: Foundations Issues, Methodological Variations, and Systems Approaches. AI Communications 7(1) (1994) 39-59
2. Bergmann, R., Wilke, W.: Building and refining abstract planning cases by change of representation language. Journal of Artificial Intelligence Research, 3 (1995) 53-118
3. Durkin, J.: Expert Systems, Design and Development. Prentice Hall International Editions (1994)
4. Fauseet, L.:   Fundamentals of Neural Networks. Architectures, algorithms, and applications. Prentice Hall International Editions (1994)
5. Gallant, S, I.: Neural Network Learning and Expert systems. Massachusetts Institute of Technology (1993)
6. Lenz, M., et al (eds.): Case-Based Reasoning Technology: from foundations to applications. Lecture notes in Computer science vol. 1400. Springer-Verlag, Berlin Heidelberg New York (1998)
7. Lucus, P.: A Theory of Medical Diagnosis as Hypothesis Refinement. 6th Conference on Artificial Intelligence. Springer-Verlag, Berlin Heidelberg New York (1997) 169-180

Knowledge Representation

A Medical Ontology Library That Integrates the UMLS Metathesaurus™

Domenico M. Pisanelli, Aldo Gangemi, Geri Steve

Istituto di Tecnologie Biomediche - CNR   Roma, Italy
Viale Marx 15, 00137 Roma, Italy
{nico,aldo,geri}@color.irmkant.rm.cnr.it

Abstract. Paper-based terminology systems cannot satisfy anymore the new desiderata of healthcare information systems: the demand for re-use and sharing of patient data, their transmission and the need of semantic-based criteria for purposive statistical aggregation. The unambiguous communication of complex and detailed medical concepts is now a crucial feature of medical information systems. Ontologies can support a more effective data and knowledge sharing in medicine. In this paper we survey the ontological analysis performed on the top-levels of some important medical terminology systems (an outcome of the ONIONS methodology) and we sketch out the ontological analysis performed on the UMLS Metathesaurus™. We show the convenience of an ontological approach in dealing with the different conceptualizations behind medical terminologies and the polysemy of terms. The multiple classification in UMLS is shown to be a phenomenon of polysemy and not one of multiple subsumption.

1 Introduction

The overwhelming amount of information stored in various data repositories emphasizes the relevance of knowledge integration methodologies and techniques to facilitate data sharing. The need for such integration has been already perceived for several years, but telecommunications and networking are quickly and dramatically changing the scenario. Physicians developed their language in order to reach an efficient way to store and communicate general medical knowledge and patient-related information. This language was appropriate for the support available for archiving, processing and transmitting knowledge: the paper.

But paper-based terminology systems cannot satisfy anymore the new desiderata of healthcare information systems, such as the demand for re-use and sharing of patient data, their transmission and the need of semantic-based criteria for purposive statistical aggregation. The unambiguous communication of complex and detailed medical concepts is now a crucial feature of medical information systems.

However, the ever-increasing demand of data sharing has to rely on a solid conceptual foundation in order to give a precise semantics to the terabytes available in different

W. Horn et al. (Eds.): AIMDM'99, LNAI 1620, pp. 239-248, 1999.
© Springer-Verlag Berlin Heidelberg 1999

databases and eventually traveling over the networks. The actual demand is not for a unique conceptualization, but for an unambiguous communication of complex and detailed concepts, leaving each user free to make explicit his/her conceptualization.

Often this task is not an easy one to be achieved, since a deep analysis of the structure and the concepts of terminologies is needed. Such analyses can be performed by adopting an *ontological* approach for representing terminology systems and for integrating them in a set of ontologies.

The role of ontologies for allowing a more effective data and knowledge sharing is widely recognized [1][2].

Recently Sowa proposed the following definition influenced by Leibniz [4]:

"The subject of ontology is the study of the categories of things that exist or may exist in some domain. The product of such a study, called an ontology, is a catalog of the types of things that are assumed to exist in a domain of interest D from the perspective of a person who uses a language L for the purpose of talking about D. "

In our perspective, an ontology is a formal theory which partially specifies the conceptualization of a lexical item as it is used in a certain domain [3]. Since lexical items are often used with more than one conceptualization in the same domain (they are "polysemous"), such different conceptualizations have to be specified and segregated within different formal contexts, or conceptualizations must have assigned distinct names within the same context. A "context" is a theory that serves as a module within a system that allows a partial ordering among its component theories.

The procedure by which the lexical items from a terminology system are conceptually analyzed and their conceptualizations are (partially) specified within a context hierarchy is what we call the "ontological analysis" of a terminology.

The sources of the ontological analysis in our project are medical terminology systems. Our analyses aim at expliciting the implicit relationships among the conceptualizations of the lexical items ("terms") included in the sources, and maintaining the reference of such relationships to a set of generic theories.

In this paper we survey the ontological analysis performed on the top-levels of the most important medical terminology systems and we sketch out the ontological analysis performed on the UMLS Metathesaurus™ [6]. We show the convenience of an ontological approach in dealing with the different conceptualizations behind medical terminologies and the polysemy of terms.

2   The ONIONS Methodology: Tools and Results

Although some notable work has been carried out in the framework of building medical ontologies [5][8], the relevance of generic (domain-independent) theories to the development of ontologies is not always recognized. There is a number of significant experiences showing that an ontological analysis can profit from theories which are philosophically and linguistically grounded [7][9]. Examples of generic theories include: "mereology" or theory of parts, "topology" or theory of wholes and connexity, "morphology", or theory of form and congruence, "localization" theory, "time" theory, "actors" theory, etc.

We developed ONIONS, a methodology for integrating domain terminologies by exploiting a "library" of generic theories [9]. Aims of ONIONS include:

- Developing a well-tuned set of generic ontologies to support the integration of relevant domain ontologies in medicine. In fact, current medical ontologies mostly lack axiomatization, or semantic precision, or ontological cleverness.
- Integrating a set of relevant domain ontologies in a formally and conceptually satisfactory ontology library to support many tasks, including information integration, information retrieval, natural language processing, computerized guidelines generation, etc.
- Providing an explicit tracing of the procedure of building an ontology, in order to facilitate its maintenance (evaluation, extensions and/or updating, and intersubjective agreement).

The tools of ONIONS include: a set of formalisms, a set of computational tools which implement and support the use of the formalisms, and a set of generic ontologies, taken from the literature in either formal or informal status and translated or adapted to our formalisms.

The main products of ONIONS are: the ON9 library of generic ontologies (available also on-line at http://saussure.irmkant.rm.cnr.it); the IMO (Integrated Medical Ontology, that represents the integration of five medical top-levels of relevant terminologies, and the relative mappings); a formalized representation of some medical repositories (mainly the UMLS Metathesaurus™ defined by the U.S. National Library of Medicine) with their classification within the IMO.

ONIONS methodology has been applied to the analysis and integration of the following top-levels of medical terminology systems: the UMLS Semantic Network [6] (1997 edition: 135 'semantic types', 91 'relations', and 412 'templates'), the SNOMED-III [10] top-level (510 'terms' and 25 'links'), GMN [11] top-level (708 'terms'), the ICD10 [12] top-level (185 'terms'), and the GALEN Core Model [13] (2730 'entities', 413 'attributes' and 1692 terminological axioms).

Conceptual integration in ONIONS is carried out as follows: all terms, templates, and axioms are formally represented. When available, natural language glosses are axiomatized; such intermediate products are finally integrated by means of a set of generic theories. We experimented a web-based tool for cooperative modeling; different modelers could experiment and face each other about the effects of ontological analysis on terminology integration [14]. For a deep explanation of the problems, considerations and methods used in the integration, see [15]. For a complete presentation of the methodology, see [9].

LOOM	SET-THEORETIC SEMANTICS
(:and B C)	$B^I \cap C^I$
(:or B C)	$B^I \cup C^I$
(:all R B)	$\{i \in \Delta^I \mid \forall j.(i,j) \in R^I \Rightarrow j \in B^I\}$
(:some R B)	$\{i \in \Delta^I \mid \exists j.(i,j) \in R^I \wedge j \in B^I\}$
(defconcept A :is-primitive (:all R C))	$A^I \Rightarrow \{i \in \Delta^I \mid \forall j.(i,j) \in R^I \Rightarrow j \in C^I\}$

Table 1.
Some Loom language constructs and their set-theoretic semantics.

An example of the outcome of such integration activity is the formalization of the concept "Body-Region" resulting from the UMLS Semantic Network, GALEN Core Model and generic theories "topology", "meronymy", "localization".

In the following we report such formalization expressed in the Loom language [16], a description logic that supports *structural subsumption*, both TBox and ABox expressions, transitively closed roles, role hierarchy, implications (non definitional axioms), default axioms, a modular organization of the namespace, etc. The most used Loom constructs are summarized in Table 1.

In its definitional axioms (after the :is-primitive keyword) the following formula states that a "Body-Region" is a "Region", which is the location of some "Anatomical-Structure", and which is a portion of an "Organism". There follow some implicational axioms (after the :implies keyword) that are not used for the subsumption calculus, but only checked for semantic coherence, and an affiliation to a module in the ontology library (after the :context keyword). For a detailed discussion, see [15].

```
(defconcept Body-Region
  :is-primitive (:and Region
    (:some location Anatomical-Structure)
    (:some portion Organism))
  :implies
    (:and (:some strictly-depends-on Organism)
    (:some connected Body-Region)
    (:some component (:or Body-System Body-Part))
    (:all near (:or Body-Region Anatomical-Structure))
    (:all location
      (:or Anatomical-Structure biologic-function body-region
        biologic-substances^body-substance))
    (:all crosses-through Body-Region))
  :context anatomy)
```

3   The Ontological Analysis of the UMLS Metathesaurus™

Apart from the generic theories and the top-levels of medical terminologies, our activity is aimed also at integrating some relevant 'bottom-level' medical terminologies. We are investigating the Metathesaurus™ [6], developed in the context of the Unified Medical Language System (UMLS) project by the U.S. National Library of Medicine [17]. It is a very significant repository, since it collects millions of terms belonging to the most important nomenclatures and terminologies defined in the United States and in other countries too. Such feature makes it a proper object of analysis and reuse, being it probably the largest repository of terminological knowledge in medicine.

Among the various sources, the National Library has singled out more than 470,000 preferred terms in English. Preferred terms are chosen among the lexical variants of terms, and are labeled by the NLM "concepts", each one having an alphanumeric "CUI" (Concept Unique Identifier). It should be pointed out that "concept" for NLM is not necessarily the same as "concept" in disciplines like logic, ontology, and conceptual modeling. In fact, a UMLS concept may have several conceptualizations, as we show in this section. Actually, the NLM "concept" means "preferred term".

Starting from the public-domain UMLS sources (made available on CD-ROM by the NLM) we built a database featuring:

- The preferred names of the CUIs (e.g. "Fibromyalgia").
- The instances of IS_A relations between different CUIs that UMLS took from its sources (e.g. "Fibromyalgia" IS_A "Muscular-diseases").
- The relationships between different CUIs that UMLS took from its sources (e.g. "COPAD protocol" USES "Asparaginase").
- The instances of IS_A relations between a CUI and its "semantic types" (e.g. "Fibromyalgia" IS_A "Disease-or-Syndrome").
- The definition of the CUIs in plain text, as reported in authoritative sources such as medical dictionaries.

It should be pointed out that UMLS stated IS_A relations between CUIs only for a minority of CUIs (e.g. "Muscular-diseases"). About 43,000 instances of IS_A relationships have been explicitly stated in the Metathesaurus, but we stated 318,385 more tuples as IS_A (i.e. "subsumed by") instances on the basis of an analysis of the available sources.

Moreover, UMLS assigned to every CUI one or more semantic types. About 604,755 assignments of a semantic type to a CUI have been stated.

Starting from the database - which systematizes the UMLS definitions without further assumptions - for each CUI we generated a Loom expression.

Cardinality	CUIs	DP	ACDP
1	357803	132	2711
2	108905	714	153
3	9262	358	26
4	331	84	4
5	4	1	4
6	2	1	2

Table 2.
UMLS patterns of semantic types: number of different semantic types in a pattern (Cardinality), number of CUIs pertaining to the patterns with such cardinality (CUIs), number of distinct patterns for that cardinality (DP), and average number of CUIs per DP (ACDP).

The 476,307 Loom expressions generated from the 1998 UMLS sources concerning CUIs were automatically classified and this process has been helpful in the creation of a consistent model. The 118,504 multi-typed CUIs (i.e. CUIs with more than one semantic type) have been analyzed. The allowed combinations of semantic types - we call them 'patterns' – result to be 1158, ranging in cardinality (i.e. number of semantic types pertaining to the pattern) from 1 to 6. Table 2 shows figures concerning such patterns. Some examples of patterns are shown in Table 3.

We found that most multi-typed patterns are not referable to an actual conjunction of subsumptions (as a logical *AND*). On the contrary, they are motivated by the polysemy of these terms, whose conceptualization can be disambiguated only by distinguishing the contexts in which they are used. For example, "Salmonella-Choleraesuis" is classified both under "Disease-Or-Syndrome" and "Bacterium", although the salmonella is only the aetiology of a disease called "Salmonellosis" (this polysemy may originate from the metonymic use of the bacterium name, e.g. in sentences like "the patient is affected by salmonella"). Another example is "Onychotillomania" which is classified under "Sign-Or-Symptom", "Individual-Behavior" and "Mental-Or-Behavioral-Dysfunction".

Pattern name	CUIs
Disease-Or-Syndrome	30601
Disease-Or-Syndrome & Acquired-Abnormality	606
Disease-Or-Syndrome & Anatomical-Abnormality	352
Disease-Or-Syndrome & Classification	15
Disease-Or-Syndrome & Congenital-Abnormality	1169
Disease-Or-Syndrome & Finding	379
Disease-Or-Syndrome & Injury-Or-Poisoning	827

Table 3.
Some patterns of "semantic types" in the Metathesaurus and number of CUIs pertaining to them.

The individuation of such patterns induces a partition in the Metathesaurus and facilitates its ontological analysis. For example, the CUIs having the pattern "Amino Acid, Peptide, or Protein & Carbohydrate", which is composed by two sibling sub-types of "Organic Chemical", have been analyzed and their pattern can be ontologized as "a protein which contains a carbohydrate". The analysis and integration procedure results in a Loom concept definition as follows:

```
(defconcept |Amino Acid, Peptide, or Protein & Carbohydrate|
    :annotations ((Suggested-Name "carbohydrate-containing-protein")
                  (onto-status integrated))
    :is-primitive (:and protein
                        (:some has-component carbohydrate))
    :context :substances)
```

More polysemous phenomena come from multiple subsumption relations among CUIs. For example, the concept "ununited fractures" has the semantic types "Finding" and "Injury or Poisoning", and the IS_A assignments: "fractures" and "malunion and nonunion of fracture". The following graph results (arrows mean IS_A, semantic types are denoted by capital letters):

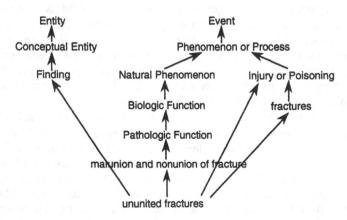

Such graph puts in evidence several ontological problems, at least if ontological analysis and integration are aimed at supporting clear identity criteria (see also [15]). Is it ontologically acceptable that "ununited fractures" is classified both under "Natural Phenomenon" and under "Injury or Poisoning", which is not a "Natural Phenomenon"? Is ontologically acceptable a concept which is classified both under "Phenomenon" and "Conceptual Entity"?

One may simply conclude that hierarchical assignments here have been decided with disregard of logical semantics. On the other hand, this would be a superficial judgment. In fact, UMLS assignments try to cover some possible polysemous senses of "ununited fractures" without creating ad-hoc distinctions (e.g. "ununited fractures-1", "ununited fractures-2", "ununited fractures-3", etc.).

An advantage provided by ontological analysis and integration is the possibility of treating such polysemy without multiplying the ad-hoc distinctions.

For example, after the application of ontological analysis, "ununited fractures" would be conceptualized as follows:

1. a fracture of a bone that necessarily *bears* a malunion (a pathology causing a morphological imprecision) or lacks integrity;
2. it necessarily *depends on* and *postdates* a fracture resulted from a fracture event;
3. it contingently may be an *interpretant* (a sign) *of* some clinical condition.

Therefore, such conceptualization shows only one classification (under "fracture") and three definitional axioms, which provide the identity criteria for the instances of "fractures, ununited".

```
(defconcept |fractures, ununited|
  :is-primitive (:and fracture
                (:some morphology
                  (:and bone (:or (:some embodies malunion)
                              (:not integral))))
                (:some dependently-postdates fracture)
                (:all interpretant clinical-condition)))
```

Further details on formal and conceptual tools used in ontological analysis are reported in [15]. For a full report about the UMLS ontologization, see [18] and [19].

4 Ontology for an Effective Information Integration

The UMLS Metathesaurus is already used in various projects aimed at the retrieval of web sites [20], the knowledge-based querying of databases [21], the development of middleware components for enterprise information management [22]. However, in order to allow an effective information integration, the Metathesaurus should have a formal and conceptually rigorous structure which can be obtained only by means of the appropriate logical and ontological tools.

In fact, heterogeneity of information in data bases schemata or in other semi-formal information repositories is due essentially to the different conceptualizations of the terms which constitute the information in the repository. Such inherent polysemy of terminological information is reflected by widespread polysemous phenomena within existing medical terminologies. As we have emphasized, polysemy is widespread in the UMLS Metathesaurus as well.

More generally, medical terminological sources show either one or more of the following issues (see the case studies in [15] for detailed examples):

- *Lack of axioms*: for example, ICD10 shows naked taxonomies, without axioms or even a natural language gloss.
- *Semantic imprecision* (cycles, relation range violation, etc.): for example, the semantic network used as the top-level of the UMLS Metathesaurus includes a set of templates for its taxonomy, but the semantics of such templates is not defined at all: after careful analysis, the best that we could do is considering UMLS templates as default axioms.
- *Ontological opaqueness* (lack of reference to an explicit, axiomatized generic ontology, or at least to a generic informal theory): for example, systems in which concepts and relations in the top-level are non-axiomatized and undocumented: they may appear to have been chosen with disregard of formal ontology: possibly no trace of mereological, topological, localistic, dependence notions is retrievable.
- *Linguistic awkwardness in naming policy*: for example, systems in which purely formal architecture considerations originate a lot of redundancy and cryptic relation and concept names.

We already pointed out that an explicit conceptualization of a terminology needs to be philosophically and linguistically grounded. We suggest the importance of the so-called "generic theories", such as "mereology" or theory of parts, "topology" or theory of wholes and connexity, "morphology", or theory of form and congruence, "localization", or theory of regions, "time" theory, "actors", or theory of participants in a process, "dependence", etc.

The debate on the relevance of generic theories to the development of domain ontologies is still open. Our position is that generic theories are essential to the development of ontologies and to a rigorous conceptual integration of heterogeneous terminologies.

For example, in the previous definition of "ununited fracture", there is a subtle connection between "ununited fracture" and "fracture": an ununited fracture must *postdate* a previous fracture occurring in the same area of a bone, which has been complicated by a malunion. Moreover, an ununited fracture *depends on* that previous fracture. According to the ontological methodology we have proposed elsewhere [9], postdating and dependence must have a definition in some generic theory, in order to be easily understood, reused, and maintained.

A "dependently-postdates" relation is actually defined in our ON9 (see section 2.) theory: "unrestricted-time", which contains the definitions of many temporal relations that hold for intervals, or for processes, or for entities in general (like "postdates"). Such distinctions in the domain and range restriction of temporal relations are motivated by the different identity criteria that different kinds of entities have over time. "Dependently-postdates" is a kind of "postdates" that also states that the second entity depends on the first for its existence. The definition of this relation makes use of the relation "strictly-depends-on", defined in the ON9 theory: "dependence".

A similar line of reasoning can be made for the other axioms in the example definitions given above: "embodies" - defined in theory: "actors" - is a special kind of actor meaning that an object is the host of some process, "component" and "portion" – defined in theory: mereology - are two kinds of part relations, etc.

Ontology integration may act as a reference activity for information integration architectures and standardization work. Our experience has proved that the ontologies produced by means of the ONIONS methodology support:
- *Formal upgrading* of terminology systems: terminological subsumptions and definitions are available in an expressive and semantically explicit formal language;
- *Conceptual explicitness* of terminology systems: term definitions are available, even though the source does not include them explicitly. Consequently, within a given module, polysemy disappears;
- *Conceptual upgrading* of terminology systems: term classification and definitions are translated so that they can be included in a modular ontology library which has a subset constituted of adequate generic ontologies;
- *Ontological comparability*, since pre-existing ontology libraries pertaining to different fields are largely reused. Moreover, the primitives of the formal language have a meta-level assignment [7], which allows easier distinction between superficially similar concepts.

5   Conclusions

Telecommunications and networking are dramatically changing the scenario of knowledge management in medicine. Traditional terminology systems are not appropriate anymore to satisfy the demand for re-use of data, unambiguous transmission and statistical aggregation. An ontological approach to the description of terminology systems will allow a better integration and reuse of these systems.
An example of such effective reuse has been provided by our analysis of the multiple classification phenomenon in UMLS in terms of polysemy and its possible account according to generic theories and general medical ontologies.
One may wonder if UMLS can be considered a "super source" to be preferred to its component sources. We believe that it should not replace the original sources, because they often embed more information than that incorporated by UMLS. We started our ontological analysis from the Metathesaurus because it has normalized the lexical variants and most synonyms and it has related the CUIs to a great amount of additional information. The ontological analysis of UMLS yielded a partition of CUIs according to the original UMLS semantic types. Such a partition allowed us to define contexts that refer to medical sub-domains and depend on a library of generic theories.
However we do not plan to limit our ontological analysis to UMLS. It is a good starting point, but it will be followed by analyses of other important sources like SNOMED, for which the top-levels have already been analyzed.

References

1. Guarino N (ed.), *Formal Ontology in Information Systems*, Amsterdam, IOS-Press, 1998.
2. Goñi A, Mena E, Illaramendi A, "Querying Heterogeneous and Distributed Data Repositories Using Ontologies", in Info. Modeling and Knowledge Bases IX, Amsterdam, IOS, 1998.
3. Guarino N, *Formal Ontology and Information Systems*, in [1].
4. Sowa J, communication to the *ontology-std* mailing list, 1997.
5. Rothenfluh TE, Gennari JH, Eriksson H, Puerta AR, Tu SW, Musen MA, Reusable Ontologies, Knowledge-Acquisition Tools, and Performance Systems: PROTEGE-II Solutions to Sisyphus-2. *International Journal of Human-Computer Studies*, 44, 1996.
6. National Library of Medicine, *UMLS Knowledge Sources*, 1997 edition, available from the NLM, Bethesda, Maryland.
7. Guarino N, Carrara M, Giaretta P "An Ontology of Meta-Level Categories" In J Doyle, E Sandewall and P Torasso (eds.), *Principles of Knowledge Representation and Reasoning: Proc. of KR94*. San Mateo, CA, Morgan Kaufmann, 1994.
8. van Heijst G, Falasconi S, Abu-Hanna A, Schreiber G, and Stefanelli M, A case study in ontology library construction. *Artificial Intelligence in Medicine*, 1995, 227-255.
9. Steve G, Gangemi A, Pisanelli DM, "Integrating Medical Terminologies with ONIONS Methodology", in Kangassalo H, Charrel JP (Eds.) *Information Modeling and Knowledge Bases VIII*, Amsterdam, IOS Press 1998.
10. Coté RA, Rothwell DJ, Brochu L, Eds. *SNOMED International* (3rd ed.), Northfield, Ill, College of American Pathologists, 1994.
11. Gabrieli E, "A New Electronic Medical Nomenclature", *J. Medical Systems*, 3, 1989.
12. WHO, *International Classification of Diseases* (10th revision), Geneva, WHO, 1994.
13. Rector A, Solomon WD, Nowlan WA, "A Terminology Server for Medical Language and Medical Information Systems", *Methods of Information in Medicine*, 34, 1995.
14. Pisanelli DM, Gangemi A, Steve G, "WWW-available Conceptual Integration of Medical Terminologies: the ONIONS Experience", *Proc. of AMIA 97 Conference*, 1997.
15. Gangemi A, Pisanelli DM, Steve G, "Ontology Integration: Experiences with Medical Terminologies", in [1].
16. MacGregor RM, "A Description Classifier for the Predicate Calculus" *Proc. AAAI 94*, 1994.
17. Humphreys BL, Lindberg DA, "The Unified Medical Language System Project", *Proc. of MEDINFO 92*, Amsterdam, Elsevier, 1992.
18. Gangemi A, Pisanelli DM, Steve G, "Ontologizing UMLS", ITBM-CNR TR 0198A, 1998.
19. Pisanelli DM, Gangemi A, Steve G, "An Ontological Analysis of the UMLS Methatesaurus", *Proc. of AMIA 98 Conference*, 1998.
20. http://www.mwsearch.com
21. http://igm.nlm.nih.gov
22. Tuttle MS, Chute MD, Safran C, Abelson DJ, Campbell KE, Panel: Enterprise Experience with a Reusable Vocabulary Component, *Proc. of AMIA 98 Conference*, 1998.

The Use of the UMLS Knowledge Sources for the Design of a Domain Specific Ontology: A Practical Experience in Blood Transfusion

Soumeya Achour[1], Michel Dojat[2], Jean-Marc Brethon[3], Gil Blain[3], Eric Lepage[1]

[1] Medical Informatics Departement, Henri Mondor Hospital, AP-HP,Creteil, France
email :soumeya.achour@hmn.ap-hop-paris.fr
[2] RMN Bioclinique, INSERM U438, Grenoble, France
[3] LIP6, Paris VI University, Paris, France

Abstract. In highly evolved medical domains, decision support systems have to be easily modified by medical experts themselves. In the field of blood transfusion, the evolution of medical knowledge and governmental regulation impose a continuous adaptation of decision support systems. Explicit domain ontologies are then a prerequisite for the construction of such extensible systems. We have chosen to have our domain ontology representation based on the entities and relations present in the UMLS knowledge sources. In this paper we detail how, in using a specific browser, we have exploited, reused and extended UMLS entities and relations to design a domain specific ontology for blood transfusion.

1 Introduction

To overcome the limitations of the first generation of medical knowledge-based systems (KBS), we must adopt a clear methodology for knowledge acquisition and knowledge representation. In practice, the knowledge engineer (KE) must represent the expert discourse using an explicit sharable domain ontology (entities and relations between them) in order to facilitate future extensibility and reuse. The support of patient care applications lead to a growing interest for controlled medical terminologies [1]. In the field of blood transfusion, the evolution of medical knowledge and governmental regulation impose a continuous adaptation of decision support systems. For the design of a KBS for blood transfusion, we have chosen to build our domain ontology representation on the entities and relations present in the UMLS knowledge sources [2]. UMLS is now a largely used system for clinical applications, [3], [4], [5], [6]. Our pragmatic goal is to introduce a part of UMLS concepts and relations, in the knowledge representation language we use, to design our KBS. For this purpose, we need to extract useful information coming from the metathesaurus and semantic network of UMLS and if necessary extent the initial kernel. In this paper we firstly report the UMLS navigator we have designed for visualization and extraction of information.

W. Horn et al. (Eds.): AIMDM'99, LNAI 1620, pp. 249-253, 1999.
© Springer-Verlag Berlin Heidelberg 1999

2   The UMLS Navigator

The UMLS project, conducted by NLM, was elaborated to facilitate integration of information from multiple biomedical sources. Three main components constitute the UMLS : the so-called Metathesaurus, which contains a collection of biomedical concepts and relationships between them, the Semantic Network, which contains semantic types that characterize the terms present in the Metathesaurus and links between them, and the Information Sources Map. The conceptual model of our navigator is the object-oriented representation of two components of UMLS: the Metathesaurus and the semantic network. Each concept has a unique identifier and different terms which with the same meaning are linked to the same concept identifier.

Our conceptual model accesses, via ODBC and SQL queries, a standard relational database (FoxPro) where the UMLS data have been previously imported. A specific User Interface has been designed to navigate between concepts through the concept hierarchy (function of the information source) and through the semantic network.

Our UMLS navigator is implemented in Smalltalk-80 language (VisualWorks, ParcPlace Ca). We use this language, previously extended with embedded inference capabilities, as the knowledge representation system for our medical applications [7].

3   Construction of Our Domain Specific Ontology

The term ontology is used in different ways and in different disciplines with various meanings. Despite these differences, computer scientists and metaphysicians use in general the term ontology to describe formal descriptions of objects in the world, the properties of those objects, and the relationships among them. In AI, according to Gruber [8] an ontology is a « specification of a conceptualization ». It defines the domain's vocabulary and constraints on the use of terms in the vocabulary.

In our use, domain ontology such as lexicons, specifies medical terms that are used to represent the medical discourse, the classes or categories attached to these terms and the relations which exist between terms and categories are specified.

Our domain of application is blood transfusion. At the Mondor Hospital (Créteil, Fr) we develop a computerized decision support system for blood transfusion. We want to provide embedded tools to allow the clinician to modify and extend the initial corpus knowledge. The first stage of this work consisted in designing an environment where the physician can create his/her domain ontology. The construction of this specific ontology requires four steps.

Step 1: Extraction of the Medical Terms

Starting from direct interviews with the medical expert, we extract all the medical terms relevant to the application. Here is an example of the medical discourse for platelet transfusion, where the relevant terms are shown in italic:

« If patient *platelets number* is $>20.10^9/l$ and $<=30.10^9/l$ and this patient has *leuke-mia myelomonocytic chronic* and has *extracorporeal circulation* then a *platelet transfusion* is necessary . » .

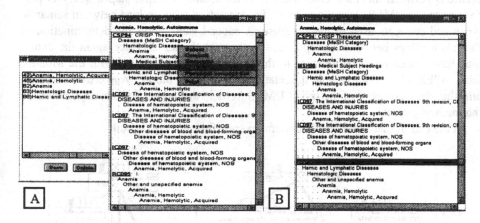

Fig. 1. Selection of the relevant hierarchy . A : a specific popup menu for the construction of our personal source hierarchic. B : a ascendant hierarchic context with our personal source.

Step 2: Finding UMLS Corresponding Terms and Establishing Contextual List

All the terms of our medical list are searched into the UMLS Metathesaurus. To facilitate comprehension and to enrich our list we determine for each concept its as-cending hierarchy i.e. its parents. Depending of the knowledge source one consider, a concept can be found at several levels into a specific ascendant hierarchy. Figure 1. shows the different possible ascendant hierarchies for « anemia hemolytic autoim-mune » term. The expert selects the hierarchy that corresponds to the semantic mean-ing he/she associates to a specific concept, or constructs his/her hierarchy by choos-ing the concepts from the different sources (Figure 1.). Because strong standardization is not always possible in medicine, the medical expert can extend the initial hierar-chies corpus to take into account particular considerations [7]. In this case, the spe-cific classification is built and saved respecting the UMLS constraints and we mark a specific label (PERSO). (Figure 1.).

Step 3: Determination of the Categories and the Semantic Types

The categories represented by the concepts, located at the top of the hierarchy of con-textual list, are selected, then the medical expert explores the UMLS semantic network to find the semantic types of concepts. Every concept has one or more semantic types. For instance, the expert may choose to consider *hematologic neoplasms* as a semantic types *Neoplastic Process* (Figure 2.).

Step 4: Extraction of the Relations

After classification of the terms according to ascendant hierarchy, all the possible relations between them are automatically determined. In a first step a query is performed to the UMLS semantic network for extracting relationships between semantic types and concepts used in the expertise. A second step allows the determination of the relationships between concepts used in the metathesaurus. Once again the expert may have added new relationships to this contextual list identified with the Mondor label «PERSO». For example the relationship between *blood transfusion* and *anemia* that does not exist in the initial UMLS kernel, was added for our application by the medical expert.

At the end of these four steps our domain specific ontology is built.

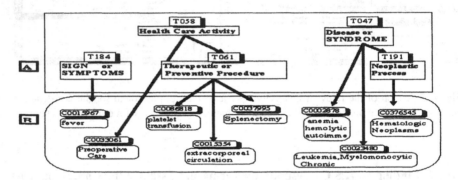

Fig. 2. Medical terms with corresponding categories. A : A part of the semantic network , B: Some concepts extracted from UMLS metathesaurus .

4   Results and Discussion

For the collection of terms present in the blood transfusion expertise part (n=108), we find a correspondence in UMLS metathesarus for 72 concepts (i.e. 70 %). A difficulty is related to composition terms. Thus we have added several terms to enrich the initial metathesaurus. Clearly, this introduction of new items could generate redundancies and conflicts with current terms in the base. Our browser should be extended to incorporate specific tools to deal with these drawbacks .

There are many projects to quantify the content coverage of the UMLS in several domains: clinical radiology [3], laboratory terminology [4], surgical procedures [5]. Similarly to our experience, all these projects indicate limitations of Metathesaurus terms in these areas or inconsistencies respect to anatomical concept representation [9]. This demonstrates the necessity to add new terms and relations for a particular use of UMLS. Nevertheless, following [10] we consider that the UMLS is a useful formal framework that provides a « precise and unambiguous description of the process of assigning meaning », that is easily available to medical institutions and is continuously updated by NLM.

5   Conclusion

In our experience, the UMLS provides a useful corpus of medical knowledge for designing a domain specific terminological knowledge base. It constitutes a first step to facilitate knowledge sharing and reuse. This terminology created will be used in the next step of our project whose objective is to build a knowledge acquisition tool using this ontology and a blood transfusion decision support system (DSS) integrated to the Henri Mondor Hospital Information System.

Acknowledgments

The authors thank the U.S. National Library of Medicine for having provided the UMLS knowledge sources.

References

1. Cimino, J., *Distributed cognition and knowledge-based controlled medical terminologies.* Artificial Intelligence in Medicine, 1998. **12**(2): p. 125-168.
2. *UMLS Knowledge Sources.* Vol. 9th Edition. 1998: National Library of Medicine.
3. Friedman, C. *The Umls coverage of clinical radiology.* in *Proc of the 17th Symposium Computer Application in Medical Care.* 1993. New York.
4. Cimino, J. *Representation of clinical laboratory terminology in the unified Medical Language System (UMLS).* in *Proc of the 15th Symposium Computer Apllication in Medical Care.* 1991. New York.
5. Burgun, A., *et al. Knowledge Acquisition from the UMLS Sources: Application to the Descriptions of Surgical Procedures.* in *MEDINFO 95 Proceedings. R.A. Greenes et al (editors)*. 1995.
6. Campbell, K.E., D.E. Oliver, and E.H. Shortliffe, *Representing Thoughts Words, and Things in the UMLS.* Journal of the American Medical Informatics Association, 1997(Special).
7. Dojat, M. and F. Pachet, *Effective domain-dependent reuse in medical knowledge bases.* Computers and Biomedical Research, 1995. **28**(6): p. 403-432.
8. Gruber, T., *A translation approach to portable ontology spécifications.* Knowledge Acquisition, 1993. **5**: p. 199-220.
9. Mejino, J.L. and C. Rosse. *The Potential of the Digital Anatomis Foundational Model for Assuring Consistency in UMLS Sources.* in *Proc Annu Symp Comp App Med Care.* 1998.
10. Campbell, K.E., D.E. Oliver, and E.H. Shortliffe, *The Unified Medical Language System: Toward A CollaborativeApproach for Solving Terminologic Problems.* Journal of the American Medical Informatics Association., 1997. **5**(1): p. 12-16.

Representing Knowledge Levels in Clinical Guidelines

Paolo Terenziani[1], Paolo Raviola[1], Oscar Bruschi[1],
Mauro Torchio[2], Marina Marzuoli[2], Gianpaolo Molino[2]

[1]Dipartimento di Informatica, Universita' di Torino,
Corso Svizzera 185, 10149 Torino, Italy
[2]Laboratorio di Informatica Clinica, Az. Ospedaliera S. Giovanni Battista,
Corso Bramante 88, 10126 Torino, Italy

Abstract. In this paper, we argue that different levels of knowledge are involved in the representation of clinical guidelines, and that distinguishing among these levels is important from both the conceptual and the methodological point of view. In particular, at the *epistemological level*, one points out different *types of actions* and distinguishes between *structural relations* and *control relations*. On the other hand, the *ontological level* specifically concerns the clinical domain, consisting in the definition of the basic *attributes* of clinical actions and in the description of some *specific types of actions*. We also show how the above distinctions are important for our formalism and for the design of our acquisition module.

1 Introduction

Clinical guidelines are one of the most central areas of research for artificial intelligence in medicine. Many different systems and projects have been developed in the last years in order to obtain a computer-assisted management of clinical guidelines (consider, e.g., [1,4,5,7,10]). In particular, the problem of representing clinical guidelines attracted a lot of attention. Most approaches faced this problem by pointing out a set of pre-defined types of entities (e.g., generic actions vs queries vs decisions), of attributes of these entities (e.g., cost, conflicts, time) and of relations between entities (e.g., sequences or alternatives between actions). This is also the approach we carried on in [6], where we described our representation formalism and compared it with other formalisms in the literature. In particular, our approach is very close to the one of PROforma [4], and its distinctive features mainly concern the enphasis on contextual aspects (e.g., costs, resources) and (as in Asgaard [9]) temporal aspects.

On the other hand, in this paper, we analyse the different types of knowledge involved in clinical medical guidelines, and propose a *methodology* for designing formalisms representing such a knowledge and for developing tools managing it. As a practical example of our methodology, we show how we applied it for defining our representation formalism and our acquisition tool.

W. Horn et al. (Eds.): AIMDM'99, LNAI 1620, pp. 254-258, 1999.
© Springer-Verlag Berlin Heidelberg 1999

2 A Methodology

The methodology we propose is based on the distinction among the different levels of knowledge one has to consider in the representation of clinical guidelines. In fact, we propose an incremental process in which each step corresponds to the representation of a specific type of knowledge.

(1) First, define the basic *epistemological primitives* for the representation of general guidelines. This step concerns:

(1.1) pointing out and distinguishing the basic types of *entities* (e.g., atomic vs. composite actions);

(1.2) representing the *structural relations* between entities;

(1.3) representing *control relations* between entities.

Structural relations are those relations which can be used to define the "structure" of the given domain, imposing some form of hierarchical relation between the entities in the domain[1]. Moreover, an essential part of each guideline and/or plan is the description of the *control relations* (e.g., which actions have to be executed next). In our opinion, these relations are not at all peculiar of the clinical domain, but are related to the general problem of representing protocols, guidelines and plans.

(2) second, devise an *ontology* to represent clinical guidelines, on the basis of the epistemological primitives. This involves at least two related problems:

(2.1) pointing out the basic attributes in the description of the entities in the given domain;

(2.2) modeling at least some of the basic and most frequently recurring entities in the domain (e.g., diagnostic vs. therapeutic decisions).

In order to give a practical example of what we mean for the different levels of knowledge, and a practical application of this methodology, in Section 3 we briefly sketch our representation formalism (see [6] for more details). Moreover, in Section 4, we sketch how such notions and such a methodology impact on the construction of an acquisition module.

3 Different Types of Knowledge in Our Formalism

3.1 Basic Types of Entities

The first step is the definition of the basic epistemological entities. We focused on the notion of action, which is a basic one for describing clinical guidelines. We distinguished between *atomic actions* (elementary steps in a guideline) and *composite actions* (actions to be decomposed into other actions). At least three different types of atomic actions can be distinguished. *Query actions* are requests of information to the

---

[1]For example, in terminological languages such as KL-ONE [2], *set containment* between classes of entities (called *subsumption*) is the basic structural relation, giving a class-subclass hierarchy (e.g., all cats are animals, all animals are animate beings and so on).

outside world (users, data/knowledge bases). *Work actions* are atomic actions which must be executed at a given point of the guideline, and can be described in terms of a set of attributes (see Section 3.4). *Decision actions* are specific types of actions which embody the criteria which can be used to select among alternative actions in a guideline/plan.

3.2 Structural Relations

In the case of plans and guidelines, the basic structural relation is the *has-part relation*, which relates each composite action to the actions composing it. On the basis of the has-part relation, each guideline can be represented as a tree, in which the root node represents the composite action denoting the whole guideline, and, recursively, each node has as childs the actions composing it.

3.3 Control Relations

In our current proposal, we distinguish among three different control relations. A *sequence relation* between two actions A1 and A2 states that A1 and A2 must be executed in sequence, i.e., the execution of A2 can only begin after the end of the execution of A1. In particular, we intend that the sequence of A1 and A2 fails if any of A1 and A2 fails, while the sequence starts when A1 starts and ends when A2 ends. A *concurrency relation* between two actions A1 and A2 states that they can be executed concurrently: the concurrent action fails if any of A1, A2 fails. A1 and A2 can start in any order, and the concurrent action ends when both A1 and A2 end. An *alternative relation* applies to a decision action DA and to n actions A1, ... An of any type (composed or atomic; n>0) representing the fact that one of the n actions A1, ... An is executed depending on the results of the execution of the decision action DA. We intend that the execution of an alternative can be cyclic. Suppose that in the execution of the decision action DA the user selects the action Ai (1=i=n), and that the execution of Ai fails. DA is proposed again to the user, who has to choose among A1, ..., Ai-1, Ai+1, ..., An. The alternative fails if all selected alternatives fail.

3.4 Attributes of Actions

Some of the attributes we used to represent the **basic description** of actions are (see [6] fore more details): **name** (compulsory; all other attributes are optional), **textual description**, **pre-conditions** (minimum and maximum **cost** and **time, resources, conflicts**), **conclusions**. Other attributes are considered to model, e.g., the patterns of repeating actions (e.g., "3 times every 2 days").

3.5 Specific Types of Actions (e.g., Decisions)

The decision process uses different forms of knowledge depending on the context. Currently, we considered two types of decisions, comparing therapeutic vs. diagnostic decisions. In the therapeutic context, physicians choose among different therapies evaluating a given (fixed) set of parameters: effectiveness, cost, side-effects, compliance, duration (which have to be specified for each one of the alternative therapies to be discriminated). Thus, we represented the knowledge involved in a therapeutic decision by considering the set of the above parameters, for each one of the alternatives. On the other hand, the set of parameters to be used in order to discriminate among different diagnoses depends on the specific diagnostic hypothesis being compared. We thus represented the knowledge used in a diagnostic decision as an open list of parameters to be introduced by the expert physician during the acquisition process. For each one of such parameters, we consider a list of values that characterizes it. Finally, we assign a score to each triple <diagnosis, parameter, value>, and consider a threshold which is relative to the sum of the scores[2].

4 Acquisition Module

The distinction among different levels of knowledge is important also for the design of the acquisition tool. Our acquisition module provides a user-friendly graphical interface and is implemented in Java. Whenever the *basic description* of an action (see section 3.4) has to be introduced, an apposite window (called *description window*) is popped out by the acquisition tool. Of course, there are different versions of *description windows*, depending on the types of actions being considered (e.g., query actions vs. decision actions). Such windows show a set of slots (each one corresponding to an attribute of the action) to be filled. Special tabular windows are used to facilitate the introduction of the decision criteria in case of decision actions. The acquisition tool provides a special window (called *structure window*) to represent the structural knowledge, which shows the tree representing the hierarchical structure (based on the *part-of* relation) of the clinical actions already introduced by the expert physician. Whenever the expert physician chooses to introduce a composite action A, a special window (called *control window*) is popped out, which provides a set of graphical primitives to describe the *control relations* between the sub-actions of A. In particular, each subaction is represented by a node in the graph, and different arcs are provided to represent *sequences*, *concurrencies* and *alternatives*.

5 Discussions and Conclusions

This paper deals with the representation clinical guidelines. We argue that different levels of knowledge[3] are involved in this task, and that distinguishing among these

---

[2]During the consultation process, the values of the parameters for the given patient will be considered, and the corresponding scores will be summed up, for each one of the alternatives. Only the alternatives whose additive score is greater than the threshold will be recommended for selection to the user.

[3]Our distinction among different types of knowledge has its roots in the Artificial Intelligence experience. In particular, KL-ONE-like [2] hybrid knowledge representation formalisms [8] proposed a restricted set of domain-independent primitives to represent knowledge at the

levels is important from both the conceptual and the methodological points of view. Moreover, the distinction among different levels of knowledge also provides a better understanding of the generality and applicability of the formalisms and tools being built. For instance, the epistemological primitives (e.g., those described in 3.1, 3.2 and 3.3 and supported by our acquisition module) are domain and task independent. Thus, e.g., we believe that our acquisition module (such as, e.g., the one of PROforma [4]) could be used in other application domains to deal with protocols, guidelines and/or plans. Moreover, the modularity obtained by distinguishing among different levels of knowledge can be advantageous also in the case one wants to deal with specific clinical tasks/domains (see the discussion on generic tasks in [3]). In such a case, our formalism can be easily extended with the introduction of other task/domain specific ontological entities.

References

1. Artificial Intelligence in Medicine 14(1,2), selected papers from AIME'97, 1-236, 1998.
2. R. Brachman and J. Schmolze, "An Overview of the KL-ONE Knowledge Representation System", *Cognitive Science 9(2)*, 171-216, 1985.
3. B. Chandrasekaran, "Towards a functional architecture for intelligence based on generic information processing tasks", Proc. 10th *IJCAI*, 1183-1192, 1987.
4. J. Fox, N. Johns, A. Rahmanzadeh, "Disseminating medical knowledge: the PROforma approach", in [1], 157-182, 1998.
5. C. Gordon & J.P. Christensen, *Health Telematics for Clinical Guidelines and Protocols*, IOS Press, Amsterdam, 1995.
6. A. Guarnero, M. Marzuoli, G. Molino, P. Terenziani, M. Torchio, K. Vanni. Contextual and Temporal Clinical Guidelines. *Journal of the American Medical Informatics Association*, Proc. AMIA Fall Symposium, 683-687, 1998.
7. S.I. Herbert. Informatics for Care Protocols and Guidelines: Towards a European Knowledge Model, in [5], 27-42.
8. B. Nebel, *Reasoning and Revision in Hybrid Knowledge Representation Systems*, LNCS 422, Springer-Verlag, 1990.
9. Y. Shahar, S. Miksch, P. Johnson, "The Asgaard project: a task-specific framework for the application and critiquing of time-oriented clinical guidelines", in [1], 29-52, 1998.
10. I. de Zehger, C. Milstein, B. Sene, A. Venot. Prescription Guidelines in OPADE: what are they, how are they used?, in [5], 199-205.

---

epistemological level, and many approaches took advantage of these formalisms to build "high-level" and/or domain-dependent ontologies [8].

Temporal Reasoning

Intelligent Analysis of Clinical Time Series by Combining Structural Filtering and Temporal Abstractions

R. Bellazzi, C. Larizza, P. Magni, S. Montani, and G. De Nicolao

Dipartimento di Informatica e Sistemistica, Università di Pavia, Italy,
ric@aim.unipv.it, http://aim.unipv.it

Abstract. This paper describes the application of Intelligent Data Analysis techniques for extracting information on trends and cycles of time series coming from home monitoring of diabetic patients. In particular, we propose the combination of structural Time Series analysis and Temporal Abstractions for the interpretation of longitudinal Blood Glucose measurements. First, the measured time series is analyzed by using a novel Bayesian technique for structural filtering; second, the results obtained are post-processed using Temporal Abstractions, in order to extract knowledge that can be exploited "at the point of use" from physicians. The proposed data analysis procedure can be viewed as a typical Intelligent Data Analysis process applied to time-varying data: Background Knowledge is exploited in each step of the analysis, and the final result is a meaningful, abstract description of the complex process at hand. The work here described is part of a web-based telemedicine system for the management of Insulin Dependent Diabetes Mellitus patients, developed within the EU-funded project called T-IDDM.

1 Introduction

Intelligent Data Analysis (IDA) is a new research field, mainly related to develop and apply methods that automatically transform data into information through the exploitation of the Background Knowledge available on the domain [1]. As a natural consequence, in all application areas, IDA collates methodological contributes that come from several disciplines, from AI to Bayesian statistics, and from cognitive science to mathematical modeling. This approach is particularly suitable in bio-medical applications, where the value of each single datum can be high (in terms of cost or of patient's discomfort) and then the capability of interpreting it, by integrating the domain knowledge in the analysis process, may be crucial. With respect to classical Knowledge Discovery in Databases and Data Mining problems [2], the number of data involved in this analysis may be low, while the complexity of the results interpretation still remains high [3].

In this paper we describe an IDA application to the interpretation of time-series coming from the home-monitoring of Insulin Dependent Diabetes Mellitus (IDDM) patients. In particular, we analyze the time-series of Blood Glucose

W. Horn et al. (Eds.): AIMDM'99, LNAI 1620, pp. 261–270, 1999.

Levels (BGL) by combining Time Series (TS) analysis and Temporal Abstractions (TA) techniques [4]. In particular, we use a Bayesian filtering technique to extract from the original TS its *structural components*, i.e. the underlying trends and cycles, that are usually buried into noise and then difficult to highlight. TAs are then applied to each extracted component, to obtain a more concise and user-friendly view of the results, as well as to provide an automated explanation of the phenomena underlying the data.

The idea of applying noise reduction techniques to the original TS in combination with TAs has been already applied by [5] in the monitoring of Intensive Care Unit patients. The novelty of our approach is the integration of *structural filtering* with TAs, so that background knowledge is exploited in each step of the analysis: first, we look for an a-priori known structure of the data, second we look for interesting abstractions through knowledge-based mechanisms. Moreover, since we look for cycles in the BGL data, we are able to cope with the extraction of strictly periodic events, by resorting to simple abstractions [6,7]. Finally, the methodology applied for structural filtering is a brand new application of Bayesian smoothing.

In this paper we will describe each step of the proposed analysis, and we provide some comments about the relationships of our work with other methods proposed in the literature. This work is part of a EU funded telemedicine project, called T-IDDM (Telematic Management of Insulin Dependent Diabetes Mellitus), devoted to provide patients and physicians with an Information Technology infrastructure for a better management of IDDM. In this project, the physician relies on a set of distributed web services, provided by a Medical Workstation. The approach described in this paper is part of the data analysis and visualization tools, that are linked with the data-management and decision support modules of the whole system. For further details see [8].

2   The Problem: A Short Summary

Diabetes Mellitus is one of the major chronic diseases in industrialized countries. Its incidence (around 5%) in the European population and its related costs, force the health care institution towards the improvement of the treatment quality; rather interestingly, Information Technology has been recognized as one of the potential means for obtaining such improvement [9]. In particular, IDDM patients (around 10% of the total diabetic population) are required to undergo an intensive treatment to increase their life-expectancy [10]. This treatment is composed by several (from 3 to 4) insulin injections per day, and a careful BGL self-monitoring before (and sometimes after) each meal. Patients are required to collect into (hand written) diaries BGL, insulin dosages, meals intakes, physical exercise and occurrence of events that may affect glucose metabolism (e.g. fever). All these data are evaluated by physicians every 2/4 months in order to assess the status of the patient's glucose metabolism. Finally, the diary data are combined with some mid-term control variables, like glycated hemoglobin, in order to revise the insulin therapy.

Since early 80's, several systems have been proposed to help patients and physicians in data collection, data analysis, decision support, and, more recently, in a telematic management of the disease [8]. Nevertheless, the analysis of data coming from home monitoring of IDDM patients still remains a rather complex task. A wide spectrum of approaches have been proposed in the literature [6,9,11,12,13]. One of the main difficulties is related to the problem that, in real clinical practice, often the only available data are the BGL measurements, that may be automatically down-loaded from blood glucose reflectometers. This practical limitation has led to the definition of decision support tools that are mainly based on the BGL TS analysis [14].

A way to judge the outcome of a certain therapy scheme starting from the analysis of BGL TS, is to check if it follows a cyclo-stationary behavior, i.e. if the daily course of glycemia is approximatively the same over the monitoring time. A cyclo-stationary behavior is therefore characterized by the absence of significant trends (stationarity) and by a periodic (with period equal to one day) course of BGL. The characteristic daily BGL pattern that summarizes the typical patient's response to the therapy is called *Modal Day* and is usually derived by the frequency histograms of BGL measurements in the different times of the day (see [6,11,12,15] for a detailed discussion).

Looking for modal days and trends can be viewed as a search for a prototypical structure in the data, and can be faced with a TS technique known as structural analysis. Structural filtering has been proposed in the Diabetes field by Deutsch et al. [11], and their experience motivated our work in this field. By itself, structural analysis is able to provide a collection of TSs that express the components of the original one. Such new collection of TSs are smoother than the original, but they may still be difficult to interpret for the final user. For this reason, we propose to post-process them with TAs, that will allow for a higher level data aggregation. The rest of the paper is devoted to the explanation of this two-step process.

3   Structural Time Series Analysis: A New Bayesian Approach

The basic assumption of structural TS analysis is that each measurement of the predicted variable can be expressed as a *sum* of separate components, that represent its underlying *structure*.

In the case of BGL TS, the structure can be chosen as a composition of a Trend component (T), a Cyclic component (C) and a stochastic component (ϵ), so that, for each measurement BGL_i (see [11]):

$$BGL_i = T_i + C_i + \epsilon_i \tag{1}$$

The goal of the TS analysis is then, starting from BGL_i, to extract T_i and C_i. This *filtering* operation can be done by resorting to a variety of approaches, comprising Kalman filtering and least squares fitting.

Before choosing the desired estimation algorithm, it is necessary to select the basic philosophy to pursue during the filtering operation: if, given a certain monitoring period, it is of interest to extract the *dominant trend* and the *dominant cycle* components, or if it is of interest to detect *local trend* and *local cycles*. For example, given 20 days of data, the first choice will lead to select the best linear regression ($Trend = BGL_0 + c \times time$), and the most probable BGL daily pattern (e.g. high BGL at breakfast and low BGL at dinner); on the contrary the second choice allows the user to detect different trends within the 20 days as well as different daily behaviors (e.g high BGL at breakfast and low BGL at dinner until day 10 and then high BGL at breakfast and dinner).

In our work we chose the second approach, that provides the physician (at the end of the IDA activity) with a more deep understanding of the original TS. In particular we have exploited a general approach for Bayesian signal reconstruction described in [16].

In order to detect local trends, the T dynamics is described by introducing an additional variable (S_i) that represents the random variation of T from one measurement to the next one, so that $T_{i+1} - T_i = S_i$. If we assume that the S_i time course is described by a Markov chain, the time evolution of the T component can be specified by the probability distribution $P(S_i \mid S_{i-1})$.

The C dynamics requires a more complex model [17]. At each measurement time, C_i is seen as a linear composition of a sine and a cosine wave, with period one day, so that, if for example, there are three measurements per day, the frequency (f) is $1/3$. The model for C is hence:

$$C_{i+1} = C_i cos(2\pi f) + R_i sin(2\pi f) \tag{2}$$
$$R_{i+1} = -C_i sin(2\pi f) + R_i cos(2\pi f)$$

The randomness of such model can be introduced by supposing that the R_i component is a stochastic variable. Given (2), the system evolution is described by the probability distribution $P(R_{i+1} \mid R_i, C_i)$.

By assuming that:

$$P(S_i \mid S_{i-1}) = N(S_{i-1}, \sigma_T^2)$$
$$P(R_{i+1} \mid R_i, C_i) = N(-C_i sin(2\pi f) + R_i cos(2\pi f), \sigma_C^2)$$
$$P(BGL_i \mid T_i, C_i) = N(T_i + C_i, \sigma_\epsilon^2)$$

where $N(\cdot, \cdot)$ denotes the Normal distribution, it is possible to estimate the couples S_i, T_i and R_i, C_i given BGL_i by resorting to a Markov Chain Monte Carlo method (MCMC) [16]. This method is also able to estimate the variances set $\{\sigma_T^2, \sigma_C^2, \sigma_\epsilon^2\}$. This capability is one of the main advantages with respect to standard Kalman filtering, since usually the "process" prior statistics, namely σ_T^2, σ_C^2 are unknown.

The final outcome of the Bayesian machinery presented above is hence the extraction of two new TS (T and C), from the BGL TS. Such TS express, at each measurement time, the trend and cycle components. Rather interestingly, this model can be easily represented and solved by using a Dynamic Bayesian Network [18], as described in [16].

4   Data Analysis through Temporal Abstractions

The approach we propose for post-processing the C and T components obtained through the structural TS analysis is based on an AI methodology called Temporal Abstraction (TA). TAs are methods used to abstract high level concepts from longitudinal data [4]. They provide an effective instrument to extract from huge amount of temporal information its most relevant features. In the medical domain, TAs are successfully used to describe patients states holding over time periods like *hypoglycemia at dinner for a week* or *hyperglycemia associated to presence of glycosuria at breakfast* [15].

In our application we resort to TAs to summarize in an abstracted and comprehensible form for the physicians the results of the TS structural analysis.

The problem solving method underlying TAs is based on an explicit ontology and a model of time adapted from [4] and described in detail in [6]. The principle of the TA method is to move from a time-point to an interval-based representation of longitudinal data. In our data model all clinical data (measures of clinical parameters, like *BGL'* or *glycosuria*, and actions, like *insulin injection'*) are time-stamped entities, called events, while TAs, which refer to situations persistent over time periods, are represented with intervals, called episodes.

The TA task is decomposed into two subtasks, each one solved by a specific mechanism:

basic TA: solved by mechanisms that abstract time-stamped data into intervals (input data are events and outputs are episodes);

complex TA: solved by mechanisms that abstract intervals into other intervals (input and output data are episodes).

Basic TAs aggregate events (time-stamped data) into episodes (intervals) by detecting clusters of adjacent observations falling within a specific set of qualitative levels or showing definite patterns. In particular, state TAs are defined to detect episodes associated to qualitative levels of time-varying variables, like *hypoglycemia* or *hyperglycemia*, while trend TAs detect patterns like increase, decrease, and stationarity in a numerical time series. Each TA mechanism requires the setting up of several parameters to give a complete specification of the episode in dependence of the characteristics of the application [6].

In our approach we exploit basic TA mechanisms to extract trends (increase, decrease or stationary patterns), and states (e.g. low, normal, high values) from the two structural components of the BGL TS. In particular, we have applied the following analyses:

1) T is analyzed by applying the trend TA mechanism. The final results of this step of the analysis are the intervals corresponding to the periods of relevant BGL increase or decrease.

2) The C component interpretation needs the following post-processing procedure:

2.1) The monitoring period is analyzed to select the intervals where C can be considered a significant component of the original TS. This task is performed by searching stationarity patterns in the C TS. The related TA mechanism aggregates adjacent observations giving rise to oscillations with amplitude lower than a threshold, determined on the basis of the available physiological knowledge (in our case 20 mg/dl). The episodes so extracted can be interpreted as periods without relevant BGL cyclic patterns. The method discharges these episodes from the successive processing and focuses the further analysis on the remaining intervals.

2.2) Over the selected periods a BGL cyclic pattern is extracted for each day. It is derived as the list of daily time measurements arranged so that the corresponding BGL level is in decreasing order (e.g. if, given three measurements per day, the maximum BGL measurement is at lunch and the minimum is at breakfast, the pattern is <lunch, dinner, breakfast>).

2.3) The days with the same BGL cyclic patterns are searched and aggregated with a state TA mechanism in order to check the persistence of each pattern.

The outputs of this phase are the collection of episodes that express the local trends during the monitoring period and the intervals corresponding to the occurrence of all the possible cyclic patterns.

5 A Training Example

In this section we will show the application of the methodology proposed above to the data coming from the home monitoring of a 14 years old male IDDM patient. Such data have been collected during the verification phase of the T-IDDM project in Pavia, at the Department of Pediatrics of the Policlinico S. Matteo Hospital of Pavia.

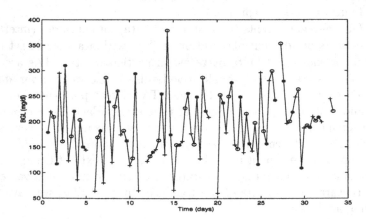

Fig. 1. Data coming from the home monitoring of a 14 years old male IDDM patient. Breakfast (stars), lunch (crosses) and dinner (circles) measurements are highlighted.

Figure 1 shows the data under analysis, corresponding to 33 monitoring days during which the insulin protocol has not been changed by physicians. The data reflect a high variability, and some missing data are present. It is difficult to extract trends and/or cycles from visual inspection, and the histogram analysis allows to detect only some hyperglycemia problems at breakfast and dinner.

When the structural TS analysis is applied, the patient's behavior is more clearly identifiable, as shown in Figure 2. Let's note, for example, the presence of relevant increasing and decreasing trends at the end of the monitoring time, corresponding to a small amplitude of the cycle component. This happens when the cyclo-stationarity assumption does not hold anymore, and the patient BGL is driven by other forces than the daily meal ingestion. Finally, the analysis of the cycles confirms that the lunch measurements (see Fig. 2 bottom) are usually the lowest in each day.

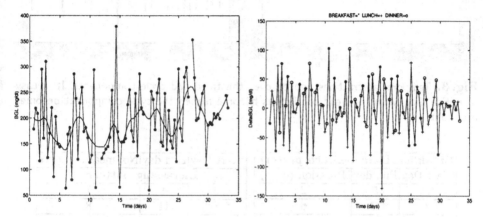

Fig. 2. The trend (left figure) and cycle (right figure). The trend is superimposed with the original data, while in the cycle breakfast (stars), lunch (crosses) and dinner (circles) are highlighted.

The results of this analysis, although quite interesting, are difficult to interpret even for statisticians, and may be useless for the final user during the clinical routine activity. For this reason, the use of TA mechanisms represents a required step towards the clinical evaluation of the data.

Figure 3 shows the result obtained after TA processing. The lack of cyclo-stationarity is highlighted by the *absence of relevant daily cycle* episode, while the extent of cyclical patterns are clearly depicted.

Table 1 shows the textual report generated from the data analysis, that describes the patient's behavior of the analyzed time period. From a clinical point of view, the analysis allows the physician to separate the last monitoring period from the first 20 days, asking the patient for additional information. Since the last period was related to a concurrent fever, it was discarded, and the therapy modification was related only to the analysis of the first part of the data set.

6   Discussion

The method that we propose in this paper presents a number of interesting advantages with respect to the standard methods reported in the literature for IDDM data analysis:

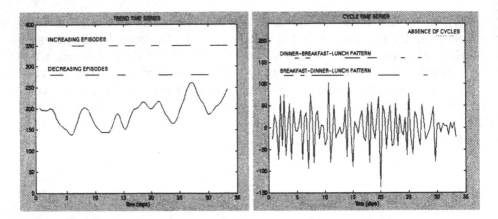

Fig. 3. Temporal abstractions applied over the trend and cycle components. It is easy to notice that when the trend oscillations become higher, the cycle component becomes irrelevant.

Breakfast-Dinner-Lunch pattern			Start Day	End day	No. measurements
Start Day	End day	Duration (days)	**Increasing pattern**		
3	5	2	2	4	7
8	14	6	8	11	8
20	24	4	14	15	5
Dinner-Breakfast-Lunch pattern			21	24	7
Start Day	End day	Duration (days)	27	30	10
14	17	3	**Decreasing pattern**		
18	20	2	6	8	7
Absence of cycles			12	14	6
Start Day	End day	Duration (days)	15	17	6
30	34	4	20	21	5
			23	27	11
			30	33	10

Table 1. Textual report of the structural analysis. Only episodes with extent grater than one day are reported.

- *Over descriptive statistics*: the method is able to explicitly take into account time, and to perform the non trivial separation of Trend and Cycle components. Moreover, the method is able to handle missing data (by estimating them).
- *Over simple structural analysis*: TAs provide the final user with results more easy to handle and to interpret; moreover, such result can be combined with other information to derive more complex patterns (Complex TAs), useful for further steps of data mining and automated reasoning.
- *Over simple TA*: the pre-filtering operation is able to provide smooth TSs with cycles separation. This allows for a more robust application of TA mechanisms, as well as for an easier extraction of information buried into noise.
As often happens with the majority of the approaches, there are not only pros.

The structural analysis method has a number of cons, that are listed below:

1) It is required that the patient follows a nearly regular sampling scheme; in other words, it is assumed that the unreported data are missing at random. If there is a systematic lack of measurements in a certain moment of the day, the structural filtering scheme may give inaccurate results [19].

2) The MCMC algorithm applied is quite slow from a computational point of view: when the monitoring period is over one month, a run of 1000 samples on a Sun Sparc station 10 may take around one hour. This means that it is necessary to run in batch the algorithm before physicians consultation. We are now working on more efficient techniques, comprising a combination of MCMC with recursive least squares estimation.

Finally, some further considerations are needed on the applicability of the proposed approach, with particular emphasis on the cycle extraction. The structural analysis is able to detect cycles with a *fixed* period (in our case 1 day) or with a period varying within a known range (like weekly events, with a period of 5/7 days). When this kind of knowledge is available, mixed approaches, like ours, can be conveniently adopted. Otherwise, it is necessary to resort to more general heuristic methods, as described in [7,20]. In these works, the notion of periodicity is extended to find out recurrent abstract episodes: in this case the time span of the period is not necessarily specified, as well as the time extent of each episode. Clearly, such methods are so general that they can also cope with the problem herein presented in a methodologically uniform fashion. Nevertheless, being interested in exploiting the data analysis results in a real clinical setting, we believe that in our problem it is more effective to resort to a hybrid approach that losses generality but gains robustness in combining quantitative and heuristic methods. In the future, we plan to investigate how the use of periodic Temporal Abstractions could be integrated in our work, in order to find recurrent events at an higher level of abstraction, such as repeating hypoglycemia patterns, or seasonal effects on BGL control.

Acknowledgements. Prof. Mario Stefanelli is gratefully acknowledged for having revised early draft of this paper. We thank Emanuela Piccolini for her contribution in the system implementation. Finally we thank sincerely Alberto Riva, without whom this work couldn't have been done. This work is part of the project T-IDDM (HC 1047), funded by the European Commission.

References

1. Bellazzi, R., Zupan, B.: Intelligent Data Analysis in Medicine and Pharmacology: A position statement. in IDAMAP 98: ECAI 98 Workshop, Brighton, 1998, 2–5.
2. Fayyad, U., Uthurusamy, R.: Data Mining and Knowledge Discovery in Databases. Communications of the ACM. **39** (1996) 24–26.
3. Lavrac, N., Keravnou, E., Zupan, B.: Intelligent Data Analysis in Medicine and Pharmacology: an overview. in: *Intelligent Data Analysis in Medicine and Pharmacology*, N. Lavrac, E. Keravnou, B. Zupan eds., Kluwer, 1997, pp. 61-80.
4. Shahar, Y.: A Framework for Knowledge-Based Temporal Abstraction, Artificial Intelligence. **90** (1997) 79–133.

5. Horn, W., Miksch, S., Egghart, G., Popow, C., Paky, F., Effective data validation of high frequency data: time-point-, time-interval- and trend-based- methods. Computers in Biology and Medicine. **27** (1997) 389–409.

6. Bellazzi, R., Larizza, C., Riva, A.: Temporal abstractions for interpreting chronic patients monitoring data. Intelligent Data Analysis - an International journal, **2** (1998), http://www.elsevier.com/locate/ida.

7. Keravnou, E.T.: Temporal Abstraction of Medical Data: deriving periodicity in: *Intelligent Data Analysis in Medicine and Pharmacology*, N. Lavrac, E. Keravnou, B. Zupan eds., Kluwer, 1997, pp. 61-80.

8. Bellazzi, R., Riva, A., Larizza, C., Fiocchi, S., Stefanelli, M. : A Distributed System for Diabetic Patients Management. Computer Methods and Programs in Biomedicine, **56** (1998) 93-107.

9. Lehmann, E.D.: Application of computers in clinical diabetes care. Diab. Nutr. Metab. **10** (1997) 45-59.

10. The Diabetes Control and Complication Trial Research Group: The effect of intensive treatment of diabetes on the development and progression of long-term complications in insulin-dependent diabetes mellitus, The New England Journal of Medicine. **329 (14)** (1993) 977–986.

11. Deutsch, T., Lehmann, E.D., Carson, E.R., Roudsari, A.V., Hopkins, K.D., Sönksen. P.: Time series analysis and control of blood glucose levels in diabetic patients. Computer Methods and Programs in Biomedicine. **41** (1994) 167–182.

12. Kahn, M.G., Abrams, C.A., Orland, M.J. et al.: Intelligent computer-based interpretation and graphical presentation of self-monitored blood glucose and insulin data. Diab. Nutr. Metab. **4** (1991) 99-107.

13. Andreassen, S., Benn, J., Hovorka, R., Olesen, K.G., Carson, E.R.: A probabilistic approach to glucose prediction and insulin dose adjustment: description of metabolic model and pilot evaluation study. Computer Methods and Programs in Biomedicine. **41** (1994) 153-165.

14. Deutsch, T., Roudsari, A.V., Leicester, H.J., Theodorou, T., Carson, E.R., Sönksen, P.H.: UTOPIA: a consultation system for visit-by-visit diabetes management. Medical Informatics. **21** (1996) 345-358.

15. Shahar, Y., Musen, M.A.: Knowledge-Based Temporal Abstraction in Clinical Domains. Artificial Intelligence in Medicine. **8** (1996) 267-298.

16. Bellazzi, R., Magni, P., De Nicolao, G.: Dynamic Probabilistic Networks for Modelling and Identifying Dynamic Systems: a MCMC Approach. Intelligent Data Analysis: an International Journal. **1** (1997) http://www.elsevier.com/locate/ida.

17. Harvey, A.: Structural Time Series Model and the Kalman Filter. Cambridge: Cambridge University Press. 1990.

18. Dagum, P., Galper, A.: Time Series prediction using belief network models. Int. J. Human-Computer Studies. **42** (1995) 617-632.

19. Ramoni, M., Sebastiani, P.: The use of exogenous knowledge to Learn Bayesian Networks from Incomplete Databases. Advances in Intelligent Data Analysis. Lecture Notes in Computers Science 1280. Berlin: Springer. 1997; 537-549.

20. Morris, R.A., Khatib, L.: Quantitative Structural Temporal Constraints on repeating events. L.Vila et al.(eds.), The Handbook of Time and Temporal Reasoning in Artificial Intelligence (to appear).

Knowledge-Based Event Detection in Complex Time Series Data

Jim Hunter[1] and Neil McIntosh[2]

[1] Department of Computing Science, University of Aberdeen, Aberdeen AB24 3UE
jhunter@csd.abdn.ac.uk
[2] Department of Child Life and Health, University of Edinburgh

Abstract. This paper describes an approach to the detection of events in complex, multi-channel, high frequency data. The example used is that of detecting the re-siting of a transcutaneous O_2/CO_2 probe on a baby in a neonatal intensive care unit (ICU) from the available monitor data. A software workbench has been developed which enables the expert clinician to display the data and to mark up features of interest. This knowledge is then used to define the parameters for a pattern matcher which runs over a set of intervals derived from the raw data by a new iterative interval merging algorithm. The approach has been tested on a set of 45 probe changes; the preliminary results are encouraging, with an accuracy of identification of 89%

1. Introduction

It is generally recognised that the ability to reason with data which has a temporal dimension is an important attribute of many medical problem solving systems. However there is no single 'temporal dimension' - many variations are possible and include:

- Is the time between data samples constant or variable?
- What is the frequency of sampling? Clearly the description of a particular frequency as 'high' or 'low' will depend on the time-scales inherent in the process being observed.
- Is one variable being sampled, or more than one? If we are sampling more than one, is the process being monitored such that we need to correlate changes in different variables? (We will use the term channel to refer to a series of samples from one variable).
- Is the primary temporal construct the point or the interval?
- Is the final system intended to work in real time or retrospectively? In real time the only data available is in the past relative to the time at which we are trying to generate an interpretation. On the other hand, we may be trying to generate an interpretation for a given time series as a whole - for a time in the middle of that series we have both 'past' and 'future' data available.
- What is the goal of the interpretation? Many goals are legitimate: real-time alarming, diagnosis, treatment planning and monitoring, summarisation, clinical audit, etc.

W. Horn et al. (Eds.): AIMDM'99, LNAI 1620, pp. 271-280, 1999.
© Springer-Verlag Berlin Heidelberg 1999

This paper is concerned specifically with data acquired from monitors in intensive care; the data come from several channels which are sampled regularly at relatively high frequencies; in the example which runs through this paper we look at two channels sampled once per second. Data samples are taken at time points, but our underlying temporal ontology is based on intervals. At present we consider our data retrospectively; however extension to real-time is one of our goals for the future.

Our current objective is the identification of specific events. By an event we mean a temporal interval over which the nature of the signal, usually in more than one channel, is characteristic of the occurrence of a particular process. The origins of the process may be external to the patient e.g. taking a blood sample or sucking out an endotrachael tube. Such events are generally referred to as artefacts in that they do not represent the true physiological state of the patient. Other events arise purely internally e.g. a pneumothorax. The distinction is not hard and fast - a blocked tube arises neither from the inherent physiological processes operating in the patient, nor is it the result of a totally external intervention. One reason for wanting to identify artefacts is to enable us to remove them from the data. However it may be of interest for audit purposes to know how often particular events take place.

In this paper we will discuss the interpretation of data from a neonatal ICU. The *Mary*[3] system has been used in the Simpson Maternity Hospital, Edinburgh, for a number of years. Over that time a large data archive of over 1000 cases has been built up. A PC is located at each cot, and Mary is used to acquire, display and archive multi-channel data from the monitors.

The particular event we have worked with is the probe change. A small probe is attached to the baby's skin, and used to measure transcutaneous oxygen and carbon dioxide. Because the technology involves the underlying skin being heated, and because neonates have very delicate skin, the probe has to be lifted and re-sited every few hours to avoid permanent scarring. When the probe is removed the measured values move rapidly towards the O_2 and CO_2 levels in the atmosphere, the O_2 rising sharply and the CO_2 falling somewhat more slowly. On being replaced, the measured levels return to those corresponding to the levels in the blood - again the CO_2 levels respond more slowly than the O_2.

The signals arising from events may be complex. However our observations in the COGNATE project shows that an experienced clinician can bring a considerable amount of background knowledge to their interpretation. The thesis developed in this paper is that although sophisticated mathematical techniques may have their place, capturing and representing expert knowledge is indispensable. However the very volume and richness of the data give rise to difficulties. Conventional knowledge acquisition normally includes sessions in which the expert is presented with a typical problem and comments on how (s)he arrives at an interpretation. When the data is sparse, individual data items can be referred to verbally ('the patient's history of anorexia'). However it is much more difficult to talk about a temporal pattern without being able to indicate which section of data is being referred to. For this reason we have developed a software tool (known as the Time Series Workbench) which

---

[3] *Mary* was developed and supplied by Meadowbank Medical Systems.

displays multi-channel data and enables the expert to identify particular intervals in one or more channels and to attach a symbolic descriptor to each interval.

The organisation of the remainder of this paper is as follows. Section 2 sets out how the expert clinician uses the workbench to interact with examples of the event being analysed and to describe the features which will be used by the event detection system. This system is presented in Section 3 - it is based on an algorithm which automatically segments the time series into intervals and then passes these to a pattern matcher implemented as forward chaining rules. Section 4 summarises our preliminary results. Section 5 compares our approach with those of others and our final conclusions are presented in Section 6.

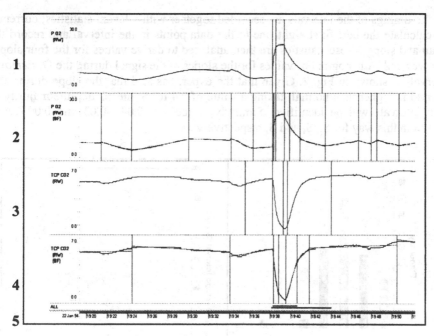

Fig. 1. Example of a probe change

2. Knowledge Acquisition

Preliminary interviews with the expert are used to identify which type of event to investigate; we then build up a catalogue of examples of such events. The next step is to specify which features characterise the event. In our approach these have to be specified as named temporal intervals with particular attributes. For probe changes our expert identified three main intervals in each of the O_2 and CO_2 channels: *Removal*, *Atmosphere* (when the probe is exposed to atmospheric levels) and *Replacement*. In addition, a preceding reference interval (*Pre-Probe-Change*) was also defined. It was further established that the slopes of the signals during the *Removal* and *Replacement* intervals were higher than normal.

We then formalised the characteristics of these features and their temporal relationships - for example the removal of a probe is defined by two overlapping intervals - an interval in which the O_2 rises with a slope of greater than S_1 and an interval in which the CO_2 falls at a rate greater than S_2. Likewise for the probe replacement with its slopes S_3 and S_4. The expert will often have a good idea as to what the values of the numerical parameters should be, but we can assist him by getting him to 'mark-up' a number of examples. Using the Workbench, he inspects the data for a particular event and drags the mouse over the data to identify, for each of the two channels, the four intervals defined above. Our expert marked up 45 probe changes in this way. Fig. 1 shows the data for a typical probe change; panels 1 and 3 show the expert's mark up. The meaning of panels 2, 4 and 5 will be explained later.

The timings of the intervals are recorded together with relevant statistics; currently we calculate the best fit straight line to the data points in the interval and record the mean and slope. These statistics are then analysed to derive values for the four slopes that we need. A histogram of values for the slopes of the signal during the O_2 *Removal* intervals is shown in Fig. 2. Given that the expert has said that the slope during this interval is higher than normal, taking a value of 0.4 for S_1 means that the majority of such intervals will be identified. Similarly, values of -0.04, -0.03 and 0.005 were chosen in this way for S_2, S_3 and S_4 respectively.

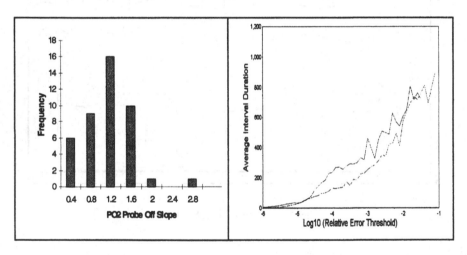

Fig. 2. The slopes (in kPa/sec.) of the 45 O_2 *Removal* intervals

Fig. 3. Average Relative Error plots for both channels (see Section 3.1)

3. Event Detection

3.1. Automatic Segmentation

Our approach is based on temporal intervals. We therefore need a way of automatically segmenting the time series into a number of intervals in a meaningful way. Since we are interested in slopes it seems natural to approach segmentation from the point of view of trying to approximate to the data with a sequence of line segments. Panels 2 and 4 of Fig. 1 present an example of the output of the algorithm that has been developed. It might be argued that higher order curve fitting would be more appropriate for some features, but linear fitting has the benefit of simplicity.

In essence the algorithm iterates by merging two adjacent intervals into a 'super-interval' until a halting condition is satisfied. It starts by converting the sequence of time points at which the samples occur into a sequence of elementary intervals. Thus if the samples are taken at times t_i, t_{i+1}, t_{i+2}, etc, we construct intervals (t_i, t_{i+1}), (t_{i+1}, t_{i+2}), etc. We then fit the best straight line to the data in each interval; since at this initial stage there are only two points per interval, the line passes through both points. The aim now is to decrease the number of intervals by selecting two adjacent intervals to merge. At each iteration we examine all pairs of adjacent intervals and calculate the regression line through the points in the super-interval that would be obtained by merging them. We define the *error* for the super-interval as the sum of the squares of the deviations of the points from the regression line (where n is the number of points in the potential super-interval):

$$\sum_{i=1}^{n}(y_i - (mx_i + c))^2$$

We now select and perform the merge that minimises this error. In principle we could explore a search tree of possible merges. We have not investigated this possibility as we believe it to be computationally intractable, and have settled for the simpler 'greedy' approach.

Merging continues until the halting condition is satisfied. If merging were allowed to continue unchecked we would obtain one interval containing all the points in the time series. This is considered to be the 'worst case' segmentation; we therefore pre-compute the error for the entire time series and use this *series error* as a reference. As we iterate, we calculate the error (as defined above) for each interval and obtain the *current error* by summing these over all intervals (taking care not to double count the errors derived from the end points). The *relative error* at any particular iteration is defined as the ratio of the current error to the series error. Clearly the relative error is 0 before merging starts (as each line segment is fitted to two points with no error) and, unless the merging is halted, would ultimately rise to 1. Merging ceases when the relative error reaches a pre-set threshold. The lower this threshold, the earlier the merging will stop, the greater will be the number of intervals left, and the closer we will approximate to the original time series. More formally this best-fit algorithm is defined as follows:

- Decide on the *relative error threshold;*
- Use linear regression to fit the best line to all points t_1 - t_N (where N is the number of points in the series);
- Calculate the *series error;*
- *FOR EACH* of the N-1 time points t_1 .. t_i .. t_N in the time series construct an interval (t_i, t_{i+1}) - call this interval I_i;

- *REPEAT*
  - For each pair of adjacent intervals I_i and I_{i+1} use linear regression to fit the best line to all the points in the potential super-interval and calculate the *error*;
  - Find the lowest error;
  - Merge the two corresponding intervals;
  - Calculate the sum of the errors over all intervals - the *current error*
- *UNTIL (current error / series error)* ≥ *relative error threshold*

We can get some indication of the appropriate value for the relative error threshold, by looking at the distribution of durations of the intervals which the expert has marked up; for probe changes this turns out to be in the range 100-300 seconds. We assume that once we have stopped merging, the average interval size should be comparable to the average interval duration as defined by the expert. The relationship between relative error and average duration can be investigated experimentally. For each example, we carry out the iterative best-fit, noting at each iteration the relative error and the average interval duration, letting the merging continue until a single interval is obtained. Fig. 3 shows the average (over 45 samples) duration for a given relative error for both channels. Once the average interval size is established we can work back to the relative error which would generate it. In this case it seems that to get an average duration in the range 100-300 seconds, we should set the relative error threshold around 10^{-4} to 10^{-3}.

3.2. Pattern Matching

Event detection now proceeds as follows. Each channel is segmented using the best-fit algorithm. The slopes for each of the intervals is calculated. The set of intervals is passed to a forward chaining rule-based system with the following basic rules:

Rule: Probe-Off
if ∃ interval, IO_2 in the O_2 channel with slope > 0.4 kPa/sec
and ∃ interval ICO_2 in the CO_2 channel with slope < -0.04 kPa/sec
and IO_2 overlaps ICO_2
then assert that an instance of Probe-Off (*POff*) occurs at the earlier of start(IO_2) and start(ICO_2)

overlaps is used in the sense of Allen's temporal relation of that name [1].
start(I) means the time that interval I starts.
Note that our definition of the timing of the event is consistent with that used for the expert's mark-up.

We have a similar rule for *Probe-On*, where *POn* occurs at the later of end(IO_2) and end(ICO_2).

The rule to construct a *Probe-Change* is:

Rule: Probe-Change
if   ∃ instance of Probe-Off, *POff*
and ∃ instance of Probe-On, *POn* such that *POff* occurs earlier than *POn*
and the time difference between *POff* and *POn* is less than all other remaining
     POff - POn sequential pairs
then assert the existence of a *Probe-Change* interval starting at *POff* and ending at
     POn and remove *POn* and *POff* from working memory.

It should be realised that there may be a number of false Probe-Off and Probe-On identifications. The test on the time difference ensures that we favour Probe-Off/Probe-On pairings which are close together. There are other rules that retract pairings which are obviously incorrect (e.g. which imply, for example, two succeeding Probe-Ons without an intervening Probe-Off).

The rule-based system returns all identified probe change intervals for display and analysis.

4. Analysis of Results

We evaluated the accuracy of the event detection system by running it on the data associated with each known probe change; somewhat arbitrarily this consisted of 60 minutes of data centred on each event. For each sample we displayed both channels with the expert's mark up, the segmentation generated by the best-fit algorithm, and probe change intervals both generated automatically and derived from the expert's mark-up. An example is shown in Fig. 1. The top bar in panel 5 (marked ALL) shows the duration of the probe change event as detected by the pattern recogniser; the bottom bar shows the same interval as derived from the expert. We say that we have a true positive when there is an overlap between the two bars – we have not yet taken into account any difference in duration.

We decided to investigate the effect of different levels of relative error threshold. The event detection algorithm was applied with different values for this, viz. 5.10^{-6}, 10^{-5}, 5.10^{-5}, 10^{-4}, 5.10^{-4}, 10^{-3} to all 45 samples.

The cumulative results for true positives are presented in Table 1. Our initial estimate for a suitable value for the relative error threshold of 10^{-4} was perhaps too high; better results are obtained in the region of 10^{-5}.

It is difficult to know how to estimate the false positive rate as we do not have a fixed number of negative examples. For the 45 hours of data we looked at, the number of false positives is given in Table 1. An additional complication was provided, in several cases, by the presence of one or more 'probe lift' events. Such an event occurs when the probe is not securely attached and, as the baby moves, the probe lifts temporarily from the skin, and the signals are perturbed briefly towards atmospheric levels before recovering. The origin and signature of such an event is very similar to a probe-change and indeed they are often followed by a probe change as the nurse re-sites the probe to get better adhesion. We felt that at this stage, since we had not asked our expert to identify probe lifts, it would be misleading to count them as false positives. We have kept a separate count of these and will investigate ways of distinguishing them from probe changes.

Table 1. Preliminary results of event detection for 45 examples

Relative Error Threshold	5.10^{-6}	10^{-5}	5.10^{-5}	10^{-4}	5.10^{-4}	10^{-3}
True positives as % of total number of examples	89%	87%	78%	73%	53%	33%
False positives over 45 hours (excluding Probe lifts)	10	9	18	20	11	6
Probe lifts over 45 hours	35	38	23	17	6	3

5. Relationship to Previous Work

Temporal reasoning in medicine has attracted a considerable attention in recent years as a number of supporting theories and technologies have been developed [2]. However there is considerable variation in the nature of the underlying data and in the goal of the reasoning. It must be emphasised that in this paper we are concerned only with the detection of low level somewhat primitive events. Ultimately our techniques must be embedded in a system which generates higher levels of abstraction for monitoring, therapy planing, etc.

The merging algorithm described in Section 3 arose from previous work in our group [3]. However Salatian's algorithm involved a more complex set of merging rules and required the setting of four numerical parameters, as opposed to our single relative error threshold.

Part of our approach is inspired by the Knowledge-Based Temporal Abstraction (KBTA) theory developed by Shahar [4]. The initial stage of our best-fit algorithm in which we construct elementary intervals from the raw data points is an instance of temporal interpolation. Similarly the merging of intervals into larger super-intervals may be considered as a form of horizontal temporal inferencing, albeit at the level of the raw data rather than at a higher level of abstraction. Finally (and somewhat obviously) the application of the event recognition rules is an instance of temporal pattern matching. The KBTA theory has been applied in a number of domains, but it would appear that these tend to be characterised by relatively large (and sometimes irregular) sampling intervals e.g. diabetes [5]. At the level at which we are working, we do not need persistence functions since we assume that data samples are always available - and the 'absence' of data is recognised as, for example, a disconnection event. However once an event has been recognised as an artefact it needs to be removed from the raw data so that incorrect inferences are not drawn, and at that point we will need to appeal to some form of higher level temporal interpolation.

We have also been inspired by the trend template approach developed as part of the TrenDx system [6,7]. TrenDx was initially developed in a domain (pediatric growth monitoring) in which the data frequency is somewhat low. It has been applied to the analysis of ICU data, but only to one patient; this makes it difficult to know how robust it will be in this type of domain. No indication is given as to how the trend templates are established - in contrast with our explicit approach to knowledge acquisition. Another major difference is that the extraction of features from the raw data by fitting regression lines and curves is an essential part of the attempt to instantiate a trend template. In our case the feature extraction (segmentation) is much more independent - the setting of the relative error threshold may depend on the event which we are trying to detect, but apart from that, feature extraction is complete before pattern matching starts.

Of obvious relevance is the VIE-VENT system for ventilator monitoring and therapy planning for neonates [8.9]. The authors rightly point out [10] that in the ICU, validation of high frequency data is a sine-qua-non for the construction of reliable interpretations. Our intensively knowledge-based approach to interval-based validation is in contrast to their more statistical methods. Also VIE-VENT is designed to operate in real time - at present our technology is retrospective.

As the number of different types of event increases and as their temporal relationships become more complex we will need to look at more general theories of temporal reasoning [11,12].

6. Conclusions

There is some way to go before we can claim that we have a robust technique for knowledge-based event detection of general applicability. However we believe that the preliminary results reported in this paper are encouraging. In particular we consider that the best-fit algorithm may be of interest to others. Our plans for the future include:

- verifying our approach on other event types (e.g. endotracheal suction, probe recalibration, etc.);
- extending the best-fit algorithm to run in real-time;
- looking at the possibility of applying machine learning techniques to the set of marked up examples; it may be that the features that our expert has selected are not the most discriminatory;
- extending the workbench so that think-aloud protocols can be recorded digitally and replayed in synchrony with the actions of the expert while browsing the data;
- applying our approach to other domains - we are looking at the analysis of data from gas turbines, refrigerated food display cabinets, and the results of ecological A-life simulations.

Acknowledgements

Much of this work was undertaken as part of the COGNATE project; we are grateful to the UK ESRC for providing funding under the Cognitive Engineering Programme. We also acknowledge the input of our co-workers on that project: Eugenio Alberdi, Peter Badger, Ken Gilhooly, Bob Logie, Andy Lyon and Jan Reiss.

References

1. Allen J.F., 'Towards a General Theory of Action and Time', Artificial Intelligence, Vol. 23, pp 123-154, 1984.
2. Keravnou E.T., 'Temporal Reasoning in Medicine', Artificial Intelligence in Medicine - Special Issue: Temporal Reasoning in Medicine, Vol. 8, No. 3, pp 187-191, 1996.
3. Salatian A. and Hunter J.R.W., 'Deriving Trends in Historical and Real-Time Continuously Sampled Medical Data', Journal of Intelligent Information Systems - Special Issue: Intelligent Temporal Information Systems in Medicine, in press , 1999.
4. Shahar Y., 'A Framework for Knowledge-Based Temporal Abstraction', Artificial Intelligence, Vol. 90, pp 79-133, 1997.
5. Shahar Y. and Musen M.A., 'Knowledge-Based Temporal Abstraction in Clinical Domains', Artificial Intelligence in Medicine, Vol. 8, No. 3, pp 267-298, 1996.
6. Haimowitz I.J. and Kohane I.S., 'Managing Temporal Worlds for Medical Trend Diagnosis', Artificial Intelligence in Medicine, Vol. 8, No. 3, pp 299-321, 1996.
7. Haimowitz I.J., Phuc Le P. and Kohane I.S., 'Clinical Modelling Using Regression-Based Trend Templates', Artificial Intelligence in Medicine, Vol. 7, No. 6, pp 473-496, 1995.
8. Miksch S., Horn W., Popow C., and Paky F., 'Therapy Planning using Qualitative Trend Descriptions', Artificial Intelligence in Medicine, Proceedings AIME-95, Barahona P. et al. Eds., pp 197-208, 1995.
9. Miksch S., Horn W., Popow C., and Paky F., 'Utilizing Temporal Data Abstraction for Data Validation and Therapy Planning for Artificially Ventilated Newborn Infants', Artificial Intelligence in Medicine, Vol. 8, No. 6, pp 543-576, 1996.
10. Horn W., Miksch S., Egghart G., Popow C. and Paky F., 'Effective Data Validation of High Frequency Data: Time-Point-, Time-Interval-, and Trend-Based Methods', Computers in Biology and Medicine, Vol. 27, No. 5, pp 389-409, 1997.
11. Chittaro L. and Dojat M., 'Using a General Theory of Time and Change in Patient Monitoring: Experiment and Evaluation', Computers in Biology and Medicine, Vol. 27, No. 5, pp 435-452, 1997.
12. Keravnou E.T., 'Temporal Diagnostic Reasoning Based on Time Objects', Artificial Intelligence in Medicine - Special Issue: Temporal Reasoning in Medicine, Vol. 8, No. 3, pp 235-265, 1996.

Abstracting Steady Qualitative Descriptions over Time from Noisy, High-Frequency Data

Silvia Miksch[1], Andreas Seyfang[1], Werner Horn[2,3], and Christian Popow[4]

[1] Institute of Software Technology, University of Technology, Vienna,
{silvia, seyfang}@ifs.tuwien.ac.at
[2] Department of Medical Cybernetics and Artificial Intelligence, University of Vienna
werner@ai.univie.ac.at
[3] Austrian Research Institute for Artificial Intelligence, Vienna
[4] Department of Pediatrics, University of Vienna
popow@akh-wien.ac.at

Abstract. On-line monitoring at neonatal intensive care units produces high volumes of data. Numerous devices generate data at high frequency (one data set every second). Both, the high volume and the quite high error-rate of the data make it essential to reach at higher levels of description from such raw data. These abstractions should improve the medical decision making. We will present a time-oriented data-abstraction method to derive steady qualitative descriptions from oscillating high-frequency data. The method contains tunable parameters to guide the sensibility of the abstraction process. The benefits and limitations of the different parameter settings will be discussed.

1 Introduction

Our application domain is the treatment planning for premature infants at neonatal intensive care units (NICUs). Many neonates need artificial ventilation for various reasons. Compared to the treatment of adults, mechanical ventilation of newborn infants is a highly sophisticated task because of the immature structure of their lungs. While medical knowledge has greatly increased over the past years [5], the integration of the data produced by today's monitoring devices into the therapy-planning process still remains an unsolved problem.

Monitoring mechanically ventilated neonates is a clinical, high-frequency domain. Various of devices yield a rather high volume of measured data – at a typical rate of one value per second – which is often faulty. Each measured data shows only a snapshot of a single aspect of the patient's situation in a particular moment.

To a physician these snapshots alone are of limited use. What she needs is an overview over a certain period of time and over various parameters which together give a more detailed and comprehensible picture of the patient's condition. Often she thinks in terms like "X is higher than normal for five minutes". Nevertheless some monitoring devices in current use show only the values measured in the previous seconds or even only the very last one. This leads to a strong need for facilities to visualize raw data as well as their abstractions.

W. Horn et al. (Eds.): AIMDM'99, LNAI 1620, pp. 281–290, 1999.

While the sensors send possibly wrong numbers at high precision that represent a parameters value at a certain point of time, human users distinguish but a few different states like very high or medium low in context with a interval of time during which such a proposition holds. To close this gap we developed an algorithm to obtain maximum intervals during which a parameter stays constant. As a vehicle to reach this we introduce a statistically motivated representation of quantitative values, called a *spread*, which shows both position and uncertainty of a value at each point of time.

The ultimate goal of the algorithm is to present the information gathered from various monitoring devices as concise as possible to the physicians in order to reduce their information overload and improve the quality of care.

Currently we are acquiring and analyzing five types of input from various sources. The ECG gives the heart rate rather reliably. The pulse oximetry gives both arterial hemoglobin saturation of oxygen in the blood (S_aO_2) and pulse rate. Small movements of the patient result in a high volume of erroneous oscillations of these values. Transcutaneous electrodes measure the partial pressure of oxygen ($P_{tc}O_2$) and carbon dioxide ($P_{tc}CO_2$). We are analyzing data off-line. It is envisioned to employ the findings obtained thereby in on-line monitoring and alarming in the future.

In section 2 we show why related approaches do not cover our problem specification. Section 3 features the three steps of our algorithm which are elimination of data errors, clarifying the curve, and qualifying the curve. In section 4 we discuss the parameters involved in the process. In section 5 we discuss application and further direction of our work.

2   State of the Art

Temporal dimensions are a very important aspect in the medical domain, particularly when dealing with the interpretation of continuously assessed data. The most common methods are time-series analysis [1], control theory, probabilistic or fuzzy classifiers. These approaches have a lot of shortcomings, which lead to applying knowledge-based techniques to derive qualitative values or patterns of current and past situations of a patient, called *temporal data abstraction*. Several significant and encouraging approaches have been developed in the past years.

Haimowitz et al. [2] have developed the concept of trend templates ($TrenD_x$) to represent all the information available during an observation process. A trend template defines disorders as typical patterns of relevant parameters. These patterns consist of a partially ordered set of temporal intervals with uncertain endpoints. Trend templates are used to detect trends in time-stamped data.

The RÉSUMÉ project [11] performs temporal abstraction of time-stamped data without predefined trends. The system is based on a knowledge-based, temporal-abstraction method, which is decomposed into five sub-tasks: temporal context restriction, vertical temporal inference, horizontal temporal inference, temporal interpolation, and temporal pattern matching.

Larizza et al. [7] have developed methods to detect predefined courses in a time series. Complex abstraction allows to detect specific temporal relationships between intervals. The overall aim was to summarize the patient's behavior over a predefined time interval.

Keravnou [6] focuses on the periodicity of events derived from the patient history.

All these approaches are dealing with low-frequency data. Therefore, the problems of oscillating data, frequently shifting contexts, and different expectations of the development of parameters are not covered.

Two promising approaches for high-frequency data are the "Time Series Workbench" [4], which approximates data curves through a series of line-segments, and the temporal data abstraction module in the VIE-VENT system [8], which focuses on high-frequency domain of artificial ventilation of newborn infants. Its abstraction module consists of five different methods to arrive at unified, context-sensitive qualitative descriptions: context-sensitive transformation of quantitative data points into qualitative values (context-sensitive schemata for data point transformation), smoothing of data oscillating near thresholds, smoothing of schemata for data point transformation, context-sensitive adjustment of qualitative values, and transformation of interval data (context-sensitive and expectation-guided schemata for trend-curve fitting). VIE-VENT's smoothing and abstraction methods are a very good starting point. However, these methods are quite ad-hoc and do not cover in-depth analysis of the data curve over a longer period of time.

3   The Temporal Abstraction Method

The temporal abstraction method obtains intervals, in which a qualitative value stays steady, from oscillating raw data. In the struggle for smooth, steady curves one is confronted with two types of disturbances: *errors, noise,* and *physiological variations.*

Most *errors* can clearly be distinguished from correct input data. The absolute values of erroneous data points or the difference to their neighbors are beyond well-defined limits. Reasons for errors comprise technical details like the automatic re-calibration of the transcutaneous electrodes every three to four hours as well as unfortunate circumstances like sensors being badly attached.

Noise consists of small rapid oscillations of the measured values that cannot be sorted out as errors. They have very different reasons which makes them hard to handle. Some of them are caused by technical details of measuring devices and can be considered as small errors. Others are medically explicable phenomena or symptoms (e.g. variability of the heart rates) which we subsume as *physiological variations* and which should not be suppressed by the abstraction process.

It is thus clear that all transformations of the curves need parameters that control the amount of abstraction or smoothing that is performed. These parameters need to be carefully adjusted to the issues of medical practice. In section 5 we will present some observations on this topic.

The following steps of processing and abstracting the data can be distinguished:

1. **Eliminating data errors**. Sometimes up to 40 % of the input data is obviously erroneous e.g. exceeding the limits of plausible values.
2. **Clarifying the curve.** Transform the still noisy data into a steady curve with some additional information about the distribution of the data along that curve.
3. **Qualifying the curve.** Abstract qualitative values, like "normal" or "high", from the quantitative data and join data points of equal values to time intervals (qualitative description).

The results of each step of processing is displayed to the physician in combinations of choice to give her a clear perception of the abstraction process. In the following we will detail these three steps.

3.1 Eliminating Data Errors

Many errors can be eliminated by defining rather strict maximum and minimum values for each type of input as well as maximum change rates. Furthermore, if two types of input (S_aO_2 and pulse) come from the same sensor and one of the two is invalid, it can be concluded that the other one is not valid either. If two sensors measure the same value (pulse and heart rate) and their inputs differ, then you can discard the less reliable one (or do some adaptation).

Still a number of faulty data points – those which fall just inside the range of allowed values – and nearly all of the noise will be left after such processing. They must be handled with in the other steps of the method. See Horn et al. [3] for a thorough discussion of error detection and correction in the domain of clinical monitoring.

3.2 Clarifying the Curve

The algorithm presented in the following seeks to derive a smooth, easy comprehensible, and stable curve from noisy and error-prone data. For a selected interval of time, e.g. one minute, we derive an abstraction representing the values within this interval. Moving along the time axis we shift this interval (*time window*) to receive continuous abstractions of the curve.

So for example, if we consider a time window of one minute and a step width of one second, we do not calculate only one value per minute but for every second in the whole period of measurement we calculate an abstraction within that time window. For each time window a linear regression model is calculated as explained below. Figure 1 shows the abstraction within one time window and the moving of this window.

Given the fact that not all deviations of data points from the main line can be considered negligible although many certainly are, it is clear that any abstraction must not only provide the mean of the curve at a certain point of time but also

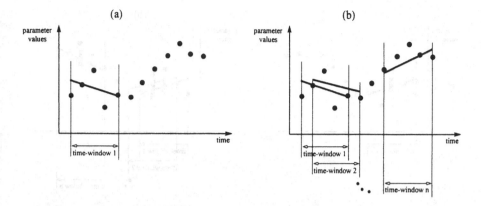

Fig. 1. The calculation of the linear regression is done for a time window of fixed size sliding over the entire curve in small steps. (a) shows a single time window and the line calculated from the data points within it. (b) shows a sequence of overlapping time windows and the resulting lines.

some measure for the certainty with which this abstraction can be done at that point. Such measures include standard deviation, standard error, quartiles, etc.

All these measures are only one-dimensional. Applying them on the x-coordinates of the data points would presume that the curve is horizontal. Since this rarely is the case, we first must find a "common line" of the data points in the considered interval. Only relative to that line we can define measures for the closeness of a point to the entity.

Among several candidates we chose the linear regression model as a well-proven technique for this task [1, 9]. We calculate overlapping lines in user defined steps which can be as small as a second. The length which is also user defined typically ranges from several seconds to one or two minutes. Figure 1 shows some of the lines in a close zoom.

The calculation yields not only the center of the distribution but also the inclination of the line optimally fitted through the data points (minimizing their squared deviations) and the standard deviation. The standard deviation is a very good measure of uncertainty unless some data points are missing (or removed by the error detection). Dividing the standard deviation by the square root of the number of data points used in the calculation gives the standard error. This value is preferable against the standard deviation since it grows with the decrease of valid data points reflecting thus growing uncertainty.

Plotting the standard deviation on the center of the distribution instead of the standard error gives a much wider band which exactly depicts the average distance of the data points to the line but is invariant to number of points involved in the calculation. To combine the advantages of both standard deviation and standard error, we multiply the standard error by the square root of the maximum number of data points possible within the interval of time considered and name it *adapted standard error*.

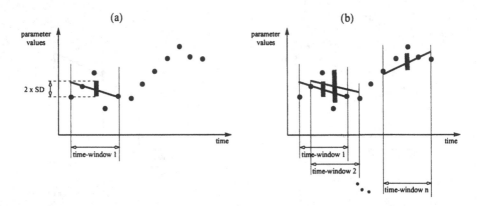

Fig. 2. To give an optical impression of the distribution of the data points around the regression line we vertically plot a measure for their distance like the standard deviation (SD) on the center of the line. (a) shows the construction of one vertical line while (b) shows a sequence of them.

Plotting the adapted standard error on the center of the distribution shows its error bar, which is a well-known means of visualizing statistical data. In the perfect case, in which all data points within the interval are valid, the width of the spread equals the (double of the) standard deviation while it will grow with an increasing number of invalid data points. Figure 2 illustrates the calculation error bars.

Connecting the upper and lower ends respectively of the error bars found for all time windows of a curve yields a band of variable width following the raw data in rather gentle bends which we call a *spread*. The narrower it is, the more concentrated the values around their mean. Figure 3 shows the final calculation of the spread.

3.3 Qualifying the Curve

Often the numerical value of a parameter is not itself interesting to the physician, but its qualitative abstraction like "very high" or "slightly low" or – most important – "normal". As indicated by the quotes, the exact definition of "normal" depends on the context in which the judgment is done [8].

A second characteristic of qualitative values in addition to being easy comprehensible is that they usually last for a longer time period. The resulting intervals are perceived for example as "S_aO_2 is high for 5 minutes". This implies that any short oscillation of the qualitative description must be avoided. While raw data typically oscillate and thus are not usable as a basis for finding reasonably long intervals wherein a qualitative value stays stable, the spread calculated above is a good ground to start at.

Figure 4 shows an example of a spread crossing borders only according to the overall tendency of the curve, skipping short-term peaks. Notice that nothing happens as long as only one margin of the spread crosses a border. Only when

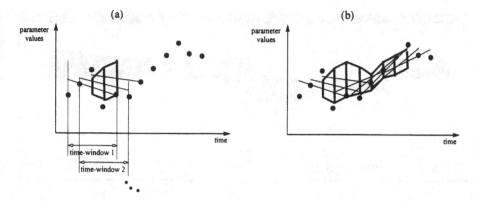

Fig. 3. Connecting all upper and lower ends respectively of the vertical lines (a) gives the upper and lower limits of a region containing most of the data points. The polygon constituted by these lines (b) gives an intuitive impression of the underlying data. The wider the band, the more uncertainty is involved in the calculation of the vertical position of the band representing the mean.

the other margin follows, the qualitative value changes. The spread is the wider, the more uncertainty is involved in calculating the mean of the time window. Thus changes to another region are less likely there. In contrast, a narrow spread strongly enforces the qualitative values to closely follow the quantitative value as it represents a sample of dense, noise free data points.

Retrospective analysis of data allows to select the time point at which the qualitative value changes. One may chose the intersection of the margin first crossing the border with that border, the intersection of the second margin with the border or the middle in between these points. In the example in figure 4 we have chosen the middle.

Another reasonable point to set the event of change is the intersection of the middle of the spread (in the value axis) – representing the average of its surrounding – with the border. Unfortunately, the middle can have several intersections with the border during the interval in question. So we need a rule which intersection should be taken: the first, the last or the middle between the first and the last intersection.

4   Parameters in the Abstraction Process

In the following we discuss the influence of different parameters on the abstraction process.

Length of Time Window. The length of the time window is the most influential parameter. It drives the amount of change of the curve which goes into the abstracted spread. The longer the considered interval, the smaller the influence of insular peaks in the raw data. If you want to get the overall estimation of a minute, the length of the time windows will be 60 seconds. If

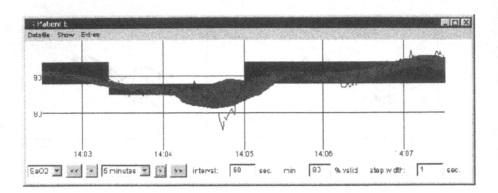

Fig. 4. The thin line shows the raw data. The red (light gray) area depict the *spread*, the blue (dark gray) rectangles represent the derived temporal intervals of steady qualitative values. Increased oscillation leads to increased width of the spread but not to a change of the qualitative value. The lower part of the screen shot shows the parameters used.

a decrease during 5 seconds is considered significant, the length should not be much longer than 5 seconds.

Permitted Gaps. In real-world situations there is always a certain amount of data points which are missing or get discarded by the error detection performed in step 1. If the amount of such points becomes too large, the linear regression calculated from the remaining points might not be too reliable and it should be visualized clearly that there is no usable input at that point. Such a situation happens frequently in daily practice.

To handle such situations we define both a maximum duration of a single gap in error-free input data, and a minimum percentage of valid data points within the time interval in which the linear regression is computed. If a gap in the (error-free) input data exceeds the maximum allowed duration, this gap is propagated through all levels of abstraction and cannot be closed by higher level abstractions. If the number of valid data points in one time window does not reach the required limit, the calculation of the regression line is skipped. Since the lines usually overlap, a gap only appears if the ends of neighboring lines do not touch. Still the reduced number of data points is visible because it leads to an increase in the adapted standard error and thus in the width of the spread.

Point of Changing the Qualitative Value. As described above the point of time at which the qualitative value of a parameter is changed can be set at will within the period in which the spread intersects the border between the old and the new qualitative value in retrospective analysis.

The point of change can either relate to the margins or to the middle (on the value axis) of the spread. Since the middle can intersect the border several times during the period between the first margin crossing the border and the second margin following, we can generally only speak of an interval between the first and the last crossing of the border by the middle of the spread.

For both intervals – defined by the intersections of the margins and by intersections of the middle – the beginning, end, and middle of the interval are possible choices. Among the more plausible ones are the last intersection of the middle of the spread and the middle between the first and the last intersection of the middle with the border.

Step Width. While as a default the algorithm calculates one linear regression within the defined time window for every data point measured, under many circumstances this can mean a lot of unnecessary computation. E.g. if the length of the considered time window is one minute, a step width of 10 seconds will still yield a smooth curve. This example shows that for best results the step width should always be some fraction of the length of the considered time window.

Position of the Error Bar. In the above text we silently presumed that it would be most suitable to visualize the entity of the data points in the considered by a vertical bar in the middle of the line produced by the linear regression. This means that one time window of the spread represents $x/2$ data points before and $x/2$ data points after the position of the time window where x is the number of data points involved in the calculation of the time window.

While this symmetrically smoothes out disturbances in the curve in retrospective analysis, it does not properly reflect the situation of on-line monitoring where the values before the actual point of time are not available of course . In such a situation one would only consider the past and deduct only from it – the left-hand side of the curve – some abstraction of the data at the current time point. While the appearance of the spread shows some difference between these two modes of visualization, differences in the qualitative intervals abstracted from the two variants are rare.

5   Discussion and Further Development

Abstracting raw data to spreads and deducting intervals, in which qualitative descriptions hold, is an important step toward better visualization and comprehension of high-frequency data. The output of the algorithm presented can be used for three distinct though related purposes.

1. **Visualization of quantitative data.** While the raw data when plotted "as it is" are rather confusing, the spread gives an intuitive impression of the data by showing both the value - by its position - and the amount of uncertainty in that value - by its width. It is thus a useful tool for visualizing the quantitative input itself.

2. **Abstracting qualitative descriptions over time intervals.** Based on the need of the practitioners we display the data as a sequence of intervals, during which the values of a parameter take one qualitative value (e.g. high).

3. **Finding suitable therapeutic actions.** The qualitative descriptions are a solid basis for recommending changes of the ventilator settings and for

intelligent alarming. These are nontrivial tasks and need a knowledge base with sophisticated temporal inference capabilities.

Our future efforts will be dedicated to the integration of the visualization tool into the bigger context of a knowledge-based system using the Asgaard framework [10] for temporal planning and developing our tool from a retrospective analyzing tool towards an on-line monitoring and alarming system.

Acknowledgments. We thank Klaus Hammermüller, Robert Kosara and Georg Duftschmid for their useful comments. This project is supported by "Fonds zur Förderung der wissenschaftlichen Forschung - FWF" (Austrian Science Foundation), P12797-INF. We greatly appreciate the support given to the Austrian Research Institute of Artificial Intelligence (ÖFAI) by the Austrian Federal Ministry of Science and Transport, Vienna.

References

[1] R.K. Avent and J.D. Charlton. A critical review of trend-detection methologies for biomedical monitoring systems. *Critical Reviews in Biomedical Engineering*, 17(6):621–659, 1990.

[2] I. J. Haimowitz and I. S. Kohane. Managing temporal worlds for medical tread diagnosis. *Artificial Intelligence in Medicine, Special Issue Temporal Reasoning in Medicine*, 8(3):299–321, 1996.

[3] W. Horn, S. Miksch, G. Egghart, C. Popow, and F. Paky. Effective data validation of high-frequency data: Time-point-, time-interval-, and trend-based methods. *Computer in Biology and Medicine, Special Issue: Time-Oriented Systems in Medicine*, 27(5):389–409, 1997.

[4] J. Hunter. Knowledge-based interpretation of time series data from the neonatal ICU. presentation, 1998.

[5] Goldsmith J.P. and Karotkin E.H. *Assisted Ventilation of the Neonates*. Saunders, Philadelphia, 1996.

[6] E. T. Keravnou. Temporal abstraction of medical data: Deriving periodicity. In N. Lavrac, et. al., editors, *Intelligent Data Analysis in Medicine and Pharmacology*, pages 61–79. Kluwer Academic Publisher, Boston, 1997.

[7] C. Larizza, R. Bellazzi, and A. Riva. Temporal abstractions for diabetic patients management. In *Proceedings of the Artificial Intelligence in Medicine, 6th Conference on Artificial Intelligence in Medicine Europe (AIME-97)*, pages 319–30, Berlin, 1997. Springer.

[8] S. Miksch, W. Horn, C. Popow, and F. Paky. Utilizing temporal data abstraction for data validation and therapy planning for artificially ventilated newborn infants. *Artificial Intelligence in Medicine*, 8(6):543–576, 1996.

[9] W.H. Press, S.A. Teukolsky, W.T. Vetterling, and B.P. Flannery. *Numerical Recipies in C*. Cambridge University Press, Cambridge, 1992.

[10] Y. Shahar, S. Miksch, and P. Johnson. The Asgaard Project: A task-specific framework for the application and critiquing of time-oriented clinical guidelines. *Artificial Intelligence in Medicine*, 14:29–51, 1998.

[11] Y. Shahar and M. A. Musen. Knowledge-based temporal abstraction in clinical domains. *Artificial Intelligence in Medicine, Special Issue Temporal Reasoning in Medicine*, 8(3):267–98, 1996.

Visualization Techniques for Time-Oriented, Skeletal Plans in Medical Therapy Planning

Robert Kosara and Silvia Miksch

Vienna University of Technology, Intitute of Software Technology
Resselgasse 3/188, A-1040 Vienna, Austria, Europe
{rkosara, silvia}@ifs.tuwien.ac.at

Abstract. In order to utilize elaborate tools and techniques (like verification) for use with clinical protocols, these must be represented in an appropriate way. Protocols are typically represented by means of formal languages (e.g., Asbru), which are very hard to understand for medical experts and lead to many problems in practical use. Therefore, a powerful user interface is needed. We identify the key problems the user-interface designer is faced with, and present a number of "classic" solutions and their shortcomings — which led to our own solution called AsbruView. Its two different views (Topological View and Temporal View) are presented.

1   Introduction and Motivation

Clinical protocols exist for many areas of medical care. Such protocols are typically represented as text, tables, or flow-charts. These representations are far from perfect, however, because they lack a clear concept of time and do not allow automation support for verification or quality assessment. In the Asgaard/Asbru[1] project [12], a number of methods are being developed that deal with problems of clinical therapy planning. The key element of these efforts is Asbru, a powerful language to represent time-oriented, skeletal plans. Asbru has a LISP-like syntax, which makes it unusable for domain experts. Powerful methods are useless, however, when they cannot be used by the people they are intended for. This is why we developed a user interface that gives physicians access to Asbru.

In section 2, we give a short introduction to the key concepts of Asbru. The main challenges in visualizing Asbru, plus some possible solutions are discussed in section 3. Our own approach, called AsbruView, is introduced in section 4. We end up with a conclusion and future plans in section 5.

2   Asbru Concepts

Asbru is a plan representation language that can capture time-oriented, skeletal plans. In order to understand the specific problems we faced in visualizing Asbru,

---

[1] In Norse mythology, *Asbru* (or *Bifrost*) was the bridge to *Asgaard*, the home of the gods (see also http://www.ifs.tuwien.ac.at/~silvia/projects/asgaard/).

W. Horn et al. (Eds.): AIMDM'99, LNAI 1620, pp. 291–300, 1999.

one must be familiar with some of its basic concepts. These will be described here briefly. For a more detailed description, see [12].

Plan Layout (Actions). The plan body contains plans or actions that are to be performed if the preconditions hold. A plan is composed of other plans which must be performed in sequence, in any order, in parallel, or periodically (as long as a condition holds, a maximum number of times, and with a minimum interval between retries). A plan is decomposed into sub-plans until a non-decomposable plan — called an action — is found. This is called a *semantic stop condition*. All the sub-plans consist of the same components as the plan itself.

Preferences constrain the applicability of a plan (e.g., select-criteria: exact-fit, roughly-fit) and describe the kind of behavior of the plan (e.g., kind of strategy: aggressive or normal).

Intentions are high-level goals that should be reached by a plan, or maintained or avoided during its execution. Intentions are very important not only for selecting the right plan, but also for reviewing treatment plans as part of the ever ongoing process of improving the treatment. This makes intentions one of the key parts of Asbru.

Conditions need to hold in order for a plan to be *started, suspended, reactivated, aborted,* or *completed.* Two different kinds of conditions (called preconditions) exist, that must be true in order for a plan to be started: *filter-preconditions* cannot be achieved (e.g., subject is female), *setup-preconditions* can. After a plan has been started, it can be suspended (interrupted) until either the *restart-condition* is true (whereupon it is continued at the point where it was suspended) or it has to be aborted. If a plan is aborted, it has failed to reach its goals. If a plan completes, it has reached its goals, and the next plan in the sequence is executed.

Effects describe the relationship between plan arguments and measurable parameters by means of mathematical functions. A probability of occurrence is also given.

Time Annotations. Time-oriented planning is centered around Asbru's *time annotations.* A time annotation is defined by seven entities: reference point, earliest starting shift (ESS), latest starting shift (LSS), earliest finishing shift (EFS), latest finishing shift (LFS), minimum duration (MinDu) and maximum duration (MaxDu). Any subset of these parameters may be left undefined. Reference points can be abstract points in time, so each reference point can be considered to be the origin of its own time axis.

3 Visualization Challenges

An enormous amount of work has been done in the field of scientific and information visualization in the last few years, but most of these approaches focus on large amounts of multi-dimensional data. For this kind of problem, a number of good visualizations exist now, that make data accessible [5, 6, 13, 19].

The challenges that the designer of a visualization of time-oriented plans faces are quite different, however. We identified five main problems: hierarchical decomposition of plans, compulsory vs. optional plans, temporal order, cyclical plans, and temporal uncertainty. A more detailed description of these problems plus possible solutions that inspired our approach are given below.

Hierarchical Decomposition. Plans can either be actions ("atomic") or consist of sub-plans. A plan can be reused as a sub-plan of another plan. A successful visualization must be able to communicate this concept.

This part is already satisfactorily solved in our Topological View (section 4.1). As an alternative, a tree view, like it is used for viewing file and directory structures, could be used.

Compulsory vs. Optional Plans. A sub-plan can be used in two different ways: it either *must* be executed (compulsory plan) or it *can* be (optional). While a compulsory plan is easy to understand (and to depict), a way of indicating that a plan is optional is a lot more difficult, especially if it must be different from the representation of temporal uncertainty (see below). A blurred depiction of plans [9] therefore cannot be used.

Temporal Order. In some cases, only the set of plans to be used is known, but not the order in which they will be performed. A way of depicting a plan has to be found where the order in which they are depicted does not necessarily correspond to the order in which they will be executed.

Flow-charts [4, 14] have been proposed for this purpose, but they do not cover parallel plans or sets of plans that can be performed in any order (the latter is possible[2], but only with considerable effort that leads to diagrams that are impossible to read). Additionally, flow-charts scale very poorly, i.e. become unreadable when a large number of plans is defined, and they do not cover the temporal aspect (see below).

Cyclical Plans. Many actions in medicine are cyclic, for example a treatment every two weeks, or blood tests every morning. It is of little value to display all the many instances of the same action when it is known to be cyclical anyway.

We tried sphere and cylinder metaphors (inspired by [5]), but that did not lead to usable representations.

---

[2] By defining one path for every possible permutation of the plans. For n plans, this means $n!$ different paths.

Temporal Uncertainty. The time a plan takes, but also time spans that are considered for the relevance of symptoms are not defined in terms of exact durations. Therefore, a way of visualizing time spans, where only part of the information (e.g. the minimum duration) is known, must be found. This information may be refined later; this is called a minimum-commitment approach [23].

A related problem is that of temporal granularity. It should be possible to tell to what accuracy a point in time has been defined (e.g. seconds, minutes).

Simple ways of indicating uncertainty can be found in [9, 23], but are very limited. These approaches only tell the reader that the data is uncertain, but not to which degree.

A very versatile, albeit difficult to understand solution to this problem can be found in [20]. While the methodology proposed there is very powerful, it is badly suited for *displaying* more than a few plans, especially when they are to be executed in parallel or when they overlap.

A time annotation in Asbru consists of seven values, and thus can be understood as a point in seven-dimensional space. There are a number of visualization approaches to this kind of problem, the most usable of which are parallel coordinates [6, 7]. They are, however, not useful here since they do not clearly indicate the relations between the different quantities.

The most promising way of visualizing temporal uncertainty are glyphs [15] (or Chernoff faces [2]), which is the solution we finally used.

Further Requirements. Following the "Visual Information Seeking Mantra" [22], an overview should be presented first, so that the user can zoom into the parts he or she wants to examine in greater detail. Details should only be displayed on demand.

Often, one works on a small part of a larger structure, but still wants to know the context this part is in. Three basic ideas are used for this: the Perspective Wall [10], FishEye Views ([3], a similar idea is used in [18]), and stretchable rubber sheets [21]. All of these methods of showing context differ from a simple "lens" in that there is no abrupt break between the magnified area and its surroundings, but a smooth transition. This, in combination with scrolling, makes the concepts very easy to understand and use.

4   AsbruView

AsbruView consists of two very different views, which complement one another. Undefined components are displayed in grey in both views. This is easy to spot because of the heavy use of color (see below).

4.1   Topological View

In the Topological View (Figure 1, [8, 11]), we use a "running tracks" metaphor. Every plan is considered a running track, which the patient runs along while the plan is being performed. When the plan completes successfully, the patient is considered to have passed the finishing line, hence a finishing flag is used to represent the *complete condition* (see section 2).

Although this view has a number of drawbacks (temporal uncertainty is practically impossible to represent), it is, due to its simplicity, very effective in communicating the basic concepts of Asbru. This was tested in a few preliminary scenario-based evaluations [1] we did with our medical experts.

Metaphors from traffic control are used for the other conditions, like a "no entrance with exceptions" sign for the *filter precondition* and a barrier for the *setup precondition*. Since the setup precondition can be fulfilled, the barrier is considered to open in this case. A traffic light stands for the *stop condition* (red light), *suspend condition* (yellow light) and the *reactivate condition* (green light).

Hierarchical Decomposition. Plans can be stacked on top of each other, representing hierarchical decomposition. The sub-plans a plan consists of are put on top of that plan. Each plan has a unique color, which makes plans easier to recognize. It also makes reused plans easier to spot.[3]

Compulsory vs. Optional Plans. Plans that may or may not be performed are displayed with a question-mark texture, while mandatory plans have a plain background. As an alternative, a dotted line can be drawn around optional plans on black-and-white displays (this line can be distinguished from the dotted line which marks the current plan, since, in the latter one, the points move).

Temporal Order. By putting plans next to each other along the time axis, one can indicate that these plans will be performed in this sequence. Parallel plans are aligned along the "parallel plans" dimension (Figure 1). Plans that may be performed in any order are put next to each other more "loosely", and the containing plan has a groove that the plans can be put into as soon as their sequence is determined.

Cyclical Plans. A circle symbol is used to indicate that a plan is a cyclical plan. The maximum number of repetions can be given, but no temporal aspects, like the minimum or maximum delay between retries.

Temporal Uncertainty is not shown in this view. Because of the perspective distortion, it would be impossible to see the temporal dimension properly.

4.2   Temporal View

For more complicated tasks, as well as for the experienced user, a more detailed view was developed. It is an extension to the "LifeLines" concept described in

---

[3] This is, of course, not true for color-blind people. For this reason, we plan to include an option in our prototype that changes the color-selection scheme so that different plans can be discriminated more easily.

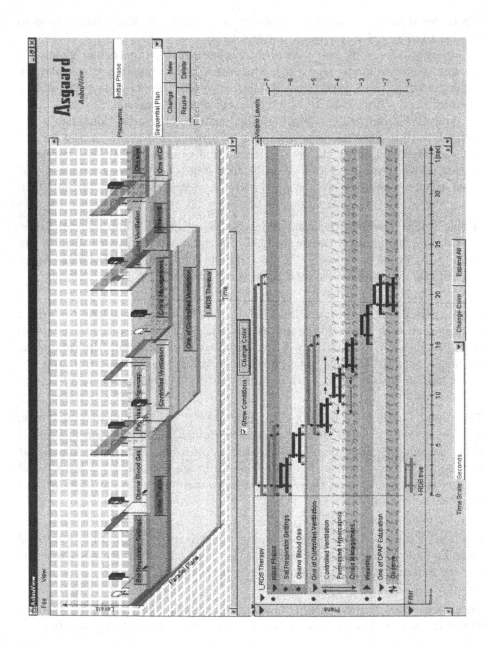

Fig. 1. A screenshot of the AsbruView program. The example depicted is from a real clinical protocol for treating infants' respiratory distress syndrome (I-RDS). The left/upper half shows the Topological View, the right/lower half shows the Temporal View. In the Temporal View, the Plans Facet plus a very small part of the Conditions Facet are visible

[16, 17]. LifeLines are an extension and application of an old concept often named timelines, and presented, for example, in [24].

The idea of LifeLines is very simple: in a diagram with time proceeding from left to right, a horizontal line is drawn for every time span. The lines are drawn in different vertical areas, with a label to the very left of the area. While events whose dates are known (i.e. past events) are captured very well by this approach, it does not deal with temporal uncertainty.

Our own adaptation of LifeLines is described here in a manner similar to section 3 (see Figure 1, lower half).

Hierarchical Decomposition. To make the hierarchical structure of the plans visible, a tree-view-like display is used on the left side. A plan's sub-plans appear as items underneath one another, bracketed by the containing plan. Similar to the Topological View, each plan has its own, unique color to make identification easier, not only between different facets, but also between the two views.

Compulsory vs. Optional Plans. The same method as in the Topological View is used here.

Temporal Order. A symbol next to every "opened" plan (i.e. a plan whose sub-plans are visible) shows its type. In the example, *I-RDS Therapy* is a sequential plan, *One of Controlled Ventilation* is an any-order plan; a parallel plan would be indicated by two parallel lines.

The order of execution is also indicated by the position of the plans along the time axis. In addition, plans that are to be executed in any order are displayed in one "time slot", with arrows pointing to other possible execution times.

Cyclical Plans. The first instance of the plan is shown, with arrows pointing to other possible occurrences. If minimum and maximum delays between retries are given, they are displayed in a manner similar to time annotations. The maximum number of retries is given as a number next to the first instance.

Temporal Uncertainty. Instead of simple lines (like in LifeLines), we use an extended version of the time annotation (see Figure 2) we proposed in [11]. The metaphor used here makes the concept of time annotation easy to grasp. All defined components of a time annotation are displayed in black; any undefined components are grey. Additionally, if the LSS or EFS are not defined, the diamonds supporting the MinDu become circles. This means, they can move if the MinDu is changed. It is also easy to understand that the MinDu cannot become shorter than the time span between LSS and EFS, otherwise the "MinDu bar" would fall down. Both MinDu and MaxDu are constrained in their maximum length by ESS and LFS: they cannot extend beyond the vertical lines.

Another problem that was not solved for LifeLines is that of different time precision. The user can select the scale of the time axis in a "logarithmic way",

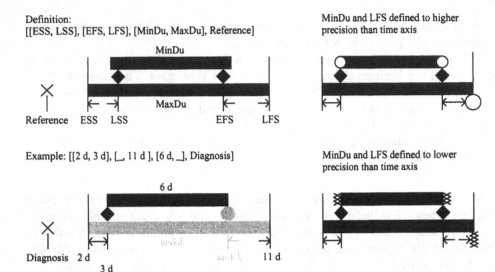

Fig. 2. Time Annotations. On the left side, the definition of time annotations is illustrated (top) and an example given (bottom). On the right side, two cases are depicted in which the time scale of the time annotations is not the same as that of the current time axis

i.e. select a granularity of weeks, days, hours, minutes, or seconds. If a point in time is defined to a higher precision than can be displayed with the current time resolution, a circle is put at the corresponding point (Figure 2, top right). If the whole time annotation is smaller than one unit of the current time axis, it is only displayed as one small circle. A similar concept is used in mathematics when one wants to draw a line from A to, but not including, B.

If a point is defined to a lower precision than the current time axis (such as "plus one hour" for a time scale of five minutes), zigzag lines are used to mark the area of "imprecision" (i.e. one half unit of the more precise unit to both sides of the point; Figure 2, bottom right).

Facets. We make heavy use of the "facet" idea [16]. A facet is a vertical region in the display (see Figure 1) that is dedicated to a certain aspect of the data. We are using facets for all of Asbru's aspects: plan layout, preferences, intentions, conditions, and effects. Facets can be opened and closed at any time, and share a common time axis. Thus, the relation between different parts of the display is very easy to understand, and problems from different views showing different parts of a plan, for example, at the same time do not arise. Vertical scrolling of the different facets is independent, however.

Since time annotations play an important role in all aspects of Asbru, the same kind of representation can be used in all facets.

5 Conclusion and Future Plans

We have given a short introduction to Asbru, and presented the main challenges in our efforts to make it accessible to medical experts. A number of possible solutions to these challenges were presented, together with their drawbacks.

The solution to the stated problems, based on many of the listed "possible solutions", was presented. It is called AsbruView, and consists of two views: the Topological View and the Temporal View, offering different ways of interaction.

Most of AsbruView has been implemented, and is currently being evaluated with medical experts.

Acknowledgements

We thank Georg Duftschmid, Klaus Hammermüller, Werner Horn, Christian Popow, and Andreas Seyfang for valuable suggestions and discussions. We also thank Clive Richards and Aaron Sloman for interesting discussions at *Thinking with Diagrams '98*.

This project is supported by "Fonds zur Förderung der wissenschaftlichen Forschung" (Austrian Science Fund), P12797-INF.

References

[1] J. M. Caroll. *Scenario-Based Design — Envisioning Work and Technology in System Design*. John Wiley & Sons, New York, 1995.

[2] H. Chernoff. The use of faces to represent points in k-dimensional space graphically. *Journal of the American Statistical Association*, 68:361–368, 1973.

[3] G. W. Furnas. The FISHEYE view: A new look at structured files. Technical Memorandum #81-11221-9, Bell Laboratories, Murray Hill, New Jersey 07974, U.S.A., 12 Oct. 1981.

[4] H. H. Goldstine and J. von Neumann. Planning and coding problems for an electronic computing instrument. Part II, vol. 1, U.S. Army Ordinance Department, 1947. reprinted in von Neumann, J., 1963. Collected Works Vol. V. New York: McMillan, pp. 80-151.

[5] M. H. Gross, T. C. Sprenger, and J. Finger. Visualizing information on a sphere. In *Proc. Information Visualization*, Oct. 1997.

[6] A. Inselberg. Multidimensional detective. In *Proc. Information Visualization*, pages 100–107, Oct. 1997.

[7] A. Inselberg and B. Dimsdale. Parallel coordinates for visualizing multi-dimensional geometry. In T. L. Kunii, editor, *Computer Graphics 1987 (Proceedings of CG International '87)*, pages 25–44. Springer-Verlag, 1987.

[8] R. Kosara, S. Miksch, Y. Shahar, and P. Johnson. AsbruView: Capturing Complex, Time-oriented Plans — Beyond Flow-Charts. In *Thinking with Diagrams '98*, University of Wales, Aberystwyth, UK, 22–23 Aug. 1998.

[9] A. M. MacEachren. Visualizing uncertain information. *Cartographic Perspective*, (13):10–19, Fall 1992.

[10] J. D. Mackinlay, G. G. Robertson, and S. K. Card. The perspective wall: Detail and context smoothly integrated. In *Proceedings of ACM CHI'91 Conference on Human Factors in Computing Systems*, Information Visualization, pages 173–179, 1991.

[11] S. Miksch, R. Kosara, Y. Shahar, and P. Johnson. AsbruView: Visualization of Time-Oriented, Skeletal Plans. In *Proceedings of the 4th International Conference on Artificial Intelligence Planning Systems 1998 (AIPS-98)*, Menlo Park, CA. Carnegie Mellon University, AAAI Press.

[12] S. Miksch, Y. Shahar, and P. Johnson. Asbru: A task-specific, intention-based, and time-oriented language for representing skeletal plans. In *Proceedings of the 7th Workshop on Knowledge Engineering: Methods & Languages (KEML-97)*. Open University, Milton Keynes, UK, 1997.

[13] S. Mukherjea, K. Hirata, and Y. Hara. Visualizing the results of multimedia web search engines. In *Proceedings IEEE Symposium on Information Visualization 1996*, pages 64–65. IEEE, 1996.

[14] I. Nassi and B. Shneiderman. Flowchart techniques for structured programming. *SIGPLAN Notices*, 8(8):12–26, 1973.

[15] A. Pang, C. Wittenbrink, and S. Lodha. Approaches to Uncertainty Visualization. Technical Report UCSC-CRL-96-21, University of California, Santa Cruz, Jack Baskin School of Engineering, Sept. 1996.

[16] C. Plaisant, B. Milash, A. Rose, S. Widoff, and B. Shneiderman. Lifelines: Visualizing personal histories. In *Proceedings of ACM CHI 96 Conference on Human Factors in Computing Systems*, pages 221–227, 1996.

[17] C. Plaisant, R. Mushlin, A. Snyder, J. Li, D. Heller, and B. Shneiderman. Lifelines: Using visualization to enhance navigation and analysis of patient records. In *Proceedings of the 1998 American Medical Informatic Association Annual Fall Symposium*, pages 76–80, 1998.

[18] S. M. Powsner and E. R. Tufte. Graphical summary of patient status. *The Lancet*, 344:386–389, 1994.

[19] W. Purgathofer and H. Löffelmann. Selected new trends in scientific visualization. Technical Report TR-186-2-97-17, Vienna University of Technology, Computer Graphics, Visualisation and Animation Group, Sept. 1997.

[20] J.-F. Rit. Propagating temporal constraints for scheduling. In *Proceedings of the Fifth National Conference on Artificial Intelligence*, pages 383–388, Los Altos, CA, 1986. Morgan Kaufman Publishers, Inc.

[21] M. Sarkar, S. S. Snibbe, O. J. Tversky, and S. P. Reiss. Stretching the rubber sheet: A metophor for visualizing large layouts on small screens. In *Proceedings of the ACM Symposium on User Interface Software and Technology*, Visualizing Information, pages 81–91, 1993.

[22] B. Shneiderman. The eyes have it: A task by data type taxonomy for information visualizations. In *Proceedings of the IEEE Symposium on Visual Languages*, pages 336–343, Washington. IEEE Computer Society Press.

[23] D. A. Stevenson, X. Guan, K. J. MacGallum, and A. H. B. Duffy. Sketching on the back of the computational envelope ... and then posting it? In *Proceedings of the Workshop on Visual Representation, Reasoning and Interaction in Design, Fourth International Conference on Artificial Intelligence in Design 1996 (AID'96)*. Stanford University, USA, June 23 1996.

[24] E. R. Tufte. *The Visual Display of Quantitative Information*. Graphics Press, Cheshire, CT, 1983.

Visualizing Temporal Clinical Data on the WWW

Carlo Combi[1], Luisa Portoni[2], Francesco Pinciroli[3]

[1] Dipartimento di Matematica e Informatica, Universita' degli Studi di Udine
via delle Scienze 206, 33100 Udine, Italy
combi@dimi.uniud.it
[2] 3D Image Processing & Synthesis Laboratory - SAIA - ISIS,
Joint Research Centre of the European Commission, Ispra - Italy
luisa.portoni@jrc.it
[3] Dipartimento di Bioingegneria, Politecnico di Milano and
Centro di Ingegneria Biomedica del CNR, Milano
pinciroli@biomed.polimi.it

Abstract. This paper deals with the visualization of complex objects on the WWW. In considering complex data our focus is in particular on temporal clinical information given at different levels of granularity or with indeterminacy. We propose some tools and graphic notations to visualize temporal data, according to two different modalities: the first one based on the time axis, displaying the absolute location of temporal data; the second one allowing the user to focus on different temporal relations among data. The designed and developed tools for visualizing temporal clinical data are part of a prototype, allowing a general practitioner to access on the WWW, from his ambulatory office or from home, clinical data related to his referred cardiological patients.

1   Introduction

The management on the WWW of complex information, often stored in object-oriented databases, has highlighted the need of suitably visualizing complex, not necessarily multimedia, data. The visualization of temporal data has been considered both from database community and from AI community [2, 3, 4, 6, 7]: reasons of this interest can be found both in the need of graphically representing and summarizing a large amount of data, often given with different levels of abstraction, and in the widespread diffusion of graphic user-interfaces and browsers. Approaches and solutions in literature are different and heterogeneous; proposals are related to specific tasks, as, for example, display of clinical data on different time scales [2], visual query of temporal data [3], visualization of video data [4], visualization of personal histories [6], display of abstractions on clinical data [7].

In the following, we focus on aspects related to complex data visualization, we faced within the project KHOSPAD - Knocking at the HOSpital for PAtient Data: the project aims at improving the quality of the process of patient care concerning general practitioner-patient-hospital relationships, merging WWW and object-oriented database technologies [5]. More precisely, this paper deals with the definition of graphic tools to suitably visualize sets of temporal objects, i.e. objects representing a

W. Horn et al. (Eds.): AIMDM'99, LNAI 1620, pp. 301-311, 1999.

piece of temporal information, with a special attention on data specified at different levels of granularity (i.e., different time units) or with indeterminacy (i.e., uncertainty in temporal location). We propose graphic notations and tools to visualize both the location, with the related indeterminacy, of objects on the absolute time line and the temporal relations between objects.

The paper is organized as follows: in Section 2 we introduce the main issues in modeling temporal clinical data and present the temporal data model we adopted; Section 3 provides a detailed description of our proposal about displaying temporal information. Section 4 briefly describes the KHOSPAD prototype. Section 5 presents the final outlines.

2   Modeling Temporal Data

In modeling temporal data we adopted the GCH-OODM (Granular Clinical History – Object-Oriented Data Model) model, described in detail in [1] and briefly sketched in the next section. This choice enables a suitable representation and management of temporal information. Let us consider, for example, the need of storing and representing the following sentences, concerning symptoms, pathologies, measured parameters, and therapies related to a patient.

1. "In 1996 the patient took a calcium-antagonist for three months"
2. "The patient had chest pain from 7 a.m. to 3 p.m., July 28, 1996"
3. "At 5:17 p.m., October 21, 1995, the patient suffered from myocardial infarction"
4. "On August 29, 1995, between 10:10 and 11:30 a.m., the physician got a blood pressure of 170/110 from the patient"
5. "At 6:15 p.m., March 3, 1994, the patient's renal colic ended; it lasted five days"
6. "The patient suffered from an episode of tachycardia lasting 130 seconds on September 17, 1994, at 4:12 p.m."

Some of the above sentences (i.e., 3 and 4) describe instantaneous events. Others refer to clinical information lasting a time span (i.e., 1, 2, 5, and 6). Different granularities and indeterminacies are present in the temporal clinical information: in sentence 2, for example, the time unit *hour* is used to identify the starting and ending instants of the chest pain; in sentence 3, the time unit *minutes* is used; in sentence 4, a temporal indeterminacy for the blood pressure measurement is represented by "..., between 10:10 and 11:30 a.m."; in sentence 5, *hours* is the time unit for the end of the renal colic, while *days* is the time unit used to express the time span of the renal colic.

Considering sentences related to a time interval (i.e., 1, 2, 5, and 6), it is not possible to represent all the specified intervals, by giving, as usually, their starting and ending instants, even with different granularity: for example, the interval of sentence 6 could not be expressed, because the duration of tachycardia episode is given at a granularity finer than that used for expressing the starting instant of the episode. Finally, we underline that in case of different granularities we have to deal with the uncertainty coming from relations between intervals: it is not possible, for example, to establish for sure if the patient took calcium antagonists (sentence 1) before having chest pain (sentence 2).

2.1   The Object-Oriented Temporal Data Model GCH-OODM

GCH-OODM is an object-oriented data model extended to consider and manage the valid time of information, i.e. the time at which the information is true in the modeled world [8]. The database schema consists of a set of *classes*. Objects are created as instances of a *class*. We will use the terms *class* and *type* as synonyms, to describe the proposed data model. An object is characterized by a *state*, described by attributes, not accessible from outside, and by an *interface*, defined by methods. GCH-OODM supports the main features of object-oriented data models applied to databases: object identity, abstract data types, single inheritance, polymorphism, management of complex objects, persistence [1].

Besides the usual types (char, char*, int, real, array, list, set, ..), GCH-OODM uses the class hierarchy *el_time, instant, duration, interval*, to model the temporal dimension of information.

The class *el_time* models time points on the basic time axis, named elementary instants. Each elementary instant is identified by the corresponding chronon, i.e. the nondecomposable unit of time supported by the temporal DBMS [8]. By the class *el_time* properties of integers are extended to the time axis. So, both time points and spans between time points are modeled in a homogeneous way: time points are identified on the basic time axis by their distance from the origin of the axis.

The class *instant* models a time point identified by the granule, i.e. a set of contiguous chronons, containing it. This class uses, by the methods *inf()* and *sup()*, two objects of type *el_time*, to represent the lower and upper bound of the granule, in which the generic time point is located. The instant 94/10/10, for example, may coincide with anyone of the time points included between the two bounds 94/10/10:0:0:0 and 94/10/10:23:59:59, represented by two objects of *el_time* type. By the class *instant* we can deal also with explicit indeterminacy: for example, the instant ≺96/12/12:12:30:0, 96/12/12:12:36:59≻ specifies a time point between 12:30 and 12:36, on December 12, 1996. The class *duration* models a generic duration, specified at arbitrary granularity. This class uses, by the methods *inf()* and *sup()*, two objects of type *el_time*, to represent the lower and upper distances between chronons, between which the value of the given duration is included. The duration 3 d, for example, stands for a time distance lasting between 3 d 0 h 0 mi 0 s and 3 d 23 h 59 mi 59 s. A duration may also be expressed by specifying the lower and upper distances, e.g. ≺3 d 4 h 6 mi 3 s, 4 d 6 h 5 mi 2 s≻, for explicit indeterminacy. Suitable methods allow the expression of relations and operations, like sum or difference, on instances of the classes *instant* and *duration* [1].

A generic interval, i.e. a set of contiguous time points, is modeled by the class *interval*. The methods *start()*, *end()* and *dur()* allow us to identify, respectively, the starting instant, the ending instant and the duration of the interval. The methods of the class *interval* permit to establish temporal relations between two intervals, specified at (possibly) different and not predefined granularity and/or indeterminacy. Relations between intervals are described in detail in [1]. We use three different notations to represent the value of an interval: (i) FROM <*instant*> TO <*instant*>; (ii) FROM <*instant*> FOR <*duration*>; and (iii) FOR <*duration*> TO <*instant*>.

GCH-OODM relies on a three-valued logic (*true, false, undefined*), modeled by the class *bool3*, allowing the management of the uncertainty coming from comparisons between temporal dimensions expressed with different granularity/indeterminacy. The classes modeling objects having a temporal dimension (hereinafter *temporal objects*) inherit from the class *t_object*: the method *valid_interval*() defined for this class, returns an object of the class *interval*, used to express valid time for a given temporal object.

3   Visualizing Temporal Information

In visualizing complex temporal information there are two different needs, to deal with: the first one is related to the visualization of the history, described by the considered temporal objects; the second one is related to the visual representation of temporal relations existing among different temporal objects. In the first case, the aim is to provide users with a concise visual description of a set of temporal objects (e.g., related to a given patient), according to the absolute time axis; in the second case, the purpose is to allow users to explore the different temporal relations existing among temporal objects (e.g., among symptoms and therapies), which can not be precisely observed with the previous history-oriented representation.

3.1   Displaying Temporal Objects on the Time Axis

This history-oriented visual representation of temporal data is offered to the user through graphic tools easily displaying the relative position among temporal objects and allowing a quick identification of the temporal extension, with its indeterminacy, of the object valid intervals. The following features have been identified as important ones when designing the graphic interface devoted to the representation of histories:

- selection of subsets of temporal objects, to allow the user to focus on a subpart of the history, described by the whole set of temporal objects;
- visualization, on the considered screen window, of the minimal interval containing the whole set of temporal objects, to provide an overall view of the considered history;
- displaying of a reference time axis, to locate temporal data;
- selection of the preferred time unit to be used in displaying information;
- selection of the part of the time axis to be displayed;
- zooming in and out on the time axis.

The structure of the visualization system, designed according to the above requirements, is represented in figure 1. The notation adopted for the visual representation of temporal data, modeled by suitable temporal objects, is depicted in figure 2. For each temporal object two elements are represented: a graphic one related to the extension of the valid interval and a textual one providing a concise description for the atemporal content.

The graphic representation is strictly related to GCH-OODM, and allows the visualization of the indeterminacy related to the object valid interval. The color of the box is associated to the specific temporal class of the database schema, the considered temporal object is instance of. The box represents the extension of the object valid interval, i.e. the segment on the time axis having as lower and upper bounds the smallest time point possibly being the start of the interval and the greatest time point possibly being the end of the interval, respectively. For example, in fig. 1 the considered box, related to the valid interval FROM <1996/2/25> FOR <7d> of the temporal object labeled as Angina, has the lower bound 1996/2/25:0:0:0 and the upper bound 1996/3/4:23:59:58 (coming from the addition of the upper distance of the duration 7 d, i.e. 7 d 23 h 59 mi 59 s, to the upper bound of the instant 1996/2/25, i.e. 1996/2/25:23:59:59, being the year 1996 a leap year). We can identify some subparts of the box representing, respectively, the starting instant, the duration, and the ending instant of the interval: in the example depicted in fig. 1, the visualized starting instant is the day <1996/2/25>; the visualized duration is <7d>; the visualized ending instant is evaluated by adding a duration of seven days to February 25, 1996.

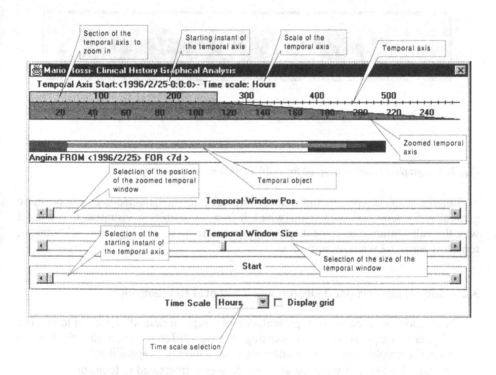

Fig. 1. The structure of the window for visualizing histories on temporal objects: squared blobs contain brief descriptions of the window details.

Subparts representing starting and ending instants are as extended as the indeterminacy related to these instants is high: the subparts representing these instants are, in fact, all the time points on the time axis, possibly being the start (end) of the considered interval: the sub-box related to the starting instant in fig. 1, for example, is bounded by the time points 1996/2/25:0:0:0 and 1996/2/25:23:59:59 on the basic time axis (having the granularity of *seconds*). The duration is represented by two sub-boxes having a dimension respectively related to the lower and the upper time span that the valid interval can have: in our example, we have 7 d 0 h 0 mi 0 s as lower time span and 7 d 23 h 59 mi 59 s as upper time span. The two sub-boxes are centered in respect with the box representing the valid interval of the considered temporal object: this way, the visual notation underlines that, while starting and ending instants of the valid interval are anchored temporal concepts (i.e., related to an absolute position on the time axis), the duration of the valid interval is an unanchored temporal concept (i.e., related to the possible distances between the starting and ending time points of the valid interval).

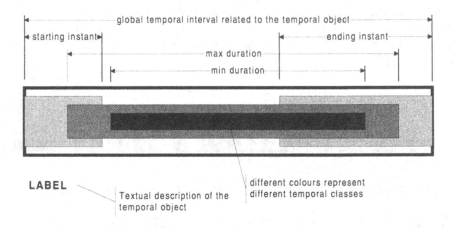

Fig. 2. The graphic notation adopted for valid interval of temporal objects.

Suitable graphic representations are defined also for instantaneous events or, more generally, for temporal objects for which it is not possible to visualize in a correct way the valid interval in some displaying conditions (e.g., too big temporal window, too short temporal window, and so on).

3.2   Displaying Temporal Objects and Temporal Relationships

The relation-oriented visual representation of temporal data allows users to explore the different temporal relations existing among different temporal objects. In designing the graphic interface we considered the following capabilities:
- selection of subsets of temporal objects, the user is interested to focus on;
- visual representation of the granularity of object valid intervals;
- displaying temporal relations between valid intervals;
- displaying the uncertainty related to temporal relations between temporal data at different granularities;
- abstract representation of the temporal location and of the global temporal extent of a given temporal object;
- selection of the temporal relations to be visualized;
- selection of the temporal entity on which to evaluate temporal relations: starting instant, ending instant, duration, or valid interval itself.

The notation adopted for the visual representation of temporal objects is depicted in figure 3. The valid interval of a temporal object is represented by a node, composed by three circular sectors: each sector corresponds to one of the dimensions of the valid interval (starting and ending instants, duration). The label at the top of each node represents, after a system-assigned number, the atemporal content of the considered temporal object (e.g., a concise description of a therapy, or of a pathology) and an abstract description of the valid interval. The valid interval is represented by the granule containing it at the finest allowed granularity. Colors (that in the black-and-white figures are depicted as different gray levels) and radial lengths of sectors are related to the granularity used in specifying the parts of the valid interval: the color ranges from cool (blue) to warm (red) tones for granularities ranging from coarser to finer ones; the radial length increases with the granularity (big radial lengths for coarse granularities). This way, the radial dimension is useful to compare granularities of different temporal objects. The angular dimensions depend on the different granularities used in expressing the valid interval related to a given node. The angular dimensions of the temporal entities given at coarser granularity are greater than the angular dimensions of the temporal entities given at finer granularity for the same interval. Angular dimensions are useful in comparing granularities used to express the temporal entities (starting and ending instants, duration) related to a single valid interval. For temporal objects having an instantaneous validity, a special notation has been defined, as depicted in figure 3. The user can also display the temporal object with some representation of the temporal location. Around the sectors, a watch-like face is visualized, showing a suitable time scale according to the given valid interval: on this scale the position of the valid interval is highlighted. For example, the node labeled as "(4) Renal Colic on Mar 1996" in figure 3 refers to a temporal object, previously stored in the database, having as valid interval FOR <5 d> TO <1996/3/26:13:12>: "Renal colic" is the part of the label describing the atemporal data of the object; "on Mar 1996" represents the smallest granule (March 1996) containing the whole valid interval; the smaller sector is in green (i.e., granularity of minutes) and represents the finest granularity, i.e. that related to the ending instant, used for the given valid interval; the sector at the bottom of the node is in cyan and represents the duration (given at the granularity of days, corresponding to cyan); the leftmost sector of the node stands for the starting instant, is depicted in magenta (i.e., granularity of months), and has an indeterminacy in its temporal location due to granularities of both the ending instant and the duration. On the external circular scale, March days are represented and the days containing the valid interval are highlighted with the color corresponding to the granularity of days.

Temporal relations are visualized by edges between the nodes; different edge colors are associated to different truth values. Each edge has some labels; they represent the different relations existing between nodes. The edges have a direction from the first operand to the second one of the relation. Bi-directional edges stand for two directional edges with the suitable labels. For example, in figure 4, two nodes are displayed, related to a pathology (strong flares of rheumatoid arthritis) and to a therapy (assumption of Lacirex, a calcium-antagonist), respectively. The first edge, labeled by "<" (before) and "O" (overlaps), stands for uncertain relations (blue color): e.g., is it possible that flares of arthritis happened before the therapy; the second one, labeled by "M(M)" (meets at granularity of months) and "F(Y)" (finishes at granularity of years), stands for true relations (black color); the third one, labeled by "F(Y)" in one direction and "M(M)", "O", and "<" in the other direction, stands for false relations (red color).

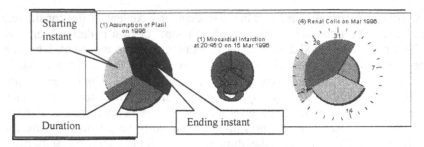

Fig. 3. Graphic notation for temporal objects (from the left to the right): main notation, instantaneous temporal object notation, extension of the main notation to represent temporal location.

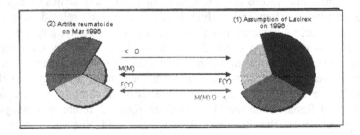

Fig. 4. Graphic notation for relations between temporal objects.

The overall structure of the designed visualization system is represented in figure 5, where from the top to the bottom are shown:

- a panel containing some controls for the visualization: (i) the selection of the temporal entities (starting instant, ending instant, duration, or valid interval) to consider, (ii) the buttons for defining how and where temporal objects must be represented, (iii) the truth values of the temporal relations to display;
- a panel containing the temporal relations which can be selected;
- a window visualizing temporal objects and temporal relations;
- a panel where the user can select the granularity used when evaluating a given relation – this window reminds also to the user of which are the different colors related to the different granularities.

4   The KHOSPAD Prototype

We implemented the visualization tools above described as parts of the KHOSPAD prototype.

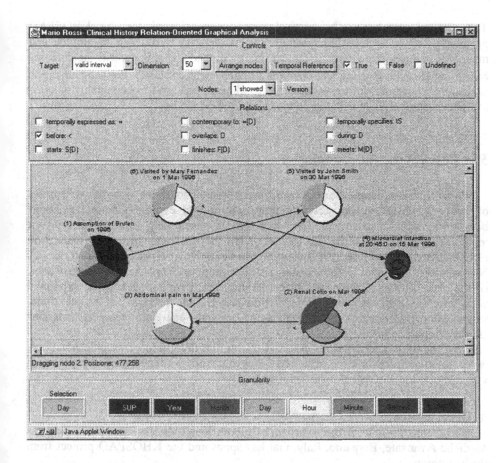

Fig. 5. The structure of the system for visualizing relations between temporal objects.

The system architecture. The KHOSPAD prototype is based on a client-server architecture. The hardware consists of client machines, a Web server machine, a database server machine and the communication infrastructure. The main software components are:

- the client application, through which the user interacts with the system. It provides a window-based graphic interface and handles remote accesses to the database according to suitable protocols; at this level are executed most of the functions to process and display data. In particular, the client application supports both the history-oriented visualization and the relation-oriented one.
- the Web server. It handles the queries coming from the client. Queries can concern the full or partial download of the client application, Hypertext (HTML) pages, or queries to be transmitted to the database server.
- the database server. To this part of the system are devoted the functions related to data management, access control, concurrency control and recovery.
- programs interfacing the Web and the database server.

Details on the web-based architecture of the KHOSPAD system can be found in [5].

The clinical database. The clinical database considered for the KHOSPAD prototype, related to a single specialty clinical setting, is devoted to archive and manage PTCA patient records in the cardiology division. In this context the database has to handle both α-numerical data and images acquired during the catheterization procedures. Temporal information related to clinical data have to be suitably handled too: the database system is based on the GCH-OODM model.

5   Discussion and Conclusions

We designed and implemented two different graphic notations to visualize histories of temporal objects on an absolute time axis and to explore temporal relations between objects, respectively. Our approach in visualizing clinical histories of temporal objects has some similarities with the personal history visualization technique called Lifelines [6] and with the time line browser described in [2]. Nevertheless, two main features distinguish our proposal from these previous works: (i) the visualization of temporal objects having their temporal dimension expressed with different granularity and/or indeterminacy; (ii) the proposal of an additional visualization tool devoted to the analysis of (possibly uncertain) temporal relations among temporal objects.

Even though clinicians were involved during the definition of graphic notations, we plan to perform a deep and detailed evaluation of benefits of the proposed visualization tools in real clinical settings.

Acknowledgments
Special thanks are due to the Accademia Internazionale di Bergamo per le Scienze Mediche Avanzate, Bergamo, Italy, that has sponsored the KHOSPAD project from the beginning.

References

1. Combi C, Cucchi G, Pinciroli F. Applying Object-Oriented Technologies in Modeling and Querying Temporally-Oriented Clinical Databases Dealing with Temporal Granularity and Indeterminacy. IEEE Transactions on Information Technology in Biomedicine, 1997, 1(2): 100 - 127.
2. Cousins SB, Kahn MG. The visual display of temporal information. In Keravnou ET (guest editor) Special Issue on Temporal Reasoning in Medicine. Artificial Intelligence in Medicine 1991; 3(6): 341-357.
3. Fernandes S, Schiel U, Catarci T. Visual Query Operators for Temporal Databases In: Proceedings fourth international workshop on temporal representation and reasoning (TIME '97). Los Alamitos, IEEE Computer Society Press, 1997, 46 - 53.
4. Hibino S, Rundensteiner EA. A Visual Multimedia Query Language for Temporal Analysis of Video Data. In: MultiMedia Database Systems: Design and Implementation Strategies. (ed. Kingsley C. Nwosu, Bhavani Thuraisingham, and P. Bruce Berra), Norwell, MA: Kluwer, 1996, 123 - 159.

5. Pinciroli F, Portoni L, Combi C, Violante F. WWW-based Access to Object-Oriented Clinical Databases: the KHOSPAD Project. In: Internet for Medicine and Health Care. Special Issue Computers in Biology and Medicine, 1998, vol. 28, n. 5, 531 - 552.
6. Plaisant C, Shneiderman B. An Information Architecture to Support the Visualization of Personal Histories. Information Processing and Management, 1998, 34 (2), 581 – 597.
7. Shahar Y, Cheng C. Knowledge-Based Visualization and Navigation of Temporal Data. 1998. SMI-98-0705 Technical Report, Stanford University - Section on Medical Informatics, 1998.
8. Tansel AU, Clifford J, Gadia S, Jajodia S, Segev A, Snodgrass R (eds.). Temporal Databases. Theory, Design and Implementation. Benjamin-Cummings, Redwood City, CA, 1993.

Machine Learning

Machine Learning in Stepwise Diagnostic Process*

Matjaž Kukar[1] and Ciril Grošelj[2]

[1] University of Ljubljana, Faculty of Computer and Information Science,
Tržaška 25, SI-1001 Ljubljana, Slovenia,
matjaz.kukar@fri.uni-lj.si,
[2] University Medical Centre Ljubljana, Nuclear Medicine Department,
Zaloška 7, SI-1001 Ljubljana, Slovenia

Abstract. Diagnostic processes for many diseases are becoming increasingly complex. Many results, obtained from tests with substantial imperfections, must be integrated into a diagnostic conclusion about the probability of disease in a given patient. A practical approach to this problem is to estimate the pretest probability of disease, and the sensitivity and specificity of different diagnostic tests. With this information, test results can be analyzed by sequential use of Bayes' theorem of conditional probability. The calculated posttest probability is then used as a pretest probability for the next test. This results in a series of tests, where each test is performed independently. Its results may be interpreted with or without any knowledge of other test results. By using Machine Learning techniques for test result evaluation, this process can be almost completely automated. The computer can learn from previously diagnosed patients and apply the acquired knowledge to new patients. Different Machine Learning methods can be used for evaluation of each test result. They may assist the physician as a powerful tool for assistance in pretest probability estimation, interpretation of individual test results and in the final decision making. The presented approach has been successfully evaluated in practice in the problem of clinical diagnosis of coronary artery disease.

1 Introduction

In general, medical diagnosis on the basis of history and physical examination alone is often difficult. Several sophisticated tests (both functional and morphological) are being developed to allow an early and more accurate diagnosis. As a consequence, making the final diagnosis is becoming increasingly complex. Many results, obtained from tests with substantial imperfections (an unavoidable evil, due to limited resources), must be integrated into a diagnostic conclusion about the probability of disease in a given patient.

---

* Parts of this work are taken from both Matjaž Kukar's and Ciril Grošelj's Ph.D. theses. This work was supported by the Slovenian Ministry of Science and Technology.

W. Horn et al. (Eds.): AIMDM'99, LNAI 1620, pp. 315–325, 1999.
© Springer-Verlag Berlin Heidelberg 1999

A practical approach to address the complexity problem is the analysis of probability. For that we need to estimate the pretest probability of a disease and then sequentially use Bayes' theorem of conditional probability to obtain the posttest probability after each test.

In recent decade many Machine Learning methods have been developed that can be used as efficient tools for the analysis of databases and extraction of the classification knowledge. Once acquired, it can be used to solve new problems from the given problem domain. There have been many successful applications of Machine Learning to medical diagnostic problems [3].

By using Machine Learning techniques, a probabilistic diagnostic process can almost automatically be run in parallel with a classical diagnostic process. The computer can learn from previously diagnosed patients and apply the learned knowledge to new patients. Different Machine Learning methods can be used for evaluation of different test results. This gives the physician a powerful tool for assistance in pretest probability estimation, interpretation of individual test results and in the final decision making.

The aim of our work was to examine the possibilities of using Machine Learning methods in stepwise diagnostic process and evaluate the approach in practice in the problem of clinical diagnosis of coronary artery disease.

Our experiments show that by using Machine Learning techniques, improvements can be expected from the pretest probability estimation as well as from the interpretation of test results. In practice, this means better performance and rationalization of diagnostic process.

2   Analysis of Probability in the Stepwise Diagnostic Process

Because many different tests (functional and morphological) can be used for similar diagnostic purposes, the physician must decide on their optimum use in terms of performance and cost-effectiveness. As a consequence, making the final diagnosis is becoming increasingly more complex. Many results, obtained from tests with substantial imperfections, must be integrated into a diagnostic conclusion about the probability of disease in a given patient.

One way to address this problem, that has been successfully applied in practice, is the analysis of probabilities. The key element in this approach is to estimate the pretest probability of disease, and the sensitivity and specificity of different diagnostic tests. With this information, test results can be analyzed by sequential use of Bayes' theorem of conditional probability. The obtained posttest probability accounts for the pretest probability, sensitivity and specificity of the test. This is then used as a pretest probability for the next test (Figure 1). This results in a series of test where each test is performed independently and its results may be interpreted with or without any knowledge of the other test results. However, previous test results are used to obtain the final probability of disease.

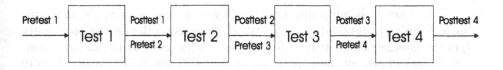

Fig. 1. "Chaining" diagnostic tests: a general principle of a stepwise diagnosis.

The *pretest* probability of disease is fundamental in deciding whether a diagnostic test should be performed. Usually, after taking a history and performing a physical examination, the physician estimates the (pretest) probability of disease, and often does so intuitively. Such an estimate is made on basis of personal experience, on the data from the literature (Table 1) and on particular features of the patient. The integration of these three sources into a single parameter represents the probability of disease [8, pp. 349].

Table 1. Pretest probabilities for the presence of CAD. Probabilities were elicited from pathological data obtained from 23996 persons at autopsy according to three parameters (age, sex, type of chest pain) and calculated as pooled means [1, 9].

Sex	Age	Asymptomatic patients	Nonang. chest pain	Atypical angina	Typical angina
Female	35-44	0.007	0.027	0.155	0.454
	45-54	0.021	0.069	0.317	0.677
	55-64	0.054	0.127	0.465	0.839
	65-74	0.115	0.171	0.541	0.947
Male	35-44	0.037	0.105	0.428	0.809
	45-54	0.077	0.206	0.601	0.907
	55-64	0.111	0.282	0.690	0.939
	65-74	0.113	0.282	0.700	0.943

However, there are several caveats that one must be aware of, e.g., the problem of different selection biases when using data from literature, which may result in not entirely reliable conclusions.

Once the pretest probability has been estimated, the physician decides which diagnostic test will reduce or increase the probability of disease, thus turning it into posttest probability. If the pretest probability is low (say under 0.10), it may not be necessary to perform further tests. If the pretest probability is high (say over 0.90), specific therapy may be started. The problem represent only the patients where the probability is intermediate. For them, further testing is indicated, with ultimate goal to decrease (or increase) the probability of disease (in our case under 0.10 or over 0.90). As usual, quality of a diagnostic test is determined by its sensitivity (Se) and specificity (Sp).

The *posttest* probability measures the degree of certainty of the diagnosis after performing a certain diagnostic test. It depends on the pretest probability (P) of the disease and sensitivity (Se) and specificity (Sp) of the diagnostic test. It can be calculated by the application of Bayes' theorem. The application of the theorem imposes several restrictions [8, pp. 353-354]., however it has been already successfully used in practice [1, 7].

In essence, we apply the Bayes' theorem to calculate the conditional probability of the disease's presence, when the result of a diagnostic test is given. After some tedious work with formulae [8, pp. 352] we get the following two equations. For positive test result the probability $P(d|+) = P(disease|positive\ test\ result)$ is calculated:

$$P(d|+) = \frac{P \cdot Se}{P \cdot Se + (1 - P) \cdot (1 - Sp)} \tag{1}$$

For negative test result the probability $P(d|-) = P(disease|negative\ test\ result)$ is calculated:

$$P(d|-) = \frac{P \cdot (1 - Se)}{P \cdot (1 - Se) + (1 - P) \cdot Sp} \tag{2}$$

The posttest probability after a diagnostic test represents the pretest probability for the subsequent test. This approach combines several test results (posttest probabilities) with data from the patient's history (pretest probability) [1].

3   Stepwise Diagnostic Process in CAD

We speak of a coronary artery disease (CAD), when a blood flow through coronary arteries is diminished due to stenosis or occlusion. It results in impaired function of the heart and may end with a myocardial infarction (necrosis of the myocardium).

During exercise, the volume of the blood pumped to the body has to be increased to several times of that at rest. This causes the blood flow through the coronary arteries to be increased several times as well. In a (low grade) CAD the perfusion of the myocardium is adequate at rest or during a moderate exercise, but insufficient during a severe exercise, when signs and symptoms of the CAD develop.

There are four diagnostic levels of CAD. Firstly, signs and symptoms of the disease are evaluated clinically and ECG is performed at rest. This is followed by sequential ECG testing during controlled exercises by gradually increasing the work load of the patient. Usually a bicycle ergometer or a treadmill is used.

If this test is not conclusive, or if additional information regarding the perfusion of the myocardium is needed, myocardial perfusion scintigraphy is performed. Radioactive material is injected into the patient during an exercise. Its accumulation in the heart is proportional to the heart's perfusion and can be shown in appropriate images (scintigrams). Scintigraphy is repeated at rest and by comparing both sets of images, the presence, the localization, and the distribution of the ischaemic tissue are determined.

If the test is inconclusive, or an invasive therapy of the disease is contemplated, i.e. the dilatation of the stenosed coronary artery or coronary artery bypass surgery, the diagnosis has to be confirmed by imaging of the coronary vessels. This is performed by injecting radio opaque (contrast) material into the coronary vessels and by imaging their anatomy with x-ray coronary angiography.

In our study [2, 7] we used a dataset of 327 patients (250 males, 77 females) with performed clinical and laboratory examinations, exercise ECG, myocardial perfusion scintigraphy and coronary angiography because of suspected CAD. The features from the ECG an scintigraphy data were extracted manually by the clinicians. In 228 cases the disease was angiographically confirmed and in 99 cases it was excluded. The patients were selected from a population of approximately 4000 patients, who were examined at the Nuclear Medicine Department, University Medical Centre, Ljubljana, between 1991 and 1994. We selected only the patients with complete diagnostic procedures (all four levels) [7]. The reason for this (narrow) selection was that a definite proof [1] of presence or absence of CAD for all patients was required. In determining the pretest probability we applied the Table 1, which we retrieved from literature [9]. For each patient, the table was indexed by a subset of "signs and symptoms" attributes (age, sex, type of chest pain).

The aim of our early studies [5, 2] was to improve the diagnostic performance (sensitivity and specificity) of non-invasive diagnostic methods (i.e. clinical examinations of the patients, exercise ECG testing, and myocardial perfusion scintigraphy in comparison with the coronary angiography as a definite proof of coronary artery stenosis) by evaluating all available diagnostic information with Machine Learning techniques. In ongoing work we aim to increase the number of reliable diagnoses after myocardial perfusion scintigraphy (posttest probability over 0.90 or under 0.10, respectively). This will reduce the number of patients that must unnecessarily be submitted to further invasive examinations (coronary angiography), that can be potentially dangerous, unpleasant and very costly.

4   A Machine Learning Approach

Machine Learning is a subfield of Artificial Intelligence that deals with learning, in our case, learning from examples (inductive learning). Each example is given by its description (a vector of attribute values) and a known outcome (a correct classification of the example). In medical diagnosis, the example is given by a description of the patient (including some test results), the classification is a confirmed correct diagnosis. From known examples (the so-called training set), Machine Learning methods are able to discover the knowledge necessary for classification of previously unseen examples. Usually, a method that uses the generated knowledge (a classifier) not only provides an answer to which class an example belongs, but it also estimates the probability that an example belongs to any class.

---

[1] A definite proof of a disease can only be obtained by autopsy or with a morphological examination, in our case, coronary angiography.

In a stepwise diagnostic process Machine Learning methods can be used both as pretest probability estimators and as (meta) test evaluators (methods that assesses raw test results and make proposals for diagnoses). For estimating pretest probabilities it is essential that the method produces probabilistic answers. It is useful to use this approach when no appropriate data exist in literature, or selection biases are too much different. A selection bias of the collected dataset may be partially compensated (or enhanced) by using cost-sensitive learning techniques [6, 7].

For evaluation of test results, categorical answers are sufficient. The characteristics of each test evaluator (in our case, a Machine Learning method) is determined by the corresponding ROC curve (Figure 2), obtained with use of cost-sensitive learning techniques [6].

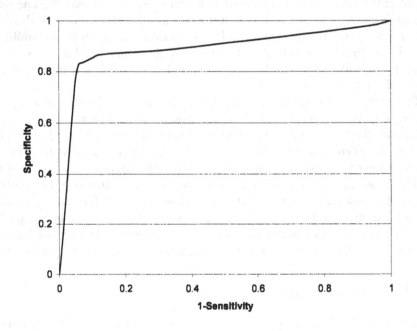

Fig. 2. A ROC curve describing the behaviour of the backpropagation neural network in the CAD diagnostic problem.

Figure 3 illustrates a possible use of Machine Learning methods in a stepwise CAD diagnosis. Pretest probability of a patient is estimated from the signs and symptoms (a set of 30 attributes). The first diagnostic result is obtained from evaluation of the exercise ECG (a set of 16 attributes). The second diagnostic result is obtained from evaluation of the myocardial perfusion scintigraphy (a set of 31 attributes). Posttest probability after the first test (exercise ECG) is used as a pretest probability for the second test (scintigraphy).

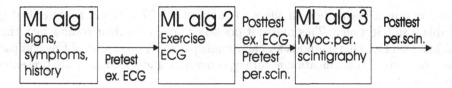

Fig. 3. Machine Learning in stepwise diagnostic process. Note that each box may contain different ML algorithm.

In our experiments we used the following well known Machine Learning methods, which are all able to give both categorical and probabilistic classifications.

- naive Bayesian classifier (sometimes also called simple or idiot Bayes) [3]
- decision trees (Assistant-I) [4]
- multilayered (with a single hidden layer) feedforward neural networks with backpropagation learning [10]

5   Experimental Results

We performed our experiments on the CAD dataset of 327 patients (Table 2). Pretest probabilities were estimated from the signs and symptoms, then exercise ECG results were assessed (first test) and then myocardial perfusion scintigraphy (second test). For the sake of learning process, the results of coronary angiography which is considered a reference method, were used as a definite proof of presence (or absence) of a disease. Since no independent testing set for evaluation

Table 2. CAD data for different diagnostic levels.

Diagnostic data	Number of attributes		
	Nominal	Numeric	Total
Signs, symptoms and history	23	7	30
Exercise ECG	7	9	16
Scintigraphy	22	9	31
Entropy of the dataset (228 pos., 99 neg.)		0.88 bit	

of our methodology was available, we performed a ten-fold cross validation, a methodology well known in Machine Learning community. All experiments were performed ten times, each time one tenth of the dataset was not used in learning but reserved for testing purposes. The presented results are averages of ten runs.

Firstly, we were interested in how well the Machine Learning methods compare with physicians in evaluation of two diagnostic tests. The physicians' results were obtained in practice on the same dataset of 327 patients as described in Table 2 and Section 3. This makes it possible to compare their results with that of Machine Learning methods for each single patient. The results of this comparison (in terms of classification accuracy, sensitivity and specificity) are presented in Table 3.

As we can see, in all cases the Machine Learning methods considerably improve classification accuracy, mostly as a consequence of significantly ($P < 0.01$) improved sensitivity of the test. The best performer is the backpropagation neural network with considerable improvements of all three criteria.

Table 3. Accuracy, sensitivity and specificity of Machine Learning methods compared with the physicians.

	Exercise ECG			Scintigraphy		
	Acc.	Sens.	Spec.	Acc.	Sens.	Spec.
Physicians	0.65	0.61	**0.75**	0.85	0.85	0.86
Backprop.	**0.77**	**0.87**	0.56	**0.91**	0.92	**0.87**
Assistant	0.73	0.87	0.40	0.90	**0.93**	0.83
Bayes	0.73	0.85	0.45	0.89	0.91	0.83

After applying the methods described above to the stepwise diagnostic process, we measured the average pretest and posttest errors on angiographically positive and negative patients. Results were compared to that of physicians, with pretest probabilities obtained from the Table 1. The results are presented in Table 4 and depicted in Figures 4 and 5. The better results are higher posttest probabilities for positive patients and lower posttest probabilities for negative patients. The improvements are a consequence of improved diagnostic performance of the methods in comparison with physicians. For estimation of pretest probabilities the best performer was (again) the backpropagation neural network. It seems that its interconnected structure is best suited for the relatively complex dependencies in the data. However its serious drawback is the inability to explain exactly why a certain probability value was assigned.

Table 4. Average pretest and posttest probabilities on positive and negative patients.

	Positive			Negative		
	Pretest	Ex.ECG	Scintig.	Pretest	Ex.ECG	Scintig.
Physicians	0.77	0.78	0.85	0.47	0.42	0.28
Backprop.	0.83	0.84	0.92	0.47	0.42	0.23
Assistant	0.84	0.83	0.91	0.56	0.51	0.26
Bayes	0.86	0.89	0.93	0.54	0.49	0.28

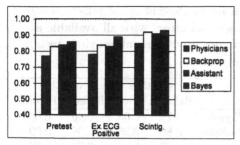

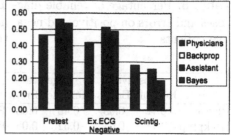

Fig. 4. Average pretest and posttest probabilities on positive patients.

Fig. 5. Average pretest and posttest probabilities on negative patients.

We also measured the percentage (share) of reliable diagnoses (with the posttest probability over 0.90 for positive patients and under 0.10 for negative patients), and errors made in this process (percentage of incorrectly diagnosed patients with seemingly reliable diagnoses). We compared the results with that of the physicians and with results obtained from Machine Learning methods when all available attributes (signs and symptoms, exercise ECG, myocardial perfusion scintigraphy) were used. The results are presented in Tables 5 and 6 and depicted in Figures 6 and 7. The best result (backpropagation neural network) shows improvements by 6% for both positive and negative patients without risk of making more errors than physicians.

Even bigger improvement can be expected when using all available attributes for classification (Machine Learning methods can efficiently deal with much larger sets of attributes than humans). The predicted class probabilities were considered as posttest probabilities with the same 0.90:0.10 criterion for reliability as before. Achieved improvements are breathtaking (Bayes: by 18% for positive and even by 35% for negative patients), however this goes hand in hand with a higher error rate (Bayes: by 4% for positive and by 3% for negative patients). Error rate could further be reduced by applying stronger criteria (i.e., 0.95:0.05) for reliable classifications. A physician must decide which tool to use either to stay safe with relatively smaller improvements (stepwise diagnostics) or to take more risk and achieve considerably higher improvements.

6 Discussion

The results of our study are promising. We have shown that Machine Learning techniques can be successfully used as an intelligent tool in a stepwise diagnostic process. Machine Learning methods can help physicians evaluate test results and improve their performance (sensitivity and specificity). They can also be very useful in determining pretest probabilities from collected datasets and therefore take in account the selection bias for a particular medical facility. The biases can be partially compensated by using cost-sensitive learning techniques.

Table 5. Percentage of reliable diag- **Table 6.** Percentage of reliable diagnoses and errors on positive and nega- noses and errors with all available at-
tive patients.   tributes used (from all previous tests).

	Positive		Negative			Positive		Negative	
	Reliable	Errors	Reliable	Errors		Reliable	Errors	Reliable	Errors
Physic.	0.72	0.03	0.46	0.08	Physic.	0.72	0.03	0.46	0.08
Backprop.	0.78	0.04	0.52	0.06	Backprop.	0.86	0.05	0.66	0.09
Assistant	0.79	0.05	0.49	0.08	Assistant	0.87	0.08	0.77	0.06
Bayes	0.79	0.05	0.46	0.03	Bayes	0.90	0.07	0.81	0.11

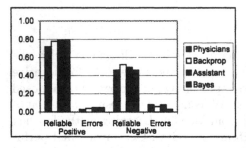 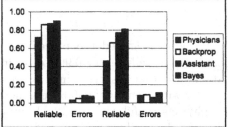

Fig. 6. Percentage of reliable diagnoses   **Fig. 7.** Percentage of reliable diagnoses
and errors with stepwise diagnost. pro-   and errors with all attributes used.
cess.

From practical use of described approaches a two-fold rationalization might
be expected. Due to higher specificity of tests fewer patients without the disease
would have to be examined with coronary angiography or other invasive high-
level examinations. Together with higher sensitivity this would also save money
and shorten waiting periods for truly ill patients

The most important result of our study are the improvements in the predictive power of the stepwise diagnostic process. The 6% of positive and 6%
of negative patients who would not need to be examined with costly further
tests, represents a considerable improvement in the diagnostic power as well as
in the rationalization of the existing CAD diagnostic procedure without danger
of incorrectly diagnosing more patients than in current practice. Even bigger
improvements may be expected by using all available attributes at once.

However, it should be emphasized that the results of our study are obtained
on a severely restricted population and therefore may not be generally applicable to the normal population, i.e. to all the patients coming to the Nuclear
Medicine Department. Further studies might be needed to verify our findings. In
particular, on-line data gathering is necessary to obtain a representative dataset.

References

[1] G. A. Diamond and J. S. Forester. Analysis of probability as an aid in the clinical diagnosis of coronary artery disease. *New Eng J Med*, 300:1350, 1979.

[2] C. Grošelj, M. Kukar, J. Fettich, and I. Kononenko. Machine learning improves the accuracy of coronary artery disease diagnostic methods. In *Proc. Computers in Cardiology*, volume 24, pages 57–60, Lund, Sweden, 1997.

[3] I. Kononenko. Inductive and Bayesian learning in medical diagnosis. *Applied Intelligence*, 7:317–337, 1993.

[4] I. Kononenko. Estimating attributes: Analysis and extensions of RELIEF. In L. De Raedt and F. Bergadano, editors, *Proc. European Conf. on Machine Learning*, pages 171–182, Catania, Italy, 1994. Springer-Verlag.

[5] M. Kukar, C. Grošelj, I. Kononenko, and J. Fettich. An application of machine learning in the diagnosis of ischaemic heart disease. In *Proc. Sixth European Conference of AI in Medicine Europe*, pages 461–464, Grenoble, France, 1997.

[6] M. Kukar and I. Kononenko. Cost-sensitive learning with neural networks. In *Proc. European Conference on Artificial Intelligence ECAI'98*, pages 445–449, Brighton, UK, 1998.

[7] M. Kukar, I. Kononenko, C. Grošelj, K. Kralj, and J. Fettich. Analysing and improving the diagnosis of ischaemic heart disease with machine learning. *Artificial Intelligence in Medicine: Special Issue on Data Mining Techniques and Applications in Medicine*, 1999. In press.

[8] M. Olona-Cabases. The probability of a correct diagnosis. In J. Candell-Riera and D. Ortega-Alcalde, editors, *Nuclear Cardiology in Everyday Practice*, pages 348–357. Kluwer, 1994.

[9] B. H. Pollock. Computer-assisted interpretation of noninvasive tests for diagnosis of coronary artery disease. *Cardiovasc. Rev. Rep. 4*, pages 367–375, 1983.

[10] D.E. Rumelhart and J. L. McClelland. *Parallel Distributed Processing*, volume 1: Foundations. MIT Press, Cambridge, 1986.

Refinement of Neuro-psychological Tests for Dementia Screening in a Cross Cultural Population Using Machine Learning

Subramani Mani[1,3,5], Malcolm B. Dick[2,3], Michael J. Pazzani[1,3],
Evelyn L. Teng[4], Daniel Kempler[4], and I. Maribell Taussig[4]

[1] Department of Information and Computer Science
{mani,pazzani}@ics.uci.edu
[2] Department of Neurology
mdick@teri.bio.uci.edu
[3] University of California, Irvine
[4] University of Southern California
[5] Center for Biomedical Informatics, University of Pittsburgh

Abstract. This work focused on refining the Cognitive Abilities Screening Instrument (CASI) by selecting a clinically significant subset of tests, and generating simple and useful models for dementia screening in a cross cultural populace. This is a retrospective study of 57 mild-to-moderately demented patients of African-American, Caucasian, Chinese, Hispanic, and Vietnamese origin and an equal number of age matched controls from a cross cultural pool. We used a Knowledge Discovery from Databases (KDD) approach. Decision tree learners (C4.5, CART), rule inducers (C4.5Rules, FOCL) and a reference classifier (Naive Bayes) were the machine learning algorithms used for model building. This study identified a clinically useful subset of CASI, consisting of only twenty Mini Mental State Examination (MMSE) attributes—CASI-MMSE-M, saving test time and cost, while maintaining or improving dementia screening accuracy. Also, the machine learning algorithms (in particular C4.5 and CART) gave stable clinically relevant models for the task of screening with CASI-MMSE-M. ...

1 Introduction

Demand is growing for brief, reliable, and sensitive methods to detect dementia, given the emphasis on cost-effectiveness in the current health care environment. Already, managed care companies are limiting access to traditional neuropsychological testing. As the number of older adults in the United States continues to increase and concern heightens about memory problems, health care professionals will need quick, effective tools to accurately separate cognitively impaired from healthy elders from a variety of cultural backgrounds. The prevalence of dementia has been estimated as ranging from 1-3% in the 65-74 age group, from 7-19% in those 75-84, and from 25-47.2% in those 85 and older [1], [2]. Neuropsychological assessment has retained its key role in the diagnosis of dementia

W. Horn et al. (Eds.): AIMDM'99, LNAI 1620, pp. 326–335, 1999.

despite improvements in neuroimaging techniques, such as magnetic resonance imaging (MRI) and single photon emission computerized tomography (SPECT). While forgetfulness has been described as America's latest health obsession [3], dementia continues to be under-recognized within community practice settings. The problem of under-recognition is even greater in minority elders [4] due to a variety of factors. The process of diagnosing dementia in minority individuals is complicated by cultural beliefs about Alzheimer's disease and similar disorders, mistrust of mainstream care providers, the cultural press to "take care of the problem" within the family, economic limitations, and, until recently, a lack of culturally sensitive neuropsychological tools. The Cross-Cultural Neuropsychological Test Battery (CCNB) was developed in response to the growing interest in and need for culturally fair measures of cognitive functioning [5].

2 Methods

2.1 CCNB and CASI

The eleven tests comprising the Cross Cultural Neuropsychological Test Battery (CCNB) assess recent memory, attention, language, reasoning, and visual spatial functioning (areas known to be impaired in Alzheimer's disease) as well as overall mental status. Mental status is assessed with the Cognitive Abilities Screening Instrument (CASI) [6]. Designed for cross-cultural application, the CASI is easier to adapt for a variety of cultural/language groups than many of the screening instruments currently used with English-speaking individuals (e.g., MMSE, BIMC). Unlike these instruments, when direct translation of an item is inappropriate, the CASI provides a culturally fair alternative. For example, as the phrase "No ifs, ands, or buts" is meaningless to non-English speaking individuals, the CASI provides alternative versions of this item, using linguistically equivalent phrases from other languages. Many of the items in the CASI are common to the Mini-Mental State Exam (MMSE) [7], the Modified Mini-Mental State Exam (3MSE) [8], and the Hasegawa Dementia Screening Scale (HDSS) [9]. Consequently, scores on subsets of the CASI are equivalent to scores on the MMSE, 3MSE, and HDSS. In the current health care environment, patients are unlikely to receive neuropsychological testing due to the cost and time involved. Application of the CCNB in clinical settings may be limited by the 90-minute administration time. Consequently, ongoing efforts are directed at finding ways to shorten the CCNB without compromising it's diagnostic accuracy.

3 Description of the Data Set

The data for this study is from the Los Angeles and Orange County areas of Southern California. Normative data has been collected on a total of 324 healthy English speaking (i.e., Caucasian, African American) and non-English speaking (i.e., Chinese, Vietnamese, Hispanic) minority elders. The investigators are currently expanding the CCNB normative database to other highly represented minority groups in the United States, beginning with Koreans, and administering the battery to cognitively impaired older adults in each of the minority groups, with a total of 57 demented patients tested to date. Using conventional statistical methods, the investigators [5] demonstrated that most of the tests in the CCNB are culturally fair. Ethnicity had a limited impact on overall test scores, affecting only certain measures (e.g., Digit Span, Category Fluency), while education played a significant role in performance on almost all of the tests. The sample consisted of the 57 mild-to-moderately demented patients of African-American, Caucasian, Chinese, Hispanic, and Vietnamese origin and an equal number of age matched controls from a cross cultural pool. The specific data entered for each subject included gender, age, education, and ethnicity plus responses to all of the items on the CASI. See Table 1 for the sample characteristics.

Table 1. Characteristics of the sample of this study

	Cases (n = 57)		Controls (n = 57)	
Attribute	Mean	Std. Dev.	Mean	Std. Dev.
Age	76.05	9.4	73.93	7.7
Education	10.33	5.2	9.11	4.9

3.1 Neuropsychological Test Data Sets

We created four datasets from the whole sample. The CASI-FULL-BATTERY (CASI-FB) has 42 attributes and the outcome variable or class (normal or demented). The CASI-MMSE—CASI-SCORED (CASI-MMSE-C) has a subset of 20 MMSE variables scored in the CASI framework plus the class. The third dataset was the CASI-MMSE—MMSE-SCORED (CASI-MMSE-M) which also had the 20 MMSE variables but scored in the MMSE framework plus the class. We also included a CASI-SHORT (CASI-SH) [6] consisting of just 8 CASI variables plus the class. In this work, we have focused on selecting sets of features corresponding to tests used in screening for dementia. More traditional approaches (e.g., forward and backwards selection procedures [10] consider adding or deleting individual features. These were not considered in this study because it was important to preserve the structure of the existing examinations as much as possible so that there was less resistance to adopting changes in procedures.

3.2 Machine Learning and KDD

Machine Learning (ML) and Knowledge Discovery from Data bases (KDD) are increasingly being applied in health care to build models, develop practice guidelines or refine guidelines for better medical decision making. They differ from traditional approaches by generating domain models such as decision trees, rules, graphs etc. from data. The KDD process involves many steps encompassing data pre-processing (attribute selection, recoding etc.), choice of datamining algorithms, experimental protocol and post-processing of the output. See [11] for a detailed discussion on this. Some recent applications of these techniques in the medical domain include differential diagnosis of abdominal pain [12], screening and severity staging models for dementia [13], [14] and learning from a database of sports injuries [15]. Using ML and KDD techniques, we are attempting to refine the CCNB with two explicit goals. First, we are interested in identifying a clinically usable subset of CASI (CASI-SUBSET) which will save time and cost retaining or improving the accuracy obtained by the full battery. Second, to generate simple and useful models for dementia screening in a cross cultural population with the CASI-SUBSET, maintaining or improving the sensitivity and specificity obtained using a total score cutoff value. Hopefully, these refinements should lead to greater utilization of the CCNB in clinical settings. As a first attempt at refining the CCNB through ML and KDD techniques, this study examined data from the Cognitive Abilities Screening Instrument (CASI; Teng et al., 1994). The CASI items cover 10 cognitive domains commonly assessed in dementia: attention, concentration, orientation, short-term memory, long-term memory, language ability, constructional praxis, verbal fluency, abstraction, and everyday problem solving skills. In most of these domains, scores range from 0 to 10 points while the total CASI score ranges from 0 to 100. Many of the CASI items are taken directly, or modified, from the Mini Mental State Exam [7]. The subset of CASI items representing the MMSE yields an equivalent score to that achieved on the MMSE itself. This raises the possibility that a shortened version of the CASI, more specifically the subset of items from the MMSE, could achieve the same level of diagnostic accuracy as the entire CASI.

3.3 Machine Learning Algorithms

Of particular interest to this study is the case where guidelines for screening must be written down and followed by an organization. In this case, automated tools that make black-box predictions are not acceptable and the human interpretability of rules and trees is a major benefit. We concentrated on decision tree learners and rule learners as they generate clear descriptions of how the ML method arrives at a particular classification. These models have the advantage that they can easily be taken *offline*, and depicted as charts representing a rule set or decision tree. They also tend to be simple and understandable models, compared with complex models such as neural networks, Bayesian networks or multiple models. Naive Bayes [16] was selected as a reference baseline classifier for comparison purposes.

C4.5 is a decision tree generator and C4.5Rules produces *if ... then* rules from the decision tree [17]. Naive Bayes is a classifier based on Bayes Rule. Even though it makes the assumption that the attributes are conditionally independent of each other given the class, it is a robust classifier and serves as a good comparison in terms of accuracy for evaluating other algorithms. FOCL [18] is a concept learner which can incorporate a user provided knowledge of two types. First, when provided with a guideline or protocol directly, FOCL has the capacity for revision if the guidelines produce better classification rules than that produced from exploration of the data. Second, FOCL can accept information on each nominal variable indicating which values of the variable increase the probability of belonging to a class (such as retarded) and information on each continuous variable on whether higher or lower values of the variable increases the probability of belonging to a class. When this facility of FOCL is used, it is termed "constrained" FOCL. For this study we used only the "unconstrained" functionality of FOCL. CART [19] is a classifier which uses a tree-growing algorithm that minimizes the standard error of the classification accuracy based on a particular tree-growing method applied to a series of training subsamples. We used Buntine and Caruana's implementation of CART, (the "IND" package) [20]. For each training set, CART builds a classification tree where the size of the tree is chosen based on cross-validation accuracy on this training set. The accuracy of the chosen tree is then evaluated on the unseen test set.

3.4   Model Building

We used MLC++ [21] to run these ML algorithms on the 4 datasets. For each of the four datasets (set Section 3.1), the whole sample was divided into 10 random partitions of equal size and a ten-fold cross validation was done. The training and test sets were created from these partitions as follows. For each of these partitions P_i, the test set was P_i and the training set was the whole sample S minus P_i i.e. all the other partitions $P_{j(j \neq i)}$. Models were generated from the training set and evaluated on the unseen test set. The classification accuracies reported are the mean scores obtained with the ten test sets. Note that cross validation evaluates each instance only once and the n which goes into the various statistics such as total accuracy, sensitivity and specificity is the size of the whole sample. This methodology is based on the approach recommended by Salzberg [22].

Table 2. Sensitivity and Specificity of the ML algorithms for dementia screening in a cross cultural population with the CASI-FB and CASI-MMSE-M

(Total sample $n = 114$, Impaired/Demented $n = 57$, Normal $n = 57$)

Algorithm	CASI-FB			CASI-MMSE-M		
	Accuracy[†]	Sensitivity	Specificity	Accuracy[†]	Sensitivity	Specificity
C4.5	82.46(10.9)	75.44	89.47	84.21(13.6)	80.70	87.72
C4.5Rules	81.58(14.2)	75.44	87.72	83.33(15.8)	77.19	89.47
Naive Bayes	85.96(10.8)	77.19	94.74	82.46(10.8)	73.68	91.23
CART	73.88(14.8)	58.77	89.06	79.33(18.9)	69.65	89.06
FOCL	84.20 (5.8)	75.44	92.98	78.10(13.4)	84.21	71.93

[†] The standard deviation is given in braces.

ML—Machine Learning, CASI—Cognitive Abilities Screening Instrument, CASI-FB—CASI full battery, CASI-MMSE-M—MMSE subset of CASI with MMSE scoring scheme

Table 3. Sensitivity and Specificity of the ML algorithms for dementia screening in a cross cultural population with the CASI-MMSE-C and CASI-SH

(Total sample $n = 114$, Impaired/Demented $n = 57$, Normal $n = 57$)					
	CASI-MMSE-C			CASI-SH	
Algorithm	Accuracy[†]	Sensitivity	Specificity	Accuracy[†]	Sensitivity	Specificity
C4.5	82.46(12.2)	77.19	87.72	78.95(10.5)	82.46	75.44
C4.5Rules	78.95(15.8)	71.93	85.96	78.95(10.5)	75.44	82.46
Naive Bayes	84.21 (9.6)	75.44	92.98	83.33(10.3)	75.44	91.23
CART	72.97(15.8)	60.58	85.42	75.94(10.1)	76.90	74.97
FOCL	84.20 (8.7)	87.72	80.70	78.90(12.9)	80.70	77.19

[†] The standard deviation is given in braces.

ML—Machine Learning, CASI—Cognitive Abilities Screening Instrument, CASI-MMSE-C—MMSE subset of CASI with CASI scoring scheme, CASI-SH—Short CASI

4 Results

Table 2 and Table 3 give the detailed results obtained with the various ML algorithms using the four different datasets—CASI-FB, CASI-MMSE-C, CASI-MMSE-M and CASI-SH. The performance of each of the different algorithms was comparable, across the four neuropsychological tests—CASI-FB, CASI-MMSE-C, CASI-MMSE-M and CASI-SH. Likewise, for the same neuropsychological test, the various algorithms reported similar accuracy figures. In general the performance using the CASI-SH was somewhat lower. Also, CART gave lower accuracy figures across the data sets. We examined the sensitivity (probability of correctly classifying cases, i.e. the demented group in our sample) and specificity (probability of correctly classifying controls, i.e. the normal group) for the testing samples. All the ML algorithms except FOCL gave higher specificity across CASI-FB, CASI-MMSE-C and CASI-MMSE-M datasets while in the case of CASI-SH sensitivity was higher with C4.5, CART and FOCL. CART gave typically simple decision trees with two to six leaves. See Figure 1 for a representative CART tree. C4.5 gave slightly larger trees with the number of leaves ranging between two and eleven. The rules generated by C4.5Rules were comparatively simpler. See Figure 2 for a typical set of C4.5 rules.

5 Discussion

CASI-MMSE-M dataset gave higher accuracies with C4.5, C4.5Rules and CART while the accuracy was slightly lower with Naive Bayes. With FOCL, accuracy was lower using CASI-MMSE-M but using CASI-MMSE-C, the performance was similar to that of the full CASI. Note that accuracy is a good metric for evaluating the different datasets since our sample had equal number of cases and controls. Hence, the accuracy is the mean of the sensitivity and specificity. Both the datasets CASI-MMSE-C and CASI-MMSE-M contain the same subset of twenty attributes from the CASI-FB, the only difference being in the scoring of

Fig. 1. Cart tree with five leaves

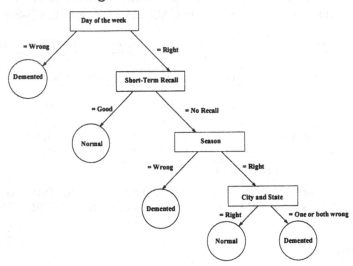

Fig. 2. A C4.5Rule Set

Rule 1: DAY-OF-WEEK = Wrong ⇒ class **demented**(95.8%)
Rule 2: SHORT-TERM-RECALL = Good *and* SEASON = Wrong ⇒ class **demented**(93.0%)
Rule 3: DAY-OF-WEEK = Right ⇒ class **normal**(71.3%)
Default: ⇒ class **demented**

Note: These rules are applied sequentially; the percentage figures in paretheses alongside each rule are the accuracy figures of the rule when it is applicable.

these tests (see Section 3.1). Since MMSE has been used extensively since 1975 and easier to score, the CASI-MMSE-M which makes it culturally fair could be substituted for MMSE in a cross cultural population. It will also save testing time and hence cost when compared to CASI-FB, while improving or retaining test accuracy. CASI-MMSE-M satisfies our *first refinement goal* of identifying a clinically usable subset of CASI saving provider time and cost without compromising on accuracy. In this case actually we improve accuracy marginally. C4.5 gave the highest classification accuracy (84.21%) and sensitivity (80.70%) with the CASI-MMSE-M but the performance of the other algorithms excepting FOCL were comparable. C4.5Rules came close with an accuracy of 83.33% and sensitivity of 77.19%. Decision trees and rule sets are considerably more understandable models when compared for example to Naive Bayes which gives a probability density function. Hence they have the potential to be much more useful in clinical practice.

The basic factors in model selection are its accuracy, comprehensibility and stability, and in medical domains comprehensibility is particularly important.

We have addressed these issues in further detail elsewhere [14]. Here we present some interesting properties of our models. In general CART models scored high on comprehensibility compared to C4.5 trees. They were smaller and had fewer domain constraint violations.

5.1   Highlights of Our CASI-MMSE-M Model

Table 2 (last 3 columns) gives the accuracy, sensitivity and specificity of the various ML algorithms using CASI-MMSE-M. The total accuracy, sensitivity and specificity of the different algorithms are clinically acceptable. The decision tree learners, C4.5 and CART also gave stable models. The attribute *Day-of-week* formed the root of C4.5 trees in nine out ten models and six out of ten CART trees. A CART or C4.5 decision tree with *Day-of-week* as root could serve as a good starting point for selecting a good screening model. The other important consideration apart from accuracy is faithfulness to domain principles and constraints. There is preliminary evidence that domain faithfulness plays a significant role in model acceptability by health care providers [23]. The CART tree in Figure 1 did not violate any domain constraints.

The CART tree selected by the expert (Figure 1) had four attributes while the C4.5 rule set in Figure 2 had just three. Though the CASI-MMSE-M is composed of twenty attributes, most models we generated comprised of four to six features. This clearly shows that all the attributes in the CASI-MMSE-M are not equally significant. Moreover, attributes such as *Day-of-week*, *Short-term-recall* and *Season* figure at the top region of the trees and rule-sets consistently. This raises the possibility of a shorter test compared to CASI-MMSE-M. Further research is required before an optimal subset of features could be advanced as a shorter test. On the other hand, a model such as the one in Figure 1 could be used in community settings for dementia screening in a cross-cultural population. This completes our *second refinement task* of identifying a clinically useful model for dementia screening in a cross cultural population with the CASI-SUBSET, the CASI-MMSE-M.

5.2   Limitations and Conclusions

The dataset which we used for our model building task came from a representative cross cultural population, but the sample size was small ($n = 114$). The study findings would have to be verified with a larger sample before adopting it. Likewise, the proportion we have used (equal number of cases and controls) is not reflective of the general population. Hence the models will have to be validated for the relevant population groups. Furthermore, for the task of dementia screening, the CASI-MMSE-M might turn out to be optimal saving provider time and cost while retaining or improving screening accuracy, but the smaller instrument might be insufficient for the task of dementia staging or differential diagnosis.

In this study, we have shown that ML algorithms can be employed successfully in refining a battery of neuro-psychological tests (CASI) suitable for a cross cultural populace. ML methods achieved two explicit goals. First, this study identified a clinically usable subset of CASI consisting of only twenty attributes (CASI-MMSE-M) saving test time and cost while maintaining or improving dementia screening accuracy. Second, the ML algorithms in particular the decision tree learners C4.5 and CART gave stable clinically usable models for the task of screening with CASI-MMSE-M. The study is also important from the perspective of the use of ML and KDD methods to the novel task of refinement of a neuro-psychological test battery.

Acknowledgements This work was supported in part by the National Library of Medicine postdoc trainee fellowship to SM. We thank the two anonymous reviewers for their helpful comments and suggestions.

References

[1] D. A. Evans, H. H. Funkenstein, M. S. Albert, P. A. Scherr, N. R. Cook, M. J. Chown, L. E. Hebert, C. H. Hennekens, and J. O. Taylor. Prevalence of alzheimer's disease in a community population of older persons. *Journal of the American Medical Association*, 262:2551–2556, 1989.

[2] Losing a million minds: Confronting the tragedy of alzheimer's disease and other dementias. U.S. Congress, Office of Technology Assessment, Washington D.C., 1987. Publication OTABA-323.

[3] G. Cowley and A Underwood. Our latest health obsession: Memory. *Newsweek*, pages 49–54, June 15 1998.

[4] G. Yeo, D. Gallegher-Thompson, and M. Lieberman. Variations in dementia characteristics by ethnic category. In G. Yeo and D. Gallagher-Thompson, editors, *Ethicity and the dementias*, pages 21–30. Taylor & Francis, Washington, D.C., 1996.

[5] M. B. Dick, E. L. Teng, D. Kempler, D. S. Davis, and I. M. Taussig. The cross-cultural neuropsychological test battery (ccnb): Effects of age, education, and ethnicity on performance. submitted, 1998.

[6] E. L. Teng, K. Hasegawa, A. Homma, Y. Imai, A. Larson, E.and Graves, K. Sugimoto, T. Yamaguchi, H. Sasaki, D. Chiu, and L. R. White. The cognitive abilities screening instrument (casi): A practical test for cross-cultural epidemiological studies of dementia. *International Psychogeriatrics*, 6:45–58, 1994.

[7] MF Folstein, SE Folstein, and PR McHugh. Mini-mental state: A practical method for grading the cognitive state of patients for the clinician. *Journal of Psychiatric Research*, 12(3):189–98, Nov 1975.

[8] E. L. Teng and H. C. Chui. The modified mini-mental state (3ms) examination. *Journal of Clinical Psychiatry*, 48:314–318, 1987.

[9] K. Hasewaga. The clinical assessment of dementia in the aged: A dementia screening scale for psychogeriatric patients. In M. Bergener, U. Lehr, E. Lang, and R. Schmitz-Scherzer, editors, *Aging in the eighties and beyond*, pages 207–218. Springer, New York, 1983.

[10] R Caruana and D Freitag. Greedy attribute selection. In W Cohen and H Hirsh, editors, *Machine Learning: Proceedings of the Eleventh International Conference*. Morgan Kaufmann, 1994.

[11] Usama M. Fayyad, Gregory Piatetsky-Shapiro, and Padhraic Smyth. From data mining to knowledge discovery: An overview. In Usama M. Fayyad, Gregory Piatetsky-Shapiro, Padhraic Smyth, and Ramasamy Uthurusamy, editors, *Advances in Knowledge Discovery and Data Mining*, pages 1–36. AAAI Press, Menlo Park, California 94025, 1996.

[12] C Ohmann, Q Yang, V Moustakis, K Lang, and van PJ Elk. Machine learning techniques applied to the diagnosis of acute abdominal pain. In Pedro Barahona and Mario Stefanelli, editors, *Lecture Notes in Artificial Intelligence: Artificial Intelligence in Medicine, AIME95*, volume 934, pages 276–281. Springer, 1995.

[13] WR Shankle, S Mani, M Pazzani, and P Smyth. Detecting very early stages of dementia from normal aging with machine learning methods. In Elpida Keravnou, Catherine Garbay, Robert Baud, and Jeremy Wyatt, editors, *Lecture Notes in Artificial Intelligence: Artificial Intelligence in Medicine, AIME97*, volume 1211, pages 73–85. Springer, 1997.

[14] Subramani Mani, William R. Shankle, Malcolm B. Dick, and Michael J. Pazzani. Two-Stage Machine Learning Model for Guideline Development. *Artificial Intelligence in Medicine*, 1998. In Press.

[15] I.Zelic, I.Kononenko, N.Lavrac, and V.Vuga. Machine learning applied to diagnosis of sport injuries. In Elpida Keravnou, Catherine Garbay, Robert Baud, and Jeremy Wyatt, editors, *Lecture Notes in Artificial Intelligence: Artificial Intelligence in Medicine, AIME97*, volume 1211, pages 138–144. Springer, 1997.

[16] RO Duda and PE Hart. *Pattern Classification and Scene Analysis*. John Wiley, New York, 1973.

[17] JR Quinlan. *C4.5: Programs for Machine Learning*. Morgan Kaufmann, Los Altos, California, 1993.

[18] Michael Pazzani and Dennis Kibler. The Utility of Knowledge in Inductive Learning. *Machine Learning*, 9:57–94, 1992.

[19] L Breiman, J.H. Friedman, R.A. Olshen, and C.J. Stone. *Classification and Regression Trees*. Wadsworth, Belmont, 1984.

[20] Wray Buntine and Rich Caruana. *Introduction to IND Version 2.1 and Recursive Partitioning*. NASA, 1992.

[21] R Kohavi, George John, Richard Long, David Manley, and Karl Pfleger. MLC++: A machine learning library in C++. In *Tools with Artificial Intelligence*, pages 740–743. IEEE Computer Society Press, 1994.

[22] Steven L. Salzberg. On Comparing Classifiers: Pitfalls to Avoid and a Recommended Approach. *Data Mining and Knowledge Discovery*, 1:317–328, 1997.

[23] Michael J. Pazzani, Subramani Mani, and W.R. Shankle. Beyond concise and colorful: Learning intelligible rules. In *The third international conference on Knowledge Discovery and Datamining*, pages 235–238. AAAI Press, Menlo Park, California., 1997.

The Analysis of Head Injury Data
Using Decision Tree Techniques

A. McQuatt [1], P.J.D. Andrews [2], D. Sleeman [1], V. Corruble [1], P.A. Jones [2]

[1] Dept. of Computing Science, University of Aberdeen, Aberdeen AB24 3UE, Scotland
{amcquatt,sleeman,vcorrubl}@csd.abdn.ac.uk
[2] Dept. of Clinical Neurosciences, Western General Hospital, Edinburgh, Scotland
{pa,paj}@skull.dcn.ed.ac.uk

Abstract. Predicting the outcome of seriously ill patients is a challenging problem for clinicians. One alternative to clinical trials is to analyse existing patient data in an attempt to predict the several outcomes, and to suggest therapies. In this paper we use decision tree techniques to predict the outcome of head injury patients. The work is based on patient data from the Edinburgh Royal Infirmary which contains both background (demographic) data and temporal (physiological) data.

1. Introduction

In most western countries, the treatment of patients with head injuries is very resource intensive and frequently involves the patient staying in a Neurological Intensive Care Unit (NICU) for an extended period. Besides dealing with the initial accident (event), the medical team has to cope with secondary events such as the swelling of the brain. As the brain is encased in the skull, treatment procedures are more limited than for the rest of the body. The primary clinical strategy appears to be alleviating extreme symptoms such as high intra-cranial pressure (ICP) and relying on the self-healing mechanisms of the organ.

Predicting the outcome of seriously ill patients is a challenging problem for clinicians. There are still many situations where it is very hard to predict whether a patient will survive given his or her state on admission to hospital. This makes it difficult to choose the best course of treatment. Head injury has the added complication that it is very difficult to devise effective clinical trials, as the brain is largely inaccessible and experimentation can have serious consequences. One alternative to clinical trials is to analyse existing patient data in an attempt to predict the several outcomes, and to suggest therapies. The focus of this study has been data from head injury patients.

In this paper we will first describe the data that was available to us (section 2). We will then discuss analyses carried out on this data by the Edinburgh DCN group and previous work involving decision tree analysis on head injury data from other researchers (section 3). This is followed by an overview of the decision tree methods used and an evaluation of these methods (section 4). Section 5 describes the analyses, and section 6 outlines the results. We will then discuss these results in section 7; section 8 discusses the conclusions.

W. Horn et al. (Eds.): AIMDM'99, LNAI 1620, pp. 336-345, 1999.
© Springer-Verlag Berlin Heidelberg 1999

2. The Data and Its Use

The data, which describes 121 patients, falls into four distinct categories: demographic data, complication data, temporal data and outcome data. The purpose of this investigation was to determine how well the first three categories, and combinations of them, can be used to predict the fourth. Experiments using complication data are not reported here.

Demographic data: Demographic data describes patients and their state on admission to hospital. The following data were used in this analysis: Grade of injury (minor to severe), Glasgow Coma Score, or GCS (a measure of verbal, motor and eye responses), Age, Pupil response, Injury Severity Score (ISS), Sex, Cause of injury, Diagnosis (type of injury to the brain), where the patient was referred from, type of skull fracture (if any).

Temporal data: During their stay in the NICU, the bedside monitors for the patients in this study were connected to a data collection system. This recorded the values of various parameters once a minute. These values could then be analysed to ascertain whether they were indicative of physiological abnormalities, or "insults", depending on their values relative to predefined "normal" and "abnormal" values. The degree of abnormality, that is the amount by which the parameter was out of range, was graded on a scale of 0 to 3. 0 being classed as normal and 3 being extremely abnormal.

The number of occurrences and total duration of each of these insult grades could then be calculated, as well as the average length of each insult grade and the percentage of monitored time for each insult, thereby forming a summary of the physiological abnormalities of the patient. It is this summary data which was used in this study. The data is described below:

- *Parameters monitored and recorded*: ICP (Intracranial pressure), BP (Blood pressure), SaO_2 (oxygen content in the arterial blood to the brain), SvO_2 (oxygen content in the venous blood from the brain), $ETCO_2$ (end tidal carbon dioxide), T1 (temperature), HR (heart rate)

- *Insult types derived from recorded data*: Intracranial Pressure (pressure exerted on the brain by the skull), Hypotension (low blood pressure), Hypertension (high blood pressure), Cerebral Perfusion Pressure (cerebral blood flow), Hypoxia (low oxygen content in the arterial blood to the brain), Cerebral Oligaemia (low oxygen content in the venous blood from the brain), Cerebral Hyperaemia (high oxygen content in the venous blood from the brain), Hypocarbia (low end tidal carbon dioxide), Hypercarbia (high end tidal carbon dioxide), Pyrexia (high temperature), Bradycardia (slow heart rate), Tachycardia (fast heart rate), Global cerebral hypoxaemia (low oxygen content in the blood in the brain), Global cerebral hyperaemia (high oxygen content in the blood in the brain)

- *Parameters derived for each insult type:* Duration (Total duration in minutes, of a grade 1/2/3 insult, and of all grades taken together), Occurrences (Total number of occurrences of a grade 1/2/3 insult, and of all grades taken together), Monitored time (Total number of minutes the parameter was recorded, Percentage of monitored time, Percentage of recorded time of a grade 1/2/3 insult, and of all grades taken together), Average insult length (Average length, in minutes, of a grade 1/2/3 insult, and of all grades taken together).

Outcome data: Data is generally available concerning the outcome of each patient at 6, 12 and 24 months. Only outcome at 12 months was used in this study. Outcome is graded using the Glasgow Outcome Scale [1], which classifies outcome into five categories:

1: Dead, 2: Persistent vegetative state, 3: Severely disabled, 4: Moderately disabled, 5: Good recovery

What Predictions Do Clinicians Wish to Make?

Clearly it would be desirable to predict the actual GOS value for patients. However, given the quantity and the quality of the data available, this has so far not been possible. On the other hand, predicting dead or alive has been done reliably. This, however, is not a very useful measure and so most studies have focussed their attention, for the moment, on predicting good or bad outcomes on the Glasgow scale.

3. Previous Analyses

3.1 Previous Analyses on a Subset of This Data

Details of the principal analysis undertaken by the Department of Clinical Neurosciences in Edinburgh are described in [2]. This study is basically a statistical analysis of the demographic and time-stamped head-injury data collected by the computerised data collection system in Edinburgh.

This study found that the important predictors of mortality (death or survival) at 12 months from the date of the injury were the duration of hypotension (significance, p=0.0064), the duration of pyrexia (p=0.0137), and the duration of hypoxaemia (p=0.0244). They found these to be "significantly better predictions than the usually described predictive factors of coma score on admission, age, or pupil response." The paper also states: "Previous studies showing important associations between ICP and mortality may be due to the fact that CPP and hypotension were not entered into the model."

When predicting morbidity (good or bad outcome), the study found duration of hypotension (p=0.0118) and pupil response on admission (p=0.0226) to be the most significant predictors of outcome.

3.2 Previous Decision Tree Analyses Using Other Head Injury Data

There have been various studies of data from head injury patients. Two such studies are by Choi et al in 1991 [3] and by Pilih et al in 1997 [4]. These have been chosen for discussion due to their use of decision tree analysis.

Choi presents a study which predicts the outcome of head-injury patients. Twenty-three prognostic factors were analyzed from 555 patients admitted to the Medical College of Virginia hospitals with severe head injuries. The factors used were: age, race, sex, motor response, pupillary response, oculocephalics, eye opening, verbal response, midline shift, intracerebral lesion, extracerebral lesion, intracranial pressure, systolic blood pressure, diastolic blood pressure, pulse, respiration, temperature, hematocrit, pCO_2, pO_2, pH, blood alcohol. All of these factors were taken at admission, except ICP which was obtained during monitoring in the neurosurgical ICU. The paper compares the result of a decision tree analysis on the data with the results of statistical analysis using logistic regression and discriminant analysis. The decision tree analysis uses the CART methodology [5]. All the analyses were to predict outcome on the Glasgow Outcome Score [1] at 12 months after the injury.

The paper claims a predictive accuracy of 77.7% for the decision tree analysis, 74.2% for logistic regression and 74.6% for discriminant analysis (although these figures appear to represent *training* set classification accuracy). The paper argues that as well as giving a higher predictive accuracy, decision trees are "visually more informative and easier to interpret". The rationale behind this is that when data is represented by a decision tree, patient sub-groups can be identified. This can result in different prognostic indicators being found for different sub-groups of patients and hence higher predictive accuracy.

Of the 23 possible predictive factors, their decision tree includes only four. These are pupillary response, age, motor response and intracerebral lesion. In all, the decision tree contains eight different sub-groups of patients.

A more recent study by Pilih et al [4], applies decision tree induction to the prediction of outcome of head injured patients six months after admission to hospital. The patient group consisted of 38 patients with severe head injury. Factors used in the study include: Glasgow coma score (GCS) [6], computed axial tomography abnormalities (CT), brainstem syndromes (BSS) [7], age, level of consciousness, motor reactions to sound stimuli, motor reactions to pain stimuli, position and motility of eyes, pupillary size and reactions to light, position of the body and extremities, motility of the body and extremities; the parameters of vegetative functions such as respiration, heart rate, blood pressure and body temperature. The BSS classification separates brain stem dysfunction into seven stages. This classification is estimated from basic clinical attributes. Decision trees were constructed from the data using Magnus Assistant [8] which uses an algorithm based on ID3 [9].

When predicting good or bad outcome, only three factors were used. These were age, CT score and either GCS or BSS. The first of these analyses, using GCS but not BSS, produced a decision tree with CT score as its root and GCS as one of the sub-nodes. Using each of the 38 patients in turn as a test case and the decision trees generated by the remaining 37 test cases (leave-one-out cross-validation), this produces a prediction accuracy of 82%. Using BSS, but not GCS, produced a tree with BSS as the root node and CT score, BSS and age as sub-nodes. This gives a predictive accuracy of 79%. However, this paper does not present its results as being prognostically reliable, mainly on the grounds of the sample size being so small; it only attempts to show that decision trees can be a useful tool for predicting outcome.

4. Decision Tree Methodology

4.1 Building Decision Trees

A definition of decision trees and their creation is as follows: "The traditional approach to constructing a decision tree from a training set of cases described in terms of a collection of attributes is based on successive refinement. Tests on the attributes are constructed to partition the training set into smaller and smaller subsets until each subset contains cases belonging to a single class. These tests form the interior nodes of the decision tree and each subset is associated with one of its leaves. An unseen case is classified by tracing a path from the root of the tree to the appropriate leaf and asserting that the case belongs to the same class as the set of training cases associated with that leaf," [10].

The decision trees used in this report were generated using the See5 environment [11]. This is a PC application that uses the C5.0 algorithm which is an upgraded version of the C4.5 algorithm. As the new facilities of C5.0 have not been utilised in this analysis, the resulting decision trees can be considered as being the same as produced by the C4.5 algorithm. There has been much work done on decision trees since the 70s, both by Quinlan [9], [12] and others in the machine learning and statistics communities [5].

The power of this methods lies in its ability to choose the value of the attribute at which the cases can be divided into the lowest entropy categories. Pruning of decision trees is useful for simplifying models which have "grown" too much and therefore "overfit" the data. Generally, when generating a decision tree there will be some misclassifications, i.e. some cases which are assigned to one class by the tree though they belong to another one. These errors are represented in the leaf nodes of the decision trees in the following way:

(n, m), where n is the total number of cases in the leaf node and m is the number of misclassified cases.

4.2 Assessing Tree Accuracy

This has been presented using the following measurements:

The *training accuracy* is a measure of how accurately the tree represents all known cases. However, these figures give little indication of how well these decision trees would predict the outcome of a new patient. Predictive accuracy calculated using ten fold cross-validation gives a better measure of predictive accuracy (see below). Also, it could be misleading to consider that, say a 80% accuracy is very good, in the situation where one of the classes represents 75% of the population. Therefore all the results reported in this paper will include the size of the biggest category (as a percentage of population) as a comparison.

Predictive accuracy is a measure of how well the tree classifies new cases. The standard method of testing the predictive accuracy of a decision tree is to use a new set of as-yet-unseen cases from the same population. The problem with this is that the predictive accuracy is very much dependent upon which cases are in the test and in the training sets. To avoid this problem, the set of cases is randomly split into a number of equally sized subsets (say, 10). Each subset in turn becomes the test set, with the remaining 9 subsets forming the training set. This, therefore, requires ten different decision trees to be generated and tested. The overall predictive accuracy is then the average of all the predictive accuracies. This method is *called cross-validation*, and as it uses 10 subsets, it is referred to as *10-fold cross-validation*. However, when the cross-validation is repeated, it will randomly choose a different 10 subsets and so produce a different overall predictive accuracy. For this reason, the average of ten 10-fold cross validation tests is used for an overall predictive accuracy measurement

5. The Analyses

Decision trees were generated for nine different combinations. They were obtained from 3 selections of data-sets (namely demographic, temporal, demographic and temporal) against 3 types of predictions (death/survival, good/bad outcome, the Glasgow Outcome Score [1]). For further details see [13].

6. Results

6.1 Accuracy of the Models

The following table gives the results for the nine combinations, in terms of training accuracy (x) and predictive accuracy (y) using the format x / y. The last column is given as an item of comparison.

Table 1: Tree accuracy (both training and cross-validated)

	Demographic	Temporal	Demographic & Temporal	*Biggest category*
Dead or Alive	90.9 / 77.6	95.0 / 82.7	98.3 / 84.2	*78.5*
Good or Bad	92.6 / 64.2	78.5 / 62.4	84.3 / 60.9	*63.6*
GOS	81.8 / 44.3	62.0 / 47.0	80.2 / 44.3	*43.0*

6.2 Decision Trees

As there were a high number of different decision trees generated by this analysis, we only show a selection here. The rest are presented in full elsewhere [13]. Figure 1 shows a decision tree for predicting death/survival that is based only on demographic data; Figure 2 predicts good/bad outcome and is based on both demographic and temporal data.

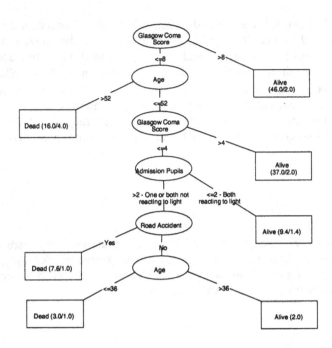

Fig. 1. Predicting Death or Survival using only demographic data

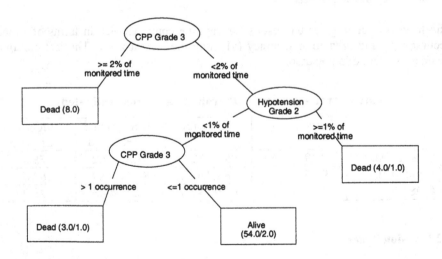

Fig. 2. Predicting death/survival for a subset of all patients using both demographic and temporal data

7. Discussion

7.1 Predictive Accuracy

Using only demographic data. Demographic data, when analysed on its own, consistently produces poor accuracy improvements or a slight reduction in accuracy, therefore the decision trees produced are no more accurate than simply predicting the largest outcome category. However, the sub-groups of patients they identify **are** of interest to the medical community. Given a larger sample of data, or perhaps additional demographic data, these accuracies would probably improve.

Using only temporal data. This is the data-set which generally produced the best accuracy.

Using demographic and temporal data together. This data produced some improvements in accuracy. However, the decision trees produced as a result of this particular analysis are probably of most interest to the medical community as they show which physiological abnormalities are most useful in summarising cases. For example, the age of a patient appears to affect recovery from a particularly low blood pressure.

7.2 Decision Trees

Taking all the decision trees generated [13], there are often *good predictors of outcome* in each of the data categories (demographic, temporal). The best predictors (i.e. those at "high" positions in the decision trees, or those which appear often in decision trees) are as follows: In the demographic data, Severity of injury, GCS, grade of injury, Age, Cause of injury, Pupil response on admission, Injury Severity Score (ISS). In the temporal data: Hypotension, Cerebral Perfusion Pressure (CPP), Bradycardia, Intracranial Pressure (ICP).

The decision trees were discussed with three experts in head injury. The findings are summarised below under three broad headings: those which confirm current medical views, those which challenge them, and those which raise issues to be resolved.

Views Confirmed

The decision trees confirm current thinking about *hypotension and pupil response being major predictors of poor outcome* and the management of blood pressure being of importance in the treatment of head injury patients.

CPP insults were found to be more significant than ICP insults. This also mirrors current clinical thinking.

Views Challenged

The way that decision trees represent the cases in *sub-groups was of great interest* to the experts. The idea of *hypothesis generation* (suggestion) rather than hypothesis confirmation was also appealing to the experts.

It was suggested that some of the insults (hypertension, tachycardia and bradycardia) are consequences of clinical actions. For example, tachycardia could be the result of a drug being administered to regulate blood pressure.

The *effect of alcohol and morphine* on the Glasgow Coma Score and pupil response on admission was discussed. If a patient is very drunk when the accident happens, their low coma score or unreactive pupils may be due to the alcohol rather than being a symptom of brain damage. Similarly, if there has been other bodily injuries to the patient, it is quite common for morphine to be given as a pain killer. This also affects GCS and pupil response. Such medication may make the patient appear to be in a worse state than they actually are and could explain some of the "better than expected" results.

The scale used for measuring *motor response* was also discussed. Point 1 on the scale means no response. This could be due to severe brain damage or possibly to external factors such as alcohol or morphine. However, point 2 on the scale shows an extension of the limbs response which is always associated with brain damage. This means that patients with a motor score of 2 may be more severely brain damaged than those with a score of 1, meaning that the scale is not a continuous one. As this score is a constituent part of the GCS score, it could explain why a patient with a score of 3 (the lowest possible score) may have better outcome that a patient with a score of 4.

Issues to Be Resolved

When considering the different grades of insult in an analysis, it is more realistic to *consider each insult grade to also include insults at a higher grade*. For example, when a patient is suffering grade 2 or grade 3 of an insult, then consider them to be suffering grade 1 of that insult as well (similarly, grade 3 is also grade 2). This would make insult durations and number of occurrences more realistic.

The experts were *interested in "mis-classified" cases*. Generally, the experts would agree with the sub-groups and expected outcomes given by the decision trees. However, they were interested in those patients who died/ had bad outcome when their expected outcome was survival/ good outcome. Perhaps if additional parameters (such as alcohol intake of the patient, whether they are sedated or not) were taken into account, the algorithm could better classify these patients.

During the final few hours before death, a patient's heart rate and blood pressure often wildly fluctuates. Usually these parameters will rise to a peak and then fall. This could explain many of the hypotension grade 3 insults and some of the hypertension, bradycardia and tachycardia insults. This "pre-morbid" data is not really useful in predicting outcome of new cases, and so should be removed.

Currently grade 3 of one insult type is not necessarily as bad as grade 3 of a different insult type. For example, grade 3 hypotension is nearly always fatal, however patients do survive small periods of grade 3 ICP insult. Perhaps the *current thresholds which define the grades of insult need to be adjusted*.

The decision trees for *prediction of Glasgow Outcome Score* were generally thought to be too big to provide useful predictions; some of the outcome classes contained too few patients to be representative. To improve these decision trees, *more training cases* would need to be provided.

8. Conclusions

The use of decision trees to predict outcomes is a useful approach to analysing medical data. The major strength of this approach is the categorisation of patients into sub-groups. Traditional statistical methods tend to treat the patient group as a single population, whereas decision tree analysis considers sub-groups of patients. The identification of subgroups allows predictions to be made for each. The clinicians also found the identification of sub-groups to be interesting and therapeutically relevant.

When comparing the predictive accuracy improvements of decision trees generated using the different types of data (demographic, temporal), experiments show an improvement over using demographic data alone. This investigation clearly shows that there are benefits from using minute-by-minute recordings of physiological data when predicting patient outcomes. Moreover, the issues identified in the analyses with the experts should enable the predictive accuracies to be improved further.

References

1. B. Jennett, M. Bond. Assessment of outcome after severe brain damage. A practical scale. The Lancet, vol. 1, pp480-484, 1975.
2. P.A. Jones, P.J.D. Andrews, S. Midgley, S.I. Andrerson, I.R. Piper, J.L. Tocher, A.M. Housley, J.A. Corrie, J. Slattery, N.M. Dearden, J.D. Miller (1994). Measuring the burden of secondary Insults in Head-Injured Patients during Intensive Care, Journal of Neurosurgical Anaesthesiology, Vol. 6, No. 1, pp 4-14, 1994
3. S.C. Choi, J.P. Muizelaar, T.Y. Barnes, A. Mamarou, D.M. Brooks, H.F. Young (1991)Prediction tree for severely head-injured patients. J. Neurosurg., Vol. 75, pp. 251-255, August 1991
4. I.A. Pilih, D. Mladenic, N. Lavrac, T.S. Prevec. Data analysis of patients with severe head injury. In Intelligent Data Analysis in Medicine and Pharmacology. Kluwer Academic Publishers, Boston. 1997.
5. L. Breiman, J.H. Freidman, R.A. Olshen, et al. Classification and regression trees. Belmont, Calif: Wadsworth, 1984.
6. G. Teasdale, B. Jennett. Assessment of coma and impaired consciousness. A practical scale. Lancet, vol. 2, pp81-84, 1974.
7. F. Gerstenbrand, L. Saltuari, M. Kofler, R. Formisano. Clinical evaluation of severe head injury. Neurologija 1990, vol 39, Suppl 1: pp71-88.
8. D. Mladenic. The learning system Magnus Assistant. BSc Thesis. Faculty of Computer and Information Sciences, University of Ljubljana, Slovenia, 1990.
9. J.R. Quinlan. Induction of decision trees. Machine Learning 1, vol. 1, pp81-106. 1986
10. J.R. Quinlan. Probabilistic Decision Trees. In Machine Learning: An A.I. Approach vol. III, Morgan Kaufmann, pp 140-152, 1990
11. J.R. Quinlan. Data Mining Tools C5.0 and See5. Rulequest Research, 1997. Web Ref: http://www.rulequest.com/see5-info.html
12. J.R. Quinlan. C4.5: Programs for Machine Learning. Morgan Kauffman, 1993
13. A. McQuatt. Using Machine Learning Techniques to Predict Clinical Outcome. MSc Thesis (forthcoming). Computing Science Department, The University of Aberdeen.

Machine Learning for Survival Analysis:
A Case Study on Recurrence of Prostate Cancer

Blaž Zupan[1,2,4], Janez Demšar[1], Michael W. Kattan[3], J. Robert Beck[4], and
I. Bratko[1,2]

[1] Faculty of Computer Science, University of Ljubljana, Slovenia,
[2] J. Stefan Institute, Ljubljana, Slovenia
[3] Memorial Sloan Kettering Cancer Center, New York City, NY, USA
[4] Baylor College of Medicine, Houston, TX, USA

Abstract. This paper deals with the problem of learning prognostic
models from medical survival data, where the sole prediction of probability of event (and not its probability dependency on time) is of interest. To appropriately consider the follow-up time and censoring — both
characteristic for survival data — we propose a weighting technique that
lessens the impact of data from patients for which the event did not occur
and have short follow-up times. A case study on prostate cancer recurrence shows that by incorporating this weighting technique the machine
learning tools stand beside or even outperform modern statistical methods and may, by inducing symbolic recurrence models, provide further
insight to relationships within the modeled data.

1 Introduction

Among prognostic modeling techniques that induce the models from medical
data, the survival analysis methods are specific in both the modeling and the
type of data required. The survival data normally include the *censor* variable that
indicates whether some outcome under observation (like death or recurrence of a
disease) has occurred within some patient specific *follow-up time*. The modeling
technique has then to consider that for some patients the follow-up may end
before the event occurs. In other words, it must take into account that for the
patients for which the event has not occurred during the follow-up period it
might have occurred just after it.

A well-accepted statistical technique that appropriately considers the follow-
up time and censoring is the Cox proportional hazards model [3]. Alternative
machine learning approaches based on artificial neural networks (ANN) have
been investigated by Ripley and Ripley [11]. Since ANNs are primarily developed
for classification tasks, the simplest way to employ them for survival analysis is
to model the occurrence of event within a specific follow-up time. This requires
the omission of patients with shorter follow-up and for whom the event did
not occur, thus potentially biasing the probability estimates of event. Another
approach proposed by the same authors but potentially suffering from similar
biasing problem is to divide survival times into a set of non-overlapping intervals

W. Horn et al. (Eds.): AIMDM'99, LNAI 1620, pp. 346–355, 1999.

in order to model each interval separately. Alternatively, one can employ the statistical techniques to estimate the survival probabilities and model them with some machine learning technique. Using this scheme, Biganzoli et al. [2] estimate probabilities with logistic regression and feed them to ANN. Similarly, Kattan et al. [5] also use ANN, but instead model the patient's null martingale residual.

Typically, given the patient's data, survival models attempt to determine the probability of event to occur within a specific time. Frequently, however, there are cases in survival analysis where the prediction of *whether* the event will eventually occur or not is of primary importance. For example, for the urologist deciding whether to operate on patients with clinically localized prostate cancer the probability of cancer recurrence is a very important decision factor. In such cases, the survival analysis requires purely classification models that classify either to occurrence or non-occurrence of event, optionally model the class probabilities, and appropriately consider the censoring.

In this paper, we propose a framework which uses selected machine learning techniques to construct classification models from survival data. To properly address censoring in the training data, a weighting technique is proposed that lowers the importance of patients with short follow-up time and for whom the event does not occur. We investigate the applicability of this framework to the problem of modeling prostate cancer survival data and compare machine learning methods to standard statistical survival analysis techniques. The potential advantages of the proposed framework stem from the advantages of the selected machine learning methods. Symbolical induction techniques can help to understand underlying relationships in the prostate cancer data. Some machine learning techniques can discover and use non-linearities and variable interactions, thus overcoming the limitations of linear statistical predictors. We use three different statistics to examine the performance of machine learning methods and compare them to statistical approaches.

We begin by describing the prostate cancer dataset used (Section 2). The applied machine learning and statistical methods are described next (Section 3), with an emphasis on computing and employing the appropriate weights for the patient's data. The same Section also describes the experimental design and statistics that were used to compare the performance of resulting models. Section 4 presents the experimental results and discusses the differences and advantages of selected prediction methods. Section 5 summarizes the results and concludes the paper.

2 Patient Data

The dataset initially consisted of records from all 1055 patients admitted to The Methodist Hospital (Houston, TX) with the intent to operate on their clinically localized prostate cancer between June 1983 and December 1996. Excluded from analysis were the 55 men initially treated with radiation, and 1 treated with cryotherapy. Sixteen men whose disease status (free of disease versus cancer recurrence) was unknown were also excluded. The mean age was 63 years and 85% of the patients were Caucasian.

We selected the following routinely performed clinical variables as predictors of recurrence: pretreatment serum PSA levels (prepsa), primary (bxgg1) and secondary Gleason grade (bxgg2) in the biopsy specimen, and clinical stage assigned using the TNM system (uicc) [9]. Treatment failure was defined as either clinical evidence of cancer recurrence or an abnormal postoperative PSA (0.4 ng/ml and rising) on at least one additional evaluation. Patients who were treated with hormonal therapy (N=8) or radiotherapy (N=25) after surgery but before documented recurrence were treated as failures at the time of second therapy. Patients who had their operation aborted due to positive lymph nodes (N=24) were considered immediate treatment failures. To accommodate for some of the modeling methods used, we additionally excluded 16 men having either primary or secondary or both Gleason grades unknown. The resulting dataset thus included 967 patients, of which 189 (19.5%) recurred. For the methods that only use discrete predictor variables (e.g. naive Bayes and association rules), the PSA level was discretized using 5 intervals by computing the quartiles from the training data.

3   Methods

Several statistical and machine learning modeling methods were used and evaluated. They include classification methods (logistic regression, decision trees, adaptation of association rules, naive Bayesian classifier, and artificial neural networks), statistical survival analysis methods (Cox proportional hazards model) and regression methods (artificial neural networks). The resulting models were compared on the basis of the weighted classification accuracy, weighted average probability assigned to the correct class and concordance index. To use the classification-based techniques, the patient's data was weighted according to follow-up time and censor (recurrence).

3.1   Weight Assignment

For the purpose of learning the classification models, data of each patient was assigned a corresponding weight. The weight of the patient that recurred is 1 (one *knows* that the patient recurred). As the certainty that non-recurrent patients will not recur grows with their follow-up time, they have to be weighted accordingly. Their weights are derived from the the null martingale residual (NMR) [12,5], which is computed from the follow-up time and the censor indicator of whether the patient recurred. Computation of the NMR is completely independent of the predictor variables and simply represents the difference between the observed and expected number of recurrences which should have been observed for that point in time (i.e., the patient's follow-up time).

NMR is interpreted as being proportional to the risk of the recurrence for the patient given only his follow-up time [5]. Intuitively, the lower the risk of recurrence, the more likely it is that the patient that is non-recurrent is also a good example for the patients that never recur. Thus, we weighted the non-recurrent patients with weights that were proportional to 1 − NMR. We also assumed that the non-recurrent patients with follow-up time of more than 5 years never recur. The weights were linearly scaled so that a patient with hypothetical follow-up time of 0 would have a weight equal to 0, and a patient with a follow-up time of 5 years or more would have a weight equal to 1.

3.2 Modeling Techniques

The following modeling techniques were used:
Decision trees: our own implementation of the ID3 recursive partitioning algorithm [10] was used that included pre- and post-pruning as proposed by [8]. Weights were used in the estimation of probabilities. The basic idea of ID3 is to divide the patients into ever smaller groups until creating the groups with all patients corresponding to the same class (recurrent, non-recurrent). The division criteria is a function computed from predictor variables.
Naive Bayesian Classifier: assuming the independence of attributes, the probability that a patient described with values of predictor variables $V = (v_1...v_n)$ recurs can be estimated by Bayesian formula

$$P(R|V) = P(R) \prod_{i=1}^{n} \frac{P(R|v_i)}{P(R)}$$

where $P(R)$ is the apriori probability of recurrence and $P(R|v_i)$ is the conditional probability of recurrence if i-th predictor variable has the value v_i; both are estimated from the training set of patients. Note that this formula can be derived from the more common form $P(R|V) = P(R)/P(V) \prod_i P(v_i|R)$ by reusing the Bayesian rule $P(v_i|R) = P(R|v_i)P(v_i)/P(R)$. The probability for non-recurrence is computed in the same way and the resulting probabilities must be normalized to sum to 1.
Association rules: introduced in 1993 by Agrawal [1], association rules search for regularities in the data as the rules of the form *precondition → consequence*. The "quality" of a rule is measured by its *support*, i.e. the proportion of patients for which the rule was observed, and the *confidence*, the proportion of patients for which the consequence hold among the patients which satisfy the precondition part of the rule. Only the rules with a reasonable support and confidence level are taken into account. In our implementation, we have restricted the preconditions to include only predictor variables, and the consequence to include only the prediction of recurrence or non-recurrence. For prediction, the voting technique is used with each rule for which the patient's data satisfy the precondition part voting with the weight proportional to its support. The probability for recurrence is then predicted as a normalized number of votes for recurrence.
Artificial neural network: feed-forward neural network with a single hidden layer as available by nnet package for S-PLUS [13] was used. The ANN either

modeled the recurrence or NMR, i.e., was used either for classification or regression.

Logistic regression: we used a logistic regression available through the command glm in S-PLUS.

Cox proportional hazards model as implemented in S-PLUS was used. Using the Cox model for prediction, the probability was estimated for the patients to recur within 5 years after the operation.

3.3   Experimental Design and Evaluation Statistics

To evaluate the modeling methods, a standard technique of stratified 10-fold cross-validation was used [7]. This divides the patient data set to 10 sets of approximately equal size and equal distribution of recurrent and non-recurrent patients. In each experiment, a single set is used for testing the model that has been developed from the remaining nine sets. The evaluation statistics for each method is then assessed as an average of 10 experiments. The same training and testing data sets were used for all modeling methods. To assess the performance of the model from the test datasets, the following statistics were derived:

Classification accuracy (CA), which is expressed in percent of patients in the test set that were classified correctly. Where induced models output probability of recurrence, a probability of higher than 0.5 was considered as a prediction for a patient to recur.

Average probability assigned to the correct class (AP). For the patients in the test set, the probabilities are assigned by the induced model for each of the classes ("recur" and "does not recur"). Knowing the "correct" class, the corresponding probabilities are averaged across the patients in the test set. AP of 1.0 would thus mean that the model always predicted the right class and assigned it the probability of 1.0.

Concordance index (CI), the measure developed by Harell [4], is interpreted as the probability that, given two randomly drawn patients, the patient who recurs first has had predicted a higher probability of recurrence. CI is computed from the testing data set as a proportion of consistent patient pairs over the number of usable patient pair. A patient pair is usable if a patient with a shorter follow-up time recurred. A pair is consistent, if the patients with a shorter follow-up time is assigned a higher probability of recurrence.

The problem with CA and AP occurs when predicting for non-recurrent patients with short follow-up times. Intuitively, if a non-recurrent patient with a short follow-up time is misclassified the error made would be smaller than in the case of a non-recurrent patients with a long follow-up time. For this reason, we weight the patients in the test sets as well (see Section 3.1) and adjust CA and AP scores accordingly. We call the resulting statistics a weighted CA and weighted AP, respectively.

Table 1. Results of performance evaluation. The best two scores for each statistics are printed in bold.

modeling technique	outcome modeled	weighted classification accuracy	weighted prob. assigned to the correct class	concordance index
default		73.1	0.606	0.500
naive Bayes	recurrence	**75.5**	**0.706**	**0.759**
association rules	recurrence	74.8	0.661	0.717
decision tree	recurrence	73.2	**0.662**	0.653
ANN	recurrence	72.5	0.639	0.729
logistic regression	recurrence	73.4	0.626	**0.769**
ANN	NMR	65.6	-	0.734
Cox	recurrence	**75.8**	0.625	0.756

4 Results and Discussion

Table 1 shows the three performance measures when different modeling techniques are applied to prostate cancer survival data. Overall, naive Bayes and Cox proportional hazards model seem to perform best. Logistic regression obtained the highest concordance index, while it performed poorer on the other two statistics used. Note that for most methods the classification accuracy is only slightly above the "default", which classifies to the majority class in the training set (non-recurrence).

The results for concordance index are very similar to those reported in Kattan et al. [5], although they have used a different validation technique (a repetitive drawing of 70% cases for training while using the remaining 30% for testing). They obtained 0.74 for Cox model and 0.76 for ANN using NMR as the outcome.

The neural network used three neurons in the hidden layer — an architecture that yielded the best overall performance. Although for other methods their parameters could be tuned for best performance as well, such study exceeds the primary intention of the paper to demonstrate the utility of machine learning tools for survival data analysis. Thus, methods were run with their default parameters instead.

A decision tree as induced from the complete dataset is given in Fig. 1. The tree is in concordance with physiological knowledge on this domain, and interestingly brings up a secondary Gleason score (bxgg2) as the most important factor for the recurrence prediction. The tree also pinpoints an anomaly in the prostate recurrence data used: a clinical stage T1ab is expected to be less severe than stages T1c to T2c, yet the tree predicts the opposite. This indicates that the data may undersample this problem subspace, and further analysis (potentially using additional data) is required to investigate this anomaly.

Association rules that predict the recurrence are shown in Fig. 2. The required minimal support was 0.05 and confidence 0.2. Note that the rules mostly involve the conditions on both Gleason scores (bxgg1 and bxgg2) requiring these to be

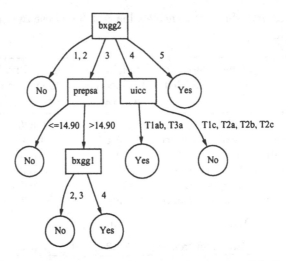

Fig. 1. Decision tree for prostate cancer recurrence prediction.

3 or higher, and PSA level (**prepsa**) being higher than 14.9. There were 25 rules (not shown here) with same requirements on support and confidence found that predict to non-recurrence. We observed that some conditions of rules from both groups overlap, making the interpretation harder but also suggesting that the rules for recurrence with conditions not found in the other groups should be considered important. An example of such rule is **bxgg2=4 -> recur**, the importance of which was also confirmed by physicians.

We additionally analyzed the performance of classifiers by means of calibration curves $q(p)$ [13], where q is the fraction of recurrent patients for which the model predicted the recurrence probability p. Ideally, a calibration curve would be a straight line $q = p$. Fig. 3 shows a calibration curve for naive Bayes and Cox model. Both models are overconfident when predicting recurrence, especially when probability goes toward 1. Similar overconfidence was observed for other classifiers as well. Naive Bayes seems more accurate when predicting lower probabilities of recurrence.

An interesting calibration curve is that for association rules: the curve is close to ideal, but shows also the major weakness of this predictor: its highest predicted probability of recurrence is about 0.7. This also indicates that the method could be improved provided more appropriate voting mechanism that decides for and against the recurrence can be found.

Finally, we show a graphical device called a nomogram [6] that uses the naive Bayesian formula to compute recurrence probability. The nomogram (Fig. 4) shows the impact of individual features on probability of recurrence (upper labels on feature lines) and non-recurrence (lower labels). The values right of zero favor (non)recurrence and the values on the left speak against it. For example observe **bxgg2** and non-recurrence: values of 5 and 4 vote against, and values 3, 2 and 1 vote for non-recurrence. Nomogram can be used to compute the probabilities of outcomes. First, the impact factors for feature values must be summed, once

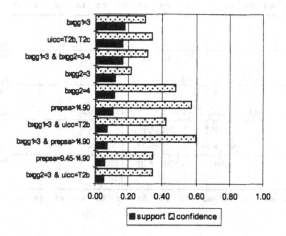

Fig. 2. Association rules for prediction to recurrence of prostate cancer.

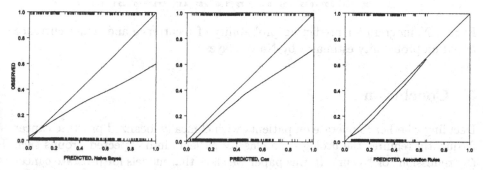

Fig. 3. Calibration curves for naive Bayes (left), Cox model (middle) and association rules (right).

for recurrence and once for non-recurrence, using the scale above (below) the table. The sums are then converted into probability estimation using the lookup graph below and, finally, normalized to sum to 1. For example, patient (`bxgg1=1`, `bxgg2=3`, `prepsa=11`, `uicc=T2a`) has the sum $-0.54 - 0.09 + 0.11 - 0.21 = -0.73$ for recurrence and $0.1 + 0.03 - 0.05 + 0.05 = 0.13$ against. Approximation by the lookup table gives 0.06 for recurrence and 1.0 against which, multiplied by $(0.06 + 1.0)^{-1}$, gives the probabilities of 0.057 for and 0.943 against recurrence.

The nomogram also points out some specifics about the recurrence domain we are modeling. It reveals that the two Gleason scores are the most important factors for the decision as their values are most dispersed through the score line that nomogram provides — an observation which is in accordance with findings by association rules and decision tree. Furthermore, the anomaly concerning the stage T1ab also pointed out by decision tree is also evident. Namely, it would be expected for T1ab to appear before T1c for recurrence ("Yes" side of `uicc` line) and after T1c for non-recurrence ("No" side of `uicc` line).

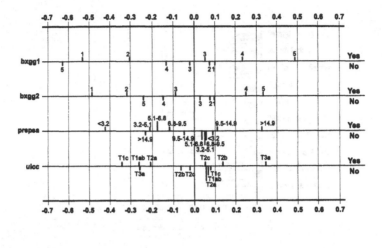

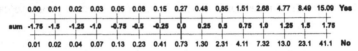

Fig. 4. Nomogram for predicting probability of recurrence and non-recurrence based on probability estimates by Naive Bayes.

5   Conclusion

Deciding whether to operate on patients with clinically localized prostate cancer frequently requires the urologist to classify patients into expected groups such as "remission" or "recur". In this paper we show that models for prostate cancer recurrence that may potentially support the urologist's decision making can be induced from data using standard machine learning techniques, provided that follow-up and censoring has been appropriately considered. For the latter, we propose a weighting technique that lessens the importance of non-recurrent patients with short follow-up times.

The case study on prostate cancer survival data shows that machine learning techniques with proposed weighting schema can, in terms of performance, stand beside or even outweigh standard statistical techniques. The additional feature of inducing interpretable models (like those of decision trees and association rules) was also found beneficial. The best models were obtained by naive Bayesian method, also indicating that for our dataset the potential discovery of non-linearities and variable interaction seems not to play a crucial part (naive Bayesian method does not include them but still outperforms, for example, artificial neural networks).

By inspecting the induced models we can conclude that, for the observed set of patients, the Gleason scores and PSA level are more powerful predictors than clinical stage. In case of Gleason grades 4 and 5 these seem to contribute most to the high probability of recurrence, which is also in accordance to their physiological meaning of "high grade".

The non-recurring patients were weighted by the null martingale residuals, i.e., proportional to their risk of recurrence. We have preliminary tested other weighting techniques (e.g., with weights as a linear or exponential function of follow-up time) and obtained poorer results. Further experimental and theoretical work is needed to gain deeper understanding of the weighting effects.

The authors strongly believe that, although tested only on prostate cancer recurrence data, the proposed methods can be applicable to general survival analysis where the sole prediction of probability of event (and not its probability dependency on time) is of interest.

Acknowledgment

This work was generously supported by the Slovene Ministry of Science and Technology and the Office of Information Technology at Baylor College of Medicine.

References

1. R. Agrawal, T. Imielinski, and A. Swami. Mining association rules between sets of items in large databases. In *Proc. ACM SIGMOD Conference on Management of Data*, pages 207–216, Washington, D. C., 1993.
2. E. Biganzoli, P. Boracchi, and L. Mariani, et al. Feed forward neural networks for the analysis of censored survival data: a partial logistic regression approach. *Statis Med*, 1998.
3. D. R. Cox. Regression models and life-tables. *J R Statist Soc B*, 34:187–220, 1972.
4. F. E. Harrell, R. M. Califf, D. B. Pryor, K. L. Lee, and R. A. Rosati. Evaluating the yield of medical tests. *Journal of American Medical Association*, 247(18):2543–2546, 1982.
5. M. W. Kattan, H. Ishida, P. T. Scardino, and J. R. Beck. Applying a neural network to prostate cancer survival data. In N. Lavrač, E. Keravnou, and B. Zupan, editors, *Intelligent data analysis in medicine and pharmacology*, pages 295–306. Kluwer, Boston, 1997.
6. J. Lubsen, J. Pool, and E. van der Does. A practical device for the application of a diagnostic or prognostic function. *Methods of Information in Medicine*, 17:127–129, 1978.
7. D. Michie, D. J. Spiegelhalter, and C. C. Taylor, editors. *Machine learning, neural and statistical classification*. Ellis Horwood, 1994.
8. T. Niblett and I. Bratko. Learning decision rules in noisy domains. In *Expert Systems 86*, pages 15–18. Cambridge University Press, 1986. (Proc. EWSL 1986, Brighton).
9. M. Ohori, T. M. Wheeler, and P. T. Scardino. The new american joint committee on cancer and international union against cancer tnm classification of prostate cancer: Clinicopathologic correlations. *Cancer*, 74:104–114, 94.
10. R. Quinlan. Induction of decision trees. *Machine Learning*, 1(1):81–106, 1986.
11. B. D. Ripley and R. M. Ripley. Neural networks as statistical methods in survival analysis. In R. Dybowski and V. Gant, editors, *Artificial Neural Networks: Prospects for Medicine*. Landes Biosciences Publishers, 1998.
12. T. M. Therneau, P. M. Grambsch, and T. R. Fleming. Martingale-based residuals for survival models. *Biometrika*, 77(1):147–160, 1990.
13. W. N. Venables and B. D. Ripley. *Modern applied statistics with S-PLUS*. Springer, New York, second edition edition, 1997.

ICU Patient State Characterization Using Machine Learning in a Time Series Framework

Daniel Calvelo[1], Marie-C. Chambrin[2], Denis Pomorski[1], and Pierre Ravaux[2]

[1] Laboratoire d'Automatique et Informatique Industrielle de Lille CNRS ESA 8021
[2] Université de Lille 2

Abstract. We present a methodology for the study of real-world time-series data using supervised machine learning techniques. It is based on the windowed construction of dynamic explanatory models, whose evolution over time points to state changes. It has been developed to suit the needs of data monitoring in adult Intensive Care Unit, where data are highly heterogeneous. Changes in the built model are considered to reflect the underlying system state transitions, whether of intrinsic or exogenous origin. We apply this methodology after making choices based on field knowledge and *ex-post* corroborated assumptions. The results appear promising, although an extensive validation should be performed.

1 Introduction

We seek to identify stable ICU patient's states within the recordings of monitored data. We propose the following framework: local, window-based models will be built using a carefully chosen modeling system. The built models will be characterized by a set of indicators. The time variation of these indicators will show stationarity violations with respect to the model class considered.

2 Machine Learning from Raw Data

The windowed approach is a classic means of dealing with non-stationarity. By carefully choosing a modeling system that focuses on relevant information, we introduce an abstraction layer on which state changes are detected.

Machine learning modeling systems [1] seem adapted to this framework:

- they span a large class of models, including hybrid numeric/symbolic;
- they are mostly non-parametric, avoiding arbitrary parameter settings;
- they offer in most cases explicit models that can be integrated in a knowledge framework.

Furthermore, the data we have at our disposal — issued from common ICU monitoring equipment and acquired by the AidDiag system [2] — contain variables that are useful indicators of the overall patient's state.[1] These can be used

---

[1] Available variables include respiratory and hæmodynamic parameters, ventilator settings, blood gas measurements — these constitute our observation variables. (As of October 1998, in the about 200 patient-days in the AidDiag database, the median number of parameters recorded per session was 22.)

W. Horn et al. (Eds.): AIMDM'99, LNAI 1620, pp. 356–360, 1999.
© Springer-Verlag Berlin Heidelberg 1999

as observation variables, as opposed to measured state variables. We thus chose to work with systems able to exploit this variable specialization, namely, we concentrated on supervised learning techniques.

Ex-post validation for our methodology would ideally rely on explicitation of the information inferred, which led us to use tree inducer systems (see [3] for an up-to-date review): they give strong explicitation in form of trees, and further transformation into rule sets enables the introduction of field knowledge [4]. We have chosen to work with the C4.5 system [5], a well-studied system for induction of decision trees.

2.1 Adapting Machine Learning to Time-Series

To properly exploit our data, it is necessary to adapt this system, designed for static classification, to a time-series dynamic modeling framework (see *e.g.* [6] and [7] for other approaches).

Introduction of lagged variables [8] has been experimentally ruled out in favor of derivative-like variables, carrying the trend information. Indeed, supplementary lagged variables result in heavily grown datasets and more complex, harder to interpret models. Furthermore, trend has been proposed [9], [10] as the preferred description means for physio-pathological processes.

2.2 Trend at Characteristic Scales

For the calculation of trend, we hypothesize the existence of a characteristic time-scale for each variable, that separates short- from long-term behavior. A linear filter, equivalent to a regression of univariate data with respect to time, is then applied at this scale. It yields both the trend and an error variance, interpreted as a stability indicator around the trend. This constitutes a projection of each variable in the two-dimensional space of trend *vs.* stability. This space provides a rich visual representation of the current and past dynamic states of each variable (see Fig.1-b).

From a learning dataset, we calculate the trends and errors for each scale, at every point. A classic test yields the count of significant regressions as a function of scale. We define the characteristic time-scale τ_r as the one beyond which no better local linear approximations can be found. Other criteria have been tested (*e.g.* the characteristic time-scale is the one where the best piecewise-linear model is first found) and exhibit other properties (*e.g.* improved robustness with respect to the size of the learning dataset), yet they don't fit as well as the τ_r criterion in producing a derivative-like variable.

2.3 Characterization of the Built Models

After filtering, we apply windowed decision tree construction and characterize the resulting models using their complexity, their intrinsic error and a presence index representing the decision tree morphology, as a summarized presence for each variable. (As a validation argument for the introduction of trend variables, the trees generated on the augmented dataset are much smaller and more accurate than in the static case.)

Window size was determined by *ex-post* validation: having chosen a window size deemed large enough to proceed to induction (which needs the estimation of joint probabilities), variations of this size, from halving up to doubling, produced the same qualitative results.

Evaluation of the methodology can be performed, partly, by exploiting data: the zones we determine must correspond to behavioral stability of the dataset. On the other hand, external actions that *a priori* change the patient's state should be correlated to transitions as we identify them.

3   Results

We illustrate the approach applied to a hand-documented dataset (Fig.1).

Data are sampled at $5s$ period for eight hours, directly from the routine monitoring of an adult ICU patient. Five seconds is the minimal period technically available for a synchronized simultaneous acquisition from the available devices.

We have used a conservative approach with respect to missing data when calculating the characteristic time-scale: missing data points, leading to missing values for any trend depending on them, are left out of the counts. Yet, we did fill the one-sample gaps with the mean of surrounding points for the calculation of the trend variables.[2] For the decision tree building itself, `missing` is a special category.

The τ_r calculated from the whole dataset show groupings by physiological subsystem: extremely fast behavior for VTe; the arterial pressures show close τ_r, smaller than the airway pressure ones (Fig.1-a). The orders of magnitude of τ_r are always comparable for the same variable between different patients (not shown here), and the relative ordering of the variables with respect to τ_r is (loosely) preserved as well.

The windowing induction of decision trees is then applied, with a window size of $1h24mn$ (1000 data points).

Expert and naïve visual inspection of the presence index map, alongside error and complexity evolution (Fig.1-c), shows temporal zones that can be correlated with observed external actions, as changes in oxygenation levels and suctions. Namely, the zones that can be visually detected (in Fig. 1 units, these are the intervals $[0; 40]$ $[40; 260]$ $[260; 500]$ $[500; 700]$ $[700; 880]$ $[880; 1020]$ and $[1020; 1070]$) correlate with suctions for the beginning of second and third; changes in incoming oxygenation occur at around point 500 (here, bedside care is also being done) and point 700; at 880, stabilization of cardiac frequency (hitherto decreasing) takes place; finally bedside care happens from around 1020 and on.

---

[2] This was done in order to minimize the number of large gaps in the augmented dataset — each missing datum forbids the calculation of trend variables for τ_r successive samples.

Besides, the cross-entropy maps between all variables within each of the aforementioned zones are definitely distinct, and stable within each zone.

The prediction errors of the locally built trees remain low within the identified zones, and grow beyond them, showing their specificity to the considered time zone.

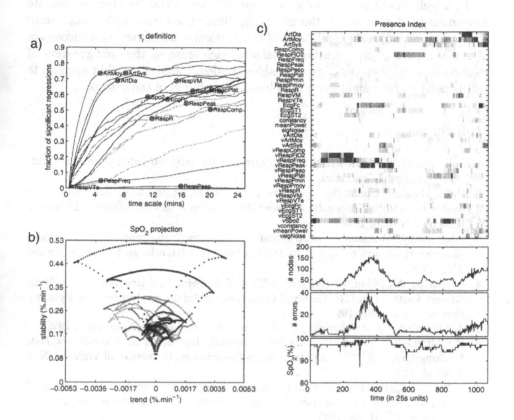

Fig. 1. Characteristic Scales and Windowed Processing of Dynamic Decision Trees
a) Count of significant trend calculations as a function of scale. Risk is $p < 10^{-2}$.
Circled crosses show the characteristic scales τ_r. They are estimated at 95% below the first maximum.
b) Projection of SpO_2 into the trend *vs.* stability plane, at its characteristic scale τ_r.
Axis are labelled in percent units by minute. Lighter points are past, darker points correspond to the end of recording.
c) From top to bottom, presence index map (darker means stronger presence), complexity, error and (for reference) time-series of the classification variable (pulse oximetry SpO_2) as a function of time.
Variables prefixed with 'v' denote supplementary trend variables. Abscissa values are the median time points of each window. Window size is 200 graphical units ($1u = 25s$).

4 Conclusion and Perspectives

The database we have now at our disposal is too irregular (patients', pathological, therapeutic characteristics) for any rigorous testing. Investigation protocols to come will provide a well-controlled individual and pathological framework in which to validate this methodology.

In a well-known experimental environment, we should be able to separate exogenous (well detected in the preceding illustration) from endogenous state shifts. This would enable the study of the particular pathology as a succession of states separated by transitions, defining each state as the configuration of relationships between measured variables. In-depth analysis within each state will hopefully give insights into the phases of evolution of the disease.

References

1. Y.Kodratoff, R.Michalski, *Machine Learning: An Artificial Intelligence Approach, Vol.III*, Morgan Kaufmann, 1990.
2. P.Ravaux, M.C.Chambrin, A.Jaborska, C.Vilhelm, M.Boniface, *AIDDIAG : Un Système d'Aide au Diagnostic Utilisant l'Acquisition de la Connaissance*, Biometric Bulletin 11(3):10, 1994.
3. S.K.Murthy, *Automatic construction of decision trees from data: A multidisciplinary survey*, to appear in Data Mining and Knowledge Discovery journal 2(4), 1999.
4. G.Holmes, A.Donkin, I.H.Witten, *WEKA: A Machine Learning Workbench*, Proc. Second Australia and New Zealand Conference on Intelligent Information Systems, Brisbane, Australia, 1994.
5. J.R.Quinlan, *C4.5: Programs for Machine Learning*, Morgan Kaufmann, 1992.
6. R.S.Mitchell, *Application of Machine Learning Techniques to Time-Series Data* Working Paper 95/15, Computer Science Department, University of Waikato, New Zealand, 1995.
7. L.Torgo, *Applying Propositional Learning to Time Series Prediction in* Y.Kodratoff *et al.*, Workshop on Statistics, Machine Learning and Knowledge Discovery in Databases, ECML-95, 1995.
8. D.Pomorski, M.Staroswiecki, *Analysis of Dynamical Systems based on Information Theory*, World Automation Congress (WAC'96), Montpellier, May 27–30, 1996.
9. I.J.Haimovitz, I.Kohane, *Managing temporal worlds for medical trend diagnosis*, Artificial Intelligence in Medicine, 8(3), 1996
10. F.Steimann, *The interpretation of time-varying data with DiaMon-1*, Artificial Intellignece in Medicine 8(4), Aug. 1996.

Diagnostic Rules of Increased Reliability for Critical Medical Applications

Dragan Gamberger[1], Nada Lavrač[2], and Ciril Grošelj[3]

[1] Rudjer Bošković Institute, Bijenička 54,10000 Zagreb, Croatia
gambi@lelhp1.irb.hr
[2] Jožef Stefan Institute, Jamova 39, 1000 Ljubljana, Slovenia
nada.lavrac@ijs.si
[3] University Medical Centre Ljubljana, Nuclear Medicine Department, Zaloška 7,
1000 Ljubljana, Slovenia

Abstract. This paper presents a novel approach to the construction of reliable diagnostic rules from the available cases with known diagnoses. It proposes a simple and general framework based on the generation of the so-called confirmation rules. A property of a system of confirmation rules is that it allows for indecisive answers, which, as a consequence, enables that all decisive answers proposed by the system are reliable. Moreover, the consensus of two or more confirmation rules additionally increases the reliability of diagnostic answers. Experimental results in the problem of coronary artery disease diagnosis illustrate the approach.

1 Introduction

Induction of reliable hypotheses is required for inductive learning applications in critical domains, like medicine and financial engineering, in which a single wrong prediction may be very costly. The general problem of the induction of reliable diagnostic rules is hard because theoretically no induction process by itself can guarantee the correctness of induced hypotheses. Additionally, in practical situations the problem is even more difficult due to unreliable diagnostic tests and the presence of noise in training examples.

Construction of redundant rules is known to be appropriate for achieving reliable predictions [3]. This approach, however, contradicts the philosophy of most inductive learning approaches that use some form of Occam's razor, aimed at minimizing the complexity of the induced hypotheses. As a consequence, standard inductive learning algorithms are not appropriate for the induction of redundant rules, except if they are used to construct different hypotheses which are then combined to get the result of the final, compound classifier. It was experimentally demonstrated that the prediction accuracy can be improved by combining different classifiers for the same domain. In most cases classifiers are combined by voting to form a compound classifier. Different classifiers can be obtained either by the application of different learning algorithms on the same training set or by the same learning algorithm on different training (sub)sets.

W. Horn et al. (Eds.): AIMDM'99, LNAI 1620, pp. 361–365, 1999.

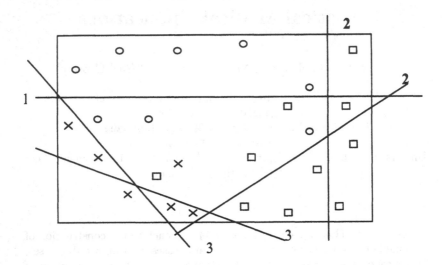

Fig. 1. The confirmation rule concept illustrated on a three-class problem.

The later approach is used in the well-known *bagging* and *boosting* approaches that employ redundancy to achieve better classification accuracy [6].

This paper presents an approach to the induction of reliable diagnostic rules called *confirmation rules*. The main difference to other standard induction approaches is that this method does not aim at giving a decisive answer in every situation. In this sense the approach follows the concept of *reliable, probably almost always useful learning* defined in [7]. This means that in the case of a two-class problem, three different possible predictions are considered: class positive, class negative, and answer not possible. By considering three possible answers it can be ensured that the method gives only reliable answers; this is the main advantage of the approach. A disadvantage of this method are indecisive answers, whose amount has to be kept as low as possible.

2   Confirmation Rules

In the concept of confirmation rules every diagnostic class is treated separately as a target class. For a given target class a rule is a conjunction of logical tests (literals). Confirmation rules have a similar form as, for example, association rules [1] and if-then rules induced by the AQ15 learning system [5]. The main difference with association rules is that confirmation rules have only the class assignment in the conclusion of a rule whereas a conclusion of an association rule is a conjunction of arbitrary attribute values. On the other hand, the main difference compared to AQ generated rules is that every *complex* (conjunction) of an AQ rule is in the context of confirmation rules treated as a separate and independent rule.

The concept of confirmation rules is graphically presented in Figure 1. Confirmation rules have the following properties. A confirmation rule has to cover (and should hence be able to reliably predict) a significant number of cases of the target class. At the same time a confirmation rule should not cover cases of non-target diagnostic classes, and when used for prediction it should exclude the possibility of classifying any of the non-target cases into the target class. The consequence is that every confirmation rule can be used independently of other confirmation rules or in combination with any subset of other confirmation rules. For a given unclassified case, the following outcomes are possible:

a) If no confirmation rule fires for the case, class prediction is indecisive (the case is not classified).

b) If a single confirmation rule fires for the case, class prediction is determined by this rule.

c) If two or more confirmation rules of the same class fire for the case, this class is predicted with increased reliability.

d) If two or more confirmation rules fire for the case and at least two of these rules are for different classes, class prediction is indecisive.

This indicates that the confirmation rules do not give a decisive prediction in every situation (cases (a) and (d)), and that a prediction of increased reliability can be achieved (case (c)).

3 Application of Confirmation Rules in Coronary Artery Disease Diagnosis

The coronary artery disease (CAD) dataset, collected at the University Medical Center, Ljubljana, Slovenia, includes 327 patients. Each patient had performed history, clinical and laboratory examinations including ECG at rest, ECG during controlled exercise, stress myocardial perfusion scintigraphy, and coronary angiography which gives the diagnosis of coronary artery disease. In 229 patients CAD was angiographycally confirmed and in 98 it was excluded. The patients' clinical and laboratory data are described by 77 attributes. This dataset was previously used for inducing diagnostic rules by a number of machine learning algorithms [4].

The dataset was used to generate confirmation rules in a series of experiments using different disjoint attribute subsets: symptoms and signs including ECG at rest, ECG during exercise, and myocardial perfusion scintigraphy. These rules may be interesting for disease prediction at various stages of the diagnostic process. This paper presents only the results obtained using the complete attribute set.

Rule induction was performed by the ILLM (Inductive Learning by Logic Minimization) system [2]. ILLM's literal selection algorithm ensures that rules are built only from the globally relevant literals, which can be advantageous in the construction of reliable confirmation rules. Table 1 lists 21 attributes that were used for induction by the ILLM algorithm. The selection of these 21

Name	Description	Possible attribute values
star	patient's age	continuous
mi	miocardial infarction	1 no, 2 yes
ap	angina pectoris (AP)	1 no, 2 nontyp. thoracic pain, 3 nontyp. AP, 4 typ. AP
ptca	percutaneous coronary angioplasty	1 no, 2 yes
kajen	smoker	1 no, 2 former, 3 up to 20 cigarettes, 4 more than 20 cig.
maxfr	max. achieved heart frequency	continuous
prsbo	thoracic pain	1 no, 2 yes, 3 strong
ciklo	achieved exercise load [in Watts]	continuous
rrobr	max. blood pressure in stress	continuous
denst	ST downslope	1 no, 2 up to 2 mm, 3 more than 2 mm
ves	ectopic beats	1 no, 2 yes, 3 frequent
hiplv	left ventricular hypertrophy	1 no, 2 yes
hprdv	right ventricular hypertrophy	1 no, 2 yes
apmaa	anterior projection rest anteroapical	1 no, 2 mild, 3 evident, 4 severe
apoan	anterior projection stress anterolateral	1 no, 2 mild, 3 evident, 4 severe
apoaa	anterior projection stress anteroapical	1 no, 2 mild, 3 evident, 4 severe
laose	45^0 oblique stress septal	1 no, 2 mild, 3 evident, 4 severe
laoin	45^0 oblique stress inferoapical	1 no, 2 mild, 3 evident, 4 severe
laola	45^0 oblique stress lateral	1 no, 2 mild, 3 evident, 4 severe
laoan	70^0 oblique stress anteroseptal	1 no, 2 mild, 3 evident, 4 severe
ompos	70^0 oblique post. diff. (stress - rest)	integer values 0-3

Table 1. Name and description of 21 attributes used in confirmation rule construction.

attributes was done according to the following criterion: the set includes only the attributes used in at least one of the confirmation rules constructed in previous experiments for different disjoint attribute subsets. For the class *not-confirmed* only one confirmation rule was generated :

$$(\text{laose} = 1)(\text{apoaa} = 1)(\text{denst} \neq 3)(\text{maxfr} > 67.50)(\text{laola} = 1) \qquad (1)$$

This rule covers none of the 229 cases of the opposite class while it covers 52 out of 98 cases (53%) of the target class. Therefore it is considered to be a reliable rule for the prediction into this class.

For the class *confirmed* a set of 8 confirmation rules was generated. These are presented in Table 2.

These rules cover none of the 98 examples of the non-target class. The number of covered target class cases is between 44 and 113 (first column), which is 19% to 49% of the total number of *confirmed* cases (second column). The last row is the total for the complete set of 8 confirmation rules. It shows that the set covers 201 cases (89% of the total of 229 target cases) and that 69 cases are covered by only one of the rules in the set. This means that 132 cases are covered by two

rule	covered	cases of the	target class
(apmaa ≠ 2)(ompos ≠ 0)	51	22%	(6)
(ompos ≠ 0)(rrobr < 205.0)	76	33%	(8)
→ (ap = 4)(mi = 2)(laoan ≠ 1)	54	24%	(11)
→ (ap = 4)(laoin ≠ 1)(ptca = 1)	113	49%	(23)
(ptca = 1)(mi = 2)(apmaa ≠ 2)(laoin ≠ 1)	53	23%	(1)
→ (ptca = 1)(mi = 2)(laoin ≠ 1)(laoan ≠ 1)	44	19%	(2)
→ (ptca = 1)(mi = 2)(laoin ≠ 1)(rrobr < 205.0)	82	36%	(4)
(ptca = 1)(laoan ≠ 1)(rrobr < 205.0)(apmaa ≠ 2)	59	26%	(14)
	201	89%	(69)

Table 2. A set of 8 confirmation rules for the class *confirmed*. A rule description is followed by the total number of covered examples, the percentage of covered examples of the target class, and the number of examples covered only by this rule and no other rule in the set. The → signs point at the rules evaluated by a medical doctor as reasonable and completely reliable.

or more rules, which results in the increased reliability of predictions. It is clear that also the complete rule set of eight rules covers none of the non-target cases.

References

1. R. Agrawal, H. Mannila, R. Srikant, H. Toivonen and A.I. Verkamo (1996) Fast discovery of association rules. In U.M. Fayyad, G. Piatetski-Shapiro, P. Smyth and R. Uthurusamy (Eds.) *Advances in Knowledge Discovery and Data Mining*, 307–328. AAAI Press.
2. D. Gamberger (1995) A minimization approach to propositional inductive learning. In *Proc. Eighth European Conference on Machine Learning*, 151–160, Springer Lecture Notes in AI 912.
3. M. Gams (1989) New measurements highlight the importance of redundant knowledge. In *Proc. European Working Session on Learning*, 71–80. Pitman.
4. C. Grošelj, M. Kukar, J.J. Fetich and I. Kononenko (1997) Machine learning improves the accuracy of coronary artery disease diagnostic methods. *Computers in Cardiology*, 24:57–60.
5. R.S. Michalski, I. Mozetič, J. Hong, and N. Lavrač (1986) The multi-purpose incremental learning system AQ15 and its testing application on three medical domains. In *Proc. Fifth National Conference on Artificial Intelligence*, 1041–1045, Morgan Kaufmann.
6. J.R. Quinlan (1996) Boosting, bagging, and C4.5. In *Proc. Thirteenth National Conference on Artificial Intelligence*, 725–730, AAAI Press.
7. R.L. Rivest and R. Sloan (1988) Learning complicated concepts reliably and usefully. In *Proc. Workshop on Computational Learning Theory*, 69–79, Morgan Kaufman.

Machine Learning Inspired Approaches to Combine Standard Medical Measures at an Intensive Care Unit[*]

Basilio Sierra[1], Nicolás Serrano[2], Pedro Larrañaga[1], Eliseo J. Plasencia[2],
Iñaki Inza[1], Juan José Jiménez[2], Jose María De la Rosa[2], and
María Luisa Mora[2]

[1] Dept. of Computer Science and Artificial Intelligence, University of the
Basque Country, P.O. Box 649, E-20080 San Sebastián, Spain,
ccpsiarb@si.ehu.es (Basilio Sierra)
http://www.sc.ehu.es/isg
[2] Servicio de Medicina Intensiva, Hospital Universitario de Canarias,
38320 La Laguna, Tenerife, Canary Islands, Spain,
nserrano@epicure.org (Nicolás Serrano)
http://www.epicure.org

Abstract. There are many standard methods used at Intensive Care
Units (ICU) in order to overview patient's situation. We present in this
paper a new method that outperforms the prediction accuracy of each
medical standard method by combining them using Machine Learning
(ML) inspired classification approaches. We have used different Machine
Learning algorithms to compare the accuracy of our new method with
other existing approaches used by ML community. The new method is an
hybrid made between the Nearest Neighbour and the Naive Bayes classification methods. Experimental results show that this new approach
is better than any standard method used in the prediction of survival
of ICU patients, and better than the combination of these medical approaches done by using standard ML algorithms.

1 Introduction

In the medical world, there are many methods (APACHE II and III [3], MPM
II [6], SAPS II [5]) being applied to an ICU patient at the ICU admission that
appear to calibrate well to predict hospital mortality from the time of ICU
admission. We use the values given by those Standard Medical Methods (SMM)
in order to improve individual accuracy of each one by combining them properly.

The data used in this study has been obtained at the 20-bed ICU at the
Hospital Universitario de Canarias (Spain). There is information about 1210
ICU patients.

* This work was supported by the Gipuzkoako Foru Aldundi Txit Gorena under
OF097/1998 grant and by the PI 96/12 grant from the Eusko Jaurlaritza - Hezkuntza,
Unibertsitate eta Ikerkuntza Saila.

W. Horn et al. (Eds.): AIMDM'99, LNAI 1620, pp. 366–371, 1999.
© Springer-Verlag Berlin Heidelberg 1999

We have been working with this datafile using ML methods trying to outperform individual SMM survival prediction accuracy. We present a new method, a Nearest Neighbour and Naive Bayes hybrid, which has obtained the best results in the experimentation process.

The rest of the paper is organized as follows. In Section 2 used Machione Learning standard algorithms are reviewed. Section 3 introduces the new proposed approach, while Section 4 presents the experimental results obtained applying the previous methodology to a database of cases. Section 5 presents the conclusions.

2 Machine Learning Standard Approaches

We briefly describe the paradigms that we use in our experiments. These paradigms come from the world of the Artificial Intelligence and they are grouped in the family of *Machine Learning or ML*.

Decision Trees: A *decision tree* consists of nodes and branches to break a set of samples into a set of covering decision rules. In our experiments, we will use two well known decision tree induction algorithms, ID3 [7] and C4.5.

Instance-Based Learning (IBL): IBL has its root in the study of k Nearest Neighbour algorithm (k-NN) in the field of Machine Learning, described in Aha [1]. In our experiments we will use two standard algorithms: IB1 and IB4

Rule induction: One of the most expressive and human readable representations for learned hypothesis is sets of *IF-THEN rules*, in which the *THEN* part gives the class prediction for the samples that carry out the *IF* part. In our experiments we use *cn2* and oneR.

Naive Bayes classifiers: In the core of this paradigm there is an assumption of independence between the occurrence of features values, that in many tasks is not true; but it is empirically demonstrated that this paradigm gives good results in medical tasks [8]. In our experiments, we use the NB and NBTree classifiers.

3 New Proposed Method

Our method is a new version of the k-NN that gives to the new point the class which k nearest points have the minimum mean distance from it. We call it k-Class Nearest Neighbour (k-CNN), and it is shown in its algorithmic form in Figure 1.

Figure 2 shows the behavior of the 3-CNN algorithm in comparison with the 6-NN for a two class example problem.

In k-NN and also in k-CNN, we can introduce more information to the method by weighting each predictor variable taking into account its relevance in the classification task. So the distance between two points Y and Z, with components $Y_1, ..., Y_n$ and $Z_1, ..., Z_n$ respectively is calculated by using the next formulae:

$$D_{XY} = \sum_{j=1}^{n} W_i(X_i - Z_i)^2$$

```
begin k-CNN
    As input we have the samples file, containing n cases (xᵢ, θᵢ), i = 1, ..., n,
    the value of k and a new case (x, θ) to be classified
    FOR each class value C DO
        BEGIN
        Select the k nearest neighbours to x from the sample file cases belonging to C
        Compute the mean distance to x of this k points D_C
        END
    Output the class Cᵢ which mean distance Dᵢ is minimal between all the classes
end k-CNN
```

Fig. 1. The pseudo-code of the k-Class Nearest Neighbour Algorithm.

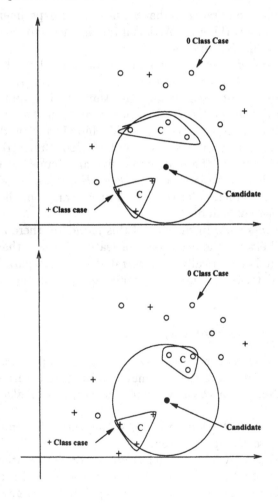

Fig. 2. 3-CNN Decision Rule compared with 6-NN. (Top) the result of 3-CNN and 6-NN is a tie. (Bottom) the result of 3-CNN is the $+$ class but the 6-NN has a tie.

Where W_i are the weight of the i-th variable, for $i = 1$ to n. We have added to this method a new technique to measure the weights of the predictor variables in the following manner: Let $X_1, ... X_n$ be the set of predictor variables. For each variable X_i, we take a datafile containing all the rest of variables and the variable to be predicted, C, and we obtain the classification accuracy of this file using the Naive Bayes classification method. In this manner, we obtain a P_i indicating the number of well classified cases obtained with the file in which there are all the variables except X_i. We call this method the k-CNN-NB approach.

Then, the weight to be used in the compute of the distance for each variable is obtained applying the following formulae:

$$W_i = \frac{P_i}{\sum_{j=1}^{n} P_j}.$$

4   Experimental Results

Four datafiles are used in these experiments. The files are divided in two categories: One focuses in the Probabilities that Standard Medical Methods give to the doctor and another takes into consideration the Scores provided by the SMM. In each category, we use two files, one containing only the measures given by the methods and the Class variable, and a second file containing the same information and some additional data referring to the patient.

In order to give a real perspective of applied methods, we use 10-Fold Crossvalidation [9] in all experiments. We have carried out the experiments with all four datafiles using MLC++ [4]. Table 1 shows some of the experimental results obtained.

As it can be seen, using ML standard approaches the best results (crossvalidated) are obtained with NBTree (a classification Tree with a Naive Bayes classifier in leaves) and oneR (a very simple Rule Inductor that searches and applies only the best rule in the datafile).

In our experiments, we have run the k-CNN with the new method to weight the attributes based in Naive Bayes (k-CNN-NB) with different k values. Table 2 shows experimental results obtained with the new proposed method. As it can be seen, with this new approach, k-CNN-NB, obtained results are significatively

Table 1. Details of accuracy level percentage obtained using standard Machine Learning algorithms

Inducer	Probabilities Only	Probabilities + Patient Data	Scores Only	Scores + Patient Data
ID3	82.07	81.49	81.25	81.07
C4.5	86.12	86.61	86.94	87.11
NB	85.70	85.21	85.87	84.63
NBTree	87.60	84.05	87.77	84.79
IB	81.82	79.34	81.07	78.76
oneR	83.97	86.12	84.28	87.77
CN2	85.65	85.71	84.80	85.94

Table 2. Accuracy level percentage of the *k*-Class Nearest Neighbour weighing the attributes using the Naive Bayes classifier (*k*-CNN-NB) method for the four databases using different *k* numbers

k	1	2	3	4	5	6	7	8	9	10
Probabilities Only	83.36	89.58	91.07	91.32	92.23	92.23	91.90	91.65	91.32	91.24
Probabilities + Patient Data	98.43	98.76	98.67	98.35	98.01	97.60	97.19	97.11	96.53	96.53
Scores Only	82.21	83.36	88.51	88.51	88.51	88.51	88.51	88.51	88.51	88.35
Scores + Patient Data	97.27	97.44	97.68	97.77	97.85	97.93	97.85	97.93	97.85	96.85

better than those obtained using previous approaches. We are not proposing the medical world to apply the exposed method, but to apply the underlying idea of combining existing methods in order to improve the individual accuracy of each one.

5   Conclusion and Further Results

A new ML inspired method is presented in this work to predict the survival of patients at ICU that outperforms existing Standard Medical Methods by combining them. The new method, called *k*-CNN-NB is a combination between *k*-CNN and NB, and it is based on the idea that probability distribution of predictor variables could have different probability distribution in each class.

This new method is used in ICU patient database, and its final results are compared with those obtained by using the MLC++ library.

As further work we are going to apply this methods taking into account the specifity or the sensibility of the data we are using.

References

1. D. Aha, D. Kibler and M.K. Albert (1991): "Instance-Based learning algorithms", *Machine Learning* **6**, 37-66
2. B.V. Dasarathy (1991): "Nearest Neighbor (NN) Norms: NN Pattern Recognition Classification Techniques", *IEEE Computer Society Press*
3. W.A. Knaus, E.A. Draper, D.P. Wagner, J.E. Zimmerman (1985): "APACHE II: A severity of disease classification system". Crit Care Med 13:818-829
4. R. Kohavi, D. Sommerfield and J. Dougherty (1997): "Data mining using MLC++, a Machine Learning Library in C++", *International Journal of Artificial Intelligence Tools* **Vol. 6, num. 4**, 537-566. [http://www.sgi.com/Technology/mlc/]
5. J.R. Le Gall, S. Lemeshow, F. Saulnier (1993): "A new Simplified Acute Physiology Score (SAPS II) based on a European/North American multicenter study". JAMA 270:2957-2963
6. S. Lemeshow, D. Teres, J. Klar, J.S. Avrunin, S.H. Gehlbach, J. Rapoport (1993): "Mortality Probability Models (MPM II) based on an international cohort of intensive
7. J.R. Quinlan (1986): "Induction of Decision Trees", *Machine Learning* **1**, 81-106

8. B. Sierra and P. Larrañaga (1998): "Predicting survival in malignant skin melanoma using Bayesian Networks automatically induced by genetic algorithms. An empirical comparision between different approachess", *Artificial Intelligence in Medicine* **14**, 215-230

9. Stone, M.: "Cross-validation choice and assessment of statistical procedures". *Journal Royal of Statistical Society* **36** (1974) 111-147

A Screening Technique for Prostate Cancer by Hair Chemical Analysis and Artificial Intelligence

Ping Wu[1], Kok Liang Heng[1], Shuo Wang Yang[1], Yi Feng Chen[1],
Ravuru Subramanyam Mohan[2], and Peter Huat Chye Lim[2]

[1] Institute of High Performance Computing, 89B Science Park Drive,
01–05/08 The Rutherford, Singapore 118261
{wuping, kokliang, yangsw, chenyf}@ihpc.nus.edu.sg
[2] Division of Urology, Department of Surgery, Changi General Hospital,
2 Simei Street 3, Singapore 529889

Abstract. Early detection of cancer may not only substantially reduce the overall health care costs but also reduce the long term morbidity and death from cancer. Although there are screening techniques available for prostate cancer, they all have practical limitations. In this paper, a new screening technique for prostate cancer is discussed. This technique applies artificial intelligence on the chemical analytical data of human scalp hair. Our study shows that it is possible to reveal relationship among hair trace elements and to establish correlation of multi element to prostate cancer etiology.

1 Introduction

Prostate cancer is one of the most common cancers among men globally. It is the 6th most frequent cancer in Singapore accounting for about 4% of all male cancers. Moreover, it shows a rapid rising trend over the last 25 years, as in many populations worldwide (average annual percent change of 1.94 in age–standardized incidence rate) [1].

Although there are screening techniques available for prostate cancer, they all have practical limitations. In this paper, a screening technique of prostate cancer by hair chemistry and artificial intelligence is introduced. Chemical analysis of hair, if established as a screening tool may be a reasonable alternative to many other traditional methods. It may serve as a monitoring tool for recurrence and play an important role as a biochemical marker for cancer prognosis.

2 Screening Technique for Prostate Cancer

Before the screening process, hair sample collection and chemical analysis are needed. Hair samples from healthy normal and prostate cancer patients are collected. In the sampling, a total of about 0.4 grams hair will be cut and collected

W. Horn et al. (Eds.): AIMDM'99, LNAI 1620, pp. 372–376, 1999.

from the occipital region of the head (close to the scalp). Each hair sample is to be 3 to 5cm long.

The obtained correlation between trace elements and prostate cancers is valid only when the origin of the trace elements measured in the sample is almost entirely endogenous. To remove exogenous contribution (contaminant) the optimal choice of sample washing procedures become crucial. Our sample washing procedure is similar to the standardized washing procedure recommended by International Atomic Energy Agency in Vienna [2], [3].

Recently an artificial intelligence software, APEX (Advanced Process Expert) [4] has been developed on the IBM SP2 supercomputer in Institute of High Performance Computing (IHPC). In our case study, APEX and a commercial software S–PLUS [5] are applied. Details of our screening technique are followed.

2.1 Pretreatment of Hair Analytical Data

Concentrations of some hair elements are significantly higher (by 2–4 magnitudes) than others. Trace elements of low concentrations may actually be more important in the development of prostate cancer than those of high concentrations. The analytical data will be normalized so that the mean and standard deviation for each element will be zero and one respectively.

2.2 Expansion of Variables

The analytical data contains concentrations of 23 trace elements for each sample. Hair trace elements may have not only linear but also complex non–linear effects to the development of prostate cancer. Nonlinear terms will be added to the original data matrix.

2.3 Reduction of Variable Dimension

In the expanded variable space, there are many useless and noisy variables. S–PLUS is used to remove the less important variables. Generalized linear models [6] of S–PLUS is applied. An initial model, which is constructed explicitly as an intercept only model, is required. S–PLUS provides an automatic procedure for conducting stepwise model selection to choose the best model in fitting predictor variables to the response variable. It calculates the C_p statistics [7] for the current model, as well as those for all reduced and augmented models, then adds or drops predictor variable that reduces C_p the most.

2.4 Selection of Variables

The model selected by S–PLUS will undergo variable selection module of APEX [8] to see if any variable will be further deleted. This module consists of Kruskal Wallis Test (KW) [7], Principal Component Regression (PCR) [9] and Partial Least Squares Regression (PLSR) [10]. Cross validation with PRESS (Prediction Errors of Squares Sum) statistics [11] is done in PCR and PLSR [8].

2.5 Two Dimensional Projection of the Screening Model

In the final reduced variable space, pattern recognition methods such as Partial
Least Square [10], Principal Component Analysis [12], Fisher Discriminant Analysis [13] and Linear Mapping [14] will be applied to generate two–dimensional
projections. On these projections, samples will be clustered into subgroups with
regards to the development of prostate cancer. One particular projection which
best separates control and cancer groups, will be automatically selected by a
genetic algorithm search among all the projections generated by the above four
methods [8].

3 Results

In earlier 1998, a study of prostate cancer prognosis has been successfully com-
pleted by IHPC in collaboration with the Division of Urology of Changi General
Hospital. A total of 100 hair samples is collected, 30 of them are from prostate
cancer patients provided by the hospital and the remains are from control group.
The 100 samples are digested and tested for 23 trace elements (B, Na, Mg, Al,
Si, P, S, K, Ca, V, Cr, Mn, Fe, Ni, Co, Cu, Zn, As, Se, Sr, Mo, Cd and Pb).
To ensure statistically valid model, outliers, if present, will be removed. A total
of 15 outliers is detected by using simple scatter plot of concentration of each
trace element versus the record index. These 15 malnutrition or contaminated
samples (either extreme low or extreme high concentration) are removed from
the sample pool before the data is input to APEX.

The 23 dimensional trace element space is expanded to include nonlinear
terms such as $\frac{x_i}{x_j}$ where x_i and x_j are the concentrations of elements i and j
respectively. The expanded data matrix is input to S–PLUS to fit a logistic
regression model between the predictor variables (original 23 variables and non-
linear terms) and the categorical response. In the expanded data space, there are
many useless and noisy variables, S–PLUS is applied to remove the less important variables. In this study, 8 of 529 variables are selected by S–PLUS. These
selected variables are then undergone APEX's variable selection module for further selection of significant variables. Since all the variables are important, they
are all kept by APEX. Next, two dimensional projection of this reduced sample
space is obtained by pattern recognition method of APEX. To avoid overfitting,
ten fold cross validation is employed. In particular, the data set (85 samples) is
partitioned into ten equal sized sets (8 samples for each set), then each set is in
turn used as the test set while the classifier trains on the other nine sets.

In this paper, Fisher Discriminant Analysis is found to best separate the
cancer and control groups in the trace element space. A 2–dimensional projection
of the best separation is shown in Fig. 1. In Fig. 1, cancer and control groups
occupy distinctly different regions, no overlap of the two groups is observed. The
average sensitivity and average specificity over ten training sets are 98.83% (254
of 257) and 96.49% (495 of 513) respectively. The aforementioned values over
ten test sets are 91.30% (21 of 23) and 91.23% (52 of 57) respectively.

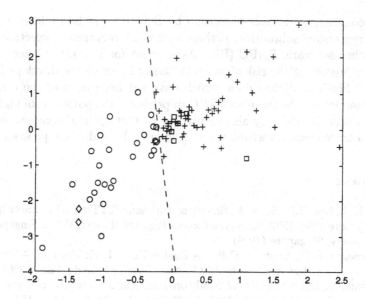

Fig. 1. Projection of hair samples (training set and test set) onto a two dimensional space. + *(healthy control group of training set)* and ○ *(prostate cancer patient of training set)* are well separated. □ *(healthy control group of test set)* and ◇ *(prostate cancer patient of test set)* are used to test the developed model

The X and Y axes in Fig. 1 are given by the following equations:

$$X = 0.13 \left(\frac{Mn}{Cu}\right)_n + 0.66 \left(\frac{P}{Cd}\right)_n - 0.42 \left(\frac{Fe}{P}\right)_n - 0.22 \left(\frac{Se}{P}\right)_n$$
$$+ 0.29 \left(\frac{Cr}{Se}\right)_n + 0.03 \left(\frac{Fe}{Cd}\right)_n - 0.43 \left(\frac{Sr}{Cd}\right)_n - 0.24 \left(\frac{K}{Cu}\right)_n$$
$$Y = -0.18 \left(\frac{Mn}{Cu}\right)_n - 0.29 \left(\frac{P}{Cd}\right)_n - 0.42 \left(\frac{Fe}{P}\right)_n - 0.56 \left(\frac{Se}{P}\right)_n$$
$$+ 0.19 \left(\frac{Cr}{Se}\right)_n + 0.31 \left(\frac{Fe}{Cd}\right)_n + 0.47 \left(\frac{Sr}{Cd}\right)_n - 0.20 \left(\frac{K}{Cu}\right)_n$$

where $\left(\frac{Mn}{Cu}\right)_n$ denotes normalized concentration of Mn over concentration of Cu.

4   Future Work

APEX is originally designed for the diagnosis and optimization of industrial process. In view that human bio–process is much different from the industrial process, we will develop new artificial intelligence software, DSCM (Development of Cancer Screening Model). DSCM will meet the special requirements of human bio–system. More reliable cancer screening models will be expected by DSCM.

The reduction of variable dimension by S–PLUS will be replaced by a new stepwise regression subroutine, orthogonalization recurrence selection (ORS) [15]. Another software, RAPC (Risk Assessment for Prostate Cancer) will be written for predicting the risk of prostate cancer by using the developed screening model. Fresh analytical data, which have not been used in the training of screening model, will be input to RAPC to predict if the patient is of high risk of prostate cancer. RAPC may also be used to predict optimal composition range of selected trace elements within which it is unlikely to develop prostate cancer.

References

1. Chai, K.S., Lee, H.P., Seow, A., Shanmugarathnam, K.: Trends in Cancer Incidence in Singapore 1968–1992. Singapore Cancer Registry Report, Vol. 4. Singapore Cancer Registry, Singapore (1996)
2. Montenegro, E.C., Baptista, G.P., De Castro Faria, L.V., Paschoa, A.S.: Correlation Factor for Hair Analysis by PIXE. Nucl. Instr. Methods. 168 (1980) 479–483
3. Obrusník, O., Bencko, V.: INAA Study on Trace Elements in Hair of Three Selected Groups in Czechoslovakia. Radiochem. Radioanal. Lett. 38 (1979) 189–196
4. Wu, P., Straughan, R., Ong, I., Heng, K.L.: Development of a Process Diagnosis and Optimization Tool for Industrial Process: A Pattern Recognition/Neural Network Code on NSRC's IBM SP2. In: Chandra, T., Leclair, S.R., Meech, J.A., Verma, B., Smith, M., Balachandran, B. (eds.): Australiasia–Pacific Forum on Intelligent Processing and Manufacturing of Materials. Australia (1997) 235–239
5. Chambers, J.M., Hastie, T.J. (eds.): Statistical Models in S. Wadsworth and Brooks Cole Advanced and Software. Pacific Grove, California (1992)
6. Nelder, J.A., Wedderburn, R.W.M.: Generalized Linear Models. J. Roy. Stat. Soc. 135 (1972) 370–384
7. Milton, J.S., Arnold, J.C.: Introduction to Probability and Statistics, Principle and Applications for Engineering and the Computing Science. 2nd edn. McGraw–Hill, New York (1990)
8. Heng, K.L., Jin, H.M., Li, Y., Wu, P.: Computer Aided Design of NiMH Electrodes. J. Mater. Chem. (1999) (in press)
9. Afifi, A.A., Clark, V.: Computer Aided Multivariate Analysis. 2nd edn. Van Nostrand Reinhold, New York (1990)
10. Geladi, P., Kowalski, B.R.: Partial Least Squares Regression: A Tutorial. Anal. Chim. Acta. 185 (1990) 1–17
11. Myers, R.H.: Classical and Modern Regression with Applications. Duxbury Press, Boston (1996)
12. Bryan, F.J.: Multivariate Statistical Methods: A Primer. 2nd edn. Chapman and Hall, London (1992)
13. Rasmussen, G.T., Ritter, G.L., Lowry, S.R., Isenhour, T.L.: Fisher Discriminant Functions for a Multilevel Mass Spectral Filter Network. J. Chem. Inf. Comput. Sci. 19(4) (1979) 255–259
14. Fukunage, K.: Introduction to Statistical Pattern Recognition. Academic Press, Boston (1990)
15. Zhu, E.Y., Yang, P.Y., Deng, Z.W., Huang, B.L.: Orthogonalization Recurrence Selection Methods and its Applications. Chem. J. Chi. Uni. 14(11) (1993) 1518–1521

Natural Language Processing

A Conversational Model for Health Promotion on the World Wide Web

Alison Cawsey[1], Floriana Grasso[2], and Ray Jones[3]

[1] Department of Computing and Electrical Engineering
Heriot-Watt University - alison@cee.hw.ac.uk
[2] Department of Computer Science - University of Liverpool
[3] Department of Public Health - University of Glasgow

Abstract. In this paper we describe a new approach to computer-based health promotion, based on a conversational model. We base our model on a collection of human-human email dialogues concerning healthy nutrition. Our system uses a database of tips and small pieces of advice, organised so that support for the advice, and arguments against the advice may be explored. The technical framework and initial evaluation results are described.

1 Introduction

The use of interactive, computer based systems for health education and promotion has a long history [6]. However, the World Wide Web (WWW) presents new possibilities for interactive health promotion (e.g., [5,7]). Materials can be developed which can be accessed by anyone with a WWW connection, and perhaps as importantly, tools and ideas easily shared among health promotion researchers.

There are now numerous WWW sites dedicated to health promotion[1]. Most combine the presentation of health information with some interactive component, and often online support groups. In this paper we focus on interactive tools for the promotion of healthy nutrition.

In nutrition education, there are two main interactive tools that are used. The first is the quiz. While good quizzes can be useful, they often presume some initial motivation of the user to study and acquire some basic nutrition facts first. The second type of interactive tool used is a nutrition assessment. Users typically enter information about their current diet (selecting from meal options), and personal facts such as weight, sex, and activity level. They then receive an assessment of the nutrients in their meal selections. While this can be very useful for relatively sophisticated users, it is difficult to develop systems that provide a useful and meaningful assessment for relatively naive users who may not understand the nutrition concepts involved.

This paper presents an alternative approach to interactive health promotion, based on a dialogue with the user centered on practical tips. In our system the users make a number of simple meal choices, then receive tips for improving the

---

[1] See http://www.arbor.com for a reviewed selection.

W. Horn et al. (Eds.): AIMDM'99, LNAI 1620, pp. 379–388, 1999.
© Springer-Verlag Berlin Heidelberg 1999

meal. They can respond to each tip in various ways, asking why it is recommended, stating objections to it, or rejecting it outright. The system is based on a simple conversational model, emulating aspects of the conversation between human dieticians and advisees. While we focus on nutrition education, the framework is designed to be easily adapted to other areas of health promotion.

In the following sections we present the background research, in health promotion, and conversational modelling. We describe our initial study of human health promotion dialogues, and show how this influenced our system design. The system itself is described in detail and a preliminary evaluation described.

2   Background

2.1   Promoting Healthy Nutrition

Health promotion can be described as "the process of enabling people to increase control over, and to improve, their health" [13]. It involves both providing information, and advocating healthier behaviours. The promotion of healthy nutrition is currently seen as particularly important – healthy nutrition can have a crucial role in decreasing the incidence of illnesses such as cardiovascular disease or cancer. Education and persuasion is only part of what is required to change people's behaviour, to be considered in combination with attempts to remove external barriers to healthy nutrition (e.g., cost and availability). Nevertheless, it is an essential part of health promotion, and one that has proved very difficult – getting people to change established behaviours is hard. Mere information provision is inadequate - interventions should take into account behavioural theories and goals, and incorporate some degree of personalisation [11].

While the best approach to the promotion of healthy nutrition may involve personal contact, there is an interest in low-cost intervention methods. Campbell *et al.* [1] demonstrated the impact that personalised leaflets could have. Leaflets, tailored according to the Stages of Change model [9], resulted in a significant (4%) reduction in fat intake. While there is interest in more interactive computer-based approaches, there are few trials to date which demonstrate their potential. One exception is Winett *et al.* [14] who describe a trial of a computer-based intervention to help supermarket shoppers alter food purchases – participants using the system decreased high fat purchases, and increased high fibre ones.

More recently, many nutrition information sites have been developed for the WWW. While in most cases, their effectiveness in health promotion has not been formally assessed, many have thousands of visitors. Though many of these may already have a good diet, the sites nonetheless provide an opportunity for new novel interventions to re-inforce suggestions for dietary change.

In our work we aim to contribute to the collection of techniques available for the development of such interactive health promotion sites.

2.2   Modelling Persuasive Conversation

We are interested in how theories of human persuasive communication and dialogue can be applied to computer-based health promotion.

We combine a model of argument structure, with a conversational framework. We use Toulmin's model of argument structure [12]. He suggested that effective human arguments share common elements:

- A claim (e.g., You should eat more fruit and vegetables.).
- Support for the claim (e.g., People who eat more fruit have less disease).
- Qualifiers, anticipating possible counter arguments or exceptions (e.g., *Most people* should..).
- Warrant, linking claim and support (often unstated).
- Concession, acknowledging part of the opposing argument. (e.g., Although you may not like all types of vegetable..).

These elements provide a useful way of organising the elements of an argument. However, the model does not provide us with guidance as to how the *conversation* with the user should be managed - how much of an argument should be presented at once, and how can we manage the interaction.

Our conversational model is informed by two complementary models of natural language discourse. The first is the dialogue game [2]. Dialogue is modelled as a sequence of moves. You can be in various game states, and from each possible state different moves are allowed (e.g., ask a question). Dialogue games can be conveniently represented as transition networks (see Fig. 4) and are widely used as a way of representing options in a dialogue, in natural language processing and HCI (e.g., [10]).

The second model emphasises the hierarchical structure of discourse. Grosz and Sidner's model [4] links the hierarchical structure of discourse to the objects in focus. In this type of model, a stack can be used to store discourse elements which should be returned to when the current element is complete. For example, given an interruption from the user we can place the previous (uncompleted) discourse goal on a stack to be returned to when the interruption is dealt with.

Our model, described in detail in Section 4, uses a representation of the underlying arguments influenced by Toulmin's model. There is an (implicit) dialogue game representing options at each state in the interaction, and a stack based model of dialogue contexts.

3   Knowledge Elicitation

Our goal was to emulate aspects of the conversation between a human advisor and advisee. As we wanted the human participants responses to be fully thought out, with no time pressure, we engaged users in email conversations concerning healthy nutrition. In the first experiment the researcher role-played different advisees, engaging in a dialogue concerning healthy nutrition with five nutritionists. In the second the researcher role-played the advisor.

We looked at the overall structure of the (email) conversation (e.g., how it was opened), the way tips and suggestions were presented and followed through, and also noted the specific tips offered. In the first experiment, all nutritionists asked, early on, for some information about current diet (e.g., "What are you

R: Have you thought of adding some fruit to your breakfast?

U: I know I should, but I'm often in a hurry to get to work that all I can do is eat what I have in my desk drawer. I buy fruit, but it just sits there until it goes bad.

R: You could have a glass of juice. It's just as quick. Or add some tinned fruit to your saltines.

Fig. 1. User objections and concerns expressed (R = researcher, U = user).

having for dinner tonight?"). They then moved on to making some suggestions, while asking for more details about the diet. Some also asked early on about current attitudes to dietary change (e.g., "Are you contemplating increasing your vegetable intake in the near future?"). These followed, sometimes explicitly, the Stages of Change model [9].

Most of the main body of the dialogue was centered on a number of tips or suggestions – one suggestion might lead to several (email) messages, as the advisor followed up on any responses of the user. While advisors never argued with the advisee, some of these follow-up messages were concerned with dealing with objections and concerns about the tips, and so can be viewed as presenting a more complete 'argument' for the suggestion in question. Figure 1 gives one example sequence from a second email experiment, showing an advisee posing an objection that needed following up.

To guide the development of our system we also looked at numerous leaflets concerned with the promotion of healthy nutrition. Most gave simple nutrition information, supplemented by practical tips and recipe/meal suggestion. The practical tips listed in these leaflets formed the core of the 'tip' knowledge base in our implementation. We have so far included 140 tips, and linked these to particular meal choices. While still restricted, this goes beyond what is likely to be found in an individual leaflet, and allows for both better linking of tip to user, and better follow-up on tips given user responses.

4 System Description

Our system uses a conversational model, and an underlying database of tips. Initially the users are asked for some information about their current diet (selecting meal components from a menu). They then receive tips about how to improve the meal they have chosen. They can respond in various ways to the tips, allowing a moderately complex 'conversation' to develop. The basic structure of the interaction, asking about meal choices, followed by tips and follow-up information, is based on that observed in the dialogues with our human nutritionists.

4.1 Tip Knowledge Base

The tips (pieces of advice and supporting facts) are organised in a uniform structure. Tips are viewed as 'arguments' that have a main claim, some support,

```
tipclaim(t002, 'Grill or bake meat, rather than frying.').
tipsupport(t002, t008, 'The fat drips off into the grill pan.').
tipsupport(t002, t15, '').
tipobjection(t002, o03).
tipobjection(t002, o09).
..
tipclaim(t008, 'You should reduce the amount of fat in your
diet.').
..
obclaim(o03, 'I definitely won't stop frying things').
obresponse(o03, t024).
..
tipclaim(t024, 'Try stir frying using a little oil.').
```

Fig. 2. Example tips and objections.

possibly a warrant, but which anticipate a number of objections (allowing concessions). Each piece of support for a tip is represented as another tip (and has its own support etc). Warrants are represented simply as optional texts linking the tip with the support. Objections are represented separately; each objection may have a number of possible responses each of which is a tip. We do not represent or reason about what the tips mean, just how they relate together. Figure 2 gives a number of (simplified) tips and objections, showing the different components. The third argument in the 'tipsupport' term is the optional warrant.

We specify when a tip is relevant. The simplest case is to make it relevant to a given selected meal component, for example:

```
relevant(t002, sausages).
```

This tip will be considered if the user has selected this item for their meal. We can also define more complex rules, for example:

```
relevantifno(t007, vegetable) :- mealtype(dinner).
```

This tip is relevant if the user has not selected anything from the vegetable category, and the current meal being considered is dinner.

4.2 Conversational Model

These tips provide the basic knowledge base behind our conversation system. Once the user has selected meal components, a relevant tip is presented. The user has then the option of responding in a number of ways (by clicking on an appropriate button). They can ask Why? the suggestion or claim is valid, select But.. and pose an objection, reject a tip by selecting No Way!, or select OK! to accept a tip and move on (see Fig. 3). The Why? button is omitted if there is no support stored for the tip.

If they select Why? the supporting information is presented. As this is represented as another 'tip' all the same options apply. If they select But.. the

You selected: a tuna sandwich.

Here's a suggestion:

If you make your own sandwiches, try to use thick cut slices of bread.

Fig. 3. Example screen.

possible objections are listed, and also a text box presented, allowing the user to enter new unlisted objections[2]. Once an objection is selected, a response to that objection is given. This is again a tip, so the above options again apply.

The options in the conversation can be represented as a transition network (dialogue game). Currently the systems responses always involve presenting a tip (possibly as support to another tip, or response to an objection), or presenting a menu of possible objections. We therefore represent the user's options as arcs, with the basic system 'states' being either T (tip) or O (objection) (Fig. 4).

4.3   Managing Responses

The above model illustrates the basic structure of the conversation, but does not show how responses are selected, or how the 'focus' of the dialogue is managed.

If the user selects But.. or Why?, the current tip is placed on a stack of tip contexts, to be returned to once the subdialogue concerning the objection or request for support is completed. The dialogue is therefore hierarchical in structure, and returns to 'higher level' contexts are made explicit. When the user has accepted a supporting tip, the system restates it (possibly in a shorter version) and reminds of the current context:

> OK, so remember: 'Eat lots of starchy food'. Let's go back to: *If you make your own sandwiches, try to use thick cut slices of bread.*

These explicit reminders appeared useful in preventing people lose track of the structure of the conversation, and ensured that all 'loose ends' in the conversation were followed up.

As the dialogue progresses, the system keeps track of which tips have been used, and which have been accepted. This is used, in a simple way, in the selection of responses and the presentation of new tips. If a previously used tip is an appropriate response (possibly in a new context), the system will remind the user of the old tip, and if possible present an alternative response as well:

> Here's why: It is recommended that you eat at least 5 portions of fruit and vegetables a day.

---

[2] These objections are recorded, and used to enhance the system in later versions.

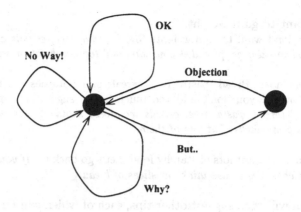

Fig. 4. Dialogue Game

> As we've seen before: Fruit and veg provide vitamins, minerals and fibre, with little fat. Another reason is: *Fruit and veg are high in what are known as antioxidants, which protect the body cells against damage that could lead to heart disease and cancer.*

Reminding the user about old tips is useful, as it provides consistency in the dialogue, and it allows old advice to be reconsidered in new context. But providing further advice allows the dialogue to move on. The new tip then provides the new context, with all the conversational options applying to it.

If the user rejects a tip (**No Way!**), then the system's response depends on whether the tip was providing a supporting argument for another. If so, it will present alternative arguments. If not, or if there are no alternative arguments, it will simply return to the previous tip context:

> OK, so you don't agree with: You should eat 5 portions of fruit and veg.
> Let's go back to: *Add salad to sandwiches, or choose ones with added salad.*

4.4 Example

The above model, although technically simple, allows for quite complex dialogues. The following is an example illustrating the various points above. The user has selected a tuna sandwich for lunch. User responses will be given in bold.

> You selected a tuna sandwich. Here's a suggestion: *If you make your own sandwiches, try to use thick cut slices of bread.*
> **Why?**
> Here's why: If you make your own sandwiches, try to use thick cut slices of bread. *Starchy food (bread, pasta, rice, cereals, potatoes) should be the main part of most meals and snacks. Eat lots of them.*
> **But..**
> Why are you unsure about: *Starchy food (bread, pasta, rice, cereals, potatoes) should be the main part of most meals and snacks. Eat lots of them*
>   - I don't want to gain weight.
>   - My diet is OK as it is.

I don't want to gain weight.
You said: I don't want to gain weight. *Bread, pasta, rice, cereals and potatoes are not high in calories, provided you don't add too much fat or sugar.*
OK!
OK, so remember: Bread, pasta, rice, cereals and potatoes are not high in calories, provided you don't add too much fat or sugar. Let's go back to: *Starchy food (bread, pasta, rice, cereals, potatoes) should be the main part of most meals and snacks. Eat lots of them.*
OK!
OK, so remember: Eat lots of starchy food. Let's go back to: *If you make your own sandwiches, try to use thick cut slices of bread.*

The system will then suggest other tips, each of which can be followed up in a similar way. At the end of a session the system lists the tips which have been accepted (by clicking OK!) by the user. These can be printed out if desired.

4.5   Implementation

The system is implemented in Prolog, with small Perl scripts providing the interface with the WWW. The HTML code is dynamically generated by the program in response to the user's selections.

The system is re-started to produce every screen. Most state information which we want to keep track of (e.g., list of tips already used, meal items selected) are stored in a file. Unique session numbers are maintained for each user, and simultaneous users' data will be kept in separate session files. However, the stack of tip contexts is passed as an argument in the URL, so that we can be sure that the use of the 'back' button on the browser does not upset this context information. The previous tip, and the user's selected button press (e.g., But..) are also passed as arguments in the URL.

The previous tip, stack of tip contexts, session numbers, and button press are passed as arguments to the main Prolog procedure that outputs the appropriate HTML. The selection of tips (etc) within this procedure will depend on the additional user data loaded from the session file.

5   Evaluation

The system was evaluated with relatively expert users, in order to obtain good feedback to guide the development of the system. Users were recruited from three sources: a mailing list on consumer health informatics; the sci.med.nutrition newsgroup; staff and students in the researchers' academic department. After using the system, they were requested to fill out a short questionnaire, containing both questions concerning their impression of the system, and personal questions on their diet etc. Altogether 152 sessions were recorded (but with some users initiating several sessions), and 40 questionnaires completed. There was a roughly equal balance of users from our three sources (newsgroup, mailing list, and department). 55% of our users were in the 20-30 age group, and 57% were

British. 95% felt that their diet was already either good or OK as it was, and 85% were at least trying a little to improve their diet. The majority (90%) of users found the system easy to use, with few navigation problems. It made 62% think about their diet, and 42% said they might improve some aspect of their diet as a result. 60% found some of the tips helpful.

The most positive comments came from those concerned with health promotion themselves, who appreciated the needs of our target audience, and the difficulties in creating simple, interactive nutrition systems. However, some users found it over simplistic, and were affronted by some apparent assumptions the system makes about their diet – they might be advised to cut out sugar in coffee for example. These tips (with implicit assumptions) were taken directly from leaflets, and needed rewriting for an interactive environment where many users expect tailored of advice.

Analysis of traces of system use revealed that many people did not press the Why?/But.. options much, so missed getting basic information supporting and reinforcing the tips. Presenting small chunks of information, and leaving the initiative with the user, has problems. Some users suggested that the system should be asking more questions as it went (keeping the initiative). This approach would mirror more closely the style of the human nutritionists dialogues, where most of the nutritionists contributions ended with a question.

Based on feedback from these users we have completed a revised version[3] with the following features:

- An initial questionnaire on attitudes to diet change, cooking habits etc.
- An initial page of personalised advice based on this questionnaire.
- Pages of advice tailored, in very simple ways, to user characteristics.
- Tips that may not apply (e.g., user may not take sugar in coffee) are now prefixed with 'Do you currently do X? If so, here's a suggestion.'.

These extensions involved adding a few further features to our tip knowledge base. For example, we now have statements such as:

```
tipfor(t036, cook).
tipif(t095, 'Do you currently take sugar in your tea/coffee').
```

While we have not yet evaluated this version formally, feedback from people accessing the site and filling in the questionnaire is positive.

6 Conclusion

We have described a new conversational model for computer-based health promotion, and an implementation for simple nutrition advice. The basic framework is simple, but can easily be extended and adapted. The tip knowledge base is separate from the dialogue module, so we can independently develop new knowledge bases in other domains, or vary the way the tips are presented in dialogue (e.g., to ask more questions of the user, or to always include supporting information).

---

[3] http://www.cee.hw.ac.uk/~alison/meals2/start.html

Our model could also be developed to allow further personalisation, such as in the arguments selected to support a tip. We have developed a more complete computational model of everyday argumentation [3], based on a theory of rhetoric [8], which could support this.

To use the model effectively in health promotion we would want to make the use of the system just one part of a healthy nutrition intervention. A conversational system such as this could be used in combination with quizzes and multimedia presentations, allowing practical and factual information to be given in a motivating and interactive manner, based on practical goals for change.

Acknowledgements

We wish to thank the staff at the Dep. of Human Nutrition of Glasgow University for their help. This research is supported by the EPSRC grant GR/K55271.

References

1. M.K. Campbell, B.M. DeVellis, V.J. Strecher, A.S. Ammerman, R.F. DeVellis, and R.S. Sandler. Improving Dietary Behaviour: The Efficacy of Tailored Messages in Primary Care Settings. *American Journal of Public Health*, 84(5):783–787, 1994.
2. L. Carlson. *Dialogue Games: An Approach to Discourse Analysis*. D. Reidel Pub. Co., Dordrecht, Holland; Boston, 1983.
3. F. Grasso. Exciting Avocados and Dull Pears: Combining Behavioural and Argumentative Theory for Producing Effective Advice. In *Proceedings of the 20th Annual Meeting of the Cognitive Science Society*, pages 436–441, 1998.
4. B.J. Grosz and C.L. Sidner. Attention, intentions, and the structure of discourse. *Computational Linguistics*, 12(3):175–204, 1986.
5. M. Hern, T. Weitkamp, D. Haag, J. Trigg, and J.R. Guard. Nursing the Community in Cyberspace. *Computers in Nursing*, 15(6):316–321, 1997.
6. C. Lyons, J. Krasnowski, A. Greenstein, D. Maloney, and J. Tatarczuk. Interactive Computerized Patient Education. *Heart and Lung*, 11(4):340–341, July 1982.
7. K. Miller and S. Wisniewski. Internet Web Resources for Anti-Tobacco Advocacy. *Wisconsin Medical Journal*, 95(11):784–785, 1996.
8. C. Perelman and L. Olbrechts-Tyteca. *The New Rhetoric: a treatise on argumentation*. University of Notre Dame Press, Notre Dame, Indiana, 1969.
9. J. Prochaska and C. DiClemente. Stages of Change in the Modification of Problem Behavior. In M. Hersen, R. Eisler, and P. Miller, editors, *Progress in Behavior Modification*, volume 28. Sycamore, IL: Sycamore Publishing Company, 1992.
10. R. Reichman. *Getting Computers to Talk Like You and Me*. The MIT Press, Cambridge, Mass., 1981.
11. Liana Roe, Paula Hunt, and Hilary Bradshaw. *Health promotion interventions to promote health eating in the general population: a review*. Health Education Authority - The Cromwell Press, Melksham, 1997.
12. S. Toulmin. *The Uses of Argument*. Cambridge University Press, 1958.
13. WHO. World Health Organization. Ottawa Charter, 1986.
14. R.A. Winett, J.F. Moore, L.A. Hite, M. Leahy, T.E. Neubauer, J.L. Walberg, W.B. Walker, D. Lombard, and E.S. Geller. Altering Shoppers' Supermarket Purchases to Fit Nutritional Guidelines: an Interactive Information System. *Journal of Applied Behavior Analysis*, 24(1):95–105, 1991.

Types of Knowledge Required to Personalise Smoking Cessation Letters*

Ehud Reiter[1], Roma Robertson[1], and Liesl Osman[2]

[1] Dept. of Computing Science, University of Aberdeen, Aberdeen, Scotland,
{ereiter,rroberts}@csd.abdn.ac.uk
[2] Dept. of Medicine and Therapeutics, University of Aberdeen, Aberdeen, Scotland
l.osman@abdn.ac.uk

Abstract. The STOP system generates personalised smoking-cessation letters, using as input responses to a smoking questionnaire. Generating personalised patient-information material is an area of growing interest to the medical community, since for many people changing health-related behaviour is the most effective possible medical intervention. While previous AI systems that generated personalised patient-information material were primarily based on medical knowledge, STOP is largely based on knowledge of psychology, empathy, and readability. We believe such knowledge is essential in systems whose goal is to change people's behaviour or mental state; but there are many open questions about how this knowledge should be acquired, represented, and reasoned with.

1 Introduction

The STOP (Smoking Termination through cOmputerised Personalisation) system generates short smoking-cessation leaflets that are personalised for different recipients. Personalisation is based on responses to a questionnaire on smoking habits and beliefs, previous attempts to quit, current medical problems, and so forth.

The goal of STOP is to change a patient's behaviour in a medically desirable way. This is different from the decision-support systems that are what many people most associate with the AI/Medicine field, especially in terms of the knowledge needed. Decision-support systems are based on medical knowledge, that is knowledge about diseases, treatments, how the body works, and so forth. But while STOP uses some medical knowledge, it is primarily based on other types of knowledge, including the psychology behind behaviour change, techniques for empathy, and rules for effective writing.

---

* Many thanks to the experts who worked with us, including Scott Lennox, James Friend, Martin Pucci, Margaret Taylor, and Chris Bushe; and also to Scott Lennox and Jim Hunter for their comments on earlier drafts of this paper. This research was supported by the Scottish Office Department of Health under grant K/OPR/2/2/D318, and the Engineering and Physical Sciences Research Council under grant GR/L48812.

W. Horn et al. (Eds.): AIMDM'99, LNAI 1620, pp. 389–399, 1999.

AI systems that attempt to change people's medical behaviour are relatively new, but they are attracting increasing attention. In part this is because the most important influence on many people's health is their behaviour (smoking, diet, compliance with treatment regimes, etc). To date, clinical trials of systems which produce personalised patient information material have been mixed, with some systems proven effective in changing behaviour of at least some patients but others showing no statistically significant effects. The challenge for the research community is to develop technology that increases the effectiveness of such systems, and also to determine the types of applications in which success is most likely.

2   Previous Work

A number of previous AI/Medicine projects have investigated generating personalised patient information that is intended to change the patient's behaviour or psychological state, of which the best known are perhaps MIGRAINE (Buchanan et al., 1995) and PIGLIT (Binstead, Cawsey, and Jones, 1995). Personalisation in these systems was primarily based on medical knowledge, in part because these systems only had access to medical information about patients; they did not have the information on attitudes and intentions available to STOP via its questionnaires. A clinical evaluation of one version of PIGLIT looked at PIGLIT's effect on patient satisfaction and patient anxiety; it showed a statistically significant effect on satisfaction, but not on anxiety (Cawsey et al., 1999).

Several systems which generate personalised patient information have also been produced by the public-health community, including at least two systems which produce smoking-cessation letters (Velicer et al., 1993; Strecher et al., 1994). These two systems base personalisation on a psychological theory of behaviour change, the Stages of Change model (Prochaska and diClemente, 1992). Clinical evaluations showed that both of these systems had a statistically significant impact on smoking cessation rates.

We hope that STOP will be more effective than previous AI/Medicine projects because it is based on knowledge about psychology (including the Stages of Change model), empathy, and readability as well as medical knowledge. We also hope that it will be more effective than previous systems developed by the public health community because it is uses AI and Natural-Language Processing (NLP) techniques.[1] A randomised controlled clinical trial of STOP is currently underway to test the effectiveness of the system; results of the trial should be available in late 1999.

---

[1] The focus of this paper is on comparing STOP to previous work in the AI community, not the public health community. But very briefly, we believe that STOP's performance is enhanced because it is based on knowledge acquired using structured AI knowledge acquisition techniques (these, for example, led to the smoker categories described in Section 4.1); and because NLG technology allows STOP to do a better job of optimising and satisfying constraints (for example, we believe it would be much harder to optimise content subject to a size constraint, as described in Section 3.1, without NLG representations and algorithms).

SMOKING QUESTIONNAIRE

Please answer by marking the most appropriate box for each question like this: ☒

Q1 Have you smoked a cigarette in the last week, even a puff?

YES ☒   NO ☐

Please complete the following questions   Please return the questionnaire unanswered in the
                                                               envelope provided. Thank you.

Please read the questions carefully.   If you are not sure how to answer, just give the best answer you can.

Q2   Home situation:

Live ☐   Live with ☒   Live with ☐   Live with ☒
alone   husband/wife/partner   other adults   children

Q3   Number of children under 16 living at home   .... boys   ....1....... girls

Q4   Does anyone else in your household smoke? *(If so, please mark all boxes which apply)*
husband/wife/partner ☒   other family member ☒   others ☐

Q5   How long have you smoked for? ...10... years
Tick here if you have smoked for less than a year   ☐

Q6   How many cigarettes do you smoke in a day? *(Please mark the amount below)*

Less than 5 ☐   5 – 10 ☒   11 – 15 ☐   16 – 20 ☐   21 - 30 ☐   31 or more ☐

Q7   How soon after you wake up do you smoke your first cigarette? *(Please mark the time below)*

Within 5 minutes ☐   6 - 30 minutes ☐   31 - 60 minutes ☒   After 60 minutes ☐

Q8   Do you find it difficult not to smoke in places where it is   YES ☐   NO ☒
forbidden eg in church, at the library, in the cinema?

Q9   Which cigarette would you hate most to give up?   The first one in the morning ☐
                                                                                              Any of the others ☒

Q10   Do you smoke more frequently during the first hours after   YES ☐   NO ☒
waking than during the rest of the day?

Q11   Do you smoke if you are so ill that you are in bed most of the   YES ☐   NO ☒
day?

Q12
Are you intending to stop   YES ☐   **Q13   If yes, are you intending to stop smoking**
smoking in the next 6   **within the next month?**
months?   YES ☐   NO ☐

                                       NO ☒   **Q14   If no, would you like to stop smoking if it was**
                                                              easy?
                                                         YES ☒   Not Sure ☐   NO ☐

Fig. 1. First page of Fiona Cameron's questionnaire

3   The System

The input to STOP is a 4-page questionnaire on smoking; the first page of a
questionnaire from a typical smoker, Fiona Cameron (not her real name), is
shown in Figure 1. STOP also gets some basic information, such as age and
sex, from the patient's medical record. The output of STOP is a small leaflet (4
pages of A5). The front page of a leaflet contains an introductory paragraph
but otherwise is not personalised; the back page is selected from one of a dozen
possible back pages, but is not personalised in detail. Most of the personalisation
happens in the two inside pages of the leaflet; the inside pages of the leaflet
generated for Fiona Cameron are shown in Figure 2.

STOP is thus a 'paper-in, paper-out' system; users fill out a paper questionnaire, and receive in response a paper leaflet. We could make STOP interactive

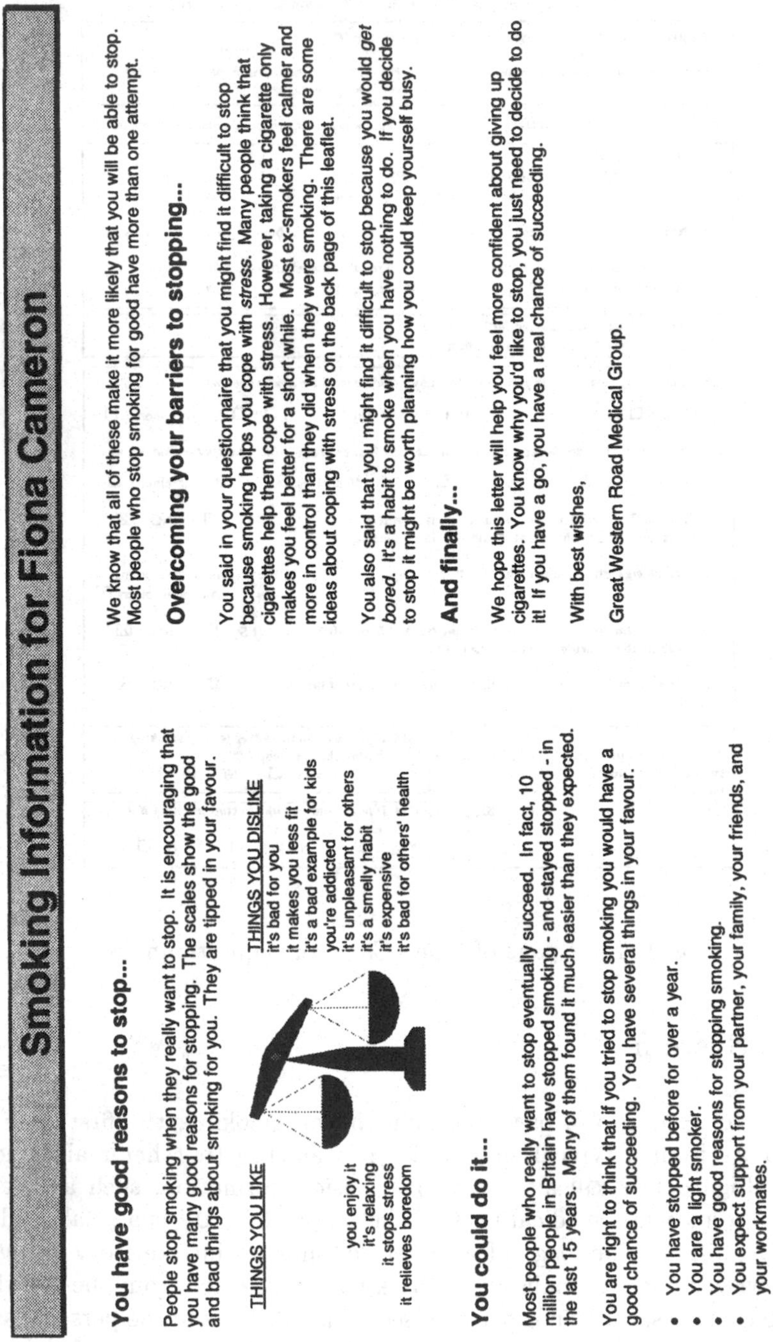

Smoking Information for Fiona Cameron

You have good reasons to stop...

People stop smoking when they really want to stop. It is encouraging that you have many good reasons for stopping. The scales show the good and bad things about smoking for you. They are tipped in your favour.

THINGS YOU LIKE

you enjoy it
it's relaxing
it stops stress
it relieves boredom

THINGS YOU DISLIKE

it's bad for you
it makes you less fit
it's a bad example for kids
you're addicted
it's unpleasant for others
it's a smelly habit
it's expensive
it's bad for others' health

You could do it...

Most people who really want to stop eventually succeed. In fact, 10 million people in Britain have stopped smoking - and stayed stopped - in the last 15 years. Many of them found it much easier than they expected.

You are right to think that if you tried to stop smoking you would have a good chance of succeeding. You have several things in your favour.

- You have stopped before for over a year.
- You are a light smoker.
- You have good reasons for stopping smoking.
- You expect support from your partner, your family, your friends, and your workmates.

We know that all of these make it more likely that you will be able to stop. Most people who stop smoking for good have more than one attempt.

Overcoming your barriers to stopping...

You said in your questionnaire that you might find it difficult to stop because smoking helps you cope with *stress*. Many people think that cigarettes help them cope with stress. However, taking a cigarette only makes you feel better for a short while. Most ex-smokers feel calmer and more in control than they did when they were smoking. There are some ideas about coping with stress on the back page of this leaflet.

You also said that you might find it difficult to stop because you would *get bored*. It's a habit to smoke when you have nothing to do. If you decide to stop it might be worth planning how you could keep yourself busy.

And finally...

We hope this letter will help you feel more confident about giving up cigarettes. You know why you'd like to stop, you just need to decide to do it! If you have a go, you have a real chance of succeeding.

With best wishes,

Great Western Road Medical Group.

Fig. 2. Inside pages of leaflet generated for Fiona Cameron (like MIGRAINE and PIGLIT), and have users fill out questionnaires and read leaflets on-line; but this would mean the system could only be used by people with access to computers. Since we want to reach as many smokers as possible, including people who do not have access to and are not comfortable with computers (such as many middle-aged and elderly people living in low-income public housing estates), we decided to use the 'paper-in, paper-out' model.

We do not expect STOP to have much effect on most smokers; smoking is a difficult habit to give up, and receiving a letter in the post is unlikely to make much difference to most people. But we hope that it will help a few people to quit. Studies show that brief discussions about smoking with a doctor will cause about 2% of people to quit smoking (Law and Tang, 1995); if we can achieve a similar effectiveness rate then STOP will be useful from a public-health perspective, since it is a very cheap intervention. Human doctors, incidentally, generally do not routinely have such discussions with patients because they find a 98% failure rate too discouraging; a computer system, of course, does not get discouraged no matter how small its success rate.

3.1   System Design

Space prohibits a detailed description of how STOP works, but a brief description follows. Questionnaires are read by an optical scanner, and processed by the core STOP system, which produces an RTF file which is printed with Microsoft Word. The core system is a Natural Language Generation (NLG) system which follows the model described in Reiter and Dale (1999). Processing is divided into the three stages of document planning, microplanning, and realisation, of which document planning (deciding what information to communicate) is the most complex. Oversimplifying to some degree, the document planner works by first classifying smokers into one of 7 categories, and then activating a schema (McKeown, 1985; Reiter and Dale, 1999) associated with that category. The combination of classification and schemas is similar at least in concept to the Exemplars system (White and Caldwell, 1998), although the implementation is quite different. The schemas produce a tree, known as a document plan. Each leaf node of the tree essentially defines one sentence in the leaflet. The internal nodes of the tree indicate how sentences are grouped, associate document structures (such as paragraphs or itemised lists) with groups of sentences, and sometimes specify discourse relations (Reiter and Dale, 1999) between daughter nodes.

Perhaps the most innovative aspect of STOP from an NLG perspective is its use of revision to optimise the content of a letter, given the size constraint (4 pages of A5). In general terms, this is done by having schemas annotate document plan constituents (both sentences and internal nodes) with importance markers. If the leaflet is too long, a revision module deletes the least important constituents until the size limit is satisfied. The microplanner and realiser convert this structure into an actual RTF document specification; the microplanner decides which discourse relations should be expressed in the text based on the outcome of the revision process, to ensure that the resulting document is rhetorically coherent.

4   Types of Knowledge

Most of the STOP project to date has focused on knowledge acquisition (KA). This was done in a structured fashion using standard techniques developed by the knowledge-acquisition community (Scott, Clayton, and Gibson, 1991), such as sorting and think-aloud protocols. These KA activities revealed that experts used several types of knowledge to produce smoking-cessation letters, including:

- psychological knowledge about how people change addictive behaviours;
- practitioner knowledge about 'empathy';
- linguistic knowledge about readability in texts; and
- medical knowledge about smoking.

Of course, experts also used knowledge about the patients, which they took from the questionnaire. Some of the expert's knowledge may be specific to Aberdeen or Scotland; this is not something we have investigated to date.

We will not further discuss medical knowledge here, as it is very common in AI and Medicine systems. It also turned out to be less important than we originally thought it would be. Most smokers are not interested in the medical details of smoking, and are well-aware of the health risks of smoking; indeed they may overestimate rather than underestimate health risks. Some of the other types of knowledge listed above are perhaps more unusual in AI/Medicine systems, and we discuss these below.

4.1   Psychological Knowledge about Addictive Behaviours

A crucial type of knowledge in STOP is psychological knowledge about how people stop addictive behaviours. All other systems we are aware of which produce personalised smoking-cessation material use the Stages of Change model (Prochaska and diClemente, 1992). This model groups smokers into five stages:

Precontemplator: not intending to quit
Contemplator: seriously considering quitting
Preparation: intending to quit
Action: in the process of quitting
Maintenance: has quit, avoiding relapse

Only the first three stages are relevant to systems (such as STOP) which target people who are currently smoking.

The Stages of Change model also specifies what type of information should be communicated to people in each stage. For example, information for precontemplators should emphasise that the disadvantages of smoking outweigh its advantages; information for contemplators should discuss specific 'barriers' to change, such as addiction or fear of weight gain; and information for preparers should present techniques for quitting.

We initially hoped to use the Stages of Change model 'off the shelf', because it is clinically validated and widely used. But we found that it often suggested content that we believed to be inappropriate, perhaps because it is a general model which is not tuned either to smoking cessation or to the task of generating individualised letters. For example, many of the people in our study (including Fiona Cameron) are precontemplators in the sense that they are not intending to quit smoking; but they also are already convinced that smoking is bad for them, so it seems redundant to stress the disadvantages of smoking in a leaflet. The reason such people are not intending to quit is that they do not think they will be able to stop smoking; the right emphasis for such people is therefore not 'smoking is bad for you' but rather 'you can quit if you really want to.'

We ended up using 7 categories for smokers instead of 3; these categories were derived from sorting KA exercises. The categories are:

Committed smoker: People who clearly want to smoke; they get short letters reminding them of the health risks of smoking, and suggesting sources of advice in case they change their mind at some future date.

Classic precontemplator: People with mixed feelings about smoking, but who are not currently intending to quit; they get letters which emphasise that the disadvantages of smoking outweigh its advantages.

Lacks confidence: People who would like to stop smoking, but don't think they will be able to quit; they get letters which emphasise confidence-boosting

Classic contemplator: People who are considering quitting but have barriers; they get letters which emphasise overcoming their barriers.

Borderline contemplator: People who have mixed feelings about smoking but are considering quitting; they get letters which emphasise the disadvantages of smoking as well as how to overcome barriers.

Classic preparer: People who are intending to quit; they get letters which emphasise techniques for quitting.

Uncertain preparer: People who are intending to quit but have ambivalent feelings about smoking (this includes people who are being pressured by someone else to quit smoking); they get letters which both stress the disadvantages of smoking and suggest techniques for quitting.

The first three of these categories are essentially refinements of the Precontemplator stage; the subsequent two categories are refinements of the Contemplator stage; and the last two categories are refinements of the Preparation stage.

While category determines the emphasis of the letter, other information may be included as well, depending on the patient's details. For example, while the emphasis of the letter shown in Figure 2 is on confidence-building, since Fiona Cameron is classified in the *Lacks confidence* class, it also includes a section reinforcing her reasons for quitting, and some advice on techniques for coping with problems (this is partially intended to boost her confidence that she can quit).

4.2 Empathy

As we worked through various KA exercises with our experts, it became clear that they were using a type of knowledge which we had not initially anticipated, which we now call 'empathy'. The purpose of empathy knowledge is to produce leaflets which people take seriously and think about, instead of tossing aside as yet another anti-smoking polemical.

The only previous work on empathy in AI/Medicine systems which we are aware of is Forsythe's work (1995) during the MIGRAINE project; she used the term 'enlistment', which may be a better name than 'empathy'. In particular, Forsythe identified the need to treat patients with respect and acknowledge their competence; this finding influenced the wording of explanations in MIGRAINE. There is also a substantial body of work on empathy in the general medical literature, but it focuses on empathy in oral face-to-face consultations, and we found it difficult to apply these ideas to written leaflets.

We acquired a set of empathy rules via KA exercises; we also used some general psychological and communication principles (Monahan, 1995). Unlike Forsythe, who observed doctors conducting oral consultations, we asked our experts to focus on empathy in written leaflets. Some of the rules which emerged from these exercises are:

- Be positive, do not criticise. For example, avoid negative constructs such as *We regret that*; use neutral constructs such as *We see that* instead. Positive constructs such as *We are very pleased that* are desirable and should be used when appropriate.
- Wherever possible, make points by repeating facts that the smoker has stated in the questionnaire. For instance, the scales graphic in leaflet shown in Figure 2 uses Cameron's questionnaire responses to emphasise to her that there are many things she dislikes about smoking.
- Use second-person (*you*) sentences wherever possible; when this isn't possible, try to use first-person plural (*we*) sentences.

One expert also felt it would be useful to relate letters to a person's expertise (for example, *As a nurse, you know that ...*) and circumstances (for example, *I know being a single mother is very hard*); and two experts suggested using humour. However, another expert felt that these techniques could backfire and antagonise people if we were not very careful. Because we were working to a tight schedule, we elected not to implement any techniques which any of our experts expressed doubts about.

We believe that achieving a better understanding of empathy rules, including some testing and validation, is essential to the success of future personalised patient-information systems. We plan to investigate this in future research.

4.3 Readability

A primary design imperative in STOP was that texts should be readable by a wide range of recipients, including people with poor reading skills. Readability rules were also acquired with KA sessions, but these used an expert on health-information leaflets instead of a doctor; we also ran some KA sessions with a graphic designer to acquire acquire visual appearance rules (layout, font, etc). In technical NLG terms, many readability rules were essentially choice rules for microplanning operations such as lexicalisation and aggregation.

Many of the rules that emerged from the KA sessions were similar to those used for AECMA Simplified English (AECMA, 1986); indeed we gave our expert a copy of the Simplified English manual, and she found that it largely agreed with her thinking. Examples of our rules are:

- Sentences should be as short as possible. Hence STOP never aggregates messages (that is, forms a complex sentence by merging two simpler sentences with a relative clause or a conjunct such as *and*).
- Common (high-frequency) words and simple syntactic structures should be used wherever possible. For example, *You may be addicted* instead of *It is likely, but not certain, that you are addicted.*
- Avoid impersonal constructs. For example, *You mentioned some good reasons for stopping* instead of *There are lots of good reasons for stopping.*
- Put bullet lists in the same font as normal text (graphic design rule).

We originally thought about varying sentence length and word choice for different patients; for example, using more complex structures and words for university-educated patients. But our experts believed it was best to always use simple language in patient-information material, and indeed this is supported by research elsewhere (Davis et al., 1996).

We would have liked to implement some of these rules declaratively within the NLG system, but this proved difficult. Some rules (such as avoiding aggregation) were trivial to implement, but others turned out to require complex domain reasoning and knowledge as well as linguistic knowledge. For example, consider the principle that high-frequency words should be used whenever possible. It is easy to get a list of word frequencies and pick the highest-frequency word when given a choice between synonyms. But exact synonyms are not common; *may* is not exactly the same as *It is likely, but not certain,* for example. In this case, as in many others, the choice is between a relatively complex linguistic construct that conveys a precise meaning, and a simple linguistic construct that conveys an approximation to this meaning. Thus, whether *may* is acceptable depends on how important it is to communicate an exact meaning, and whether approximation is acceptable; and this is a fairly deep content decision which is difficult to encode declaratively.

5 Conclusion

AI systems which change people's behaviour in medically desirable ways have tremendous potential to improve health, since behaviour is the largest influence on health for many people. Given their psychological goals, we believe it is essential that such systems be based on knowledge of psychology, empathy, and readability, as well as more 'conventional' medical knowledge. We have made an initial attempt at understanding some of the issues in acquiring, representing, and reasoning with such knowledge in AI systems; but it is very much an initial attempt, and much more work needs to be done in this area.

References

AECMA. 1986. A guide for the preparation of aircraft maintenance documentation in the international aerospace maintenance language. Available from BDC Publishing Services, Slack Lane, Derby, UK.

Binstead, Kim, Alison Cawsey, and Ray Jones. 1995. Generated personalised patient information using the medical record. In Pedro Barahona, Mario Stefanelli, and Jeremy Wyatt, editors, *Proceedings of the Fifth Conference on Artificial Intelligence and Medicine Europe (AIME-1995)*, pages 29–41. Springer.

Buchanan, Bruce, Johanna Moore, Diana Forsythe, Guiseppe Carenini, Stellan Ohlsson, and Gordon Banks. 1995. An interactive system for delivering individualized information to patients. *Artificial Intelligence in Medicine*, 7:117–154.

Cawsey, Alison, Ray Jones, Janne Pearson, and Kim Binstead. 1999. The design and evaluation of a personalised health information system for patients with cancer. *User Modelling and User-Adapted Interaction*. Submitted.

Davis, T, J Bocchini, D Fredrickson, et al. 1996. Parent comprehension of polio vaccine information pamphlets. *Pediatrics*, 97:804–810.

Forsythe, Diana. 1995. Using ethnography in the design of an explanation system. *Expert Systems with Applications*, 8(4):403–417.

Law, Malcolm and Jin Tang. 1995. An analysis of the effectiveness of interventions intended to help people stop smoking. *Archives of Internal Medicine*, 155:1933–1941.

McKeown, Kathleen. 1985. *Text Generation*. Cambridge University Press.

Monahan, Jennifer. 1995. Using positive affect when designing health messages. In Edward Maibach and Roxanne Parrott, editors, *Designing Health Messages: Approaches from Communication Theory and Public Health Practice*. Sage, pages 81–98.

Prochaska, James and Carlo diClemente. 1992. *Stages of Change in the Modification of Problem Behaviors*. Sage.

Reiter, Ehud and Robert Dale. 1999. *Building Natural Language Generation Systems*. Cambridge University Press. In press.

Scott, A. Carlisle, Jan Clayton, and Elizabeth Gibson. 1991. *A Practical Guide to Knowledge Acquisition*. Addison-Wesley.

Strecher, Victor, Matthew Kreuter, Dirk-Jan Den Boer, Sarah Kobrin, Harm Hospers, and Celette Skinner. 1994. The effects of computer-tailored smoking cessation messages in family practice settings. *The Journal of Family Practice*, 39:262–271.

Velicer, Wayne, James Prochaska, Jeffrey Bellis, Carlo diClemente, Joseph Rossi, Joseph Fava, and James Steiger. 1993. An expert system intervention for smoking cessation. *Addictive Behaviors*, 18:269–290.

White, Michael and Ted Caldwell. 1998. EXEMPLARS: A practical extensible framework for dynamic text generation. In *Proceedings of the Ninth International Workshop on Natural Language Generation (INLG-1998)*, pages 266–275.

Small *Is* Beautiful — Compact Semantics for Medical Language Processing

Martin Romacker[1,2], Stefan Schulz[1,2], and Udo Hahn[1]

[1] Text Knowledge Engineering Lab, CLIF Group, Freiburg University
[2] Department of Medical Informatics, Freiburg University Hospital
http://www.coling.uni-freiburg.de/

Abstract. We introduce two abstraction mechanisms by which the process of semantic interpretation of medical documents can be simplified and optimized. One relates to the linguistic generality, the other to the inheritance-based specification of semantic rules. The proposed methodology leads to a parsimonious inventory of abstract, simple and domain-independent semantic interpretation schemata whose effectiveness has been evaluated on a medical text corpus.

1 Introduction

Medical language processing (MLP) deals with the automatic free-text analysis of discharge summaries, finding reports, etc. When MLP methodologies are combined in a system for automatic knowledge capture from these medical narratives – rather than merely for the retrieval of the source documents – the need for some form of natural language understanding arises. This usually requires parse trees resulting from syntactic analysis to be mapped to a content-oriented representation format, either a semantic or a knowledge representation language.

While some consensus has been reached in the past with respect to the proper design of grammars, parsers, and knowledge representation devices, almost no standards have emerged for the formulation of semantic interpretation rules. The lack of an adequate methodology results in an unwieldy growth of the number of rules for large-scale MLP systems. This causes many problems, because the rules' compatibility, mutual interactions, side effects, order constraints, etc. are likely to run out of control.

To avoid these problems, we introduce two abstraction mechanisms by which the process of semantic interpretation can be simplified and optimized. The first abstraction increases the linguistic generality of descriptions for semantic interpretation. The criteria we use address configurations within dependency graphs rather than hook on particular language phenomena. These configurations have a natural graph-theoretical reading in terms of minimal connected subgraphs of a syntactic dependency graph. This way, we are able to cover a variety of linguistic phenomena by few and general interpretation *schemata*. The second abstraction relates to the way how these schemata are specified. By integrating them into an *inheritance hierarchy*, we further increase descriptional economy and supply a parsimonious semantic interpretation system.

W. Horn et al. (Eds.): AIMDM'99, LNAI 1620, pp. 400–410, 1999.

2   Knowledge Sources for Semantic Interpretation

Grammatical knowledge for syntactic analysis is based on a fully lexicalized dependency grammar [7]. Lexical specifications of concrete words form the leaf nodes of a lexicon tree which are further abstracted in terms of word class specifications at different levels of generality. This leads to a word class hierarchy, which consists of word class names W = {VERB, VERBTRANS, DETERMINER, ARTICLE, ...} and a subsumption relation isa_W = {(VERBTRANS, VERB), (ARTICLE, DETERMINER), ...} $\subset W \times W$, which characterizes specialization relations between word classes.

In essence, a dependency grammar captures binary valency constraints between a syntactic head (e.g., a noun) and one of its possible modifiers (e.g., a determiner or an adjective). These include restrictions on word order, compatibility of morphosyntactic features and semantic criteria. In order to establish a dependency relation D = {*specifier, subject, dir-object, ...*} between a head and a modifier, all valency constraints must be fulfilled. Fig. 1 depicts a sample dependency graph in which word nodes are given in bold face and dependency relations are indicated by labeled edges. For example, the syntactic head *"zeigt" (shows)* governs its modifier *"Partikel"* via the *subj(ect)* dependency relation. At the parsing level, lexicalized processes, so-called *word actors*, perform corresponding constraint checking tasks.

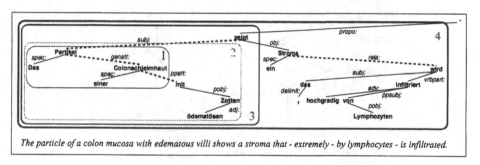

The particle of a colon mucosa with edematous villi shows a stroma that - extremely - by lymphocytes - is infiltrated.

Fig. 1. A Sample Dependency Graph

Conceptual knowledge is expressed in a KL-ONE-like terminological representation language [11]. It consists of concept names F = {SHOW, COLON-MUCOSA, ...} and a subsumption relation on concepts isa_F = {COLON-MUCOSA, DIGESTIVE-MUCOSA), (DIGESTIVE-MUCOSA, MUCOSA), ...} $\subset F \times F$. The set of conceptual relations R = {SHOW-PATIENT, HAS-ANATOMICAL-PART, ...} is also organized in a subsumption hierarchy isa_R = {(HAS-ANATOMICAL-PART, HAS-PHYSICAL-PART), (HAS-PHYSICAL-PART, HAS-PART), ...}. Associated with a specific conceptual class C (e.g., PARTICLE) may be concrete instances $C.n$, e.g., PARTICLE.1. A semantic interpretation of the dependency graph from Fig. 1 in terms of this terminological language is depicted in Fig. 2.

Conceptual linkages between instances are determined by different types of dependency relations that are established between their corresponding lexical

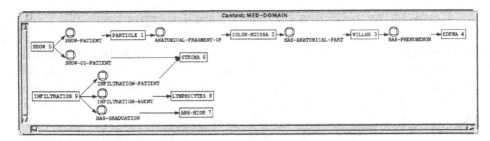

Fig. 2. The Corresponding Concept Graph

items. *Semantic interpretation rules* mediate between both levels in a way as abstract and general as possible. An illustration of how we relate grammatical and conceptual knowledge is given in Fig. 3. On the left side, at the syntactic level proper, a subset of the dependency relations contained in $\mathcal{D}$ are depicted. Those that have associated conceptual relations are shown in italics. For instance, whenever the dependency relation *dir-object* has to be tested it must conceptually be interpreted in terms of PATIENT or CO-PATIENT. *gen(itive)att(ribute)*, however, has no fixed conceptual counterpart as this dependency relation does not restrict conceptual interpretation at all.

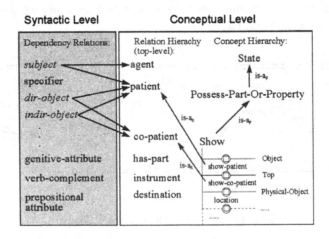

Fig. 3. Relating Grammatical and Conceptual Knowledge

At the conceptual level, two orthogonal taxonomic hierarchies exist, one for relations, the other for concepts (cf. Fig. 3, right side). Both are organized in terms of subsumption hierarchies ($isa_\mathcal{F}$ and $isa_\mathcal{R}$). Also, both hierarchies interact, since relations are used to define concepts. The concept SHOW is a subconcept of STATE. It has a role SHOW-PATIENT whose filler's type must be an OBJECT. SHOW-PATIENT itself is subsumed by the more general relation PATIENT.[1]

---

[1]   Note that with PATIENT we here refer to the general linguistic notion "somebody/something that is affected by an action or a state". This may or may not be a human patient who receives medical treatment from a doctor.

3   Methodological Framework for Semantic Interpretation

In the dependency parse tree from Fig. 1, we can distinguish lexical nodes that
have a conceptual correlate (e.g., *"Partikel"* (particle), *"zeigt"* (shows)) from
others that do not have such a correlate (e.g., *"mit"* (with), *"von"* (by)). This is
reflected in the basic configurational settings for semantic interpretation:

- **Direct Linkage:** If two lexical nodes with conceptual correlates are linked
  by a *single* edge, a *direct* linkage is given. Such a subgraph can immediately
  be interpreted in terms of a corresponding conceptual relation. This is illustrated in Fig. 1 by the direct linkage between *"Partikel"* (particle) and *"zeigt"*
  (shows) via the *subj(ect)* relation, which gets mapped to the SHOW-PATIENT
  role linking the corresponding conceptual correlates, *viz.* PARTICLE.1 and
  SHOW.5, respectively (see Fig. 2).
- **Mediated Linkage:** If two lexical nodes with conceptual correlates are
  linked by a *series* of edges and none of the intervening nodes has a conceptual correlate, a *mediated* linkage is given. This subgraph can be interpreted
  indirectly in terms of a conceptual relation using lexical information from intervening nodes. In Fig. 1 this is illustrated by the syntactic linkage between
  "Colonschleimhaut" (colon mucosa) and *"Zotten"* (villi) via the intervening
  node *"mit"* (with) and the *ppatt* and *pobj* relations, the result of which
  is a conceptual linkage between COLON-MUCOSA.2 and VILLUS.3 via the
  relation HAS-ANATOMICAL-PART in Fig. 2.

To account for both cases in the most general way and to preserve the simplicity of semantic interpretation, we introduce a unifying notion: Two content
words (nouns, adjectives, adverbs or full verbs) stand in a *mediated syntactic
relation*, if one can pass from one to the other along the connecting edges of
the dependency graph without traversing, if necessary, nodes other than prepositions, modal or auxiliary verbs. In Fig. 1, e.g., the tuples (*"Partikel"*, *"zeigt"*),
(*"Colonschleimhaut"*, *"Zotten"*), (*"infiltriert"*, *"Lymphozyten"*) stand in mediated syntactic relations, whereas, e.g., the tuple (*"Partikel"*, *"Zotten"*) does not,
since the connecting path contains *"Colonschleimhaut"*, a content word.

We then call a series of contiguous words in a sentence S that stand in a
mediated syntactic relation a *semantically interpretable subgraph* of the dependency graph of S. So, semantic interpretation will be started whenever two word
nodes with associated conceptual correlates are dependentially connected so that
they form a semantically interpretable subgraph. In some cases the dependency
structures we encounter will have no constraining effect on semantic interpretation (e.g., genitives). There are other cases (e.g., prepositions, the subject of
a verb), however, where constraints on possible interpretations can be derived
from dependency structures and the lexical material they embody.

This constraint knowledge is basically encoded at the lexical grammar level.
Consider Fig. 4, which depicts a fragment of the lexicon tree. The information
we focus on here are constraints for semantic interpretation that can already be
specified at the level of *word classes*. For instance, transitive verbs (denoted by

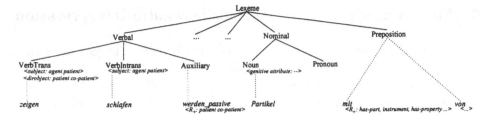

Fig. 4. Hierarchical Encoding of Constraints on Semantic Interpretation

the word class VERBTRANS) carry the constraint that the *subject* dependency relation is always mapped to the conceptual AGENT or PATIENT role (cf. also Fig. 3). As a consequence, every transitive verb, such as *zeigen (show)*, inherits this interpretation constraint. In contrast, there are also *lexical items* (all from closed word classes like prepositions, auxiliary or modal verbs), which carry specific conceptual constraints that cannot be generalized to the word class level. Rather than being bound a priori to particular dependency relations these constraints will interact with others that are associated with lexical items which are checked for establishing a dependency relation. Such constraints are illustrated for the auxiliary verb *werden (be)* in its passive reading that imports the conceptual relations PATIENT and CO-PATIENT, as well as for the preposition *mit (with)* that carries along the relations HAS-PART, etc. (cf. Section 4). Interestingly, constraints at the word class level account for direct linkage, while those at the lexical level account for indirect linkage, only.

In order to account for these varying degrees of abstraction we introduce a general *semantic interpretation schema* (1) that can be constrained on the fly by the occurrence of particular word classes or even lexemes. *si* describes a mapping from the conceptual correlates, $h.C_{from}$ and $m.C_{to}$, of the two dependentially linked lexical items, h and m, respectively, to connecting relation paths R_{con}. A relation path $rel_{con} \in R_{con}$ composed of n relations, $(r_1, ..., r_n)$, is called *connected*, if for all its n constituent relations the concept type of the domain of relation r_{i+1} subsumes the concept type of the range of relation r_i.

$$si : \begin{cases} \mathcal{F} \times 2^{\mathcal{R}} \times 2^{\mathcal{R}} \times \mathcal{F} \to 2^{R_{con}} \\ C_{from} \times R_+ \times R_- \times C_{to} \mapsto \widetilde{R_{con}} \end{cases} \tag{1}$$

As an additional filter, *si* is constrained by all conceptual relations $R_+ \subset \mathcal{R}$ a priori permitted for semantic interpretation, as well as all relations $R_- \subset \mathcal{R}$ a priori excluded from semantic interpretation (several concrete examples will be discussed below). Thus, $rel \in \widetilde{R_{con}}$ holds, if rel is a connected relation path from C_{from} to C_{to}, obeying the restrictions imposed by R_+ and R_-. For ease of specification, R_+ and R_- consist of general conceptual relations only. Prior to semantic processing, however, we expand them into their transitive closures, incorporating all their subrelations in the relation hierarchy. So we may define, $R_+^* := \{ r^* \in \mathcal{R} \mid \exists r \in R_+ : r^* \ isa_{\mathcal{R}} \ r \}$ (correspondingly, R_-^* is dealt with).

If the function *si* returns the empty set (i.e., no valid interpretation can be computed), no dependency relation will be established. Otherwise, for all resulting relations $\text{REL}_i \in \widetilde{R_{con}}$ an assertional axiom is added by the proposition $(h.C_{from} \; \text{REL}_i \; m.C_{to})$ where REL_i denotes the ith reading.

4 Sample Analyses

We will now discuss some configurations of semantically interpretable subgraphs. We start from the interpretation of direct linkage, and then turn to mediated linkage patterns by considering increasingly complex configurations in dependency graphs as given by prepositional phrases and passives in relative clauses.

Interpreting direct linkage. When the first content word in our sample sentence, *"Partikel"*, is read, its conceptual correlate PARTICLE.1 is instantiated immediately. The next content word, *"Colonschleimhaut"*, also leads to the creation of an associated instance (COLON-MUCOSA.2). The word actor for *"Colonschleimhaut"* then attempts to bind *"Partikel"* as its syntactic head via the *gen(itive)att(ribute)* relation (cf. Fig. 1, Box 1), which introduces no restrictions whatsoever on semantic interpretation. Hence, we may proceed in an entirely concept-driven way. So, we extract all conceptual roles associated with the concept definition of PARTICLE (cf. Fig. 5), *viz.* HAS-WEIGHT, HAS-PHYSICAL-DIMENSION, ANATOMICAL-FRAGMENT-OF, etc., and iteratively check for each role whether COLON-MUCOSA might be a legal role filler. This is the case for the relation ANATOMICAL-FRAGMENT-OF, since only ANATOMICAL-SOLID-STRUCTURE subsumes COLON-MUCOSA. We, therefore, assert PARTICLE.1 ANATOMICAL-FRAGMENT-OF COLON-MUCOSA.2 (cf. also Fig. 2).

Another direct linkage configuration occurs when *"zeigt"* *(shows)* attempts to govern *"Partikel"* *(particle)* via the *subj(ect)* relation (cf. Fig. 1, Box 3). Unlike *genatt*, *subj* constrains the semantic interpretation involving SHOW and PARTICLE to those conceptual relations that are subsumed by AGENT and PATIENT (cf. the hard-wired mapping from *subject* to AGENT and PATIENT in Fig. 4). From Fig. 3 it can be derived that this narrows the set of possible conceptual relations down to SHOW-PATIENT. Since PARTICLE is subsumed by OBJECT – the type restriction of SHOW-PATIENT – SHOW.5 SHOW-PATIENT PARTICLE.1 may be asserted (cf. Fig. 2). Note that the constraints for the computation of conceptual relations originate from the *dependency relation* under consideration. Hence, particular dependency relations specialize the general interpretation schema previously described. This approach is rather general as it covers diverse linguistic phenomena (e.g., subjects, (in)direct objects, genitives) by a single schema at the specification level. During run-time this schema gets instantiated by the actual content words and the particular dependency relations to be tested.

Interpreting mediated linkage. For interpreting mediated syntactic relations, lexical information supplied by the *intervening nodes* is available in terms of a list R_+ which contains high-level conceptual relations in order to constrain the semantic interpretation. This information (cf. Fig. 4) is attached to specific lexical exemplars from closed word classes (e.g., prepositions). Hence, after the specialization induced by dependency relations in the previous subsection, we here focus on specialization effected by particular *lexical items*.

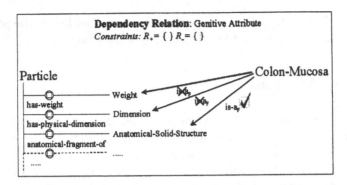

Fig. 5. Instantiation of the Genitive Schema

Consider Fig. 1, Box 2, where a semantically interpretable subgraph consisting of three word nodes, (*"Colonschleimhaut"* — *"mit"* — *"Zotten"*), occurs. In particular, the word actor for *"mit" (with)* tries to determine its syntactic head. We treat prepositions as relators supplying conceptual constraints for the corresponding instances of their syntactic head and modifier. The "meaning" of a preposition is encoded in a set $R_{Prep} \subset \mathcal{R}$, for each preposition in *Prep*, holding all permitted relations in terms of high-level conceptual relations. For the preposition *"mit"*, we have $R_{mit} = \{$HAS-PART, INSTRUMENT, HAS-PROPERTY, HAS-DEGREE, ...$\}$ (cf. also Fig. 4). When *"mit"* attempts to be governed by *"Colonschleimhaut" (colon mucosa)* the mediated linkage results in the instantiation of a specialized interpretation schema which applies exclusively to PP-attachments. The conceptual entities to be related are denoted by the leftmost and the rightmost node in the actual subgraph (i.e., *"Colonschleimhaut"* and *"Zotten" (villi)*). By extracting all conceptual roles and checking for sortal consistency (cf. Fig. 6), only HAS-ANATOMICAL-PART $isa_{\mathcal{R}}$ HAS-PART yields a valid interpretation that is sanctioned by the constraints imposed by *"mit"*, one which directly relates COLON-MUCOSA and VILLUS (cf. also Fig. 2).

To convey an idea of the generality and flexibility of our approach, consider, in Fig. 1, Box 4, the already analyzed relative clause *"das hochgradig von Lymphozyten infiltriert wird" (that is extremely infiltrated by lymphocytes)*. In particular, LYMPHOCYTES.8 figures as INFILTRATION-AGENT of INFILTRATION.9 (cf. Fig. 2). Since the *subj* valency of the passive auxiliary *"wird" (is)* is occupied by a relative pronoun (*"das" (that)*), the interpretation of this dependency structure must be postponed until the pronoun's referent becomes available.

Passive interpretation is performed by another specialization of the general interpretation schema. As with most prepositions, constraints come directly from a positive list $R_{passaux} = \{$PATIENT, CO-PATIENT$\}$ (cf. Fig. 4, the constraints attached to $werden_{passive}$). The items to be related (cf. Fig. 1, Box 4) are contained in the semantically interpretable subgraph spanned by *"das" (that)* and *"infiltriert" (infiltrated)*. The referent of the relative pronoun *"das"* becomes available once the syntactic head of the relative clause (*"wird"*) has determined its head. Choosing among the two alternatives, *"Partikel" (particle)* and *"Stroma"*, the

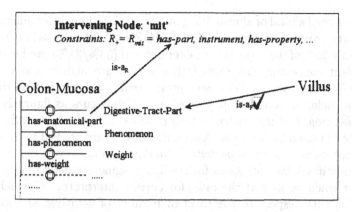

Fig. 6. Instantiation of the PP-Attachment Schema

appropriate one, the missing argument for the semantic interpretation of the passive is fixed. The choice of *"Stroma"* leads to the instantiation of the specialized passive interpretation schema. This schema inverses the argument structure, i.e., inserts STROMA as a role filler of INFILTRATION by bringing the role restrictions, PATIENT or CO-PATIENT, into play. The final interpretation is depicted in Fig. 2. Obviously, integrating intra- and extra-sentential anaphorical phenomena [6] necessitates a slight extension of our notion of a semantically interpretable subgraph. In case pronouns are involved, such a subgraph is interpretable *iff* all referents are made available.[2]

The semantic interpretation schemata we supply currently cover declaratives, relatives, and passives at the clause level, complement subcategorization via prepositional phrases, auxiliaries, tenses at the verb phrase level, pre- and postnominal modifiers at the noun phrase level, and anaphoric expressions. We currently do not deal with control verbs, coordination and quantification.

5   Evaluation

We deviate from the tradition that sample analyses are considered sufficient to motivate a particular approach to semantic interpretation (for a notable exception, cf. [2]) and report on the empirical assessment of our methodology.

The ontology we used in our experiments consists of more than 3,000 concepts and relations. Also, the concepts had to be linked to associated lexemes in the lexicon. We took a random selection of 29 finding reports (comprising 4,300 words) from the clinical information system at the Freiburg University Hospital. For evaluation purposes we concentrated on the interpretation of genitives (direct linkage), PP-attachments and auxiliary as well as modal verbs (both variants of mediated linkage). In the following, we will focus on the discussion of the results from the semantic interpretation of genitives and auxiliary constructions.

---

[2]   There is an ambiguity at this stage of analysis, because PARTICLE.1 can be related to INFILTRATION.9, too. We just mention that heuristics are applied to select the most plausible reading based on preferential criteria [9].

We considered a total of almost 100 genitives (GEN) and 60 auxiliaries (AUX) in these texts, from which about 67%/69% (GEN/AUX) received an interpretation. Roughly 20% of the total loss we encountered (33%/31%) can be attributed to insufficient conceptual coverage. Other misses are mainly due to domain-external references such as *"rice-corn-grain-sized"*, which refers to the size of a biopsy particle, as well as sloppy wording which occurs as figurative speech, e.g., in *"the biopsy of the gastric mucosa shows ..."*, which actually refers to the particle obtained by a biopsy. Also notoriously hard to deal with are overly generic concepts as *"a form of gastritis"*. No doubt, whatsoever, that conceptual coverage constitutes *the* bottleneck for medical language understanding. This becomes clear when we look at the rates for correct interpretation, which amount to 64%/66% with respect to the total of number of genitives and auxiliaries, respectively, but appear in a different light, both 95%, when the accuracy of semantic interpretation is measured, given sufficient domain knowledge.

6 Related Work

In MLP, there exist basically two approaches to semantic interpretation. The first one either encodes the regularities how lexical items may combine syntactically and semantically in a *single* set of rules, thereby adhering to concepts from semantic grammars [5], or combine semantic and syntactic criteria in a *major subset* of rules [10]. However, the tight coupling of syntax with semantic constraints at the grammar level leads to a proliferating number of rules, since structurally equivalent syntactic patterns may encode a multitude of semantic interpretations. Also, portability to other (sub)domains is impeded, as for new (high-level) conceptual categories entirely new rules must be defined. Finally, these kinds of rules mix in an indistinguishable way grammar knowledge and ontological knowledge of the medical domain in a single representational format.

Within the second approach, conceptual knowledge is encapsulated at an independent layer of MLP systems. During analysis, inferences are made as to whether certain lexical items can combine according to the underlying domain model. Baud *et al.* [1] cluster complex nominal groups on the basis of concept descriptions available from the GRAIL domain model in a semantics-first strategy, but still use many "semantic compatibility rules". The results are represented at an intermediate layer, whereas our system directly operates on conceptual structures. The most advanced work related to a modularized semantic interpretation in MLP by Ceusters *et al.* [3], however, has still several limitations compared to our approach. It is restricted to the analysis of complex noun phrases, and focuses exclusively on a concept-driven coupling of syntactic and conceptual knowledge.

Abstraction mechanisms for the specification of semantic rules were first introduced by Charniak and Goldman [4] and Jacobs [8]. We differ, however, in that we specify semantic interpretation *schemata* rather than *rules* based on the notion of configurations. Jacobs [8] even ties syntactic role specifications completely into conceptual ones and, so, mixes knowledge levels.

7 Conclusions

We proposed a principled approach to the design of compact, yet highly expressive semantic interpretation schemata. They derive their power from two sources. First, the organization of grammar and domain knowledge, as well as semantic interpretation mechanisms, are based on inheritance principles. Second, interpretation schemata abstract from particular linguistic phenomena in terms of general configuration patterns in dependency graphs.

Underlying these design decisions is a strict separation of linguistic from conceptual knowledge. A clearly defined interface is provided which allows these specifications to make reference to fine-grained hierarchical knowledge, no matter whether it is of linguistic or conceptual origin.

It should be clearly noted, however, that the power of this approach is, to a large degree, dependent on the fine granularity of the knowledge sources we incorporate, the domain knowledge base, in particular. Given such an environment, the formulation of the regularities at the semantic description level can be kept fairly general. Also since the number of schemata at the semantic description layer remains rather small, their execution is easy to trace and thus supports the maintenance of large-scale natural language understanding systems.

Acknowledgements. We would like to thank our colleagues in the CLIF group, especially Katja Markert, and the Department of Medical Informatics for fruitful discussions. M. Romacker and St. Schulz are supported by a grant from DFG (Ha 2097/5-1).

References

[1] R. H. Baud, A. M. Rassinoux, J. C. Wagner, C. Lovis, C. Juge, L. L. Alpay, P. A. Michel, P. Degoulet, and J.-R. Scherrer. Representing clinical narratives by using conceptual graphs. *Methods of Information in Medicine*, 34(1/2):176–186, 1995.

[2] C. Bean, T. Rindflesch, and C. Sneiderman. Automatic semantic interpretation of anatomic spatial relationships in clinical text. In *AMIA'98 – Proceedings of the 1998 AMIA Annual Fall Symposium*, pages 897–901. Hanley & Belfus, 1998.

[3] W. Ceusters, P. Spyns, and G. De Moor. From natural language to formal language: when MULTITALE meets GALEN. In *MIE'97 – Proceedings of Medical Informatics Europe 97*, pages 396–400. IOS Press, 1997.

[4] E. Charniak and R. Goldman. A logic for semantic interpretation. In *Proceedings 26th Meeting of the Association for Computational Linguistics*, pages 87–94, 1988.

[5] C. Friedman, P. Alderson, J. Austin, J. Cimino, and S. Johnson. A general natural-language text processor for clinical radiology. *Journal of the American Medical Informatics Association*, 1(2):161–174, 1994.

[6] U. Hahn, M. Romacker, and St. Schulz. Discourse structures in medical reports - watch out! The generation of referentially coherent and valid text knowledge bases in the MEDSYNDIKATE system. *International Journal of Medical Informatics*, 53(1):1–28, 1999.

[7] U. Hahn, S. Schacht, and N. Bröker. Concurrent, object-oriented natural language parsing: the PARSETALK model. *International Journal of Human-Computer Studies*, 41(1/2):179–222, 1994.

[8] P. Jacobs. Integrating language and meaning in structured inheritance networks. In J. Sowa, editor, *Principles of Semantic Networks. Explorations in the Representation of Knowledge*, pages 527–542. Morgan Kaufmann, 1991.

[9] K. Markert and U. Hahn. On the interaction of metonymies and anaphora. In *IJCAI'97 – Proceedings of the 15th International Joint Conference on Artificial Intelligence*, pages 1010–1015. Morgan Kaufmann, 1997.

[10] N. Sager, M. Lyman, N. T. Nhan, and L. J. Tick. Medical language processing: applications to patient data representation and automatic encoding. *Methods of Information in Medicine*, 34(1):140–146, 1995.

[11] W. Woods and J. Schmolze. The KL-ONE family. *Computers & Mathematics with Applications*, 23(2/5):133–177, 1992.

Speech Driven Natural Language Understanding for Hands-Busy Recording of Clinical Information

D.J. Barker[1], S.C. Lynch[1], D.S. Simpson[1], W.A. Corbett[2]

[1] School of Computing and Mathematics, University of Teesside, Middlesbrough,
Cleveland, TS1 3BA, United Kingdom
d.j.barker@tees.ac.uk
[2] Endoscopy Center, South Cleveland Hospital, Middlesbrough,
Cleveland, United Kingdom

Abstract. The hands-busy nature of many clinical examinations means that keyboard and mouse driven interface paradigms are unable to capture medical information at source. The impact of compromised data integrity when using such systems and their inability to serve the needs of clinicians in an endoscopic context is examined. A speech driven application has been developed to serve the clinical process of endoscopy and record data at source. The system exploits the power of a natural narrative to capture and generate consistent visual and textual clinical information.

1 The Problem Domain

The capture of medical information using keyboard and mouse driven interface paradigms by clinicians at the Gastrointestinal Unit (GIU) at South Cleveland Hospital has failed to gain acceptance. Immediately after a patient encounter a paper form is used to document observations made during an endoscopy. Clinicians may also draw a pictorial representation of their findings to provide important spatial information about a given observation or procedure, within the context of the whole Gastrointestinal (GI) anatomy being examined. As well as providing a clinician with information for selecting the most effective treatment and investigation plan, data recorded plays an essential role in the care process itself through clinical audit[1]. The information recorded on the paper form is transferred to a relational database held within the department to aid this process. However, the task of transferring data is not undertaken by the clinician performing the endoscopy, but by data entry personnel. The delay between the original endoscopic examination and the transfer process may be many months and a diverse set of clinical terms presented on the paper form must be mapped to a limited set of terms available on the computer system. A limited knowledge of the clinical domain when transferring information must always raise questions about the integrity of any data stored and can only serve to undermine the quality and cost of patient healthcare. Grasso[2] observes that end users are likely to abandon an application if it does not improve or possibly interferes with their work and this is a view supported by clinicians from the department. Although they accept the value of recording data onto the computerized system, they

W. Horn et al. (Eds.): AIMDM'99, LNAI 1620, pp. 411-415, 1999.
© Springer-Verlag Berlin Heidelberg 1999

feel that the keyboard driven text based application is difficult to learn and difficult to use. Tange[3] suggests that clinicians are far more positive about the quality of the paper based record. Although clinicians acknowledge the inherent problems with manual systems, they do provide a mechanism for the representation and communication of medical information that is not always available with electronic systems. This is certainly true with the current GIU system. Clinicians cannot express information in a visual way, nor does it allow them to use their own preferred clinical terms.

Attempts have been made by the department to introduce more modern technologies in an effort to address the problems associated with transferring clinical information from a paper record to the electronic system. Endoscopic Reporting Interface for Clinical Audit (ERICA) was one such project, using a purely mouse driven GUI with pre-defined graphical representations to record endoscopic findings[4]. Textual information was extracted from the graphical representation and stored in the department's database. Using pre-defined graphical images provided a more consistent visual and textual description of observations made, but the system was not adopted by clinicians. The application had freed clinicians from the limitations of a text based system and the change in interface metaphor had provided additional clinical functionality required by clinicians. However, the increased flexibility of the application had brought a complexity that was a product of the interface paradigm itself. Like the text based system it tried to replace, the application was thought difficult to learn and difficult to use.

The interval of time between a clinician making an observation and actually recording it can also compromise the integrity of data documented. A video camera was used to record a number of endoscopy sessions, which included both upper and lower GI examinations. During filming, clinicians were asked to provide a narrative of any observations made or procedures carried out. Some examinations may only last ten minutes, but even within this small time frame, important information communicated through the narrative was often failing to appear on the paper form. For example, multiple biopsies had been taken during one endoscopic encounter but had not been recorded. Distance measurements, used to express important positional information about a finding or key endoscopic landmarks, were forgotten. Clinicians sometimes requested assistance from nursing staff to confirm measurements after the examination, as they had become unsure of their original observation. Even if the ERICA system had been adopted by clinicians, it is clear that a keyboard or mouse driven GUI would be unable to record clinical information at source, within the constraints imposed by the hands-busy nature of an endoscopic examination.

If a patient has been referred by a General Practitioner (GP), an interim or full discharge summary is dictated after the examination for later transcription by a medical secretary. The completed letter is then referred back to the clinician to review and sign, before being sent out to the GP. A number of GPs from the Cleveland area were interviewed and expressed dissatisfaction with the timeliness of discharge summaries. Delays in the transmission of such letters have been previously acknowledged[5] and many of the GPs interviewed would ideally like to see an interim discharge within forty eight hours and a full discharge within seven days. Limited resources and the dictate-transcribe bottleneck means that many interim and final discharge letters are taking up to two and a half and three to four weeks respectively. In the worst instance, some letters do not arrive at all.

Berghgraeve[6] defines three primary characteristics of general practice: accessibility of care; continuity of care; comprehensiveness of care. Continuity of care includes keeping good medical records. Discharge summaries that never arrive cannot provide continuity of care. Comprehensive care can only exist if the whole human being is considered and not just the physical patient. GPs are acutely aware of the significant distress that many patients experience when waiting for examination results. Asking patients to make another appointment because letters have not arrived undermines the GPs ability to provide comprehensive care and in extreme cases may actually damage the GP-patient relationship.

The problems identified at South Cleveland GIU are not unique. Berwick[7] says that every system is perfectly designed to achieve the results it achieves. His central law of improvement re-frames performance from a matter of effort to a matter of design and stresses the need for a change of a system, not change in a system. Apart from the patient, the only other source of information available is contained in the Patients Medical Record (PMR). The integrity and availability of information contained within the PMR is central to the delivery of efficient and effective clinical care. Change of a system requires modern applications to capture data at source. The acceptance of an application will be defined by its ability to meet the clinical needs of the user and also provide a transparent interface through which the clinical domain is viewed. It is only then that a clinician in a secondary healthcare environment can deliver a quality service to the primary healthcare market.

2   Change of a System

During the filming of endoscopic examinations, it was seen that observational and procedural narratives were a natural way for clinicians to communicate clinical information. The language used does not exhibit the same complexity as a language used for general endoscopy. Complex verb tenses are rarely used and ambiguity seldom occurs at the sentence level. Consider the following observational narrative for an endoscopic finding: *there is a 6 centimetre gastric ulcer located at 10 centimetres from the cardio oesophageal junction. It is benign and positioned on the anterial wall close to the greater curve.* The narrative provides a rich set of information about an ulcer. It communicates three dimensional spatial information using both textual descriptors and relative numeric locators. It describes the finding type and its size. For a clinician, the utterance represents an observation in a simple, clear and unambiguous way. However, the inability of the current system to record information at source can pollute the purity of such an observation.

The Clinical Support Systems Research Group at the University of Teesside, together with clinicians from South Cleveland GIU, have developed a prototype speech driven language understanding interface for the recording of information obtained during an endoscopic examination. The system will accept natural spoken input from a clinician and immediately capture the data at source, preserving the integrity of the information contained within the narrative. Preferred clinical terms are automatically mapped onto a set of agreed endoscopic terms. A pictorial representation of the narrative is generated in real time, showing the observation within the context of the whole GI anatomy being examined. The information recorded by the system is both visually and textually consistent.

The application communicates meaningful clinical information using both speech and text output. For example, by confirming a finding and giving a preliminary diagnosis. More complex verbal interactions can exist between the system and the user. For example, a clinician can obtain additional details on a particular system response by asking for an explanation. Communication and interaction with the system supports the clinical process. It is a working tool and not merely an application front end to a relational database. Observations made or procedures undertaken are immediately available at the end of the examination for review. A discharge summary can be generated automatically and signed.

2.1 Implementation Overview

The speech recognition module used is derived from an inexpensive propriety package. Its accuracy is improved considerably by providing a word-usage model obtained from the grammar and lexicon used by the language processor. The output of the speech module is processed by the language processor using a small lexicon and domain-specific or semantic grammar. The grammar rules are expressed in the style of a Definitive Clause Grammar (DCG) which specify rules of semantic transformation as well as syntax. The rules are built around domain specific phrase types rather than typical abstract categories. It had been observed during filming that the narratives used during an examination were closed and well specified, even in the context of a general clinical language used in endoscopy. The inability of a system to exploit this type of language will miss the opportunity to effect positive change in the quality and cost of patient healthcare. By ignoring complex issues of language analysis which do not exist in the target domain, it is possible to construct a spoken language interface within a short period of time.

Knowledge representation is achieved in two distinct ways. Domain item knowledge is structured into a slot-filler notation termed item frames. An individual item frame refers to a specific type of endoscopic object. Domain anatomy knowledge is structured into a hierarchical model of anatomical features. The hierarchical model allows the physical characteristics of features and their spatial relationships to change when anatomical deformations have been observed. Changes in spatial relationships caused by anatomical deformations can distort slot values for item frames. For example, a hiatus hernia is an anatomical deformation which describes the movement of the stomach up into the thoracic cavity. As the size of the hiatus hernia increases, more of the stomach will move into the chest. The legality of the observation *gastric ulcer at 20 centimeters from the diaphragm* will depend on the amount of anatomical deformation that has actually taken place.

The two styles of knowledge representation reflect the different ways in which a clinician may describe the medical domain. For example, a purely textual description can be used to describe an endoscopic object. Many of the elements contained within the description map directly onto slot-filler values contained within an item frame. However, a clinician will often use pictorial representations to depict anatomical features and indicate their spatial relationships for a domain anatomy. These visual representations can be mapped directly onto the hierarchical model.

3   Results

Implementation of the prototype system has now been completed. An informal evaluation using a small but complete set of gastrointestinal findings has shown that the system can: record clinical information at source using a natural spoken input; accept preferred clinical terms and map them onto agreed endoscopic terms; generate a visual representation of observations made in real time; record and generate consistent clinical information; provide meaningful communication and interactions to support the examination process. The confidence expressed by clinicians over the prototype system has been acknowledged with their commitment to actively support the additional acquisition process and a full operational trial has been planned for April 1999.

4 Conclusions

The hands-busy nature of endoscopic examinations means that keyboard and mouse driven applications are unable to record clinical information at source. These paradigms have failed to support the needs of clinicians during endoscopy because they are considered difficult to use and difficult to learn. Processing data after a patient encounter compromises the integrity of clinical information in secondary healthcare and undermines the ability to provide a quality service to the primary healthcare market. The development of a speech driven application to support endoscopy has shown that clinical information can be recorded at source and preserve data integrity. It provides a transparent interface to the clinical domain by allowing users to use a natural narrative, making it easy to use and easy to learn.

References

1. Bakker, AR.: Presentation of electronic patient data and medical audit. Int J Biomed Comput. 35 (1994) 65-69
2. Grasso, MA., Ebert, D., Finin, T.: Acceptance of a speech interface for biomedical data collection. Proc AMIA Annu Fall Symp (1997) 739-743
3. Tange, HJ.: The paper-based patient record: is it really so bad? Comput Methods Programs Biomed. 48 (1995) 127-131
4. Barker, D. et al. A graphical endoscopy reporting program in a client server environment. Current Developments in Medical Computing. June (1995)
5. Westerman, RF. et al.: A study of communication between general practice and specialist. Br J Gen Pract. 40 (1990) 445-449
6. Burghgraeve, P., De Maeseneer, J.: Improved methods for assessing information technology in primary healthcare and an example in telemedicine. J Telemed Telecare. 1 (1995) 157-164
7. Berwick, D.: A primer leading to the improvement of a system. BMJ. 9 (1996) 619-622

Automatic Acquisition of Morphological Knowledge for Medical Language Processing

Pierre Zweigenbaum and Natalia Grabar

Service d'Informatique Médicale, AP–HP &
Département de Biomathématiques, Université Paris 6, Paris, France
{pz,ngr}@biomath.jussieu.fr, http://www.biomath.jussieu.fr/

Abstract. Medical words exhibit a rich and productive morphology. Morphological knowledge is therefore very important for any medical language processing application. We propose a simple and powerful method to acquire automatically such knowledge. It takes advantage of commonly available lists of synonym terms to bootstrap the acquisition process. We experimented it on the SNOMED International Microglossary for pathology in its French version. The families of morphologically related words that we obtained were useful for query expansion in a coding assistant. Since the method does not rely on a priori linguistic knowledge, it is applicable to other languages such as English.
Keywords. Natural language processing, knowledge acquisition, acquisition of linguistic knowledge for information retrieval.

1 Introduction

Medical words exhibit a rich and productive morphology. The decomposition of a word into its component *morphemes* is useful to get at its elementary meaning units. This is a key to more relevant and more principled semantic processing of medical utterances. In an even simpler way, this allows finer-grained indexing of medical texts and terms, and potentially better accuracy for information retrieval and coding assistants [1].

Medical morphology has been studied by many researchers for several different languages [1,2,3,4,5,6]. Most of this work relies on labour-intensive coding of morphological knowledge for specific languages, although some tools have been used in some instances to help collect data or organize knowledge [4,6]. We propose a simple, automatic method to help acquire such knowledge. It bootstraps the acquisition process on synonym terms found in medical terminologies, and expands it on attested word forms found in a large reference list of medical words. These two constraints result in a very low level of noise.

For this experiment, we used the French Microglossary for Pathology [7] of SNOMED International as a source of synonym terms (table 1a). It includes 12,555 terms for 9098 different concepts, among which 2344 have synonyms, totalling 5801 terms. Our second sample of language data is a reference list of word forms. We worked with the words in the 10797 main terms of the French ICD-10, to which we added words found in the French Microglossary for Pathology. The resulting word list contains 7490 distinct word forms.

W. Horn et al. (Eds.): AIMDM'99, LNAI 1620, pp. 416–420, 1999.

2   Methods

We consider as *morphologically related* a pair of words that are derived from a common root and, therefore, share a more or less large part of their meanings. A pair of such words quasi-universally share a common set of characters. In many languages, including French and English, this set of characters is most often a string of contiguous characters, *e.g.*, **symbio** in the pair *"symbiosis"* / *"symbiotic"* (this is not generally true, for instance, of semitic languages). Very often too, this string is found at the beginning of each word, as in the above example. A simple way to find a clue that two words are potentially morphologically related is to examine their longest common prefix. If this prefix is "large enough", they might belong to the same morphological paradigm.

Such a simple approach might however lead to much noise. Consider for instance the pair of words *"administrative"* / *"admission"*, found in our word list. Although they share a four-character prefix, they are not morphologically related: they are not obtained by morphological rules operating from a common root. Even with a higher threshold on the minimal length of the longest common prefix, one still finds word pairs such as *"antidiabetic"* / *"antidiarrhea"* (common prefix length = 7) which are not derived from a common root.

2.1   Bootstrapping: Inducing Derivation Rules in a Selected Context

The idea put forth in this paper is to apply this simple approach *in a very specific, favourable context*, that focusses the comparison of word pairs on words which have a high chance of sharing some meaning. We found such a favourable situation in pairs of synonymous terms, as are included in medical vocabularies such as SNOMED. Examples such as those in table 1a show that in the restricted context of pairs of synonymous terms, morphologically related word pairs can be found: *e.g.*, *"symbiosis"* / *"symbiotic"*. Since most of the terms are multi-word expressions, potentially related words must be aligned by comparing their longest common prefix. We set experimentally the threshold on minimal common prefix length to 3, *i.e.*, two words are considered related in this context iff they share at least their first three letters. The advantage of working with pairs of synonymous terms is that given this alignment procedure, there is very little risk of finding morphologically similar but semantically unrelated word pairs. Word pairs organised around the same prefix are joined into morphological families, for instance *"cardiaque"* / *"cardio"* / *"cardiomégalie"* / *"cardiopathie"* / *"cardite"*.

The word pairs identified as morphologically related are instances of potentially *more general derivation rules* akin to those described in [4]. We therefore hypothesize the existence of these rules, and register each of them. Since we do not work here on syntactic categories, we adopt an even simpler notation than [4] for these rules. A morphological rule consists of a pair of suffixes, such as *"sis/tic"*. It allows to transform a word ending in *"-sis"* into another word where the suffix *"-sis"* has been replaced with the suffix *"-tic"* (*e.g.*, from *"stenosis"* to *"stenotic"*).

2.2   Expanding the Morphological Families with Attested Word Forms

The next step of the procedure attempts to apply these rules to an additional language sample to identify more related words. However, there is a high risk that many of the resulting word forms simply do not exist in the language studied. This is all the more expectable as some of the rules have one empty suffix. For instance, the rule "/al", which relates inter alia "ombilic" to "ombilical", can add the suffix "-al" to any word form. Therefore, it is important here again to constrain the application of this simple method. Our rationale is to *relate attested word forms*. We accept a derivation produced by our rules on the reference list when the derived word is also found in this list. For instance, the rule "/al" only succeeded on three word pairs in our reference list: "médiastin" / "médiastinal", "vagin" / "vaginal", and "ombilic" / "ombilical".

The new word pairs discovered in this second step are added to the initial families collected in the first step, resulting in extended morphological families. For instance, the initial family "**alvéolaire**" / "**alvéolaires**" gets expanded and refined into "**alvéol**aire" / "**alvéol**aires" / "**alvéole**". Families that share a common word form are joined.

3   Results

We implemented this method using perl programs, sed and awk scripts and Unix sort. The resulting figures for the experiment on the French Microglossary and ICD-10 are listed in table 1b. We performed a manual review of the morphological rules. It may be useful to make a difference between the rules that preserve meaning, possibly allowing only slight variations (inflection rules and a part of derivation rules) and the rules that modify meaning, generally by adding some information (other derivation rules and compounding rules). 1029 morphological families produced (79 %) contain words that were only related by the first kind of rules. 212 (16 %) include words related through the second kind of rules, possibly in combination with rules of the first type.

The remaining 63 families (5 %) each contain at least one pair of words that we think should not have been related. A few cases are clear errors. For instance, "chrome" / "chronique" is produced by rule "me/nique" induced from the aligned forms "polyembryome" / "polyembryonique". The other cases concern words that are actually based on different roots and only share a *prefix*. For instance, "auto-" in "**auto**greffe" / "**auto**logue" / "**auto**plastique".

The above morphological families have been used to enhance the matching capabilities of a simple, information-retrieval type, prototype coding assistant of the kind described in [8]. The schematic usage scenario of this assistant is the following. The user types in an expression, and the system presents ICD-10 codes whose terms contain the largest number of words present in the expression. With the addition of the above-acquired morphological families, used in a query expansion step, the user can use words or word forms that are not present in

Table 1. Input language data and output morphological knowledge.

a. Preferred and synonym SNOMED terms. b. Morphological knowledge acquired.

Code	Class	French term	English term
F-00470	01	symbiose	symbiosis
F-00470	02	commensalisme	commensalism
F-00470	05	symbiotique	symbiotic
F-00470	05	commensal	commensal
T-51100	01	palais, SAI	palate, NOS
T-51110	02	voûte palatine	roof of mouth
T-51110	05	–	palatal

Knowledge elements	Number
Morphological rules	566
Initial families	755
Words per family	3.39
Families after expansion	1304
Words per family	3.67

the relevant terms (for instance, *"aortic stenosis"* in place of *"stenosis of the aorta"*). We collected 220 different queries typed in by various users presented with the prototype, and used them as a test set: query expansion increased recall by 12 % and decreased precision by 2.5 %.

4   Discussion and Perspectives

This method relies on very little a priori linguistic knowledge. The only hypotheses made are that (*i*) a segmentation of a word into base + suffix is relevant; (*ii*) setting a minimum length for a base sufficiently reduces noise while not bringing much silence (the 3-character threshold was set and can be changed); and (*iii*) empty bases should be avoided in the expansion step. These hypotheses are probably as true of many other languages as they are of French.

The evaluation of noise depends to a large extent on the task in which the acquired knowledge will be used. If a fairly strict semantic equivalence is necessary, one should be able to separate out the grammatical suffixes from the semantic suffixes, which our method currently does not cater for. Distinguishing part of the semantic suffixes might be possible, *e.g.*, by trying to identify known words used as suffixes. If on the contrary semantic proximity is sufficient, as may be the case for information retrieval, then our method, with 95 % accurate families, provides a directly usable resource.

The simple segmentation of words into base and suffix limits the kinds of morphological rules that can be identified. First, only suffixes are looked for, whereas prefixes should be relevant too. Second, a more complex morphological alternation such as *"détruire"* / *"destruction"* cannot be found, since it would involve a one-character length base. Finally, combined prefix and suffix variation (*e.g.*, *"strangulation"* / *"étranglement"*) cannot be coped with since we only deal with one decomposition into base + affix. More elaborate morphological models [9] could help overcome a large part of these limitations.

Our bootstrapping step relies here on sets of synonymous terms found in the SNOMED Microglossary for Pathology. Other sets of synonyms are available in other medical vocabularies and in other languages. In similar work on English

420 P. Zweigenbaum and N. Grabar

[10], we showed that this method could find 92 % of the inflected forms and 79 % of the derived forms generated by the UMLS lvg tool in the same conditions.

Other sources of constraining contexts may be found elsewhere to bootstrap the method, for instance in corpora instead of thesauri [11], and by matching thesaurus terms to variant corpus occurrences [12]. Besides, once morphologically related pairs are found, more elaborate rules could be learnt based on more sophisticated morphological models [13].

5 Acknowledgements

We wish to thank Dr. RA Côté for graciously providing us a pre-commercial copy of the French version of the SNOMED Microglossary for Pathology.

References

1. Wingert, F., Rothwell, David, Côté, Roger A. Automated indexing into SNOMED and ICD. In: Scherrer, Jean Raoul, Côté, Roger A., Mandil, Salah H., eds, *Computerised Natural Medical Language Processing for Knowledge Engineering*. North-Holland, Amsterdam, 1989: 201–39.
2. Pacak, M. G., Norton, L. M., Dunham, G. S. Morphosemantic analysis of -ITIS forms in medical language. *Methods Inf Med* 1980; 19: 99–105.
3. Dujols, Pierre, Aubas, Pierre, Baylon, Christian, Grémy, François. Morphosemantic analysis and translation of medical compound terms. *Methods Inf Med* 1991; 30: 30–5.
4. McCray, Alexa T., Srinivasan, S., Browne, A. C. Lexical methods for managing variation in biomedical terminologies. In: Proc Eighteenth Annu Symp Comput Appl Med Care, Washington. Mc Graw Hill, 1994: 235–9.
5. Spyns, Peter. A robust category guesser for Dutch medical language. In: Proceedings of ANLP 94 (ACL), 1994: 150–5.
6. Lovis, Christian, Baud, Robert, Rassinoux, Anne-Marie, Michel, Pierre-André, Scherrer, Jean-Raoul. Medical dictionaries for patient encoding systems: a methodology. *Artif Intell Med* 1998; 14: 201–14.
7. Côté, Roger A. Répertoire d'anatomopathologie de la SNOMED internationale, v3.4. Université de Sherbrooke, Sherbrooke, Québec, 1996.
8. Lovis, Christian, Baud, Robert, Michel, Pierre-André, Scherrer, Jean-Raoul. A semi-automatic ICD encoder. *J Am Med Inform Assoc* 1996; 3(suppl): 937–.
9. Koskenniemi, Kimmo. *Two-level morphology: a general computational model for word-form recognition and production*. PhD thesis, University of Helsinki Department of General Linguistics, Helsinki, 1983.
10. Grabar, Natalia, Zweigenbaum, Pierre. Language-independent automatic acquisition of morphological knowledge from synonym pairs. TR 99-211, DIAM - SIM/AP-HP, 1999. Submitted to AMIA'99 Fall Symposium.
11. Xu, Jinxi, Croft, Bruce W. Corpus-based stemming using co-occurrence of word variants. *ACM Transactions on Information Systems* 1998; 16(1): 61–81.
12. Jacquemin, Christian. Guessing morphology from terms and corpora. In: Actes, 20th Annual International ACM SIGIR Conference on Research and Development in Information Retrieval (SIGIR'97), Philadelphia, PA. 1997: 156–67.
13. Theron, Pieter, Cloete, Ian. Automatic acquisition of two-level morphological rules. In: ANLP97, Washington, DC. 1997: 103–10.

Image Processing and
Computer Aided Design

A Multi-agent System for MRI Brain Segmentation

Laurence Germond[1], Michel Dojat[2], Chris Taylor[3], and Catherine Garbay[1]

[1] Laboratoire TIMC-IMAG, Institut A. Bonniot
Faculté de Médecine, 38706 La Tronche, France
Laurence.Germond@imag.fr,
[2] INSERM U438 "RMN" Bioclinique, CHU de Grenoble,France
[3] Department of Medical Biophysics, University of Manchester (UK)

Abstract. In this paper we present an original approach for the segmentation of MRI brain images which is based on a cooperation between low-level and high-level approches.

MRI brain images are very difficult to segment mainly due to the presence of inhomogeneities within tissues and also due to the high anatomical variability of the brain topology between individuals.

In order to tackle these difficulties, we have developped a method whose characteristics are : (i) the use of **a priori knowledge** essentially anatomical and model-based ; (ii) a **multi-agent system** (MAS) for low-level region segmentation ; (iii) a **cooperation** between *a priori* knowledge and low-level segmentation to guide and constrain the segmentation processes. These characteristics allow to produce an automatic detection of the main tissues of the brain. The method is validated with phantoms and real images through comparisons with another widely used approach (SPM).

1 Introduction

The development of modern magnetic resonance imaging (MRI) has been driven by the necessity of providing radiologists with high contrast and noise free images. Such a technique provides a powerful tool for brain structures visualisation and diagnosis.

Currently, a major issue for the development of several neurological applications of MRI (quantitative analysis, surgical operation planning or functionnal mapping) is the elaboration of specialised image processing techniques, and more specifically automatic segmentation techniques. Segmentation is particularly difficult due to low-contrasts between tissues, which even renders their manual delineation difficult, and also to high topologic variations of the structures amongst individuals. As a consequence, the main requirements for a segmentation system are the following. The system should be : (i) as automatic as possible to avoid errors due to user interaction, (ii) adaptable to intensity variations essentially due to magnetic field inhomogeneities and (iii) able to cope with shape and topology variations of the brain structures.

W. Horn et al. (Eds.): AIMDM'99, LNAI 1620, pp. 423–432, 1999.

In this paper, we present a method to cope with the previous requirements and based on :
- the use of **a priori knowledge** essentially anatomical and model-based.
- a **multi-agent system** (MAS) for low-level region segmentation. Each agent is locally specialised to provide runtime adaptativity to local intensity variations.
- a **cooperation** between *a priori* knowledge and low-level segmentation to guide and constrain the segmentation process.

The method is validated through comparisons with SPM, a largely used tool for brain MRI analysis. The validation involves phantoms, i.e synthetic images of the brain and real images.

We present a short review of the previous work on brain segmentation (Section 2), the method proposed (Section 3), the implemented system (Section 4). We present results on phantoms and on real data (Section 5). Finally (Section 6), we discuss our approach.

2   Previous Work

Segmentation consists in classifying pixels in different classes corresponding to different tissues. The approaches proposed to this end can be classified under different viewpoints depending whether the goal is region or edge detection and whether the method is purely data-driven or guided by high-level knowledge.

As regards region segmentation, one main difficulty is to isolate the brain from the other components (muscles, skull,...). It has been solved in [1] and [2] by performing a bayesian classification of the tissues followed by techniques of erosion/dilation. These approaches are only based on pixels intensities (low-level information).

To drive the segmentation process, high-level information can be used. For instance, it is known that gray-matter forms a ribbon of nearly constant width surrounding white-matter. Based on this anatomical knowledge, gray-matter is automatically segmented as a layer of 2 pixels around previously segmented white-matter [3]. However, intensity of pixels are not taken into account in addition to this fixed anatomical knowledge.

A priori knowledge on tissue localisation is used in [4] by mapping a reference brain onto the image to segment. This assumes that it is possible to find a deformation map between the brain to be segmented and the reference.

As regards edge detection, an approach is proposed in [5] to extract the boundary of gray-matter in the images, based on the definition of thresholds to isolate gray-matter (GM) from white-matter (WM) and cerebro-spinal fluid (CSF). However, the thresholds are manually introducing non-reproductibility into the method.

A model of ribbon (high-level information) is proposed in [6] for mapping the cortex. The difficulty of using an energy minimizing approach for the cortex search is the existence of deep convolutions at the brain surface. Indeed, minimizing energy is more adapted to the detection of smooth edges.

In general, for each class, approaches rely exclusively on either low-level methods or high-level knowledge. Because of intensity inhomogeneities and differences in image acquisition, low-level methods, based only on pixels intensities, can lead to missclassifications. A method based on an E/M classification has been proposed in [7] to cope with this difficulty.

Furthermore, the use of high-level knowledge alone is not sufficient to cope with high variability of shapes and appearance. However, we consider that low-level methods and high-level knowledge can be viewed as complementary and should be combined. Thus we propose to introduce a cooperation between high-level structural information (a priori knowledge), and low-level information (region segmentation agents) to enhance their mutual strenghts of these approaches. Such a cooperation provides capacities for adaptativity and also a mean to perform simultaneously segmentation and interpretation of the results.

3   Method Presentation

3.1   A Priori Knowledge

As seen in section 2, the use of a priori knowledge appears necessary to obtain an accurate segmentation. To introduce high-level structural information, we use two kinds of a priori knowledge :
- **Explicit** a priori knowledge : this is introduced through a statistical deformable model of the cortex convex hull. The model allows for the automatic detection of the brain in the images.
- **Implicit** a priori knowledge : this is represented through anatomical spatial relationships between the brain components. More precisely, the brain is considered to be composed of WM, surrounded by a ribbon of GM of nearly constant width ($\approx 2mm$), and lying within CSF. Pixels belonging to CSF have lower intensities than GM and WM. This anatomical knowledge is used to guide the segmentation process.

3.2   Cooperation

In the system, cooperation is used to derive constraints for the low-level segmentation processes and occurs at two different levels. The gray-matter detection agents occur under constraints derived from the cortex detection. Similarly, the white-matter detection agents operate under constraints derived from the gray-matter agents. Indeed, the model position allows for the initialisation of a locally specialised population of gray-matter agents (seeds) (see figure 1). Then, white-matter agents are initialised in the remaining parts of the brain and specialised locally.

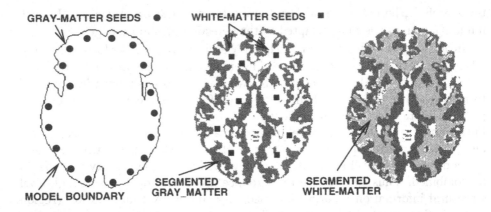

Fig. 1. The cooperative process for segmentation. (Left) Initialisation of gray-matter agents from the model position. (Middle) Segmentation of the gray-matter and subsequent initialisation of white-matter agents. (Right) Final result of the segmentation.

3.3 Runtime Adaptativity

The adaptativity of the method is essential for the segmentation of regions. Indeed, the intensities of pixels within a tissue are variable, and it is not possible to know in advance what values will occur for a given tissue. As a consequence, the processes for region segmentation have to be specialised at runtime, independently for each tissue. This principle of specialisation is a way of extracting new knowledge at runtime, and thus to introduce more knowledge in the system.

4   System Implementation

4.1 Statistical Deformable Model

The statistical deformable model [8] is built from a set of training examples representing the convex hull of the brain. The slices are selected at the AC-PC level. The mean example $\bar{X}$ is calculated and a principal component analysis of the matrix of the deviations from the mean gives the modes of variations of the model. New shapes can then be generated using equation $X = \bar{X} + \mathbf{P}\mathbf{b}$ where $\mathbf{P}$ is a matrix of a subset of the modes of variations and $\mathbf{b}$ a vector of weights.

The main modes of variation of the model and the result of the search in a new image are presented in figure 2.

4.2 Generic Model of Agent

Each agent of the system behaves as a locally specialised process of region growing. The principle is to aggregate pixels, starting from a seed, and following an aggregation criteria depending on (μ_i, σ_i) calculated at runtime.

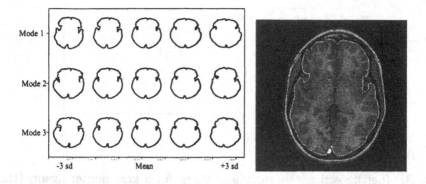

Fig. 2. (Left) Modes of variations for the statistical deformable model of the brain convex hull. (Right) Result of the model search for a new occurence.

| Agent i |
| Seed i |
| Behaviour $F_i(\mu_i, \sigma_i)$ |

A pixel p will be aggregated to agent A_i if either it has 3 neighbours belonging to A_i, or the equation (1) is verified, where the coefficient 1.5 is set according to experimental considerations.

$$\mu_i - 1.5 * \sigma_i < I_p < \mu_i + 1.5 * \sigma_i \qquad (1)$$

4.3 Gray-Matter Agents

- **Initial seed position** The initial position of a gray-matter agent is derived from a set of points associated to the result of the deformed model boundary. For each selected point, a displacement of 2 pixels towards the inside of the brain is performed, and the seed of each agent placed at the resulting position. A gray-matter seed is initialised every 5 pixels alongside the model boundary.
- **Specialisation** A sample of tissue is selected alongside the model boundary, centered at a seed position. The sample contains 2 types of tissues (GM and CSF) which are separated with an E/M algorithm. The resulting gaussian with the highest mean is used to specialise the corresponding agent (see figure 3).

4.4 White-Matter Agents

- **Initial seed position** The white-matter agents are initialised in the remaining part of the brain after gray-matter segmentation. In order to avoid seeds in CSF, the seeds can only have gray-levels higher than the mean gray-level of GM. They are equally placed in the remaining space. The number of seeds is set to 20.

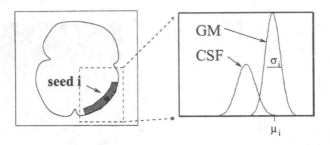

Fig. 3. (Left)Selection of a sample of tissue for a gray-matter agent. (Right) Separation of the sample into 2 tissue classes with a gaussian modelisation. The parameters of the agents are the mean and variance of the gaussian on the right.

- **Specialisation** The specialisation of white-matter agents is done locally on a 5x5 window. The mean gray-level and variance over the window are calculated, and used to specialise the agent.

4.5   Global Architecture

The agents are executed under control of a generic scheduler, having no knowledge of the application. The scheduler's goal is to manage all the agents of the system. It is built like an internal operating system [9] (see 4).

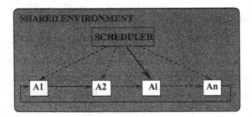

Fig. 4. System distribution. Each agent is allocated a time for execution and then stored in a queue. Ai is the current active agent in this figure (solid line).

5   Evaluations

5.1   Evaluations Using Phantoms

Gold standards are necessary to perform accurate evaluation. Such standards are provided by the Montreal Neurologic Institute under the form of series of "simulated" MRI images (**http://www.bic.mni.mcgill.ca/brainweb/**). These simulations are built on a realistic geometrical model of the brain and the gray-levels are simulated with sophisticated models of the MR imaging processes (see fig. 5). Moreover, noise has been added, at various levels (0%, 3%, 9%), together with varying levels of intensity non-uniformity (0%, 20%, 40%). The phantoms histograms are presented in figure 5 (bottom) in addition to the histogram of a real image. The separation between tissues is difficult for the real image and for the phantom with 9% of noise.

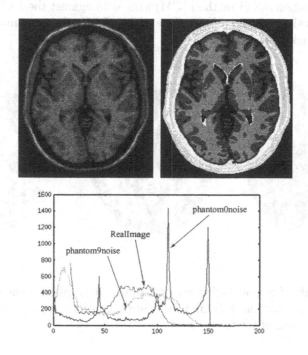

Fig. 5. (Left) Original gray-level images for phantoms MNI with 3% of noise. (Right) True segmented reference. (Bottom) Histograms of gray-level images for the 3 phantoms and a real image.

We tested the quality of our segmentation algorithm in comparison with the ground truth given by the simulations. We also compared another segmentation method provided with the SPM package [10] to the simulated data, in order to evaluate the respective performances of the methods. SPM proceeds with an iterative probabilistic estimation of classification using gaussian models of the tissue distributions. We calculate the positive prediction value PPV and the negative prediciton value NPV, according to the following equations (TP : true positives, TN : true negatives, FP : false positives, FN : false negatives) :

$$PPV = \frac{TP}{TP+FP} \qquad NPV = \frac{TN}{TN+FN}$$

Image	Method	PPV GM	NPV GM	PPV WM	NPV WM	PPV all
0%	CM	0.74	0.95	0.98	0.90	0.88
0%	SPM	0.68	0.99	1	0.87	0.87
3%	CM	0.83	0.94	0.95	0.93	0.90
3%	SPM	0.90	0.98	0.99	0.93	0.93
9%	CM	0.71	0.95	0.97	0.91	0.88
9%	SPM	0.85	0.92	0.96	0.90	0.86

Fig. 6. Evaluation of our method (CM) and SPM against the truth of the MNI phantom for values of noise of 0%, 3% and 9%. PPV all represents the PPV for GM+WM+background.

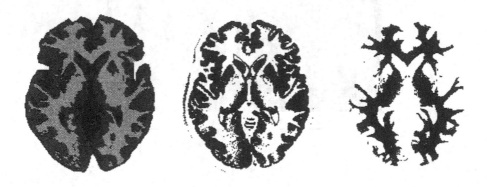

Fig. 7. Result of segmentation on (3% noise, 20% inhomogeneity) phantom. (Left) Our segmentation. (Middle) SPM segmentation for gray-matter. (Right) SPM segmentation of white matter.

A decrease of PPV corresponds to an over-segmentation of a tissue and a decrease of NPV corresponds to an under-segmentation of a tissue. The results are presented in figure 6. CM is our Cooperative Method. We note that the PPV values for GM are globally lower than the PPV for WM and this confirms the hypothesis that WM is easier to segment than GM. The results are globally comparable between our method and SPM and close to the ideal 1. Figure 7 presents an example of segmentation of a simulation with the results for our method and SPM.

5.2   Results on Real Data

In figure 8, segmentations on real data are presented for our method. These show that even if the tissue distributions are not easily separated from a histogram analysis (fig. 5), our method is able to automatically extract knowledge and then process a correct segmentation.

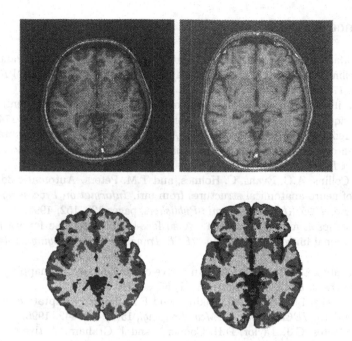

Fig. 8. (Top) Real gray-level images. (Bottom) The corresponding segmentation results with our method. The systems is adaptive to variations of shape and intensities.

6   Discussion

The originality of our method is to combine low-level primitives and high-level knowledge. Low-level primitives are represented as a multi-agent system. High-level knowledge, which constrains the multi-agent system, mixes implicit knowledge and model-based knowledge.

The initial manual design of the deformable model requires an amount of user interaction ; however this effort is compensated for the quantity of information generated by the model. As a comparison to SPM we require less *a priori* knowledge, and our system is able to extract automatically new knowledge at runtime.

Thanks to our distributed architecture, the system could be implemented in parallel, and we study the possibility of transfering information between agents for segmentation.

The results we obtained with phantoms and real images in 2D are very promising. Currently we pursue our experimental studies to demonstrate the validity of our method. We will extend it to several slices in 2.5D and then to 3D.

References

[1] J.F. Mangin, J. Regis, I. Bloch, and V. Frouin. A mrf based random graph modelling the human cortical topography. *Proc. First Int. Conf. CVRMed, Nice*, pages 177–183, 1995.

[2] C. Barillot, B.Gibaud, and G. Le Goualher X. Morandi. Représentation mixte numérique/ symbolique des sillons corticaux. *RFIA 98*, pages 165–174, 1998.

[3] P.C. Teo, G. Sapiro, and B. Wandell. Anatomically consistent segmentation of the human cortex for functional mri visualization. *Hewlett-Packard Labs. Technical Report HPL-97-03*, 1997.

[4] D.L. Collins, A.C. Evans, C. Holmes, and T.M. Peters. Automatic 3d segmentation of neuro-anatomical structures from mri. *Information Processing in Medical Imaging, 1995 Kluwer Academic Publishers*, pages 139–152, 1995.

[5] P. Thompson and A. W. Toga. A surface-based technique for warping three-dimensional images of the brain. *IEEE Trans. on Med. Imaging.*, 15(4):402–417, 1996.

[6] C. Davatzikos and J.L. Prince. An active contour model for mapping the cortex. *IEEE Trans. on Med. Imaging.*, 14(1):65–80, 1995.

[7] W.M. Wells, L. Grimson, R. Kikinis, and F.A. Jolesz. Adaptive segmentation of mri data. *IEEE Trans. on Med. Imaging.*, 15(4):429–442, 1996.

[8] T.F. Cootes, C.J. Taylor, D.H. Cooper, , and J. Graham. Active shape models-their training and application. *Computer Vision and Image Understanding*, 61(1):38–59, January 1995.

[9] A. Boucher, A. Doisy, X. Ronot, and C. Garbay. A society of goal-oriented agents for the analysis of living cells. *Artificial Intellignce in Medecine, Elsevier Science*, 14:183–199, 1998.

[10] K. J. Friston, A. P. Holmes, J. B. Poline, C. D. Frith, and R. S. J. Frackowiak. Statistical parametric maps in functional imaging: a general linear approach. *Human Brain Mapping*, 2:189–210, 1995.

Modelling Blood Vessels of the Eye with Parametric L-Systems Using Evolutionary Algorithms

Gabriella Kókai[1], Zoltán Tóth[2], and Róbert Ványi[2]

[1] Department of Computer Science, Programming Languages
Friedrich-Alexander University of Erlangen-Nürnberg
Martensstr. 3. D-91058 Erlangen, Germany
kokai@informatik.uni-erlangen.de
[2] Institute of Informatics, József Attila University
Árpád tér 2, H-6720 Szeged, Hungary
h531714|h531774@stud.u-szeged.hu

Abstract. In this paper the *GREDEA* system is presented. The main idea behind it is that with the help of evolutionary algorithms a grammatical description of the blood circulation of the human retina can be inferred. The system uses parametric *Lindenmayer systems* as description language. It can be applied on patients with diabetes who need to be monitored over long periods.
Keywords: Computer vision, image and signal interpretation, evolutionary algorithms

1 Introduction

In this paper the *GREDEA* (*Grammatical Retina Description with Evolutionary Algorithms*) system is presented. The main idea behind *GREDEA* was to develop patient-specific monitoring programs for examining the blood circulation of the human retina. The system can be used for on patients with diabetes who need to be monitored over long periods. The regular checkup of patients with this disease is an essential task, because the change of the vision quality is a direct consequence of the deterioration of the vascular tree caused by diabetes.

In recent years some earlier systems ([2], [5] and [13]) have been developed but these systems employed computer graphics methods. They require comparison of various images spaced over time. To make a diagnoses based on these images is a difficult task and needs a lot of expertise. Another attempts to use a syntactic approach is the system developed by Hesse et al. [4]. Here fractal modelling was applied but the authors concentrated on simulating the typical growth pattern of the retinal artery and so this work has no real diagnostic benefit.

In *GREDEA* an individual description of the blood circulation of the human retina is created for each patient. To derive it the process starts from fundus images recognized by scanning laser ophthalmoscope (*SLO*) and preprocessed. These images are referred to later as *destination images*.

Then a parametric *Lindenmayer system* (*L-system*) is picked up which creates the pattern closest to the vascular tree of the patient. This *L-system* can be stored (needs less memory than storing a picture) and used later to make comparison.

W. Horn et al. (Eds.): AIMDM'99, LNAI 1620, pp. 433–442, 1999.

The *L-systems* are parallel grammatical rewriting systems. They contain an initial axiom and one or more rules. With the help of such a grammar complex objects can be described starting from the axiom and using the productions [9]. When choosing the representation form, the fact that *L-systems* can be evolved using evolutionary algorithms [6] was taken into consideration.

The evolutionary algorithms can be briefly described as follows: a model of natural evolution [1] is often used as a way of solving optimization problems. These algorithms are based on the collective adaptation and learning ability of *individuals*. Individuals form a *population*, and each individual represents a possible solution of the problem. At the beginning, the individuals in the population are initialized randomly, and then they can be modified by the operators *selection*, *mutation* and *recombination*. These modifications lead to the evolution of the individuals; during the process better and better individuals appear. Thus, in later generations individuals that represent better solutions are more likely to appear.

Since parametric L-systems are evolved, two kinds of evolutionary algorithms are applied: genetic algorithms [3] are used on the rewriting rules of the evolved L-system, and evolution strategies [12] are applied on the parameters of the rules.

We proceed as follows. First in Section 2 and 3 a brief introduction to the recognition of the vascular tree in the retina and some details about the L-systems is given. The evolution process is presented in Section 4. In Section 5 an example for the experiments is discussed. Finally Section 6 contains a summary and some comments on future work.

2   The Retina

The retina is the light sensitive surface at back of the eye [7]. The retina contains a vast number of specialized nerve cells called rods and cones that convert light rays into nerve signals. The cones provide color vision, and are most concentrated at the fovea. The fovea can be see in Figure 1 as the region on the side without any blood vessels crossing it. Because of their dense concentration, the cones in the fovea provide the finest resolution vision. The rods are much more sensitive to light than the cones but they only provide black and white vision. All of the rods and cones connect with nerves whose signals exit from the eye via the optic nerve. The optic nerve along with the retinal artery, joins the eye at the optic disk. The optic disk is visible in Figure 2 on the right side. There are no rods or cones in the optic disk which creates a small blind spot on the retina. The vessel system of the eyebackground consists of two types of blood vessels, arteries and veins. The part where the vessels (arteries and veins) enter the eye is called papillary. Arteries and veins may have some crosspoints in the background of the eye but arteries never cross arteries and veins never cross veins, The blood vessels can be described with a binary tree because from a knot point a vessel can branch off only in two directions. The vessels starting from the papillary surround the macula. The macula does not contain any vessels

When diabetes affects the eyes, it often affects the retina lining the back of the eye, specifically the small blood vessels (see in Figure 3) which nourish this membrane. This condition is called diabetic retinopathy. Diabetic retinopathy often has no symptoms in its early, most treatable stages. Improving awareness of the importance of early detection and treatment is imperative if one is to reduce visual loss from this disease. A minimal evaluation of the diabetic retina consists of regular examinations by a qualified practitioner though dilated pupils.

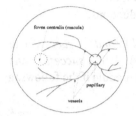

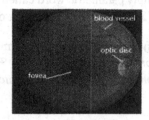

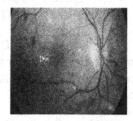

Fig. 1. The structure of the retina

Fig. 2. Fundus image of the retina

Fig. 3. Diabetic retinopathy

3   The Lindenmayer Systems

Lindenmayer introduced special kinds of descriptive grammars in order to describe natural development processes [8]. These are called Lindenmayer grammars or *Lindenmayer systems* (*L-systems*). The most important characteristic of *L-systems* compared with Chomsky grammars is *parallel rewriting*. In Lindenmayer systems rewriting rules are applied in parallel and simultaneously replace all letters in a given word.

Different *L-system* classes are introduced, such as deterministic or nondeterministic *L-systems*. The distincion can be made between context free and context sensitive *L-systems*. The definition of these classes is similar to the definition of Chomsky language classes. In this paper only *deterministic context free L-systems*, (*D0L-systems*) are used. To enlarge the number of described objects *L-systems* can also be associated with parameters.

3.1   Parametric D0L-Systems

With the idea of parametric *L-systems* the concept of parallel rewriting to parametric words instead of strings of symbols can be applied. Following the notation of Prusinkiewicz [10] the word "module" as a synonym for "letter with associated parameters" is used.

The alphabet is denoted by Σ, and the set of parameters is the set of real numbers R. A module with letter $a \in \Sigma$ and parameters $p_1, p_2, \ldots, p_n \in R$ is denoted by $a(p_1, p_2, \ldots, p_n)$.

The real-valued *actual* parameters appearing in words have a counterpart in the *formal* parameters which may occur in the specification of *L-system* productions. Let Π be the set of formal parameters. The combination of formal parameters and numeric constants using the arithmetic operators $(+, -, *, /)$, the relational operators $(<, <=, >, >=, ==)$, the logical operators $(!, \&\&, ||)$ and parentheses $(())$ generates the set of all correctly constructed logical and arithmetic expressions with parameters from Π. There are noted $C(\Pi)$ and $\mathcal{E}(\Pi)$.

Definition 1. A *parametric D0L-system* an ordered quadruple $G = (\Sigma, \Pi, \alpha, P)$, where

- $\Sigma = s_1, s_2, ..., s_n$ is the alphabet of the system,
- Π is the set of formal parameters,
- $\alpha \in (\Sigma \times R^*)^+$ is a nonempty parametric word called the axiom,
- $P \subset (\Sigma \times \Pi^*) \times C(\Pi) \times (\Sigma \times \mathcal{E}(\Pi)^*)^*$ is a finite set of productions.

A production in a *D0L-system* is given in the form *pred* | *cond* → *succ*, where *pred* $\in \Sigma \times \Pi^*$ denotes the *predecessor*, *succ* $\in ((\Sigma \times \mathcal{E}(\Pi)^*)^*$ is the *successor* and *cond* $\in C(\Pi)$ describes the *conditions*. A production *matches* a module if the following conditions are met:

- the letter in the module and the letter in the production predecessor are the same
- the number of actual parameters in the module is equal to the number of formal parameters in the production predecessor
- the condition evaluates to true if the actual parameter values are substituted for the formal parameters in the production.

If a production is matching a module then it can be *applied* in order to create a string of modules specified by the production successor. The actual parameter values are substituted for the formal parameters according to their position.

There is no essential difference between *D0L-systems* that operate on strings with or without brackets. In our implementation brackets are used: However, in this case productions involving brackets are restricted to the following forms:

- *pred* | *cond* → *succ*, where *pred* and *cond* are as before, but *succ* $\in ((\Sigma \times \mathcal{E}(\Pi)^* \cup \{[,]\})^*$, and *succ* is well nested;
- [→ [, or] →].

A string S is called well-nested if and only if for all S' substring of S the number of '[' symbols is not less than the number of ']' symbols, and the number of these symbols is equal in S. More details and examples of parametric *D0L-systems* can be found in [11].

3.2 Displaying Images Defined by L-Systems

To display an image defined by an *L-system* the well-known turtle graphics is used. The turtle is an object in space such that its position is defined by a vector and its orientation is defined by a coordinate-system. The coordinate-system determines the heading (h), the left(l) and the up (u) directions. Using these vectors the turtle can be moved in space. There are several turtle operations, also known as turtle commands. The most important ones are drawing ('F'), and turning left and right ('+' and '−'). There are special turtle operations, called stack operations. These are denoted by '[' and ']', and used to save and restore turtle position and orientation. Using stack operations branching structures can be produced.

To use turtle graphics with *L-systems* turtle commands as the elements of the alphabet are applied.

4   The Evolution Process

If an image is given and one wants to find the grammar that describes it, this is called the inverse problem of L-systems. Evolutionary algorithms are used to solve this problem are descriebed here in detail

4.1   Initial Population

The first step is define the structure of the initial population and the individuals them-selves. For the first examination the initial population is randomly created, but if the patient returns for a check-up, the previously generated L-system is used to create the initial population. This makes the convergence speed greater and makes comparison easier.

4.1.1 The Structure of the Population

As it was mentioned the individuals are represented by *L-systems*. It is easier to handle *L-systems* if it is assumed that the axiom is constant and contains only a single symbol. Let the axiom be *S*. It can be proved that every *L-system* can be transformed into such form, without changing the described image. It is also assumed that the number of the rules is constant.

Because the shape of the generated image depends both on the rewriting rules and on the parameters, the representation can be divided into two important parts. The right sides of the rules are represented as strings while the parameters are described as a vector of real values. Usually it is more important to find the appropriate right sides. Changing the parameters is used for the fine-tuning of the image. *L-systems* with the same rules are considered as an *L-system group*. In an *L-system group* the rules are con-stant, but the parameters can be variated. To find the best parameters *evolution strategies* (*ES*) are used inside the *L-system group*. Therefore an *L-system* group works as a *sub-population*. A subpopulation can be represented by rewriting rules. Because the number of the rules, and also the left sides are constant, an *L-system group* can be represented by an array of strings. To find the rewriting rules, genetic operators are applied on the string arrays representing an *L-system group*. So the *L-system groups* make up the population. The structure of the population can be seen in Figure 4.

To calculate the fitness value, the images described by the L-systems are created, then the distance between these generated images and the destination image is calcu-lated with a suitable function. This function will be discussed in section 4.2. Using this fitness value *evolution strategies* are applied on the parameter vectors several times. The number of the evolution steps (denoted by S_{ES}) is defined at the very beginning of the process. When the ES steps are finished, the best individuals in each subpop-ulation are selected. The parameters and the fitness value of these *L-systems* will act as the parameters and the fitness value for the whole subpopulation. Using this fitness value, selection can be applied to the subpopulations to generate new subpopulations using *genetic algorithms* (*GA*). It is important that selection applied on subpopulation is a *GA-selection*, which is *fitness proportional*. Thus choosing the best individual in the subpopulation as the representing individual does not mean that the L-system group with the best L-system will be selected. The detailed description of the applied ES and GA operators can be found later in section 4.3. Earlier we mentioned that ES is usually applied on real valued vectors, however GA is used with words over a finite alphabet. Therefore in this process both of them are used.

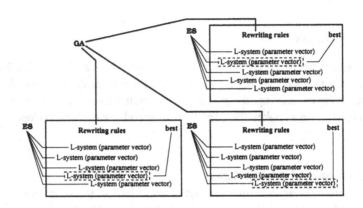

Fig. 4. The structure of the population

4.1.2 The Form of an Individual

The base *L-system* used as an individual is the following:

> alphabet: $\Sigma = \{S, F, +, -, [,]\}$
> axiom: $\alpha = S$
> rewriting rule: $S \rightarrow u$, where $u \in \Sigma^*$ is a well-nested string.

Using this approach it can be noticed that this type of *L-system* sometimes generates *unnecessarily long words* (*ul-words*). For example the image described by the word $F + - - + + F - +$ can be also generated by the word $F + F$ which is much shorter. To solve this problem, sequences of symbols can be defined, such that these sequences always start with a drawing symbol and do not contain unnecessary turtle movements (e.g. $+ - - +$). If *regulated evolution* is used to *preserve sequences* those ul-words can be avoided. During regulated evolution sequences cannot be broken, so genetic operators must be applied on substrings and not single symbols. But this makes the genetic algorithm more difficult. The other solution employs the specialties of the problem. Examining the blood vessel in the eye, a better *L-system* can be defined which itself includes the sequences:

> $\Sigma = \{S, F, +, -, [,], B, Y, T\}$
> $\alpha = S$
> and rewriting rules:
> $S \rightarrow v$, where $v \in \{S, B, Y, T, [,]\}^*$ is a well-nested string.
> $B \rightarrow F + S$
> $Y \rightarrow F[+S][-S]$
> $T \rightarrow F[+S]S$

Note that the vascular tree can contain only the following parts: *bending* (B), *branching* (Y) and *forking* (T). Using this *L-system*, only the first rule will be modified during the evolution process. The initial F symbols of the other three rules ensure that ul-words will not be created. So this *L-system* will produce better words, just like the *L-system* with sequences, without making the use of genetic operators difficult.

4.2   The Fitness Function: The Distance of Two Images

There are many possibilities to define the distance between two images. A very simple method to calculate the distance d_q between two images I_1 and I_2 is the quadratic error of the images. During the definition we assume that the sizes of both pictures are the same: $N \times M$.

The distance is the sum of quadratic errors of two corresponding pixels:

$$d_q(I_1,I_2) = \sum_{x=0}^{N-1} \sum_{y=0}^{M-1} (I_1(x,y) - I_2(x,y))^2$$

For binary images, where $I_1^B(x,y)$ and $I_2^B(x,y)$ are two pixels the quadratic error is:

$$d_p(I_1^B(x,y), I_2^B(x,y)) = \begin{cases} 1 & \text{if } I_1^B(x,y) \neq I_2^B(x,y) \\ 0 & \text{otherwise} \end{cases}$$

So let the distance between two binary pictures be defined like this:

$$d_q(I_1,I_2) = \sum_{x=0}^{N-1} \sum_{y=0}^{M-1} d_p(x,y)$$

In this paper an extended version of this definition is used because in our evolutionary process we wanted to make a distinction between the following four cases for an arbitrary (x,y) point:

- The point (x,y) is 0 on both images, it is not important for the fitness calculating.
- The point (x,y) is 1 on both images. In this case a match is found; this means positive fitness.
- The point (x,y) is 0 on the destination image, but 1 on the generated image. This means point that is not part of the vascular tree is covered.
- The point (x,y) is 1 on the destination image, but 0 on the generated image. So there is a missing point.

Let us denote the pixels with $p_d = I_d^B(x,y)$ and $p_g = I_g^B(x,y)$, where p_d means the pixel value on the destination image I_d and p_g means the value on the pixel in the generated image I_g. In this case the weighted distance of two pixels can be defined:

$$d_p'(x,y) = \begin{cases} 0 & \text{, if } p_d = p_g = 0 \\ W_1 & \text{, if } p_d = p_g = 1 \\ -W_2 & \text{, if } p_d < p_g \\ -W_3 & \text{, if } p_d > p_g \end{cases}$$

So the fitness function φ is the weighted distance between two images:

$$\varphi = d'(I_1,I_2) = \sum_{x=0}^{N-1} \sum_{y=0}^{M-1} d_p'(x,y)$$

Using this definition a missing point will cost more than an unnecessary one if W_2 is set to greater than W_3. These parameters can also be used to fine-tune the fitness function.

4.3   The Used Operators

Since parametric L-systems are evolved, two kinds of evolutionary operators are applied; evolution strategies are applied on the parameters of the rules and genetic algorithms are used on the rewriting rules of the evolved L-system. In this section these are described.

4.3.1 The ES Operators

Let us denote two parameter vectors with $u = u_1 u_2 \ldots u_n$ and $v = v_1 v_2 \ldots v_n$. During the evolution of parameter vectors two ES operators are used:

- *ES mutation.* If the u vector is mutated, the resulting vector will be u' where $u'_k = u_k$ if $1 \leq k < i$ or $i < k \leq n$ and $u'_i = u_i + \xi(R_{ES})$ for a randomly selected i. $\xi(R_{ES})$ represents the Gaussian derivation with deviation R_{ES}. This R_{ES} parameter is called the *radius* of the mutation, and is defined before the evolution process.
- *ES recombination.* If the u and v vectors are recombined, the resulting vector will be w, where $w_i = (u_i + v_i)/2$.

4.3.2 The GA Operators

Let us denote two strings with $u = u_1 u_2 \ldots u_n$ and $v = v_1 v_2 \ldots v_m$. To evolve these strings two GA operators are used which are similar to the operators used for ES. These operators are:

- *GA mutation.* If the u vector is mutated, the resulting vector will be u' where $u'_k = u_k$ if $1 \leq k < i$ or $i < k \leq n$ and $u'_i = T$ for a randomly selected i position, and a randomly selected T character.
- *GA recombination.* If the u and v vectors are recombined, the resulting vector will be w, where $w_i = u_i$, if $i \leq k$ and $w_i = v_i$, if $k < i$ for a randomly selected k.

4.4   Halting Criteria

Because our image is a finite set of discrete points there is an upper bound for the fitness value: $\varphi_{max} = (N \times M) \cdot W_1$. Therefore after a finite number of steps there will be a population such that its fitness is the same as of the previous one. The process can be stopped if the maximum fitness is reached, or nearly reached, or the fitness value was unchanged during the previous S_{GA} steps.

4.5   Choice of the Evolution Parameters

There are several parameters that can be changed before the process and also during the evolution. The *GREDEA* system can currently be used to find L-systems for simpler retina images. An example for it is presented in section 5. To find L-systems for more complex retina images, the starting parameters of the process must be set more carefully. In order to do, more retina images must be analyzed. This analysis is currently being carried out in our project.

- *General parameters.* The user can change the number of the subpopulation and the number of individuals in a population.
- *EA parameters.* To control the evolution strategy parameters are defined as previously mentioned: S_{ES}, W_1, W_2, W_3 and R_{ES}.
- *GA parameters.* The genetic algorithm has only one parameter: S_{GA}.

5 Evolution Result

Here we present an example of finding a Lindenmayer-system that describes a given retina image. In Figure 5 an *SLO* recognized and preprocessed retina image can be seen with the structure created by the L-system described below. The preprocessing part is discussed in the literature (see for example [13]) therefore we do not go into detail. The L-system describes the structure of the top-right quarter of the retina image.

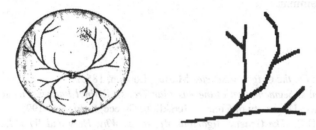

Fig. 5. An example for a retina image and an L-system that describes it

The rules of the above L-system are:

- S→;(2)B(37,0) [B(0,38) B(16,0) [B(0,27) B(11,14) B(12,6) B(19,0) [B(0,47) B(19,0)] B(0,-6) B(17,0)] B(0,-14) B(22,37) B(19,0) [B(0,-6) B(12,34) B(18,32) B(14,0)] B(0,-43) B(24,0)] B(37,0) [B(0,-7) B(8,43) B(24,0)] B(0,-14) B(26,0)
- B(a,b)→ F(a)+(b)

The turtle commands ($B[BB[BBBB[B]$ ...) determine the main shape of the structure, but the segment lengths and angles depend on the parameters $(37, 0, 0, 38, \ldots)$. (The ;(2) turtle command sets the initial line width.) Later this evolved description can be used to establish the change in a patient's eye: The patient comes again for a checkup and pictures are recorded again. From these *L-systems* are also generated and the previous grammars can be compared automatically with the newly evolved grammars. For example the shortening of the segments or the growing of the angles can be detected easily from the parameter vector. For the comparison different algorithms may be used but the detailed description of this process is beyond the subject of this paper.

To find the appropriate L-systems for more complex images needs more evolution steps. However more steps mean more computing. The evolution steps are time-consuming, because the operators work with parametrized strings and the fitnes function works with a matrix. For a complex image the resolution also has to be increased which means a greater matrix, so the computational time grows quadratically.

The convergence speed can be increased by choosing better starting parameters. They can be determined by statistical methods after analyzing more images. For the time being we do not have the adequate number of pictures, and getting new medical images has legal connection also. Our experiments showed that using evolutionary algorithms, grammatical description of the retina can be determined, but perfecting the method needs more experiments. This is our current project.

6   Conclusion

The program *GREDEA* developed by us can be applied in diabetic retinopathy for diabetic retinal disease. It solves the problem of describing the blood vessels of the eye using parametric *Lindenmayer systems* (*L-systems*). To find the most suitable description evolutionary algorithms are applied.

A further possibility of the application is that if the picture generated from the *SLO* was imperfect the incomplete part of the vascular system can be reconstructed using the description grammar.

References

1. Darwin, C.: *On the Origin of Species* Murray, London, 1859.
2. C. Georgiadis, *Segmentation of the Vascular Tree in Retinal Images*, Department of Computer Science, University of Crete at Heraklion, Greece, September 1995.
3. Goldberg, D.E.: *The Genetic Algorithm Approach Why, How and What Next* In: Narenda 1986
4. Hesse, L., Chofflet, J. and Le Mer, Y.: *Simulating of the growth pattern of the central retinal artery using fractal modeling technique* In German Journal of Opthalmology 2:116-118 1993
5. John Hipwell: *Digital Angiography in Ophthalmology* Ph.D research at the Department of BioMedical Physics at Aberdeen University
6. Jacob, C.: *Genetic L-system Programming* PPSN III - Parallel Problem Solving from Nature, International Conference on Evolutionary Computation, Lecture Notes in Computer Science 866, Springer-Verlag, Berlin, 1994, pp. 334 - 343.
7. L'Esperance, F. A. Jr: *Ophthalmic Lasers: Photocoagulation, Photoradiation and Surgery.* 2nd ed. The C. V. Mosby Company St. Louis. 1983
8. Lindenmayer, A.: *Mathematical models for cellular interaction in development* In: Journal of Theoretical Biology 18: 280-315 1968.
9. Rozenberg. G., Salomaa A.:*The book of L* Springer Verlag 1985
10. Prusinkiewicz, P., Hammel, M., Hanan, J., Měch, R.: *Visual models of plant development* From G. Rozenberg and A. Salomaa, editors, handbook of formal languages Springer-Verlag, 1996.
11. Prusinkiewicz, P., Hanan. J.: *Lindenmayer systems, fractals and plants* Lecture Notes in Biomathemathics vol 79. Springer-Verlag, 1989.
12. Rechenberg, I.: *Evolutionsstrategie '94, Werkstatt Bionik und Evolutionstechnik* Band 1, Fromman-Holzboog, Stuttgart, 1994.
13. Zana, F.: *Registration of Retinal Images with Occlusion under a Weak Affine Hypothesis, Multimodal and/or Temporal Registration.* In the Proc. The 13th International Conference on Digital Signal Processing (DSP97), on the island of Santorini, Greece, July 2-4, 1997

Animating Medical and Safety Knowledge

Peter Hammond[1], Paul Wells[1,2], and Sanjay Modgil[1]

[1] Department of Informatics,
Eastman Dental Institute for Oral Health Care Sciences,
University College London,
256 Gray's Inn Road, London WC1X 8LD, U.K.
{P.Hammond,P.Wells,S.Modgil }@eastman.ucl.ac.uk
http://www.eastman.ucl.ac.uk/~dmi/DECADE
[2] Team Management Systems Ltd, Aylesbury, U.K.
P.Wells@tmsdental.co.uk

Abstract. DECADE is an environment for building CAD applications with embedded expert or regulatory design knowledge. Several medical applications are being built with DECADE, one of which has been launched commercially and is being evaluated formally in a primary healthcare setting.

1 Background

The DECADE environment can be used to build computer-aided design and decision support systems that apply a range of pre-declared constraints and animate their violation by critiquing the user. For graphically oriented design applications, constraints can include common sense spatial reasoning and expressed design knowledge such as rules of expert design, technical standards, and codes of practice such as statutory fire and safety regulations. The pre-declared constraints are applied each time the graphical depiction is altered and when they are contravened a critique is offered. Sometimes a more acceptable alteration can be proposed. Meta-programming techniques are used to implement a logic database describing the artefact being designed or the data being entered graphically. DECADE augments the underlying PROLOG environment with facilities for defining both symbolic and graphical representations of designs of artefacts or their configuration. It also supports the description of graphical tools for amending designs and for linking such amendments with integrity constraints.

2 Abstract and Interactive Models Underlying DECADE

An artefact being designed in a DECADE application has two representations, one symbolic and one graphical. A logic database of facts represents subcomponents of the artefact and relationships between them. Requirements constraining any amendment of these facts are represented as integrity constraints by the application builder. The logic database is amended as a result of direct manipulation of the graphical representation by the end user of the application. The

W. Horn et al. (Eds.): AIMDM'99, LNAI 1620, pp. 443–447, 1999.

underlying model in DECADE is that a design is built by an end-user so that its description and the background domain knowledge of component shapes and their conformation remain consistent with the integrity constraints expressing rules of regulated design.

A design window in a DECADE application has a CAD style interface with a pane of design tools and a drawing area (see figure 1). The invocation of a tool arises from its selection in the tool pane and the execution of a single click, or series of clicks, in the drawing area. It is convenient to associate an initial attempt to use a design tool with a preliminary constraint that checks if the tool is being used appropriately. Such an immediate evaluation of tool use can avoid tedious situations where complex component manipulations are undertaken only to result in error messages criticising the first tool action undertaken. Whenever an error is trapped, an appropriate critique can be generated. Otherwise, the user is allowed to continue to manipulate icons to specify the intended alteration. On completion of the update, all relevant constraints are checked. Constraints which can never be broken (hard constraints) are checked before softer ones, which can. In some applications, it is necessary for users (for example, in clinical domains) to be able to override constraints, hence the terminology soft and hard constraint. The user is informed of integrity constraints that may have been contravened. Depending on the kind of constraint and the user's reaction to the critique, the design amendment may be rejected or may be executed, the latter resulting in both the graphical depiction and underlying database being updated. The exact form of these changes is pre-determined by meta-predicate descriptions defined by the application builder. The rejection of a design amendment may also result in some reconfiguration of the interface to return a design's graphical representation to its previous state.

3   Developing a Simple DECADE Application

A complete specification of graphical tools is provided by a DECADE application builder. Each tool requires a bitmap icon for the tool pane, a description of its graphical, manipulative effect and also its effect on the underlying logic database capturing the design. The action of a design tool and the constraints to which its use is subject are described by a set of meta-predicates. The predicate **prelim_condition(+Invocation, +Design, −Constraint, −HardOrSoft, −Error)** defines a preliminary constraint check on the invocation of a design tool. Its input parameters are a description of the tool invocation and the design name; the output parameters are a constraint to check (interpreted as a denial), an indication of whether the constraint is absolute (hard) or heuristic (soft), and a term describing the error that arises should the constraint be contravened. For example, **prelim_condition(link(Obj,Pt), Design, type(Obj,box), hard, no_box_links)** would disallow an initial attempt to link an object of type box to any other object. The meta-predicate **determine_alteration(+Invocation, +Design, −Update)** consumes a token +**Invocation** describing the initial invocation of a tool and converts subsequent manipulations of icons into a term −**Update** capturing the user's intended alteration to the underlying logic database. For example, the clause

```
determine_alteration(link(Obj1,Pt1), Design, link(Obj1,Obj2,Pt1,Pt2)) :-
    line_marqui(Design, Pt1, Pt2),
    find_pict(Design, Pt2, Obj2).
```

employs built-in graphical primitives in a procedural fashion to draw a line between **P1** on **Obj1** and **P2** under **Obj2**. To disallow linkages to boxes we define an instance of the meta-predicate **precondition(+Update, +Design, −Constraint, −HardOrSoft, −Error)** such as **precondition(link(Obj1, Obj2, Pt1, Pt2), Design, type(Obj2, box), hard, no_box_links)**.

This consumes the output update description from **determine-alteration** and passes any declared constraint description for checking, in this case the second object must not be a box. Following the critique, any temporary icons are removed. If a design amendment passes all constraint checking, then the design and graphical databases are updated according to declarations in the meta-predicate **record_alteration(+Update, +Design, −Changes)**. The **Changes** argument is represented, for technical convenience, as a difference list. For example, the linkage update might record a fact representing the linkage and pass a term to the graphics subsystem to generate its permanent representation:

```
record_alteration(link(Obj1,Obj2,Pt1,Pt2),Design,
    [add_fact(links(Name Obj1,Obj2)),
    add_pict(Name,linkage(Pt1, Pt2))|Z]-Z) :-
genobjname(Design, linkage, Name).
```

DECADE maintains a database of facts recording the objects and links between them. The application builder must define the graphical representation of the objects and links using built-in primitives.

4   DECADE Design Applications

A number of medical design applications are under construction. The most developed is RaPiD, recently released commercially by a collaborating company, Team Management Systems Ltd. Below we give a brief description of RaPiD and a similarly brief summary of a recently initiated design assistant, CaRiS, aimed at the animation of radiological safety regulations.

4.1   RaPiD: Designing Removable Partial Dentures

A removable partial denture (RPD) replaces missing teeth in partially dentate patients and has the important functions of restoring the patient's appearance, improving speech, assisting mastication and maintaining a healthy, stable relationship between the remaining natural teeth. The design of RPDs is a clinical responsibility, yet there is ample evidence that this responsibility is commonly delegated by dentists to dental technicians with recognised design failure. The RaPiD project was initiated to address this problem and the results so far have shown the approach to be viable and effective. RaPiD contains the consensus, expert design knowledge of a large group of domain experts [2, 1]. The graphical output from RaPiD is in the form of an annotated 2D diagram and written description which is given by the dentist to a dental technician as a prescription for the construction of the denture (see figure 1).

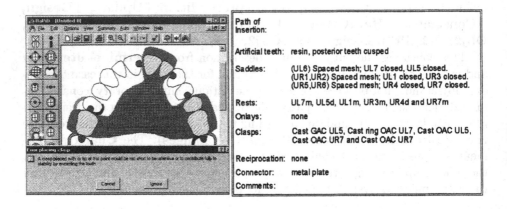

Fig. 1. (a) a developing design in RaPiD with associated critique; (b) a design description generated from the underlying logic database of components

4.2   CaRiS - Checking and Animating Radiation Safety

The UK Health & Safety Commission issues advice on how to comply with the law on ionising radiation [3] in the form of a code of practice [4]. The Regulations contain the fundamental requirements needed to control exposure to ionising radiation, whereas the Code details acceptable methods of meeting those requirements. The duty is on designers, manufacturers, suppliers and installers of x-ray equipment to undertake their work in such a way so as to reduce unnecessary radiation exposure as far as is reasonably possible. CaRiS is a prototype drafting tool, enforcing radiation hazard codes of practice on the installation of x-ray equipment, initially in dental practice, but subsequently to be generalised to other settings. Fig 2 illustrates how a user might interact with an architectural like design system which undertakes a variety of checks on the installation of x-ray equipment with respect to the safety of patients, dental practice staff as well as the person controlling the equipment. The Guidelines address a range of issues, including what is an acceptable room for undertaking dental radiography, what is a safe distance from an x-ray source for an operator, how to protect waiting areas with shielding and how to ensure restricted access to the area during

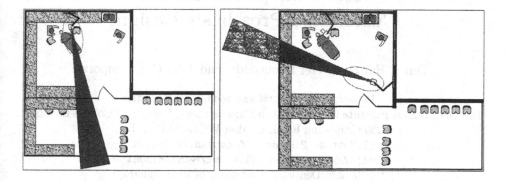

Fig. 2. (a) simulation of unattenuated x-ray beam(left); (b) beam partly attenuated

radiation. As well as catching errors of design as they occur, CaRiS can be more proactive and give an indication of x-ray beam extent and its attenuation by animating the movement of a source as illustrated in Fig 2.

5 Future Work and Concluding Remarks

A rationalised and extended version of the Graphics Description Language will form an important focus in further developments of DECADE. Extensions could also include the generation of multiple plan and elevated views from symbolic three dimensional representations, and meta-tools for defining new applications. Most DECADE applications will demand both spatial reasoning, on the one hand, and reasoning about function on the other. For example, the shape of a component can sometimes be computed automatically from topological requirements alone, but the description of some constraints requires an ability to describe the function of components. Thus, multiple representations of a design may need to be referred to simultaneously.

References

[1] J.C. Davenport and P. Hammond. The acquisition and validation of removable partial denture design knowledge - I. *Journal of Oral Rehabilitation*, 1996.
[2] P. Hammond, J.C. Davenport, and F.J. Fitzpatrick. Logic-based integrity constraints and the design of dental prostheses. *Artificial Intelligence in Medicine*, 5:431–446, 1993.
[3] HSC. *The ionising radiation regulations*. HSE Books, 1985.
[4] HSC. *The protection of persons against ionising radiation arising from any work activity*. HSE Books, 1985.

Active Shape Models for
Customised Prosthesis Design*

Tim J. Hutton[1], Peter Hammond[1], and John C. Davenport[2]

[1] Department of Dental and Medical Informatics,
Eastman Dental Institute for Oral Health Care Sciences, University College London,
256 Gray's Inn Road, London WC1X 8LD, U.K.
{T.Hutton, P.Hammond}@eastman.ucl.ac.uk
http://www.eastman.ucl.ac.uk/~dmi/MINORI
[2] School of Dentistry, University of Birmingham,
St. Chad's Queensway, Birmingham B4 6NN, U.K.
J.C.Davenport@bham.ac.uk

Abstract. Images and computer graphics play an increasingly important role in the design and manufacture of medical prostheses and implants. Images provide guidance on optimal design in terms of location, preparation and the overall shape and configuration of subcomponents. Direct manipulation of a graphical representation provides a natural design environment. RaPiD is a CAD-like knowledge-based assistant for designing a dental prosthesis known as a removable partial denture (RPD). The expertise embedded in RaPiD encourages optimal subcomponent configuration, but currently supports only minor customisation. This paper describes how oral images and Active Shape Models (ASMs) are being used to address this limitation.

1 Background

Images and computer graphics are important in the design, manufacture and fit of many medical implants and prostheses. Typically they are involved in:

- optimising the location of the implant/prosthesis
- minimising bone/tissue removal for insertion and fit
- maximising accuracy of overall fit
- configuring and designing sub-components for optimal shape, fit and function
- determining and recording shape variation in relevant patient populations

For example, conventional radiographs and CT/MR images are all used in selecting the best location for a dental implant [9]. Radiographs are manually digitised in two dimensions to configure parameterised 3D models and provide

---

* The authors wish to acknowledge the funding provided for the RaPiD project by the Higher Education Funding Council and the DTI/EPSRC Teaching Company Scheme. Also, the authors wish to thank Paul Taylor of the Centre for Health Informatics and Multiprofessional Education, UCL for his help and guidance.

W. Horn et al. (Eds.): AIMDM'99, LNAI 1620, pp. 448–452, 1999.

input to CAD/CAM manufacture of hip and knee prostheses [3]. Nails, screws and plates for bone fixation following trauma [7] and spinal implants [4] all rely on imaging data. Extendible endoprostheses require accurate graphical design and expert configuration [10].

RaPiD is a knowledge-based assistant for designing a dental prosthesis known as a removable partial denture (RPD). Embedded design expertise encourages the correction, selection and configuration of subcomponents in a 2D CAD style and incorrect design is critiqued [8]. Manufacture takes place on a physical model according to the printed design specification.

RaPiD has undergone and is undergoing considerable validation and evaluation ([5],[6]). It has also recently been commercialised under UK government funding in co-operation with a specialist dental software company, Team Management Systems Ltd. Consequently, there is some confidence that RaPiD is well designed and will be of benefit to general dental practitioners. However, designs in RaPiD are still produced on a set of generic tooth icons and although some graphical tools support rotation and translation of teeth icons, this remains inadequate for customised design for individual patients. In the MINORI project (Model-based INterpretation of ORo-facial Images) we are addressing this problem.

2   The MINORI Project

2.1   Requirements

Hand-digitising of images can be slow and requires expert knowledge of the imaging method and the structures being identified. Computer vision techniques provide an alternative, automatic method. If such a system is to replace manual digitisation successfully, it must satisfy certain criteria. It must be able to work with available images, it must be sufficiently robust to work largely unsupervised and the measurements it provides should be sufficiently precise for the prosthesis designed.

2.2   Image Acquisition

Within a few years, most dental practices will have access to some form of digital image acquisition. Many commercially available systems already enable intra-oral pictures to be taken and stored on computer. Alternatively, digital cameras that are widely available and inexpensive can also be used to take pictures of casts of patients' jaws. To extract the dentition of a patient from such images, we restrict them to occlusal views only, where the arch of teeth is seen from above. Pictures of casts or intra-oral views can be used.

There is considerable variation in patient dentition: teeth can tilt, move, rotate and change shape. Additionally, in the case of RPD design, the images presented will have teeth missing. A successful approach will have to model all of these variations. As with any image analysis, the pictures should have sufficient contrast between the objects we want to segment and the background. Thus some care must be taken when acquiring the images to avoid artefacts such as varying shadows and background clutter being introduced.

2.3   Deriving the Active Shape Model (ASM)

RaPiD uses a two-dimensional polygon to represent each tooth boundary. 20-40 points per tooth boundary provide enough flexibility to model changes in shape, as well as position, rotation and scale variation. MINORI uses the same set of polygons to build an ASM, as described by Cootes et. al. [2]. The natural variation in shape is learned from a training set of manually digitised oral images. Together with the mean shape, this is then used to direct the search of a new image for similar structures. A few examples from the training set are shown below (Fig. 1). The model has 444 vertices in each complete set of tooth boundaries.

Fig. 1. Some examples from the training set

Each training shape example yields a shape vector. We compute the eigenvectors and eigenvalues of the covariance matrix of the shape vectors. The eigenvectors each represent a deformation of the mean shape, the eigenvector with the largest eigenvalue accounting for the major changes in shape seen over the training set. The first four modes of variation are shown below (Fig. 2).

The number of modes required to represent most of the variation seen in the training set is typically much smaller than the number of points in the shape vector; we have extracted a very compact representation of the deformations seen in natural teeth shapes. By varying the strength of each of the modes of variation we can synthesise new dentitions. As long as we restrict our deformations to within 3 standard deviations of the mean then the shapes are plausible.

2.4   Extracting Tooth Icons from New Images

Having computed a model of how dentition varies, we can use it to fit shapes to new images. The modes of variation reduce the search space from potentially a thousand dimensions to perhaps only twenty. Many schemes are possible to implement this search. Cootes et. al. describe a simple local optimisation strategy that proves very effective. Each vertex of the shape polygon is pulled towards any nearby strong edges in the image. From these pull vectors, the ideal translation, rotation, scaling and deformation are computed. The transformation is applied

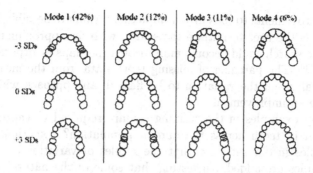

Fig. 2. The first four modes of variation. In each column the mean shape *(middle row)* is deformed by one of the eigenvectors. Mode 1 has captured the change in arch width from wide to narrow and explains 42% of the variation seen in the training set. The other modes explain the remaining variation, together the first four modes explain 71% of the total variation

and the process is repeated until convergence. Given a suitably close initial placement, the shape converges on the teeth in the image, typically within fewer than fifty iterations.

A prototype version of MINORI has been implemented in Visual C++. The graphical user interface (GUI) is used both for hand-digitising the training set and for fitting to new images.

3 Conclusions and Future Work

It can be seen (Fig. 3) that a customised dentition can alter the design of an RPD so it is important to have a reasonable method for acquiring the dentition of the patient. The approach we have put forward here requires no specialist hardware other than the ability to digitise images and is therefore attractive to the general practitioner.

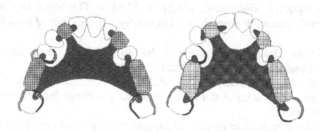

Fig. 3. A design produced in RaPiD using the generic tooth icons *(left)* and a design using the icons derived from MINORI *(right)* demonstrating the difference in design when the dentition is customised to the patient

Many improvements to the current implementation are possible. The removal of the need for the user to initiate the search with an approximation is highly desirable. The search could become more robust, perhaps incorporating some of the ideas in [1]. The patching of missing teeth data from the mean causes the statistical analysis of the variation to be flawed, an approach which overcame this would be an improvement.

How many examples in the training set are required to capture all of the variation seen in teeth across the human population? Experiments with the thirty examples in our set show that the modes of variation are fairly stable as new examples are added, suggesting that some of the natural variation has already been captured. Further evaluation of the training set is ongoing.

The automatic digitisation of medical images has many potential applications: for planning surgery, to quantify the results of cosmetic surgery, for cephalometric measurements and as here, for designing customised prostheses. The use of ASMs is an approach capable of compactly encoding knowledge about the natural variation in shape for use in searching an image. We expect that the use of ASMs in customised prosthesis design applications like ours will become increasingly widespread.

References

[1] T.F. Cootes, G.J. Edwards, and C.J. Taylor. Active appearance models. In H. Burkhardt and B. Neumann, editors, *Proc. European Conference on Computer Vision*, volume 2, pages 484–498. Springer, 1998.

[2] T.F. Cootes, C.J. Taylor, D.H. Cooper, and J. Graham. Active shape models - their training and application. *Computer Vision and Image Understanding*, 61(1):38–59, 1995.

[3] H.V. Crawford, P.S. Unwin, and P.S. Walker. The CADCAM contribution to customized orthopaedic implants. In *Proc. Inst. Mech. Eng.*, volume 206:1, pages 43–6, 1992.

[4] B. Dahl, P. Gehrchen, P. Blyme, T. Kiaer, and E. Tondevold. Clinical outcome after spinal fusion with a rigid versus a semi-rigid pedicle screw system. *Eur. Spine J.*, 6(6):412–6, 1997.

[5] J.C. Davenport and P. Hammond. The acquisition and validation of removable partial denture design knowledge - I. *Journal of Oral Rehabilitation*, 1996.

[6] J.C. Davenport, P. Hammond, and M. de Mattos. The acquisition and validation of removable partial denture design knowledge - II. *Journal of Oral Rehabilitation*, 1996.

[7] A.H. Elkholy. Design optimization of the hip nail-plate-screws implant. *Comput. Methods Programs Biomed.*, 48(3):221–7, 1995.

[8] P. Hammond, J.C. Davenport, and F.J. Fitzpatrick. Logic-based integrity constraints and the design of dental prostheses. *Artificial Intelligence in Medicine*, 5:431–446, 1993.

[9] A.B. Reisken. Implant imaging: status, controversies and new developments. *Dental Clinics of North America*, 42:47–56, 1998.

[10] P.S. Unwin and P.S. Walker. Extendible endoprostheses for the skeletally immature. *Clin. Orthop.*, 322, 1996.

Author Index

Springer
and the
environment

At Springer we firmly believe that an
international science publisher has a
special obligation to the environment,
and our corporate policies consistently
reflect this conviction.
We also expect our business partners –
paper mills, printers, packaging
manufacturers, etc. – to commit
themselves to using materials and
production processes that do not harm
the environment. The paper in this
book is made from low- or no-chlorine
pulp and is acid free, in conformance
with international standards for paper
permanency.

Lecture Notes in Artificial Intelligence (LNAI)

Lecture Notes in Computer Science